SHAKESPEARE STUDIES

SHAKESPEARE STUDIES

SHAKESPEARE STUDIES

An Annual Gathering of Research, Criticism, and Reviews

VIII

Editor

J. Leeds Barroll III

Associate Editors

Barry Gaines

Ann Jennalie Cook

Burt Franklin & Co., Inc.

Published by Burt Franklin & Co., Inc.

All editorial correspondence concerning *Shakespeare Studies* should be addressed to: The Editorial Office, *Shakespeare Studies*, Department of English, University of Tennessee, Knoxville, Tennessee 37916. Correspondence concerning orders and subscriptions should be addressed to: Burt Franklin & Co., Inc., 235 East 44th Street, New York, New York 10017 U.S.A.

ISBN: 0-89102-068-3
Library of Congress Card Catalog Number: 66-4496
Library of Congress classification PR2885.S64
Manufactured in the United States of America

Contents

Contributors

Gates K. Agnew
Associate Professor of English, Indiana University

John F. Andrews
Director of Research Activities, Folger Shakespeare Library

J. Leeds Barroll III
Deputy Director, Research Division, National Endowment for the Humanities

Roy Battenhouse
Professor of English, Indiana University

David N. Beauregard
Institudo N.S. Di Fatima, Rome

G. E. Bentley
Professor Emeritus of English, Princeton University

Dennis Biggins
Associate Professor of English, University of Newcastle, New South Wales

Diana Bornstein
Assistant Professor of English, Queens College of the City University of New York

J. A. Bryant, Jr.
Professor of English, University of Kentucky

Maurice Charney
Professor of English, Rutgers University

John Scott Colley
Associate Professor of English, Vanderbilt University

Richard L. DeMolen
Visiting Lecturer, University of Maryland

R. W. Dent
Professor of English, University of California, Los Angeles

Harry Epstein
Assistant Professor, University of Kentucky

Oliver H. Evans
Assistant Professor of English, Dakota State College

Charles R. Forker
Professor of English, Indiana University

Dean Frye
Associate Professor of English, McGill University

C. J. Gianakaris
Professor of English, Western Michigan University

William Leigh Godshalk
Professor of English, University of Cincinnati

Joan Hartwig
Associate Professor of English, University of Kentucky

R. Chris Hassel, Jr.
Associate Professor of English, Vanderbilt University

Michael L. Hays
Ph.D., University of Michigan

Sidney Homan
Associate Professor of English, University of Florida

Charles B. Lower
Assistant Professor, University of Georgia

Michael Manheim
Professor of English, University of Toledo

Robert P. Merrix
Associate Professor of English, University of Akron

Robert L. Montgomery, Jr.
Professor of English and Comparative Literature, University of California, Irvine

Barbara A. Mowat
Assistant Professor of English, Auburn University

Michael Neill
Professor of English, University of Auckland, New Zealand

Vincent F. Petronella
Professor of English, Boston State College

David Riggs
Associate Professor of English, Stanford University

Jeanne Addison Roberts
Professor of Literature, American University

Philip Rollinson
Associate Professor of English, University of South Carolina

Christopher Spencer
Professor of English, University of North Carolina, Greensboro

Grant L. Voth
Assistant Professor of English, Northern Illinois University

Frederick O. Waage, Jr.
Assistant Professor of English, Douglass College

Chauncey Wood
Professor of English, McMaster University

Preface

This volume of *Shakespeare Studies* initiates a change in editorial staffing. Professor John F. Andrews, for several years the Assistant Editor, has gone from Florida State University to the Folger Shakespeare Library, where he now serves as Director of Research Activities and as Editor of *Shakespeare Quarterly*. Professor Barry Gaines, of the University of Tennessee, and Professor Ann Jennalie Cook, formerly at the University of South Carolina, have been named Associate Editors. Their appointment will ensure a smooth functioning of the publication process and a continuation of our policy of careful attention to all manuscripts submitted, despite a marked increase in submissions. Finally, the editorial offices of *Shakespeare Studies* have moved to the Department of English, the University of Tennessee, Knoxville, Tennessee 37916.

Because Volume X marks the end of the first decade of publication for *Shakespeare Studies*, the editors and the advisory board are seeking articles of more than usual significance for the future of Shakespearean scholarship. Writers with fresh insights, seminal ideas, and genuinely valuable criticism are again encouraged to submit their work for this volume and the ones that follow. Contributors need not include abstracts of their papers, but they are urged to take care to have their manuscripts conform to the following specifications to avoid the inevitable delays occasioned by return for alterations. Articles and reviews may be of any length deemed appropriate by the authors, consistent with economy of expression. Pages should be typed double-spaced (including extracts), leaving an inch or so of margin on either side. Double-spaced footnotes should follow at the end of the article or review; do not place them at the foot of the individual page. Thus they should be numbered consecutively. For other mechanical details, authors should consult the second edition of *The MLA Style Sheet*, which is the style manual for *Shakespeare Studies*, and should observe the play abbreviations for the canon agreed upon for citation in Shakespearean journals and in the computer-generated concordances of Professor Marvin Spevack and of Professor Trevor Howard–Hill.

SHAKESPEARE STUDIES

The Structure of a Shakespearean Tragedy

J. Leeds Barroll III

The *Poetics* of Aristotle provides an extremely useful model—although not the only one—for describing the manner in which a tragedy may be structured, especially a Shakespearean tragedy. For if we consider Aristotle's argument that "poetics" constitutes one element of a class of artificial objects, and if we also follow him in his differentiating "poetry" from other fine arts through the proposition that poetry has a different "object," "means," and "manner" of imitation than other fine arts, we have not yet destroyed any fundamental or widely-held notion of the nature of English Renaissance tragedy. It is not, after all, necessary to argue that Shakespeare himself read the *Poetics* any more than it would be necessary to assume that an asteroid in its wanderings has read a table of orbital calculations. Aristotle, we remind ourselves, was not writing an *Ars Poetica*: he was attempting not to evaluate but to describe the structure of one of the classes of artificial objects which man tends to produce. And although individual cultures may differ among themselves, an attempted description in one culture of the principles underlying the structure of a dramatic offering is not necessarily inapplicable to the dramatic offerings created by another culture. This is especially so when a description has attempted (if not succeeded in) objectivity: one thinks of Shaftesbury on metaphor.

If we accept also Aristotle's classification of "tragedy" as one kind of "poetry"—agreeing with the proposition that, in this context, tragedy may be spoken of as a "whole" consisting of "parts"—we can also accept that reasoning which categorizes the (Athenian) "parts" of a tragedy according to which "object," "means," or "manner" of imitation according to which "poetry" differs from other fine arts. And when Aristotle indicates that the "manner" of imitation in tragedy is through "visual adornment," that the two "means" of imitation are "verbal expression" and "song composition," then chronological extrapolations allow us to apply such principles to the drama of the Renaissance. We have only to adopt the emendations of a more neutral wording. Clearly, Elizabethan stage, costume, and dramatic positioning we could understand as "visual adornment," and, obviously, spoken words were "verbal expression." Perhaps there was much less emphasis on the choric, but "song composition" is a concept to which *Twelfth Night*, *Othello*, and *King Lear* are not alien.

I argue, however, that such a statement cannot be made about Aristotle's approach to what he considered to be one of the "objects" of imitation in tragedy. Aristotle styled these "objects" as character, thought, and plot. But while "character" and even "thought" are certainly viable concepts in a critical dialectic, the concept of "plot" is a much more dubious proposition. It is not only dubious for the purposes of the confirmed neo-Aristotelian, but, much more importantly, it is generally useless as the conceptualization of some supposed aesthetic entity which we have always taken for granted. "Of course there is such a thing as 'plot,' " we say: "a plot is something that every drama has. A plot is . . . well . . . the plot!" No. "Plot is a *theory*, not a fact. To argue this, I wish to examine those sections of the *Poetics* from which all later criticism has ultimately derived its notion of this concept "plot," and I shall argue that the theoretical bases of this idea are insufficient to establish "plot" as a useful concept in itself. In fact, I shall go so far as to urge that what we mean by "plot" has very little relevance or utility to any study of the structure of Shakespeare's tragedies.

I

There is, of course, something to be said for the relevance to certain tragic modes of some elements in Aristotle's definition of what constitutes *mŷthos*, or "plot."[1] No one, for instance, would argue too strenuously against the suggestion that "recognition," "reversal," and "peripety," when placed into some kind of relationship with the mistake committed by a dramatic figure, might produce some kind of "structure" theoretically evoking certain emotions the particularities of which we need not dwell upon, questions of "pity," "fear," etc., best being left to anthropology and psychology. But if we are concerned with the utility of Aristotle's basic approach for critical analysis, we must be aware of the constant danger of constructing a quasi-Aristotelian system which has as its terminology words simply borrowed from Aristotle without the informing concepts.

For example, Francis Fergusson may speak of "recognition" in *Hamlet*, or of "peripety" in *Macbeth*, but for these terms to be meaningful in the Aristotelian sense that we might expect when we begin to read "Macbeth as the Imitation of an Action," they must derive from that system in the *Poetics* which requires a "mistake," not wickedness, to make probable or necessary *anagnorisis* and *peripeteia*.[2] There would be a considerable difference, too, between forcing (as Fergusson does not) a "recognition" on Macbeth at that point, say, where he sees the woods moving, or realizes the fulfillment of the witches' prophecy in the person of Macduff.[3] And because the problem becomes even more complicated as we seek for "recognition" in a *Lear* or a *Julius Caesar*, we are made only the more aware that to adopt Aristotle's vocabulary without his system is merely to construct a completely different system which uses the ancient and familiar words. The alternative is either to change terms, or, if Aristotle's basic premises are accepted (or Plato's or Hegel's), to define carefully when any divagation of corollaries subtly alters the referential-value of the consequent terminology. It is from this viewpoint that, when I consider the Aristotelian concept of the "objects" of imitation ("character," "plot," and "thought"), I take issue with his differentiation of two of these three "objects" from each other: "character" as distinct from "plot," or *mŷthos*.[4]

Surface adjustments are of course necessary. Aristotle sought to account for a phenomenon which he himself knew of as, and his contemporaries termed, "tragedy," while my concerns are for an English Renaissance drama which offers data not available to the Greek philosopher-scientist. Yet when Aristotle distinguishes *praxis* or *mŷthos* from "character," he raises difficulties resulting not entirely from cultural differences. The fact is that his distinctions do not necessarily follow from his own premises. And if some critics not only believe in the term "plot" but also wish to use his epistemology as a basis for approaching the problem of analyzing tragedy, it is the internal consistency of his system which must concern us. For example, when Aristotle regards "plot" as more important than "character," he allows the judgmatic to enter his work, and at a point when the shaping axiom has already been established. His distinction between the two concepts is an evaluative one based on his personal notions of how tragedy relates to an audience. Yet if a critic opts for consistency in method the ultimate purpose of which is not to discover the "end" of poetry but merely to recover the "intention" (in Aristotelian terms)[5] of the poet as maker (*poiêtês*), he must avoid that final prescriptiveness whereby Aristotle can term tragedies "better" or "worse" than each other (54a25–54b15). He must examine closely that point in Aristotle's argument which, separating the "constituent forms" of tragedy (50a15), enunciates the importance of *mŷthos* over "character."

"The greatest of these elements [plot, character, thought, visual adornment, verbal expression, song composition] is the structuring of the incidents [*systasis tôn pragmatôn*].[6] For tragedy is an imitation not of men but of a life, an action [*praxis*], and they [the dramatic persons] have moral quality in accordance with their characters, but are happy or unhappy in accordance with their actions; hence they [dramatic figures][7] are not active in order to imitate their character, but they include the characters along with the actions for the sake of the latter. Thus the structure of events, the plot [*ta pragmata kai ho mŷthos*], is the goal of tragedy, and the goal is the greatest thing of all" (50a15–20). So goes the basic statement, which presents difficulties even if we agree with the sense of the translation. When Aristotle argues that "a tragedy cannot exist without a plot [*praxis*], but it can without characters," we are immediately reminded of the broader assumptions of the *Poetics.*

By *mŷthos,* Aristotle implies some pattern of activity which does indeed exist. But concepts of value are the link between "tragedy" and *mŷthos*, a link ultimately consistent with Aristotle's general theory about means and ends. "The most powerful means tragedy has for swaying our feelings, namely the peripeties and recognitions," he argues, "are elements of plot [*mŷthos*]." This psychologistic notion, coupled with the statement as to the relevance of the term *mŷthos* to "means," will inevitably attest for Aristotle to the validity of his well-known remark that "plot [*mŷthos*] is the basic principle, the heart and soul, as it were, of tragedy, and the characters came second." *Mŷthos* is "the imitation of an action and imitates the persons primarily for the sake of their actions." It is the "pleasure derived from pity and fear by means of imitation that the poet should seek to produce," and these qualities "must be built into constituent events [*en tois pragmasin*]" (53b14). Such is the "end" of tragedy. And since pity and fear are primarily effected by peripety and recognition, it follows, of course, that having defined peripety and recognition as "elements of plot," Aristotle will naturally regard *mŷthos* as the most important element of "tragedy"—"for the goal is the most important thing of all."

Aristotle himself furnishes us with a number of synonymous concepts for *mŷthos*—a number of dimensions, if we wish.[8] He speaks of the "whole" (*holon*), he speaks of "action" (*praxis*), and he speaks of "change" (*metabolê*). I shall begin with this last, as I indicate the divergence of my view from his, for from a consideration of where *metabolê* might lead us, I will be able to focus my objections to the other synonyms more clearly. Here is Aristotle on *metabolê* or "change." "The artistically made plot must necessarily be single rather than double, as some maintain, and involve a change not from bad fortune to good fortune but the other way round, from good fortune to bad" (53a13–16). Basically, then, Aristotle is implying a situation comprising two states, state one being a situation of "good fortune," state two being a situation of "bad fortune." In these terms, let us imagine a hypothetical sequence which involves such "change." Scene one depicts Oedipus as happy, or, if we will, as in "good fortune" (it is not important how we define this now); scene two depicts Oedipus as unhappy, or as in "bad fortune." What principle can actually *relate* the two scenes, aside from the presence of the same character? For "change" is used to indicate that *one* particular phenomenon is under discussion. Thus, in terms of "change," what enables us to say something besides, "Here is a happy instance plus/and an unhappy instance, not related to each other by anything except the conception of one and the same 'Oedipus' as in one presentation happy and in another presentation unhappy?" Or, to put matters in another way, why would we object to such a statement about the incidents as "Here is Oedipus in bad fortune; now here is Oedipus in good fortune"?

One principle which enables us to evade the concept of mere juxtaposition and to speak meaningfully of "change" would be some illusion of "causation": the construction of an understanding in the audience that the bad fortune of scene two derives from, is a hypothetical result of, is a "probable" (?) derivation from, the good fortune, the happy state, of Oedipus in scene one. But if one admits to such a principle of relationship, then the definition of "good" and "bad fortune" will be extremely important, since the "good fortune," in this particular context, can only be "good" in the sense that it contains probabilities for "bad" fortune: the very quality of "good fortune" in Aristotle's own dialectic must make "probable" the "bad."[9] We must accordingly define "change" itself (from good fortune to bad) with more precision, and we can attempt to do so by approaching the situation from another direction, since quibbles about the precise "meaning" of "change" could be merely verbal.

Let us observe that for Aristotle it is an important event merely when a character realizes the true state of things, because the author of the *Poetics* is extremely concerned with the psychological impact of modes such as "recognition" and "reversal." And these modes, in turn, he defines as elements of *mŷthos*. But I would argue that any psychological reaction deriving from these elements of *mŷthos* is a function of the attitude and knowledge of the character concerned. His knowledge "changing" (according to some function of the laws of "probability" or "necessity"), his *attitude* consequently changes, and "recognition" (with "pathos") is a concomitant of the *new* attitude. That is to say, "recognition" or "reversal" has no existence unless attitude one of some character becomes attitude two. But if the sequence, attitude one . . . attitude two, therefore has something to do with a "change from good fortune to bad," we must ask ourselves whether this change of attitude implied by "recognition" or "reversal" is not an admission, in Aristotle's theory, that *character* orientation also must "change" according to the laws of "probability or necessity."

The kind of "tragedy" with which Aristotle emerges becomes clearer when we consider his own conclusions as to the role of "character," however, since these conclusions are themselves not inconsistent with his premises, despite my own foregoing question as to distinctions. When Aristotle first differentiates poetry from history, we learn that "character" itself [*êthos*] will come to have quite a specialized meaning and function in his system. "Poetry speaks more of universals, history of particulars. 'Universal' [*ta katholou*] in this case is what kind of person is likely to do or say certain kinds of things, according to probability or necessity; that is what poetry aims at, although it gives its persons particular names afterwards." But "probability or necessity" in this context of "person" (51b1–15) is theoretically subject to such versions of human reality as are posited by particular cultural or artistic convention, or by whatever other equating assumptions give rise to a notion of the "probable or necessary" in human activities. The foregoing concept of "person," moreover, is further limited by the kind of man Aristotle will describe as appropriate to "tragedy" in his own section on "character" (54a10), which we need not review more closely than to observe that the philosopher, by speaking of characters as having to be "good" [*krêstos*], is taking moral quality as an absolute element, one independent of any structural configurations of *ethical* emphasis in a drama itself.

This important and significant gesture indicates a concept of the intrinsic in Aristotle's approach to human morality. Thus, when he observes that dramatic persons in a tragedy "have moral quality in accordance with their characters, but are happy or unhappy in accordance with their actions," this analytic act of defining happiness or unhappiness as a function not of "character" but of "action" in turn specifies the "imitation" of "character" according to certain standards which have nothing to do, logically, with general propositions about psychology. For we could argue that "happiness" does not *necessarily* come to certain kinds of "characters" as a result of certain events. But when we learn from Aristotle that the artistically made plot must "involve a change not from bad fortune to good fortune, but the other way around, from good fortune to bad, and not thanks to wickedness [*dia mokthêrian*] but because of some mistake [*hamartia*] of great weight and consequence, by a man such as we have described" (53a15), we are confronted with a particular kind of attitude toward how the term "character" is to be used.

Certain distinctions concerning the proposition of "character" may not have been important to Aristotle because of his reliance on a kind of *consensus gentium* in the matter of human psychology.[10] for it is as though he assumes that some "natural" human reaction will follow "bad fortune." This assumption is logical if what Aristotle is after in "tragedy" is solely a depiction, say, of horror and despair in archetypal terms. We may perhaps think of *Joseph Andrews*, wherein the drowning of Parson Adams' youngest child is reported to him so that Adams can react in an exaggeratedly distracted way, thus vitiating his own previous moralizing to the desperate Joseph about the futility of grief and fulfilling Fielding's satire purpose.

If Aristotle had an interest in making the change in *attitude* of the character —the terms of his "recognition"—occur according to any theory of probability or necessity, however, then the author of the *Poetics* might logically have concerned himself with what would otherwise seem merely a quibble. To be specific, if a king were to discover that he caused a plague in his country because he inadvertently married his mother after killing his father, would this king "necessarily" react by putting out his eyes? Or is this act rendered more "probable" by previously depicted attitudes? And if the latter is so, is it the "structuring" of the "plot," as Aristotle defines it, or the structuring of "attitudes" which is the principle informing *anagnorisis* or "recognition"?

Aristotle's familiarity with what he terms "the old stories" may in itself have been a handicap for him. If everyone knew the story of Oedipus, there may have been a deceptive gradient of "inevitability" for Aristotle in what "Oedipus" would do. But if we observe the *Oedipus Tyrannus* from our own distance, it seems clear that Sophocles himself did not depend on Aristotle's generalized universal principles to effect "recognition." In the tragedy, Oedipus' reaction—"attitude two"—can indeed be taken as a "probable" (in Aristotelian terms) ramification of "attitude one." The king's unrelenting insistence on justice, punishment, and exile for the offender while the identity of the offender is yet unknown makes "probable" the phenomena of "recognition," "reversal," "peripety," and "pathos," which are to cause "pity and fear" when the offender is known.

If the reader does not agree with my interpretation of the play, however, let me enunciate Aristotle's problem in another way. Given Oedipus' rigid sense of justice and given the dramatist's desire, as Aristotle might see it, to build a recognition, reversal, and peripety, can the news which must reach Oedipus be that, say, locusts are ravaging the land because the farmers have not sacrificed sufficiently to the gods? If we answer that the news must be patterned so as to affect Oedipus' own situation and attitude for any "recognition," "reversal," or "peripety" to take place at all, this is as much as to say that if the "change" has to be an imitation of such events as are most likely to affect a given dramatic figure, we cannot isolate "a change from good fortune to bad" from the proposition of "character," however "character" may be conceived. Thus if Aristotle insists on principles of "probability" and "necessity," it is more probable that "characterization" is the "soul of tragedy," in that it dictates the structuring of those happenings external to the dramatic figure if they are to affect him in such a way as to make Aristotle's *mŷthos* elements (recognition, reversal, etc.) *applicable.*

There is another way to examine Aristotle's proposition about *mŷthos* if we take as our hint, not his statements about tragedy, but his implications as to comedy. For Aristotle's approach to tragedy was allied to what he thought about comedy in his initial definition of what poetry as opposed to history, strives for. The "universal" in poetry "is what kind of person is likely to do or say certain kinds of things, according to probability or necessity; this is what poetry aims at, although it gives its persons particular names afterwards; while the 'particular' is what Alcibiades did or what happened to him. In the field of comedy this point has been grasped; our comic poets construct their plots [*mŷthos*] on the basis of general probabilities and then assign names to the persons quite arbitrarily, instead of dealing with individuals as the old iambic poets did" (51b1–15).[11]

If we waive such defining entities as Aristotle's "pity" and "fear," substituting such neutral terms as "emotion x" and "emotion y" as the "end" of drama, Aristotle's concept of *mŷthos* in tragedy shows its relationship to the manner in which he saw the comic poets grasping the situation. In "tragedy," reversal, peripety, and recognition, "properly handled," as it were, operate as the "probable or necessary" functions of a "mistake" by a man, functions which involve a change from good fortune to bad, the whole arrangement producing "emotion x" and "emotion y." By the same token it might be said, without too much outrage to the spirit of Aristotle's treatise, that (Aristotelian) comedy has as its end the inducing in the audience of "emotion a" and "emotion b" through *mŷthos*, which, among other things, must involve a change from *bad* fortune to *good.*[12]

This is all we would need for our purpose if we also recall that comedy, as regards character, is "an imitation of persons who are inferior; not, however, going all the way to full villainy" (49a34).[13] For the sake of argument, we will grant that an audience of comedy will be more prepared to regard values as "intrinsic" though accepting conventions of the "universal" as applied to "character." We can thus observe, without *a priori* insistence on the validity of "character," some operations of the concept *mŷthos* as "change" when it is applied to a species of drama which Aristotle considered more mature in its grasp of the principles of dramaturgy, and thus possibly closer to the principles which he may have derived from this species, comedy, in the first place.

In the comedy change-sequence "bad fortune to good fortune," let us define the latter as a social or psychological state for which the dramatic figure enunciated a desire, the other mimetic conditions of the play having established for the audience the proposition that this object of desire would indeed be a source of satisfaction to the dramatic figure(s) in question. For example, in some hypothetical New Comedy, the *adulescens* desires a woman, and no other character offers the audience any notion that the young man may regret attaining her.[14] This manner of speaking may seem circumlocutory, but it avoids as far as possible the assumption of "good fortune" as an intrinsic entity, as a state which one would expect an audience to assume as "good" on the basis of its own desires and experiences, if only because we do not know how Aristotle would have defined "good fortune" beyond what he says about the ending of the *Odyssey*.

With such definitions in mind, let us then suppose a case wherein the dramatic figure attains a "good fortune" which he has not been depicted as seeking. The good fortune is not a function of his own direct efforts as is, for example, Odysseus' slaying of the suitors, where we observe how the consciously-attempted attainment of "good fortune" implies, for the sake of the principle of the "probable or necessary," a rather considerable effort at establishing those traits whereby the character's success is not considered absurd. We know what Odysseus can do, because we have been informed at some length. But in the hypothetical situation which I have delineated, when we consider the possible effect of a dramatic figure attaining that "good fortune" which he did *not* seek, the audience can theoretically react in two ways. It can be momentarily surprised, or it can be gratified: certainly both reactions may be combined, but this need not deter us from analyzing each separately.

As concerns "surprise," I describe it as "momentary" to differentiate the situation from one of utter astonishment, such as might occur if something happened which had not previously been established in the play as at least a remote probability, the dramatic figure, say, turning into a grasshopper. "Momentary surprise" seems to stem from two kinds of dramatic situations. One such is that in which an audience, having accepted the author's premises regarding the psychological possibilities in all his dramatic figures, may not be able to predict all of the probable ramifications of this psychological system. Having been presented with a specific derivative thereof, the audience, however, comprehends, and accepts, in retrospect. An irritable old man performs occasional kindnesses which sometimes seem irrational. He suddenly dies and his will leaves all of his money to an indigent young man with whom the elder had always adopted a disapproving and crusty tone. The audience may be "surprised" by the sudden "change" in the young man's fortunes, but the incident will be saved from the purely random, the surprise of the audience will be "momentary," in direct proportion to the terms of the relationship between the younger and the older man. The old man, that is, may have talked to many of the other characters, but his relationship with the young man may have been depicted in such a way that the youth is a "probable" recipient of the will. Or, the old man could as easily have left his money in equal portions to all the characters, one result of the wholesale generosity being also the change in the fortunes of the particular young man in whom the audience may be especially interested.

What is significant in all this, however, is that the discussion of "surprise" has become a discussion of "characterization" as it pertains to one or two or more characters in relationship to each other. The "probable" has made surprise "momentary," but "momentary surprise" in this case operates as a function of the traits of the characters.

For a second kind of dramatic situation eliciting "momentary surprise" we can eliminate from the young man's activities the problem of a donor (i.e., of another character). Let us suppose the probabilities of a comedy are such that the indigent young man in whom the audience is interested and who is not specifically seeking money has stumbled over a treasure-trove, the location of which is already known to the audience and thus not a source of astonishment per se. In such a situation, "momentary surprise" will be minimal except under certain conditions. The indigent young man may himself astonish the audience by the manner in which he reacts to his find. For example, he may reject the treasure even though the probabilities have led the audience to assume the opposite. In such a case, surprise will be a function of the author's maneuver to make the treasure-trove serve as an instrument to evoke something not as yet known about the young man's character-traits.

It would seem, then, that if we have posited a category wherein a change from "bad fortune" to "good" has not come about through the agency of the dramatic figure, and wherein the dramatic figure himself has not sought the specific change, the problem of "character" continues. We have not, that is, been able to isolate "character" from "plot," or *mŷthos.*

Considering some element other than "surprise," in a "change" from bad fortune to good, let us now inquire into matters attendant on such a concept as audience "gratifications," which might serve as an analogy to something such as "pity and fear" in tragedy. "Gratification" is often preceded by suspense, which may be defined here as the presence in the audience-mind of certain kinds of unanswered questions. Can the dramatic figure extricate himself from his unpleasant predicament? Can he defeat his opponent? If suspense is *absent,* if the answer to these questions has already been surmised by the convention of the genre (i.e., "comedy"), an audience may then wonder "how" the change to "good fortune" will come about, and this matter is a simple one to deal with in terms of previous discussion, because "how" obviously has to do with our expectations of the "probable" in terms either of the character-traits of the hero or of the traits of those with whom he deals. If suspense is *present,* however, the matter is rather more complex.

Let us grant the point that an audience "favors" some dramatic figure over others in the play. To accede to this proposition, however, we must for the moment abandon the intrinsic, the Aristotelian notion that "goodness" and "badness" are donnés, by recalling that an audience may favor a dramatic figure because the author has, by certain procedures, established an "ethical climate" according to which, say, a *choros* leads us to disapprove of Agamemnon's murder and does not encourage us to contemplate the first part of the *Oresteia* with high praise for Clytemestra, despite her own speeches on the subject of Iphigenia. By the same token, in comedy, too, an audience will not rejoice at the good fortune of the dramatic figure unless it "likes" him, and he cannot be liked unless societal convention or dramatic technique have established him as the figure to be favored. When we then deal with the matter of suspense in the former kind of question—will the hero triumph?—we observe that the unanswered questions which constitute suspense are a function of the anxiety of the audience regarding the reaffirmation of those ethical premises according to which they favored the dramatic figure in the first place. Thus, a dramatist may bring forward a "bad" character and endow him with traits and powers which allow him to dominate the hero for a time, but by so doing the dramatist is actually teasing the audience into fearing that its sense of "rightness" or "sense of justice" will be outraged by the possible triumph of the evil dramatic figure. "Gratification" will therefore arise when "justice" finally prevails—when the favored character's fortunes change from "bad" to "good."

But in these foregoing terms, we note that a "change of fortunes" which offers "gratification" to an audience is the function of several prior conditions. There is a manipulation of the "probable" in the dramatic figures, but, more importantly, we observe the "probable" in character being related to some activity having to do with ethical premises. I accordingly conclude that "comedy," a "change from bad fortune to good," is quite dependent for its effect, if "character" is waived as a primary consideration, not on the "change" itself which is implied in *mŷthos,* but on the problem of "ethical manipulation."

Thus if, in Aristotle's definition of tragedy as a change from good fortune to bad, he has not sufficiently differentiated *mŷthos* from "character," it could also be argued that the reversed situation, the change from *bad* fortune to *good,* does not sufficiently differentiate *mŷthos* from Aristotle's definition of *dianoia* or "thought," which is concerned with "the stimulation of feelings such as pity, fear, anger, and the like" (56b1). For if we wish to be evaluative, it could be argued that "thought" itself may be the "soul" of comedy. But since a number of critics have taken Aristotle's concept of the "change of fortune" as a way of describing poetics in general, I suggest that even *comedy* cannot be described in Aristotle's own terms by recourse to the concept of *mŷthos* until we have achieved a viable differentiation of *mŷthos* not only from "character" but from "thought" too.

I cannot here take *dianoia* as my concern. The immediate subject is the distinction inherent in Aristotle's statement that tragedy "cannot exist without a plot, but it can without character," for if one "strings end to end speeches that are expressive of character and carefully works in thought and expression, he still will not achieve the result which we said was the aim of tragedy; the job will be done much better by tragedy that is more deficient in these other respects but has a plot, a structure of events [*mŷthos kai systasis pragmaton*]" (50a24–29).

Much of this statement derives from Aristotle's insistence on the tragic act as the unknowing one. There can accordingly be no real dialogue with his position unless one accepts the concept of the act performed in ignorance. "Better to perform it [the act] in ignorance and recognize what one has done afterward . . . for the repulsive quality does not attach to the act, and the recognition has a shattering emotional effect." This ignorance, of course, simply *must* exist if the end of tragedy is to be the evocation of such emotions in the audience as are precipitated through the contemplation of "reversal" and "recognition." Yet any disagreements with what Aristotle takes to be "tragic" need not deter us from examining his concept of *mŷthos*.

II

Aristotle has offered other implicit definitions than those connoted by "change in fortune." There is, for example, the concept of the "imitation of an action." The "action" (*praxis*) itself is then defined as an entity which is a "whole" (*holon*) with a "beginning, middle, and end" (*archê, meson, telos*). Does this formulation of *mŷthos* serve to establish a viable differentiation from "character"? The matter is more complicated "grammatically" than former considerations because of the various kinds of language which this terminology has tended to precipitate.[15] It has often led critics to ask such a question as, "What is the role of Polonius in forwarding the action?" It is as if some element, Aristotle's *praxis*, exists independent of Polonius, exists to be "forwarded" in the first place. Again, there is a tendency, in such a context, to describe the "action" as comprising a "sequence of events" linked to each other by "probability or necessity": consequent discussions accordingly evolve a terminology of "plot-lines" and "subplots."

For all this kind of terminology to be descriptive of any elements in drama, however, certain conceptual difficulties must be settled. One might wish, for instance, that Aristotle himself had pursued the remark which he made when he distinguished the historian from the poet. He made this distinction not in terms of their uses of language but by virtue of the fact that "the historian speaks of what has happened, the poet of the kind of thing that *can* happen" (51a36–37). History speaks of "particulars" while poetry "speaks more of universals." "Universal," Aristotle continues, "in this case is what kind of person is likely to do or say certain kinds of things, according to probability or necessity" (*eikos . . . anakaion*).

At stake here is a consideration no less important than the difference between the real and the fictive. The whole question of "causation" is implied in the concept of "probability or necessity."[16] The question of "causation" is a problem, furthermore, whenever we speak of the fictive in the first place. For it is not by identity with but only by analogy to history that the concept of "causation" applies to events in a drama. The causes, in history, which may have led to the death of Julius Caesar, for example, were manifold, presumably involving so many factors that, to comprehend all "causes" of this assassination at such a time in the life of the Roman Republic, we should have to perform extensive studies in the political, sociological, economic, and psychological aspects of the total situation. Such a particular view of "causation," however, can hardly be brought to an examination either of Shakespeare's tragedy about Caesar or, for that matter, of Sophocles' play about Oedipus.

The truth is that concepts of "cause" in history and concepts of "cause" in art are very different structures. For the "causes" of events in history always exist, regardless of the historian. Whether or not he can discover the reasons for a specific event, the reasons still existed: after all, the event indeed occurred. If the narrator of history cannot himself produce the causes for the events which happened in a given period, the events themselves were nevertheless present. Their causes existed, too, independently of any historian's attempt at establishing them. With fiction—"imitation," if we wish—the concept of "causation" is, however, of such a nature as to require the critic to react in a manner different from an historian. For if the critic cannot locate the "reasons" for "events" in a tragedy written by a dramatist, then the critic can actually dismiss these events from "reality." The fictive situation can be rejected, that is, as events in history cannot be, on the grounds of a kind of "improbability" very different from the kind of "improbability" pertinent to the language of historical investigation. Aristotle could "reject" (54b31–34) Iphigenia's recognition of Orestes in the tragedy even though an historical event might have happened in just that manner. Conversely, events in drama can be created which could not have happened in history but which "imitation" renders acceptable through recourse to certain *kinds* of laws of "probability or necessity."

When we lose sight of such distinctions, confusing the two modes of "causation," one frequent result of this blurring is the attempt to study the "action" of a play by establishing the "chain of causation" or the "plot-line" as if in an *analogy* to historical process. Perhaps "plot-line" is the more misleading term of the latter two, because a "chain of causation" might be used simply to refer to every phenomenon occurring from the instant the play began until the instant it ended. If we wish to be more discriminating than this, however, we must be able to define what principle underlies our concept of "chain," just as we need to know what we mean when we speak of a "line" in a "plot-line." Otherwise, the misapplied analogy to historical process becomes the only defining characteristic of such a critical dialectic.

Let me, in illustration, momentarily employ such a way of speaking to describe the "chain of causation" leading to Othello's suicide. (The first maneuver, we already note, has been an arbitrary choice. Why should Othello's suicide be taken as the final event in this "chain"? The last speech in the play, or Iago's final exit, could itself operate as such a final event. This critical prejudgment having been made, no matter the reason, we now attempt to reconstruct a "chain.") To exist in "chain," the events must be "interlinked" by something, and we can bring forward a concept of "probability" to reconstruct, say, a chronological/causative system. Thus, Cassio's promotion has made "probable" Iago's hatred for Othello. This hatred in turn has made it "probable" that Iago will seek some kind of revenge. Iago thus attempts to persuade Othello that Desdemona is unfaithful. We then accept the "probability" of Othello's being swayed to the point that he infuriatedly kills his wife, and we consequently accept the "probability" that his reflection on his act, or his discovery of Desdemona's innocence, will motivate him to suicide.

This, then, can serve as a bare outline of the "chain of causation" in the tragedy, but even as bare outline it is a very incomplete description of what, even in Aristotelian terms, is "imitated" in the play. For such a description has waived the characterizations which themselves established the degrees of "probability" for each incident in the "chain": Iago's complex hates, Othello's sense of himself and of others, Cassio's proclivities, and the like. Accordingly, dissatisfied with this approach to "action" or "plot," we could define a "chain of causation" more specifically in terms of "plot-lines" which "converge" or "diverge," suggesting that "If you diagram a plot and find two or more lines of action stemming from a single cause or incident, this is divergence. If you find chains of causation concurring in a single effect or situation, this is convergence. If they are wholly independent of each other, they are parallel."[17] We could thus use Roderigo's infatuation for Desdemona to construct a "line" wherein his activities are frequently commingled with those of Iago to foster further probabilities. We could also use Cassio's weak head for drink as a way of embarking him on an independent "line" of action so that a whole network of such lines ultimately could construct for us a consistent chain of "causations."

One odd result of such a diagram, however, is that since Cassio's promotion "caused" Iago's hatred, we arrive at the interesting proposition that Othello's promotion of Cassio "leads to" the Moor's suicide, that the promotion "forwards the action" to Othello's death. There are, one realizes (and to remain properly Aristotelian), kinds of "causes," and by such tokens one might readily enough agree that Roderigo's love for Desdemona could be taken as only a certain level of "cause" for Cassio's downfall, just as the attack of the pirates in *Hamlet* leading to Hamlet's return is a certain level of "cause" for Claudius' death.[18] And by such reasoning, in terms of "probabilities" and "necessities," Othello's promotion of Cassio, or Iago's hatred of Othello, may be a "nearer" cause for Iago's persuading Othello to kill Desdemona than the pirates are for the death of Claudius, even though Iago's plot depends on Desdemona. Considering the complexity of motivations which Shakespeare interweaves to precipitate incident in Othello, a "chain of causation" is a highly ambiguous concept.

Finally, when we speak of "plot-lines," we are forced to establish distinctions. If we wish to describe a tragedy by means of a network of "lines" whereby any given line correlates in some manner with the performance of some act by a character, the resultant diagram is merely an attempted linear description of relationships and events made probable by characterizations. It is important to state matters in just this way; otherwise, the "lines" might then be taken as purporting to describe history, or analogy with history, and this they cannot possibly do. For any analogy with "history" as such would have to be an account which pretends to be an historical investigation. And the "lines" of *Othello* cannot achieve this effect. For I would ask how the dispersal of the Turkish fleet in the storm was more "probable" than the wreckage of Othello's own naval force. Or again, the attack by the pirates on the ship bearing Hamlet to England would, if this were history, have to be linked to prior events in the life of the pirate crew and to the state of training of a Danish crew bearing a royal person, etc. And to assert that such considerations are not relevant because they are not raised as problems in their respective plays is to abandon a concept of general historicist "causation" for a principle of selective causation.

To aver that an Elizabethan audience would have accepted a pirate-attack on the sixteenth-century high seas as "probable" and therefore that the attack is a satisfactory "device" for returning Hamlet to Denmark is, however, to speak a different conceptual language. For if the poet interested in making "possible" an encounter between Hamlet and Claudius, the pirate attack is acceptable as a way of returning Hamlet to Denmark. We have seen Hamlet's impetuosity with the ghost and can accept the "probability" that the prince might have led the attack on the pirates. But again, this is as much as to say that, strictly speaking, it is the concept of "characterization," not of "events," which is dominating the shape of causation-structures.

In the confused definitions of "causation" whereby a plot-line may be said to describe an element isolable from "character," we encounter such dilemmas again and again. If we assert, as in an historical analogy we must, that since Cassio's promotion caused Iago's active hatred, then Othello's promotion of Cassio was the ultimate "cause" of his own suicide, we recognize two facets of the statement. In one sense, the statement is absurd; in another sense, it is not so, if we qualify it by averring that the same lack of judgment which led Othello to promote Cassio is of a pattern with Othello's other decisions. If we accept this qualification, however, we are again speaking of "character" and, in effect, stating that Othello's promotion of Cassio was used by the author to make "probable" the quality of Othello's later judgments as well as to offer Iago an incident which his own "characterization" has made "probable" that he would accept. Or again, if we must plot a "line" which will "lead to" Aemelia's exposure of Iago, we find that "causation" here is also sparse. We have observed some unpleasant interchanges between husband and wife, but we have neither seen Aemelia acting impulsively before nor seen extended demonstrations of her devotion to Desdemona to the point where she might risk the death of her husband. Her revelations are certainly not improbable, but they are not an activity which is the end product of a series of causes. But other elements in her "characterization" may allow us to accept her reaction.

If "plot-lines" are not a satisfactory differentiation, neither is the (historical) concept of a "sequence of events," unrelated except by imagined chronology. For we are familiar with the debates about imagined time in *Othello*, some critics by their objections to the "speed" of Othello's reactions ultimately attesting to the fact that they are speaking of "character." And we will agree that an imagined chronology must begin in one of two ways. It can begin with the first moment of the play. But if imagined chronology begins with the first moment of the play, then to trace chronology from the first moment of the presented drama to the last moment is simply to rewrite the drama verbatim. The concept of a "sequence of events" operates in this case merely as a synonym for the total play itself.

On the other hand, imagined chronology can begin with the "oldest" piece of information presented to us: Desdemona has scorned the wealthy young men of Venice, or Othello was smiting the circumsised dog in Aleppo. In such cases, however, the imagined chronology does not define an element isolable from "character." We are presented with an element no more nor less relevant than, say, imagined geographic location or imagined weather. The past events in the lives of Desdemona and Othello are obviously evoked to illustrate their characters, not to establish a time-sequence as such.

To state this in another manner, we might think of the "beginning" of *Hamlet* as the duel between Hamlet senior and the elder Fortinbras and the "end" as the burial of Hamlet by the younger Fortinbras, who then ascends the throne of Denmark to which his father aspired. On this basis, one could then suggest that the "action" of the play is that sequence of probabilities according to which the younger Fortinbras finally avenged his father by realizing his aim to win what the elder Fortinbras had not succeeded in obtaining. But though this train of happenings is indeed suggested by activity depicted in the play, most critics would agree in feeling that this is not what the play is "about." Rather, they would probably aver that though the motivation of Fortinbras may indeed have some relevance to the "story," it is the motivation of Prince Hamlet which may "define the play more closely." And if this same critical view will also refuse to accept a description of *King Lear* as an "action" which begins with Gloucester's commentary on his bastard son and ultimately leads to the end of the play with the possible accession to the throne of Gloucester's other son, then the alternative effort to find the "action," in some quasi-historical sense, elsewhere in the play, offers difficult methodological implications, for it is as if the sense of an "historical flow" *qua* flow seems to have little to do with a sense of the "action," the "structure of events."

We can refuse to cope with this problem in distinguishing "plot" from "character" and "thought" by isolating elements at pleasure, positing something as "action" or "plot" and then suggesting that all events not "causally" related to the "main plot" are not part of it. One may perform a maneuver which establishes diverging and converging plot-lines, or speak of "single," "multiple," and "parallel" plots. But what will have happened, dialectically, is that all elements lying within an arbitrarily chosen area will simply have been segregated from elements lying outside of it. And this is as much as to differentiate "plot" from "character" by stating, in some terms, that "whatever it is, 'plot' is differentiable from 'character' and 'thought.' " Dubious epistemology.

III

We might wish to insist, however, that something like *mŷthos*, as conceived by Aristotle, can indeed be isolated from "character"—that, call it what we like, there does exist in drama a sense of "events following each other." Aristotle himself offered an approach which lends some articulation to this view when he spoke of "that which has a beginning, middle, and end." But, in answer, I must inquire what is the nature of this "action" which has a beginning, middle, and end, or how these terms are being used to differentiate some element in tragedy from "character" and "thought."

Aristotle speaks of an action in tragedy as a "whole" action, in turn defining a "whole" in this context as "that which has beginning, middle, and end" (50b25 ff). But we become aware that the definition of the "whole" in this context has serious consequences. In fact, some awareness of the consequences is implicit in Aristotle's own crucial omissions, for he himself never defined "necessary" or "probable" in relationship to poetics, although the terms have a meaning in his general philosophy, nor was Aristotle ever specific about how an "action" is indeed "imitated."[19]

Aristotle himself did demonstrate an awareness that there might be some difference in poetics between temporal cause-effect systems and logical ones, for he is quite interested in that device of Homeric "lying" whereby something established as a *result* in poetics can lead an audience to assume the truth and validity of the posited "cause" of that result (60a20–30).[20] It would have been interesting if this observation had been expanded upon, because further argumentation might have led Aristotle to establish his "whole" action as a wholeness of logical structure rather than as a "wholeness" probably inferred from the fact that dramatic performance has a specific chronological dimension in the very time consumed by the enacting. For, indeed, why is it necessary to define a "whole" (with reference to "action") as that which has "beginning, middle, and end"? Can I not define a "whole" just as easily as "that which has a top, middle, and bottom," or "that which has a left, middle, and right," or "that which has a surface, cortex, and core"? This is not simply to play with words but to call attention to a fundamental problem in one of Aristotle's own justifications for the primacy of "*mŷthos*" over "character" and "thought" as the main object of "imitation."

In his argument as to this primacy, we recall Aristotle's statement that random speeches may constitute "character" but do not serve to make an "action." Yet even in Aristotelian terms, we deal here, not with definition, but with a question of taste similar to that implicit in his comment that figures of humans pictured in black and white will give more "pleasure" than "the most beautiful pigments smeared on at random" (50m30). That is to say, it would seem as if his sense of "wholeness" in art operates according to certain kinds of analogy to life which may be quite arbitrary. His concept of the wholeness of an "action" as beginning-middle-end may derive, as we have suggested, from the possibility that the sense of the chronological lapse required in our own lives for absorbing the stage-presentation of a tragic performance acts as an agent in inducing in us an illusion of historical "motion."[21] For a "whole" *qua imitation* to have some analogy with life, however, this analogy need not operate as a function purely of chronological considerations. There are obviously other kinds of logical structures in terms of which one might accept phenomena as related. One may speak of the "progress" of a representational painting which hangs on the wall, a "progress" from what would seem to be the "foreground" to what seems to be the most distant object directed to us by the laws of perspective. Or, in all painting, one may "proceed" from the simplest looking object to the most complex. But if, in such a mode, one smiles at the child who would touch the "real"-looking object which seems so "solid," painted as it is according to adroit use of shadows, colors, and perspective-laws, may we not perhaps be reminded of ourselves speaking of the action of a tragedy as that which has a "beginning, middle, and end" joined to each other by probability or necessity? Especially if our definition is informed by some impressions of real temporal sequence other than that of the time elapsed in performance? Cannot the illusion of "historical motion" be itself simply a technique, a *manner*, not an *object*, of "imitation"?

A useful parallel to our dilemma is the situation in which we find ourselves when, analyzing sonata form, we "follow" the exposition, modulation, and resolution to the appropriate key. Because a measurable time is required for the seriatim enunciation of component sounds, it is easy to think of a "progress," of a beginning and end (the term "middle" always being logically derivable from the other two by ultimate analogy to mathematics). But as a single line of music proceeds through time, there is the harmonic simultaneity of chord "progression" and the orchestrational simultaneity of changing and repeating combinations of instruments which may suggest other modes of "beginning, middle, and end." We also remind ourselves that if we follow the flicker of the eyelids, measurable time is applicable to the viewing of a painting, a piece of sculpture, or even a ten-line lyric. Modern novels are often described as circular, as is *Finnegan's Wake*, or in terms of "depth," as is *The Sound and the Fury*, but, unless principles are established, how far the concepts of "beginning and end" may apply in these cases becomes merely an exercise in language.

These distinctions are recognized by many aestheticians, and, in these terms, the critic who would wish to approach poetics by way of Aristotelian assumptions about reality must give sufficient attention to contemplating the true difficulty of Aristotle's own attempt to differentiate, within his own system, the concept of *mŷthos* from other possibly differentiable phenomena in a literary work.

Something like *mŷthos* might be isolable from "character" or "thought" if only by virtue of our concept of "story," which does seem to have some relevance to the totality of a drama.[22] But if the subjective sense of something called "story" alludes to anything, I have already suggested that it may allude to some aspect of "manner," or, if we wish, "technique." Comparing *Doctor Faustus* with *Hamlet* in these respects is possibly instructive, for Marlowe's play is often regarded as "episodic," and hence "contrived." But given the momentary assumption that Marlowe indeed wished to present all the scenes on stage which occur in either the A or B text, *Faustus* may differ from *Hamlet* not in terms of its "episodic" nature, but according to such considerations as "profundity of characterization" and the like. "Let us go to Rome and tease the Pope," says Faustus, as it were, and when such a scene follows, we think of the "episodic." But Shakespeare's play, though it may differ from *Faustus* in our sense of its "wholeness," is equally gratuitous in many respects. The difference is that the author of *Hamlet* goes to the effort of offering a different kind of "probability-system" for the existence of most of the scenes on stage. If, for instance, we compare the beginnings of *Othello* with that of *Hamlet*, we find Iago and Roderigo on the street just because they *are*, while, at the beginning of *Hamlet*, the guard is on duty because of . . . a number of elaborately presented reasons. If we reply that being on a street is more "natural" but that being a member of a guard on guard-duty at night is slightly more unusual, we are directing our arguments rather to the *terms* of imitation than to a statement that a scrupulous attention to (historical) causation-theories must exist to effect probabilities.

To observe this matter in *Hamlet* more closely, we might consider the activities of the younger Fortinbras. They make *plausible*, but not inevitable, the guard-scene at the beginning of the play. Later, they also allow Claudius to demonstrate poise and administrative skill, even though these activities could have been elicited by some other invasion-threat, or by some such event as Laertes' (improbable?) ability to stir up a mob with enough strength to invade the king's very chamber. But Fortinbras is again used when he passes through Denmark on his campaign, for his army's progress and goal prompt Hamlet's soliloquy, just as a similar soliloquy was prompted by the (probable?) appearance of a troup of actors, one of whom just happens to remember the Hecuba speech. Later, the return of Fortinbras with his accession to the throne of Denmark results in the creation of a tone of obvious irony, especially retrospective of the guard-scene where, at the beginning of the play, the role of the soldiers was directed toward preventing just this occurrence. But if we tend to think of the uses of Fortinbras as an example of the "tightly-knit plot," we must not neglect to ask ourselves how good were the chances that his troops would cross Hamlet's path just at the moment of his departure for England and, again, at the moment of his death?

From one viewpoint, if Shakespeare had merely wished the guard-scene to make "probable" a private encounter between Hamlet and the ghost, if he had wished a gravedigger scene to make "probable" an encounter with Laertes, and if he had wanted a mad-girl scene for general effects, there were other opportunities for the "probable." Ophelia never talks to Hamlet when she is mad, so that as a mad-figure she could easily have been an escaped Bedlamite, Ophelia herself drowning offstage. The gravediggers could have been working on the burial of Polonius, and the army which prompts Hamlet's soliloquy could have been the Danish army off to guard the borders. We may feel a sense of loss at the contemplation of such a *Hamlet*, but is the loss one of coherence as regards "probabilities" or one of our own sense that "everything seems to fit into place"?

Whatever the case, the pirate-sequence to which we have previously alluded, as well as the very presence of Yorick's skull, sufficiently attests to the possibility that Shakespeare may have been concerned with analogy to historical process only in cases which were to serve purposes other than those of "forwarding" a "plot." For specific purposes, it would seem, the poet is scrupulous concerning "cause-and-effect," but in other cases, and in the *same play*, he is not. Therefore, if the manner of Shakespeare's strategy in *Hamlet* makes us wonder about his specific theory of "verisimilitude," it may also lead us to comment upon his technique. For we could regard Shakespeare's careful little "history" of the doings of the family of Fortinbras less as an effort at establishing probabilities than as a maneuver to indicate in microcosm many of the elements of Hamlet's situation. The problem of avenging one's father, the problem of activity, the problem of politics are all observable in Laertes, but, from a different viewpoint, they are observable in the Fortinbras-sequence too. And if something in the tragedy is meant to suggest that internal dissension and, if we like, "sin," can expose a country to dangers from the outside, Fortinbras' "progress" towards Hamlet's own rightful throne is not an irrelevant process. We may also agree that the "progress" of Ophelia from the state of a young girl jesting with her brother to the state of a corpse whose funeral is ugly affects the nature of the total offering which is the play.[23]

Shakespeare's tragedies, are, however, amenable to Aristotelian analysis, in the sense that such analysis is basically a set of principles of observation, not a group of conclusions. Thus, the foregoing examples offer a way of maintaining that effort at differentiation for those to whom Aristotle's basic approach seems to accord with the nature of their own presuppositions about literary "observation." For if we adhere to our subjective sense that something does "happen" in a play, that there is, as it were, a "story," we can articulate this sense of process in terms other than those which frequently realize one kind of adherence to Aristotle's *mŷthos* by speaking of "plot." We need not commit ourselves to the connotations evoked by purely historical process which might describe the Battle of Waterloo as having a beginning, middle, and end, or which might seek to determine the chains of causation leading to the fall of Constantinople. Rather, from the simple examples in *Hamlet*, or merely from our recollections about "progress" in other art-forms, we can confine ourselves to maintaining the "sense of process" itself as the basic generality, using, if we like, Brower's sense of the term "sequence" in order to describe this phenomenon. For "sequence" may indeed exist as an element in drama isolable for analysis, as long as the concept is applied not to only one, but to all matters which may be subject to sequential considerations.

This is not merely to evolve an elaborate way of using the concept *mŷthos*, however. For we can separate, say, the rendering of the traits of a character in each individual instance from the *order* in which these traits are presented to an audience, and when we do so, we do not have *mŷthos* any more than we do when we speak of "emerging image-patterns." For "sequence" subsumes *mŷthos* by including it as only one of many constituent elements. When a character departs from the stage and then, when the audience next sees him, is presented as having returned again to his imagined geographical location some longish time ago—we think of Anthony's comings and goings between Rome and Egypt—then "change" is the product of a specific illusion whereby the audience is asked to assume that the "progress of time" was itself enough to make "probable or necessary" a difference of attitude. A similar device occurs in *Macbeth*, for the interval of the audience's attention to Malcolm and Macduff in England is used to enable us to believe that "as time has progressed," Macbeth has steadily deteriorated into a kind of "monster." His first appearance on stage after his last exit thus presents him almost as "a different person," the probabilities of this difference established by a specific kind of sequential technique. On the other hand, that kind of "time" invoked by the chorus of *The Winter's Tale* not only contributes to the probability of Leontes' repentance, since he has not remarried for "so long," but the imagined interval may render "probable" the reconciliation of the two enemy kings through the actual presence of a younger generation which has had the "time" to grow up.

There are, of course, other functions which illustrate "sequence," functions comparable to those which convey illusions of temporal process. Macbeth seems to "recede" from the audience gradually as he becomes increasingly steeped in blood, and we can analyze this process as a function of sequential technique which allows us to see him less frequently in soliloquy and less frequently in conversation with his wife; rather, we begin to see him simply announcing to us (and to Lady Macbeth) what he has already decided to do or what he has already done. In another dimension, we may think of such devices as that in *Troilus* whereby the large number of actors impersonating Greeks on stage alternates constantly with a smaller number of the actors impersonating Trojans. The resultant impression is that the Trojans are "outnumbered," even though the number of characters in the play on each side is roughly similar. If we also adduce the problem of act-division, which may serve to suggest either elapsed time or aesthetic demarcations within the whole, we may agree that the whole concept of "sequence" does indeed exist as an element isolable in drama.

It is in this sense that we amend Aristotle's differentiation of "character" from "*mŷthos*" by assuming as our own interpretational principle that, in the class of things imitated, two of the three objects of such imitation are "character" and "sequence" (rather than "plot").[24] For process is an imitable dimension of life, but it is not necessarily confined to its realization in what is implied by *mŷthos*, even by Aristotle's own standards.

Notes:

1. All translations, unless otherwise specified, derive from *Aristotle's Poetics*, trans. G. F. Else (Ann Arbor: Univ. of Michigan Press, 1967)—hereafter cited as *Poetics*. This translation differs slightly from that in Else's more detailed *Aristotle's Poetics: The Argument* (Cambridge, Mass.: Harvard Univ. Press, 1957)—hereafter cited as *Argument*. Line references to Aristotle throughout this paper adhere to the divisions of Immanuel Bekker in the edition of Aristotle prepared for the Berlin Academy. For the *Poetics*, line references are abbreviated as follows: 1450a15 becomes 50a15.
2. The emphasis on error is supported by the terms Aristotle uses, *eutychia* and *dystychia* (sometimes *atychia*) for "good fortune" and "bad fortune" respectively. *Eutychia* of course appears in the *Rhetoric* (1391b), where it is defined not as a function of "character" but of chance, as in the possession of noble birth, bodily goods, etc. Yet "fortune" is to some extent a determinant of "character" here in that good fortune "does indeed make men more supercilious and more reckless; but there is one excellent quality that goes with it—piety, and respect for the divine power, in which they believe because of events which are really the result of chance." The translation is that of W. Rhys Roberts in Aristotle, *The Basic Works*, ed. Richard McKeon (New York: Random House, 1941). This view places us in disagreement with S. H. Butcher's well-known discussion, *Aristotle's Theory of Poetry and Fine Art* (New York: Dover, 1951), p. 336. For him, few elements of "plot" are a function of "change." In fact, *eutychia* does not appear in Butcher's index, his own discussions being confined to the concept of *tyche* as "disorder."
3. See Francis Fergusson, *The Human Image in Dramatic Literature* (Garden City, N.Y.: Doubleday, 1957), pp. 115–25, and *The Idea of a Theater* (Princeton: Princeton Univ. Press, 1949), Ch. iv, passim.
4. Throughout this section we adhere to the term *mŷthos*, waiving such possible synonyms as "fable," "plot," *argumentum*, or *Handlung*. From the viewpoint of formal Renaissance criticism, *fabula* or "fable" would be the more appropriate term, Giorgio Valla having established it as the Latin translation of *mŷthos* and Maggi also equating the Greek with the Latin: see Bernard Weinberg, *A History of Literary Criticism in the Italian Renaissance* (Chicago: Univ. of Chicago Press, 1961), pp. 362, 381. Indeed, *fabula*, with or without Aristotelian connotations, had wide dispersion, its use in connection with Terence

suggesting, too, that *fabula* was often synonymous with a sense of the total work. The bilingual *Terence in English*, seeing six editions between 1598 and 1641, constantly translates *fabula* as "comedy," as in, e.g., the rendering of the Terentian prologues to *Adelphi* and *Eunuchus*. Presumably, *fabula* derives from Horace's *Ars Poetica*, and in England the point is clear from comparing the Latin text of Horace (ll. 819–90) as reproduced in Johnson's 1640 Folio with line 270 of Jonson's translation, which renders *fabula* as "fable" (for the nature of Jonson's Horatian text, see *Ben Jonson*, ed. Herford and Simpson [Oxford: Clarendon Press, 1947], XI, 110 ff.). *OED* cites such usages of "fable" dating back to Chaucer. For the transmission of *fabula* as a critical term without necessarily Aristotelian connotations, see T. W. Baldwin, *William Shakspeare's Five-Act Structure* (Urbana: Univ. of Illinois Press, 1947), esp. Chs. xiii, xvi. Marvin T. Herrick, *The Fusion of Horatian and Aristotelian Literary Criticism, 1531–1555* (Urbana: Univ. of Illinois Press, 1946), pp. 69–73, contains samples of the fusion between *fabula* and *mŷthos* in formal criticism, but for a different view of the matter, see Madeleine Doran, *Endeavors of Art* (Madison: Univ. of Wisconsin Press, 1954), Ch. x, which does not distinguish between "fable" and *mŷthos* as such. The English word "plot" is more difficult. *OED* cites scattered and dubious instances but does demonstrate that the word in its modern sense was occasionally used. The matter is complicated by the specialized theatrical connotations of the term: see W. W. Greg, *Two Elizabethan Stage Abridgements*, The Malone Society: Extra Volume (Oxford: Oxford Univ. Press, 1922), pp. 21 ff. T. W. Baldwin, *On Act and Scene Division in the Shakspere First Folio* (Carbondale, Ill.: Southern Illinois Univ. Press, 1965), Ch. ii, cites other relevant discussions. Shakespeare's own uses are, however, specific. In the speeches of his characters and in his poems, "fable" suggests either Aesop or *Märchen*, while "plot" conveys the notion of "a portion of ground," of an "evil scheme," or of building-blueprints. In fact, the word which is *always* used in specific connection with plays is *argument* (see *1H4*, II.iv.310; *2H4*, IV.v.199; *TC*, Prol. 25; *Ham.*, III.ii.149,242). The implications of this use of *argumentum*, a term from rhetoric, and its classical connotations are explored in later chapters.

5. In so asserting, we are in disagreement with René Wellek and Austin Warren, *Theory of Literature* (New York: Harcourt, Brace, & World, 1962), pp. 142–57, where discussions about "intention" offer many arguments against, but none for, the concept.
6. The nominative of each Greek term is given except when the direct quotation of phrases dictates otherwise.
7. See Else, *Argument*, p. 256, n. 120.
8. The basis for this point cannot, however, be Kenneth Burke's (*A Grammar of Motives* [New York: Twayne Publishers, 1952], pp. 477–78), for Burke's allusion to an alternative definition of Aristotle's concepts of the parts of a tragedy derives from a passage which Else (*Argument*, pp. 360–63) and others have regarded as spurious. For the alignment of scholars *pro* and *contra*, see loc. cit., n. 1.
9. This reasoning about "good" and "bad" fortune accords with Aristotle's own principle that everything changes from that which is "potentially" to that which

is "actually." See *Metaphysics*, 1069b15. Change (*metabolê*) itself accords with the concept of "cause" suggested in n. 18 below. See also *Physics*, 225a.

10. For this concept of a "*consensus gentium*" see, for example, *Topics*, 100b20 ff.
11. Ben Jonson "grasped this point" too, for his discussion of the structure of comedy is a close paraphrase of the *poetics*. In this discussion, incidentally, Jonson uses "fable" for *mŷthos* consistently. See *Timber or Discoveries*, ed. Ralph S. Walker (Syracuse, N.Y.: Syracuse Univ. Press, 1953), pp. 89, 92–96. See also n. 4 above.
12. Even though we do not have Aristotle's own section on comedy, analogies may to some extent be admissible. He speaks (53a35) of the "double" structure of the *Odyssey* as second best for the *mŷthos* of tragedy, for the *Odyssey* has "opposite endings for the good and the bad" and "this particular pleasure is not the one that springs from tragedy but is more characteristic of comedy." This suggestion brings together "comedy" and a change to good fortune, by implication.
13. It might be possible to suggest Aristotelian comedy as the depiction of an inferior character going from good to bad fortune, but again, the implication is that some other kind of character concomitantly goes from bad fortune to good, or at least attains better fortune. The reference to the *Odyssey* (n. 12 above) suggests this. In any case, it is well to remember that, to Aristotle, an "inferior" character is not necessarily a rogue. "Good character exists, moreover, in each category of persons: a woman can be good, or a slave, although one of these classes (*sc.* women) is inferior and the other, as a class, worthless" (54a20). But cf. 49a35 ff.
14. Such a term as *adulescens* is employed intentionally, for we agree with W. K. Wimsatt, Jr., and Cleanth Brooks, *Literary Criticism, A Short History* (New York: Knopf, 1959), pp. 46 ff., that perhaps Aristotelian theories of comedy seem "even better satisfied by later Helenistic new comedy and the Roman translations of Terence and Plautus." For some other views of Aristotle and comic theory, see Lane Cooper, *An Aristotelian Theory of Comedy* (New York: Harcourt, Brace, 1922), passim. This also, we recall, prints a translation of the so-called *Tractatus Coislinianus*.
15. The term "grammatical" is used here in the sense indicated by Ludwig Wittgenstein, *Philosophical Investigations*, trans. G. E. M. Anscombe (New York: Macmillan, 1953), secs. 244–57, where Wittgenstein employs the word "die Grammatik" (p. 92^{e}). Kenneth Burke's definition is roughly similar, at least in implication: see *Grammar of Motives*, pp. 465–66.
16. For further definitions of "probability" see *Metaphysics*, 1027a; *Rhetoric*, 1357a25 ff. For "necessity" in art, see *Parts of Animals*, 639b24–640a10, and *Physics*, 200a–200b10, all of which suggest that "hypothetical necessity" is what Aristotle has in mind for poetics, his example of such hypothetical necessity being that, in such a sense, it is "necessary" for a saw to be made of iron, not because of its antecedents, but because of the purpose for which it is to be used. For Valla and Robortello on "probability," see Weinberg, pp. 365, 391 ff. In his allusions to *Macbeth*, *Othello*, and *Richard III*, R. S. Crane does not, I think, take such distinctions sufficiently into account, observing about *Othello*,

for example, that it embodies "a tragic plot-form in the classic sense of Aristotle's analysis in *Poetics* 13," *Richard III* embodying a plot-form that Aristotle "rejected as non-tragic" and *Macbeth* involving elements of both. See R. S. Crane, *The Languages of Criticism and the Structure of Poetry* (Toronto: Univ. of Toronto Press, 1953), pp. 170 ff.

17. Elder Olson, *Tragedy and the Theory of Drama* (Detroit: Wayne State Univ. Press, 1961), p. 43.

18. For Aristotle on "cause," see *Physics*, 194b20 ff. We follow his sense of the complexity of the term, generally using his third kind of "cause": the primary source of the change or coming to rest (194b30).

19. As Olson points out, Aristotle "never tells us how to imitate; never tells us how to make likenesses of this or that action, this or that character. He tells us that characters must be likenesses, but never how to give them likeness— as he tells us that actions must be necessary or probable, but not how to make them necessary or probable." Rather, he presupposes such matters. See Elder Olson, "The Poetic Method of Aristotle" in *Aristotle's "Poetics" and English Literature*, ed. Elder Olson (Chicago: Univ. of Chicago Press, 1965), p. 189.

20. Else, both in *Argument*, pp. 624–26, and in *Poetics*, p. 111, points out the possible difficulty that he and other commentators have found here. The passage, as translated by *Argument*, reads (p. 622): "But Homer more than anyone else has taught the other poets also how to tell untruths in the right way. This is a matter of false reasoning. Namely people think that if a certain thing (B) exists or happens when another thing (A) exists or has happened, then if the second thing (B) is true, the first (A) must be true or be happening also (but it is untrue); hence they feel, if the first item is untrue but something else must necessarily be true or happen if it *is* true, <that they> must add it (A); for because we know that the later thing is true our mind reasons falsely that the first one is true also. An example of this is the incident in the Foot-bath."

Ch. xvi, which Else omitted from discussion in *Argument*, would seem, however, to furnish an answer toward which Else himself implicitly points in n. 115 of *Poetics*. Aristotle refers to two kinds of recognition, one inferior to the other, both dealing with Odysseus' scar. The superior kind of recognition is that which occurs, presumably, when Eurycleia discovers the scar by accident while bathing his feet; the inferior recognition is that in which Odysseus has to point to his scar to prove his identity to someone else. Aristotle has already referred to the incident on Mount Parnassus (51a25ff.)—see Else's discussion of it in *Argument*, pp. 298–299—and it seems clear that the point about telling "untruths" is as follows. Aristotle will reject a work which contains every known episode in the life of Odysseus, such as the Parnassus episode, which occurred when he was a youth. On the other hand, the elaborate recounting of the episode furnishes element A to make believable B, the presence of the scar to which Eurycleia reacts so violently, she having been Odysseus' nurse all his life, etc.

21. For a discussion on problems of "cause" in art more detailed than that allowed for by the scope of this chapter, see L. Wittgenstein, *Lectures and Conversations on Aesthetics, Psychology and Religious Belief*, ed. Cyril Barrett (Oxford: Blackwell, 1966), pp. 13–17.

22. The attempt to cope with this problem characterizes Tomashevsky's distinction between "fable" and *sujet* in *Teoriya literatury* (Leningrad, 1931): see Wellek and Warren, p. 218 and n. 15.
23. Brower's suggestion for a "redefinition of plot as dramatic sequence perceived in the progress of meanings" may be considered an essay analogous to this argument in that he is concerned with differentiating "plot" from what we would here term "diction." See Reuben A. Brower, "The Heresy of Plot" in *English Institute Essays*, 1952 (New York: Columbia Univ. Press, 1952), pp. 44–69.
24. For Aristotle on "thought," see Richard McKeon, "Aristotle's Conception of Language," in *Critics and Criticism*, p. 213.

Richard Mulcaster: An Elizabethan Savant

Richard L. DeMolen

From his cradle
He was a scholar, and a ripe and good one,
Exceeding wise, fair-spoken, and persuading;
Lofty and sour to them that loved him not,
But to those men that sought him, sweet as summer.
Henry VIII (IV.ii.50–55)

The octogenarian life of Richard Mulcaster (ca. 1531–1611) spanned an especially productive period in English history. The age pulsated with human achievement and creativity: there were stirring adventure, brilliant literature, and unforgettable personalities—a chameleon world with something for every taste. Blazing at the heart of this swirl of activity lay London with its powerful guilds and inspiring façades. Londoners had successfully managed to sever their political and religious bonds with the continent in the course of the sixteenth century and to promote a profitable strain of insular chauvinism. It was to enterprising citizens like Richard Mulcaster that they looked for inspiration and leadership. Positioned squarely within the dynamic hub of the English capital, this London sage released the creative instincts of his students and appealed to the burgeoning patriotism of their parents.

For nearly four decades Richard Mulcaster was the headmaster of two of London's prestigious grammar schools: Merchant Taylors' School (1561–86) and St. Paul's School (1596–1608).[1] His reputation as a classicist and a scholar earned for him the headmastership of the former. Later on, his renown as a schoolmaster and educational theorist won him the high mastership of St. Paul's at an age when most pedagogues are laid to rest. Although sixty-five, Mulcaster managed to hold on to this prominent post for twelve years, during which he strove to restore John Colet's enlightened ideas to a school which had been defamed by his predecessor, John Harrison.

The reasons for Mulcaster's success as a teacher and administrator were many. Possessing an infectious energy and a creative mind, he saw his role and that of his students in terms of service to England. He lauded his country and his monarch, who personified the commonwealth, and cultivated like sentiments among his students. As a patriot he strove to make his fellow countrymen more aware of their responsibilities to English culture and believed that England's future depended on cooperative effort. He therefore promoted the enrichment and extension of the English language and encouraged the dramatic efforts and poetical samplings of his students. Poetry, pageantry, and drama served his needs just as royal proclamations, the pulpit, and the press served those of the crown. It was through educational institutions, at every level, that Englishmen could be made aware of their obligations as loyal citizens. Everyone could learn to serve, and such service would contribute to England's permanent greatness.

As a sixteenth-century headmaster, Mulcaster held a unique and enviable position in English society. His office put him in a privileged milieu. Almost daily, he came in contact with the city fathers and the leading guildsmen of London. He held equal favor at court, intermingling with the literati and waging war on those "rackers" of orthography. And in the end, Richard Mulcaster achieved a measure of immortality: he succeeded in establishing himself as the leading schoolmaster of the Elizabethan age.

But this long life that was to culminate in uncommon attainment began far from the heart of London, in the borderlands of northern England. During the years preceding the Henrician reform, Richard Mulcaster was born in 1531 or 1532 in the city of Carlisle.[2] Located some three hundred miles north of London and eight miles south of the Scottish border, Carlisle was one of the principal northern garrisons. Richard, the eldest surviving son of William and Margaret Mulcaster, was a proud scion of prominent Cumberland landowners. At least two known brothers, Abraham and George, and a sister, Eleanor, helped to frame the nucleus of his family life.[3]

Mulcaster was by birth and heritage an English gentleman. The cradle of his family lay in southern Cumberland,[4] where one can trace its descent from Sir Richard Mulcaster in the eleventh century. The family pedigree notes that "This Sr Richard was commanded by King W'm Ruffus in the 6 yere of his Raigne to Reside at Brakenhull . . . [with] foure other Knights against the Scotts."[5] A border family for centuries, the Mulcasters had maintained defenses in the northernmost counties against their warring neighbors.[6]

Although our knowledge of Richard's parents is limited, we do know that his father held at least two political offices: William Mulcaster served as one of the nine members of the Carlisle "counsale" in 1561[7] and a year later represented the city in Parliament.[8] As the son of a leading Carlisle family, Richard Mulcaster took justifiable pride in his ancestry. On a brass plate dedicated to his deceased wife in 1609, he wrote of himself: "by ancient parentage and linnial descent, ann esqvier borne. . . ."[9]

Having spent his childhood in Carlisle, Richard was expected to attend the university and to carry on the family name with proud distinction. For this reason he was groomed for a life of leadership and service and was sent to Eton College, which had been founded a little over one hundred years earlier by King Henry VI. The principal purpose of Eton College was to prepare the sons of the governing classes for the university by teaching them a thoroughly classical curriculum. Richard attended the school from about 1544 to 1548.[10] While there, he was a classmate of three future schoolmasters: Christopher Holden, surmaster at St. Paul's (1561–78); William Malim, headmaster at Eton (1561–71) and high master at St. Paul's (1573–81); and Ralph Waddington, master of Christ's Hospital (1564–1612).[11] These three headmasters received their first taste of teaching as pupils in the seventh form. For purposes of both instruction and discipline, the Eton College faculty relied upon the senior boys to assist them. As "student teachers," they were styled as "praepositores" and supervised their juniors.

We know a good deal about Richard Mulcaster's schooling at Eton, because the curriculum from 1528 to 1534 has fortunately been preserved in a document drawn up when Richard Cox was master.[12] The document describes the daily activities of the seven forms and includes a timetable. Although Mulcaster attended Eton a decade later, he undoubtedly followed a curriculum very similar to that prepared by Cox.[13] The timetable required students to be present six days a week at 6:00 A.M. Classes ran uninterruptedly until 9:00 A.M., when students were given a short recess for breakfast. At 9:15 A.M. class resumed and continued until 11:00 A.M. After about an hour for lunch, Etonians studied the classics until 5:00 P.M., when they were dismissed for dinner. Though formal classes were now suspended, it is likely that a two-hour period of preparation and study followed dinner from 6:00 to 8:00 P.M. A similar timetable, even if rigorous by present standards, was generally followed in the other grammar schools of the sixteenth century.[14] In the summer months and on special holidays, however, more time was allowed for recreation.

The Eton curriculum devoted special attention to the mastery of Latin, but neither Greek nor Hebrew was studied at this time.[15] In all the forms, the emphasis was on rote memory, especially the "renderying of rules." Of the classical authors, Etonians read Cato, Terence, Virgil, Sallust, Horace, and Cicero. Furthermore, they used the texts of such contemporary northern humanists as Juan Luis Vives, William Lily, Erasmus, Despautier of Ninove, and Peter Schade of Leipzig. As a student at Eton, Mulcaster based his written compositions on classical models, especially those of Cicero and Horace. Later on, he wrote Latin poetry that showed a familiarity with the style of Martial.[16] Mulcaster and his peers were taught to read and write Latin because the 1540s demanded it. Latin, after all, was the language of business and letters, and those

Englishmen who were ultimately to assume positions of leadership studied Latin grammar in preparation for their adult lives. Under the watchful eye of William Barker, Mulcaster soon mastered the rules of grammar, taught his first classes, and developed a lasting appreciation for poetry.

In addition to receiving the elements of a classical and humanist education, Mulcaster perhaps developed at Eton his later enthusiasm for drama. According to William Malim, it was an established custom at Eton for the school to present a play during the Christmas season. The headmaster selected the play around the feast of St. Andrew (November 30) "according to the schoolmaster's choice, which seems best and most appropriate to him, which the boys may act, not without the elegance of Roman plays, before a popular audience sometime during the Christmas season. Occasionally he may also present dramas composed in the English tongue which have cleverness and wit."[17] Because of their popularity the academic comedies of Nicholas Udall must have been included in the Eton repertory even after this headmaster left the school in 1541.

Mulcaster's scholastic success can be surmised from his honorable passage from Eton to Cambridge University on the Eton foundation: on August 14, 1548, Richard entered King's College, Cambridge, as a King's scholar.[18] His name appears in a list of fourteen "learned youths," ranging in age from fifteen to seventeen. Each of the young men took the "corporal oath before the aforesaid Vice-Provost [Henry Bissel] . . . to wit that . . . each one of them for his part would observe in all things the statutes before read and all other statutes in so far as they concerned them."[19] During Mulcaster's brief residence at King's (1548 to about 1550), Sir John Cheke served as provost.[20] As a classical scholar, Cheke played a prominent role in the revival of Greek learning in England, and Mulcaster recalls in his *Positions* that Cheke personally presented him with the works of Euclid and Xenophon: "My selfe am to honour the memorie of that learned knight, being partaker my selfe of his liberall distribution of these Euclides, with whome he ioyned Xenophon, which booke he wished, and caused to be red in the same house, and gaue them to the students, to encourage them aswell to the greeke toungue, as he did to the mathematikes."[21] Moreover, Cheke was instrumental in bringing to King's William Buckley,[22] whose presence must have been a horror to the boys, for this mathematician had arranged the rules of arithmetic into Latin verses which he distributed to his students.[23]

Mulcaster left King's College about 1550[24] for Peterhouse, Cambridge, where he received his B.A. in 1553/4.[25] The reason for his departure from King's remains unknown. The Cambridge statutes required students of the various colleges to be resident for four years. At the time of Mulcaster, a Cambridge scholar would have attended lectures in mathematics, rhetoric, dialectic, and philosophy. In addition, throughout twelve terms of residence, he would have been expected to engage in scholastic disputations. As part of the qualifications for the B.A., for example, students participated in two formal Lenten disputations.[26] Discovering that his particular forte was languages, Mulcaster took with him an appreciation of the debater's art, which was to increase in succeeding years.

Master Cheke and John Caius[27] were probably most responsible for stimulating Mulcaster's interest in Greek. Caius must have been especially influential. After translating two treatises by Nicephorous Callistus and Chrysostom into Latin at the age of twenty-one, he displayed an impressive knowledge of Greek. Between 1544 and 1551, he published five Latin translations of works by Galen.[29] Later, in a treatise titled *De Pronunciatione Graecae et Latine Linguae cum scriptione nova libellus*,[30] Caius criticized that method of pronouncing Greek which had been introduced at Cambridge during his student days. Following his own graduation from Cambridge, Mulcaster acted as Latin secretary to Dr. Caius. From his daily contacts with the learned physician, he was inspired to continue his classical studies. Unfortunately for both of them, their relationship was suddenly terminated late in 1555, when Mulcaster was accused of robbing Caius.[31] Mulcaster's decision not to return to Cambridge University for the master's degree in 1555 may also have been the result of this unfortunate incident. At the time, Caius was an influential alumnus and former fellow of Gonville College, Cambridge. In 1559 he was to become Master of Gonville Hall.

Pursuing an interest in the classics, Mulcaster left Cambridge for Oxford in 1555 and applied for admission to Christ Church in May of 1556. He was "incorporated" the following June 5, and on December 17, 1556, he was awarded an M.A.[32] Quite probably Mulcaster remained at Oxford from 1557 to 1558, for according to Anthony Wood and Henry Ellis[33] it was when Mulcaster was at Oxford that he became distinguished for his knowledge of Greek and Hebrew. So eminent was his reputation that the "English Rabbi," Hugh Broughton, described Mulcaster as one of the most capable Hebraists in England.[34] Later as headmaster of Merchant Taylors' School, Mulcaster regularly taught Hebrew.

After leaving Oxford, Mulcaster combined an interest in the classics with politics. The family name and his father's influence were undoubtedly responsible for Mulcaster's election to the Parliament of 1558/9 as one of the two members from Carlisle.[35] Although he served in Elizabeth's first parliament from January 23 to May 8, 1559, almost nothing is known of his activities there. Moreover, it seems certain that he never sought reelection, since he began teaching in London in the fall of 1559.[36] Partly because of his political office and his religious sympathies, Mulcaster was commissioned by the architects of Queen Elizabeth's entry pageant, Richard Hilles, a fellow member of parliament, Lionel Duckett, Francis Robinson, and Richard Grafton,[37] to prepare a précis of the royal passage through London. The précis, which exists in two issues, appeared in 1559, although the London publisher, Richard Tottel, printed both issues with a 1558 date on their respective title pages.[38] For what particular reason Mulcaster found favor with these men is not certain; no doubt, he had impressed Richard Hilles and his circle of friends while serving in Parliament. Hilles knew of his reputation as humanist and poet and made these talents known to the court and the city. Therefore, it is not surprising that London's city fathers summoned Mulcaster to this literary task. What ought to be emphasized in this context is the importance of the commission itself. To begin with, the précis of the 1559 pageant is the first of Mulcaster's known literary efforts,[39] which was to be followed by other contributions to pageantry and poetry. In addition, it represents the beginning phase of Elizabeth's patronage that finally culminated in the dramatic productions of the Merchant Taylors' boys. Simply by offering this remarkable pageant in abridged form, Mulcaster secured a place for himself at court and in the minds of the city guildsmen. Even without knowing the actual identity of the author of the précis, Sir John Neale made some remarkable observations about him: "What can be said with assurance is that the passage concerning the Queen's unrehearsed actions and remarks must have come from someone close to her throughout the procession; and he must have been statesman or courtier. . . . But who the gifted author was seems beyond speculation—save that he may have been one of the Marian exiles, returned to his homeland to share in the building of the New Jerusalem."[40] We may conclude that the pageant is important because it was more than a popular spectacle. In all probability it was devised under Parliament's aegis as an instrument of persuasion for those of Elizabeth's subjects who were present at the spectacle. London by 1559 was a hotbed of religious radicalism. Many inhabitants longed for extended reforms after the five-year reign of Mary Tudor and prepared for a return to Protestantism. Those Englishmen who had been exiles under Mary had come under the influence of Geneva, Zurich, or Frankfurt and returned home filled with admiration for a thoroughgoing Protestantism.

In an atmosphere conducive to reform and seething with opportunity, Mulcaster began his teaching career. And marriage followed profession. Soon after assuming a position in an unknown London school, he married "Katheryne Asheleye" on May 13, 1560, in the parish church of St. Michael, Cornhill.[41] Katherine, who was the daughter of a London grocer named William Asheley,[42] must have been noticeably impressed by the gifted Cumbrian gentleman turned schoolmaster. The marriage itself proved to be enduring. According to the General Register of the church of St. Laurence Pountney, Richard and Katherine were in time the parents of three sons and three daughters.[43] With the exception of the following few details, however, almost nothing is known about these Mulcaster children: Margery, the oldest, was baptized on September 11, 1562; and on February 22, 1585, she married John Minter. A year and a half after Margery's christening, Silvan was baptized on March 12, 1564. He lived less than ten years and was buried January 28, 1574. The third child, Anne, was baptized on July 8, 1566. At the age of twenty, she married Edward Johnson on December 21, 1586. Peter, who survived his father and was to live in Stanford Rivers, was baptized August 11, 1572. The youngest daughter, Katherine, was baptized on November 26, 1573, and was buried on September 19, 1576.[44] Twenty years after Richard and Katherine's marriage, a sixth child, Walter, was baptized July 17, 1580.[45] Richard's family life, which was centered in London, must have been a rewarding shelter because he speaks with obvious tenderness of his wife and with paternal affection toward children in general.

In spite of being encumbered by the demands of a large family, Mulcaster devoted his teaching and administrative talents for twenty–five years to the school founded by the Merchant Taylors. By 1560 the Merchant Taylors' Company was one of the most prominent guilds in London. It was devoted to charitable work, especially education. Since the founding of Stephen Jennings' school at Wolverhampton (ca. 1512), the guild had been serving as its principal patron. But now they wanted a school of their own. Hesitating to endow such an institution because of the large investment required,[46] they nevertheless suppressed their fears and established a school in London "for the better education and bringing up of children in good manners and literature."[47] They housed their school in a part of the Manor of the Rose, located in the parish of St. Laurence Pountney.[48] Sir John Pulteney, who had been the Lord Mayor of London for five terms, built this spacious mansion during the reign of Edward III. At the time of the founding there were about twenty-four members of the court of the Merchant Taylors' Company. One of the most prominent members, and the one to whom the school owed its origin, was Richard Hilles, then serving as master of the company. From his own resources, he contributed £500 toward purchasing the school property, which was to cost nearly £567.[49] Because of his religious beliefs, Hilles had spent thirteen years of his early manhood living on the continent,[50] mostly in Strasbourg.[51] Upon his return to London in 1549, he joined in a conspiracy to place Lady Jane Grey on the throne. Pardoned by Mary Tudor for his treasonable conduct, he nevertheless maintained contact with the Protestant exiles in the Rhineland and turned his energies to education. As the principal founder of the school of the Merchant

Taylors, Hilles searched for a headmaster who exhibited erudition and promised success, someone who would combine the trivium and the quadrivium and breathe new life into the old curriculum of St. Paul's School. Richard Mulcaster was his first choice.

The same day that Mulcaster accepted the headmastership, September 24, 1561, the company drew up the statutes of the school. There were to be seven forms. The enrollment was to be limited to 250 students.[52] Of this number one hundred were to be educated without fee, fifty were to pay two shillings and a sixpence per quarter, and the remaining one hundred were to be charged five shillings per quarter. Furthermore, the statutes outlined a schedule of instruction that departed somewhat from the one Cox described at Eton: "The children shall come to the schoole in the mornyng at seaven of the clock both winter & somer, & tarry there until eleaven, & return againe at one of the clock, and depart at five. . . . Let not the schoolemaister, head ussher, nor the under usshers, nor any of them, permytt nor lycence their schollers to have remedy or leave to play, except only once in the weeke, when there falleth noe holliday. . . ."[53] It is obvious that these statutes did not emphasize physical education. The boys had only the gloomy cloisters of the Merchant Taylors' School in which to play.[54] Such confinement may have prompted Mulcaster to offer dramatic productions as a supplement to the limited outdoor activities of his students, for the records indicate that Mulcaster promoted play acting at Merchant Taylors' Hall in order to teach "good behavior and audacity." These productions enjoyed such popularity that his boys were in "great favour at Court."[55] From 1572 to 1582, Mulcaster's boys gave eight recorded performances before Elizabeth I. Within a demanding and diverse schedule, academic standards were high at Merchant Taylors'. Before a boy could be formally admitted to the school, he had to satisfy rigid entrance requirements and pass through a probation period of one month.[56]

The company also gave considerable attention to the staff. In addition to a high master, who was to be in charge, they approved the appointment of a chief usher and two underushers to assist him.[57] The high master was expected to be discreet, virtuous, and learned. Furthermore, they hoped that he would possess a knowledge of Greek. The minutes of the company described the candidate of their choice for the position of first headmaster in these words: ". . . it is agreed and decreed by the foresaid Maister Wardens and Assistants that Mr Richard Mulcaster Maister of Arte for the good reporte that hath bene made of him to this howse of divers and sundry well learned men That he is not only excellently learned in the latyn tongue but also in the Greeke tongue and very apt and meete to teach shall haue the roome and place of Cheif Maister of the foresaid school. . . ."[58] Mulcaster was appointed headmaster of Merchant Taylors' School because of his "proficiency in learning"[59] and because of "his extraordinary accomplishments in philology."[60] He formally accepted the office on September 24, 1561, delaying his decision for about three weeks. The reasons for the company's choice seem obvious. Since Hilles had been associated with Mulcaster in the Parliament of 1559 and in the devising of the Elizabethan entry pageant, one may assume that he was familiar with Mulcaster's character and religious convictions and found them to be in harmony with his own. But, as F. W. M. Draper has suggested, Mulcaster hesitated at first to accept the position because of the quality and nature of the emolument.[61] Even though headmaster, he was offered no more than his assistants: an annual salary of £10 and a place of residence for him and his wife. In order to persuade Mulcaster to accept the offer, Hilles during the "tyme of respit" proposed to supplement the company's stipend with £10 from his own income.[62]

The statutes (which are unique among public school documents in that they remain in force) show traces of the influence of John Colet's statutes for St. Paul's School.[63] But, unlike St. Paul's, the school of the Merchant Taylors was supported out of the corporate revenues of the company, rather than from trust funds administered by a city company. Note the similarity of language in the following excerpts taken from the statutes of the two schools:

St. Paul's Statutes	*Merchant Taylors' Statutes*
This high maister in doctrin lernyng and techyng shall direct all the scole.[64]	This high maister in doctrine, learning, and teaching, shall direct all the schoole.[65]
There shalbe taught in the scole Children of all nacions and countres indifferently. . . .[66]	There shalbe taught in the said schoole children of all nations & countryes indifferently. . . .[67]
The Children shall come vnto scole in the Morning at vij of the Clok boith wynter and somer and tary ther vntill a xi and retourne ageyn at one of the cloke and depart at v. . . .[68]	The children shall come to the schoole in the mornyng at seaven of the clock both winter & somer, and Tarry there untill eleaven, and returne againe at one of the clock, and departe at five. . . .[69]

Within a year of its founding, Merchant Taylors' School was visited by the Bishop of London, accompanied by a number of distinguished scholars. The examination was held in the chapel, a room so designated because at one time, when the manor was used as a town house, services had been held in it.[70] The visitors not only examined the students in order to determine their academic attainments but also questioned the headmaster and his assistants. It was their conclusion "that the schole master of the said schole, which then lay sick in his bed, had moche profyted the schoolers there and therefor worthy of greate commendacion."[71] The force of the compliment was diminished, however, by the following criticism. Without identifying the persons accused, the examiners found fault with the "Cumbrian accents" of the masters and students. This was due largely to the presence of masters who "were Northern men borne, and therefore did not pronounce so well as those that be brought vp in the scholes of the south partes of the Realme."[72] Mulcaster, it seems, surrounded himself with his boyhood friends.

It is clear from the list of eminent examiners who agreed to visit the school in its early years that Merchant Taylors' soon established a worthy reputation for itself. Among the prominent churchmen who served on the panel of examiners were Edward Grindal, Bishop of London and successively Archbishop of York and Canterbury; Alexander Nowell, Dean of St. Paul's Cathedral and author of the official catechism of the Church of England; and Miles Coverdale, Bishop of Exeter and the translator of the first printed English Bible (1535).

Moreover, two events in particular illustrate the growing prestige of the school. In 1567, Sir Thomas White established forty-three scholarships at St. John's College, Oxford, exclusively for boys from Merchant Taylors'.[73] By doing so, he was following a practice established by other founders. Merchant Taylors' School became to St. John's what Winchester was to New College and Eton was to King's: a closely allied preparatory school. A second illustration of its increasing prominence occurred in 1571 at the time of the founding of Jesus College, Oxford. Dr. Hugh Price, who had established this college, prevailed upon Queen Elizabeth to select a certain number of former Merchant Taylors' students, now enrolled at Pembroke Hall, Cambridge, to become the first scholars of Jesus College. One of the four thus selected was the erudite Lancelot Andrewes, afterward Bishop of Ely and Winchester and one of the principal translators of the Authorized Version. These honors placed Merchant Taylors' on a level with the great public schools and served to attract large numbers of boys to its ranks.

Moreover, in order to ensure the quality of instruction, the company decreed in 1563 that the annual examination, which was suspended that year, would be enforced thereafter. Accordingly, in November of 1564, a second visitation was held. Prominent among the students enrolled at the time were Edmund Spenser, Lancelot Andrewes, Thomas Dove, Thomas Heath, Ralph Huchenson, and Giles Thompson. As Draper relates, "What latent drama marked a day on which the translator of the Bible of 1535 confronted three future translators [Andrewes, Huchenson, and Thompson] of the Authorized Version and the man who trained them!"[74] For it was Mulcaster who regularly taught Latin and Greek and introduced Hebrew into the curriculum.[75]

So quickly did the enrollment increase that the number of students allowed by the statutes was soon attained, and Mulcaster, probably seeing an opportunity to raise his meager income, began to accept additional students into his home. Writing in his *Elementarie* (1582), Mulcaster described, in part, the nature of the school he was maintaining in his home:

> For the performance thereof in the bringing vp of children, I haue all the principles there named on foot, within mine own house, vnder excellent maisters. Wherein I do more than mine Elementaire requireth. For mine Elementarie course is to haue the principles perfited, before the childe deal with grammer: Mine execution now is by finding out of times, without losse of learning (which I maie easilie do hauing the hole train within mine own sight) to help those principles forward in such children, as wanted them before, or had som vnperfit. . .[76]

Mulcaster was in effect conducting a private elementary school in his own residence. He offered a preparatory curriculum which probably served as a model for other private schools in sixteenth-century London. For keeping students beyond the stated limits approved by Statute XLIII, Mulcaster was severely reprimanded by the company in 1569 and was compelled to dismiss the unauthorized number which he kept in his home.[77]

The first examination and election of scholars to St. John's College took place in 1572.[78] The feast of St. Barnabas, June 11, became by school custom the day of election. Like elections at Eton and Winchester, the examination itself emphasized the student's mastery of the classical languages. On the morning of June 9, the examiners were received at the school "and aboutte a quere of paper [was given to them] in written verses."[79] Dean Nowell of St. Paul's began by testing the students on their knowledge of Horace, "requiringe diversytie of phrases and varietie of wordes and fynally obmyttinge nothinge which mighte seme neadfull for the tryall of their lerninge in the Latyn tonge."[80] Archdeacon Watts proceeded to examine the forms on the Greek of Homer, while the Bishop of Winchester questioned them on their comprehension of the Hebrew Psalms. The visitation was concluded when the Dean of Westminster examined the sixth form on Cicero. From the above, it seems clear that the course of study at Merchant Taylors' School in 1572 was narrowly tied to the classics. Latin, Greek, and Hebrew were the alpha and omega of the seven forms. One suspects, moreover, that even under Mulcaster the curriculum was more preoccupied with form than content and tended to emphasize language at the expense of literature.

In the years following, frequent quarrels between the Merchant Taylors' Company and the fellows of St. John's College occurred over the financing of elections. Each year as the time of the election drew near, the college would postpone the examination, once complaining ". . .yt is myserable to see howe the poor schollers of our howse this deare season are pynched."[81] At length, however, an agreement was reached in which St. John's promised to send the necessary examiners and the company stated its willingness to defray the cost of their traveling expenses.

Meanwhile, Mulcaster continued to annoy the company by not adhering to their admonitions and by demanding more money. He was charged before the company's officials with disregarding its orders and showing disrespect to the school's examiners by refusing ". . . to here his Former doyngs in that behalf recyted, willinge the sayde master, wardens, and assistants, to procede agaynst him angerly or otherwise, as they listed, so as he mighte have a copie of their decree."[82] A tardy apology closed the rupture for a while, but even during the respite Mulcaster continued to complain bitterly that his salary was unequal to his financial obligations. By 1575, Hilles had stopped supplementing Mulcaster's salary, even though he knew that Mulcaster personally paid his chief usher £10 a year. Something now had to be done. In December 1575, if not before, the court took notice of Mulcaster's embarrassment and met to consider a remedy. Mulcaster was confident that Hilles would attend the meeting and plead his cause. But on December 12, when Mulcaster formally presented his claim to the company for the unpaid £10 stipend, Hilles was absent and no defense was offered. It seems strange that Mulcaster's patron should have suddenly stopped the headmaster's subsidy without a letter of request to the company for a salary increase. Surely Hilles must have been aware that Mulcaster could no longer afford to meet his own obligations and continue to pay his chief usher. The record states,

> Richard Mulcaster, Schoolmaster of the St. Laurence Pountney, required the Master, Wardens, and Assistants to have consideration of the decay £10 wages allowed by Mr. Richard Hills, a benevolent brother of this mystery, unto the Chief Usher now decayed five years and more, and also of his charges in controversy the said allowance though the same were decayed, whereupon it was answered unto him that a time should be appointed to consider thereof.[83]

Eventually the company took an adverse view of Mulcaster's claim and denied his motion. Since they now expected him to resign, they sought an appropriate successor. At a meeting of the company on May 25, 1575, it was determined that upon Mulcaster's resignation the vacancy would be filled with "a mann or fellow of St. John's." But Mulcaster kept uncharacteristically silent and turned to another form of redress.

During this prolonged dispute with the Merchant Taylors' officials, Mulcaster served as one of the churchwardens of St. Laurence Pountney with John East from 1575 to 1577. His duties included the collecting of contributions and the preparing of a financial report at the end of his term. Through falsification of the 1578 records, he was able to pocket part of the church's revenues. Moreover, it appears that he had successfully deceived his colleagues for a few years, but a subsequent audit of his account on June 25, 1583, revealed that Mulcaster, while churchwarden, had misappropriated £9 15s. 1d. for his personal use.[84] In addition, £2 of the sum had been requested and accepted by Mulcaster in 1582 as a recompense "for my churchwardenship according as the lease holdeth," because it was his opinion that the efforts of the churchwardens should be rewarded with an annual stipend. The parish auditors, however, denied the validity of both transactions in their review of his account in 1583. Ultimately, Mulcaster must have accepted their decision, for a further entry in the churchwarden's account of 1599 reveals that the parish "received of Mulcaster, in part of his debt, £4."

In the face of heated confrontations with church and school officials, Mulcaster does not appear to have neglected the academic preparation of his boys. He seems instead to have been praised regularly. For example, on June 11, 1576, his students were commended for their knowledge of languages by the examiners of St. John's: ". . . which saide scholers were examined in the Lattyn, Greeke, and Hebrue grammars, and founde in the Lattinge tounge especially, and also competentlie in the Greeke and Hebrue tounges, for scholers of a grammar schole. . . ."[85]

Partly as an expression of their gratitude for his gifted leadership and partly in an effort to relieve Mulcaster of his financial ills, the Merchant Taylors' Company offered to provide a house and board for his wife should he die while in service to the school. The minutes read,

> . . . for and in consideracion of his longe and paynefull service taken to and with the schollers of our saide schole nowe almost xx yeres synce, and for the proffytt that he hathe don unto the schollers of the same, That yf yt shall fortune the saide Mr. Moncaster to departe this presente lyfe in the service of the saide schole, as scholemaster of the saide schole, then wee will provide for his wife some mete and convenyent house of ours to inhabite in duringe the tyme of her widdohoode for her owne dwellinge. . . .[86]

But this was not nearly enough. Forced to borrow £50 from the company in 1585, Mulcaster by June of 1586 had developed such distaste for his financial position that, even after some attempts had been made to dissuade him, he gave formal notice of his resignation. At the same time he promised to remain at the school another year if the company could not procure an immediate successor.[87]

Mulcaster's resignation from the school of the Merchant Taylors was hardly an impulsive act. After repeated confrontations, he had many compelling reasons for wishing to sever his connection. In addition to long hours and a meager salary, he was entrusted with the care of 250 schoolboys and the supervision of three assistants. There was little satisfaction in such an environment. But one suspects that Mulcaster's resignation was also due to continual frustration. After two decades of attempting to persuade the Merchant Taylors to put into operation a variety of educational reforms, he met failure. For it seems almost certain that he had urged the governors of the school to adopt a less classically oriented curriculum, a shorter school day, and a rural location. What must have galled him most, however, was the realization that, even after his twenty-five years of devoted service, his employers were willing to sacrifice him for Henry Wilkinson, an untried and unknown successor. Licking his wounds, perhaps he derived some satisfaction from hurling invectives. Thomas Fuller has recorded that Mulcaster prepared the following Latin barb for his "jailers" after tendering his resignation: "*Fidelis servus, perpetuus asinus.*"[88]

Although the active headmaster of a large school and the father of six children, Mulcaster managed to find the time necessary to compose two lengthy works on education.[89] Both the *Positions* (1581) and the *Elementarie* (1582) are very English books. Their tone is often pleading and their style is homely rather than elegant. Writing to Abraham Ortelius on April 24, 1581, Mulcaster displayed a cautious nature concerning the public's reception of the *Positions*:

> For I now begin, though late yet seriously (*serus sed serio*) to think of going to press, from which hitherto I have shrunk, conscious of my slender merit. . . . Vautrollier is printing my book, which I have written in English, and which, if our English public approves of it, I will send to you in Latin; but if it is not approved, I desire my errors to be confined to my own island. Meanwhile, however, I send some Latin verses in this letter, which I have prefixed to the book, that you may perceive how cautiously I proceed.[90]

To see Mulcaster in the context of the Elizabethan age is to understand better his ideas and contributions. Mulcaster wrote his principal treatises against a background of history and with an explicitly patriotic motive. He stood between two worlds: the conservatism of Sir Thomas Elyot and Roger Ascham on the one hand and the enlightened caveats of John Locke on the other.[91] Mulcaster's views on children and their education were remarkably practical and sagacious. He realized that the true starting point of education is the child and his needs, and he emphasized again and again the importance of observing children and of planning their education in the light of those observations. He expected that every teacher would stimulate learning by appealing to the individual's curiosity and interests. Indeed, what he said about the potential influence of education was carefully balanced by his recognition of the child's innate qualities. Mulcaster also carefully counseled against excessive punishment which might inhibit learning or thwart progress. He prescribed a flexible combination of firmness and kindness. In general his methods were judicious: example and practice were preferable to precept and compulsion.

Whereas the mission of Richard Mulcaster's predecessors was often one of narrow discrimination, his own criticism was distinguished for the breadth of its sympathies and the size of its appetite. He enjoyed the advantage of being in a position to appreciate what this older generation of theorists had made possible. Moreover, he exploited this advantage with an uncommon energy and almost prodigal intelligence. His energy, however, was frequently undisciplined, and his intelligence was often maddening in its excursions and digressions. Indeed, Mulcaster exercised a freedom, not only in taste and emphasis but even in such matters as vocabulary, syntax, and comprehensibility, that would have been unthinkable to an earlier generation. Yet, despite the difficulty which this freedom might sometimes cause, it was essential to the mode of criticism which Mulcaster chose to practice. For he was, above all, an enthusiast. He placed no distance between himself and his writing. Rather, he immersed himself in it totally, without apology or fear of reprisal. Mulcaster also wrote as an advocate, an impassioned insider. Even though in his role as cartographer he was not always clear and occasionally indulged in vanities, Mulcaster entered into lively debate and tried to steer a less dogmatic course than his contemporaries, conscious of the effects of a comprehensive educational theory. Moreover, it is of interest to note that he turned to a prominent Calvinist for the publication of his major works: Thomas Vautrollier, the Blackfriars bookseller, printed both of them.[92] A Huguenot exile from Antwerp, Vautrollier had issued popular editions of Calvin's *Institutes* and between 1564 and 1587, according to John C. Whitebrook, produced a steady stream of books "sometimes distinctly, and dangerously Puritan, and occasionally tinged with the more hazardous speculations of Dickson, and the other followers of Bruno."[93]

II

In his spirited defense of the English language, Richard Mulcaster is acknowledged as one of the chief promoters of the vernacular in sixteenth-century England. He shares this accolade with Sir Thomas Smith, John Hart, and William Bullokar but has little in common with them. Mulcaster wrote *The Elementaire* for the Elizabethan schoolmaster and parent. His book is a manual on the teaching of reading and writing at the elementary school level. It is filled with precept and advice. Smith, Hart, and Bullokar were less practical in their approaches to vernacular studies. They wrote for an adult audience in an effort to promote a phonetic system of spelling. Mulcaster's concern with orthographic reform was secondary to his interest in teaching boys and girls how to read and write well. After devoting sixteen chapters of his *Elementarie* to the subject of writing, which included spelling, he indicated his overwhelming desire to return to reading, which "is the first principle of the hole Elementarie." Mulcaster's perspective was greater than that of contemporary orthographers. In offering *The First Part of the Elementarie* in 1582, Mulcaster envisioned the publication of additional books on drawing (i.e., arithmetic), music, and physical education, which constituted the core of his curriculum for the elementary school. But before entering into these discussions, he felt compelled to defend the established spelling against such innovators as Smith, Hart and Bullokar. Mulcaster was especially anxious to "rip vp the hole certaintie of our English writing . . ."[94] to "wipe awaie that opinion of either vncertaintie for confusion, or impossibilitie for direction, that both the naturall English[95] maie haue wherein to rest, & the desirous stranger maie haue whereby to learn."[96] Mulcaster was the first Englishman to perceive clearly the uses of his native language. He asserted that English was as capable of expressing a profound idea or emotion as Latin or Greek. This equality was owing to the evolutionary nature of language, which cyclically enjoyed stages of productivity and sterility. Mulcaster described three such "Golden Ages": "Such a period in the Greke tung was that time, when *Demosthenes* liued, and that . . . period in the Latin tung, was that time, when *Tullie* liued, and . . . Such a period in the English tung I take this to be in our daies, for both the pen and the speche."[97]

Since he considered the English language of his day to be in a period of great promise, Mulcaster condemned those predecessors of his who chose to reform the language by introducing new letters or by altering old ones. He illustrated the folly of their schemes by presenting an allegorical history in which four characters—sound, reason, custom, and art—participate. Languages, he stated, passed through three stages of development with regard to their spelling. At first, spelling was entirely phonetic, and the invention of new symbols to express sounds was the prerogative of all. As a consequence, both confusion and uncertainty developed. Later on, "reason and custom" altered the original phonetic forms, creating a system of spelling based on sound, reason, and custom.

But error persisted because there was no authoritative standard, and the need for a standard or norm became urgent. Slowly, a modified phonetic system of spelling developed. In cooperation with sound, reason, and custom, "art" as an authoritative norm contributed to the formation of spelling rules.

In tracing the origins of variant spellings, Mulcaster argued that uninhibited "sound" was largely responsible for introducing chaos into the language. Differences in vocal cords, which contributed to differences in pitch, resulted in confusion for the hearer. Mulcaster was here opposing the exclusively phonetic system of Smith, Hart, and Bullokar. Nevertheless, as Eric J. Dobson has rightly pointed out, Mulcaster misinterpreted and misunderstood the aims of these reformers. He mistakenly assumed, for example, that Hart and Smith sought to represent the individual differences of each man's voice when both of them recognized the futility of such an effort.[98]

Mulcaster's greatest virtue was his moderation. He saw the futility of attempting to win acceptance for a scientifically phonetic spelling. It was inevitable, he thought, that the same letter would sometimes be used for different sounds, but this was no worse than to give the same word a different meaning or purpose. Language, Mulcaster explained, resisted innovation. Custom and reason were much too ingrained in the nation to permit ambitious changes: "For theie considered not, that whereas common reason, and common custom haue bene long dealers in seking out of their own currant, themselues wilbe councellers, and will neuer yeild to anie priuat conceit. . . ."[99]

Furthermore, Mulcaster argued that there was no need for increasing the number of letters in the alphabet. It was his opinion that we could expand our vocabulary by making greater use of the twenty-four letters available in different combinations: ". . . what nede we mo letters to vtter our minde? . . . neither is it anie discredit to our peple to rest content with those letters, and with that number, which antiquitie hath allowed, and held for sufficient."[100] Smith and Bullokar, on the other hand, had advocated the development of more letters in order to fit each sound with an individual symbol. Discounting their thesis, Mulcaster stated that individual letters did not have, intrinsically, a corresponding sound. The sound of a particular letter had been arbitrarily determined in the past. Thus it became the purpose of "reason" to restore order by recommending the enforcement of certain rules based on "custom" and the experience of "sound." Under the guiding spirit of "reason," exceptions to the general rules could be made when such situations arose. Unfortunately, in times past these rules were never recorded, and error resulted from the failure to develop an authoritative set of standards.

In addition to his influence on orthography, Mulcaster deserves to be remembered for his expressions on the vitality of the English language. He emphasized the importance of giving language a free rein to grow and expand; and he praised English for its boundless energies and potential power: "Bycause no banks can kepe it in so strait, bycause no strength can withstand such a stream, bycause no vessell can hold such a liquor. . . ."[101] In this and other passages, Mulcaster spoke of the English language with unreserved praise. He regarded its possibilities for rhyme and alliteration as infinite, and ultimately he attributed the strength of the language to its sounds as well as its varied vocabulary. In praising the merits of English, Mulcaster stressed four characteristics: first, its fine lyrical quality; second, its strong and forcible endings; third, its "pithie" terms for purposes of translation; and, fourth, its economy of words.[102] Summarizing his view, he suggested that the language contained "commonesse *for euerie man*, beawtie *for the learned*, brauerie *to rauish*, borrowing *to enlarge our naturall speche*, & rediest deliuerie."[103] He also asserted that the English language was in a period of greatest promise: "I take this present period of our English tung to be the verie height thereof, because I find it so excellentlie well fined, both for the bodie of the tung itself, and for the customarie writing thereof, as either foren workmanship can giue it glosse, or as homewrought hanling can giue it grace."[104]

With compelling logic, Mulcaster pleaded for vernacular literature. He argued that the English language was fully capable of literary expression. English had remained underdeveloped because it had been neglected by those most capable of providing it with eloquence and learning. All that it needed was an inspired writer. In a spirited defense, Mulcaster argued for the independence of the English language:

> For is it not in dede a meruellous bondage, to becom seruants to one tung for learning sake, the most of our time, with losse of most time, whereas we maie haue the verie same treasur in our own tung, with the gain of most time? our own bearing the ioyful title of our libertie and fredom, the *Latin* tung remembring vs, of our thraldom & bondage? I loue *Rome*, but *London* better, I fauor *Italie*, but *England* more, I honor the *Latin*, but I worship the *English*.[105]

Nevertheless, it was foolish to expect that all the qualities of one language would be inherent in another. For this reason, he said, two considerations have special weight in the study of Latin: first, the wealth of knowledge contained in it, and, second, its diffusion through so many nations. To give up the study of Latin would cause confusion in the world of learning. Yet, again and again, Mulcaster maintained the view that the quality of the ideas contained in classical literature, rather than any one special quality in the language itself, accounted for the superiority of the classics.[106]

Although Mulcaster acknowledged the importance of acquiring a mastery of the classical languages, he regretted the loss of time which was required to learn them. With prophetic confidence he looked forward to the day when the English language progressed to such an extent that it would no longer be necessary to require the study of the ancient languages.[107] To achieve this end, he suggested that the study of the English language should take precedence over the study of Latin grammar. In this connection, it is interesting to note that the first English grammar by William Bullokar appeared after Mulcaster had pointed out its necessity. Yet despite his preference for the study of English grammar, Mulcaster also discussed the urgency of having a Latin grammar and even promised to write one.

Mulcaster's enthusiasm for the use of English greatly exceeded that of his predecessors.[108] Although both John Palsgrave and Roger Ascham had earlier advocated the study of English, they did so only as a basis for the teaching of Latin. Writing in 1545, Ascham even found it necessary to apologize for writing in the vernacular. Mulcaster, on the other hand, showed none of this hesitancy. Instead, he exhibited uncompromising pride in his native language.

For his strong defense of English, Mulcaster must be credited with an important share in the dethronement of Latin in favor of vernacular languages as a medium of scholarly communication. The initiative in this matter goes back, of course, to the time of Dante. But even with the examples of Du Bellay, Rabelais, and Vives to suggest the change, it was a difficult task to replace Latin with English because of the tenacious hold of the classical tradition. It should be pointed out that Mulcaster was not the first Englishman to use the vernacular. Thomas More, Roger Ascham, and Thomas Elyot had anticipated him in practice and surpassed him in style. Nonetheless, it can be fairly claimed that Mulcaster was the first of his nation to provide a justification for the teaching of English in the elementary school. He was convinced that English had the capability of fulfilling both literary and scholarly purposes. Moreover, though there may be comparatively little value in his judgments on vocabulary and spelling,[109] it is significant that at a time when linguistics was at an elementary level, Mulcaster pursued the study of language and the conditions surrounding its growth and decay.

In his attitude toward language and literature, Mulcaster departs clearly from the tradition of purist humanism that had characterized such English educators as John Cheke and Roger Ascham. A detailed comparison of the relationship of Mulcaster's linguistic theories to those of Du Bellay and Ronsard has been made by W. L. Renwick, who suggests that Spenser's acquaintance with "the prose as well as with the poetical work of Du Bellay" was, quite possibly, nurtured by Mulcaster at Merchant Taylors'.[110]

But it was not only in the matter of linguistic theory that Mulcaster was indebted to Du Bellay; he also borrowed the manner, the forthright exhortations, and the pithy, categorical statements on the value of the vernacular: "that our hole tung was weined long ago, as hauing all her tethe."[111] With the intense conviction of a patriot, Richard Mulcaster wanted to demonstrate to his countrymen the boundless opportunities for poetical expression inherent in the English language. Moreover, his confidence and trust in the vernacular were amply rewarded by the influence he exerted on the greatest of the Elizabethan poets, Edmund Spenser. The vibrant nationalism and profound confidence in the future of the language, which he expressed in the *Elementarie*, soon found its justification in Spenser, just as Du Bellay's devotion to French found its justification in Ronsard.[112]

III

Richard Mulcaster was above all else a professional teacher. For some fifty years he devoted considerable energy to the instruction of boys and quickly established a reputation as a leading educationalist. Even so, during his many long years of residence in London, Mulcaster also maintained an active interest in literature, concentrating on three literary forms in particular. Beginning in 1559, he developed a taste for pageantry, poetry, and drama, but not from a purely literary motive. He preferred to use these literary genres for particular purposes. Pageantry became for him a means of conveying adulation or a device for persuasion. Poetry functioned in still other ways. It might either convey personal sentiment or acknowledge a debt or aid learning. Drama, on the other hand, performed a purely educational service. It could teach boys both grace and good speech. In the following pages, we shall explore how and why Mulcaster made use of these literary forms and note, when appropriate, his influence on a particular genre.

Pageantry, like other forms of artistic expression in the sixteenth century, reflected an Elizabethan's interest in this world and its pleasures. Elizabethan pageantry "grew up around the procession, drawing to itself elements from folk-custom, the miracle-play, historical, allegorical, chivalric, and classical literature, and adapting them to the occasion for which they were borrowed."[113] It was the intent of English pageantry to illustrate a particular theme by means of an entertaining spectacle rather than through the exclusive use of either narrative or dramatization. In order to achieve this end, Elizabethan pageants included dramatic episodes, music, dancing, and processions. Moreover, pageant-makers used both mobile and stationary sets, which generally supported historical and allegorical figures.

Essentially, there were three types of civic pageantry flourishing in Elizabethan England, and Mulcaster with a yen for public spectacles expressed an interest in each of them. The first was the Royal Entry Pageant, by tradition a procession along a prescribed course. Preceding the day of coronation, the sovereign was led through the city of London to Westminster. Along the way, the city companies organized entertainments and prepared elaborate vignettes in honor of the royal visit. The second type of pageantry was the Lord Mayor's Pageant. On the occasion of the inauguration of a new mayor of London, after taking his solemn oath of office at Westminster, the Lord Mayor began his return trip to Guildhall and was greeted by the pageantry of the city companies. The final type was the Royal Progress. At the monarch's invitation, certain noblemen organized elaborate entertainments on their country estates, generally including masques and pageants. In 1575, Mulcaster participated in the Kenilworth fetes when Leicester hosted Queen Elizabeth during her royal visit. But these "progresses" were often held for very practical reasons. Faulty sanitation and the danger of plague frequently necessitated a retreat to the country.[114] All three types of civic pageantry shared one thing in common. Their creators made an open and concerted effort to flatter, and flattery was an insured means to advancement. As all burghers and nobles knew only too well, city and court favors were earned and not freely offered.

Poetry likewise caught Mulcaster's fancy. Perhaps no period in English literature has ever equalled the Elizabethan age. The versatility and boundless exuberance of its poets have amazed even the most discerning critics of the past. Yet it must never be forgotten that the Spensers and Shakespeares were what they were, wrote what they wrote, because other men preceded them—men who often wrote painfully and haltingly, men who were willing to experiment. Such pioneers were beset by the limitations of the vernacular, particularly problems related to orthography and prosody: "and the poet who could turn out a deft song at one moment might very well fall, on another occasion, into the crudest jog-trot or the most wooden kind of labored regularity."[115] A large part of this experimental group of poets has escaped notice. One member of the group is the subject of this study.

Richard Mulcaster influenced sixteenth-century poetry largely through his contact with students, but he also tried his hand at composition. He wrote poems in Latin and English, although the output and quality were very modest indeed. Because English had not yet established a reputation as a literary medium, no scholar felt comfortable writing in the vernacular. "English was still the language of familiar intercourse, poetry, and prayer—a tongue rather than a written language."[116] It was not until after the appearance of Spenser's *Faerie Queene* in 1590 that Englishmen in any great number turned their pens to vernacular literature. Following English custom, Mulcaster employed the language of the Romans in composing most of his poetry: ". . . I would haue sollicited my request in the latin tung, bycause the kinde of people, which I reuerence most, and whose frindlie opinion I do couet most, both desireth and deliteth to be dealt with in that tung, as being learned themselues."[117] In essence, Mulcaster wrote only three kinds of poetry: occasional, commendatory or dedicatory, and didactic. His *Catechismus Paulinus* and *Cato Christianus* illustrate this last type.[118] Examples of Mulcaster's occasional verse, which were written either in Latin or English, can be found in the pageants of 1559, 1561, and 1568, in the unpublished poem in the Van Meteren Album of 1577, and in the "Comforting Complaint" of 1603. He chose the occasional poem as the means to express his devotion to learning, the liberal arts, monarchy, and England. In addition, he wrote commendatory and dedicatory verses for certain of his contemporaries and for his own publications. Over a period of twenty-five years (1574–98), he dedicated some ten poems to his friends.

Mulcaster's poetry reveals a good deal about his continuing interest in education and his abiding love for England. Of Mulcaster the English poet, very little can be said; but we might introduce his poetry by observing that although he did not write more than a few poems in English, he succeeded through his teaching and his educational treatises in exercising a creative impact on succeeding generations of poets. To read Mulcaster is to obtain a new sense of the didactic and hortatory purpose that he constantly had in view when writing his poetry. He led poetry forward by taking it backward to its primal origins. He showed Englishmen how poetry could gain in resourcefulness and power by incorporating in its own artistic processes those natural principles of growth and adaptation which govern our everyday speech and give it its peculiar tang and expressiveness. Mulcaster's theory of poetry was strikingly like Spenser's practice: when poets write soberly without disguise, declared Mulcaster, they are not true poets. They become so only when they "couer a truth with a fabulous veele."[119]

Like those of many of his contemporaries, the poetic labors of Mulcaster preached the gospel of thrift, work, and morality. Life was modeled upon a heavenly standard. To accomplish his hortatory purpose, Mulcaster employed a style which was obviously influenced by the classical poets: his use of one of Martial's devices has already been noted. Moreover, his style, like his themes, did not come from any specific source. He owed many debts. Despite certain classical influences, however, much of Mulcaster's poetry, especially his English verses, lacks literary merit. Its significance must depend upon its effects. One may suggest, therefore, that Mulcaster played a humble part in spreading the necessity of obedience to God and Queen and in stimulating English nationalism. Mulcaster also regarded poetry as the art of word selection. It was far more important for him to enlarge and enliven the English vocabulary than to stimulate the heart. At the same time, Mulcaster's poetry proved to be utilitarian. It could honor his patrons and flatter his friends. In the final analysis, what more could an Elizabethan expect from a few hurried lines of poetry than a measure of security and peace of mind?

As a playwright, Richard Mulcaster's contribution to Elizabethan drama remains unknown. It seems almost certain, however, that some of the plays presented before Queen Elizabeth and the Merchant Taylors' Company in the course of the sixteenth century were adapted by Mulcaster to the age and ability of his young actors. On the basis of a company edict issued in 1573/4,[120] Mulcaster at an early date introduced play production into the Merchant Taylors' curriculum. Moreover, plays were regularly given at the company hall on a commercial basis with the public admitted. Mulcaster adopted acting as a means to cultivate stage presence and proper behavior. Sir James Whitelocke, who was a student at Merchant Taylors' School from about 1575 to 1588, acknowledged Mulcaster's use of drama as a pedagogical device:

> I was brought up at school under mr. Mulcaster, in the famous school of Marchantaylors in London, whear I continued untill I was well instructed in the Hebrew, Greek, and Latin tongs. His care was also to encreas my skill in musique, in whiche I was brought up by dayly exercise in it, as in singing and playing upon instruments, and yeerly he presented sum playes to the court, in whiche his scholers wear only actors, and I on among them, and by that meanes taughte them good behaviour and audacitye.[121]

During the years immediately preceding and following his resignation from the school of the Merchant Taylors', Mulcaster also caught the attention of the playwright and the professional actor. Since his boys had assumed so active a role in dramatic productions between 1564 and 1583, he was identified with their cause and blamed for their successes. It was not until the last quarter of the sixteenth century that the men's companies were in a position to offer any kind of competition to the boy actors. Until then, they looked with jealousy upon the school plays, which enjoyed wide popularity. As Frank W. Wilson has remarked, "there was no Hamlet or King Lear to show up their [the boys'] limitations."[122]

Shakespeare, writing in the late 1580s, likewise must have felt the rivalry of the Merchant Taylors' troupe. In an effort to discredit their productions and to enlist popular support for his own plays, he may have leveled an attack on Mulcaster in *Love's Labour's Lost* by characterizing him as Holofernes. Without identifying Holofernes with Mulcaster, Alfred Harbage has offered a most convincing argument as to the date and first performance of *Love's Labour's*

Lost, suggesting that it was first written for a company of boys about 1588/9 and that it was presented in a revised version before Elizabeth I at Christmas in 1597:[123] "Let me propose that Shakespeare's *Love's Labour's Lost* in its original form was written for Paul's in 1588/9 and see what the hypothesis suggests."[124] Employing a troupe from St. Paul's, Shakespeare perhaps launched his *Love's Labour's Lost* and in the process may have sought to ridicule his worthy rival from Merchant Taylors', who had only recently resigned from the headmastership in 1586. Indeed, such timing was perfect. Since Mulcaster had dissociated himself from the school of the Merchant Taylors, an attack upon Mulcaster in 1589 would not have offended that powerful London guild. At fifty-eight, therefore, Mulcaster would have been an ideal target for the barbs of a twenty-five-year-old playwright and poet, and a waspish, wordy, and whimsical Holofernes was the result.

The grammar schools of Eton, Merchant Taylors', and Westminster and the choir schools of the Chapel Royal and St. Paul's continued far into Elizabeth's reign to give performances at court alongside the growing companies of royal servants. It was not until the professional actors called upon the university playwrights and began to intermingle the literary with the popular elements of sixteenth-century society that the future of drama passed securely into their hands. Most of the boy companies, such as Merchant Taylors' and St. Paul's, died out about 1590. A decade later, however, St. Paul's and the Chapel Royal companies were revived. For the revival at St. Paul's, Mulcaster, who began his high mastership there in 1596, was largely responsible.[125] Even though Edward Pierce (Pearce) is generally given credit for reintroducing acting at St. Paul's, he arrived there several years after the revival had already begun.[126] The Stationers' Register names, for example, at least three plays which were "diuerse tymes Acted by the Children of Paules" prior to Pierce's presence at the school.[127]

Evidence of Mulcaster's prominence in the revival at St. Paul's is further strengthened by the following court record. The name of the distinguished actor and playwright, Nathan Field, is recorded in the *Star Chamber Proceedings* as being a student of Mulcaster at St. Paul's in about 1601, when he was "most wrongfully, vnduly & uniustly taken"[128] by Nathan Giles *et alia* to the Blackfriars Theatre.[129] It can be assumed from this account that as Mulcaster's dramatic efforts began to rival those of the professional companies, they sought to reduce this competition by the kidnapping of boy actors from St. Paul's.

Although Pierce was not responsible for reintroducing drama into the school, it seems certain that both he and Edward Kerkham, as masters at St. Paul's, assisted Mulcaster in play production. Later on, as Mulcaster advanced in age, they gradually replaced him. Mulcaster's use of drama was immensely practical. Since he was convinced of its educational value, he saw play production as a means of improving oral communication and of developing social grace. But aside from this pedagogical purpose, his dramatic efforts were also successful as entertainment. Both Queen Elizabeth and King James I found pleasure in the performances of Mulcaster's boys; and the general popularity aroused by these productions, when held for brief periods at the Company Hall of the Merchant Taylors' and at St. Paul's, is even more revealing. However, Mulcaster was to leave his permanent mark on dramatic literature as mentor to two of the period's distinguished playwrights: Thomas Kyd and Nathan Field. Mulcaster was a teacher par excellence, whose wide interests and diverse talents inspired many of his students to literary and artistic endeavors.

IV

During his twenty-five years as headmaster, Mulcaster had served Merchant Taylors' School with distinction. In recognition of this service, but principally as a means of avoiding a future pension, the company ordered "that the some of £50 shallbe geaven unto the said Mr Mulcaster, onelie in respect of his longe service and painefull teaching of ther said grammar-schole, as a friendlie farewell vnto him; and soe his obligacon to be canceled, uppon condicon that the said Mr Mulcaster shall geve his generall release unto this howse, for all matters from the beginning of the world unto this daye."[130] Certainly there was no generosity here.

Despite occasional rewards, Mulcaster continued to be plagued with recurrent financial difficulties throughout his long life. As the father of a large family and as the recipient of a small headmaster's income, he found it almost impossible to meet the economic demands which his social position imposed. It was indeed difficult to travel in the company of successful and well-to-do friends, when he had the smallest of annual revenues. Even as a young man, if the entry in the Privy Council Register is true, Mulcaster began an unfortunate pattern of theft in order to meet his needs. He was also guilty of stealing from his parish church while serving as churchwarden, and he devised an illegal method of increasing his income by admitting students beyond the prescribed number to the two public schools he served. But what must surely be labeled his major transgression was the selling of the office of underusher at St. Paul's School. Mulcaster, it seems, was constantly forced to borrow money and beg for loans. Later on, as the result of an unsuccessful attempt to establish a private school, he was overwhelmed by the persistence of his creditors and died nearly a pauper. And such economic struggles left their mark. As his debts mounted and his conscience weakened, Mulcaster grew increasingly irascible and directed a number of impassioned speeches to his employers. Seeking financial security, he began demanding church benefices, which he saw as a reward rather than a responsibility.

Despite Mulcaster's choleric temperament, which was in part responsible for his quarrels with the Merchant Taylors, there is no doubt that his reputation as a teacher and scholar had attracted many worthy students to the school. So famous and important had it become that the company had no difficulty in finding a successor to Mulcaster. Henry Wilkinson, who had been chief usher at the school in 1573, was ultimately selected as the next headmaster; but in the appointment of Wilkinson, Mulcaster had no influence. He had recommended William Burd.[131]

During the decade that intervened between his resignation from Merchant Taylors' School and his appointment to St. Paul's in 1596, very little is known of Mulcaster's activities.[132] It must have been a period of reflection and innovation. Writing in 1586, Johann van der Does (1545–1604)[133] dedicated an ode to Alexander Nowell in which he asks of the present whereabouts of Mulcaster: ". . . from what imaginable retreat may the delightful Mulcaster be enticed."[134] Van der Does would have been pleased to learn that Mulcaster was contemplating in that very year the establishment of a school of his own to which he would devote his talents and his reputation for nearly ten years.

To realize his ambition, Mulcaster in 1588 petitioned the Court of the Merchant Taylors' Company to grant him "certen arrerages of ten poundes a yeare . . . for the space of XVII^{ten} yeares." He was represented at the court on February 13 by Peter Osborne, the Queen's "remembraser," and won a partial victory. But because he was neither present at the hearing nor living in London, the court decreed that he would be recompensed (£100) "when he cometh to towne."[135] With this money, Mulcaster purchased a country estate (where, we do not know), which he transformed into a boarding school. Here, he was to admit both elementary and grammar school students from the ranks of the affluent. Freed from the confines of the city and the jurisdiction of the Merchant Taylors' Company, he hoped to put into practice some of his educational objectives.[136] The task proved to be beyond his ability.

In an effort to furnish this country school, Mulcaster became heavily indebted to four London creditors and turned to the Privy Council for assistance.[137] Writing to the Lord Mayor of London on his behalf, the council presented a plea for a "respite for one yeeres space, in regard of his present wante, for the paymente of his serverall debtes due unto them." They based their petition of delay on his record of public service: "whereas one Richard Mulcaster havinge heretofore well deserved of that Cittie of London for his travaile and paines taken in the carefull instructinge and bringing up of such youthes as have beene recommended to his charge and tuicion . . . ys now, by reason that his welth is not answerable to his virtue, growen indebted to certain persons within the said Cittie."[138] His lack of funds at this time may also explain why he was petitioning John Puckering for the prebend of Yatesbury in 1593.[139]

Moreover, cases in the Courts of Chancery and Requests for the period make it clear that Mulcaster, "being a schoolmaster in London and giving up the keeping of the sd. school in London [Merchant Taylors']," [140] had established a private school in the country "where he should teach (as he said) certain noble men's children,"[141] and needed money "to make provision for the better furnishing of his house in the country."[142] For this reason, he borrowed £200 from Thomas Tyrrell, a London grocer, who required him to pawn plate worth £300 as security.[143] When Mulcaster failed to make payment on the day appointed, Tyrrell brought him to court. Later on, he was to borrow another £100 from Tyrrell, repaying him £45 and what he was allowed for "the boarding and teaching of Thomas his son."[144] But he was never entirely able to satisfy his creditor and asked him to retain the plate in lieu of his debt. Toward the end of 1599, Sir Julius Caesar, one of the Masters of Requests, determined that Mulcaster's indebtedness had been satisfied and constrained Margaret, Tyrrell's widow, and his son, Thomas, not to bring further suit.[145]

To what extent Mulcaster succeeded in realizing his educational aims in this private venture cannot be determined. Nevertheless, the following incident gives testimony to his ability to attract students. Having already established a worthy reputation as schoolmaster, on February 8, 1592, "Mr. Muncaster" was instructed by the office of the Lord Treasurer to take charge of "Mr. George and Edward Jerninghams, two yong gentlemen, to be brought up as s[c]hollers in learning and instructed in manners and religion."[146] In a later letter, the Lord Treasurer ordered Mulcaster to "deliver the said two yong gentlemen to such as their father shal appoint to receave them of you. . . ."[147] The plague, then raging in London, necessitated this action.

During the period of time which elapsed between his resignation from Merchant Taylors' and his appointment to St. Paul's School,[148] Mulcaster held two recorded benefices. John Whitgift, Archbishop of Canterbury,[149] appointed him vicar of Cranbrook[150] in Kent on April 1, 1590, and on April 29, 1594, he received the prebend of Yatesbury in the diocese of Salisbury.[151] In order to receive final confirmation for the latter benefice, Mulcaster had written to Edward Heyborn begging him to intervene on his behalf with John Puckering, the Lord Keeper.[152] At the same time he addressed a letter of his own to the Lord Keeper, requesting confirmation of the benefice.[153] The combined effect of the two letters won him the prebend, but the office was undeserved. He had little interest or aptitude for pastoral work. One strongly suspects that Mulcaster sought ordination so as to be able to enjoy ecclesiastical revenues in absentia and as a means of raising additional income. Toward the end of this decade, it appears that he maintained a fairly active "calling" in London, using his license to preach in order to augment his income. Between November 25, 1593, and November 20, 1594, Mulcaster, "clerk," received twenty shillings for two sermons preached in the chapel at Lincoln's Inn. Thus by 1595, Richard Robinson[155] was able to describe Mulcaster and Thomas Buckminster as "preachers in London."[156]

The date on which Mulcaster closed his private school in the country and opened his school on Milk Street, Cheapside, where the students from St. Paul's were sent, is unknown. It seems certain, however, that during the final years of John Harrison's high mastership at St. Paul's (1581–96), when the Mercers' Company charged him with incompetence, neglect of duty, and insolence and demanded his resignation,[157] Mulcaster instructed Paulines. Consulting the financial accounts[158] of the school for the year after he became high master (1597), one learns that he found it necessary to employ additional teachers in order to instruct properly those students who had been sent to his school by the Company of Mercers.

It is a matter of some surprise that Mulcaster should have even considered the high mastership of St. Paul's, having earlier expressed dissatisfaction with a similar experience in a guild school and having noted the strife between the Mercers and Harrison. But age was against him. At sixty-five, Mulcaster may have been attracted to St. Paul's by the provision in the statutes for his care in case of sickness or old age. Since financial difficulties were a continuing source of worry, St. Paul's School could at least offer him a sense of security.

Mulcaster's appointment to the high mastership of St. Paul's on August 5, 1596,[160] was probably due to the recommendation of his former student and friend Lancelot Andrewes, who was then prebend of St. Paul's and a school examiner.[161] But even before Harrison's forced resignation, Mulcaster had acted as high master in absentia. In his new position, he displayed impartiality and clemency: despite Richard Smyth's sympathetic support of Harrison, during the latter's dispute with the Mercers, Mulcaster retained him as surmaster. Christopher Johnston, an assistant of Mulcaster at Milk Street, was appointed to succeed Francis Herring as the underusher.[162]

Since the days of John Colet, the curriculum at St. Paul's had reflected both classical and Christian ideals. Humanism influenced both form and content. Moreover, the dictum "aut doce, aut disce, aut discede" (either teach, or learn, or depart) influenced the study habits and conduct of sixteenth-century Paulines.[163] Upon assuming the high mastership, the sixty-five-year-old Mulcaster introduced no major educational reforms. By now, he was a contented disciple of the noble Colet, preferring the security of an orderly classroom and the higher salary of the Mercers to experimentation and the hostility of creditors. During his twelve-year tenure, Latin and Greek continued to reign undisturbed as the major academic disciplines.

Continually plagued with debts, Mulcaster was constrained on several occasions to request money from the Mercers' Company. He even appealed to Archbishop John Whitgift to persuade the company to loan him £100. In the course of six and a half years, the Court of Assistants loaned him nearly £300.[164] To insure the process of repayment, quarterly payments were deducted from his salary. In addition, the company required his son Peter to cosign the bond as further security. By this point, one may conjecture, the burdensome costs of purchasing and equipping his two private schools had forced Mulcaster to seek financial aid in order to satisfy his creditors.

Acting in defiance of the recently amended statutes and in imitation of a previous course of action, Mulcaster, moreover, sought to increase his income by admitting boys into the school beyond the prescribed limits. The Court of Assistants reprimanded him for this violation of the rules, reminding him that the number of students was not to exceed 153. Mulcaster ceased this practice,[165] but he cultivated an even more disagreeable means of improving his salary: he sold nominations for the post of underusher at St. Paul's on at least two occasions.[166]

In addition to conflict with the Mercers, Mulcaster faced administrative and academic problems during his tenure at St. Paul's. In the preface to his Pauline catechism,[167] he spoke of the difficulties he met as high master. He referred to the school's reduced enrollment and regretted the fact that needed improvements could not be made immediately. In order to raise the standards of admission, he insisted upon adhering to that statute which required all students to read and write competently and to know the catechism. He warned that unless such actions were taken, the school would lose its prestige and value to the community.[168]

Although there is ample evidence to indicate that Richard Mulcaster was an able and conscientious headmaster, Thomas Fuller, who is occasionally more witty than reliable, has recorded for posterity Mulcaster's "method of teaching" at St. Paul's:

> His method of teaching was this. In a morning he would exactly and plainly construe and parse the lessons of his scholars; which done, he slept his hour (custom made him critical to proportion it) in his desk in the school; but woe be to the scholar that slept the while. Awaking, he heard them accurately; and Atropos might be persuaded to pity, as soon as he to pardon, where he found just fault. The prayers of cockering mothers

> prevailed with him as much as the requests of indulgent fathers, rather increasing than mitigating his severity on their offending child. In a word he was *plagosus Orbilius*,[169] though it may be truly said (and safely for one out of his school) that others have taught as much learning with fewer lashes. Yet his sharpness was the better endured, because unpartial; and many excellent scholars were bred under him. . . .[170]

It seems clear from this account that Fuller believed Mulcaster was a severe disciplinarian, who freely used the lash. In contrast to this opinion, and in keeping with the recommendations of Sir Thomas Elyot and Roger Ascham, Mulcaster in his *Positions* deprecates the use of punishment by the teacher, except for the purpose of correction and inspiring awe:

> My selfe haue had thousandes vnder my hand, whom I neuer bet, neither they euer much needed: but if the rod had not bene in sight, and assured them of punishment if they had swarued to much, they would haue deserued. . . .[171] For gentlenesse and curtesie towarde children, I do thinke it more needefull then beating, and euer to be wished, bycause it implyeth a good nature in the child, which is any parentes comfort, any maisters delite.[172]

This would suggest that Mulcaster was a moderate disciplinarian who whipped only those boys who ignored their studies and their classroom responsibilities. It also indicates that he displayed at times considerable affection toward his students. Would a severe and undiscriminating "beater" have said: "And euer the maister must haue a fatherly affection, euen to the vnhappyest boye . . ."?[173] Nevertheless, the typical Elizabethan schoolmaster was generally a severe taskmaster, who often relied upon the rod to inspire his students.[174] As Frederick Seebohm has argued, "the common run of schoolmaster described by Erasmus" were "too ignorant to teach their scholars properly, and had to make up for it by flogging and scolding, defending their cruelty by the theory that it was the schoolmaster's business to subdue the spirits of his boys!"[175]

During the course of his high mastership at St. Paul's, Mulcaster published in London, in addition to his catechism, a collection of Latin poems and a Latin grammar in verse form. The first work, which is no longer extant, was titled *Poemata* and appeared in 1599.[176] The second work, *Cato Christianus*,[177] appeared about 1600 and was used as a textbook at St. Paul's. Its purpose was to teach piety and the fundamentals of Latin composition and to Christianize Cato by offering the wisdom of that ancient in more acceptable dress.[178] Dissatisfied with the pagan tone of classical literature, Mulcaster presented his *Cato Christianus* as a more appropriate text for impressionable grammar school boys. Following an introduction of twenty-two pages, he composed a poem of eighty-four pages in which he urged his young readers to live the good, Christian life. The poem itself consists of a series of moral injunctions, supported by Biblical citations. Like Colet, Mulcaster sought to build character by emphasizing gentlemanly manners and Christian ethics. Above all, he insisted that students should practice what they were taught.

At this time, Mulcaster also became embedded in a controversy concerning the treatment of Hebrew history in the Authorized Version. In two sketchy letters, we learn that he befriended Hugh Broughton (1549–1612), the Biblical scholar and Puritan divine who had earlier written to the Lord Treasurer in defense of his scriptural studies. Siding with Broughton, Mulcaster agreed to take "a full declaration of the controversies" between Dr. Reynolds and Broughton to John Whitgift, the Archbishop of Canterbury. Broughton had long wanted to organize a small committee of scholars to produce a new English version of the Bible, but when in 1604 James I set up a panel of translators to prepare what was to become the Authorized Version, Broughton was deliberately excluded on account of his eccentric views and Puritan outlook. His works propound views characteristic of his general position: the complete internal consistency of the Old and New Testaments and the absolute incorruptness of Scripture as handed down.[179] Having fulfilled his promise, Mulcaster returned to Broughton a favorable commendation from the archbishop: "how his Grace had determined: with what honourable speaches: how he said: that he knew my studies earnest, then twentie yeares, in a path untroden since the Apostles time: to cleare the narrations of Scripture: by time, place, and person: wherein he that crossed me once, would be caught in a thousand absurdities." The debate continued, however, with the archbishop eventually siding with Dr. Reynolds. In a second letter to the Lord Treasurer, Broughton explained that his recent departure from England was due to the actions of the archbishop against him: "WHEREAS I am straungely injured (Right Honourable) by the Archbishop of C. his Grace, I thought good to leave our soyle, and all promised preferment, rather than putt up such injuries done to God's word at his hand. . . ."[180] Nor did the controversy end here. The testy Broughton, no doubt angered by the archbishop's stubborn defense of Dr. Reynolds, issued a polemic "against the Lord Archbishop of Canterbury, about Sheol and Hades. . . ."[181] As he had already sought refuge on the continent, there was little danger that this treatise would threaten his security.[182]

Mulcaster's relations with the Merchant Taylors' Company during these years appear to have been ambiguous. Despite the cavalier manner in which he had left the school, he was invited to attend the annual election to St. John's, as an examiner or guest, in 1595, 1596, 1601, and 1602.[183]

In addition, Mulcaster enjoyed great rapport with an elite segment of sixteenth-century society. Like Roger Ascham, Mulcaster was fond of archery and belonged to a prominent society of archers who styled themselves "Prince Arthur's Knights."[184] Membership in the society was considered a privilege, and both Ascham and Mulcaster proudly acknowledged their association. Mulcaster digressed on this subject in his *Positions* (1581):

> In the middest of so many earnest matters, I may be allowed to entermingle one, which hath a relice of mirth, for in praysing of *Archerie,* as a principall exercise, to the preseruing of health, how can I but prayse them, who professe it thoroughly, & maintaine it nobly, the frindly and franke fellowship of prince *Arthurs* knightes in and about the citie of London, which of late yeares haue so reuiued the exercise, so countenaunced the artificers, so enflamed emulation, as in themselues for frindly meting, in workemen for good gayning, in companies for earnest comparing, it is almost growne to an orderly discipline, to cherishe louing society, to enrich labouring pouertie, to maintaine honest actiuity. . . .[185]

Although evidently fond of the physical exercise which the club's activities afforded, Mulcaster showed greater enthusiasm for the opportunity to join his companions in "frindly meting," from which, no doubt, he derived much satisfaction. As Charles Millican has suggested,[186] Mulcaster speaks of "the fellowship, which I am of," of "those wel known knights," and of "our next meeting," with evident familiarity and gives us reason to believe that the "fellowship of prince Arthurs knightes" was prominent in the social life of Elizabethan London. The society met regularly and was addicted to spectacles. John Nichols[187] gives us an account of an assembly of three thousand archers sumptuously apparelled, 942 having chains of gold around their necks, who assembled at Merchant Taylors' Hall and marched down Broad Street on September 17, 1583.

Along with enjoying membership in the socially prominent archers' club, Mulcaster welcomed the requests of London's intellectuals for his poetical efforts. While headmaster of two distinguished grammar schools, he frequently contributed Latin verses to the literary efforts of men at home and abroad. In 1577, for example, he composed a poem in the "Album Amicorum"[188] of Emanuel Van Meteren (alias Demetrio).[180] The poem expresses Mulcaster's friendship for Van Meteren, who, like Abraham Ortelius and Jan van der Does, had been an Antwerp geographer. What is more, the album itself reveals the names of that circle of friends in which Van Meteren moved. In addition to Mulcaster, they included such persons as Richard Thompson, the biblical scholar; Andrew Melville, the great Scottish theologian and poet; William

Camden, headmaster of Westminster; Abraham Ortelius, the Flemish geographer;[190] William Whitaker, the Calvinist theologian; and Alexander Dickson, a secret political agent.[191] Because of Spanish religious persecution, Van Meteren had left Antwerp and settled in London. Here, apparently, he lived the life of a merchant-scholar. Then on April 15, 1578, Van Meteren asked Mulcaster to act as godfather to his newborn son, Paul, in a christening service at the Dutch Church in London. Mulcaster returned the compliment by presenting the child with a silver-gilt spoon.[192] Moreover, Mulcaster wrote commendatory verses or prose in works by John Baret (1573, 1580), Thomas Tallis and William Byrd (1575), George Gascoigne (1576), Christopher Ocland (1582), Claude Desainliens (1583), Richard Robinson (1595),[193] and Richard Hakluyt (1598). The dedications and poems reflect Mulcaster's abiding interest in grammar, music, exploration, and Queen Elizabeth.[194]

Mulcaster enhanced his reputation as a poet and pageant-maker when the Earl of Leicester invited him in 1575 to participate in the Kenilworth celebrations for Queen Elizabeth. Leicester designed an eighteen-day festival as a formal welcome to the monarch and as a sign of his devotion. Among the other poets who contributed to the fete were the celebrated George Gascoigne,[195] Robert Laneham,[196] William Hunnis,[197] and George Ferrers.[198] Needless to say, the favor of Leicester's patronage enhanced their respective positions. Out of gratitude, Mulcaster may have been moved to dedicate his *Elementarie* to Leicester in 1582. In this dedication, Mulcaster refers to Leicester as "so good a patron," who has extended to him for "these manie years" a "speciall goodnesse, and the most fauorable countenance."[199]

Much of Mulcaster's prominence also depended on the quality of the families who sent their children to him, though few of Mulcaster's students who later earned reputations in literary circles came from prominent families. Certainly the most notable student was Edmund Spenser, one of his earliest charges. He also counted the dramatist Thomas Kyd, author of *The Spanish Tragedy,* and the poet-playwright Thomas Lodge, author of *Rosalynde,* among his distinguished students. From the first, Shakespeare adopted some of the devices for *Hamlet,* and from the second he developed the plot for *As You Like It.* Moreover, of the forty-seven translators of the King James Bible, six studied under Mulcaster: Lancelot Andrewes, successively Bishop of Chichester, Ely, and Winchester; Ralph Huchenson, President of St. John's, Oxford; John Peryn, Regius Professor of Greek at Oxford; John Spenser, chaplain to James I; Giles Thompson, Bishop of Gloucester; and Ralph Ravens, fellow of St. John's. Five of Mulcaster's students were consecrated bishops: in addition to Andrewes and Thompson there were John Buckeridge, Bishop of Rochester and Ely; Thomas Dove, Bishop of Peterborough; and Rowland Searchfield, Bishop of Bristol.

Perhaps some of Mulcaster's success as a teacher may be inferred from the fact that the learned Lancelot Andrewes, when Bishop of Winchester, showed such esteem for the first headmaster of Merchant Taylors' School that he hung Mulcaster's portrait above the door of his own study and later left an inheritance to his mentor's son, Peter.[200] Another eminent Merchant Taylors' alumnus, Nicholas Hill, wrote treatises supporting atomism. Two court physicians were also schoolboys at Merchant Taylors' during Mulcaster's mastership: Robert Jacob, physician to Queen Elizabeth, and Sir William Paddy, physician to James I. In addition, three Mulcaster boys distinguished themselves as scientists: Matthew Gwinne,[201] physician and first professor of physic at Gresham College; Thomas Heathe, astronomer and mathematician; and Thomas Hood, physician and mathematician. The statesman and colonizer Edwin Sandys was also educated under Mulcaster at Merchant Taylors' School. So was Sir James Whitelocke, who served as justice of the Common Pleas and King's Bench.

Under Mulcaster, the school of the Merchant Taylors became noted both for the size of its enrollment and the quality of its alumni. In comparison to the records of the Merchant Taylors' School, which preserve the identity of over six hundred of Mulcaster's students, those of St. Paul's, for nearly half as long a period, reveal the names of only about forty. The most distinguished of his students at St. Paul's was the actor-playwright, Nathan Field. While still a student at St. Paul's, Field was compelled by Nathaniel Giles, Henry Evans, and James Robinson (or their agents), under authority of the Queen's commission, to serve "in playes and interludes" as one of the children in the Chapel at Blackfriars.[202] From the complaint of Henry Clifton, father of one of the boys so impressed, we learn the identity of seven others. Third in this list is the name of "Nathan Field, a scholler of a gramer schole in London, kepte by one Mr. Monkaster."[203] Later on, Field played Humphrey in *The Knight of the Burning Pestle* (1607), in which there appear these lines: ". . . were you never none of Master Monkester's scholars?"[204]

In view of this evidence, it seems apparent that Mulcaster's boys were associated with the revival of the theater at St. Paul's. During the opening decade of the seventeenth century, the Children of Paul's participated in plays specially written for them by Thomas Middleton, Thomas Dekker, John Webster, John Marston, Francis Beaumont, and George Chapman. It was a fruitful period and serves as a tribute to Mulcaster's abiding interest in the English theater.

Toward the end of his tenure at St. Paul's School, Mulcaster leveled a parting shot at educational decadence in the seventeenth century. He wrote the following oration, which was presented by one of his boys during the entry pageant of James I in 1604. Mulcaster pleaded for the creation of a system of schools under royal supervision:

> Our Schooles of *England*, are in many lims deformed whose crookednesse require the hand of a King, to set them straight: least out of these young nests, those that are there bred, flying without their fethers into Vniuersities, shold afterward light vpon the branches of the common wealth, more naked, than at first, by reason they were not perfectly fledgd. Which euil hath bin discouered by the obseruation of our Teacher: who now by the space of more than 50.4. yeeres (both publiquelie and priuatelie) hath instructed youth, and with no little griefe of his own hath both here and abroad sifted out these grosse vices, that are mingled amongst Schooles. O how happy therfore should this our Nursery of learning be, if (after hauing first met with *Collet*, a fownder so religious, and secondly the Mercers our patrons men so faithfull, and vertuous,) our Lord the King would now at last also be pleased (considering many Kings of *England* by doing so haue won wonderfull loue from their subiects) to suffer his Royall name to be rolled amongest the Citizens of *London*, by vouchsafing to be free of that worthie, and chiefest Society of Mercers! What glorie should thereby rize vp to the City? what dignity to that Society? to this our Schoole what infinite benefite? what honour besides our Souereigne himselfe might acquire. . . .[205]

Mulcaster retained his mastership at St. Paul's until 1608, when, at the age of seventy-eight, he retired to the rectorship at Stanford Rivers. On the retirement of Mulcaster, Alexander Gill[206] was elected high master in obedience to a royal decree.[207] The Mercers, who managed the financial affairs of St. Paul's School, gave Mulcaster a generous pension of one hundred marks a year.[208] A request for a similar recompense from the Merchant Taylors' Company was rejected on the grounds that their school was not so well endowed as St. Paul's.[209] In his declining years, Mulcaster's financial difficulties appear to have increased,[210] for after his death, his son Peter petitioned the Merchant Taylors' Company for financial assistance in order to meet the demands of his father's creditors.

The remainder of Mulcaster's life, some three years, was spent as a country parson. Although he had succeeded Richard Vaughan[211] in the rectorship of Stanford Rivers on February 23, 1596,[212] Mulcaster held the benefice in absentia for nearly the whole period. He had been appointed to this office directly by the Queen.[213] At the visitation held by Archdeacon Samuel Harsnett of Essex[214] in 1606, the churchwardens described Mulcaster as follows: "Our parson is not resident, neither that give the X pt. of his benefice to our knowledge; the chancel was out of repair, both glass and stonework of the windows being broken, the walls filthie and fowle and the seatt thereabout it unboarded."[215] Because Mulcaster chose to devote nearly fifty years of his life to teaching, we may assume that neither his interests nor his talents were especially suited to the active ministry. Of his preaching, Thomas Fuller relates: ". . . I have heard from those who have heard him preach, that his sermons were not excellent, which to me seems no wonder; partly because there is a different discipline in teaching children and men; partly because such who make divinity not the choice of their youth, but the refuge of their age, seldom attain to eminency therein."[216]

Since no intimate letters or autobiographical details have survived, there are no indications whatever of Mulcaster's personal beliefs. All we know with certainty about his religious life is that he was sympathetic to the cause of the Marian exiles, that he accepted the Elizabethan settlement, and that he later received priestly orders from the Church of England. It is also worth noting that his life spans most of the religious controversy which plagued England in the last three quarters of the sixteenth century. In the generation before Mulcaster, men had grown to maturity in a relatively secure environment. Even nonconformists like Thomas More and John Fisher were able to face the religious debate with the spirit of tolerant humanism. In contrast, the generation after Mulcaster, that of Richard Hooker, recognized the durability of the religious split from Rome and acted to preserve it. To Mulcaster and his contemporaries, however, the religious issues were not so clearly defined, and the outcome was wholly uncertain. Hence, their religious stands were less firm. Mulcaster's personal convictions probably lay somewhere between the reforming spirit of Calvinism and the orthodoxy of Anglicanism.[217]

Mulcaster's years of retirement must have been a cruel disappointment to him. Ill-suited to pastoral work, he probably grew to resent the demands of his parishioners, which he found both humiliating and unrewarding. The loneliness of widowerhood[218] and the infirmities of old age combined to break the spirit of both teacher and scholar. Death, no doubt, came as a welcome relief to this octogenarian.

A life spent in the pursuit and diffusion of knowledge was ended on April 15, 1611. Richard Mulcaster was buried in the chancel of his church at Stanford Rivers on the twenty-sixth day of the same month. In that church, he had earlier placed a brass plate commemorating his wife's death:

> HERE LYETH BVRIED THE BODIE OF
> KATHARINE MVLCASTER, WIFE TO RICHARD
> MVLCASTER, BY ANCIENT PARENTAGE AND
> LINNIAL DISCENT, ANN ESQVIER BORNE:
> BY THE MOST FAMOVS QUEEN ELIZABETH'S
> PREROGATIVE GIFT, A PARSON OF THIS

CHVRCH: WITH WHOM SHE LIVED IN
MARRIAGE FIFTIE YEARE,[219] AND DYED
THE 6 DAY OF AVGVST, 1609. A GRAVE
WOMAN, A LOVEINGE WIFE, A
CAREFVL NVRSE, A GODLIE CREATVRE,
A SAINCT IN HEAVEN IN THE PRESENCE
OF HER GOD AND SAVIOR, WHOM SHE EVER
DAILIE AND DEARLIE SERVED.

The concluding years of this memorable Elizabethan schoolmaster were far from idyllic. Poverty successfully stalked its wounded prey. As Harry B. Wilson has remarked, "Above all it is to be lamented that one who had been so successful in imparting the treasures of learning to others, and thereby 'making many rich,' was suffered, and that without any imputation of vice or extravagance, to die in embarrassed circumstances. . . ."[220]

Those who wish to estimate the character and influence of Mulcaster will do best to study the whole range of his writings. In the letters and works that have survived, Mulcaster remains something of an enigma: a strange compound of stubbornness and perspicacity, of vanity and zeal, of commendable aspirations and unworthy actions. Furthermore, one can trace in the court and corporation records, which disclose his activities as headmaster, qualities of strength, scholarship, and devotion, and at the same time a considerable number of unfortunate actions and judgments.

On the basis of available sources, Mulcaster appears to have had a mind of extraordinary grasp, and he was clearly one of the most learned men of his age. In the art of teaching, he was both a supremely able administrator and a creative genius who could keep his eye fixed upon the lodestar. Not once, but twice, did he secure and advance the educational plans of great corporations. In both these undertakings, one observes the same thorough methods, the same fine grasp of detail. Perhaps the greatest testimony to his abilities as a teacher and administrator is the praise of his former students, who respected him because of his adherence to a high ideal of discipline and a clear conception of duty.

In English history, Mulcaster is of significance to us as the greatest of Elizabethan schoolmasters, among whom were such men as William Camden, Edmund Coote, and William Kempe. Recognized as a dominant personality in the England of his day, he directed the minds of his students to ideas of responsibility and service to England.

Such were some of Mulcaster's admirable qualities. He had others less suited to his office and his profession. Without question, he was personally ambitious.

He desired power and independence, not principally for some higher end but for themselves. Almost from the moment that he entered into administrative work, he placed himself in a compromising position from which no amount of sagacity or moderation could extricate him. Mulcaster's high-handed and selfish actions while headmaster were totally without justification. His persistent and often successful efforts to obtain benefices and his little less than outrageous schemes for improving his financial position are but two examples of several unfortunate involvements.

We are in one respect at a disadvantage in judging Mulcaster. While his figure meets us at every turn for over half a century and while evidences of his activities are numberless, no collection of his personal letters has been preserved, nor does any portrait exist. Such remnants are the best of all mirrors of a man's character, mind, and motives. Lacking these, we can but imperfectly judge him by his actions.

Disappointment, frustration, and waste can be detected throughout much of Mulcaster's life. Yet his influence, his achievements, his abilities, all combine to make him an extraordinary personality. More than a man of his age, Richard Mulcaster proved to be the archetype of the Elizabethan schoolmaster.

Notes:

1. For Mulcaster's views on the teaching profession, see my article "Richard Mulcaster and the Profession of Teaching in Sixteenth-Century England," in *JHI*, 35 (1974), 121–29.
2. King's College, Cambridge, Protocollum Book for 1500–1578, ff. 132–33. The Protocollum Book is of particular importance here because it establishes with a measure of certainty both the year and place of Mulcaster's birth. The document, dated August 14, 1548, reads in part: ". . . there were assembled together in person Richard Mulcaster sixteen years of age born in the city of Carlisle. . . ." Translated from the Latin.
3. The first name of Mulcaster's mother and those of a brother and sister are in the Public Record Office, Req. 2/239/81. See Rawlinson MS. B/429/118, ff. 116^{v}–17, Bodleian Library, Oxford, for the name of another brother, "George Mulcaster, of Charlwood, co. Surrey."
4. The pedigree for this family is incomplete, giving no dates and generally providing only the names of the eldest sons. See British Museum, Harleian MSS. 1561 (ff. 131^{v}, 132, 133^{v}), 1554 (f. 20), 1046 (ff. 41^{v}–42); Bodleian Library, Oxford, Rawlinson MS. B/429/118 (ff. 116^{v}–17); and William Berry, *Berry's Kentish Genealogies* (London: Sherwood, Gilbert & Piper, 1830), pp. 62–63. For a discussion of the family, see T. H. B. Graham, "The Family of de Mulcaster," *Transactions of the Cumberland & Westmorland Antiquarian & Archaeological Society*, NS 17 (1918), 110–24.
5. "Mulcaster [Pedigree]," *Harleian Society Publications*, 43 (1899), 130.

6. [Henry Ellis], "Biographical Anecdotes of Richard Mulcaster," *The Gentleman's Magazine*, 70 (May 1800), Part I, p. 419.
7. Richard S. Ferguson and W. Nanson, *Some Municipal Records of Carlisle* (Carlisle: C. Thurman & Sons, 1887), p. 86.
8. *Return of Members of Parliament* (London: House of Commons, 1878), Part I, p. 403.
9. This brass plate and inscription can be found in the Church at Stanford Rivers, Essex.
10. *The Eton College Register, 1441–1698*, ed. Wasey Sterry (Eton: Spottiswoode, Ballantyne, 1943), p. 241.
11. Ibid., pp. 177, 222, 346.
12. "Eton and Winchester in 1530," *Etoniana* (22 May 1907), pp. 131–36. Richard Cox (1500–81) served as headmaster of Eton College from 1528 to 1534. Later he became Archdeacon of Ely (1541–53), Dean of Christ Church, Chancellor of Oxford (1547–52) and Dean of Westminster in 1549. During the Marian exile, he lived in Frankfort, Strasbourg, and Worms. Following Elizabeth's coronation, he was appointed Bishop of Ely (1559–81).
13. "Except in the matter of certain religious observances and in the use of particular text-books, there was probably little change in the routine of the School between the years 1528 and 1560. . . ." See Henry C. Maxwell-Lyte, *A History of Eton College* (1440–1910), 4th ed. (London: Macmillan, 1911), p. 138.
14. Both the statutes of St. Paul's (founded in 1509) and Merchant Taylors' (founded in 1561) required students to be present for class six days a week from seven in the morning until five in the afternoon with a two-hour recess at noon. See J. Howard Brown, *Elizabethan Schooldays . . .* (Oxford: Basil Blackwell, 1933), pp. 89–92.
15. Sir Thomas Pope (ca. 1507–59) suggested that during the second and third decades of the sixteenth century, Greek was actively studied at Eton, but by 1556 it was "much decaied." See Martin L. Clarke, *Classical Education in Britain: 1500–1900* (Cambridge: Cambridge Univ. Press, 1959), pp. 17–18. Later, Greek was added to the curriculum. According to William Malim's "Consuetudinarium Etonense" of 1560 (Christ College, Cambridge, MS. 118, ff. 477–89), Greek grammar was studied in the sixth and seventh forms. Nevertheless it is clear from Malim's account of the work done at Eton around 1560 that Latin was treated almost as though it was the only object of study.
16. For examples, see App. E of my "Richard Mulcaster: An Elizabethan Savant," Diss. Michigan 1970.
17. Malim, "Consuetudinarium Etonense" of 1560, f. 483. Translated from the Latin.
18. Protocollum Book, King's College, Cambridge, f. 132.
19. Ibid., f. 133.
20. John Cheke (1514–57), both scholar and statesman, had served as tutor to Prince Edward. Elected provost of King's College in 1548, he held that office until 1553. As a vocal Protestant, Cheke lived in Basle, Padua, and Strasbourg during the years of Mary's reign; but before his death, he returned to England, was imprisoned in the Tower, and was forced to recant.

21. *Positions vvherin those primitive circvmstances be examined, which are necessarie for the training vp of children, either for skill in their booke, or health in their bodie* (London, 1581), pp. 243–244.
22. William Buckley was the author of *Arithmetica memorativa, sive brevis, et compendiaria arithmeticae tractatio . . .* (London, 1567).
23. *Positions*, p. 243.
24. Sterry, *Eton College Register, 1441–1698*, p. 241.
25. *Alumni Cantabrigienses*, ed. John Venn and J. A. Venn (Cambridge: Cambridge Univ. Press, 1924), III, Pt. 1, p. 276. From a sixteenth-century record of the University, we learn something of Mulcaster's years at Cambridge. The *Grace Book* (*containing the records of the University of Cambridge for the years 1542–89*, ed. John Venn [Cambridge: Cambridge Univ. Press, 1910], p. 93), for 1553–54 states that while at Cambridge, Mulcaster "studied for twelve terms [i.e., from 1550 to 1554], during which he attended lectures called ordinary and was permitted, not entirely according to the form of the statutes, to participate in the required debates which were sufficient for him to complete his work for the B.A. degree, whereupon he was examined and aproved by the procurators and examiners during the present academic year." Translated from the Latin.
26. See James Heywood, ed., *Collection of Statutes for the University and the Colleges of Cambridge* (London: William Clowes & Sons, 1840).
27. John Caius (1510–73), Greek scholar and court physician, was awarded an M.A. from Gonville College, Cambridge (1535), and an M.D. from the University of Padua (1541). Beginning in 1547, Caius practiced medicine in London, where he was for several years president of the College of Physicians.
28. John Aikin, *Biographical Memoirs of Medicine in Great Britain* (London: Joseph Johnson, 1780), pp. 103–4.
29. John Venn, *John Caius* (Cambridge: Cambridge Univ. Press, 1910), pp. 50–51.
30. London, 1574.
31. Under the date of December 4, 1555, the Register of the Privy Council reports that by order of the Privy Council, Sir Henry Bedingfield, Lieutenant of the Tower, was directed to "receive the bodie of Richard Mulcaster, servant to Doctor Caius, vehemently suspecte for robbing his master, and by the best means he can to examyne him hereof and to bring hym to the racke and put him in feare of the torture if he will not confesse." See Public Record Office, Register of the Privy Council, P.C. 2/7, f. 326. An inaccurate transcript of this entry was printed in the *Acts of the Privy Council of England*, ed. John R. Dasent (London: Eyre & Spottiswoode, 1892), NS, V (1554–56), 198. In this transcription, the name of "Caius" is spelled "Canis."

    Although it may be argued, Mulcaster's guilt in this incident cannot be established. Certainly there is no evidence to indicate that Dr. Caius' accusation was later proven or that Mulcaster admitted his guilt. What is historically important here, however, is not Mulcaster's guilt or innocence but the fact that this official entry connects Mulcaster with Dr. Caius. See David Jardine, *A Reading on the Use of Torture in the Criminal Law of England* (London: Baldwin & Bradock, 1837), pp. 18–19.

32. *Register of the University of Oxford*, ed. Charles W. Boase (Oxford: Oxford Historical Society, 1885), I, 232.
33. See Anthony Wood, *Athenae Oxonienses*, ed. Philip Bliss (London: F.C. & J. Rivington, 1813–20), II, cc. 93–95, and Henry Ellis (op. cit., note 6), pp. 420, 512.
34. See Ellis, p. 512.
35. Public Record Office, Exchequer Originalia Roll, E/371/402, f. 1. In part it reads: "[Carlisle] [Edward?] Egleanbye, gen. Richard Mulcaster, gen." Since the order of constituency has a set pattern in earlier and later scrolls, it was possible for Alan M. Mimardière to identify the mutilated sections of this roll. It is to be noted that Mulcaster ranked second in the constituency to a man named [Edward?] Egleanbye, gen. Serving in the same Parliament was Richard Hilles, the moving spirit behind the founding of Merchant Taylors' School in 1561.
36. That Mulcaster was engaged as a schoolmaster in London by 1559 is established by a passage from his *Positions* (p. 2) in which he speaks of having been employed as a teacher for twenty-two years. He wrote, "I have taught in publike without interrupting my course, now two and twentie yeares. . . ."
37. John A. Kingdon, *Richard Grafton . . .* (London: Rixon & Arnold, 1901), p. 105.
38. The major difference between the two editions is to be found in the wording of the title. See *The Quenes Maiesties Passage Through the Citie of London to Westminster the Day before her Coronacion*, ed. James M. Osborn (New Haven: Yale Univ. Press, 1960), pp. 17–22. A second edition of this pageant, published in 1604, is to be found in the British Museum. It is titled *The Royall Passage of her Maiesty from the Tower of London, to her Palace of White-hall, with all the Speeches and Deuices, both of the Pageants and otherwise, together with her Maiesties seuerall Answers, and most pleasing Speaches to them all.* Another issue differs from the above only in the imprint, "London: S.S. for Ione Millington," instead of "London: S.S. for John Busby."
39. Although this work was published anonymously, Mulcaster's authorship of the précis of the 1559 pageant was established by Charles R. Baskervill in a letter he wrote to *The Times Literary Supplement* (15 August, 1935, p. 513). The document which supports his view was found in the Corporation Record Office, Guildhall, Repertory Book XIV, f. 143. Dated April 4, 1559, the town clerk recorded the following: "Item yt was orderyd and agreyd by the Court here this day that the Chamberlyn shall geue vnto Rychard Mulcaster for his reward for makyng of the boke conteynynge and declaryng the historyes set furth in and by the Cyties pageauntes at the tyme of the Quenes highnes commyng thurrough the Cytye to her coronacion xls. which boke was geuyn vnto the Quenes grace." Roy C. Strong has mistakenly assumed that he was the first to discover Mulcaster's authorship. See Strong's "Elizabethan Pageantry As Propaganda," Diss. Univ. of London 1962, p. 12. Despite these identifications of authorship, John M. Osborn edited the summary of the 1559 pageant in 1960 without knowing that Mulcaster wrote it.
40. *The Quenes Maiesties Passage*, p. 15. Although Mulcaster was not a Marian exile, it must be pointed out that much of the responsibility for devising the pageant went to Richard Hilles, a prominent Marian exile, and Richard Grafton,

the printer of the English Bible. For Mulcaster's contribution to pageantry, see my article, "Richard Mulcaster and Elizabethan Pageantry," *SEL*, 14 (1974).

41. *The Parish Registers of St. Michael, Cornhill, London, Containing the Marriages, Baptisms, and Burials from 1546 to 1754*, ed. Joseph Chester (London: Mitchell & Hughes, 1882), p. 8. The manuscript entry in the Guildhall Library (MS. 4061) reads: "The xiiith daye [May 1560] weave marryed Rycharde Monckestre & Katheryne Asheleye." That this marriage bond proved to be financially rewarding later on can be determined from the following documents. According to the Hustings Deeds in the Corporation of London Record Office, Mulcaster inherited property, located in the parish of St. Michael, Cornhill, from his wife's father. Between 1566 and 1599, this property was deeded by Mulcaster to various owners in five separate transactions.
42. Corporation of London Record Office, Hustings Deeds, Roll 255 (91) [9 Eliz. 1567]. The entry reads in part: "Richard Mulcaster, gent. and Katherine his wife, dau. of William Asheley alias Astley late grocer."
43. Guildhall Library, MS. 7670.
44. Perhaps in honor of young Sylvan and Katherine, Edmund Spenser selected their names for his own two children.
45. For a genealogy of Mulcaster's children, see App. A-1 of my dissertation.
46. Minutes of Court, 19 April 1564, and 29 December 1566, in the Muniment Room, Merchant Taylors' Hall, London.
47. Minutes of Court, 24 September 1561.
48. The exact site of the school was on Suffolk Lane, which leads from Lower Thames Street to Cannon Street. Nothing now remains to mark the spot except a tablet placed there by the City Corporation of London.
49. Harry B. Wilson, *The History of Merchant-Taylors' School* (London: Marchant & Galabin, 1812), I, 2.
50. Richard Hilles (ca. 1514–88) was a prominent member of the Henrician reform group. While an apprentice tailor, he addressed a treatise "against justification by works" to Thomas Cromwell, which resulted in his seeking exile. In 1535, Hilles made peace with the government, but the passage of the Six Articles forced him into a second exile at Strasbourg. Beginning in 1539, he corresponded intermittently with Henry Bullinger. See Charles M. Clode, *The Early History of the Guild of Merchant Taylors* (London: Harrison & Sons, 1888), pp. 58–64, 68–87, 139–49, and 150–72. His correspondence with Bullinger is printed in *The Zurich Letters* [1558–79], ed. Hastings Robinson for the Parker Society (Cambridge: Cambridge Univ. Press, 1842), Vol. L.
51. Marshall M. Knappen, *Tudor Puritanism* (Chicago: Univ. of Chicago Press, 1939), p. 58.
52. Statute XXV. Minutes of Court, 24 September 1561. At the same time, St. Paul's statutes limited the number of its students to 153.
53. Minutes of Court, 24 September 1561. The wording of these statutes is taken almost verbatim from John Colet's statutes for St. Paul's School. See Joseph H. Lupton, *A Life of John Colet* (London: George Bell & Sons, 1887), App. A, pp. 271–84.

54. Charles J. Robinson, *A Register of the Scholars . . . Merchant Taylors' School . . . 1562 to 1874 . . .* (Lewes: Farncombe, 1882), I, xii.
55. Ellis, p. 603. For a discussion of Mulcaster's contributions to the theater, see my "Richard Mulcaster and the Elizabethan Theatre," *Theatre Survey*, 13 (May 1972), 28–41.
56. Statute XLII. Minutes of Court, 24 September 1561. The formula of acceptance for the students read as follows: "Sir, this shalbe to signify unto you that wee have admytted (N) the sonne of (M) the bearer hereof, to be of the number of those hundreth of the poore men's children, which should be taught freely in the said schoole, upon condition that the said (N), within one moneth next ensuing, shalbe by you thought apt & meete to learne, &, being found not apt & meete to learne, as aforesaid, that then this our admyssion of him to stand as void. . . ."
57. The major responsibility of the assistants was to give religious instruction (Statute XX).
58. Minutes of Court, 24 September 1561. Mulcaster's appointment in 1561 to the headmastership at Merchant Taylors' School almost certainly meant that he had some previous teaching experience, but where he taught is unknown.
59. Thomas Fuller, *The Worthies of England*, ed. John Freeman (London: George Allen & Unwin, 1952), p. 600.
60. Ellis, p. 419.
61. Frederick W. M. Draper, *Four Centuries of Merchant Taylors' School, 1561–1961* (London: Oxford Univ. Press, 1962), p. 10. In addition, Mulcaster may have been apprehensive about Statute II, which made a headmaster liable to dismissal on "reasonable" notice but required him to give twelve months' notice of his own intention to resign.
62. Even with the £10 increment, Mulcaster's salary was less than two-thirds that of the high master of St. Paul's. See Michael McDonnell, *A History of St. Paul's School* (London: Chapman & Hall, 1909), p. 145. The high master of St. Paul's received £34 13s. 4d. per year, together with gown, quarters at the school, and a country house at Stepney. At the same time, the headmaster of Westminster received the equivalent of £27 11s. 8d. a year. See Draper, p. 10. Moreover, it seems certain that Hilles personally paid Mulcaster his £10 increment from 1561 to 1575, for the payment, if made by the common clerk, was never entered in the accounts against the company. This view of the transaction, however, was ignored by Mulcaster, who, after the death of Hilles in 1587, presented a claim to the company for continued payment of this compensation (Minutes of Court, 13 February 1588). From the will of Hilles, made 20 August 1587, it appears that he had some years before been obliged to create a trust fund for the benefit of his son, Gerson. This fund, no doubt, accounts for the withdrawal of Mulcaster's subsidy in 1575 (Wilson, I, 93).
63. In this connection, it is significant that Sir Thomas Offley, a former Pauline, was a member of the court of the Merchant Taylors' Company in the year in which they founded their school. On the bases of statutes XXV and XXVIII, Arthur Freeman (*Thomas Kyd: Facts and Problems* [Oxford: Clarendon Press, 1967], p. 7) has incorrectly concluded that the school of the Merchant Taylors'

"was considerably less conservative than St. Paul's or Eton" and that the Merchant Taylors' statutes of 1561 are "notably liberal in temper and letter." In point of fact, the very two statutes which Freeman cites to indicate a notably liberal temper at Merchant Taylors' School can also be found, word for word, in the statutes of St. Paul's (see Lupton, pp. 277, 278). Merchant Taylors' School may indeed have been less conservative than St. Paul's, but its statutes cannot be used to substantiate such an opinion.

64. "Statutes of St. Paul's School," in Lupton, p. 272.
65. "Statutes of Merchant Taylors' School," in Draper, p. 241.
66. Lupton, p. 277.
67. Draper, p. 246.
68. Lupton, p. 277.
69. Draper, p. 246.
70. After 1561, the chapel does not appear to have been used for any distinctly religious purposes. The statutes did provide, however, that "The children . . . thrice in the day, kneeling on their knees, shall say the prayers appointed with due tract and pawsing, as they be, or shalbe hereafter conteyned on a table sett up in the schoole . . ." (Minutes of Court, 24 September 1561). This pious exercise undoubtedly took place in the classroom.
71. Minutes of Court, 16 August 1562.
72. Ibid.
73. Minutes of Court, 27 April 1573.
74. Draper, p. 14.
75. Clode, *Memorials of the Guild of Merchant Taylors* (London: Harrison & Sons, 1875), p. 443.
76. *The first part of the Elementarie vvhich entreateth chefelie of the right writing of our English tung* (London, 1582), p. 233. It seems clear from this quotation that Mulcaster had begun to incorporate some of his educational ideas into actual practice.
77. The minutes read: "Fyrste at this daye, it is agreed by the master, wardens, and surveyors, of there late erected schole, founded within the parysshe of St. Lawrens Pountney, of London, That Mr. Richarde Mulcaster, scholemaister there, shall not in enywyse upon payne of dysmyssing of and avoydynge of hym oute and frome the room and place of scholemaistershippe of the sayde schole, take or resceive any scholler or schollers to be taughte within the sayde schole, or in any other place or rooms annexed to the sayde schole, after the 25th daye of March now nexte ensuynge, But onely such scholler or schollers as shalbe firste admytted to be taughte within the saide schole, by the master and wardens of this misterye for the tyme beynge . . . And, also, it is further agreed, by the saide master, wardens, and surveyors, aforesaid; that where he, the sayde Mr. Mulcaster hathe at this present daye resceived and taken into the sayde schole a nombre of schollers over and above the nombre that is there lymitted and apointed to be taughte within the sayde schole, which were now admytted by the saide master and wardens, that he, the sayde Mr. Mulcaster, shall, before the Feast of thannunciation of our lady now nexte comynge, clerely dyssmyse and dyscharge oute and from the sayde schole, all suche scholler and

schollers as be there now above the sayde nombre that is lymitted to be taught within the sayde schole, and were not admytted by the sayde master and wardens on payne of his dyssmyssing oute and from the sayde roome of scholemaistershippe of the said schole, if hee shall doo contrary to the true intente, effecte, and meanynge hereof." Minutes of Court, 15 January 1569.

78. Mulcaster's pupils who went to St. John's College were so numerous that contemporary writers referred to that institution as having been "filled with plants" from his school. See Wood, I, 94.
79. Minutes of Court, 10 June 1572.
80. Ibid.
81. Minutes of Court, 8 June 1573.
82. Minutes of Court, 26 November 1574.
83. Minutes of Court, 12 December 1575.
84. Guildhall Library, Churchwardens Accounts, 1530–1681, St. Laurence Pountney, MS. 3907/1.
85. Minutes of Court, 11 June 1576.
86. Minutes of Court, 29 April 1579.
87. Minutes of Court, 28 June 1586.
88. Fuller, p. 600.
89. *Positions* appeared at the outset in two issues with typographical variants. One issue has the imprint "Imprinted at London by Thomas Vautrollier dvvelling in the blacke Friers by Ludgate 1581." The other has "Imprinted at London by Thomas Vautrollier for Thomas Chare. 1581." Ames and Herbert reported that there also existed a 1587 edition. No copy of this edition has survived. See Joseph Ames and William Herbert, *Typographical Antiquities* (London, 1786), II, 1073. Furthermore, Lowndes and Bohn noted the existence of a 1591 edition. Like the 1587 edition, however, this edition is apparently no longer extant. See William T. Lowndes and Henry G. Bohn, eds., *The Bibliographer's Manual of English Literature* (London: Bell & Daldy, 1869), III, 1628. There is incorrect pagination in some copies of the *Positions* bearing the imprint "Thomas Vautrollier dvvelling in the blacke Friers by Ludgate"; e.g., p. 301 is followed by p. 303. In his dedication to Queen Elizabeth, Mulcaster stated that his *Positions* was "my first trauell, that ever durst venture vpon the print." He seems to have erred here, however, since the précis of the entry pageant for Elizabeth I, referred to above, appeared in 1559. But Mulcaster may have refrained from claiming complete authorship of the précis because the pageant itself was the joint effort of four other men. There is also incorrect pagination in the *Elementarie*; e.g., in some copies, p. 98 is followed by p. 95; p. 129 by 128; p. 134 by p. 133; p. 136 by p. 136; p. 167 by p. 169; p. 176 by p. 176; p. 178 by p. 180; p. 201 by p. 102; p. 203 by p. 123; p. 215 by p. 219; p. 235 by p. 246; and p. 253 by p. 253.
90. Mulcaster to Ortelius, 24 April 1581. See John H. Hessels, ed., *Ecclesiae Londino-Batavae Archivum. Tomus Primus. Abrahami Ortelii . . . Epistulae . . .* (Cambridge, 1887), I, pp. 249–252. For an examination of the contents of the *Positions*, see my introductory essay in *Richard Mulcaster's "Positions"* (New York: Teachers College Press, 1971).

91. For a discussion of "Mulcaster's Philosophy of Education," see my article in the *Journal of Medieval and Renaissance Studies*, 2 (Spring 1972), 69–91.
92. For a fuller account of his life, see William R. LeFanu, "Thomas Vautrollier, Printer and Bookseller," *Proceedings of the Huguenot Society of London*, 20 (1959), 12–25.
93. See Whitebrook, *Calvin's Institute of Christian Religion in the Imprints of Thomas Vautrollier* (London, 1935), p. 10 (reprinted from the *Transactions of the Congregational Historical Society*). Alexander Dickson (1558–1604) was a supporter of Mary, Queen of Scots. For a biographical sketch, see John Durkan, "Alexander Dickson and S.T.C. 6823," *The Bibliotheck* (Glasgow University Library), 3 (1962), 183–90. Giordano Bruno (1548–1600) was an Italian priest who expressed pantheistic ideas; convicted of heresy, he was burned at the stake.
94. By saying "rip vp the hole certaintie of our English writing," Mulcaster is offering a challenge to the current opinions on English orthography.
95. By the phrase "naturall English" Mulcaster is referring to native speakers, contrasting them, later on in the passage, with foreign speakers.
96. *Elementarie*, p. 53.
97. Ibid., p. 75.
98. E. J. Dobson, *Early English Pronunciation, 1500–1700* (Oxford: Clarendon Press, 1957), I, 122.
99. *Elementarie*, p. 79.
100. Ibid., p. 90.
101. Ibid., p. 161.
102. Ibid., p. 268.
103. Ibid.
104. Ibid., p. 159. See p. 75.
105. Ibid., p. 254.
106. Ibid., pp. 253–54.
107. Ibid., p. 255.
108. Edward R. Adair has suggested in a chapter on "William Thomas" in *Tudor Studies . . . to Albert F. Pollard . . .*, ed. R. W. Seton-Watson (London: Longmans, Green, 1924), p. 158, that the credit for being the first to advocate the teaching of English in grammar schools belongs to William Thomas. The basis of Adair's argument is the existence of an unpublished diary (Egerton MS. 837 in the British Museum, dated ca. 1551) in which Thomas states, "But if the maister wolde first teache his scholer tundrestande well his owne tonge . . ." (p. 159). Probably Thomas' unpublished diary had very little effect on the teaching of English in the schools. Mulcaster's *Elementarie*, on the other hand, is the earliest textbook on the teaching of English at the elementary level. It is emphatically a teacher's book of method for the teaching of the vernacular. The author's consciousness of the possibilities of the English language, a few years before the appearance of the major works of Spenser and Shakespeare, makes the book unique.
109. In evaluating Mulcaster's contribution to orthography, E. J. Dobson (*Early English Pronunciation, 1500–1700*, I, 122) concludes: "He appears not to realize that the letters were originally sufficient to express the sounds of the language

for which they were devised (Latin), and that it is because the reformers wish to use them consistently and as nearly as possible in the original way that it is necessary to invent new letters for sounds which did not exist in Latin. He has not the scientific conception of the development of pronunciation and spelling which Hart and Smith had." Nevertheless, one is tempted to conclude with C. S. Lewis (*English Literature in the Sixteenth Century Excluding Drama* [Oxford: Clarendon Press, 1954], p. 348) that, after reading the *Elementarie,* "we become aware that we are dealing with a learned, an original, and almost a great mind."

110. W. L. Renwick, "Mulcaster and Du Bellay," *MLR,* 17 (July 1922), p. 287.
111. *Elementarie,* p. 80.
112. See Renwick.
113. Robert Withington, *English Pageantry: An Historical Outline* (Cambridge, Mass.: Harvard Univ. Press, 1918), I, 197.
114. Ian Dunlop, *Palaces & Progresses of Elizabeth I* (London: Jonathan Cape, 1962), pp. 115–16.
115. David Daiches, *A Critical History of English Literature* (New York: Ronald Press, 1960), I, 165.
116. Muriel C. Bradbrook, "St. George for Spelling Reform . . . ," *SQ,* 15 (Summer 1964), 130.
117. *Elementarie,* p. 230.
118. See p. 42.
119. *Elementarie,* p. 230.
120. Merchant Taylors' MS., Minutes of Court, 16 March 1573.
121. James Whitelocke, *Liber Famelicus,* ed. John Bruce (London: Camden Society, 1858), LXX, 12.
122. Frank W. Wilson, *The English Drama: 1485–1585,* ed. G. K. Hunter (London: Oxford Univ. Press, 1969), p. 151.
123. Alfred Harbage, "*Love's Labor's Lost* and the Early Shakespeare," in *Stratford Papers on Shakespeare,* ed. B. W. Jackson (Toronto: W. J. Gage, 1962), pp. 119–20.
124. Ibid., p. 125.
125. Robert H. Quick (ed., *Positions* . . . [London: Longmans, Green, 1888], p. 304) does not share this conclusion: "Mulcaster no doubt had had a great share in keeping the playing of boy actors in fashion; but he probably had nothing to do with 'the children of Powles' whose acting was stopped by edict from about 1589 to 1600, and then started again with increased popularity. . . ." It is a complicated question as to who is meant by the 'children of Paul's" in the frequent accounts of interludes, plays, etc., during the reigns of Henry VIII and his successors down to the time of James I. There is evidence to indicate that on occasion reference is being made to John Colet's school and at other times to the cathedral choir school. See John Payne Collier, *The History of English Dramatic Poetry to the Time of Shakespeare* . . . (London: J. Murray, 1831), I, 34, 159, 172–73, 190, 281.
126. Pierce accepted the mastership of the choir school at St. Paul's around August 15, 1600. See Edmund K. Chambers, *The Elizabethan Stage* (Oxford: Clarendon

Press, 1923), II, 19. Harold N. Hillebrand (*The Child Actors* . . . [Urbana: Univ. of Illinois Press, 1926], p. 138), on the other hand, suggests 1601 as the year in which Pierce became choirmaster. In addition, Chambers has suggested that several plays produced by the Paulines antedated Pierce's mastership at the school," and one of them, Marston's *I Antonio and Mellida*, can hardly be later than 1599" (II, 19).

127. Edward Arber, *A Transcript of the Registers of the Company of Stationers: 1544–1640* (London: E. Arber, 1877), III, 172–76.
128. Public Record Office, Court of Star Chamber Proceedings, C 46/30 ("Clifton vs. Robinson et al.").
129. William Perry, *The Plays of Nathan Field* (Austin: Univ. of Texas Press, 1950), p. 4.
130. Minutes of Court, 8 November 1586.
131. Wilson, p. 75.
132. It was Theodor Klähr's conclusion (*Leben und Werke Richard Mulcaster's* [Dresden: Bleyl & Kaemmerer, 1893], p. 29) that Mulcaster was "ohne Amt" from 1586 to 1596. John Stow (*A Survey of the Cities of London and Westminister* . . . , ed. John Strype [London, 1726], p. 168) suggests that Mulcaster remained at Merchant Taylors' until 1596. On the other hand, Howard Staunton (*The Great Schools of England* . . . , new ed. [London: S. Low, Son, & Marston, 1869], p. 176) reports that Mulcaster was appointed headmaster of St. Paul's as early as 1586, and Wilson (p. 77) says that Mulcaster was "Surmaster of St. Paul's" in 1586.
133. Johan van der Does (alias Janus Dousa) was a Dutch patriot and scholar who corresponded with many of his contemporaries.
134. "Ode V: Celebratio Natalis Regii," in Janus Dousa, *A Noortvvick odarvum Britannicarvm Liber* . . . (Lvgdvni Batavorum, Ex Officina Plantiniana, 1586), p. 26. Trans. from the Latin.
135. Minutes of Court, 13 February 1588.
136. In his *Positions* (1581), Mulcaster had expressed dissatisfaction for schools located in the city. He preferred a country environment "both for mine owne, and for my scholers health (p. 232). Having finally set out to print his own ideas on education, Mulcaster was unquestionably anxious to win approval for them. No doubt, he also faced considerable opposition from the Merchant Taylors' Company, who were ultimately responsible for the curriculum and the direction of the school. Thwarted by negative reaction, Mulcaster decided to establish a school of his own—one which would provide both elementary and grammar school instruction. See *Elementarie*, p. 233.
137. As recorded in the *Acts of the Privy Council of England* (NS XVII [1588–89], 258), the names of the creditors were Henrie Parris, Augustyne Grafina, John Dyver, and Anthonie Sewell.
138. Ibid.
139. British Museum, Harleian MS. 6996, ff. 33, 35.
140. Public Record Office, Chancery Proceedings, C3/227/48 (16–24 October 1590).
141. Ibid., answer of Thomas Tyrrell, 24 October 1590. Elias Newcomen, in applying for the position of headmaster at Merchant Taylors' in 1586, revealed the fact that Mulcaster "obtayned some better preferment" upon leaving Merchant

Taylors' School. "Soe it is, righte worshipfull, that when I was advertysed by my frends that Mr. Mulcaster woulde geave over his place, havinge obtayned some better preferment, it pleased God, after long deliberacon with myself and some conference with my frends, to make me your worships' humble sewtor for the roome." See Minutes of Court, 13 February 1588.

142. Public Record Office, Court of Requests, Req. 2/149/53.
143. Ibid.
144. Ibid. Valued at £16. It can be determined from this passage that Mulcaster conducted a private boarding school at this time.
145. Ibid. Tyrrell's widow and son brought suit against Mulcaster at Common Law on 31 January 1602.
146. *Acts of the Privy Council of England,* NS, XXIV (1592–1593), 56. George and Edward were two of the sons of Henry and Eleanor Jerningham (or Jernegan). The grandfather of these boys was an ardent supporter of Queen Mary. For his labors on her behalf, he was appointed to the Privy Council and remained in high favor throughout her reign. On Elizabeth's accession, however, he was deprived of his seat on the Privy Council, and his name no longer appeared in state affairs. See Thomas Wotton, *The Baronetage of England . . . ,* ed. Edward Kimber and R. Johnson (London: G. Woodfall, 1771), I, 215–19.
147. Ibid., pp. 472–73. "At the Court at Windzour Castle, the 19th of August, 1593."
148. Although records of his two benefices exist, there is no evidence to indicate when Mulcaster was ordained.
149. Ibid. Whitgift received his B.A. from Peterhouse in the same year as Mulcaster.
150. Charles H. and Thompson Cooper, *Athenae Cantabrigienses* (Cambridge: Bowes & Bowes, 1913), III (1609–11), 41.
151. Bodleian Library, Willis MS. 61, f. 90ᵛ. Anthony Wood (*Athenae Oxonienses,* II, c. 93) states that in 1596 Mulcaster "succeeded one Joh. Harrison in the chief mastership of St. Paul's school in London (being then prebendary of Yatesbury in the Church of Sarum). . . ." How long he retained this benefice is unknown. He was, very probably, requested to resign this living before beginning his duties as high master. The statutes of St. Paul's School required the high master to be "A man hoole in body honest and vertuouse and . . . that hath no benefice with cure nor seruyce that may lett his due besynes in the Scole." See Lupton, p. 272.
152. British Museum, Harleian MS. 6996, f. 33.
153. Ibid., f. 35.
154. *The Records of the Honorable Society of Lincoln's Inn,* The Black Book, II (1586–1600), 38. "Account of Thomas Spencer, Treasurer from November 25, 1593 to November 29, 1594."
155. This Richard Robinson, who generally styled himself "citizen of London," is not to be confused with the poet Richard Robinson of Alton, who is best known for "The Reward of Wickednesse" (1574) and "A Golden Mirrour" (1589). For "citizen" Robinson, see George M. Vogt, "Richard Robinson's *Eupolemia* (1603)," *SP,* 21 (1924), 629–48.
156. British Museum, Additional MSS. 24, 491, ff. 159–60.
157. Harrison, having the support of the Dean of St. Paul's, steadfastly refused to resign, even under threat of legal suit. See Mercer's Company MS, Acts of

Court, 1513–1622, f. 223. While the dispute between the Mercers and Harrison raged, the latter was able to retain possession of the school buildings and to withstand eviction from the residence of the high master. Nevertheless, the Mercers prevented him from instructing the boys by sending them to Mulcaster. See McDonnell, p. 143. The company recovered its school property in February of 1597 as the result of legal action. See Acts of Court, 1513–1622, f. 266.

158. Mercers' Company MS., Accounts of St. Paul's School:

Paid to Christopher Johnson for his pains in teaching under Mr. Mulcaster, till Lady Day in Lent last . . .

Paid to John Bevane for reward for teaching the scholers of Poules one quarter, under Mr. Moncaster in Mylk Street . . .

To Mr. Mansfield, late Mr. Moncaster's ussher.

159. The statute reads: "Yf the Maister be syk of sekenes incurable, or fall into suche age that he may not conveniently teche, and hathe beene a man that long and laudably hath taught in the scole . . . lett ther be assigned to the olde maister a reasonable levyng of x^{li} or other Wyse as it shall seme convenient. . . . Yf the Maister be syk of sekeness curable, yett neuerthelesse I will he shall haue his wages. . . ." See the Statutes of St. Paul's School, in Lupton, p. 273.

160. Acts of Court, 1513–1622, f. 263.

161. Acts of Court, 1513–1622, f. 261[v].

162. McDonnell, p. 148.

163. David Masson, *The Life of John Milton . . .*, 3rd ed. (New York: Peter Smith, 1946), I (1608–39), 77. This Latin injunction was inscribed on the window panes of St. Paul's School.

164. Acts of Court, 1513–1622, ff. 270, 275, 279, 282[v].

165. Acts of Court, 1513–1622, f. 271[v].

166. Acts of Court, 1513–1622, ff. 284, 287 and Acts of Court, 1595–1629, ff. 202–6[v]. For a discussion of Mulcaster's high mastership, see Michael F. J. McDonnell, *The Annals of St. Paul's School* (Cambridge: Printed for the Governors, 1959), pp. 164–82.

167. *Catechismvs Pavlinvs, In vsum Scholae Paulinae conscriptus, ad formam parui illius Anglici Catechismi qui pueris in communi precum Anglicarum libro edijcendus proponitur* (London: Iohannes Windet, 1599). A second edition was published in 1601. A copy of it is to be found in the Bodleian Library, Oxford University. Apparently no copy of the 1599 edition has survived, but evidence of its former existence is established by the date of the preface in the 1601 edition. See p. [A5[v]]. The preface is dated "Nouemb. 17. An. 1599." The 1599 edition has also been recorded by Lowndes and Hazlitt (see note 176, below). The Pauline Catechism sheds some light on its author's religious and pedagogical ideas. The work was intended for use in St. Paul's School in conformity with the *Book of Common Prayer*. Written in Latin verse form to aid the student's memory, Mulcaster's catechism sought to combine good grammar with stimulating format. Although the primary purpose of most catechisms is to make the reader better acquainted with the principles of the Christian faith, Mulcaster devoted practically the whole of his preface to a discussion of the teaching of Latin grammar. The body of the catechism is divided into five

parts: discussions of the baptismal vows, the Creed, the Ten Commandments, the Lord's Prayer, and the two sacraments. The text is in the form of a dialogue: "Quaerens . . . Respondens."

168. Ibid., p. [A5v].

169. Orbilius Pupillus was a Roman grammarian and schoolmaster who was given the epithet *plagosus* by Horace because of the flogging received by his pupils, the poet being one of them.

170. Fuller, p. 600. Cornelie Benndorf, *Die Englische Pädagogik im 16. Jahrhundert* (Wien: Wilhelm Braumüller, 1905), p. 34, and Klähr (p. 22) are of the opinion that Fuller was describing that method of teaching which Mulcaster employed at Merchant Taylors' School. The account by Fuller, however, appears to describe an older man—one who "slept his hour (custom made him critical to proportion it) in his desk in the school. . . ." Mulcaster, who served Merchant Taylors' from about the age of thirty to the age of fifty-five, was appointed to the high mastership of St. Paul's at the age of sixty-five, retiring twelve years later. As Draper observed, "A man of sixty-six may well have slept his hour at his desk. One of thirty certainly did not" (p. 22).

171. *Positions*, p. 283.

172. Ibid., p. 282.

173. Ibid., p. 284.

174. Ansel M. Stowe, *English Grammar Schools in the Reign of Queen Elizabeth* (New York: Teachers College, Columbia University, 1908), p. 141.

175. Frederick Seebohm, *The Era of the Protestant Revolution* (London: Longmans, Green, 1874), p. 84.

176. The title of the work is recorded in the bibliographical works of William T. Lowndes (*The Bibliographer's Manual of English Literature*, rev. Henry G. Bohn [London: H. G. Bohn, 1861], Pt. VI, p. 1628) and William C. Hazlitt (*Hand-Book to the Popular, Poetical, and Dramatic Literature of Great Britain* . . . [London: John Russell Smith, 1867], p. 404) as "Poemata. Lond. 1599, 12 mo." This edition of the *Poemata* was also part of the library collection of Benjamin H. Bright. See Sotheby's *Catalogue of the Valuable Library of the late Benjamin Heywood Bright, Esq.* . . . ("Which will be sold by auction by Messrs. S. Leigh Sotheby and Co. on Monday, March 3, 1845"), p. 291.

177. *Cato Christianus. In quem conijciuntur ea omnia quae in sacris literis ad parentum, puerorumque pietatem videntur maxime pertinere* (London, [1600]). The only known copy of this work is to be found in the library of Magdalene College, Cambridge. It is of interest to note that the printer's device found on the title page of *Cato Christianus* also appears in the same state (i.e., broken on the left side) on the title pages of the first quartos of *2H4* and *Ado*. Both plays were entered in the Stationers' Register on August 23, 1600, and all three works were printed by Valentine Sims.

178. Dionysius Cato is the reputed author of a collection of moral apothegms, titled *Catonis Disticha de Moribus ad Filium*, which are monotheistic in character but not specifically Christian. William Caxton published a translation of the work in 1477. See *Parvus Cato: Magnus Cato*, trans. Benet Burgh (Cambridge: Cambridge Univ. Press, 1906).

179. Ben Jonson ridiculed Hugh Broughton's beliefs in *The Alchemist*. For a bi-

ographical sketch of Broughton, see the preface to *The Works of the Great Albionean Divine, renown'd in many nations for rare skill in Salems & Athens tongues, and familiar acquaintance with all Rabbinical learning, Mr. Hugh Broughton . . .* , ed. John Lightfoot (London, 1662).

180. Ibid., p. 367.

181. See Joseph Ames and William Herbert, *Typographical Antiquities* (London, 1786), II, 1073. The entry reads, "Master Brovghtons Letters, Especially his last Pamphlet to and against the Lord Archbishop of Canterbury, about Sheol and Hades, for the descent into Hell, answered in their kind . . . Imprinted by him, 1600. . . ." This tract was published by John Wolf.

182. Broughton lived for many years in Middelburg, the capital of Zeeland, where he was minister to the English community.

183. Wilson, pp. 118, 123, 143, 145.

184. Ascham promoted the cause of archery in *The Schoolmaster* (1570), ed. Lawrence V. Ryan (Ithaca, N.Y.: Cornell Univ. Press, 1967), pp. 58–59: 'For if but two or three noblemen in the court would but begin to shoot all young gentlemen, the whole court, all London, the whole realm would straightway exercise shooting."

185. *Positions*, pp. 101–2.

186. Charles Millican, "Spenser and the Arthurian Legend," *RES*, 6 (April 1930), p. 168.

187. John Nichols, *The Progresses and Processions of Queen Elizabeth* (London, 1788–1805), II, 411.

188. "Album Amicorum Emanuelis de Meteren," Bodleian Library, MS. Douce 68.

189. Emanuel Van Meteren (or Demetrius) was born at Antwerp in 1535 and died in London in 1612. While in London, he appears to have been a merchant. He is the author of a valuable history of the Low Countries written by him in Latin and translated into English, French, and Dutch.

190. In a friendly and erudite letter, Richard Mulcaster wrote to Abraham Ortelius (1527–98) on April 24, 1581, seeking information on how best to instruct youths in the art of drawing. This letter is important because it discloses a warm relationship between Mulcaster and Ortelius at a time when the latter was serving as royal geographer to King Philip II of Spain. For a microfilm copy of the letter, see M/457 in the British Museum.

191. For a discussion of the "Album Amicorum," see Jan A. Van Dorsten, *Poets, Patrons, and Professors: Sir Philip Sidney, Daniel Rogers, and the Leiden Humanists* (Leiden: Leiden Univ. Press, 1962). Mulcaster might also have been a member of Sir Philip Sidney's circle. For Wilson (p. 88) has suggested "Among the letters at Penshurst, is one from Mulcaster to Sir Philip Sydney, in Latin, dated 3 Nov. 1575, the year Sir Philip went upon his travels." If this be true, Mulcaster enjoyed a correspondence with one of England's most distinguished men. Unfortunately, no such letter has been located.

192. The "Webeck Manuscript" (autobiographical sketch of Van Meteren), *Proceedings of the Huguenot Society of London*, 19 (1953–59), No. 4, pp. 136–45.

193. Addressing "the curteous Reader," Mulcaster inscribed his only prose dedication in Victorinus Strigelius' *A Third Proceeding in the Harmony of King Dauids Harp . . .* , trans. Richard Robinson (London, 1595), p. [A4^{v}]. The dedi-

cation reads, "THis booke hath many and great recommendations; The text is warranted by God himselfe; The pen is king Dauids, as great a Prophet as a Prince. The originall Latine Commentarie made by a man of great learning and iudgement, *Victorinus Strigellius,* in the Vniuersitie of Lypsia in Germanie, which you see; what accompt is to be made of M. Robinsons great paines in the translating of such a worke so well warranted, and thereby of most assured profit to the Christian and aduised Reader."

194. For examples of Mulcaster's poetry, see App. E of my dissertation.

195. Gascoigne (ca. 1525–77) was a skilled poet and writer who sat in parliament as M.P. for Bedford in 1557–58 and 1558–59. It is of interest to recall that Mulcaster was elected M.P. from Carlisle in 1558. See Charles T. Prouty, *George Gascoigne: Elizabethan Courtier, Soldier, and Poet* (New York: Columbia Univ. Press, 1942).

196. Laneham, in a letter to "Humfrey Martin, Mercer," described himself as a "mercer, merchant, adventurer, clerk of the council chamber door, and also keeper of the same." For a copy of the letter, see Nichols, I, pp. 426–523. However, Laneham was also a poet and orthographist. For his contribution to poetry, see Nichols, ibid. For his orthographic ideas, see Dobson, I, 88–93.

197. Hunnis (d. 1597), a musician and poet, was appointed master of the children of the Chapel Royal by Queen Elizabeth in 1566. For an account of his life and works, see Charlotte C. Stopes, *William Hunnis and the Revels of the Chapel Royal* (Louvain: A. Uystpruyst, 1910).

198. Ferrers (ca. 1500–79) was a poet and politician who sat as M.P. for Brackley in 1554 and 1555 and for St. Albans in 1571.

199. *Elementarie,* p. iii.

200. John Buckeridge, "A Sermon Preached at the Funeral of . . . Lancelot, Late Lord Bishop of Winchester . . . ," *XCVI Sermons by . . . Lancelot Andrewes,* ed. William Laud and John Buckeridge, 5th ed. (London, 1661), p. 791.

201. In addition, Gwinne was author of two Latin plays, *Nero, Tragaedia nova* (London, 1603) and *Vertumnus, sive annus recurrens* (London, 1607). He also served as professor of music at Oxford.

202. For a discussion of this incident, see Charles W. Wallace, "The Children of the Chapel at Blackfriars, 1597–1603," *University of Nebraska Studies,* 8 (1908), Nos. 2 and 3.

203. Public Record Office, Star Chamber Proceedings, Elizabeth, C46/39 ("Clifton v. Robinson and others"). A transcription may be found in Frederick G. Fleay, *A Chronicle History of the London Stage, 1559–1642* (London: Reeves & Turner, 1890), pp. 127–32.

204. Act I, ll. 95–96, in Francis Beaumont, *The Knight of the Burning Pestle,* ed. John Doebler (Lincoln: Univ. of Nebraska Press, 1967), p. 17.

205. 'The Oration delivered at Paules Schoole by one of Maister Mulcasters Schollers," trans. from the Latin. See Fredson Bowers, ed., *The Dramatic Works of Thomas Dekker* (Cambridge: Cambridge Univ. Press, 1955), II, 294. For this indiscretion Mulcaster was "called in and required to submitt himself to the companies examacon touching his demeanor and to resigne his place as accustomed wch he utterly refused to doe. . . ." See Acts of Court for 1513–1622, f. 284.

206. Gill served as high master of St. Paul's from 1608 to 1635. John Milton was among his students from 1620 to 1625.

207. *Calendar of State Papers, Domestic Series . . . James I. 1603–1610 . . .*, ed. Mary A. E. Green (London: Longman, Brown, 1857), p. 497.

208. Acts of Court, 1513–1622, f. 296ᵛ.

209. Minutes of Court, 29 April 1609. A letter was read from Robert Dow, desiring from the company a sign of grateful recognition for Mulcaster's years of service.

210. Poverty was not uncommon to the teaching profession. There are numerous letters in the British Museum which deal with the subject of teachers' poverty. See the letters of Nicholas Udall (Cotton MS. Titus B VIII, f. 371) and Christopher Ockland (Lansdowne MS. 161, f. 4 and Lansdowne MS. 65, art. 55).

211. Vaughan (ca. 1550–1607) was successively Bishop of Bangor, Chester, and London.

212. London County Hall, Admonition, 26 April 1611, Vicar-General's Book (under "Crampton," 1607–11), DL/C339/178ᵛ. This benefice was held *in absentia* until 1608.

213. *Repertorium Ecclesiasticum Parochiale Londinense . . .*, ed. Richard Newcourt (London: C. Bateman, 1710), II, 547: "Patroni: Eliz. Reg." Elizabeth also expressed special favor toward Mulcaster by granting him "for diverse causes and considerations . . ." seven acres of land "in Laleham" in the county of Middlesex and one "toft" of land called "Brodegateshaw" . . . for the term of twenty-one years and the annual fee of six shillings and eight pence . . ." (Public Record Office, Originalia Roll, E 371/507/xiii [26 Elizabeth], translated from the Latin). In gratitude for these and other favors, Mulcaster wrote a lengthy commemorative poem in both Latin and English at the time of Elizabeth's death. Titled *In Mortem Serenissimae Reginae Elizabethae . . .* , it was published in 1603.

214. S. Harsnett (1561–1631) was successively Bishop of Chichester and Norwich and Archbishop of York.

215. Essex Record Office, Chelmsford, Archdeaconry Register, D/AEV.4/(f. 64ᵛ).

216. Fuller, p. 600.

217. Without citing any evidence, Joseph Wilson (*Memorabilia Cantabrigiae . . .* [London: Edward Harding, 1803], p. 115) suggests that Mulcaster was "a warm Protestant, but does not seem to have been engaged in any of the busy controversies of the Reformation."

218. Katherine died on August 6, 1609.

219. Richard and Katherine Mulcaster would have been maried fifty years on May 13, 1610.

220. Although Mulcaster died without benefit of will, his son Peter was named administrator of the estate. An inventory disclosed that Mulcaster had left an estate valued at £89 17s. 7d. (For a copy of the administration, see App. A-8 of my dissertation.) But Mulcaster also left an undisclosed number of debts, for which his son was responsible. To help him meet these expenses, Peter petitioned the Court of the Merchant Taylors'. See Harry B. Wilson, p. 91.

Venus and Adonis: Shakespeare's Representation of the Passions

David N. Beauregard

In the past thirty-five years or so, various attempts have been made at defining the meaning of Shakespeare's *Venus and Adonis*. Lu Emily Pearson early claimed that the poem portrays Venus as sensual love and Adonis as rational love, the final meaning being that "when Adonis is killed, beauty is killed, and the world is left in black chaos." Similarly, T. W. Baldwin concluded that "Adonis is Love and Beauty, and when he dies Chaos is come again," adding that Venus in arguing for procreation so that "Love-Beauty-Adonis may not die" is a benevolent figure (though oddly she is also made out to be Lust). Don Cameron Allen has more recently read the poem in terms of the double hunt: "Venus hunts Adonis; Adonis hunts the boar. The first hunt is the soft hunt of love; the second is the hard hunt of life." And finally, A. C. Hamilton has explained it as a treatment of the mystery of creation and the Fall: Adonis, the perfection of unfallen Nature, blunders in ignoring the good counsel of Venus, who is Love seeking to preserve him against "all the enemies of Beauty," and by his own will he goes to his ruin.[1]

Along with these attempts at allegorical interpretation, there has arisen a triad of opinion concerning our affective responses to the poem, particularly to the figure of Venus. Some commentators have seen Shakespeare as supporting the claims of Venus against Adonis. Thus John Dover Wilson found the poem an example of the Elizabethan "fleshly school of poetry" in its acceptance of what Rossetti called "the passionate and just delights of the body." And Kenneth Muir referred to its "daring sensuality" and maintained that in the first half "we feel that the poet supports the goddess in her designs on Adonis."[2] This strain is also evident in Douglas Bush's criticism of the poem's failure to achieve its intended sensuality, and in Muriel Bradbrook's recent comment that "*Venus and Adonis* is . . . a justification of the natural and instinctive beauty of the animal world against sour moralists and scurrilous invective, a raising of the animal mask to sentient level, the emancipation of the flesh."[3]

Opposed to this attitude, there is the tendency to take Venus as a comic or reprehensible figure. For Lu Emily Pearson, as I have already mentioned, Venus is "the destructive agent of sensual love." For Rufus Putney, she is the comic type of the "frustrated, voracious woman." Along more historical lines, R. P. Miller identifies her with the flesh and sensuality, which wars against the spirit and reason, and Franklin Dickey views her as Plato's *Aphrodite Pandemos* or Ficino's *amor vulgaria,* as the personification of the "mysterious stimulus for propagating offspring," which is good only within limits.[4]

In the face of such opposed attitudes toward *Venus and Adonis,* it is perhaps predictable that there should arise a third tendency in interpretation, one which sees Venus as a "complex" figure and the poem itself in terms of "ambivalences," "opposing points of view," and "antinomies." Miller himself, in spite of his identification of Venus with the flesh, concludes:

> I do not suppose that Shakespeare intends us to *choose between* Venus and a sober Fulgentius. We are meant, rather, to delight in the playful ironies and wit which result from the interplay of two opposed attitudes. But in any case the conflict remains—the battle of attitudes which informs the entire poem. . . . *What* Shakespeare is treating and *how* he treats it should not be confused. What he deals with in *Venus and Adonis* is the psychomachic "interior warfare" between two contradictory aspects of human nature.[5]

The problem with this conclusion is that it conflicts with Miller's main thesis: that the Mars-Venus fable ironically undercuts Venus' courtship of Adonis. If the fable expresses the struggle between reason and sensuality, *virtus* and *libido,* and if Venus as sensuality is ironically dealt with, then it would seem that Shakespeare means at the very least humorously to deflate Venus' claims. What irony there is serves a moral function; it is not there for the sake of mere delight or for the sake of a "sophistication" that puts us above the conflict between good and evil. If Shakespeare does not intend us to choose between Venus and Adonis, he does intend us to form an attitude toward Venus.

The same tendency to view the poem in terms of polarities and oppositions appears more prominently in other critics. Kenneth Muir, in his later comment on the work, argues:

> Although an interpretation that seeks to show that Shakespeare was writing a sermon against lust is clearly impossible, it is equally impossible to assume that the poem is a straightforward eulogy of sexual love. Almost everything in the poem appears to be ambivalent.

He concludes that Shakespeare sees "the situation from both points of view, so that we feel the force of Venus' arguments for love, as well as the reluctance of the unawakened adolescent. Both use reason to justify an irrational position."[6] A somewhat similar reaction, stressing more the subjective response of the reader, occurs with A. C. Hamilton, who, in pointing out that Venus adopts various roles, maintains,

> Which aspect dominates in our total impression becomes a deeply personal question, and indeed that may be Shakespeare's point in centering the myth upon her. Not much adverse criticism, or praise, of Venus manages to go beyond the revelation of a critic's struggle with his *anima*. Our response to her must remain profoundly ambivalent.
>
> The erotic element in *Venus and Adonis* is designed to turn the poem toward us; for Venus' temptation is not directed against Adonis—he is no more capable of responding than a flower—but against the reader. How can we answer her frank question:
>
> 'What am I, that thou shouldst contemn me this?
>
> Or what great danger dwells upon my suit?' (ll. 205–206) A simple moral response is as irrelevant here as it is to Chaucer's Wife of Bath.[7]

Even more overtly, Norman Rabkin argues that Shakespeare views love as "hopelessly paradoxical" and based on "tragic antinomies," and so he represents in Venus and Adonis two separate and opposed principles, two "incompatible views." Art "explores reality by imitating its complexity," and *Venus and Adonis* is "a convincing and searching mirror of a view of life that makes great poetry because it cannot be reduced to a critical formula."[8] What the proponents of this third position have in common, of course, is their belief that Shakespeare is of two contradictory minds toward Venus. In this sense, he is "complex." Thus, it is not surprising to find them trying to avoid "shallow literalism" (Miller) and "a simple moral response" (Hamilton) in interpreting the poem. Shakespeare becomes something of a modern, tragically aware in being open to opposing "points of view" or "antinomies," morally neutral (possibly even confused) in being ambivalent toward them. The reader is reduced to either delighting in the "interplay" of these contraries, or tragically contemplating them, or falling back on his own subjective impression.

Perhaps the strongest answer to such a critical position has been made by Rosemond Tuve and D. W. Robertson, Jr. Miss Tuve has reminded us that Renaissance poets sought not merely to delight but to move the will toward good and away from evil.[9] And Robertson, in speaking of the Middle Ages, has dealt with the matter of "antinomies":

> the medieval world was innocent of our profound concern for tension. We have come to view ourselves as bundles of polarities and tensions in

> which, to use one formulation, the ego is caught between the omnivorous demands of the id on the one hand, and the more or less irrational restraints of the super-ego on the other. . . . But the medieval world with its quiet hierarchies knew nothing of these things. Its aesthetic, at once a continuation of classical philosophy and a product of Christian teaching, developed artistic and literary styles consistent with a world without dynamically interacting polarities.[10]

This is not to say, obviously, that tension and opposition may not exist within Medieval and Renaissance poems; it is merely to maintain that the final "view of life," the psychological or metaphysical assumptions underlying such poetry, contain no irresolvable "tragic antinomies." Reason and the passions may in fact be at odds, but they ought not to be.

If the aforementioned criticism has not dealt successfully with *Venus and Adonis*, it has raised some crucial questions. What is the allegory informing the poem? Is Shakespeare's intention in fact "erotic," or does he condemn sensuality? And, finally, what response in the reader does Shakespeare seek to engender? All of these questions are closely linked, especially the last two, but the first is more easily separable from the others.

The allegory of *Venus and Adonis* presents something of a problem. None of the proposed interpretations seems entirely satisfactory, though each seems to have its partial truth. Adonis has a rational conception of love, and yet if he is Reason itself, it is difficult to see why he should be made immature. Again, he can be identified with Beauty or with unfallen Nature, but in that case the cause of his ruin seems inadequately explained. Venus does indeed seem to represent Lust, but why then does Shakespeare have the boar destroy Adonis? If Venus pursues the soft hunt of love, why is Adonis killed after having taken up the more virtuous hard hunt? Each of these interpretations fall short of explaining the poem, if we take the allegory to consist of a set of philosophical or theological symbols translatable into a statement like "Adonis is Love and Beauty, and when he dies Chaos is come again." This kind of allegory may exist, but I should like to suggest that Shakespeare is working in a different mode, a mode quite apparent in Renaissance criticism. Certainly Sir Philip Sidney's definition of poetry is applicable here: it is an "arte of imitation," by which term he means "a representing, counterfetting, or figuring foorth." The question of what is represented he answers by differentiating between nature and art; he asks whether nature "haue brought foorth so true a louer as *Theagines*, so constant a friende as *Pilades*, so valiant a man as *Orlando*, so right a Prince as *Xenophons Cyrus*, so excellent a man euery way as *Virgils Aeneas*." And speaking of the art of painting, after describing poetry as a "speaking picture," he points out that the true painter paints not the actual

Lucrece but, rather, "the outwarde beauty of such a vertue," the virtue being constancy. In other words, the poet figures forth "notable images of vertues, vices, or what els"; he represents in concrete form the abstract philosophical definitions of the virtues and vices.[11] Edmund Spenser's letter to Sir Walter Ralegh is in obvious accord with this, Spenser maintaining that the intention of his epic is "to fashion a gentleman or noble person in vertuous and gentle discipline," which, as he goes on to explain, means to represent in the epic hero a specific virtue. More applicable to Shakespeare's poem, but along the same lines, is George Puttenham's description of the poetic form most appropriate to the "utterance" of "amorous affections":

> it requireth a forme of Poesie variable, inconstant, affected, curious, and most witty of any others, whereof the ioyes were to be vttered in one sorte, the sorrowes in an other, and, by the many formes of Poesie, the many moodes and pangs of louers throughly to be discouered; the poore soules sometimes praying, beseeching, sometime honouring, auancing, praising, an other while railing, reuiling, and cursing, then sorrowing, weeping, lamenting, in the ende laughing, reioysing, & solacing the beloued againe, with a thousand delicate deuises, odes, songs, elegies, ballads, sonets, and other ditties, moouing one way and another to great compassion.[12]

The function of amorous poetry here, described rather empirically as "discouering" the "many moodes and pangs of louers," is easily aligned with Sidney's more Platonic statement about the poet "fayning" images of the virtues and vices, both of which have to do with the affections and passions.[13] And, indeed, Puttenham's statement aptly summarizes the essential characteristics of Shakespeare's poem: its structure, intention, style, and rhetorical effect. In particular, Shakespeare's intention would seem to be that of his contemporaries. He is, in fact, holding the mirror up to nature, "to show virtue her own feature, scorn her own image." Within *Venus and Adonis* itself there is some oblique evidence of this in the painting simile used by the narrator in the digression:

> Look, when a painter would surpass the life
> In limning out a well-proportioned steed,
> His art with nature's workmanship at strife,
> As if the dead the living should exceed—
> So did this horse excel a common one
> In shape, in courage, color, pace, and bone.[14]
>
> *(289–94)*

The immediate sense of this passage is clear enough: the painter "limns out" the portrait of a horse more excellent in physique than a "common one" actually found in nature. But when applied to the wider context of the digression, the passage takes on a different meaning: if the poet for the moment can be likened to the painter, then he is "limning out" not merely the physical points of the horses but their passionate antics, in Puttenham's phrase, their "moodes and pangs." And if extended to the still wider context of the whole poem, the passage would suggest that Shakespeare is "limning out" the "moodes and pangs" of the figures parallel to the horses, namely, Venus and Adonis. The problem in explaining the allegory, then, is to determine precisely which "moodes and pangs" or virtues and vices are being represented. What I shall try to show is that the poem delineates the affections arising from the concupiscible and irascible powers of the sensitive soul.

The threefold nature of the human soul, its division into three parts or powers, was commonly held in the Renaissance. In "A Treatise of the Soul," Sir Walter Ralegh concisely describes the vegetative, sensitive, and rational appetites:

> The appetite and affection and desire of man is rooted in the soul also; our appetite, of what kind soever it is, is given to preserve us, and to make us avoid those things that hurt us. It is of three sorts: the first is natural, by which we desire (when we are hungry) meat, and when we are thirsty drink, and rest when we are weary; the second is that which we have in that we are endued with sense; and this is given, as by which we should first desire that which is good, even for that it is good, and avoid that which is evil; and to this end it maketh us love or hate, desire or shun, rejoice or be sorrowful; or else it is given us that we should strive for good things, and against evil things, as they are hard and difficult: to this end by it we have in us hope and despair, boldness and fear and anger. The third kind of appetite is that by which we desire that good which the understanding comprehendeth to be such indeed or in appearance, and flieth the contrary: This is our will, which we use to stir us up to seek God and heaven, and heavenly things, by which we rest also in these things, and are delighted and satisfied in them, being gotten. This is a part of the reasonable soul.[15]

The sensitive soul, then, has two parts or powers: concupiscible and irascible. The former desires the good, and in so doing gives rise to love, desire, and joy; it also avoids evil, and thus provokes hatred, aversion, and sorrow. The irascible part has as its object good or evil insofar as it is "hard and difficult"; the respective emotions springing from it are hope and despair, courage and fear, and anger. Such a twofold division explains the structure of *Venus and Adonis.* The poem falls obviously into two parts: in the first Venus is a comic figure who pleads with the reluctant Adonis; in the second she is a pathetic figure who fears and then laments the death of Adonis. In the first part, all the aspects of the concupiscible power are "figured forth." Venus is the concupiscible power in pursuit of the good, the beautiful Adonis; Adonis is the concupiscible power attempting to avoid evil, the voracious and lustful Venus. Thus, the affections that arise in the concupiscible power with respect to good and evil are those expressed by Venus and Adonis: the former displays love, desire, and joy; the latter hatred, aversion, and sadness. In the second part of the poem, the irascible power is represented. Adonis, formerly a present good, becomes an absent good which Venus must strive for because it is now "hard and difficult"; and the boar, the exact contrary of the beautiful, rose-cheeked boy in part one, brings in the hard reality of present evil, which Venus strives against. Consequently, Venus displays the emotions corresponding to the irascible power: fear, boldness, hope, despair, and anger. In terms of the objects of the concupiscible and irascible powers, then, the presence of the three main figures in the poem can be explained. Adonis and the boar are not univocal symbols (though certainly Adonis is beautiful and the boar is deadly, ugly, hard, etc.); rather, they exist primarily as objects which provoke the concupiscible and irascible affections. Venus exists as the subject experiencing (in Sidney's terminology, "figuring forth") these affections or emotions in relation to these objects, except where she becomes the object and Adonis the subject in order to complete the "representation." To apply the quotation from Puttenham: in the first part of the poem, where Adonis is the beautiful object of Venus' passion, the joys of love predominate, and we see her "praying, beseeching, sometime honouring, auancing, praising." In the second part, we see the sorrows "uttered," with Venus "railing, reuiling, and cursing, then sorrowing, weeping, lamenting." In short, the "many moodes and pangs" of Venus are "throughly . . . discouered."

It remains to show that the affections of the sensitive soul are actually depicted within the poem. Generally, their differences depend on the nature of their objects, whether good or evil, present or anticipated. Thus Robert Burton remarks:

> They are commonly reduced into two inclinations, *irascible,* and *concupiscible.* The Thomists subdivide them into eleven, six in the *coveting,* and five in the *invading.* Artistotle reduceth all to pleasure and pain, Plato to love and hatred, Vives to good and bad. If good, it is present, and then

> we absolutely joy and love: or to come, and then we desire and hope for it: if evil, we absolutely hate it: if present, it is sorrow; if to come, fear.[16]

St. Thomas provides perhaps the most comprehensive and clear analysis of the passions, one with which sixteenth-century sources very often agree.[17] Moreover, the Thomistic scheme of the passions seems to explain the poem best. Love, according to St. Thomas, is the root of all the passions. It is initially a simple change in the appetite, an immediate experience of pleasure or complacency in some desirable object because of a natural affinity. It is caused by the good and by the beautiful.[18] Thus, three salient characteristics of Venus' relationship with Adonis are intelligible. She praises him as beautiful, as "the field's chief flower, sweet above compare." She "makes amain unto him" in the second stanza, wooing him immediately and without delay. And she is described as "sick-thoughted" in loving a "tender boy," her love being disordered in that Adonis lacks the required natural affinity of sexual maturity. Moreover, in discussing hatred, St. Thomas maintains that "absolutely speaking" love is stronger than hatred, because the movement toward a good is stronger than the aversion to an evil (*ST*, II, i, 29, 3). Venus' superior strength in pinning down Adonis can therefore be accounted for: she is pursuing a good, while he in trying to flee from her is simply avoiding an evil.

The distinction between love, desire, and joy is clarified by St. Thomas in the following passage:

> In the first place . . . good causes, in the appetitive power, a certain inclination, aptitude of connaturalness in respect of good; and this belongs to the passion of *love*. . . . Secondly, if the good be not yet possessed, it causes in the appetite a movement towards the attainment of the good beloved: and this belongs to the passion of *desire* or *concupiscence*. . . . Thirdly, when the good is obtained, it causes the appetite to rest, as it were, in the good obtained: and this belongs to the passion of *delight* or *joy*.
>
> (ST, *II, i, 23,* 4)

Desire occurs, then, when the object is unpossessed, the object in Venus' case being sexual fulfillment with Adonis. Lacking this, Venus desires and "moves toward" its attainment by elaborate pleading and physical aggressiveness. Finally, however, after she has pulled Adonis down on top of her, she is not able to "rest" in the possession of her object; in Shakespeare's words, "worse than Tantalus' is her annoy, / To clip Elizium and to lack her joy" (ll. 599–600). If Venus displays joy, it is only in a visual sense, her eye finding repose in Adonis' beauty; insofar as her object is sexual gratification, she finds only frustration, a fact underlined by the humorous grapplings and falls in the action of the first half. Her initially disordered love of Adonis calls forth desire but does not culminate in joy.

Adonis' various reactions to Venus—his disdain, his coldness, his pouting, his frowning—are probably not all ultimately traceable to hatred, but his general attitude expresses its essential marks.

> So . . . in the animal, or in the intellectual appetite, love is a certain harmony of the appetite with that which is apprehended as suitable; while hatred is dissonance of the appetite from that which is apprehended as repugnant and hurtful. Now, just as whatever is suitable, as such, bears the aspect of good; so whatever is repugnant, as such, bears the aspect of evil.
>
> . . . Consequently love must needs precede hatred; and nothing is hated, save through being contrary to a suitable thing which is loved. And hence it is that every hatred is caused by love.
>
> (ST, *II, i, 29, 1–2*)

Venus is apprehended as repugnant by Adonis for two reasons: first, he is too young for love and so is unsuitable for Venus (he twice protests that he is "unripe"); second, he loves to hunt the boar, an activity contrary to Venus' sport, and so he possesses a prior love which provokes his hatred of Venus. This hatred naturally causes aversion in Adonis, aversion being to hatred what desire is to love, namely, a flight from an unrealized evil, as opposed to a movement toward an unpossessed good (*ST*, II, i, 23, 4). Thus Adonis resists Venus' proposals and tries actively to leave her presence. Unable to do so until midway in the poem, he experiences sorrow or sadness: "sorrow is caused by a present evil: and this evil, from the very fact that it is repugnant to the movement of the will, depresses the soul, inasmuch as it hinders it from enjoying that which it wishes to enjoy" (*ST*, II, i, 37, 2). Adonis wishes to hunt the boar, but he is hindered from doing so by Venus and thus he becomes markedly sad.

> And now Adonis with a lazy sprite,
> And with a heavy, dark, disliking eye,
> His louring brows o'erwhelming his fair sight,
> Like misty vapours when they blot the sky:
> Souring his cheeks, cries, "Fie, no more of love!
> The sun doth burn my face, I must remove."
>
> (*181–86*)

The second half of the poem, beginning approximately at Adonis' mention of the boar (l. 588), ushers in the irascible passions: fear and daring, hope and despair, and anger. Their distinguishing characteristic is that with the exception of anger they spring from a good object not yet obtained or an evil object not yet present. The first of these, fear, arises from the imagination of future evil difficult to avoid (*ST*, II, i, 41, 2). Venus is obviously fearful in these terms when she excitedly describes the boar in an attempt to persuade Adonis not to hunt him. She remarks that her jealous love of Adonis

> . . . presenteth to mine eye
> The picture of an angry chafing boar,
> Under whose sharp fangs on his back doth lie
> An image like thyself, all stain'd with gore;
> Whose blood upon the fresh flowers being shed,
> Doth make them droop with grief and hang the head.
>
> (*661–66*)

Later, in order to discover what has happened to Adonis, Venus must conquer her fear with the opposite passion of daring or boldness. Aquinas mentions that "the movement of daring towards evil presupposes the movement of hope towards good," which nicely explains Venus' movement toward the boar in the hope that Adonis is still alive. He also distinguishes between daring and fortitude: the daring man turns on a threatening object in hopes of overcoming it, not like the courageous man "on account of the good of virtue," but, rather, "on account of a mere thought giving rise to hope and banishing fear" (*ST*, II, i, 45, 4). Venus does as much when, after giving way to thoughts of despair, she hears a huntsman's cry, believes that it is Adonis' voice, and runs toward it, the narrator remarking that hope flatters her "in thoughts unlikely" (ll. 973–90).

Implied in Venus' daring are two other passions, despair and hope. The former is defined as a withdrawal in the face of a future good considered unobtainable, and the latter by contrast as an attraction of the appetitive power toward a future good difficult but obtainable (*ST*, II, i, 40, 1–4). Venus' two successive addresses to Death, the one arising out of her despair at seeing the boar's bloody tusks and the other arising out of her hope upon hearing the huntsman's cry, elicit the narrator's comment that

> O hard-believing love, how strange it seems
> Not to believe, and yet too credulous!
> Thy weal and woe are both of them extremes;
> Despair and hope makes thee ridiculous:
> The one doth flatter thee in thoughts unlikely,
> In likely thoughts the other kills thee quickly.
>
> (*985–90*)

Indeed, Shakespeare's manipulation of the situation seems designed to point up Venus' vacillation from one emotion to the other. First, apprehending the bloodied boar and several bleeding hounds, Venus despairs, declaims against Death, and breaks into tears and "variable passions." But then she hears the huntsman's cry, which she takes as Adonis' voice, and she is moved to hope, taking back all she has said against Death. The future good at first seems unobtainable when Venus sees the boar's bloody tusks, and so she is stimulated to "likely thoughts" of despair. With the mistaken apprehension that the huntsman is Adonis, she is moved to "unlikely thoughts" of hope, to the belief that the future good is difficult but obtainable, and so she moves toward that good: "As falcons to the lure, away she flies" (l. 1027).

The final passion, anger, arises both out of sorrow at an evil already present, and out of desire for vengeance (*ST*, II, i, 46, 1). Two additional observations must be made. If the evil is an injury done to us through ignorance or passion, then anger is lessened, and to some extent mercy and forgiveness are called for. And, of all the passions, anger presents the greatest hindrance to "the judgment of reason" (*ST*, II, i, 47, 2; 48, 3). When Venus comes upon the dead Adonis and is stunned by what she sees, she obviously grieves over a present evil. But, instead of retaliating against the boar, she imagines that it has acted out of ignorance.

> But this foul, grim, and urchin-snouted boar,
> Whose downward eye still looketh for a grave,
> Ne'er saw the beauteous livery that he wore;
> Witness the entertainment that he gave.
>   If he did see his face, why then I know
>   He thought to kiss him, and hath kill'd him so.
>
> (*1105–10*)

Consequently, Venus' anger at the boar is lessened and irrationally directed at future lovers. The final prophecy that "sorrow on love hereafter shall attend" occurs twice in conditional form and seems vindictive: because Adonis is dead, in the future love will be a sorrowful matter (ll. 1135–36, 1163–64). Thus, Venus' angry resentment hinders "the judgment of reason," which should find the boar at fault, and leads her to punish the wrong object.

If, then, *Venus and Adonis* portrays the "moodes and pangs" of the goddess of love, or more specifically the concupiscible and irascible passions, the question of the proper response to the poem remains. The researches of D. C. Allen, Robert Miller, and Franklin Dickey have, I think, conclusively established Venus as the representative of an inferior love, whether in Platonic or other terms. In the poem's first stanza, moreover, she is called "sick-thoughted," and in the light of that epithet her desire for the young Adonis can only be taken as unnatural and disorderly. Her arguments urging Adonis to procreate, though they might be proper when addressed to the young man of the *Sonnets*, are quite inapplicable in Adonis' case; he is simply not ripe for love. The obvious literary parallel occurs in *Hero and Leander* with its long persuasion to love spoken by the "bold, sharp sophister," Leander (l. 297). In both poems, because of the obviously immoral intentions of the orators, the ingenious persuasions are not to be taken seriously. In short, the conventional significance of the figure of Venus, the generally comic-pathetic situation, the convention of the persuasion to love, the unfavorable imagery used to characterize Venus, all point to the impossibility of taking the poem as an "emancipation of the flesh." To take it as such, to assume that Shakespeare intended to produce a "sensual orgy," that he "fiddles on the strings of sensuality . . . without even being robustly sensual,"[19] is to do violence to the right order of the poem. The artifice and much of the detail must then become offensive and confusing, because they do not serve the intention. The response of C. S. Lewis is a case in point:

> . . . *Venus and Adonis* reads well in quotation, but I have never read it through without feeling that I am being suffocated. I cannot forgive Shakespeare for telling us how Venus perspired (175), how "soft and plump" she was, how moist her hand, how Adonis pants in her face, and so forth. I cannot conceive why he made her not only so emphatically older but even so much larger than the unfortunate young man. She is so large that she can throw the horse's rein over one arm and tuck the "tender boy" under the other. She "governs him in strength" and knows her own business so badly that she threatens, almost in her first words, to "smother" him with kisses. The word "smother," combined with these images of female bulk and strength, is fatal: I am irresistibly reminded of some unfortunate child's efforts to escape the voluminous embraces of an effusive female relative. . . . Shakespeare shows us far too much of Venus' passion as it would appear to a third party, a spectator—embarrassed, disgusted, and even horrified as any spectator of such a scene would necessarily be.[20]

The source of Lewis' confusion and puzzlement is his assumption that Shakespeare means to portray Venus in flattering terms. Thus, Venus' strength, her comparative size and age, her sweating—even, I might add, her comparison to a predatory eagle—her aggressiveness, her vacillations, and her sophistry, cannot be accounted for except as "mistakes" on the part of the author. In spite of this confusion, however, Lewis indicates another possible response to Venus, that of a mildly disgusted spectator. Something of the same reaction is recorded by Coleridge, though it is accounted for differently.

> . . . Hence it is, that from the perpetual activity of attention required on part of the reader; from the rapid flow, the quick change, and the playful nature of the thoughts and images; and above all from the alienation, and, if I may hazard such an expression, the utter *aloofness* of the poet's own feelings, from those of which he is at once the painter and the analyst; that though the very subject cannot but detract from the pleasure of a delicate mind, yet never was poem less dangerous on a moral account. . . . Shakespeare has here represented the animal impulse itself, so as to preclude all sympathy with it, by dissipating the reader's notice among the thousand outward images, and now beautiful, now fanciful circumstances, which form its dresses and its scenery; or by diverting our attention from the main subject by those frequent witty or profound reflections, which the poet's ever active mind has deduced from, or connected with, the imagery and the incidents. The reader is forced into too much action to sympathize with the merely passive of our nature.[21]

Here the central intention of the poem is correctly apprehended: Shakespeare is representing the feelings attached to the "animal impulse," and the function of various aspects of the poem—the similes, situations, narrator's comments—are seen in their right relation as moving us away from sympathy with Venus. Thus, though the subject is erotic, the poem itself is not dangerous "on a moral account."

Howsoever accurate is Coleridge's reading of the poem, it is not completely satisfactory. The modern intuition of the poem's "complexity" has a certain substance to it, and I suggest that although the effects on the reader intended by Shakespeare are locally multivarious, two in general stand out. Francis Bacon in his essay "Of Love" remarks that "love is ever a matter of comedies and now and then of tragedies; but in life it doth much mischief, sometimes like a syren, sometimes like a fury." *Venus and Adonis,* in its first half, is certainly matter for comedy, but, to depart from Bacon somewhat, in its second half it is more matter for "the lamenting Elegiack," to use Sidney's phrase, in that what is depicted is not the "tirannicall humors" of kings but, rather, the passions that follow on the absence and death of a beloved. The poem, then, moves us to laughter at the ridiculous antics of Venus and to compassion for her sufferings. The intricacies of such a twofold affective response are described by Timothy Bright in terms which fit *Venus and Adonis*:

> . . . the affection which moueth vs to laugh . . . we cal merinesse wherewith we with some discontentment, take pleasure at that, which is done or sayd ridiculously: of which sort are deeds, or wordes vnseemely or vnmeet, and yet moue no compassiõ; as when a man scaldeth his mouth with his potage or an hote pie, we are discõtented with the hurt, yet ioye at the euent vnexpected of the partie, and that we haue escaped it; frõ whence commeth laughter: which because it exceedeth the mislike of the thing that hurteth, bursteth out into vehemency on that side, and procureth that merie gesture. If on the other side the thing be such as the mislike excedeth the ioy we haue of our freedome from that euill, then riseth pity and compassion.[22]

In the first half of the poem, Venus' "vnseemely" words and deeds move us to laughter and amusement, with such details as the predatory-eagle simile serving to prevent us from sympathizing with her; in the second half of the poem, the object of our "mislike" becomes the greater evil of Adonis' death, and we are made to pity the grief-stricken Venus, with a corresponding shift in detail (Venus is sympathetically compared to a "milch doe" aching to get to her fawn, to a snail whose tender horns have been hit, and so on, though it should be noted that a strong sense of detachment is preserved in the narrator's comment that Venus' emotional vacillations make her ridiculous). The supposed "ambivalence" discerned by modern commentators has therefore some basis in the shift of rhetorical intention between the two part of the poem, but if Shakespeare is "ambivalent" he is not so in the modern sense of being afflicted with emotional contradictions and divided against himself. Rather, through laughter and then pity, he intends to free us from the absurdities and evils attached to passionate love; like Coleridge and Lewis, we become detached spectators viewing the affections of love in two different situations. Certainly, Shakespeare's epigraph suggests the desirability of such detachment:

> *Vilia miretur vulgus: mihi flavus Apollo*
> *Pocula Castalia plena ministret aqua.*
> Let base conceipted witts admire vilde things,
> Faire *Phoebus* lead me to the Muses springs.[23]

Notes:

1. Lu Emily Pearson, *Elizabethan Love Conventions* (Berkeley: Univ. of California Press, 1933), p. 285; T. W. Baldwin, *On the Literary Genetics of Shakespeare's Poems and Sonnets* (Urbana: Univ. of Illinois Press, 1950), pp. 73, 84; Don Cameron Allen, "On *Venus and Adonis*," in *Elizabethan and Jacobean Studies:*

Presented to Frank Percy Wilson, ed. H. Davis and H. Gardner (Oxford: Clarendon Press, 1959), p. 106; A. C. Hamilton, *The Early Shakespeare* (San Marino, Calif.: Huntington Library, 1967), pp. 155–56.

2. Wilson is quoted in *Shakespeare: The Poems*, ed. Hyder Rollins (Philadelphia: Lippincott, 1938), p. 515; Kenneth Muir and Sean O'Loughlin, *The Voyage to Illyria* (London: Methuen, 1937), pp. 51–55.
3. Douglas Bush, *Mythology and the Renaissance Tradition in English Poetry*, rev. ed. (New York: Norton, 1963), p. 145; Muriel C. Bradbrook, "Beasts and Gods: *Greene's Groats-Worth of Witte* and the Social Purpose of *Venus and Adonis*," in *ShS*, 15 (1962), 70.
4. Pearson, loc. cit.; Rufus Putney, "Venus *Agonistes*," *Univ. of Colorado Studies*, No. 4 (July 1953), p. 58; Robert P. Miller, "The Myth of Mars's Hot Minion in *Venus and Adonis*," *ELH*, 26 (December 1959), 470–81; Franklin M. Dickey, *Not Wisely but Too Well* (San Marino, Calif.: Huntington Library, 1957), pp. 47–48.
5. Miller, pp. 480–81.
6. Kenneth Muir, "*Venus and Adonis*: Comedy or Tragedy," in *Shakespearean Essays*, ed. Alwin Thaler and Norman Sanders, *TSL*, Spec. No. 2 (Knoxville: Univ. of Tennessee Press, 1964), pp. 9–13.
7. Hamilton, p. 164.
8. Norman Rabkin, *Shakespeare and the Common Understanding* (New York: Free Press, 1967), p. 162.
9. Rosemond Tuve, *Elizabethan and Metaphysical Imagery* (Chicago: Univ. of Chicago Press, 1947), pp. 398–400.
10. D. W. Robertson, Jr., *A Preface to Chaucer* (Princeton: Princeton Univ. Press, 1963), p. 51.
11. G. Gregory Smith, ed., *Elizabethan Critical Essays* (London: Oxford Univ. Press, 1904), I, 158, 156–57, 159, 160.
12. Smith, II, 47.
13. See also George Chapman's dedication to his continuation of *Hero and Leander*: "I present your Ladiship with the last affections of the first two Louers that euer *Muse* shrinde in the Temple of *Memorie*. . . . I can, and will, ere long, single, or tumble out as brainles and passionate fooleries, as euer panted in the bosom of the most ridiculous Louer," *The Poems of George Chapman*, ed. Phyllis Bartlett (New York: MLA, 1941), p. 132.
14. All quotations are from *The Poems*, ed. F. T. Prince (London: Methuen, 1960).
15. *The Works of Sir Walter Ralegh, Kt.* (New York: Burt Franklin, 1964), VIII, 586–87.
16. Robert Burton, *The Anatomy of Melancholy*, ed. Floyd Dell and Paul Jordan-Smith (New York: Tudor, 1927), p. 224. The quotation occurs in the First Partition, Sect. 2, Memb. 3, Subs. 3.
17. My reliance upon Aquinas is perhaps rhetorically unwise, but the quotation from Burton indicates an English awareness of Thomistic tradition, and the quotation from Ralegh is undeniably Thomistic. Lily B. Campbell, in *Shakespeare's Tragic Heroes* (1930; rpt. London: Methuen, 1961), p. 69, maintains that Aquinas' division of the passions was generally popular. Though Pierre de la Primaudaye's *The French Academie* (trans. 1586) and Timothy Bright's *A Treatise of Melan-*

cholie (1586) are closer in time to the composition and publication of *Venus and Adonis,* they are not as thorough and clear as Aquinas; like St. Thomas, however, they both define the various passions in terms of the object being good or evil, present or to come, and with la Primaudaye at least the list of passions is essentially that of Aquinas.

18. All quotations of Aquinas are from *The Summa Theologica of St. Thomas Aquinas,* trans. Fathers of the English Dominican Province, 2nd. ed. (London: Burns Oates &Washbourne, 1927), Pt. II, 1st pt; the relevant section on the passions includes questions 22–48, a clear and accurate summary of which is available in Etienne Gilson's *The Christian Philosophy of St. Thomas Aquinas* (London: Victor Gollancz, 1957), pp. 271–86. On love, see *ST,* II, i, 26–28; Gilson, pp. 272–78.
19. Bush, pp. 145, 148.
20. C. S. Lewis, "Hero and Leander," in *Elizabethan Poetry: Modern Essays in Criticism,* ed. Paul J. Alpers (New York: Oxford Univ. Press, 1967), pp. 236–37.
21. S. T. Coleridge, *Biographia Literaria,* ed. J. Shawcross (1907; rpt. London: Oxford Univ. Press, 1962), II, 15–16.
22. Timothy Bright, *A Treatise of Melancholie,* ed. Hardin Craig (1586; facsimile rpt. New York: Facsimile Text Society, 1940), pp. 82–83.
23. Marlowe's translation of Ovid is from *The Works of Christopher Marlowe,* ed. C. F. Tucker Brooke (1910; rpt. Oxford: Clarendon Press, 1964), p. 580.

Shakespeare's Halle of Mirrors: Play, Politics, and Psychology in *Richard III*

Michael Neill

> Here the King is, in the first half of the tragedy, the mastermind of the Grand Mechanism, a demiurge of history.[1]
>
> God in love with His own beauty frames a glass, to view it by reflection.[2]

Richard III is the most stridently theatrical of all of Shakespeare's plays. The superb histrionic insolence of Richard, his stagy relish in confidential soliloquy and aside, is matched by a self-conscious patterning of plot, spectacle, and language, as if Shakespeare's artistry were being flaunted like Richard's own. And the connection is insistently underlined by the use of stage metaphors: poet, actor, and protagonist unite in a Marlovian pageant of self-display.[3] This ostentatious theatricality, while it has a lot to do with the play's continuing success on the stage, has presented critics with problems almost as intractable as those faced by Sir Laurence Olivier when he attempted to translate *Richard* into the alien conventions of cinema. E. A. J. Honigmann, prefacing his recent edition of the play, shows a characteristic unease about its Senecan melodrama and the rhetorical rigidities which embody a "primitive" psychological technique working "at a level not much superior to that of *The Spanish Tragedy*."[4] Criticisms of this sort may seem inevitable if *Richard III* is placed beside *Macbeth*, the mature tragedy which it most obviously anticipates, and no one would contest the fact that the style of the early histories is incapable of "the intellectual and emotional insights of the tragic period."[5] Nevertheless, what is impressive about *Richard III* is the dramatic intelligence with which Shakespeare makes his limitations work for him, and this is an aspect of the play which can be brought out if one thinks of *Richard III* less as an immature version of the pathological horrors of *Macbeth* and more as a preliminary investigation of ontological problems like those explored in *Hamlet*.

At first sight the connection between *Hamlet* and *Richard III* may seem tenuous. It does, however, occur to Honigmann himself, who writes of Richard's "curious, inverted affinity to the Prince of Denmark, the other Shakespearean hero with a connoisseur's sense of theatre" (p. 39). Anne Righter similarly sees *Richard III* as being "like Hamlet . . . a tragedy filled with assertions of the actor's power," to the point that Richard himself emerges "more as an example of the power wielded by the actor than as a figure of treachery and evil" (p. 88). And Jan Kott's essay on the histories, operating from very different premises, insists on the necessity of interpreting *Hamlet* in the light of *Richard III* and *Richard III* in the light of *Hamlet*."[6]

Richard's confidence in the efficacy of acting as a mode of action certainly stands at the opposite pole from Hamlet's metaphysical agonies, but it, too, is the product of something much deeper than mere connoisseurship—just as Shakespeare's own assertions of the actor's power are more than an extravagant mannerist flourish. Hamlet sets out to obey the philosopher's precept "know thyself," and the play is about the vertiginous terrors concealed by that deceptively simple injunction. Richard, with none of Hamlet's moral sensibility, but poised on the edge of the same ontological abyss, sets out, rather, to *create* himself. His methods are those of the theater. Crucial to both plays is the familiar quibble on "acting" and "action": it is through action that we realize what we are; it is through acting that we make real what we are not. Trapped by his awareness that this apparently absolute distinction is, in existential terms, unviable, Hamlet finds significant action impossible. He can redeem himself only by an act of nominalist faith, a magical proclamation of his selfhood—"This is I, Hamlet the Dane"—a proclamation that works only because it is rooted in a larger faith that makes the quest for intellectual self-knowledge an irrelevance.[7] Richard begins and ends with a similar proclamation of his integral selfhood—"I am myself alone;" "Richard loves Richard: that is, I am I." But the blasphemous self-sufficiency of his "I am" belongs to the rhetoric of despair. The tragic paradox of Richard's position is that only action can validate the self he proclaims; and yet just because that self can be located only in action—because it is otherwise null, a chaos, unformed and unknowable—action must take the form of acting, must become a way not of proving but of concealing the self, the void at the center of being. And when the external motives for action are removed, "Richard," literally, disintegrates.

I

Of course, both the metaphors which invite us to view historical events in a theatrical perspective and the characterization of Richard as a diabolic actor-hypocrite have a basis in the traditional materials on which Shakespeare was building. The world of *Richard III* is figured as a Wonderful Theater of God's Judgments, and men are depicted as mere puppet-actors, their movements dictated with a nice regard for witty symmetry by the Cosmic Ironist. Margaret, the furious prophetess, is the Chorus for His tragedy of blood. In Act IV, scene iv, which she describes as a "dire induction" to a tragedy (ll. 5–7), she recalls the murder of her son Edward as a "frantic play," with Hastings, Rivers,

Vaughan, and Grey as its sadistic audience (ll. 68–69); and she goes on to type the reign of Edward of York as a kind of May Game pageant, with Elizabeth as a Summer Lady:

> I call'd thee then vain flourish of my fortune;
> I call'd thee then poor shadow, painted queen,
> The presentation of but what I was;
> The flattering index of a direful pageant;
> . . . . .
> A queen in jest, only to fill the scene.
>
> (*IV.iv.82–91*)

The impotence she ascribes to the pageant-actors is confirmed by the Duchess of York's abstraction of herself as "Woe's scene"—a passive spectacle of grief (l. 27). And that image in turn looks back to Elizabeth's sorrow at her Edward's death:

> *Duch.* What means this scene of rude impatience?
> *Q. Eliz.* To make an act of tragic violence.
>
> (*II.ii.38–39*)

Though she sees herself as the maker of her own play, the best that Elizabeth and her fellow mourners can do is to compose an inert tableau of grief in a pageant they cannot direct:

> . . . . .
> *Q. Eliz.* Ah for my husband, for my dear Lord Edward!
> *Chil.* Ah for our father, for our dear Lord Clarence!
> *Duch.* Alas for both, both mine, Edward and Clarence!
> *Q. Eliz.* What stay had I but Edward? and he's gone.
> *Chil.* What stay had we but Clarence? and he's gone.
> *Duch.* What stays had I but they? and they are gone.
> *Q. Eliz.* Was never widow had so dear a loss.
> *Chil.* Were never orphans had so dear a loss.
> *Duch.* Was never mother had so dear a loss.
>
> (*II.ii.71–79*)

Those who fancy themselves as directors of the theatrical procession find themselves in turn caught up in its inexorable movement. Hastings rejoices in the downfall of the Queen's party in III.ii—"I live to look upon their tragedy" (l. 59)—but before two scenes are out, the plot has come full circle: "They smile at me who shortly shall be dead." (III.iv.107). Death changes partners in a dizzy reel: God calls the tune. Buckingham, envisaging heaven as no more than the auditorium for God's brutal theater of revenge (V.i.3–9), squarely confronts its terrible ironies:

> That high All-Seer, which I dallied with,
> Hath turn'd my feigned prayer on my head,
> And given in earnest what I begg'd in jest.
> Thus doth he force the swords of wicked men
> To turn their own points in their masters' bosoms. . . .

One thinks of Beard's Marlowe, gouging his own eye with the hand of blasphemy.

A God of the kind implied by these play metaphors will do well enough for a Puritan fanatic like Thomas Beard or a propagandist like Halle, and his activities accord with the providential scheme defined by Tillyard. But he presents problems for a dramatist—witness the didactic clumsiness of *The Atheist's Tragedy*. Seen from the viewpoint of Shakespeare's supposed "official self," the play belongs to an impressive but drastically limited kind of ritual theater, plotting the ironic symmetries of providence with equally exact schemes of action, spectacle, and rhetoric. The limitations are both moral and dramatic. Moral, because providence too easily appears, if not a mere instrument of human faction,[8] then a model for its vicious plots; dramatic, because in denying the possibility of significant moral activity, it tends to reduce human action to a meaningless writhing.

Of course, Richmond's triumph appears to give official endorsement to this grand scheme—it could hardly do otherwise. But the play's total poetic statement is another matter. It is significant that the most humanly moving of Margaret's speeches is not among the cursings by which she marks the progress of nemesis but is her agonized questioning of the whole fatal process in Act I, scene iii:

> Did York's dread curse prevail so much with heaven
> That Henry's death, my lovely Edward's death,
> Their kingdom's loss, my woeful banishment,
> Should all but answer for that peevish brat?
> Can curses pierce the clouds and enter heaven?
>
> (*I.iii.190–94*)

By the end of the scene she has convinced herself otherwise:

> I will not think but they ascend the sky,
> And there awake God's gentle-sleeping peace.
>
> (*I.iii.286–87*).

But even here the violent yoking of gentleness and savagery creates an ambiguity. The endless spectacle of death glutting on life can hardly be other than sickening, and Margaret's question forces us to ask by what scale God distributes justices—if indeed He concerns Himself with it at all. Elizabeth's despairing retort to Richard in Act IV, scene iv suggests a heaven which denies justice to the victim, just as it cuts the oppressor from the sun:

> What good is cover'd with the face of heaven,
> To be discover'd, that can do me good?
>
> (*IV.iv.240–41*)

It is as though God (at best) has withdrawn His light from the fallen world and left it for the devil, Richard, to bustle in.

What finally raises the play's theater of revenge above mere ritual is the character of Richard himself—dramatist, producer, prologue, and star performer of his own rich comedy.

II

The way in which the character of Richard is developed out of a combination of More's Machiavellian "deep dissimuler" with the self-delighting witty Vice of the Moralities is perceptively traced by Anne Righter in her section on "The Legacy of the Vice."[9] Here I am concerned with the surprising psychological insights which Shakespeare manages to produce from the manipulation of such thoroughly traditional material. Because the shaping of Richard's character is a process substantially begun in *3 Henry VI*, any full account of it must take that play into account, although *Richard III* as a dramatic structure is perfectly able to stand on its own.

Richard's delight in his prowess as an actor, the bustling energy of his performances, makes him in a sense the only lively moral positive in the play. His most sustained virtuoso exercise comes in the second scene, where it is tellingly placed against the embodiment of orthodox virtue—a corpse—the "poor, key-cold figure of a holy king" whom even Margaret recalls contemptuously as "Holy Harry" (IV.iv.25). Clearly it was this quality of style in Richard—what Honigmann calls his "glamour"—which attracted the citizen's wife to Burbage, and has excited audiences ever since. It's the same quality that stirs us in a Barabbas, a Volpone, or a Vindice. Just as it is the quality which wins Anne herself, who falls to Richard precisely because she is *not* deceived, because (as he intends) she is bowled over by the nerve, the *sprezzatura*, of the performance itself:

> Arise, *dissembler*! Though I wish thy death,
> I will not be thy executioner.
>
> (*I.ii.184–85*; italics mine)

What is perhaps less obvious is the subtle psychological realism which lies behind the compelling staginess of Richard's character: the way in which his titanism is shown as the reflection of a most appalling emotional weakness and deformity.

Two important soliloquies in *3 Henry VI* contain all that is necessary for the development of Richard's character in the last play of the sequence.[10] Like most of Richard's monologues, both take the form of extended asides to the audience, and both are ostensibly expressions of his naked, all-consuming ambition. But in fact they are much more than merely signposts to the plot. In the first (III.ii.124 ff.), Richard sketches the development of his ambition in a pseudo-dialectical form: too many lives stand between him and the crown he desires, and therefore he would be wiser to direct his energies to private satisfactions; but his physical ugliness appears to make this gratification of sexual lust a vanity even more absurd than lust for dominion, so that he is forced back again on his political aspiration. Trapped in this logical impasse, he concludes that the politician's formula of violence masked by smooth deceit offers his best release. The structure of Machiavellian rationalism is not, however, sufficient to contain the confused emotional impulses behind the speech. Richard broods obsessively on the theme of sexual love and his own deformity, the whole speech grows out of his bitter reflections on Edward's carnal prodigality, and one senses that the means of the curse he invokes—the grotesque tortures of syphilis—are imaginatively more important than its ends: to open Richard's pathway to the crown. The wanton multiplication of claimants to the throne—"Clarence, Henry, and his son young Edward, / And all the unlook'd-for issue of their bodies" (ll. 131–32)—is as much an affront to his sexual capacity as to his ambition. He posits an alternative to political enterprise only to provide an excuse for further masochistic flagellation. The unstable combination of self-pity, savage irony (tending always towards brutal self-parody), and an almost masturbatory relish in his own wickedness becomes the keynote of Richard's descants on his own deformity:

Well, say there is no kingdom then for Richard;
What other pleasure can the world afford?
I'll make my heaven in a lady's lap,
And deck my body in gay ornaments,
And witch sweet ladies with my words and looks.
O miserable thought! and more unlikely
Than to accomplish twenty golden crowns!
Why, love forswore me in my mother's womb;
And for I should not deal in her soft laws,
She did corrupt frail nature with some bribe,
To shrink mine arm up like a wither'd shrub,
To make an envious mountain on my back,
Where sits deformity to mock my body;
To shape my legs of an unequal size,
To disproportion me in every part,
Like to a chaos, or an unlick'd bear-whelp
That carries no impression like the dam.

(*3H6, III.ii.146–62*)

It is the strident self-assertion of an ego monstrously enlarged to protect an inner self pitiably warped and enfeebled. Physical deformity is felt as the outward manifestation of an inner formlessness, a mirror of psychological chaos. And the ontological vacuum is located in a profound emotional alienation: Richard cannot know himself because he cannot love himself, and he cannot love himself because he has never been loved—"love forswore me in my mother's womb." It is not only in a physical sense that Richard resembles the unlicked bear-whelp "that carries no impression like the dam": his relation with his mother, whose loathing is displayed with admirable economy in *Richard III*, has failed to provide Richard with the necessary locus for his sense of self.[11]

The second of the two *3 Henry VI* soliloquies returns to this theme of love and maternal alienation:

Indeed 'tis true that Henry told me of;
For I have often heard my mother say
I came into the world with my legs forward.
. . . . .
The midwife wonder'd and the women cried,
"O, Jesus bless us, he is born with teeth!"

And so I was, which plainly signified
That I should snarl, and bite, and play the dog.
Then since the heavens have shap'd my body so,
Let hell make crook'd my mind to answer it.
I have no brother, I am like no brother;
And this word "love," which greybeards call divine,
Be resident in men like one another,
And not in me: I am myself alone.

(*3H6, V.vi.69–83*)

Richard here conceives of love in the terms set out in Ficino's *Commentary on Plato's Symposium:*

> Likeness generates love. Similarity is a certain sameness of nature in several things. If I am like you, you are necessarily like me; therefore, the same similarity which compels me to love you, forces you to love me. . . . Moreover, a lover imprints a likeness of the loved one upon his soul, and so the soul of the lover becomes a mirror in which is reflected the image of the loved one. Thereupon, when the loved one recognises himself in the lover, he is forced to love him.[12]

Ficino, significantly, insists on love as a mode of self-realization: "When you love me, you contemplate me, and as I love you, I find myself in your contemplation of me; I recover myself, lost in the first place by [my] own neglect of myself, in you, who preserve me. You do exactly the same in me. . . . I keep a grasp on myself only through you as a mediary" (II.viii; p. 145). And the highest form of self-realization is naturally through love of God, of which all other loves are but shadows: ". . . we shall seem first to have worshipped God in things, in order later to worship things in God; and shall seem to worship things in God in order to recover ourselves above all, and seem, in loving God, to have loved ourselves" (VI.xix; p. 215). Love, the creative mirror by which we realize ourselves, has been withdrawn from Richard. A child, says Winnicott, "needs one person to gather his bits together," a mirror to establish his sense of integral identity;[13] Richard, the unlicked bear-cub, carries no impression like his dam and so identifies his self as a chaos. Without form he can be "like" no one, and no one can be "like" him: he is "himself alone," with all the horror of isolation which that arrogant despair implies.

In the prologue-soliloquy with which he opens *Richard III*, Richard plays again on the theme of physical deformity and emotional alienation:

But I, that am not shap'd for sportive tricks,
Nor made to court an amorous looking-glass;
I, that am rudely stamp'd, and want love's majesty
To strut before a wanton ambling nymph;
I, that am curtail'd of this fair proportion,
Cheated of feature by dissembling nature,
Deform'd, unfinish'd, sent before my time
Into this breathing world, scarce half made up,
And that so lamely and unfashionable
That dogs bark at me as I halt by them—
Why, I, in this weak piping time of peace,
Have no delight to pass away the time,
Unless to see my shadow in the sun
And descant on mine own deformity.

(*I.i.14–27*)

The glass which Richard mockingly rejects is the old icon of vanity, displaying the narcissistic image of the physical self. But since the body in turn is only an image or shadow of soul and mind, the inner self,[14] the icon also doubles as an emblem of self-knowledge. And one is aware that Richard is as much concerned with psychological reality as with physical appearance. The solution to his anguish is a paradoxical one: "to see my shadow in the sun, / And descant on mine own deformity." He makes himself into a kind of travesty Narcissus, creating a false self to be the object of his consuming need for love. Ficino's account of Narcissus is helpful:

> A certain young man, Narcissus, that is the soul of bold and inexperienced man, does not see his own countenance, he never notices his own substance and virtue, but pursues its reflection in the water, and tries to embrace it; that is, the soul admires the beauty in the weak body, an image in the flowing water, which is but the reflection of itself. It deserts its own beauty and never catches its shadow. . . .

(*VI.xvii; p. 212*)

Richard's narcissim is in fact precisely a strategy to avoid the contemplation of his own true countenance. He sublimates his tearing consciousness of inner formlessness by concentrating on its outward image, which he creates as something outside himself, a shadow. Like an actor's shadow-self, it is a role whose recognition involves no necessary acknowledgment of self-knowledge, being part of the self-consciously adopted persona of a Machiavellian villain:[15]

And therefore, since I cannot prove a lover
To entertain these fair well-spoken days,
I am determined to prove a villain
And hate the idle pleasures of these days.

(*I.i.28–31*)

It is characteristic of Richard's mode of histrionic self-consciousness that he regards even the wicked self concealed by his pious performances as itself a role, something to be "played:"

And thus I clothe my naked villainy
With odd old ends stolen forth of holy writ,
And seem a saint, when most I *play* the devil.

(*I.iii.335–37*; italics mine)

And the broad element of self-caricature, which is never more apparent than when he is ostensibly laying himself naked—"dogs bark at me as I halt by them"—is a reflection of this self-divisive strategy.

III

In that long soliloquy from *3 Henry VI* where Richard contemplates his own chaos, he imagines his political struggle in terms which powerfully suggest his agony of psychological confusion:

And I—like one lost in a thorny wood,
That rents the thorns, and is rent with the thorns,
Seeking a way, and straying from the way
Not knowing how to find the open air,
But toiling desperately to find it out—
Torment myself to catch the English crown;
And from that torment I will free myself,
Or hew my way out with a bloody axe.

(*3H6, III.ii.174–81*)

The implication of self-division in the self-torment, and of self-destruction in the self-division, unconsciously anticipates the horrors of Richard's last night at Bosworth Field. And the method by which he proposes to end his torment is also, ironically enough, a method of self-division:

Why, I can smile, and murther whiles I smile,
And cry "Content" to that which grieves my heart,
And wet my cheeks with artificial tears,
And frame my face to all occasions.
. . . . .
I can add colors to the chameleon,
Change shapes with Proteus for advantages,
And set the murtherous Machevil to school.

(*3H6, III.ii.182–93*)[16]

It is the method of the actor—a creator of multiple selves—and it is as an actor that Henry contemptuously sees him—"What scene of death hath Roscius now to act?" (*3H6,* V.vi.10). On the level of simple plot Richard emerges as the perfect actor-hypocrite, identifying himself in the last scene of *3 Henry VI* with the archetypal figure of Judas:

To say the truth, so Judas kiss'd his master,
And cried "All hail!" when as he meant all harm.

(*3H6, V.vii.33–34*)

In *Richard III* we are constantly being reminded of Richard's theatrical virtuosity in perhaps a dozen different roles, by his self-congratulatory asides, by the games he plays with Buckingham, and even by the extravagant energy of the performances themselves, his sensuous delight in histrionic rhetoric:

Because I cannot flatter and look fair,
Smile in men's faces, smooth, deceive, and cog,
Duck with French nods and apish courtesy,
I must be held a rancorous enemy,
Cannot a plain man live and think no harm,
But thus his simple truth must be abus'd
With silken, sly, insinuating Jacks?

(*I.iii.47–53*)

In one sense, of course, Richard's flair makes him only the most accomplished performer in a court of hypocrites, as the pageant of dissimulation in II.i shows. Indeed, the logic of political corruption ensures that the self-division of hypocrisy is paralleled beyond the court: in the First Murderer's denial of conscience—"My voice is now the King's, my looks my own" (I.iv.170)—and in the pathetic evasions of Brakenbury and the Scrivener:

I will not reason what is meant hereby,
Because I will be guiltless from the meaning.
(*I.iv.93–94*)

Who is so gross
That cannot see this palpable device?
Yet who['s] so bold but says he sees it not?
(*III.vi.10–12*)

The scrivener's death warrant, beautifully engrossed for an execution which has already taken place, is an epitome, at once horrible and absurd, of a political charade in which all become passive, but nevertheless guilty, actors. All, that is, except Richard. For what gives him his demonic power is the way in which he seizes the freedom which an actor's function normally denies. The selves he creates are, or (at least until Act IV) appear to be, independent of any plot-mechanism but those which he himself devises; and, more than that, they are actually agents in determining the roles others must perform within his plots.

The prologue-like speech with which Richard opens his play, summarizing previous action and outlining the shape of that to come, creates for him a kind of extra-dramatic status which is borne out in his running commentary of asides through the first four and a half acts. In the speech itself the presenter-function is conflated with that of playmaker:

Plots have I laid, *inductions* dangerous,
By drunken prophecies, libels, and dreams,
To set my brother Clarence and the King
In deadly hate the one against the other.
(*I.i.32–35*; italics mine)

The puns are appropriate both because, until the end of IV.iii, the plot of the play is virtually indistinguishable from Richard's plotting and because his characteristic way of working out his plots is theatrical: consequently, the action tends to resolve itself into a series of plays within the play with Richard as author-actor.[17] Of these, the most breathtaking is that with Anne in I.ii, the play of "The Witty Lover."

The purpose of playing, as Hamlet tells us, is to hold a mirror up to nature, and Richard's theatrical magic works by mirrors. Hamlet's performance for Gertrude in the closet scene sets up a glass to show her her inmost self; Richard's performance for Anne works by more confusing sleights. If there seems to be something unconvincingly histrionic about Anne's first two big speeches, we soon find out why. Seeming to accept her role of grief-enraged wife and daughter, Richard draws Anne through a mirror-maze of stichomythia, where speech reflects speech in apparently innocent antithesis for eighty lines, until she is made to feed him precisely the cue he wants:

. . . . .
Anne. Out of my sight, thou dost infect mine eyes!
Glou. Thine eyes, sweet lady, have infected mine.
Anne. Would they were basilisks, to strike thee dead!

(*I.ii.148–50*)

Disastrously—but inevitably—her gibe recalls a thousand Petrarchan clichés on the killing beams of the lady's eyes, and it enables Richard to slip into the full routine of the Rejected Lover. By a further mirror-trick his speech becomes an inverted image of her opening salvo of curses: the revenge invoked then is offered her now—but in terms which render it farcically irrelevant. Anne may have his life, but only if she consents to close his play in a final tableau of the Cruelty of Love: the earthly Venus plunging her sword into the humble heart of her servant. And yet, in the rhetorical labyrinth into which she has wandered, the only conceivable alternative is the grant of mercy:

Glou. But shall I live in hope?
Anne. All men, I hope, live so
[*Glou.*] Vouchsafe to wear this ring.
[*Anne.* To take is not to give.]

(*I.ii.199–202*)

However she looks, Anne finds her image fatally defined in the mirrors of Richard's art: a looking glass world in which joke becomes reality and reality a player's sour jest, where Anne's curses reflect back, as Richard has mockingly warned (l. 132), upon herself—

If ever he have wife, let her be made
More miserable by the [life] of him
Than I am made by my young lord and thee!

(*I.ii.26–28*)

—where Margaret in turn will be made to curse herself, Hastings to pronounce his own sentence of death, and the citizens of London to implore a tyrant's accession.

Act I, scene ii ends as it began, in monologue—Richard's epilogue balancing

Anne's prologue. And in this concluding flourish of the theatrical mirror, Richard himself returns to the icon of the looking glass:

> My dukedom to a beggarly denier,
> I do mistake my person all this while!
> Upon my life, she finds (although I cannot)
> Myself to be a marv'llous proper man.
> I'll be at charges for a looking-glass
> And entertain a score or two of tailors
> To study fashions to adorn my body:
> Since I am crept in favor with myself,
> I will maintain it with some little cost.
> . . . . .
> Shine out, fair sun, till I have bought a glass,
> That I may see my shadow as I pass.
>
> (*I.ii.251–63*)

The scene we have just witnessed has been just such a glass. For if its immediate end has been the conquest of Anne, its true purpose, like all of Richard's performances, has been to reflect, and to realize, himself—to call a self into being out of the nothing, the chaos within: "And yet to win her! All the world to nothing!" (I.ii.238). The shadow of his nothing falls upon all that is.

The sun which Richard invokes is the heraldic sun of York, but it is also the sun of majesty in whose light he may cast his long shadow upon the world, a world which will thus become a gigantic reflector of his own reality. And at a further remove it may suggest the Sun of Divinity, which his shadow seems to cut from the world,[18] Plato's inner light on which all human understanding and commerce depends:

> The sun generates eyes and it bestows upon them the power to see. This power would be in vain, and would be overwhelmed by eternal darkness if the light of the sun were not present, imprinted with the colours and shapes of bodies. . . . In the same way, God creates the soul and to it gives mind, the power of understanding. The mind would be empty and dark if it did not have the light of God, in which to see the principles of everything.[19]

The suggestion somberly deepens the resonances of his threat to Clarence at the end of *3 Henry VI*:

Clarence, beware! thou [keep'st] me from the light,
But I will sort a pitchy day for thee.

(*3H6, V.vi.84–85*)

Clarence's death in Act I, scene iv is made into a grotesque mirror image of the sacrament with which he entered the world, the symbolism of rebirth horribly realized in a literal new-christening in the Tower. So that the golden time of Richard, the third sun of York, becomes the reign of a terrible anti-Christ:

For thou hast made the happy earth thy hell,
Fill'd it with cursing cries and deep exclaims.

(*I.ii.51–52*)

K. Rich. And came I not at last to comfort you?
Duch. No, by the holy rood, thou know'st it well,
Thou cam'st on earth to make the earth my hell.
A grievous burthen was thy birth to me,
Tetchy and wayward was thy infancy;

(*IV.iv.165–69*)

Not only does Richard appear as an antitype of the Comforter, but also as a kind of travesty Creator, making a new earth in the image of his own deformity, like the clumsy and malign demiurge of Gnostic myth. In Platonic accounts of creation, God, "in love with his own beauty, frames a glass to view it by reflection"; that glass is the universe:

> The desire of a thing for the propagation of its own perfection is a kind of love. Absolute perfection consists in the supreme power of God. This perfection the divine intelligence contemplates, and hence the divine will desires to generate the same perfection beyond itself; because of this love of propagation everything was created by Him.[20]

And it is this creation by love which gives the world its coherent order:

> . . . if Love creates everything, He also preserves everything, for the functions of creation and preservation always belong together. Certainly like things are preserved by like, and moreover, Love attracts the like to the like. Every part of the earth, joined by mutual love, links itself with other parts of earth like itself.
>
> (*III,ii; p. 149*)

Richard's creation by hate, on the other hand, can only be a creation of disorder: a mirror of his own psychological chaos. Where Love joins the universe together in mutual attraction—"a circle of good, revolving from good to good perpetually"[21]—Richard's self-propagating "I am" sets up an apparently endless cycle of division in which "sin will pluck on sin" (IV.ii.63) as "wrong hath but wrong, and blame the due of blame" (V.i.29), a cycle through which the desperate incoherence of Richard's inner state is at last resolved in annihilating self-division—"Myself myself confound!" (IV.iv.399)—the serpent of evil gnawing at its own tail.

IV

Richard's kingdom is built "on brittle glass" in more than the sense he intends at IV.ii.60. It is a kingdom of mirror-plays and actor-shadows in which he manipulates the lens. Mirror images register in the consciousness of other characters, too, but purely as metaphors for passive observation and reflection, metaphors which tend by their stylized remoteness to suggest an impoverishment of human relations. For Anne, the corpse of her father-in-law is contracted to a kind of mirror-emblem:

> If thou delight to view thy heinous deeds,
> Behold this pattern of thy butcheries.
>
> (*I.ii.53–54*)

For the bereaved Duchess of York, her dead sons are recalled as reflections of their father; and Richard, seen as a distorting mirror of these dead, is also a reflector of her own shame:

> I have bewept a worthy husband's death,
> And liv'd with looking on his images;
> But now two mirrors of his princely semblance
> Are crack'd in pieces by malignant death,
> And I for comfort have but one false glass,
> That grieves me when I see my shame in him.
>
> (*II.ii.49–54*)

Shadows, shades, ghosts, and finally distorted reflections—the living are only images, good and bad, of the dead, or (more accurately) of one's own passion of loss.

The way in which relationships are reduced to mere perspectives of solipsist mirrors in this corrupted world is powerfully dramatized in certain "mirror scenes," notably II.ii and IV.iv. In the antiphonal patterns of the language (and in the staging such patterns appear to invite) one grief reflects another in apparently infinite recession. Elizabeth, for Margaret in I.iii, is merely a spurious image of herself, the true Queen—"Poor painted queen, vain flourish of my fortune!" (l. 240); by Iv.iv., Elizabeth, Margaret, and the Duchess of York have become exact mirror-images of one another's sorrow:

.....

Q. Mar. [Tell over your woes again by viewing mine:]
I had an Edward, till a Richard kill'd him;
I had a [Harry], till a Richard kill'd him:
Thou hadst an Edward, till a Richard kill'd him;
Thou hadst a Richard, till a Richard kill'd him.
Duch. I had a Richard too, and thou didst kill him;
I had a Rutland too, thou [holp'st] to kill him.
Q. Mar. Thou hadst a Clarence too, and Richard kill'd him.
(*IV.iv.39–46*)

"Shadow," "presentation," "pageant," "dream"—the terms of Margaret's speech beginning at line 82 point to the way in which the fantasies of the glass have become reality. But the elaborate parallelism asserts the identity of their situations only, since the formalism denies any identity of feeling, any sympathy. Their relationship is displayed as a mere epitome of the remorseless mechanical formula by which human lives are organized in the first tetralogy —"wrong hath but wrong, and blame the due of blame."

Perhaps the most terrible of the play's mirror figures appears in the complex symbolism of Clarence's dream; cast haphazard among the other emblems of mortal vanity are jewels:

Some lay in dead men's skulls, and in the holes
Where eyes did once inhabit, there were crept
(As 'twere in scorn of eyes) reflecting gems,
That woo'd the slimy bottom of the deep,
And mock'd the dead bones that lay scatt'red by.
(*I.iv.29–33*)

It is as though the eyes, travestying their traditional function as "windows of the soul," have become mere mirrors, at once mocking their owners' humanity and denying the possibility of communication with that humanity. The image anticipates Buckingham's irony in the council scene—

> We know each other's faces; for our hearts,
> He knows no more of mine than I of yours,
> Or I of his, my lord, than you of mine.
>
> (*III.iv.10–12*)

—and Richard's subsequent rejection of Buckingham:

> none are for me
> That look into me with considerate eyes.
>
> (*IV.ii.29–30*)

Buckingham—"respective," "circumspect,"—attempts to see beyond the mirrors, and dies for it.

Clarence's gems reflect only the slimy bottom of the deep upon itself, as Richard's mirror-play ultimately shows Anne only the image of her own corruption. Her eyes which pour their balm on Henry's wounds and which she repeatedly tries to make reject the image of Richard—"mortal eyes cannot endure the devil" (I.i.45) and "Out of my sight! Thou dost infect mine eyes" (I.ii.148)—become the metaphorical agents of her fall, as Richard's verbal mirror turns her rhetoric back upon herself:

> *Glou.* Thine eyes, sweet lady, have infected mine.
> *Anne.* Would they were basilisks, to strike thee dead!
> *Glou.* I would they were, that I might die at once;
> For now they kill me with a living death.
> Those eyes of thine from mine have drawn salt tears,
> Sham'd their aspects with store of childish drops:
> These eyes, which never shed remorseful tear—
> No, when my father York and Edward wept
> To hear the piteous moan that Rutland made
> . . . . .
> —in that sad time
> My manly eyes did scorn an humble tear;
> And what these sorrows could not thence exhale,
> Thy beauty hath, and made them blind with weeping.
>
> (*I.ii.149–66*)

The love-dazzled eyes in Richard's mirror are a monstrous parody, but the brilliance of the reflection blinds Anne's moral vision; and what it reveals to her is a kind of truth. These lovers' eyes get no babies, but they get, in different ways, themselves. In the moment of triumph Richard repeats his offer to kill himself in lines which mimic the mirror-ironies of divine justice:

> This hand, which for thy love did kill thy love,
> Shall for thy love kill a far truer love.
>
> (*I.ii.189–90*)

V

Richard III, as critics from Moulton to Tillyard have observed, continues the ironical pattern of nemesis established in the three plays which precede it: punishment follows crime in apparently endless sequence, as though Justice held a mirror to every act. But in this play there is an increasing tendency for the ironies to become self-reflexive: the biter bit becomes the biter bitten by himself. Buckingham's death speech reechoes the familiar "measure for measure" theme—"Wrong hath but wrong, and blame the due of blame" (V.i.29)—but recognizes a special malicious wit in the means:

> Why then All-Souls' day is my body's doomsday.
> . . . . .
> This is the day wherein I wish'd to fall
> By the false faith of him whom most I trusted;
> . . . . .
> That high All-Seer, which I dallied with,
> Hath turn'd my feigned prayer on my head,
> And given in earnest what I begg'd in jest.
> Thus doth he force the swords of wicked men
> To turn their own points in their masters' bosoms.
>
> (*V.i.12–24*)

There is an obviously ironical echo here of Richard's mock offer to Anne; and indeed God's modus operandi seems all too close to Richard's own. As Richard made Clarence's death a new baptism, so God makes All Soul's Day Doomsday for Buckingham. As Richard's mirrors turned Anne's and Margaret's curses, so God turns Buckingham's prayer back upon himself.[22]

Richmond's concluding speech (which by its self-conscious appeal to the loyalties of the audience becomes a kind of epilogue, corresponding to Richard's "prologue") expresses the theme of self-division in political terms:

England hath long been mad and scarr'd herself:
The brother blindly shed the brother's blood,
The father rashly slaughtered his own son,
The son, compell'd, been butcher to the sire.
All this divided York and Lancaster,
Divided in their dire division.

(*V.v.23–28*)

The events of the fifteenth century are seen as a history of progressive self-division—in the body politic; in its model, the family; and at last within the individual members of the physical body. Thus the motif of the divided self in *Richard III* is in a sense only the ultimate extension of the political argument. But what makes this a richer play than its predecesors is its new psychological focus. In the Duchess of York's lament in Act II, it is as though civil dissension were now reduced to a mere mirror of the inner crisis of the psychomachia:

themselves, the conquerors,
Make war upon themselves, brother to brother,
Blood to blood, self against self.

(*II.iv.61–63*)

England, "this sickly land," as the citizens call it in II.iii, is infected by Edward's fatal sickness, a sickness which Richard mockingly describes as self-consumption:

Now by Saint John, that news is bad indeed!
O, he hath kept an evil diet long,
And overmuch consum'd his royal person.

(*I.i.138–40*)

Edward destroys himself as surely as the courtiers who gather about his death bed in II.i and call down vengeance with their false oaths of friendship. And Margaret's warning to Elizabeth amid the bitter feuds of I.iii has a general application: "Fool, fool! Thou whet'st a knife to kill thyself" (I.iii.243). It is a warning which Elizabeth may recall in her final encounter with Richard in the second wooing scene:

Q. Eliz. Shall I forget myself to be myself?
K. Rich. Ay, if yourself's remembrance wrong yourself.

(*IV.iv.420–21*)

As the play develops, we are presented with the reality of the self-division that Elizabeth is talking about. Self-forgetfulness, the suppression of the moral self, leads at last to self-abandonment, to despair, as character after character is confronted by the consequences of his abdication:

Q. Eliz. Ah, who shall hinder me to wail and weep,
To chide my fortune, and torment myself?
I'll join with black despair against my soul,
And to myself become an enemy.

(*II.ii.34–37*)

Anne. . . . . .
Lo, ere I can repeat this curse again,
Within so small a time, my woman's heart
Grossly grew captive to his honey words,
And prov'd the subject of my own soul's curse.

(*IV.i.77–80*)

Buck. . . . . .
That high All-Seer, which I dallied with,
Hath turn'd my feigned prayer on my head,
And given in earnest what I begg'd in jest.

(*V.i.20–22*)

But the most potent version of the motif is once again in the scene of Clarence's murder. The politic self-division of Brakenbury, the pathetic moral stratagem of the murderers, the dramatized contest by which they attempt to objectify conscience as something outside themselves, all help to realize the process of self-division which has led to Clarence's condition of despair:

Ah, Keeper, Keeper, I have done these things
(That now give evidence against my soul).

(*I.iv.66–67*)

The first murderer's "Come, you deceive yourself" (I.iv.245) reminds us that Clarence before, like the murderers now ("to their own souls blind," l. 255) has denied a part of himself. Such a denial is a kind of self-murder, and the drowning in Clarence's dream becomes a vivid metaphor for the suffocation of the moral self:

and often did I strive
To yield the ghost; but still the envious flood
Stopp'd in my soul, and would not let it forth
To find the empty, vast, and wand'ring air,
But smother'd it within my panting bulk,
Who almost burst to belch it in the sea.

(*I.iv.36–41*)

The imagery recalls Richard's self-torment in *3 Henry VI*:

And I—like one lost in a thorny wood,
That rents the thorns, and is rent with the thorns,
Seeking a way, and straying from the way,
Not knowing how to find the open air,
But toiling desperately to find it out—
Torment myself to catch the English crown.

(*3H6, III.ii.174–79*)

Clarence's dream-death, however, proves to be a moral rebirth, just as the dream itself, like Richard's later, is a moral awakening: he dies, not to find the "empty air" of annihilation, but to be confronted by the ghosts of Warwick and Prince Edward—as much the shadows of his murdered conscience as the shades of his murdered enemies.

If Clarence's dream becomes the chief imaginative symbol for the agonies of the divided self, it is in the character of Richard that the process of division is most fully embodied. Richard's perverted self-obsession—at once self-love and self-loathing—leads him to create a whole theater of false selves to conceal his true self from himself, a glass to contemplate his physical deformity in order to forget his inner formlessness. Ficino's *Commentary* again appears to throw some light upon the nature of this split. Ficino is seeking to explain Aristophanes' myth of the cloven man as a version of the Fall:

> "Men" (that is, the souls of men) "originally" (that is, when they were created by God), "were whole" and equipped with two lights, one natural, the other supernatural. . . . "They aspired to equal God"; they reverted to the natural light alone. Hereupon "they were divided", and lost their supernatural light, were reduced to the natural light alone, and fell immediately into bodies. "If they become too proud, they will again be divided"; that is, if they trust too much to natural ability, that innate and natural light which remains to them will also be extinguished in some way.
>
> (*IV.ii; p. 155*)

What has been debased is called, and correctly so, broken and "split" ["fractum . . . scissumque"].

(*IV.v; p. 165*)

Richard's proclamation of his self-sufficiency ("I am myself alone") is nothing if not a revelation of the pride against which Ficino warns—"God alone, in whom nothing is lacking, above whom there is nothing, remains satisfied in himself and sufficient in himself, and therefore the soul made itself the equal of God, when it wished to be content with itself alone." (IV.iv; pp. 158–59)—and its consequence is the extinction of the natural light of conscience. Perhaps the cruelest of the many ironies at Richard's expense is that the very acts by which he attempts to assert his moral self-sufficiency are those which in fact declare his moral annihilation.

With Anne, Richard can make a game of the sort of self-division by which the murderers seek to excuse themselves (I.ii.89–98) and a game of the final self-division of despair ("By such despair I should accuse myself," l. 85); and he can shrug off her attempts to remind him of the consistent relation of the self and its actions (ll. 99, 120). His insouciance is possible because, for Richard, the "self" has no moral continuity but is wholly defined in and by the immediate act, or performance—it is a projection, an image, a shadow in a glass.[23] As there is no stable self to which responsibility can be referred, the deed can be acknowledged or denied as the dynamics of performance dictate: "Say that I slew them not?" (I.ii.89). The last theatrical offer—"Then bid me kill myself, and I will do it." (I.ii.186)—is in a sense perfectly genuine: for there is no self to kill, except a part. In his closing soliloquy, as he contemplates the imaginary mirror, Richard presents an almost infinitely refracted image of himself, as though reflected in the facets of a prism:

> *I* do not mistake *my person* all this while!
> Upon *my life*, she finds (although *I* cannot)
> *Myself* to be *a marv'llous proper man.*
> *I'll* be at charges for a looking-glass,
> And entertain a score or two of tailors
> To study fashions to adorn *my body*:
> Since *I* am crept in favor with *myself*,
> *I* will maintain it with some little cost.
> But first *I'll* turn yon fellow in his grave,
> And then return lamenting to *my* love.
> Shine out, fair sun, till *I* have bought a glass,
> That *I* may see *my shadow* as *I* pass.

(*I.ii.252–63*; italics mine)

The vertiginous *trompe l'oeil* multiplication of himself is meant as nothing more than a last exuberant display of his rhetorical sprezzatura, but it anticipates, with ironical precision, the appalling mirror-maze of his agony before Bosworth.

In Act I, scene iii, Richard again mocks the notion of self-enmity in his prayer for the pardon of Clarence's enemies:

> So do I ever—(*speaks to himself*) being well advis'd;
> For had I curs'd now, I had curs'd myself.
>
> (*I.iii.317–18*)

Of course there is a sense in which Richard is already quite self-consciously his own enemy, as the following soliloquy suggests: "I do the wrong, and first begin to brawl" (I.iii.323). The extent of his control over the action means that the other characters appear increasingly as pawns in an elaborate game played with himself. Making it his heaven to *dream upon* the crown rather than to actually possess it, Richard, like his kinsman Volpone, takes more pleasure in the cunning purchase than in the glad possession. Even Buckingham emerges as a kind of extension of Richard,[24] "my other self" as Richard calls him (II.ii.151). But Buckingham, too, conforms to the logic of the split self, and he turns against the king precisely at the point when Richard's own disintegration begins. The board at last swept clean of pieces, the player is left confronting . . . himself, the image in the glass.

Already in the first scene of Act IV, Anne has given hints of shadows not in the sun:

> For never yet one hour in his bed
> Did I enjoy the golden dew of sleep,
> But with his timorous dreams was still awak'd.
>
> (*IV.i.82–84*)

And in the following scene we become aware of the first conscious stirrings of Richard's suppressed moral self:

> But I am in
> So far in blood that sin will pluck on sin.
>
> (*IV.ii.63–64*)

It is as if the grotesque incest in butchery catalogued by Margaret in IV.iv has been pursued to the point where Richard himself is its only remaining object, the last of the issue of his mother's body on which the carnal cur may prey (IV.iv.56–57). His self, in Elizabeth's sarcastic retort (IV.iv.374) is "self-misus'd"; and when Richard picks up her gibe with a repetition of the self-cursing motif, there is behind the willed mockery an hysterical seriousness:

> Myself myself confound!
> Heaven and fortune bar me happy hours!
> Day, yield me not thy light, nor, night, thy rest!
> (*IV.iv.399–401*)

The confusion of the episode with Ratcliffe and Catesby, where for the first time the comedy is turned against Richard himself, immediately confirms the descent into psychological chaos, "the blind cave of eternal night."

Act V, scene iii is the last and physically most obvious of the play's mirror-scenes (recalling in its diagrammatic precision Act II, scene v of *3 Henry VI*, the episode of the son-who-has-killed-his-father and the father-who-has-killed-his-son). Now, however, the careful parallels in action and staging serve only to show how much the world is no longer Richard's mirror. The sun, which Richard greeted in the opening lines of the play and in which his shadow has sported for so long, makes its symbolic setting, and for Richard, at least, it is not to rise again. The last scene of his life is played in shadow.

In itself, as many critics have felt, the dream sequence is less than fully satisfying: it is probably the one point in the play where the mirror motif becomes obtrusively clumsy. The sequence is constructed as a kind of didactic mirror for magistrates, in which the false king is presented as the distorted mirror-image of the true. But at the same time it has to serve as an image of Richard's psychological torment, and the two functions are incompatible. As long as the ghosts are in Richard's dream, we can take them (like those in Clarence's dream) as shadows of his murdered conscience. The awkwardness arises when they appear in Richmond's, where, if they are not to appear as projections of a smug self-righteousness, they have to be taken as literal specters. The most telling part of the scene, however, is not the dream itself but the agony which follows it, in a speech which is at once the culmination and the fullest expression of the theme of the divided self.

Richard wakes in a sweat of terror from a dream prefiguring (shadowing) his death—"Give me another horse! Bind up my wounds!" (V.iii.177)—and the terror gives a voice to self heard nowhere else in the play: "Have mercy, Jesu!" (l. 178). That cry in the dark has a poignancy absent from the conventional pieties of any of the apparently more virtuous characters. The voice, however unfamiliar, is one which Richard, like the murderers before him, recognizes well enough: "O coward conscience, how thou dost afflict me!" (l. 179) "Conscience" here has the full sense of "consciousness" as well as "moral awareness" and implies a total suppression of the inner life and hence of any true self:

> What do I fear? Myself? There's none else by.
> Richard loves Richard, that is, I [am] I.
>
> (*V.iii.182–83*)

We are back here in the mirror world of the soliloquy at the end of I.ii. The reassertion of the old blasphemy, "I am I," is a despairing attempt to proclaim his self-sufficient integrity: "Richard loves Richard," the name is one with the namer; the image in the mirror is one with the self that sees it.

> Is there a murtherer here? No. Yes, I am.
> Then fly. What, from myself? Great reason why—
> Lest I revenge. What, myself upon myself?
> Alack, I love myself.
>
> (*V.iii.184–87*)

But the struggle to remake the emblem of self-love (the lookingglass of I.ii) inevitably collapses because Richard, the chameleon actor who has created himself only in his fleeting changes, can locate no stable self to love, no self solid enough to be loved:

> Alack, I love myself. Wherefore? For any good
> That I myself have done unto myself?
> O no! Alas, I rather hate myself
> For hateful deeds committed by myself.
>
> (*V.iii.187–90*)

Indeed it proves impossible to find a locus for his self-loathing:

> I am a villain; yet I lie, I am not.
> Fool, of thyself speak well; fool, do not flatter.
>
> (*V.iii.191–92*)

The self disintegrates into a babel of self-conflicting voices:

> My conscience hath a thousand several tongues,
> And every tongue brings in a several tale,
> And every tale condemns me for a villain.
>
> (*V.iii.193–95*)

The cracked mirror becomes a fragmenting prism. And for a self so lost the only outlet is despair, because no single, integrated focus of consciousness exists, the only sound, the baying of a thousand several tongues:

> I shall despair; there is no creature loves me,
> And if I die no soul will pity me.
> Nay, wherefore should they, since that I myself
> Find in myself no pity to myself?
>
> *(V.iii.200–204)*

Richard, who from the beginning has denied his kinship to the rest of humanity ("I am like no brother"), has thereby alienated himself from his own humanity: he is not like himself and therefore cannot love himself.

"A dream itself is but a shadow," and Richard's is a dream of shadows, refracted images of his own self, seen not by the artificial sun of his parody of godhead ("Shine out, fair sun") but looming in the blind cave of night:

> *Rat.* Nay, good my lord, be not afraid of shadows.
> *K. Rich.* By the apostle Paul, shadows to-night
> Have strook more terror to the soul of Richard
> Than can the substance of ten thousand soldiers.
>
> *(V.iii.215–18)*

It is the last trick of God's dissembling mirror that Richard, who makes himself in shadows, is destroyed by shadows:

> I think there be six Richmonds in the field;
> Five have I slain to-day instead of him.
>
> *(V.iv.11–12)*

The best that Richard can manage in his last performance is a reincarnation of himself in the act. But while, even now, the energy is all his—"Come, bustle, bustle! Caparison my horse!" (V.iii.289)—Richard is far from being (as Olivier gleefully announced) "himself again!" In the willful denial of conscience at the beginning of his oration to his army there must be a self-contradiction:

> Let not our babbling dreams afright our souls;
> Conscience is but a word that cowards use,
> Devis'd at first to keep the strong in awe:
> Our strong arms be our conscience, swords our law!
>
> *(V.iii.308–11)*

In the bravado of "A thousand hearts are great within my bosom" (l. 347), we can hardly fail to hear an echo of the babbling of conscience in its "thousand several tongues."

Act V, scene iii has been regarded, somewhat slightingly, as a theatrical tour de force. Of course, if one sets it beside the dramatizations of conscience in *Hamlet* or even *Macbeth,* it is certainly that. But what is so impressive is the sure dramatic instinct by which Shakespeare makes the limitations of his immature style work for him. The theatricality of Richard's conscience soliloquy becomes a positive strength because it corresponds so exactly to his own limitations. Where the inner self has been so systematically oppressed, there is no possibility of complex introspection. Richard's interior is a kingdom of night, a blind cave of shadows, at best a hall of mirrors, reflecting endlessly the insubstantial shadows of the lost self: a self he vainly tries to capture with the hopelessly inadequate tools of his old word-games. The cunning vice, Iniquity, moralizing two meanings in one word, is lost in the labyrinth of his own puns.

VI

If the conclusion of *Richard III* has a weakness, it is not in the dramaturgy of Richard's moral collapse but in the dramatist's moralization of his fall, in his refusal to confront the real issues which the play raises—though the refusal is, I suppose, inevitable. The ironies of the end are God's, and in their light the whole plot with its complex of witty peripeties is evidently the masterwork of a Cosmic Ironist. This being so, one finds oneself asking, despite Richmond's complacent pieties, isn't God only a greater and more competent Richard, fulfilling his fantasies of omnipotence, a malign demiurge delighting in the monstrous shadow of his own ugliness and obliterating it when it attempts to walk alone? Richard tries to declare his independence of the Ironist's tragic farce, to assert himself by making the world in his own image, a mirror-play of his own chaotic deformity, a glass to hold his shadow as he passes. His greatest sin lies in his attempt to become equal to God: the disturbing trouble is that, morally speaking, he appears to succeed.

Notes:

1. Jan Kott, *Shakespeare Our Contemporary* (London: Methuen, 1964), p. 44.
2. A. E. Waite, ed., *The Works of Thomas Vaughan* (New York: Univ. Books, 1968), p. 5.
3. Cf. Anne Righter, *Shakespeare and the Idea of the Play* (London: Penguin, 1967), pp. 81–91.

4. E. A. J. Honigmann, ed., *King Richard the Third,* New Penguin Shakespeare (London: Penguin, 1968), p. 37.
5. Honigmann, p. 37.
6. Kott, pp. 13, 27–28.
7. I have argued this point at greater length in an article, "The Matter of Denmark and the Form of Hamlet's Fortunes," forthcoming in *SQ*. All citations are to *The Riverside Shakespeare,* ed. G. Blakemore Evans (Boston: Houghton Mifflin, 1974).
8. The point is well made by Wilbur Sanders, *The Dramatist and the Received Idea* (Cambridge: Cambridge Univ. Press, 1968), p. 94.
9. Righter, pp. 86–91. Richard's descent from the Vice is most fully expounded in Bernard Spivack, *Shakespeare and the Allegory of Evil* (New York: Columbia Univ. Press, 1958). Spivack, however, makes a low estimate of Shakespeare's ability to transform the medieval convention. Of Richard's theatrical displays he writes: "Through them we shall look in vain for anything in the temper of his performance that corresponds to a passion for sovereignty, *or to any other motive that is morally intelligible*" (p. 403; italics mine).
10. Olivier's film of *Richard III* acknowledged their importance (perhaps naively) by grafting parts of both into Richard's opening soliloquy.
11. Cf. D. W. Winnicott, "Mirror-role of Mother and Family in Child Development" in Peter Lomas, ed., *The Predicament of the Family* (London: International Universities Press, 1967), pp. 26–33; and David Holbrook, "R. D. Laing and the Death Circuit," *Encounter,* 31 (Aug. 1968), 35–45. Writing on the childhood bases of ontological security, Winnicott remarks on the mother's essential "role of giving back to the baby the baby's own self" (p. 33): "in individual development *the precursor of the mirror is the mother's face*" (p. 26). The failure of the mother to provide such a mirror results in "a threat of chaos. . . . a baby so treated will grow up puzzled about mirrors and what the mirror has to offer. If the mother's face is unresponsive, then the mirror is a thing to be looked at but not into" (p. 28). R. D. Laing's studies of schizoid and schizophrenic experience provide poignant illustrations of the inner "chaos" of which Winnicott writes. Certain of Laing's remarks seem especially illuminating with regard to Richard III:

   > There are men who feel called upon to generate even themselves out of nothing, since their underlying feeling is that they have not been adequately created or have been created only for destruction.
   >
   > *The Politics of Experience* (London: Penguin, 1967), pp. 36–37.
   >
   > If the individual cannot take the realness, aliveness, autonomy, and identity of himself and others for granted, then he has to become absorbed in contriving ways of trying to be real, of keeping himself . . . alive, of preserving his identity, in efforts, as he will often put it, to prevent himself losing himself.
   >
   > *The Divided Self* (London: Penguin, 1965), pp. 42–43.

12. S. R. Jayne, ed. and trans., *Marsilio Ficino's Commentary on Plato's Symposium* (Columbia: Univ. of Missouri Press, 1944), II, viii, p. 146. Ficino's argument

goes back to the discussion of the relation between likeness and love in the *Lysis,* the negative side of which is also relevant: ". . . the good are like and friendly with the good, but . . . the bad . . . are not ever even like themselves, but are variable and not to be reckoned upon. And if a thing be unlike and at variance with itself, it will be long, I take it, before it becomes like to or friendly with anything else" (*Lysis,* 214 c–d, quoted from *The Collected Dialogues of Plato,* ed. Edith Hamilton [New York: Pantheon, 1961], p. 157). There is a remarkable resemblance between Plato's argument and Laing's recognition that "a firm sense of one's own autonomous identity is required in order that one may be related as one human being to another" (*The Divided Self,* p. 44). Jayne notes that the *Lysis* topic was a frequent subject of debate in Renaissance courts (p. 149 n.). Spenser's *Hymnes* are often close to Ficino, and *Love* and *Beautie* must have been circulating in manuscript when Shakespeare was writing *Richard III. Beautie,* lines 190 ff., deals with Platonic ideas of love and likeness.

13. Holbrook, p. 39. The image of the mirror in *Richard III,* with which this essay is much concerned, has been briefly discussed by J. P. Cutts in *The Shattered Glass: A Dramatic Pattern in Shakespeare's Early Plays* (Detroit: Wayne State Univ. Press, 1968), pp. 129–34. Some of Professor Cutts's arguments touch on my own.
14. See, for instance, Ficino, *Commentary,* II, iii, p. 136.
15. The adoption of such a persona seems to be a well-documented schizoid strategy. A case history recorded by Laing makes an interesting comparison: "The sense Brian made of his sudden inexplicable abandonment by his mother was: *because* I am bad. To be bad was his credo. He lived by it. It was the rock on which he built his life. 'Since I am bad, there is nothing but to *be* bad' " (*Self and Others* [London: Penguin, 1971], p. 94). Richard's diabolic despair, in fact, corresponds very closely to the schizophrenic experience: "The schizophrenic is desperate, is simply without hope. I have never known a schizophrenic who could say he was loved, as a man, by God the Father or by the Mother of God or by another man. He either *is* God, or the Devil, or in hell, estranged from God" (*The Divided Self,* p. 38).
16. It is interesting to compare the theatrical personality projected here with the schizophrenic self described by Laing:

> it was on the basis of . . . exquisite vulnerability that the unreal man became so adept at self-concealment. He learnt to cry when he was amused, and to smile when he was sad. He frowned his approval, and applauded his displeasure. "All that you can see is not me," he says to himself. But only in and through all that we do see can he be anyone (in reality). If these actions are not his real self, he is irreal; wholly symbolical and equivocal; a purely virtual, potential, imaginary person, a "mythical" man; nothing really.
>
> *The Divided Self,* p. 37.

17. "The Loving Brother," "The Loyal Friend," "The Witty Lover," "The Loyal Subject," "The Good Protector," "The Reluctant Prince," "The Bluff Soldier"—to name only some of the most obvious. Cf. Sanders, p. 89.

18. Compare the exchange with Margaret, I.iii.263–75:

Glou. Our aery buildeth in the cedar's top
And dallies with the wind and scorns the sun.
Q. Mar. And turns the sun to shade—alas, alas!

19. *Commentary*, VI, xiii, pp. 206–7.
20. *Commentary*, III, ii, p. 149. Compare, for instance, Spenser's *An Hymne of Heavenlie Love*, ll. 29–35, 110–19; *An Hymne of Love*, ll. 195–96. For discussion of the relationship between Love and political Concord in Renaissance thought, see John Erskine, "The Virtue of Friendship in *The Faerie Queene*," *PMLA*, 30 (1915), 831–50; and Charles G. Smith, "Spenser's Theory of Friendship: An Elizabethan Commonplace," *SP*, 32 (April 1935), 158–69.
21. *Commentary*, II, ii, p. 134.
22. The mysterious episode of Hastings' encounter with the Pursuivant in III.ii is symbolically suggestive. The Pursuivant, "also named Hastings," is a kind of mirror figure; and the meeting itself ironically mirrors the occasion of Hastings's previous visit to the tower. The suggestion of unwitting self-division is appropriate; Hastings is putting his own head in the noose. The irony is complicated by the *déjà vu*, as though God were playing tricks with time.
23. Cf. Laing, *Self and Others* (p. 51): "the schizophrenic does not take for granted his own person (and other persons) as being an adequately embodied, alive, real, substantial and continuous being, who is at one place at one time and at a different place at another time, remaining the 'same' throughout." Rosalie Colie's witty and subtle examination of certain ontological paradoxes is also suggestive in this context:

> it is true, in grammar at least, that "nobody" can know himself, especially if he has no context within his disrupted and fragmentary environment. Nobody himself does not exist, in an environment existing only to change. Even if a man might recognize himself in a true mirror, he never can in a false one: if he himself is false, even a true mirror will not reflect a true man.
>
> The psychological effect of mirrors is that they both confirm and question individual identity—confirm by splitting the mirrored viewer into observer and observed, giving him the opportunity to view himself objectively, as other people do; question, by repeating him as if he were simply an object, not "himself," as he so surely knows himself to be, by repeating himself as if he were not (as his inmost self insists that he is) unique. . . . The re-created self, the separated and objectified self, may turn out, one fears, to do instead of one's self, may replace the original and originating self. The re-created self is a threat to the self.
>
> *Paradoxia Epidemica* (Princeton: Princeton Univ. Press, 1966), pp. 297–98, 355–56.

24. Buckingham's argument on sanctuary (III.i.44 ff.), for instance, precisely echoes the sophistry of Richard's advice to York regarding his oath to King Henry (*3H6*, I.ii.18–27). He speaks, in effect, with Richard's voice.

Trial by Combat and Official Irresponsibility in *Richard II*

DIANE BORNSTEIN

The trial by combat scene in Act I of *Richard II* relates to a contemporary controversy on duels and honor and suggests a negative political judgment of King Richard. In allowing a trial by combat to take place, Richard is acting against the "Christian service and true chivalry" (II.i.54) that John of Gaunt identifies as once having been the heritage of Englishmen.[1] He is revealing himself as a "young hot colt" (II.i.70), as the Duke of York calls him. The purpose of this essay is to discuss the controversy that centered around duels and trials by combat, to analyze a type of literature that probably influenced Shakespeare's portrayal of the combat scene, and to show the significance of the scene.

In scene i of Act I, the speeches of Bolingbroke and Mowbray focus on the theme of honor and reputation, which was the point at issue in the controversy regarding duels and combats. Christian humanists and exponents of the neo-chivalric cult of honor held opposing views as to the nature of honor. According to the Christian humanists, honor was based on moral virtue and public service; it was not something that could be injured by mere words. On the other hand, followers of the neo-chivalric cult of honor were less concerned with virtue than with reputation. They were extremely sensitive to anything that might be considered an insult. The cult was based on the sixteenth-century Italian code of honor, and attacks on it were associated with satires on the Italianate Englishman.[2]

Shakespeare shows familiarity with this controversy in a number of his plays. The character who most dramatically embodies the spirit of the neo-chivalric cult of honor is Tybalt in *Romeo and Juliet*. Mercutio uses the jargon of the dueling treatises in describing Tybalt and mocks him as an Italianate courtier (although the play is set in Verona, Shakespeare sacrifices verisimilitude to get in a comment on a contemporary social issue):

> Oh, he's the courageous captain of compliments. He fights as you sing prick song, keeps time, distance, and proportion; rests me his minim rest, one, two, and the third in your bosom. The very butcher of a silk button, a duelist, a duelist, a gentleman of the very first house, of the first and second cause. Ah, the immortal passado! The punto reverso! The hai! . . . The pox of such antic, lisping, affecting fantasticoes, these new tuners of

> accents! "By Jesu, a very good blade! A very tall man! A very good whore!" Why, is not this a lamentable thing, Grandsire, that we should be thus afflicted with these strange flies, these fashionmongers, these perdonami's, who stand so much on the new form that they cannot sit at ease on the old bench? Oh, their bones, their bones!
>
> (*II.iv.20–27, 29–37*)

In *As You Like It*, Touchstone satirizes the elaborate ritual set forth in the dueling treatises in regard to the giving and answering of insults:

> Oh, sir, we quarrel in print, by the book, as you have books for good manners. I will name you the degrees. The first, the Retort Courteous; the second, the Quip Modest; the third, the Reply Churlish; the fourth, the Reproof Valiant; the fifth, the Countercheck Quarrelsome; the sixth, the Lie with Circumstance; the seventh, the Lie Direct. All these you may avoid but the Lie Direct, and you may avoid that too, with an "If." I knew when seven justices could not take up a quarrel, but when the parties were met themselves, one of them thought but of an "If," as, "If you said so, then I said so," and they shook hands and swore brothers. Your "If" is the only peacemaker, much virtue in "If."
>
> (*V.iv.94–108*)

Only once does Shakespeare exhibit a favorable attitude toward duels or combats, and that is in the contest between Edgar and Edmund in Act V, scene iii of *King Lear*. But there the circumstances are entirely different. The sophisticated formalities of a combat within the lists are not followed. The combat is not arranged by any worldly authority but appears to be brought about by divine providence. Therefore, the participants are not guilty of demanding a revelation from God.

The Christian humanists considered dueling and trials by combat to be against religion, morality, reason, and patriotism. This is the viewpoint of Lodowick Bryskett in his dialogue *A Discourse of Ciuill Life*, in which he makes his friend Edmund Spenser a participant:

> Such as come to the combat vpon points of honour, as men do now a dayes for the most part, make not any shew of their fortitude, but onely of their strength and abilitie of body, and of their courage: whereas true fortitude, is to vse these gifts well and honestly according to reason. And what honestie or reason can there be in this so mischeuous and wicked a fight? which neuertheles these men so farre allow and commend, as they are not

> ashamed to say (moued surely by some diuellish spirit) that a man for cause of honour may arme himselfe against his country, the respect whereof is and euer was so holy; yea euen against his father. . . . What iniuries can a father or a mans country do vnto him that may make him not to acknowledge his countrey, which ought to be deerer vnto him then his life, or to cast off the reuerence due to his father?[3]

Bertrand de Loque's *Discourses of Warre and Single Combat* makes several points that relate directly to *Richard II.* Loque states that it is immoral and unjust for a prince or king to grant a trial by combat, particularly if he has a grudge against one of the participants:

> The first question, touching the single Combat, that is, betweene two men, to the end to discide and end any matter in controuersie, is this: whether the king or soueraigne Prince may grant and accord with safe conscience the combat. I say and hold, he may not, and proue it by these reasons. First, because *th*e affection of the king or Prince, who grantith the combat, can not bee good and right, but contrary to charity and to the deuoire of iustice and equity: For either hee hateth both the combatants, or he loueth them both, or else he loueth and hateth the one more then the other. If he hate them both, ouer and besydes that he is a murtherer in his hart, hee doth not well to make them away by such meanes. For if the Prince be ordained of God, but to minister and execute law and iustice, and cannot put to death any but those whom the law condemneth to die: and moreouer, if it bee not lawfull to reuenge his owne quarrell, not by the way of iustice (for that the law saith) that a Judge cannot be iudge in his owne cause: how shall it then be lawfull for him to reuenge himselfe by the way of combat, wherein the innocent and the faulty person are both alike exposed to the danger of death. . . . the Prince, who is minister of iustice, cannot with a good conscience grant the combat, to voide any controversy betweene two. And that is *th*e cause why it is in expresse and plaine termes defended and prohibited as well in the ecclesiasticall lawes, as in the ciuill.[4]

In scene iv of Act I, it is revealed that Richard exiled Bolingbroke in order to get him out of the way since he was becoming too popular. He thus had hostile feelings toward Henry when he granted the combat. Loque criticizes the prince who believes he can grant a trial by combat because he is a law unto himself. This is the position taken by the arrogant Richard, who attempts to play God at the beginning of the play:

> First they say, that *the* king or soueraigne Prince is a law unto himselfe and unto his subiectes, and therefore, because hee will discide and auoide any different in this sort by combat, hee may, and will do it with iustice. I make answere, that the King or Soueraigne Prince is not God, but a man, who ought to confesse and acknowledge himselfe to be but a seruant of God, as the holy Scripture calleth him.
>
> (*sig.* G4^v^)

Loque also comments on the foolishness of trying to know the secret counsel of God:

> Secondly they say that God doth direct and guide all things to their right end, and that he that is vanquished, should be vanquished, as hee that is also victor, should also be victor. I answere, that here we do not speake of the secret counsaile of God, but of that which God hath of his owne wil reuealed vnto vs in his word. For albeit that God disposeth & gouerneth all things, and that nothing bee done against his will: yet so it is, that hee hath prescribed certaine rules in his word, and especially for the order of iustice, within the irreuocable limits whereof, hee bindeth and commaundeth vs to contain our selues.
>
> (*sig.* H)

The attitude of the Christian humanists goes back to the Christian values of the chivalric code and to views that were expressed in medieval works. One of the most comprehensive medieval treatises on war and trials by combat was the *Arbre des batailles* written in 1387 by Honoré Bonet or Bouvet, a Benedictine adviser to Charles VI of France.[5] Bonet discusses the legality of trials by combat in Chapter 1 of Part III, where he states that combats are illegal, unreliable, and unjust. In Chapters 110 through 137 of Part IV, he again reproves trials by combat as unjust, tells how they have been conducted according to the laws of Lombardy, describes the oaths taken by participants, and gives advice on how to handle various technical and legal problems that may arise. Even though Bonet offers a full description of combats, he views them with strong disapproval. A copy of the *Arbre des batailles* was in the Royal Library and could have been seen by Shakespeare. It was contained in a manuscript that Sir John Talbot had given to Queen Margaret as a wedding present when she married Henry VI in 1445.[6]

A source for material by Bonet that would have been more accessible to Shakespeare was Christine de Pisan's *Livre des fais d'armes et de chevalerie.* This work was also contained in the manuscript that had belonged to Queen

Margaret. But what is more important, William Caxton had translated and printed it in 1490, at the command of Henry VII, as *The Book of Fayttes of Armes and of Chyvalrye*. Books III and IV of the *Fayttes of Armes* are based mainly on Bonet's *Arbre des batailles*. Chapters 7 through 13 of Book IV deal with trials by combat. Issues discussed include the illegality of trial by combat, causes for trial by combat according to the Lombard law, how a trial by combat should be conducted and judged, oaths to be taken by participants, the replacement of broken weapons, and the duties of a prince who judges the combat. In the condemnation of trial by combat, those who allow them to take place are said to deserve the most blame:

> Emonge the other thingis of armes, after diuine ryght & also after right humayne bothe canon & ciuyll, to giue a gage of champ of bataille, or to receyue hit for to fyght, is thing repreued & condempned, & amonge the other decrees that forbedeth þe same, is acursed by the ryght canon aswel he that gyueth hit, as he þ*at* receyueth hit, & moche more they þ*at* suffren & byholden them.[7]

Expecting God to reveal his will in a trial by combat is attacked as presumptuous:

> For men wil knowe yf god shall helpe the ryght, & also as by thyre temptyng þ*at* god shulde doo myracle, the whiche thinge is vndue as for to experimente the wille of god & it apiereth, for we saie that for to aske a thynge ayenst nature or aboue nature is presumpcyon & it displeaseth god, & for to trowe that the feble shalle ouercome þe stronge, & the olde the yonge or the sike the hole, by strengthe of goode right, to haue, as haue had & haue confidence they that therto putte hemself, such a thinge is but atemptyng of god & I saye for certeyn þ*at* yf it happe them to wynne, it is but an aduenture, & not for the gode ryght that they thereto haue.
>
> *(p. 259)*

Combats are said to be against civil and canon law:

> The lawe cyuyl hathe ordeyned iuges & iugement for to doo as raison requyreth in place & that noone be taken for a witnes in his owne cause, but a man that thus wyl make a proue by his body forceth him self for to breke this lawe. Item by ryght canon it is yet more reproued, for it comaundeth expresly that men shal obeye the pope & hys comaundementes,

> & he by a good rayson hathe comaunded expresly that men shal neuer fyght by suche a manere of wise.
>
> *(p. 260)*

Thus, a critical attitude toward trials by combat goes back to the Middle Ages and appears in a fifteenth-century translation by Caxton that Shakespeare easily could have known. References in his plays show that he certainly was familiar with contemporary works on the subject, such as the dueling treatises.

An entirely different standpoint appears in the dueling treatises, which express the views of followers of the neo-chivalric cult of honor. The writers of these works pay lip service to the Christian ideals of peace and humility. But they are quick to state that man is an imperfect, sinful creature, who needs rules and rituals for channeling his violent impulses; these treatises provide such rules without a trace of reprobation. The attitude expressed by Vincentio Saviolo,[8] an Italian fencing master whose patron was the Earl of Essex, is typical. He claims that dueling is necessary to defend one's honor:

> It doth many times come to passe that discords and quarrels arise amongest souldiers and gentlemen of honor & account, the which (when they cannot be accorded & compounded by lawe, learning, and perswasion) must bee determined, and the truth thereof tried by armes and combat. And therefore he that is wise, carefull of his safetie, and provident against danger, will be at all times stored and furnished with this honorable urgent necessity, and instant shortnes of time, he shal be constrained to expose himselfe unto evident danger.[9]

Saviolo discusses both duels and trials by combat.

A sixteenth-century treatise on trials by combat that may have a closer relationship to *Richard II* is *The Booke of Honor and Armes* (1590) by Sir William Segar. Segar was Somerset King of Arms until 1606 and Garter King of Arms, chief herald of England, after that date. He was a scholar in the field of heraldry and chivalric lore.[10] He wrote a later treatise on chivalry entitled *Honor, Military and Civil* (1602), which he dedicated to Queen Elizabeth. Heralds played an important role in the pageants, tournaments, and entertainments of the court. Therefore, it is possible that Shakespeare could have known Segar.

Shakespeare may have used Segar's *Booke of Honor and Armes* as a source for *Richard II*, which he wrote between 1594 and 1595, a few years after the publication of Segar's work. Even if Shakespeare did not use this particular work, it provides valuable background since it offers a detailed account of the customs and ceremonies that were the basis for his combat scene. Book I describes the origin and nature of trials by combat as well as the "nature and diversitie of lies" that lead to such contests. Segar justifies trials by combat but makes several remarks that point to the official disapproval of them:

> True it is, that the Christian lawe willeth men to be of a perfect patience, as not onlie to indure iniurious words, but also quietlie to suffer euerie force and violence. Notwithstanding, forsomuch as none (or very fewe men) haue attained such perfection, the lawes of all Nations, for avoyding further inconueniences, and the manifestation of truth, haue (among many other trials) permitted, that such questions as could not bee ciuilie prooued by confession, witnesse, or other circumstances, should receiue iudgement by fight and Combat, supposing that GOD (who onelie knoweth the secret thoughts of all men) would giue victorie to him that iustlie aduentured his life, for truth, Honor, and Iustice. . . . And albeit I am not ignorant that publique Combats are in this age either rarelie or neuer graunted; yet for that (as is before said) no prouidence can preuent the questions and quarrels that daylie happen among Gentlemen and others professing Armes, it shall not be amisse, but rather behouefull that all men should be fullie informed what iniurie is, and how to repulse it, when to fight, when to rest satisfied, what is Honor and good reputation, how it is gained, and by what meanes the same is kept & preserued.[11]

Book II discusses causes for combat, choice of weapons, and ways in which victory is gained. Book III takes up the question of who may engage in combats, different kinds of insults, and means of pacification. Book IV concerns the nature of nobility, quarrels between kings, judgments in trials by combat, jousts and tournaments, and the manner of conducting trials by combat in former times. Book V deals with knighthood, knighting ceremonies, and orders of knighthood.

The material in Book IV relates most directly to *Richard II*. In Chapter 9, Segar lists "certeine combats graunted by the Kings of England." Among them is the combat between Henry Bolingbroke and Thomas Mowbray:

> Henry Duke of Hereford accused Thomas Mowbray Duke of Norffolke of certeine words by him spoken, as they rode betweene London and Brainford, tending unto the Kings dishonor. Thomas Duke of Norf. denied to have spoken any such word, but Henrie affirming his accusation, the King graunted the Combat to bee performed at Couentrie the 7 of September, 1398, Anno Rich. 2.
>
> *(sig. M4)*

In Chapter 8, Segar discusses "the manner of Combats in England, as I found them recorded in the French tongue, and written in an auncient booke, shewed me by Master Garter her Maiesties chiefe Herehault" (sig. L). Segar's description of a trial by combat closely parallels the procedure that is followed in *Richard II*. Holinshed also offers a full description of the combat between Bolingbroke and Mowbray.[12] But his narrative does not account for all the details of the formal ceremony in the play, or for the large part played by the heralds. Shakespeare's scene was probably modeled on the kind of ceremony described in *The Booke of Honor and Armes*:

> The Challenger did commonlie come unto the East gate of the Listes, and brought with him such Armour as were appoynted by the Court, and wherewith he determined to fight. Being at the gate, there he staied untill such time as the Conestable and Marshal arose from their seate, and went thether. They being come to the said gate of the Listes, and beholding the Challenger there, the Conestable said, "For what cause art thou come hether thus armed, and what is thy name?" Unto whom the Challenger answered thus. "My name is A. B. and am hether come armed and mounted, to perfourme my challenge against C. D. and acquite my pledges. Wherefore I humblie desire this gate may bee opened, and I suffered to performe my intent and purpose." Then the Conestable did open the visor of his Headpeece to see his face, and thereby to knowe that man to be he who makes the Challenge.
>
> These ceremonies ended, the Conestable commanded the gate of the Listes to be opened, whereat the armed man with his necessaries and councell entered. From thence he was brought before the king, where hee remained untill such time as the Defender was come thether. In like manner, the Defender being appeared, did make request unto the Conestable & Marshall, desiring they would bee pleased to deliuer and discharge his pledges. Whereupon the said Conestable and Marshal did humblie desire the King to release them, because the Defender is already come, and presented before his Majestie, there to performe his duetie. . . . It was also auncientlie used, that the Conestable moued the King in fauour of the Fighters, and knowe whether his Majestie were pleased to appoynt any of his nobilitie or other seruants of reputation, to assist them in combat.
>
> The Conestable and Marshall did suruay the Launces and other weapons, wherewith the Combat should bee performed, making them equall and of euen measure. The Conestable also appoynted two Knights or Squires unto the Challenger, to keepe the place free from impediments; the like was also done for the Defender. . . . The Combatters being againe

called, were commanded by the Conestable to take one the other by the hand, and lay their left hands upon the booke: which done, the Conestable said. "I charge thee A. B. Challenger, upon thy faith, that thou doo thine uttermost endeuour and force to proue thine affirmation, either by death or deniall of thine aduersarie, before he departeth these Lists, and before the Sunne goeth downe this day, as God and the holie Evangelists shal help thee." The verie same oath in like manner used was offered unto the Defender, and that done, the Fighters returned unto their places, friends and councellers.

These ceremonies ended, an Herehault by commandment of the Conestable and Marshall, did make proclamation at foure corners of the Lists thus. Oiez, Oiez. We charge and commande in the name of the King, the Conestable and Marshal, that no man of what state, title, or degree soeuer, shall approach the Listes nearer than foure foote in distance, nor shall utter any speach, word, voyce or countenance, whereby either the Challenger or Defender may take aduantage uppon paine of losse of life, liuing and goods to be taken at the Kings good pleasure. . . .

After these orders taken, the Conestable and the Marshall did auoyd the listes of all sorts of persons, saue onlie one Knight and two Esquires armed, to attend on the Conestable, and the like number to await on the Marshall, either of them hauing in his hand a Launce without head readie to depart the Fighters, if the King did command. . . .

The Conestable thus set, did pronounce this speach with a loude voyce: Let them go, let them go, let them go and doo their best. Upon which words pronounced, in the Kings presence, the Challenger did march towards the Defender to assaile him furiouslie, and the other prepared himself for defence soberlie. In the meane time, the Conestable and Marshall with their Liutenants stood attentive to heare and see if any words, signe, or voyce of yielding were uttered by anie of the Fighters, and also to be readie if the King should command the Launces to bee let fall to depart the fight.[13]

Although Shakespeare portrayed the ceremonies described by Segar, his attitude toward combats was more critical. This is shown by his satirical references to the dueling treatises in *Romeo and Juliet* and *As You Like It,* and by his unflattering portrait of the King in *Richard II.* Shakespeare shared the point of view of the Christian humanists, who condemned duels and combats. In having Richard allow a trial by combat, Shakespeare shows the king to have an attitude that is presumptuous, unjust, unpatriotic, and un-English. Richard's negative qualities are contrasted with the positive ones of John of

Gaunt and Henry Bolingbroke. In setting up a trial by combat, Richard expects God to perform a miracle on demand. On the contrary, John of Gaunt states that it is necessary to leave a quarrel "to the will of heaven / Who, when they see the hours ripe on earth / Will rain hot vengeance on offenders' heads" (I.ii.6–8). Henry Bolingbroke does not attempt to play God but insists on due process of law. When Bagot, Aumerle, Fitzwater, Percy, Surrey, and other lords all accuse each other of lying and throw down their gloves in challenge, Bolingbroke insists that they wait "till we assign you to your days of trial" (IV.i.106). His legalistic language suggests that he is talking about trials in court rather than trials by combat. This scene suggests the kind of disorder that combats could encourage. Since combats were officially condemned by the Tudors, Richard's condoning one would have been seen by many people as unpatriotic. This fault is also shown by the way in which he "farms the royal realm" (I.iv.45) to support his unpopular war in Ireland. Richard's lack of patriotism contrasts with the rousing patriotic speeches of John of Gaunt and Henry Bolingbroke. Finally, criticism of combats was associated with satires on the Italianate Englishman. Richard's support of combats suggests that he is such a figure. The Duke of York remarks that Richard's ear is open only to flattery and "report of fashions in proud Italy / Whose manners still our tardy apish nation / Limps after in base imitation" (II.i.21–23).

Consequently, the trial by combat scene in Act I serves as an emblematic tableau that symbolizes a good part of the criticism Shakespeare is directing against Richard. The King becomes wiser in the course of the play. Upon returning home from Ireland, he expresses feelings of patriotism. When he "tells sad stories of the death of kings" (III.ii.156), he shows awareness of his limitations as a mortal man. This amelioration allows him to become a suitable spokesman for the majesty of the crown, even though he had been a worthy candidate for deposition earlier in the play. But his wisdom comes too late. His earlier irresponsibility unleashed the spirit of rebellion that would lead to the "unquiet times" and the "troublous season" of the War of the Roses.

Notes:

1. *The Complete Works of William Shakespeare,* ed. George Lyman Kittredge (1936; rpt. New York: Spencer Press, 1958), p. 515. All subsequent Shakespeare quotations are cited from this edition.
2. Paul N. Siegel, "Shakespeare and the Neo-Chivalric Cult of Honor," *The Centennial Review of Arts and Science,* 8 (Winter 1964), 39–46.
3. Lodowick Bryskett, *A Discourse of Ciuill Life,* ed. Thomas E. Wright (Northridge, Calif.: San Fernando Valley State College, 1970), pp. 57–58.
4. Bertrand de Loque, *Discourses of Warre and Single Combat,* trans. John Eliot (London, 1591), sigs. G3–G4ᵛ.

5. Honoré Bonet, *The Tree of Battles*, trans. G. W. Coopland (Cambridge, Mass.: Harvard Univ. Press, 1949).
6. George F. Warner, *Catalogue of Royal and Kings Manuscripts in the British Museum* (Oxford: Oxford Univ. Press, 1921), II, 177–79.
7. William Caxton, *The Book of Fayttes of Armes and of Chyvalrye*, ed. A. T. P. Byles (London: Early English Text Society, 1937), p. 258.
8. For a discussion of Saviolo, see Lewis Einstein, *The Italian Renaissance in England* (New York: Columbia Univ. Press, 1935), p. 71.
9. *Vincentio Saviolo, His Practise in Two Bookes* (London, 1595), sigs. B1^{v}–B2^{v}.
10. Sir Anthony Wagner, *Heralds of England: A History of the Office and College of Arms* (London: Stationery Office, 1967), pp. 210, 229.
11. Sir William Segar, *The Booke of Honor and Armes* (London, 1590), sigs. A2–A3.
12. For Holinshed's description of the combat, see *Holinshed's Chronicles of England, Scotland, and Ireland in Six Volumes*, III (1807–08; rpt. New York: AMS Press, 1965), 846–47. Matthew W. Black discusses the sources for the play in "The Sources of Shakespeare's *Richard II*," in *Joseph Quincy Adams Memorial Studies*, ed. J. G. McManaway, G. E. Dawson, E. E. Willoughby (Washington, D.C.: Folger Shakespeare Library, 1948), pp. 199–216. The play draws for incident and interpretation of character upon the following works: Holinshed, Hall, Froissart, two versions of the *Chronique de la traïson et mort de Richart Deux roy d'Engleterre* by Jean Créton, the anonymous play *Thomas of Woodstock*, and Samuel Daniel's *Civil Wars*. Holinshed was the main source. Peter Ure expresses skepticism regarding Shakespeare's use of the French sources in "Shakespeare's Play and the French Sources of Holinshed's and Stow's Account of Richard II," *N&Q*, 198 (October 1953), 426–29. The parallels could have come indirectly from Holinshed, who used Créton's *Histoire* and a fragmentary translation of the *Chronique.*
13. Segar, sigs, L2–M1^{v}.

The Merry Wives Q and F: The Vagaries of Progress

Jeanne Addison Roberts

Literary studies tend to divide into those which show progress toward some objective factual description of a work of art and those which, rather, change, amplify, challenge, or support one's understanding and appreciation of the work. Both types of study have their merits, and they are, indeed, frequently overlapping and interdependent. But there is a special "scientific" satisfaction in studies which seem to show progress toward the discovery of facts; and particular cumulative pleasure derives from tracing over several hundred years the slow, erratic, but apparently sure progress in studies of particular problems. Such progress can, I believe, be discerned if one traces the history of critical theories about the relationship of the Q and F versions of *The Merry Wives of Windsor.*

If such progress toward fact can indeed be recorded, it is of obvious value in providing the necessary foundation for intelligent interpretation and appreciation of this play. It ought to force critics to discard theories based on false or highly questionable assumptions. It might well stimulate new, if still variable, critical exploration of the literary merits of the play. And, I hope, delineating the progress of textual theory in regard to this play may have some implications for other works in the canon as well.

Since the time of the earliest eighteenth-century Shakespeare editors, it has been known that *The Merry Wives of Windsor* exists in two quite different versions: the Q version of 1602, reprinted in 1619, and the F version of 1623. The progress of the plot is essentially the same in both versions, but the lengths are notably different: 1,624 lines in Q as opposed to 3,018 lines in F according to the count of W. W. Greg recorded in his introduction to *The Merry Wives: 1602* (London: Oxford Univ. Press, 1939). Q omits four scenes found in Act V of F and throughout omits parts of scenes and speeches. Even where the ideas of speeches are parallel in the two versions, the language is frequently very different, although occasionally the agreement is close, especially when the speaker is the Host. Q writes as verse many prose speeches. One Q scene, the final one, is quite different from F, but much of Q's scene is rejected as non-Shakespearean by many critics. Where F has act and scene divisions and lists characters in massed entries, Q has no such divisions and lists characters as they enter. Charlotte Porter describes the peculiarity of the stage directions of Q, noting that they appear to be "an observer's rather than an author's or manager's directions" and that some of them seem to show rather than order the action.[1] F has no stage directions except one in the last scene and the massed entries and exits.

Although differing in their judgments of the merits of Q in itself, everyone who has studied the problem agrees that the Q version is inferior to that of F. The chief problem arises from the fact that Q cannot be totally rejected, for in a few cases it provides readings unquestionably superior to those of F. Arthur Quiller-Couch describes the dilemma:

> [Q is] . . . so eminently a Bad Quarto that every editor finds himself inflexibly driven back upon the Folio version. . . . And yet he must be constantly collating: since, bad though it so obviously is, at any moment out of the Quarto's chaos some chance line, phrase or word may emerge to fill a gap or correct a misprint in the better text.[2]

The effort to explain the puzzling relationship between the two versions of the play has occupied critics since the time of Pope.

The early editors, probably assuming that Q was issued by Shakespeare, supposed the later edition to represent revision by the author himself. Alexander Pope is clearly of this opinion as he cites the "entirely new writ" *Merry Wives* as evidence of the falsity of the statement that Shakespeare "scarce ever *blotted a line.*" And he says again of the play,

> This play was written in the Author's best and ripest years, after Henry the Fourth, by the command of Queen Elizabeth. There is a tradition that it was compos'd at a fortnight's warning. But that must be meant only of the first imperfect sketch of this Comedy, which is yet extant in an old Quarto edition, printed in 1619. This which we here have, was alter'd and improved by the Author almost in every speech.[3]

John Roberts in his answer to Pope agrees that Shakespeare "frequently revised and altered," though he does not specify which plays.[4]

Samuel Johnson in 1765 accepts Pope's estimate, referring to "the first sketch of this play, which, as Mr. Pope observes is much inferiour to the latter performance. . . ."[5] And George Steevens, too, accepts the revision theory without question. He says that people who like to see the first sketch of an artist as well as his finished masterpiece in order that they may trace "the progress of the artist from the first light colouring to the finishing stroke" will welcome the earlier editions of *King John, Henry the Fifth, Henry the Sixth, The Merry Wives of Windsor,* and *Romeo and Juliet.* In these earlier editions, he says, "we may discern as much as will be found in the hasty outlines of the pencil"; and in each case these may be compared with the "fair prospect of that perfecting to which he brought every performance he took pains to re-touch."[6] Edward Capell, in 1768, seems to suggest a possible alternate theory for Q. Mentioning Qq of *Henry V, King John, The Merry Wives,* and *The Taming of the Shrew,* he says they are "no other than either first draughts, or mutilated and perhaps surreptitious impressions of those plays, but whether of the two is not easy to determine. . . ." But in his notes to *The Merry Wives,* he refers to "the true play," saying that it "appears to have been writ more deliberately, and some time after. . . ."[7] This implication that he classes *The Merry Wives* with "rough draughts" is borne out in his later notes, published in 1779–83, although he seems to recognize some not-wholly-accountable authority in Q as well as F.[8] Joseph Warton also subscribes to the theory of authorial revision, saying that the 1602 and 1619 Qq are only "so far curious as they contain Shakespeare's first conceptions in forming a drama, which is the most complete specimen of his comick powers."[9]

Like Capell, Edmond Malone is somewhat undecided about the relation of the two texts. Generally speaking, he is inclined to give more credit to the skill of Shakespeare's printers than is Johnson. He tends to reject the theory of stolen copies and yet admits this as a clear possibility in the case of *The Merry Wives.* Writing against Pope, Malone emphasizes the imperfect and mutilated quality of many of the quartos. Again he makes special reference to *The Merry Wives,* but now he quotes it as an example of a case where the author has revised and not as an example of a stolen early text. This seems to be his final conclusion.[10] (Although it is not inconceivable that Q could be *both* a rough sketch and a stolen text, Malone does not discuss this possibility.)

As early in the nineteenth century as 1826 comes the first unequivocal statement of an alternative to the revision theory. Samuel Weller Singer cites the opinion of Mr. Boaden, who thinks the gaps in Q indicate that it is a version which was "imperfectly taken down during the representation."[11] The idea that the divergences between F and Q were due not to the author's revision but to some sort of mutilation of the original in the Q version gained rapid acceptance and acquired strength through the century from the support of successive eminent critics. The idea of revision was not immediately rejected, however, and the theory has continued to have adherents up to the present time, although none of its modern supporters continues to predicate the relatively simple sort of authorial change envisaged by the eighteenth century.

The development of modified revision theories was gradual. In 1835, William Mark Clark's comment differs little from Malone's. He finds Q a "meagre and imperfect sketch" in comparison with the "finished drama" of F.[12] In 1843,

Charles Knight refers to Q as the "original sketch," pointing out that except for one variation, the order of scenes is the same in both versions but that the "speeches of the several characters are greatly elaborated in the amended copy, and several of the characters not only heightened, but new distinctive features given to them."[13]

Barry Cornwall in 1843 notes that Q is "comparatively meagre," and, when compared with F, reveals "that considerable labour was employed by the poet in bringing it to maturity."[14] In the 1850s H. N. Hudson considers the problem of the two texts in some detail, and, though he seems to lean toward the idea of some revision in F, he sees Q as probably fraudulently obtained. He adds that the printing of prose as verse suggests that the play was taken down as it was spoken and made up from memory, concluding that Q may be a mangled edition of an early version of the play. He supports this by noting that there are passages in Q which have no corresponding version in F and that people stealing or reporting would be more likely to omit or alter than add. He also points out that some passages in F suggest revision in the reign of James, adding that "many" of Shakespeare's plays were apparently revised.[15]

Because he himself held both the earlier and the later view, James O. Halliwell provides perhaps the best example of all of the changing attitudes toward the two forms of the play. Greg says of him that he simply assumed Q was a first sketch.[16] And William Bracy declared that Halliwell changed his mind only after he had read the work of Daniel.[17] But, in fact, Halliwell could not have read Daniel until 1881, and he had actually changed over by 1853 from the revision theory to the theory that Q is merely an imperfect copy. Although his study is not detailed, his new stand is unequivocal:

> For several years, I adopted the opinion, so ably supported by Mr. Knight, in favor of Johnson's quarto being a transcript of the poet's first draught of the comedy; but subsequent research has convinced me that this view of the subject is liable to great doubt, and that this earlier edition must be considered in the light of an unfair and fragmentary copy of the perfect drama, possessing in all probability, unauthorized additions from the pen of some other writer.

He points out that even if Q were a sketch, there would still be passages worthy of Shakespeare. Instead he finds that it has "merely imperfect transcripts, not sketches of speeches to be found in the perfect drama." The scenes which are found only in Q are inferior, he says, and sometimes "poor and despicable." In attempting to account for Q, he favors the idea of some sort of reportorial or memorial transcript. Because of the "many deceptions . . . practiced by the booksellers in Shakespeare's day," he is doubtful about the precise origin of the "piratical edition" represented by Q, but he guesses that it was "taken either from notes made at the theatre," or made up "from the imperfect memoranda of one of the actors." He adds that one can only conjecture about which portions are original.[18]

Although Halliwell may be seen as representative of a general critical change, a few later critics of the century still speak of the "first sketch" and assume revision by the author. Alexander Dyce, citing the "unquestionable" revision of *Romeo and Juliet*, asserts his belief that Q is the original play and F "altered and amplified by Shakespeare.[19] Algernon C. Swinburne clearly sees revision, referring to the "raw rough sketch" and the "enriched and ennobled version."[20] And as late as 1882, William J. Rolfe says that the Qq "appear to be a pirated version of the play as first written by Shakespeare, probably in 1599." He finds that "internal evidence" shows that the "revised and enlarged" version was probably made about 1605.[21]

By the turn of the century, critics had ceased to attribute the differences between Q and F solely to authorial revision. The chief twentieth-century theories deserve consideration in some detail, but the preparation for all of them can be seen in the work of a few perceptive critics of the nineteenth century who restudied the texts without the preconceived notion of revision and found evidence for new conclusions. In fact, a rather cursory comparison of the two texts shows abundant examples of difference, but rarely the sort of difference that could be reasonably attributed to revision. Where the ideas of the two versions are roughly parallel, the wording is frequently different, but different in a way that seems almost random and cannot conceivably be attributed to the revision of an author. The following passages will provide examples:[22]

Q. *Shal.* Sir *Iohn*, sir *Iohn*, you have hurt my keeper,
kild my dogs, stolne my deere.
F. *Shal.* Knight, you have beaten my men, kill'd my
Deere, and broke open my Lodge.

(I.i.115)

Q. *Doc.* . . . go you all over the fields
to Frogmore?
F. *Host.* . . . go you through
the Towne to *Frogmore.*

(II.iii.77)

Q. *Host.* He is there: goe see what humour hee is in,
F. *Host.* He is there, see what humor he is in:

(II.iii.80)

Q. *Fal.*	Do *I* speake like Horne the hunter, ha?	
F. *Fal.*	Speake I like *Herne* the Hunter?	
		(*V.v.31*)
Q. *Sir Hu.*	Where is mine Host of the Gartyr?	
F. *Ev.*	Where is mine *Host*?	
		(*IV.v.73*)

Evidence of this sort, and the apparent incompleteness of Q, led to the development of new theories to explain the relation of the two texts. I have mentioned Boaden above. The editor of the 1836 edition of the play accepts his view that Q was "surreptitiously obtained" and not a rough draft. He cites as evidence the gaps in Q and also the fact that the "faulty and imperfect play" was reprinted in 1619, after the supposed revision.[23] J. Payne Collier sees Q as an edition brought out in haste to take advantage of a temporary interest in the play, adding that "the most minute examination" has led him to reject the idea that it is a first sketch. His conclusion is that it belongs in the same category as Q *Henry V*, having been "made up, for the purpose of sale, partly from memory" and that it does not show evidence even of the use "of any of the parts as delivered out by the copyist of the theatre to the actors." He supposed on the other hand that F was "printed from the play-house manuscript in the hands of Heminge and Condell. . . ."[24] Richard Grant White calls Q "a mangled version of an early sketch." He considers the F text to be of "tolerable purity," and although he thinks Q supplies "some passages which accident or haste excluded from the folio," he notes that F received (presumably from Shakespeare) "important additions and underwent . . . modifications."[25] W. W. Lloyd argues that Q is too poor for Shakespeare's mature years—after *Romeo and Juliet*, *As You Like It*, and *A Midsummer Night's Dream*—and therefore cannot be even an early draft.[26]

In 1881 came the work of P. A. Daniel, considered by Greg to be "the first serious contribution to the discussion."[27] Disturbed by the inconsistencies in the time scheme of both versions and finding several cases where F needs Q, Daniel[28] rejects both versions as not truly representative of the original. He asserts that even F shows, especially in its time inaccuracies, "some unintelligent tampering with the play which could hardly be charged on the author himself." And he believes that neither form "can be accepted as a perfect representation of its original." Whether the imperfections of both forms can be explained as departures from a common original, or whether a sketch and an original actually existed, he finds it "perhaps impossible with certainty to decide." Daniel believes, however, that the idea of a first meager sketch later laboriously amended is inconsistent with Shakespeare's reputation for "marvellous facility"; and, as plays were known to be subject to mutilation, he prefers this explanation for Q.

He offers several pieces of new evidence. The first five lines of scene xii in Q he rejects as non-Shakespearean, suggesting that if some parts are not by Shakespeare, this considerably weakens the case for revision in F. In addition, he advances the idea that some of the scenes which might be thought to have been added in F are actually omitted in Q. In F IV.v, for example, Simple wants to consult "mother Pratt" about two things: (1) the chain "of which Slender has been cozened" and (2) the suit of Anne Page. John's reply leads Simple to believe that his master will win Anne, and he leaves, saying, "I shall make my Master glad with these tydings." In Q, however, there is no mention of Anne, and Simple's line is absurd. As a second example of omission in Q, Daniel cites F I.iv, where Caius challenges Hugh to the duel and Simple acts as the parson's messenger. In scene iv of Q both the challenge and the anger are unintelligible because the audience does not know that Simple is Hugh's messenger. Daniel adds, building on this evidence, that if any omissions in Q can be proved, then all its deficiencies are "liable to fall under that category."

Finally Daniel argues that certain passages which seem to be transposed in F are actually misplaced in Q. He gives two examples. First, there is the proposal of Slender which comes suddenly and without warning in Q, scene i, but is found suitably prepared for in F III.iv. Second, Daniel notes that in the first lines of F V.i, Falstaff tells Mrs. Quickly that he will meet her at Herne's Oak. In Q the scene is absent, but the lines, altered and corrupted, are found in scene xviii, where Falstaff is awkwardly made to say he *will* venture when in fact he has already done so.

Daniel concludes, then, that Q probably represents a corruption of a version of the original which had been shortened for stage representation. He suggests that some portions of Q may have been taken down at the performance pretty accurately, either in shorthand[29] or with assistance of someone connected with the theater. However, he believes that most of it must have been reconstructed from notes and from memory. He points out also that the "elaborate descriptive stage directions" in Q support the idea that it was taken down at the theater. In summarizing his position, he makes clear his hypothesis of an original play which lies behind both extant versions. Of this original play he finds F "the truer, though not perfect representation," while Q shows but its "mutilated and corrupted form."

H. B. Wheatley, in 1886, follows largely the same line as Daniel, taking for his edition readings from both texts. He refers to the "once popular" revision theory as completely outmoded, giving his view of Q as corrupt, incomplete, and marred by some "rubbish" added by the pirate.[30]

There are two particular problems in regard to *The Merry Wives* which have never been completely solved. One received some critical notice from the time of the early editions, and the other began to be seriously discussed only in the mid-nineteenth century. The first problem is posed by the two very different versions of the final scene given in the two texts of the play, and the second grows out of the presence in both versions of a sketchily developed incident involving the stealing of some horses and the curious phrase, found only in Q, referring to "cosen garmombles."

In the final scene of the play, Q is both notably inferior and notably unrelated to F. F alone contains a reference to "our radiant Queen," and a passage which quotes the motto and refers to the colors of the Order of the Garter. As early as 1790, Malone (*Poems and Plays,* I, Part I, 329) thought these lines a possible reference to the Feast of the Garter in 1603, but the idea was not very seriously discussed until our own century.

On the question of the subplot involving the post horses, the nineteenth century had relatively little to say. No one seems to have realized that there was any problem until Knight in 1846 announced a friend's discovery of the record of the visit of a German Count, later (in 1593) to become Duke, to England and to Windsor in 1592. "In 1592, A German Duke did visit Windsor . . . [he] travelled under the name of "The Count Mombeliard". . . . We have little doubt that the passages which relate to the German duke . . . have reference to the Duke of Wurtemburg's visit to Windsor in 1592. . . ." The name of the German count was seen as represented in anagram in the phrase "cosen Garmombles" of Q, and the story fitted in with Knight's idea that the play was composed in 1592.[31] In 1842, Halliwell mentions the account described by Knight, regretting that he has not been able to find it; but by 1853 (*Works,* II, 243 ff.) he has apparently seen it, and he takes it as evidence of an earlier date for the play than has been generally supposed. He notes that the very names of two places the count visited—Reading and Brentford—are mentioned in both texts, that his visit would have presumably attracted some interest, and that humorous references to the visit would have probably had some relish for the court within a year or so.

Daniel (Intro., *Wiv.* pp. xii, ix) has nothing but scorn for this theory. He classes it with the long-popular legend of Sir Thomas Lucy and Shakespeare's deer-stealing, a legend which he also rejects. Daniel does feel sure that some underplot was projected but says that "if it ever had existence," it is now "irrecoverably lost."

Like Halliwell, Frederick Fleay, in 1886, was so impressed with the necessity of explaining the supposed Mompelgart references that he, too, attempts to connect the play with 1592, the year of the Count's visit. Instead of supposing the F version to have been written then, he connects Q with a *Jealous Comedy* performed by Shakespeare's company in 1593.[32] He is not clear about whether he thinks this early play was written by Shakespeare, but he does speak of the poet's "final version" as though he thinks that some revision took place. He says of Q:

> My own opinion is that the . . . Quarto is printed from a partly revised prompter's copy of the older version of the play, which became useless when Shakespeare had made his final version. I believe also that this older version was produced soon after the visit of the Count of Mumplegart (Garmombles) to Windsor in August 1592; that it was probably the *Jealous Comedy*, acted as a new play by Shakespeare's company 5th January 1593; that when Shakespeare revived this old play, he accommodated the characters to Henry IV, as best he could.[33]

It remained for the twentieth century seriously to attempt an analysis of the horse-stealing scenes, to bring general acceptance to the Mompelgart theory, to pursue the idea of a Garter reference, and to evolve more definite and detailed theories of the relation between the two forms of the play.

With the development of interest in scientific bibliography has come a great deal of new study of the difficult problem of the relation of Q of *The Merry Wives* to F. Certainly the specific impetus and much evidence was supplied by H. C. Hart in his study of the problem.[34] Greg (*Wiv.*, p. xv) says of his introduction that it is "at almost every point, an admirable piece of work." He praises Hart's examination of the relation of the two texts and also the detailed attention given to the peculiarities of Q, and the "lucid criticism" of their implication.

Although they do not come always to the same conclusion, all the major theorists of our time go back in one way or another to Hart's work. His careful and detailed study of the two texts left him with more reverence for the authenticity of F than any previous editor had shown. He adopts in his texts only three Q readings and those with reluctance. He supports his view of F with evidence from Daniel of omissions in Q which render its meaning unintelligible and show, Hart feels, in F an "undoubted seniority, which is palpable in many places."

He believes Q to have been reported by a "surreptitious notetaker" and "purloiner" from a shortened form of the play. He accepts F as a good text marred by "press errors" and actor's changes. His curious idea of "corruptions due to actor's innovations" in F is dealt with in more detail below. His simple description of what he found in Q was to be of great help later to Greg. He notes that the rather drastic omissions in the first scene appear more purposeful and more skillful than those later in the play, concluding that their purpose was to reduce the role of Slender. He is careful to compare the respective amount of space given to each character in the two versions. He concludes that Caius and Evans receive due attention in Q but that Mrs. Quickly's role is greatly cut and mangled and the wives' importance lessened. Falstaff is somewhat mangled but receives due proportion. Finally Hart points out, "the Host in the Quarto receives his full allowance of space. He is but slightly curtailed in any place from his proper position in the Folio, so that he is even more in evidence, comparatively in the Quarto." He concludes from this fact that the Host must have been a most popular stage character.

In spite of his respect for F, Hart was very much disturbed by its confusion of times, which he attributed to "undoubted garbling," and by needless repetitions which he found in the fourth and fifth acts. His conclusion about these characteristics is the most tenuous part of his argument and a part not fully accepted by any later critic. He suggests that in addition to the complete version of the play there was an authorized short version for occasional use and that the two forms became blended by the actors, causing the confusions apparent in F. Although it is conceivable, it is not easy, as Greg points out, to imagine how inconsistencies in actors' copies could have crept into the printed text of the play unless one supposes the play printed from actors' copies. This possibility was later suggested by A. W. Pollard and J. D. Wilson and is dealt with below.

To the Mompelgart business Hart contributes serious and detailed study. He outlines a plausible plot for the horse-stealing, deduced from the sketchy evidence of the plays. He accepts Knight's theory, saying that it helps somewhat to account for "what has all the appearance" of a topical reference and that since no other explanation has been suggested, "all the commentators appear to agree that the view has 'something in it.'" At another point, perhaps remembering Daniel, he says, "I am quite aware that some commentators will not admit this allusion though wholly unable to explain it away. . . . I believe in it." He supports his belief with cumulative evidence of both texts. In addition, he suggests, without proof, that Mompelgart may have irritated the queen and that the horse-stealing may have occurred. Hart also suggests a reason for the difference in the F version: "The alteration of the word "garmombles" (a thin disguise for "Mumpellgart") to "cozen-germans" in the F° was perhaps intentionally made to remove a personal allusion, either because it had lost its pith or because it was objected to." Noting that only F contains the line "Germans are honest men," he imagines that F was toned down because Q was "too plain-spoken." He points out that F relieves the Duke of any responsibility for dishonesty by suggesting that the trick was carried out by those supposed to be his servants. But again he concludes that "there can hardly be a question the allusion is to the visit of Count Mumpellgart." Hart is the first to suggest of the final scene that the different speeches in Q and F were intended for different audiences. He guesses that the F lines with their references to Windsor Castle and the Garter may indicate that the play "was adopted expressly for Windsor" and perhaps acted there. He describes the Q lines "which replace the Windsor Castle speech" as "very inferior" and says that they "sound pure London."

Hart's contribution to the study of Q and F is chiefly important because of its emphasis on F, its clear hypothesis of both stage abridgment and reportorial mangling in accounting for Q, its suggestion of the outlines of the horse-stealing plot, and its pointing up of the peculiar position of the Host.

Porter, in writing her introduction to a 1909 edition (*Wiv.*, ed. with Clarke, pp. 126, 130, 134–35) of the play, was clearly familiar with Halliwell and Daniel, though possibly not with Hart. She considers the first sketch theory to be finally dead, and hypothesizes that Q "presents the play in a mangled form." She supposes Q to be undoubtedly pirated and "surreptitiously secured in order to sell." She accepts as partial evidence the simultaneous entry and transfer of the play in the Stationers' Register—a process now generally thought to have been perfectly legal. Porter accepts Halliwell's hypothesis that the Q text was made up from "notes taken at the production or from the imperfect memoranda of actors." She supposes that imperfect parts and missing scenes were added later by the copyist or by the "person in charge of the whole." But she rejects Daniel's contention of omissions in F. She examines the particular lines cited by him and in each case finds omission not proven. Daniel's evidence of what he considers incompleteness in the time sequence and the horse-stealing plot she also fails to find convincing. And she concludes that "since no weightier evidence than this of incompleteness has been adduced," no omissions can be said to have been proven in F.

A. W. Pollard in the same year established his category of "bad quartos," including *The Merry Wives* as one of them and reaching the conclusion that the Q text was a piracy based on a reported version. He supports the idea of piracy by noting the use in Q of descriptions of the action rather than stage directions and mentions also the fact that both John Busby, who entered *The Merry Wives* in the Stationers' Register before assigning it to Arthur Johnson, and Thomas Creed, who printed the play, were associated with the supposedly pirated edition of *Henry V* in 1600. Pollard supposes that the Chamberlain's Men were in ill repute in 1601–2 because of their recent production of *Richard II* and were little able to defend themselves from such piracies.[35]

The major contribution to the study of the relation of the two texts was made by Greg. On some points he seems never to have been completely satisfied, but the progress of his thought may be traced in three major works: his edition of the Quarto in 1910; *The Editorial Problem in Shakespeare* (Oxford: Clarendon Press, 1951); and *The Shakespeare First Folio* (Oxford: Clarendon Press, 1955). In his original analysis,[36] Greg, finding Daniel's "proofs" of omissions in Q strong but not conclusive, still considers Q unquestionably corrupt. Even if no comparison is made to F, he says that Q is in itself "so garbled and corrupted" that the extent of its "possible mutilation" is unlimited. He adds, "The most cursory examination of the text shows that there is everywhere gross corruption, constant mutilation, meaningless inversion and clumsy transposition." He considers F to have derived "from an altogether independent source" and judges it "distinctly good though demonstrably not perfect. . . ." He notes the unusual use of massed entries and act and scene divisions, characteristics not typical of either prompt or private copies of plays, and attributes these to "a painstaking but hardly intelligent devil" who modeled his copy on Jonson.

Greg points out that in accounting for the difference between Q and F there could be three possible operations involved. Differences could be attributed to three possible causes:

> (i) the garbling, by a *reporter*, of the play as actually performed on the stage; (ii) the cutting and possible rewriting of the text for acting purposes by a stage *adapter*; and (iii) the working over, by an authorized *reviser*, of the original text (underlying the quarto) and the production of a new version (substantially represented by the folio text).

Regarding the reporter, he concludes, "Of his presence there can be no manner of doubt." Although Daniel has supposed that the reporter used shorthand and a notebook, Greg thinks that there is "nothing to suggest that the reporter relied as a rule on anything but his unaided memory." Observing, as has Hart, that the agreement between the two forms is much higher, except in two scenes involving the horse-stealing, when the Host is speaking, and when he is on or near the stage, than in other parts of the play, Greg concludes that the reporter was the actor who played the part of the Host. He finds that the facts are "exactly accounted for by supposing that the version was compiled by an actor who has learned his part imperfectly and very likely by ear." The agreement between the two versions is lowest in the last act, where the Host does not appear and where the actor might well have left the theater. At this point Greg admits that Q could have been compiled by an actor and reporter, but he sees no need to hypothesize two people where one would do.

In dealing with the question of a possible stage adapter, Greg considers in detail evidence that the play was deliberately shortened. Finding some rather strong indications, but rejecting many possible cases, he concludes that some adaptation is "highly probable," but that "the idea that the play was seriously altered or shortened is unsupported by evidence."

Considering the possible presence of a reviser, Greg supposes that his tendency would be to lengthen, and again he considers the evidence in detail. He supposes that the change from Brooke in Q to Broome in F was probably the author's. And he observes that at some period, possibly not until F was prepared for press, the oaths were omitted or toned down. He concludes, however, that except for the final scene there is no evidence that the difference between the two forms is appreciably due to revision.

Greg credits Hart with unravelling the true plot of the horse-stealing incident. He agrees with Hart and Daniel that what we have cannot represent the original because of the almost unintelligible loose ends of plot. Hart's attempt to account for the F version he considers inadequate:

> My own feeling is that the whole of the latter part of the play has been worked over at some time or other, and that probably by a hand different from that of the original author. The horse-stealing plot must once have occupied a far more prominent position than that now assigned to it, and it seems to me in the highest degree probable, from the indications that remain, that its solution was intimately bound up with that of the main plot. If that was so, then, when circumstances . . . led to the modification and, indeed, almost the suppression of this episode, a very considerable amount of reconstruction must have become necessary. What remained of the fourth and fifth acts had to be altered and expanded in such a manner as to form an intelligible and not too summary conclusion. This I think will amply account for the clumsy repetitions and the inferior composition which attracted Hart's attention in so unfavourable a manner.

For him at this stage it is clear that the F ending "must decidedly be condemned as unoriginal," although it represents the "authoritative text current in the playhouse. . . ."

Specifically in regard to the final scene, he repeats that neither quarto nor folio is original. He supposes then that after the original was cut, the remainder was twice worked over, possibly by the same hand, once for the popular stage and once for the court. Some scandal over the horse-stealing parts may have been involved, and the actors may have been lazy about learning their new lines. This would account for the Host's poor reporting in the two horse-stealing scenes, and possibly for the slipping in of such gags as the "'garmombles" line in Q. Greg is apparently not happy over the results, and he concludes in 1910 rather wistfully, "Would there were some chance of recovering the play as Shakespeare wrote it."

Greg's discussion of the two forms in 1951 (*Editorial Problem*, pp. 71 n., 72–73) is considerably more concise, and his view has changed in some particulars. He is more specific about the origin of F: "In fact F appears to have been probably printed from a transcript by Ralph Crane, most likely of foul papers. . . ."[37] But he is no more ready than before to accept the idea of extensive revision. And he is still dissatified with even F, referring to it as a "hastily written piece."

His new discussion leans somewhat more definitely toward the view that deliberate shortening of the play did take place in the preparation of the Q text:

> The text of Q is of course much abridged. This may mean that it is a report of a shortened performance: but in view of the frequent occurrence, in what remains, of displaced fragments from what is omitted, it seems on the whole more likely that the performance was substantially a full one and that the abbreviation is the reporter's due either to his inability to produce anything more adequate or to a deliberate intention of shortening the play. If the latter, the piracy was presumably made for acting. There is no proof one way or the other; but the heavy cutting of the opening, of which however a fragment is used later, suggests it, and so does the excision of two boys' parts; it is also noticeable that directions, though descriptive, seem to have the regulation of the action in view.

On three points, however, Greg seems to have changed his mind. First, he admits that the greater agreement between Q and F in scenes where the Host appears is not quite uniform and that some of the errors in the Host's speeches in Q seem due to mishearing. As a result of these problems, Greg now adds to his theory the previously excluded independent reporter.

His new theory is indeed safer in that it does explain the lack of complete uniformity in the superiority of the lines of the Host and in that it apparently permits a simplification of theory in regard to the horse-stealing (see below), but the question of errors due to mishearing is less clear. The example he quotes seems to me almost certainly due not to mis-hearing but to some sort of misreading. He quotes the line which appears thus in Q and F:

Q. *Host.* I am cosened Hugh, and coy Bardolfe,
F. *Host.* Huy and cry (villaine) goe:

(*IV.v.93*)

If the transcript the Q compositor had before him read "Huy and cry Bardolfe," or "Hue and cry Bardolfe," the normalization of the spelling of the name and the misreading of one letter in "cry" would be quite conceivable. But to suppose that anyone could have heard "Hue and cry, Bardolfe" and written down what occurs in Q is to imagine a total alteration of intonation and juncture patterns which seems to me inconceivable. That such a "mishearing" should occur in a speech of the Host, who was supposedly assisting with the piracy, seems particularly unlikely. However, there is at least one mishearing in Q, I believe, where the two versions run as follows:

Q. *Host.* Is a dead bullies taile. . . .
F. *Host.* . . . is he dead bully Stale. . . .

(*II.iii.31*)

Greg's earlier suggestion that the Host learned his part "very likely by ear" may have been an attempt to account for such mishearings; and if he did learn by ear, the Host's dictation of the play to someone either in the pirating play company or in the printer's shop would have provided new occasion for mishearing.

The second point on which Greg had changed his mind by 1951 is so sketchily developed as to leave his new position far from clear. He seems to say that he now considers the horse-stealing episode complete, but poorly reported because of the joint efforts of the Host and the reporter. Why the two people should have done less well in these scenes than others, he simply does not say. By 1955 (*Sh. First Folio*, pp. 336–37) he seems to have gone back to the idea that something may have been cut, and he develops the idea in more detail. Accepting the Mompelgart reference, he says,

> His importunity [to be awarded the Order of the Garter] seems to have roused some resentment at court and possibly some amusement in wider circles. He was eventually elected in 1597, but in spite of two further embassies failed to obtain the insignia till after the Queen's death. . . . There is . . . no hint of shady dealing on the part of the Count or his agents . . . but we can easily imagine that among other gossip some scandalous tales became current. The horse-stealing episode is curiously fragmentary and is indeed hardly intelligible in either version as it stands. It may be that it played a more important part in the play as originally written and that it was thought advisable to cut the more obviously libellous passages on the stage. Bad reporting of the Host's part hereabouts suggests that the text may have been altered subsequent to the original production. If so, the

'garmombles' allusion, which must in any case be a bit of actor's gag that got into the report, may be a sly reference to the forbidden topic.

The third difference between Greg's 1910 view and his later, apparently final conclusion relates to the last act of the play. He simplifies his cumbersome and unnecessarily complicated hypothesis of two originals for this part of the play. In 1951 (*Edit. Prob.*, p. 72) he apparently feels that at least some of the changes in Q were made deliberately with an eye to the audience for which the version was intended: "I no longer feel convinced that in the last act Q goes back to an original different from F, though the latter assumes a courtly, the former a popular, audience: this would be a necessary alteration if the piracy was made for acting." But in 1955 (*Sh. First Folio*, pp. 334–35) his supposition seems to be that the version of Q was created to supply the place of what was missing in the reported version. This hypothesis is much more plausible since it is impossible to imagine that anyone who *had* the F version deliberately substituted that of Q. Even if the reporters had desired to remove the Garter references from a form intended for a popular audience, this goal could have been accomplished much more simply. Greg's final word seems also rather definitely to allow room for a stage adapter and to assume that the reporter could have had the assistance of Falstaff.

> The last act is much confused. The omission of the first four scenes is, no doubt, like that of I.i, deliberate, but the denouement itself in V.v is woefully inadequate and bears little resemblance to the corresponding scene in F. The Host takes no part in it in either text, and it is clear that, in spite of the presence of Falstaff, the reporter was unable to recover more than the barest outline, and that he rewrote part of the scene in doggerel verse, incorporating in it what appears to be a fragment of a London ballad.

Greg's 1951 (*Edit. Prob.*, p. 337) conclusion that F "appears to have been probably printed from a transcript by Ralph Crane, most likely of foul papers. . . ." was also modified in 1955 when he concluded very tentatively that the Crane transcript was of the prompt book. The evidence, however, is not decisive, and Brock, after reexamining the problem in 1956 (Diss. Virginia 1956, pp. 26–35), favors the theory that the copy behind the transcript was Shakespeare's foul papers. In 1951, Greg (*Edit. Prob.*, p. 334) is still dissatisfied with F, but now seems more willing than before to attribute inadequacies to haste and carelessness rather than to mangling of original copy. Finally, his description of Q in 1955 makes clear that he considers the text a memorial reconstruction by a reporter who had access to both the Host and Falstaff and that he believes the text to have been deliberately shortened: "The abridgement . . . appears to have been done in the course of preparing the report, whence we may conclude that this was intended for acting, presumably in the country, and only later and incidentally found its way to press."

Although the main outlines of Greg's theory of a reported text have been accepted by most scholars, there have been a number of suggested modifications and a few serious challenges.

In a series of articles in the *Times Literary Supplement* of 1919, Pollard and Wilson made some new suggestions about the derivation of the "bad quartos," devoting one article to *The Merry Wives*, and claiming that their theory involved little more than "a combination and reconciliation" of Daniel, Greg, and Robertson.[38] In fact their hypothesis goes back to Fleay's effort to relate the Q version to the *Jealous Comedy* of 1593. They believe that all the bad quartos represent stage abridgements made for the provinces and that they either go back to early dates or have been preceded by earlier plays on the same subjects.[39]

The Merry Wives Q they consider an "undoubted piracy" based on "a much earlier play, abridged for provincial representation and expanded again by a pirate who was probably an actor." The assumption of the relation to the earlier play is based on the loose ends the authors see in both Q and F, on the fact that they find Falstaff an uneven mixture of the fat knight and "a simpering lady-killer of quite un-Falstaffian demeanour, much more akin to Joseph Surface," and finally on the "garmombles" reference. They strengthen their argument by noting that Shakespeare's company did have a *Jealous Comedy* on their books in 1593 and somewhat circularly ask, "is it likely that Shakespeare's company had two such comedies on the stocks in January, 1593?" Admitting that there is "not a tittle of direct evidence" to connect *The Merry Wives* and the *Jealous Comedy*, they nonetheless insist on the connection, citing Shakespeare's known borrowing habits and the supposed need for haste in providing a play at the command of the Queen.

They reject on literary grounds parts of both Q and F as non-Shakespearean and find F to represent revision of Q rather than Q to represent a corruption of F. They cite Fenton's speech in III.iv.13–18 as a case in point:

> Q. Thy father thinks I love thee for his wealth,
> Tho I must needs confesse at first that drew me,
> But since thy vertues wiped that trash away,
> I love the *Nan*, and so deare is it set,
> That whilst I live, I nere shall thee forget.

F. Albeit I will confesse, thy Fathers wealth
Was the first motiue that I woo'd thee (Anne:)
Yet wooing thee, I found thee of more valew
Then stampes in Gold, or summes in sealed bagges:
That now I ayme at.

They add the dubious conclusion, "Is it not clear that the second is an uninspired revision of the wooden original? And will anybody contend that the author of the Balcony Scene in *Romeo and Juliet* wrote either?"[40]

Pollard and Wilson assume, following Greg, that an actor was assistant for the pirated Q edition. "The theory that a traitor-actor was engaged by shady publishers to make what additions he could to the 1593 abridgements serves to explain all the phenomena of the Bad Quartos." They assume that the actor was a member of the company playing in a revived and revised version of the play. His purpose was to make the old stage abridgement as much as possible like the current play. They even suggest that "at times the pirate . . . could . . . copy out his 'players part' and take it to the printer."[41]

Pollard and Wilson find that the theory of pirate actor is not alone sufficient to account for the relation of Q and F. Attempting to explain the imperfections of F, the presence of actors' gags, the lack of stage directions, and the massed entries, they suggest that for some reason, perhaps because of the haste of revision, the F editors had "little but players' parts to go upon" and that F represents an "assembled text."[42] R. Compton Rhodes in 1923 supports this theory;[43] but in 1927, F. P. Wilson ("Ralph Crane," p. 214), although as puzzled as other critics by the massed entries, finds that the "assembled text" theory does not adequately explain them. He notes that they occur in only two plays of F and that Ralph Crane usually gives entries in their proper places. To do this, he says, "even if he was transcribing from the players' parts . . . was not beyond Crane's capacity." R. C. Bald continues the discussion in his introduction to Middleton's *A Game at Chesse* in 1929 (pp. 28–29, 40–42). Comparing two MSS of this play, both by Crane (MS. Malone 25 and MS. Lansdowne 690), Bald finds the former considerably shorter than the latter and also characterized by paucity of stage directions and by massed entries, although Crane seems to have made the cuts in the longer version with Middleton's consent and was apparently not working from parts. Bald concludes that the massed entries must be considered "an occasional idiosyncrasy" of Crane's, "possibly copied from Ben Jonson's neo-classical habit." Both Greg (*Edit. Prob.*, pp. 134 ff.) and E. K. Chambers[44] have rejected the idea of an "assembled text" as unlikely, unnecessary, and certainly not proven.

The Pollard-Wilson articles also insist, although they do not give supporting examples, that there are bibliographical links between the two forms of *The Merry Wives.* "A good patch in a pirated text is frequently linked by identity of misprints, identity of capital letters, or identity of spelling with its parallel in the better text."[45] My own examination of the two texts simply does not support the view that they are "frequently" identical in the ways listed. There are a few cases of parallelism, but one may always suppose that the editors of F were free to consult the published Q to assist them in difficult passages.

In summary, then, the Pollard-Wilson view of 1919 was that before 1592 there was an old play about London middle-class life. At the end of 1592 some dramatist or dramatists added the horse-stealing plot to satirize Mompelgart and perhaps attempted to link the play with the early Oldcastle cycle by changing the name of the philanderer. In 1593 this play was given as the *Jealous Comedy.* Then came the plague, when the company toured with a shortened version. After the success of *Henry IV* in 1598, the old play was brought out to meet a royal command and revised by several people. Shakespeare worked on Oldcastle, and collaborators did the rest. The horse-stealing plot was cut, as it was no longer timely. It seems evident that this theory is needlessly complicated and that it hangs tenuously on literary evidence and conjecture. Wilson himself in 1947 mentions his work with Pollard on the "bad quartos" as "later abandoned."[46]

In the Cambridge edition of *The Merry Wives* in 1921,[47] Wilson's note on the text expands his theory somewhat and gives some examples—especially to support his idea of revision. He still assumes some bibliographical link between the plays, but the evidence is no longer "frequent" but now "faint and scanty." He develops the idea of the "assembled text" for F but adds that the single indication of internal entry in the Fairy scene suggests the possibility that it "may have been set up from a scrap of author's manuscript."

Wilson's evidence for revision comes chiefly from an examination of disturbances in verse-arrangement—admittedly difficult in a prose play. But he finds the four verse-scenes full of signs of revision suggesting "that the original drama, if not wholly in verse, contained many more verse-scenes than the text as we have it, and that it was the intention of the revisers to rewrite the whole thing in prose, except perhaps the fairy-episode in 5.5., an intention which lack of time forbade them to realise." The outlines of the theory here are the same as those given in the 1919 articles. Wilson does insist also, as in fact have most of the editors before him, on giving some authority to Q and in addition seems to suggest, without advancing his reasons, that Q, too, was "assembled" from players parts.

The discussion of the Q-F problem by Quiller-Couch, also in the 1921 Cambridge edition, is clearly based on the work of Pollard and Wilson. He accepts both the idea of the Host as reporter and the use of the early play, saying that the Q version was given to the printer "by a rascal actor, who possessed some kind of text of the earlier 'jealous comedy' to fall back upon when his memory gave out." Quiller-Couch, however, mentions only Shakespeare as reviser of the abridged early play. He also emphasizes the haste of preparation of the F version and accepts the idea that Falstaff is two separate characters rolled into one. In insisting on the relation of the play to the *Jealous Comedy,* he gives a very misleading impression of unanimity among the critics who have preceded him: "the labours of P. A. Daniel, and more recent critics conclusively prove the Quarto to be no first sketch, but a compressed, 'cut down' version of some pre-existent play, and the Folio a later, still imperfect, but far better version of the same."

In 1924, Chambers spoke against the various critics responsible for what he calls the "disintegration" of Shakespeare. He describes verse and vocabulary tests as inaccurate and untrustworthy, and he doubts the notion of Pollard and Wilson that copy was continuously changed even when a play was revived.[48] In his *William Shakespeare,* published in 1930 and reprinted in 1951, Chambers makes some further evaluation of theories concerning the two forms of the play.[49] He feels no doubt that the "Bad Quartos" are those referred to by Heminge and Condell as "surreptitious." He discounts the likelihood that the play was taken down by shorthand and notes that the various "anticipations" and "recollections" imply a knowledge of the whole play. He accepts Greg's theory of the Host as reporter and, like the Greg of 1910, seriously doubts the possibility of deliberate cutting, although he admits that the parts of the two boys may have been dropped and allows the possibility that the Latin scene may have been intended only to please Elizabeth. By and large, however, he attributes omissions to the Host's carelessness or his absence from the stage.

On one point Chambers rejects the early Greg theory. He does not believe there was any revision of the horse-stealing plot but thinks that Q is a perversion of F. Chambers doubts that there was ever more to this plot, noting that the slightly developed plot with Shallow is also left hanging. He also doubts, as Greg came to do, the idea that someone, not Shakespeare, deliberately made two different endings to the play. Chambers thinks that F is Shakespeare and Q the attempt of someone else to supply a lack in Q.

In dealing with the theory of Pollard and Wilson, Chambers denies the presence of "bibliographical links" between the two versions of the play. He does not think the idea of "assembling" inconceivable but points out that he does not find the kind of error he would expect to find if this had occurred. Chambers rejects the idea of an earlier comedy adapted by Shakespeare. He indicates that efforts to connect this play with 1592 are tenuous and unproven, adding that he finds the objections of Pollard and Wilson to the "euphuistic" Falstaff hypercritical.

Also published in 1930 is the article of Henry D. Gray called "The Roles of William Kemp." Working on the premise that both the Host and Falstaff acted as reporters for Q, Gray tries to guess why the actor who played Falstaff, surely a leading member of Shakespeare's company, might have been willing to help pirate the company's play. Starting with the hypothesis that William Kemp was Shakespeare's Falstaff, Gray suggests that the character does not appear in *Henry V* because Kemp had left the Chamberlain's Men by the autumn of 1599, although he had signed a lease with the sharers of the Globe on February 21, 1599. Gray supposes that Kemp got angry during rehearsals for *The Merry Wives*, left the company in a rage, and helped pirate the play which he had rehearsed, though not enough to master the last scene. Gray's idea is interesting but almost entirely conjectural. It does not allow for the now generally agreed on date of 1597 for *The Merry Wives*, nor does it prove Falstaff a necessary accomplice to the Host as pirate.[50]

The main purpose of Leslie Hotson's *Shakespeare versus Shallow* (Boston: Little, Brown, 1931) was to advance a new theory of the identity of the original of Justice Shallow. In so doing, however, he sets new limits for the possible dates of *The Merry Wives* and suggests a specific occasion for the production of the play. Hotson accepts the reference to Mompelgart but points out that he, by now the Duke of Wurtemberg, was finally elected to the Order of the Garter (in absentia) on April 23, 1597, at the same time as Shakespeare's patron, Lord Hunsdon. He suggests, rather convincingly, that Shakespeare wrote the play for this occasion. I shall discuss this suggestion later in more detail. Suffice it for now to observe that it offers no new light on the Q-F relationship, but it does seem to vitiate efforts to tie the Q "garmombles" to Count Mompelgart's visit in 1592.

Clearly familiar with the work of his predecessors, J. Crofts advances in *Shakespeare and the Post Horses* (Bristol: Arrowsmith, 1937) a new set of complicated and ingenious suggestions.[51] Like Fleay and Pollard and Wilson, Crofts assumes that Shakespeare built on an older play by another author. He does not insist, however, on associating it with the *Jealous Comedy* of 1593, and he considers that some lines indicate rather strongly that the name Oldcastle appeared in the earlier form. He conjectures that the plot of the old play was essentially that of *The Merry Wives* and that Shakespeare altered it little except to make room for his "irregular humours" characters. The play may have been, he guesses, one on bourgeois life, based on Italian sources, with a euphuistic and priggish hero of whom he, like Quiller-Couch, finds traces in *The Merry Wives*.

In regard to the problem of the relation of Q to F, Crofts's hypothesis represents, like Pollard's and Wilson's, a variation of the revision theory. His startling innovation is that he thinks he has found sufficient evidence to reconstruct the hypothetical manuscript behind both forms of the play. This manuscript he calls *MS and reproduces in full. Crofts accepts Greg's idea that Q is a reported text and agrees that in some places it "offers a version not only inferior to that of the Folio but distinct from it." He insists, however, that at least four Q readings and possibly as many as a dozen are manifestly preferable to those of F. And he differs from Greg in feeling that no reporter who knew F would omit or rewrite popular scenes of the play.

Starting, then, with a number of good Q readings considerably larger than most critics have been willing to allow, he advances an ingenious but inadmissible hypothesis. Examining the position on the page of the "good" readings of Q, he finds that more often than is attributable to chance their position follows a pattern. He suggests that there lies at some remove behind it a folio manuscript containing about sixty-two lines to a page, a manuscript which has had the bottom of various pages worn away by use or by accident and therefore lacks certain passages. This manuscript (Crofts's *MS), later revised by the author, was the copy for F, while Q is reported by actors (the Host and Falstaff) who had learned their parts before the damage to *MS. This reconstruction of events leads him to the very tenuous conclusion that "At every point where the texts differ sharply, and a crux exists, the most natural explanation will be found to be that the Quarto represents a corrupted original, and that the Folio reading is a reckless attempt to patch it."

Crofts conjectures, without any real basis, that the order of scenes in Q was designed to allow audience participation in a real ducking of Falstaff. This idea, added to his other efforts, leads him to a rather high estimate of the authority of Q:

> We can find no reason to doubt that it represents the version of the play current in 1597; and the fact that the order of scenes points to a piece of horse-play which would have been impracticable in a public theatre but was probably quite feasible at Windsor, suggests that it may represent that first version of the play which according to tradition, was prepared for a court performance.

This estimate is based, however, on the conviction that F represents a revised form. Concerning the problem of which form is earlier, he says, "If even one page of our *MS, can be shown to have existed we shall be able to conclude with confidence that the Quarto represents the earlier version of the play, and that the Folio is a hasty but unusually interesting revision of the text which the Quarto represents." The assumption of "hasty" authorial revision leads him in at least one case to the manifestly absurd conclusion that Shakespeare wrote a line which he himself did not understand. He also deduces that the author did not recopy the whole manuscript but occasionally inserted pages without restoring lacunae or correcting errors. Concluding that *The Merry Wives* is not a play in which Shakespeare took much pride or pleasure, Crofts nonetheless takes it as a clear example of his methods as reviser.

The entire elaborate superstructure of Crofts's theory is built on a literary preference for approximately ten Q readings. If only two or three or four of these readings are admissible, as most critics since Hart have agreed, the superstructure simply collapses. The theory itself is needlessly complicated and full of precise conjectures which cannot be substantiated.

Crofts does raise one question which deserves some attention, however. It concerns the "garmombles" reference. He claims, apparently with justice, that there is no evidence connecting the 1592 visit of Mompelgart with any misunderstandings with English postmasters or indicating that there was anything mysterious or sinister about his free post-warrant. He notes further that if there had been a scandal in 1592, it could hardly have been obscure if was still good for a laugh five years later. He also dismisses Hotson's suggestions that the references in the play might be related to the Duke's failure to appear at his Garter installation in 1597. Crofts claims that such absences were not at all uncommon and could not be taken as subject for satire.

Like Greg, Crofts feels that the post-horses scenes in their present form must be fragmentary and that they are only explicable as allusive. Discounting the supposed allusion to Mompelgart, he uncovers two posting scandals which he feels may have relevance. One involves the Governor of Dieppe, de Chastes, who came to England on a mission from France and caused considerable disturbance on the Dover road on September 4, 1596. The second is an apparently hushed up scandal involving post-horses and a probably illegitimate post-warrant signed by Lords Thomas Howard and Mountjoy presented at Chard in November 1597. Either incident he considers possible as a reference, and he evolves a fanciful story which includes both of them. Building on three facts—(1) that Slender's beard is described in the play (he thinks unnecessarily, as it would have been seen by the audience); (2) that there is a reference to Slender's fight "with a Warrener"; and (3) that the Chief Waterman on the Thames was named Warner or Wardener—Crofts even imagines a wild and totally unsubstantiated story of a beard-pulling which he thinks may be referred to in the play.

Crofts admits that his theory depends on the validity of Hotson's date and on the lack of any evidence that Mompelgart stole horses. The possibility of a reference to de Chastes opens up a new field for inquiry, later picked up by William Green. But Crofts's elaborations of what happened are inadmissible, and his theory fails to offer any satisfactory explanation of the word "garmombles."

In his study of the textual history of the play in 1942,[52] David M. White supports Greg's ideas of memorial reconstruction by the Host. In fact he attributes almost all the differences between the two forms to this reporter. He disallows any deliberate abridgment for provincial performance except possibly the omission of the two boys. His reason is that some trivial scenes are allowed to remain while relatively important parts are omitted. Although Q is "compressed," he thinks this is the result of necessity rather than of deliberate shortening by the author. He assumes that the reporter is to be blamed for anticipations, recollections, and non sequitur passages and is to be credited with revision at least in the color scheme of the dresses in the last scene. White believes that the actor who played the Host may have been dropped from Shakespeare's company during the war of the theatres in 1601 and may have made his prompt book from memory for provincial players. White accepts the Mompelgart reference but assigns it to April 1597, using Hotson's date of composition.

In attempting to explain the Brooke-Broome variant, White ties the charge to the abortive Bye Plot, which led to the disgrace of Lord Cobham and the execution of his brother, George Brooke, on December 5, 1603. He guesses that the name Brooke was dropped from the original before the performance of the play at James's court on November 4, 1604. The name is so common, the applicability so slight, and the interval so long as to make this suggestion seem unlikely.

On the whole, White considers F the authentic play, somewhat marred by printer's errors. Because of the "classical form," he accepts the idea of Wilson and Rhodes that F was printed from an "assembled" text. He argues that no one would deliberately have imposed such a form on a copy which already had the usual indications of entrances and exits and other stage directions. He finds no need to posit any Shakespearean revision in F.

A new insistence on the validity of Q is seen in the work of the next two writers on the subject of Q and F: John H. Long and William Bracy. Long deals only with the masque in the final scene. He argues that Shakespeare wrote both versions of the masque, the Q form for a command performance before Queen Elizabeth and the F form for the performance before King James in 1604. Q he thinks was intended as a satire of such writers as Lyly and F as a topical reference to a recent Garter installation. While granting that F is a better example of the formal masque, he finds Q more appropriate to the rollicking spirit of the farce and suggests that it should be used in modern editions of the play. He makes no effort to explain the other differences between Q and F except as the result of piracy.[53]

Bracy, in *"The Merry Wives of Windsor"—The History and Transmission of Shakespeare's Text,*[54] in 1952, sets out to prove that the idea of memorial reconstruction is absurd and that Q is an authorized stage abridgment of F in a form intended for provincial tour. The effort is valiant but for the most part unsuccessful. He does amass a rather formidable amount of evidence which makes the idea of abridgment for the stage seem very likely—as Greg himself had said in 1951. Like Chambers, Bracy discounts the possibility that the play was taken down in shorthand. "The shorthand theory is certainly incapable of accounting for the variety of textual phenomena in the *Merry Wives* Quarto. The dramatic integrity of text is too great, the evidence of conscious revision and careful abridgment too convincing to admit such a view. The close similarity of certain Quarto and Folio passages and the accurate handling of dialectic jargon in the roles of the French doctor and the Welsh priest represent textual transmission not within the range of shorthand reporting of this early period." He also doubts the whole idea of widespread printer-piracies, contending that "if there were any reconstruction of text they must have been made, at least in most cases, for the purposes of performance; that it was the work, not of a single actor, but of a group; that fragments of manuscript or players' 'parts' may have been sometimes used as indicated by bibliographical links with 'good' texts; that authorized stage abridgments must have been intermediary in most cases between the 'good' and 'bad' versions." This statement is in clear opposition to the conclusions of Greg that "parts" were not used and that the short text was abridged by the reporter or reporters and not taken from an abridged version.

Bracy further opposes Greg on the whole idea of Host as reporter, accusing him of starting from an "initial prejudice" and "preconceived conclusions." He claims that if all facts are considered, the role of the Host is not more faithfully reproduced than are those of other characters. This assertion is supported only by the author's pointing out that the Host has a minor role and short speeches and that Greg does not explain why he would have assigned his own lines to other characters. "There are difficulties," as Greg has said, but Bracy's reductio ad absurdum of the memorial reconstruction theory certainly does not live up to its title. The theory of Host as reporter, quite likely with assistance, remains the most satisfactory explanation suggested to date.

Bracy's own efforts to account for the differences between Q and F are based chiefly on proving stage adaptation. His evidence of deliberate stage abridgment is convincing, and this point seems to be one on which critics are now generally agreed.

But the theory of adaptation is far from explaining all the differences between the two texts. Bracy simply does not seem to admit the high incidence of random variation and pointless inversion—in fact the degree of "mangling" to be found in Q. He attempts to explain some errors in terms of handwriting:

> There are many errors and variants throughout both texts of Shakespeare's *Merry Wives* which involve handwriting and printing. In such cases the Folio and Quarto are often equally at fault. This point is definitely damaging to Greg's pirate-actor theory. . . . It is at least suggestive that the printers were working directly from playhouse manuscript in both cases.

Part of this may be true, but again we must leave him at the end of his argument. Even a pirate-actor would presumably have made or dictated some sort of manuscript to be used by the printer, and no necessary implication of "playhouse manuscript" seems to be involved. Further variation, Bracy suggests, may be due to the Renaissance mind, with its "natural tendency toward variation," and to the process of adaptation which he supposes involved certain insertions, transpositions, and omissions in the manuscript, as well as recopying.

Bracy finds evidence of Shakespearean revision negligible in both forms, and he accounts somewhat vaguely for the needless repetitions and inconsistencies of F by supposing revival and adaptation or printers working from a poor manuscript. His accumulation of evidence for stage abridgment is valuable, but his examination of the bibliographical relationship between the two plays is inadequate and his dismissal of the theory of memorial reconstruction cannot be accepted. Greg in his review of the book[55] predictably rejects Bracy's arguments, finding the author not lacking in learning but deficient in logic and judgment.

A new variation on the revision theory and a renewed effort to vindicate the authority of Q is found in Albert Feuillerat's *The Composition of Shakespeare's Plays* (New Haven: Yale Univ. Press, 1953; pp. 40–43, 52–78). The author rehearses the difficulties of accepting the Host as reporter of *The Merry Wives* Q, mentioning the lines which are better when he is offstage than when he is on, and the horse-stealing scenes. Feuillerat suggests that it is odd that all actor-reporters should make similar mistakes and report inconsistently, and he concludes that the theory of memorial reconstruction is as disappointing as that of stenographic reconstruction. His own view is that F has been often tampered with and is not to be relied on; but, at the same time, he finds it reasonable to suppose that it has been augmented and improved, asserting that in every case what has been taken as a proof of corruption in Q can be viewed equally well as a proof of corruption in F. Feuillerat has found, then, a way of accepting what he likes and rejecting what he dislikes in the two forms of the play. He makes some effort to discover the nature of the MSS involved, but his tests for revision are similar to J. D. Wilson's and seem very dubious. He interprets prose written as verse and incomplete lines as signs of revision, and he considers variation between generic and specific speech headings for the characters (e.g., *Father* and *Capulet* in *Romeo and Juliet*) to be an indication that Shakespeare was working from an old play of a type close to the moralities. Feuillerat goes on to develop extremely questionable verse tests to separate Shakespearean from non-Shakespearean poetry, but he does not apply this technique to *The Merry Wives.*

In 1956, Brock reexamined the Q-F question in her history of the text.[56] Like Greg, she concludes that F is the "only authoritative text" and that Q was memorially reconstructed, with the Host at least part contributor, and that it was probably prepared for acting. She finds some, though not conclusive, evidence that a Ralph Crane manuscript lies behind the F version, and she leans toward the idea that the manuscript was made from Shakespeare's foul papers rather than from the prompt copy. Also, like Greg, she finds the *Brooke-Broome* change the only indubitable sign of revision, and she accepts the conclusion of Chambers and David White that this change was made at the time of the court performance of the play in 1604 because of the political situation. On the horse-stealing question, she feels that revision or excision is not necessarily indicated and that the fragmentary nature of the plot may be due to haste. Admitting the puzzling inconsistencies of the final scene, she accepts the idea that the difference in Q is due to the Host's absence from the stage and supposes the Q scene put together by the reporter.

The presence of the reporter is still not universally accepted, however. In 1961, Hardin Craig followed the line of argument advanced by Bracy. The "bad" Q, he protests, is not bad at all but a "stage version of such a kind as would be made by intelligent actors." He continues: "In reality, the quarto text, apart from its being an abbreviated stage version of the original so altered as to dispense with several actors, is not a bad quarto at all."[57] He considers the state of Q such as could have been produced by touring, stage revivals, and passing through the hand of a London printer and calls the text "both good and Shakespearean." He accepts Bracy's idea of shortening and indicates that the title page's announcement that the play has played before the Queen "and elsewhere" implies that the play in this form has been "on the road." He does not develop this theory, but he seems to suggest a lingering trace of the idea of revision: "Q, allowing for cuts and rearrangements, is simpler than F, and so far as it extends and escapes mutilation, it is possibly closer to Shakespeare's first version than is F."

Although Craig admits that an editor must use F as the original, since there is no other way of guessing at the text, he is not happy with it. He finds it "full of errors, misreadings of manuscript, and omissions" and calls it "shaky" and "often inferior to the much despised quarto of 1602." Accepting Hotson's date of composition in the spring of 1597, Craig suggests that the shortened form was made before Shakespeare's company went on tour in August and September of that year. Like Greg, Craig finds evidence of different authors in the final scene, but he objects to the suggestion that any "breaking down" takes place in Q. "One cannot say that Q breaks down in the last scene, since it is, with slight exceptions, perfectly clear and characteristically direct. One can only say that, where both texts of the play are preserved, Q differs from F more widely at the end of the play than at any other place." Again, as with Bracy's discussion, one feels that the critic has simply not explained the extent and the random quality of the difference between Q and F.

A recent extended study of the composition of this play is William Green's book (Princeton: Princeton Univ. Press, 1962) called *Shakespeare's Merry Wives of Windsor.*[58] Accepting Hotson's date, Green focuses his attention on "the events surrounding [the play's] composition and the manner by which those events shaped the text."

Green's thesis, convincingly defended, is that *The Merry Wives* was "Shakespeare's Garter play," written on commission from George Carey, Lord Hunsdon, newly appointed Lord Chamberlain, favorite of the Queen and patron of Shakespeare's company, for the Garter celebration at Whitehall on April 23, 1597, at which Hunsdon knew he was to be elected Knight of the Garter. Green argues that the setting of the play at Windsor is the installation ceremony to be held two months later at Windsor, a town widely known in England and abroad as the home of the Order of the Garter. He notes in F five separate references to the court and the celebration to which Dr. Caius is invited at court.

In attempting to account for Q, Green finds that the idea of unauthorized memorial reconstruction is the only theory that can explain its corruption and concludes that abridgment of the original was made for an unauthorized production by provincial troupes. For the provinces, he supposes that the court references were deleted but the horse-stealing scenes left because of their appeal to current English anti-German feeling. The parts in Q that Hart has called "pure London" he finds equally appropriate to the provinces. He accepts Greg's identification of the Host as reporter but rejects the suggestion that Falstaff might have helped on the grounds that a major actor would not have contributed to the piracy. Green wonders why Shakespeare's company did not issue a good copy of *The Merry Wives* after the publication of Q, as they did with other plays; he concludes that they could not because Q had been entered in the Stationer's Register and because this gave a printer control of a work no matter how the work had been obtained.

Although he doubts the relation of F to the *Jealous Comedy*, Green believes that some earlier play does lie behind Shakespeare's version. Some of the errors in F he attributes to scribe and compositors, but most to the author's haste.

All previous efforts to work out complete and logical outlines of a horse-stealing plot are rejected by Green. He finds it not convincing as a working out of the revenge either of Pistol and Nym or of Evans and Caius. Like Chambers and Brock, he assumes that what we are given is really all that the audience needed, and though he finds the sequence an obvious artistic failure, he assumes that its purpose was to please the Knights of the Garter. Following Hotson, Green cites a long series of letters and emissaries from Mompelgart to the Queen and nobles of the court between 1592 and 1597 supporting and pressing his desire to become a member of the Order of the Garter. He says, "in this—and in this matter only—did Frederick achieve notoriety in the English Court."

Assuming, like Hotson, that Mompelgart's absence from the ceremonies and his unpopularity at court would have made him a natural butt for jokes, Green accepts "garmombles" as a reference to Mompelgart. But, like Crofts, he feels that the horse-stealing scenes have no relevance. He picks up Crofts's suggestion of the de Chastes incident as inspiration and hypothesizes that six months after this posting scandal (which had a very slight association with the investiture of Henry IV of France as a member of the Garter) Shakespeare, in writing *The Merry Wives*, thought of joining this incident with a satire of Mompelgart. The idea is sheer guesswork; and though it is conceivably what happened, it does not seem especially probable. One is left with the feeling that the horse-stealing plot is as far as ever from a really satisfactory explanation.

Green believes that "garmombles" was in the original text and that the reporter remembered and used it even though the reference may have had no specific meaning to a provincial audience. He supposes that it was changed in the F copy in 1604 after the Duke's installation, when relations with the Germans were more amicable. Like Hart, he thinks the line "Germanes are honest men" may have been added at that time. In the absence of other evidence of revision, however, it seems that one might well suppose this line, as well as the "cozen-Iermans" in place of "cozen Garmombles," was in the original play. If so, the one may have been dropped either by accident or design by the reporter and the other, the "garmombles" line, may have been substituted as an actors' gag and remembered by the reporter.

Green offers what seems to me a useful suggestion concerning the *Brooke-Broome* revision. Considering the various suggestions—(1) Crofts's notion that the change was due to the publisher's trouble with the York Herald in 1619; (2) White's idea that the change was related to the Bye Plot in 1603; and (3) Hotson's supposition that the name *Brooke* was intended as an affront to Cobham, the Lord Chamberlain in early 1597, who was thought to be anti-theatrical —Green rejects all these possibilities. He thinks the name *Oldcastle* was changed in the *Henry IV* plays between July 1596 and March 1597 after a complaint from William, Lord Cobham, then Lord Chamberlain. In writing *The Merry Wives,* he thinks, Shakespeare used the name *Brooke* as the obvious alias for Ford, without thought of affront. In rehearsal someone noticed the family name of Cobham, now recently deceased, and in order to avoid offending the family, changed the name. Since the name *Brooke* appears forty-two times in Q, the pirate-actor would certainly have remembered it and employed it as a better reading in the provinces, where it could cause no trouble. *Broome* would, of course, have remained in the written form behind F.

About the last scene Green says little except to add the conjecture, following White, that the reporter of Q changed the mixed up color scheme of F in an effort (which Green seems to think successful) to clear up the confusion. He sums up his view of the variation between the texts:

> Divergence between the Q and F texts can therefore more properly be explained by the fact that certain alterations such as *garmombles* to *Cozen-Iermans*—had been made in the original text after 1601 . . . that certain other alterations—such as *Brooke* to *Broome*—had been made especially for the 1597 productions [and restored by the traitor-actor] . . . and that still others—such as the elimination of confusion in costume color in V.v. —had been placed directly in the provincial company script. . . .

At the end of his discussion, he summarizes his conclusions about the two texts: "there is no basis for the supposition that both the Q and F texts stem from a common original. The F text is, with minor modifications, the authoritative version of *The Merry Wives,* and basically represents the script played at the 1597 Feast of the Garter."

The new Arden edition of *The Merry Wives,* edited by H. J. Oliver, (London: Methuen, 1971, pp. xiii–xxxvii) contains in the introduction a detailed discussion of the problems of the theory of reported text. Oliver concludes that both the Host and Falstaff were probably responsible for the reporting and that behind the Q text was a version designed for a popular rather than an aristocratic audience.

Oliver accepts an early 1597 date but goes back to the idea (pp. lvi–lviii) that the *Brooke-Broome* change was made in 1604 in connection with the Bye plot execution of 1603, rejecting as "desperate" Green's suggestion that it may have been made in rehearsals of *The Merry Wives* in 1597. Green's hypothesis is simpler, and I find it plausible. To suppose that two name changes were made in *The Merry Wives* characters, both names relating to the same family, and that these changes were made seven years apart is unnecessarily complicated and coincidental. The name Brooke is a common one, and it seems unlikely that its use would have disturbed the King. Probably neither the King nor anyone else would even have thought of a possible reference to the Cobhams in the use of the name in 1604, eleven months after the execution of George Brooke. But in 1597, when *Oldcastle* was changed to *Falstaff*, the possibility of related reference would have been obvious, and the precaution makes some sense. Both name changes might well have been made during rehearsal of *The Merry Wives*.[59]

Except for this one point, however, Oliver's introduction represents a judicious analysis of problems raised by the two texts.

Because of the great complexity of the problems, an overview of the theories of the relation of Q to F may seem to compound confusion and to uncover the exploration of countless blind alleys rather than to reveal orderly progress. And yet certain accumulated conclusions may now be presented with considerable confidence. The major insight has surely been the one gradually evolved in the nineteenth century, that F is not a revision of Q—an insight now almost completely and apparently finally accepted. The second major insight is seen in Greg's enunciation of the idea that Q is a memorial reconstruction of F prepared chiefly by the Host—a view that has been developed and challenged but appears to hold its ground quite firmly. The idea of any notable revision in F, except the probable toning down of oaths and the Brooke-Broome change, now seems unlikely. The third important development is the evidence gathered chiefly by Hotson and Green concerning the date of the play's composition.[60] The final scene of F is now rather definitely associated with the 1597 Garter celebration and that of Q seen as a reporter's effort to reconstruct for provincial audiences a scene of which he remembered almost nothing. It is certainly true that problems remain. The mystery of "garmombles" and the post-horses continues at least partially obscure, and the hypothesis of an old play behind F is still, in my mind, unnecessary and unproven. But overall the progress is gratifying, and one can feel a sound basis for moving on to less factual problems of interpretation and evaluation.

Notes:

1. Edited with Helen A. Clarke, *The Merry Wives* (New York: Crowell, 1909), p. 132.
2. Edited with John Dover Wilson, *The Merry Wives* (Cambridge: Cambridge Univ. Press, 1921), p. xi.
3. *Works* (London: J. Tonson, 1725), I, viii, 223.
4. *An Answer to Mr. Pope's Preface to Shakespear* (London, 1729), p. 28.
5. Ed., *Plays* (London: J. & R. Tonson, 1765), II, 557 n.
6. Ed., *Twenty of the Plays* (London: J. & R. Tonson, 1766), p. 7.
7. Ed., *Comedies, Histories and Tragedies* (London: Dryden Leach, 1768), I, 12; *Notes*, II, 74.
8. *Notes and Various Readings to Shakespeare* (London: Henry Hughes, 1779–83), II, 78–79.
9. In *Plays*, ed. by Samuel Johnson and George Steevens (London: C. Bathurst, 1785), I, 227.
10. Ed., *Poems and Plays* (London: H. Baldwin, 1790), I, Part 1, x, 140–41 n., 328.
11. Ed., *Dramatic Works* (Chiswick: Wittingham, 1826), I, 182 n. James Boaden, 1762–1839, was a playwright and author of biographies of David Garrick, Mrs. Siddons, and other actors and actresses. He is also well known for a letter to George Steevens expressing his doubt of the authenticity of the Ireland papers.
12. Ed., *Plays* (London: Clark, 1835), V, 7.
13. Ed., *Works* (London: Knight, 1843), III, 3.
14. Ed., *Works* (London: Robert Tijas, 1843), I, 77.
15. Ed., *Works* (London: James Munroe, 1851–59), I, 209–10.
16. Ed., *The Merry Wives—1602* (Oxford: Clarendon Press, 1910), p. xv.
17. "The Merry Wives," *The History and Transmission of Shakespeare's Text* (Columbia: Univ. of Missouri Press, 1952), p. 36.
18. Ed., *Works* (London: Adlard, 1853), II, 211. For further discussion of Halliwell's position, see my "James O. Halliwell-Phillipps on the Relation of Q and F Versions of *The Merry Wives*," *N&Q*, 18 (April 1971), 139–41.
19. Ed., *Works* (London: Edward Moxon, 1857), I, vii.
20. *A Study of Shakespeare* (London: Chatto & Windus, 1895), p. 121.
21. Ed., *The Merry Wives* (New York: Harper, 1882), p. 10.
22. Quotations are taken from Greg's 1910 edition of the 1602 Q and from F.
23. *Dramatic Works* (Boston: Hilliard, Gray, 1836), p. 63.
24. Ed., *Works* (London: Whittaker, 1842–44), I, 174.
25. Ed., *Works* (Boston: Little, Brown, 1857–66), II, 199, 209.
26. *Essays on the Life and Plays* (London: Whittingham, 1858), p. 4.
27. Introduction, *The Merry Wives—1602*, p. xv.
28. Introduction, *The Merry Wives* (London: Griggs, 1881), pp. iv–xiv.
29. For a detailed discussion of systems of shorthand known to be in existence in 1603, see George Ian Duthie, *Elizabethan Shorthand and the First Quarto of "King Lear"* (Oxford: Blackwell, 1949).
30. Ed., *The Merry Wives* (London: Bell, 1886), p. xiii–xiv.
31. Ed., *Works* (London: Knight, 1846), II, 143.

32. Listed by Henslowe as "the Gelyous Comedy" produced by Alleyn's company. E. K. Chambers suggests that this could be the *Comedy of Errors.* See *William Shakespeare* (Oxford: Clarendon Press, 1951), I, 61; II, 312.
33. *A Chronicle History of the Life and Work* (London: Nimmo, 1886), pp. 211–12.
34. Ed., *The Merry Wives* (London: Methuen, 1904), pp. xi–xxiv, xli–xlix; lxxv–lxxvi.
35. *Shakespeare's Folios and Quartos* (London: Methuen, 1909), pp. 72–73.
36. Pp. xvi–xvii, xx–xxvii, xxxii, xxxv, xl–xliv.
37. For detailed discussion of the habits of Ralph Crane, see F. P. Wilson, "Ralph Crane, Scrivener to the King's Players," *The Library,* 4th Ser., 7 (Sept. 1927), 194–215; R. C. Bald, ed., *A Game At Chesse* (Cambridge: Cambridge Univ. Press, 1929); and Elizabeth Brock, "Shakespeare's *The Merry Wives,*" Diss. Virginia 1956.
38. "Stolne and Surreptitious Texts," *TLS,* 7 Aug. 1919, p. 420.
39. *TLS,* 9 Jan. 1919, p. 18.
40. *TLS,* 7 Aug. 1919, p. 420.
41. *TLS,* 16 Jan. 1919, p. 30.
42. *TLS,* 7 Aug. 1919, p. 420.
43. *Shakespeare's First Folio* (Oxford: Blackwell, 1923), pp. 95–100.
44. *William Shakespeare,* I, 430.
45. *TLS,* 16 Jan. 1919, p. 30.
46. Ed., *Henry V* (Cambridge: Cambridge Univ. Press, 1947), p. 113.
47. Pp. xii, xxii, xxvi, 25, 94, 96, 100.
48. *The Disintegration of Shakespeare* (London: Oxford Univ. Press, 1924), pp. 7, 16–22.
49. I, 155–57, 227, 429–33, 435–37.
50. *MLR,* 25 (July 1930), 266–68.
51. Pp. 13–20, 46–55, 78, 92–94, 108, 140; chapters 2, 3 passim.
52. "The Textual History of *The Merry Wives,* Diss. Iowa 1942, p. 7, 58 ff., 75 ff., 85, 92, 97, 104, 120, 185.
53. "Another Masque for *The Merry Wives,*" *SQ,* 3 (Jan. 1952), 39–43.
54. Pp. 27, 39–41, 53, 63, 70, 79, 96–97, 138–39.
55. Review of William Bracy's *The Merry Wives, SQ,* 4 (Jan. 1953), 79.
56. Pp. 1, 13–15, 18–35.
57. *A New Look at Shakespeare's Quartos* (Stanford, Calif.: Stanford Univ. Press, 1961), pp. 65–68, 74–75.
58. Pp. 4, 23, 87, 95–98, 100–103, 109–19, 123 ff., 162, 168–69, 172–76.
59. See my "*The Merry Wives* as a Hallowe'en Play," *ShS,* 25 (1972), 107–12, for elaboration of this suggestion.
60. J. M. Nosworthy in *Shakespeare's Occasional Plays* (London: Arnold, 1965), p. 88, continues to hold out for a date of 1600 or later, but he is decidedly in the minority.

Romeo and Juliet, IV.v: A Stage Direction and Purposeful Comedy

Charles B. Lower

Juliet takes the potion. Subsequent discovery of her body, apparently dead, elicits expressions of grief from the Capulets, Juliet's Nurse, and Paris:

Enter Frier and the Countie.

Fri. Come, is the Bride ready to go to Church:
Fa. Ready to go but never to returne.
O sonne, the night before thy wedding day
Hath death laine with thy wife, there she lies,
Flower as she was, deflowred by him,
Death is my sonne in law, death is my heire,
My daughter he hath wedded. I will die,
And leaue him all life liuing, all is deaths.
Par. Haue I though loue to see this mornings face,
And doth it giue me such a sight as this?
Mo. Accurst, vnhappie, wretched hatefull day,
Most miserable houre that ere time saw,
In lasting labour of his Pilgrimage,
But one poore one, one poore and louing child,
But one thing to reioyce and solace in,
And cruell death hath catcht it from my sight.
Nur. O wo, O wofull, wofull, wofull day,
Most lamentable day, most wofull day
That euer, euer, I did yet behold.
O day, O day, O day, O hatefull day,
Neuer was seene so blacke a day as this,
O wofull day, O wofull day.
Par. Beguild, diuorced, wronged, spighted, slaine,
Most detestable death, by thee beguild,
By cruell, cruell, thee quite ouerthrowne,
O loue, O life, not life, but loue in death.
Fat. Despisde distressed, hated, martird, kild,
Vncomfortable time, why camst thou now,
To murther, murther, our solemnitie?

O childe, O childe, my soule and not my childe,
Dead art thou, alacke my child is dead,
And with my child my ioyes are buried.

(Q2,IV.v.)[1]

The mode and mood of this passage is my present concern.

Its tone is comic, resulting from the cacophony of four characters wailing simultaneously. This mode is found in the stage direction *All at once cry out and wring their hand*[s] from Q1, the bad quarto.[2] From textual considerations, this Q1 stage direction is part of the authorial "final intent"; critically, the consequent effect of laughter at such hyperbolic hubbub is dramaturgically purposeful.

To propose the editorial appropriation of the Q1 stage direction demands proof of the integrity of this rubric to the Q1 dialogue, explanation of the relationship of Q1 and Q2 in IV.v, and (the first concern here) demonstration of the necessity of the action found in the Q1 stage direction to the integrity of the authoritative Q2 text, lacking such a direction. We must seek more than merely reflection of staging contemporaneous with Shakespeare, albeit such potential gives special interest to all bad-quarto rubrics; we must find the substance of this particular Q1 stage direction to reflect Shakespeare's intent.

An incontrovertible verbal portion of Q2 is the crux: in Q2 the Friar, immediately subsequent to the experience of grief, begins,

Peace ho for shame, confusions care liues not
In these confusions heauen and your selfe
Had part in this fair maide, now heauen hath all.

The Friar's command "Peace ho for shame" presupposes a literal ("physical") dimension to "these confusions." No preceding verbal unit serves as the grammatical referent for "these confusions," in modern editions left either unglossed or unsatisfactorily glossed.[3] This Q2 phrase requires a nonverbal "antecedent," presumably of performance: the Friar's lines demand that something be happening that can cease at his command. A possible objective correlative for the Friar's phrase, visually and audibly, is available in the Q1 "*All at once* [i.e., together] *cry out and wring their hand*[s]," producing speech denotatively incoherent to both the Friar and a theater audience. The substance of this stage direction, if otherwise defensible, places the least possible strain on the Friar's lines. The verbal detail of the bibliographically authoritative Q2 needs the reciprocating theatrical mode available from the bad-quarto stage direction.

In proposing, in effect, that the substance of the Q1 rubric is "lost" from Q2, I am not suggesting that its presumed presence in Shakespeare's foul papers can be deduced and that its disappearance in the transmission from that manuscript to the Q2 text can be explained: there is no bibliographical evidence for such a fancy.[4] But sometimes in the absence of a stage direction, a performance feature is, in generic terms, reconstructable from the dialogue as unmistakably authorial: for example, the dialogue "Come hither, little kinsman; hark, a word" and "Come hither, Hubert" without a stage direction demonstrates the momentary separation of characters in *King John* as convincingly as the stage direction *"They draw themselves aside"* found in *The Devil's Charter*.[5] The generic action represented in such a stage direction is implicit in and applicable to the dialogue of *King John*. *Romeo* IV.v is analogous: we have evidence of the necessity of staging embedded in "these confusions" in Q2 and a bad-quarto stage direction supplying a suitable staging (otherwise less certainly reconstructable).

If "these confusions" the Friar commands to stop are the simultanoeus cries of the Capulet pair, Juliet's Nurse, and Paris, then their preceding dialogue, lines 41–64, is denotatively incoherent. But the verse here is not of superb poetic quality; surely no one would cite it as even characteristic of Shakespeare's poetic accomplishments. The substance here is likewise slender fare. Discussions of the thematic and narrative wholeness of the play have given the scene short shrift, and image patternings, both sound and ingenious, have found the passage devoid of relevance. Apparently, therefore, we lose little if anything in positing the incoherence of simultaneity.

In Q2, Paris, Lady Capulet, Capulet, and the Nurse are each given six lines of disjointed, prosaically direct verse, such as "O woe! O woeful, woeful, woeful day! Most lamentable day, most woeful day. . . ." For the poetic dramatist, this absence of verbal distinction would be appropriate to the chaos of simultaneous delivery: why write quality if intent is reflected in *"All at once cry out"*? On the other hand, the symmetry—six lines each from the four lamenting speakers—would be appropriate to simultaneous delivery, providing each actor roughly the same temporal demand prior to the Friar's interrupting, silencing "Peace ho."[6] Poetic drabness, minimal substance, and the symmetry of length in these lines accord with the crucial Q2 feature requiring extraverbal explanation: "these confusions." All are compatible with the intrusion into the Q2 dialogue of the action in *"All at once cry out."*

Attention can, therefore, turn to Q1, the integrity of its IV.v stage direction to its corrupt text, and its relationship to Q2 in this scene. Harry Hoppe has demonstrated that Q1 is a memorial reconstruction of an abbreviated form of the copy used for Q2.[7] This still widely accepted account has unmistakable implications for editing *Romeo*, as expressed by Richard Hosley: ". . . where Q1 varies from a corrupt Q2 reading, the editor should, because of the chance that Q1 may also be corrupt, make use of the Q1 variant only after he has exhausted the possibilities of emending the Q2 error within its own textual and bibliographical contexts without reference to Q1."[8] George Walton Williams similarly observes that, "knowing the memorial nature of Q1, we should suspect it of error at all points . . . [and] that even though Q2 is manifestly corrupt and Q1 offers an acceptable reading, it may be wiser to emend the Q2 error than to adopt the Q1 reading."[9] These are bibliographically sound conclusions, so long as one's concern is dialogue. But for rubrics, for matters of theatrical production within the text, considerable weight must be given to the 1597 bad quarto. Greg concluded that "Whoever wrote the Q1 stage-directions had an intimate knowledge of the play and of the traditional stage-business" of the Elizabethan public theater,[10] a judgment editor after editor has concurred with by using some stage directions unique to Q1. Most modern editions include "*Tybalt under Romeos arme thrusts Mercutio*" (III.i), "*They whisper in his eare*" (I.v), and "*somewhat fast*" as a descriptive supplement to "*Enter Juliet*" (II.vi). Modern editions, on the other hand, rarely contain "*All at once cry out.*"[11]

Deserving, a priori, comparable considerations, it bears the apparent handicap of an extremely corrupt context. Hoppe found IV.v one of the two most inadequate scenes in Q1, hardly justifying editorial inclusion of its stage direction. Hoppe assessed the IV.v text as so inferior and so without parallel to Q2 as to be merely a "reporter's patchwork":

> The first speech after [Paris and Friar Lawrence's] entry (though assigned in Q1 to Paris instead of Lawrence) is substantially exact: 'What (Q2 *Come*), is the bride ready to go to church?' (l. 33). The first two lines of Capulet's reply are identical, but the remainder of the speech degenerates rapidly to mere summary, 'to him I give all that I have' being the gist of the reporter's remembrance of
>
> . . . Death is my heir;
> My daughter he hath wedded: I will die
> And leave him all; life, living, all is Death's.
>
> This progressive deterioration suggests that only the first two or three lines had been spoken in the shortened play. But after Paris's line, 'Have I thought long (Q2 *love*) to see this morning's face,' the Q1 text ceases to bear any direct resemblance to Q2, until we come to the Friar's instructions concerning Juliet's burial (ll. 79–81), beginning 'Dry up your tears.'[12]

Hoppe finds the dialogue in IV.v based not upon the performance being reported but rather upon a mixture of a reporter's hazy memory of a much earlier performance and of that reporter's own invention. If an adequate explanation, this disparaging report on IV.v serves as appropriate basis for editorial exclusion of the unique Q1 stage direction. Is there an explanation for the textual inadequacy other than Hoppe's, one that then vindicates this stage direction? Hoppe's standard is the "good line," defined as "one that differs from Q2 by no more than one important word (noun, verb, adjective, or adverb), disregarding variants in particles and in singular-plural forms."[13] This criterion is, I think, insufficiently subtle to contrast various poorly reported passages.

Hoppe's tabulation of the percentage of good lines (relative to the total Q2 lines) reveals, within IV.v, little contrast in quality of reporting.[14] Looked at more closely, two portions of the scene, the Nurse's opening speech (the only sustained speech while Paris is offstage in IV.v) and the lament speeches (lines 41–64 in Q2), display a sharp contrast in nature and degree of badness.

In the Nurse's speech, Q1 in prose contains the substance of nine of the sixteen Q2 lines, if we include, for example, "That you shall rest but little, God forgive me" (Q2) as reproduced in substance by "that you shal rest but little" (Q1), even though Q1 falls short of Hoppe's standard (both "God" and "forgive" being absent). Using a looser demand than Hoppe's, one appropriate only to poorly reported passages, Q1 has a "reminiscence of substance" of 68% of the Q2 lines. Even without equivalents to five Q2 lines, Q1 provides a decent reconstruction of the narrative substance of the Nurse's speech, despite a mere 12% of "good lines." Instead, the Q1 deficiency is primarily stylistic.[15] A second method, looser than Hoppe's criterion, provides parallel: of the 134 vocabulary units in the Q2 passage, Q1 reproduces *in syntactic sequence* 52 (plus five in the line belatedly found in Q1)—42%.[16]

This analysis provides for poorly reported passages a norm with which to examine the lament speeches afresh. In them, of the 176 substantive words in Q2, Q1 reproduces one line ("Have I thought long [Q2 love] to see this mornings face") and a pair of words in a series (Q2, "*accurst, unhappie,* wretched, hateful day"; Q1, "*Accurst, unhappy,* miserable man"), in which, since the two series modify different nouns, the syntactic reproduction of vocabulary may be accidental. Including this pair, Q1 totals eleven words with syntactic parallel, 4% of the substantive words of Q2 (contrasted with 42% in the Nurse's speech). The relative badness of the reporting in the lament speeches is more emphatic than Hoppe's assessment, the statistically inconsequential difference of 8% and 12% of "good lines."

The lament speeches in Q1 and Q2 together total ninety-three different substantive words (whatever their form), excluding linking verbs. Of these, Q1 and Q2 share only nineteen.[17] Words appearing in only one quarto include some surprises. Q2 does not use *destiny*, whereas Q1 uses the singular and plural four times. Q1 has five instances of forms of *hope* without a single correspondence in Q2. Only Q1 has *sad, slave, sorrow, unfortunate,* and *unjust*: all could readily be invented by a reporter to fill in a memory gap, for all are clearly appropriate either to the narrative or to lamentation.[18] As even more significant evidence of the almost complete breakdown in reporting in this passage, Q1 lacks such distinctive Q2 diction as *Pilgrimage, loving, child, hateful, black, slain, martird, kild, solemnitie,* and *solace.*

Yet, despite the vocabulary dissimilarity, the Q1 reporter used techniques paralleling ones in the Q2 laments, such as

> Q1, "Cruel, unjust, impartiall distinies"
> Q2, "Despisde, distressed, hated, martird, kild"
>
> Q1, "and being dead, dead sorrow nips us all"
> Q2, "Flower as she was, deflowred by him"
>
> Q1, "This day, this unjust, this impartiall day"
> Q2, "O day, O day, O day, O hatefull day
> O wo, O wofull, wofull, wofull day."

Although Q1 has substantive correspondence with Q2 in only the single line in the laments, here it strikingly approximates, in contrast to the Nurse's opening speech and much bad memorial reconstruction, the flavor and tone of the reliable Q2.

Romeo IV.v in Q1, a badly reported scene (radically inferior, say, to II.ii, which Hoppe found to have 66% good lines), contains clear contrasts in degree of badness.[19] Yet the reporter failed utterly with sustained speech only in the laments (Q2 lines 41–64). Why? Hoppe's narrow range of allowance for accurate reporting does not invite one to seek special cause. But secondary methods reveal considerable contrasts, contrasts inviting explanation in terms of the Q1 stage direction. "*All at once cry out and wring their hand*[*s*]" would make impossible the task of a reporter (on stage, backstage, or in the audience), and it probably would even negate an actor's responsibility to memorize his own part accurately. The lament speeches in Q1 and Q2 have only minuscule correspondence in substance, yet are remarkably parallel in tone; this situation seems strange until we see that it may be accounted for by the cacophony of simultaneity in performance.[20]

The Q1 stage direction is reinforced by two lines in Q1 without Q2 parallel: "And all our ioy, and all our hope is dead. / Dead, lost, vndone, absented, wholy fled." The speech identification is *"All Cry."* Apparently, most vividly remembering the mode of delivery, the Q1 reporter(s) or the adaptors of the abbreviated performance being reported provided this redundant method of indicating simultaneity. Although it has no bibliographical defense, for us the presence of this two-line passage confirms the literal appropriateness of *"All at once cry out."*

The textual knot is tied. Counter to Hoppe's disparaging assessment of "patchwork," the nature of the poor reporting in Q1 IV.v is explicable from the mode of its theatrical presentation: the Q1 stage direction and the quality of reporting are inseparable; the stage direction is a necessary aspect of the Q1 dramatic script. In the authoritative Q2, the symmetry of the four lamenting speakers and the poetic ineloquence of their speeches are compatible with the import of the Q1 stage direction. Moreover, in Q2, the Friar's "Peace ho" command that "these confusions" cease assumes the stage occurrence of simultaneous delivery (to such a degree that if *"All at once cry out"* had appeared in Q2, it would now be described as "redundant"). This particular Q1 stage direction belongs to Shakespeare's play: Capulet, Lady Capulet, Juliet's Nurse, and Paris grieve contrapuntally, in denotatively incoherent speeches, until silenced by the Friar.

II

What dramaturgically is achieved? Most criticism ignores the episode and its language. It is true that Granville-Barker treats it at some length, but this usually perceptive spokesman of the theater here misleads us by his troubled exploration. Although admitting that the laments are "competition in mourning," even that the situation "mocks at the mourners," he emphatically rejects the implications of those remarks: he insists that the lament situation is not a "deliberate burlesque" but rather a "long-spoken threnody," thus granting the passage the dignity of a dirge. To resolve his self-created dilemma, Granville-Barker weakly resorts to "artistic failure":

> The passage does jar a little; but we must remember that [Shakespeare] is working here in a convention that has gone somewhat stale with him, and constrainedly; and that he can call now on no such youthful, extravagant passion as Juliet's or Romeo's to make the set phrases live. The situation is dramatically awkward. . . . Shakespeare comes lamely out, but went sincerely in.[21]

Granville-Barker's influence is in evidence in Richard Flatter's description of the passage as "a four-part madrigal of wailing" and Harry Levin's comment that Capulet's lamentation—in Levin's words "a litany"—joined by those of wife, Nurse, and Paris, "reasserts the formalities by means of what is virtually an operatic quartet."[22] Such views of the ritualistic stature of the passage—expressed without Granville-Barker's honest discomfort—are hard to swallow in the face of the bleakness of the imagery and the simplistic syntax of the passage itself. And hearing the simultaneity, we are exposed to babble rather than dignity. It is difficult, I believe, to think that a theater audience accustomed to poetic drama would find these verbal "confusions"—incoherent and unpoetic—other than humorous, other than belonging to what has appropriately been called the "burlesque" mode.[23] But reasonable decision about a comic effect depends upon determining its purposeful function within the play.

The immediately subsequent episode in IV.v is innocuously humorous. At the exeunt of the Friar and wailers, Peter and the musicians engage in word-wit and actions indecorous for the bereavement on stage. They pun, obtusely dissect the meaning of a love ditty (itself a comic reduction of the presumed loss of Juliet), and concern themselves with their hunger. The audience can join in whatever fun is here and be bemused rather than appalled, because of the dramatic irony: the audience (or reader) knows of the potion and its qualities and is confident that Juliet is not yet dead. In fact, the comedy itself acts as an assurance of the rightness of that confidence: that the play offers comedy assures an audience (or reader) that any bereavement now is unwarranted.[24]

This mode of assurance is not trivial. To the extent that we find the Friar trustworthy, we have assurance that Juliet in IV.v is not actually dead, for he has explained the properties of the potion. But subsequent to hearing the Friar's assurances, we have experienced Juliet's poignant expressions of fear and doubt. Primarily her speeches testify to the depth of Juliet's commitment to Romeo. Yet, to be impressed by this devotion, we must necessarily appreciate her uncertainty: her impassioned soliloquy articulates the possibility of the potion's being fatal. Thereafter the dramatist has at hand no explicit means of giving the audience knowledge of the nonfatal efficacy of the potion (for example, Juliet cannot wink). Because of our familiarity with the entire play, we tend to overlook the dramatist's problem of providing a means of our knowing that Juliet is actually alive in Act V. How in the continuous experience of performance is this knowledge provided? By laughter: the play encourages, even forces, us to laugh while viewing the bed containing Juliet's body—and such laughter would be offensively intolerable if the young heroine were in fact dead. Believing Juliet dead and laughing are mutually exclusive. We receive this indirect assurance through the humor of the Peter episode and, earlier, in the ironic juxtaposition of the curtain containing Juliet with the frenetic behavior of Capulet and servants in last-minute wedding preparation. Their blatant absurdity produces laughter, which requires and creates our conviction of the potion's success, its being temporary rather than fatal.

But between these two episodes is the pièce de résistance, the babble of the grieving foursome in their noisy, incoherent cacophony, which turns topsy-turvy the values of the very form "poetic drama." Experiencing "*All at once cry out*" reinforces, determines an audience's confidence that the potion deceived, not murdered. The stage presentation produces laughter (1) by caricaturing the Capulet wedding preparation, (2) by parodying the solemnity of grieving, and (3) by concluding the scene with the idle quibbling of musicians and clown; the stage presentation thus assures us of Juliet's survival and preserves us from the tragic sense. It is important to note that any expression of grief responded to with empathy in Act IV would rival and thus endanger the tragic experience of Act V. To have rendered the lamentation seriously here would have been to make the proper place for such a response (likely) anticlimactic.

The play manipulates audience response through the redundancy of comic situation, so that we gain perspective in recognizing that all three situations invite audience laughter. To recognize this buttressing repetitive technique is to give primacy to the large dramatic effects. For example, in attempts to deny a burlesque quality to the laments, both Granville-Barker and Flatter are restricted in perspective. Granville-Barker argued that "Burlesque, of a sort, comes later with Peter and the musicians; Shakespeare would not anticipate this effect, and so equivocally."[25] The weakness of this view is that it treats the clown exchange as an end in itself, not (or at least also) as serving larger interests, such as informing the audience of values beyond these characters themselves. Flatter contended that the wailers "behave as the situation demands: they wail and, being Italians, they do so in an unrestrained manner. Weeping and wailing is infectious—and thus it is that what we hear is a four-part madrigal."[26] Flatter's assumption of cultural accuracy (reminiscent of Thomas Rhymer) is dramaturgically dubious at best. But even if Flatter's observations are accepted, they are of only incidental value dramaturgically: realistic Italian wailing would be a means rather than an end. Surely the thrust of the play here is not "what a remarkable portrait of Italian behavior." Instead, whatever "realism" of such Italianate excess there is would produce laughter, laughter functional for the larger spheres of value and narration.

Much more severely a victim of restricted focus, Robert Evans accepts as fact "Juliet's feigned deathbed" without any attention to the dramaturgical epistemology. In accord with the thesis of his book, he concentrates on the rhetorical figures used by the Friar, designed, according to Evans, to "emphasize his shortcomings. . . . the trouble well intended bunglers can cause." Evans concludes that "If we listen to this speech with attention to its figures, it must be with a rising sense of horror,"[27] a view without perspective about a hierarchy of values and effects. Is *Romeo* an exposé of a priest? Evans is content with style—"The speech begins with a simple *epanalepsis* (repetition at the end of a clause of the word or phrase with which it begins): 'Confusion's cure lives not / In these confusions' "—without attention to content, specifically the meaning and dramatic appropriateness of "these confusions."[28] Attention to such nuance as *epanalepsis* needs the context of larger dramaturgical concerns, here including the redundant use of a comic mode. A narrowed perspective, such as that of Granville-Baker, Flatter, or Evans, imperils itself by ignoring the prominence of comedy in IV.v, in the dramatic action following Juliet's taking the potion.

Comedy is prominent in earlier portions of *Romeo and Juliet*. One recalls the prominence of the garrulous, earthy Nurse and the witty Mercutio, as well as recurrent comic details, such as, in the opening scene, the servants with their cumbersome, obsolete "swords and bucklers" and the two enfeebled heads of household thwarted from joining the fray. Much recent criticism (comfortable with the seeming incongruity of the comic in a tragedy without retreating to the hackneyed, inadequate "comic relief") has seen the purposeful presence in *Romeo* of echoes of romantic comedy, of young love momentarily thwarted. This pattern stands, of course, under the shadow of the Prologue, with its announcement of the denouement. In Act III, this tragic shadow has been vividly reinforced with the finality of the deaths of Mercutio (and what comedy would so irrevocably deprive itself of its "wit"?) and of Tybalt, creating such an obstacle to the success of young love. Yet, as the present discussion of *"All at once cry out"* demonstrates, the play continues thereafter to employ laughter.

I wish to offer just one specific suggestion about the broader implications of this laughter in Act IV. Noting that the characters laughed at in the cacophony of grieving cannot be damaged by ridicule (that is, they are not recipients of our admiration or sympathy earlier in the play), I suggest that the mode of presentation in IV.v adds to the play's emphasis on the isolation of the title pair, both physically and in quality of character. The aural dimension of the grief in Act IV is further illustration for a recent suggestion of an image-pattern made by James Calderwood:

> If one charted the private/public range of language in *Romeo and Juliet*, at the furthest private extreme would come 'silence,' a nominalistic tendency so rigorous as to still speech entirely. . . . [For example,] the lovers' language within the orchard—self-cherishing, insular, answerable only to private feeling. At the extreme public end of the chart opposite silence is

> noise, disturbance, disquiet. . . . (The Prince is significantly more concerned with 'peace' as quiet than as cessation of hostilities; the greatest threat to the play is sheer noise, its consistent goal harmonic sound.)[29]

Capulet, Lady Capulet, the Nurse (though a go-between, constitutionally uncomprehending of the nature of Juliet's love), and Paris (as the "wooden" rival wooer) are outsiders to the world of Romeo and Juliet's love that we share. As such, these four characters belong to the world of noise, sometimes a threat to and sometimes absurdly incongruous with the beauty and near-silence of the world of the lovers. Their noise in IV.v is absurdly incongruous as we view Juliet's marriage bed and her inert body, vivid testimony to her quiet devotion to Romeo.

III

Whatever worth such a suggestion may have, the two comedic purposes for which this paper is answerable justify finding the simultaneity humorous and lend critical attractiveness to a textual decision to include the Q1 stage direction within authorial intent. First, our laughter, provoked irresistibly from the stage, would be intolerably dishonest dramaturgy if Juliet were in fact dead: that laughter is indirect assurance to us of the efficacy of the potion. Secondly, as a comic interlude, the fourth-act grief stands as a foil to the finale, offering no rivalry, not threatening to make the fifth-act grief seem emotionally or aesthetically anticlimactic. Expressed in positive terms, this relationship means that the fourth-act cacophony and our laughter in response to it provide a context enhancing our experience of the tragic in the last act.

The prerequisite for possible widespread appreciation of the comedy in IV.v is editorial inclusion of the mode of the laments. The critical edition of *Romeo* (based, of course, on Q2) should, on textual grounds, include "*All at once cry out and wring their hand*[s]." I suggest that the text here appear as follows:

Capulet.

Ready to go but never to returne.
O sonne, the night before thy wedding day
Hath death laine with thy wife: there she lies,
Flower as she was, deflowred by him,
Death is my sonne in law, death is my heire,
My daughter he hath wedded. I will die,
And leave him all life living: all is deaths.

All [Capulet, Lady Capulet, Paris, and Nurse] *at once* [simultaneously] *cry out and wring their hand*[s] Q1

Lady Capulet.

Accursed, unhappy, wretched, hateful day!
Most miserable hour that e'er time saw
In lasting labor of his pilgrimage!
But one, poor one, one poor and loving child,
But one thing to rejoice and solace in,
And cruel Death hath catched it from my sight.

Nurse.

O woe! O woeful, woeful, woeful day!
Most lamentable day, most woeful day
That ever ever I did yet behold!
O day, O day, O day! O hateful day!
Never was seen so black a day as this.
O woeful day! O woeful day!

Capulet.

Despised, distressed, hated, martyred, killed!
Uncomfortable time, why cam'st thou now
To murder, murder our solemnity?
O child, O child! my soul, and not my child!
Dead art thou—alack, my child is dead,
And with my child my joys are buried!

Paris.

Have I thought long to see this morning's face,
And doth it give me such a sight as this?
Beguiled, divorced, wronged, spited, slain!
Most detestable Death, by thee beguiled,
By cruel cruel thee quite overthrown.
O love! O life! not life, but love in death!

Friar [interrupting].
Peace ho for shame: confusions cure lives not
In these confusions. . . .[30]

A given editorial format may permit the editor to do less than I have suggested; he may decide merely to include the literal Q1 stage direction in the text, plus glosses of "*at once*" and "these confusions." The exact means he adopts is an individual editor's decision, but the investigation here should indicate the need to adopt some means. A critical edition of *Romeo* should acknowledge the authority of the Q1 stage direction and explain it.

An issue larger than this one portion of *Romeo* has to do with what an editor may learn from theatrically informed criticism when it is textually responsible. Frequently modern editing of Elizabethan drama reflects very little familiarity with sound theater reconstruction and theater criticism. On the other hand, regrettably, seldom is theater criticism written with an objectivity sufficient to permit serious consideration from the Shakespearean editor, for theater criticism is often concerned only with "the possible." Hopefully, what the present discussion of *"All at once cry out"* has demonstrated will encourage theater scholars to work within a more confined modus operandi and will alert editors to supplement their textual awareness with an enlarged understanding of the dimension of performance.

Notes:

1. The Q2 text is reproduced unaltered because its details are subsequently under consideration here. Authorities concur that Q2 is the appropriate copy-text for any modern edition of *Romeo;* Q1, also substantive, is a radically inferior text, and F is derivative. See, e.g., W. W. Greg, *The Shakespeare First Folio* (Oxford: Clarendon Press, 1955), pp. 225–35.
2. The basic textual suggestion made here—the authority of the Q1 stage direction—has been briefly presented earlier in Richard Flatter, *Shakespeare's Producing Hand* (New York: Norton, 1948), pp. 69–71, in a section entitled "Simultaneousness," which presents nine other instances (pp. 55–72). None of these, however, parallels the *Romeo* instance. In each case, one speaker offers only a brief competing comment in the midst of another speaker's sustained speech. For example, Flatter cites *Richard III,* I.iii.135 ff.

   Glo. Poor Clarence did forsake his father, Warwick,
   Ay, and forswore himself—which Jesu Pardon!—
   Marg. Which God revenge!
   Glo. —to fight on Edward's party for the crown.

   Flatter's own comment, "An interjection, unnoticed or at least unheeded by Gloucester, who speaks without interruption" (p. 56), describes only the realism of a heated narrative situation, certainly not the sustained simultaneous dialogue from several speakers resulting in unintelligibility, such as we find in the *Romeo* passage. In other instances (e.g., *Othello,* II.iii.164 ff), Flatter's suggestion depends upon the dubious premise of sustained versification within speeches of each character (and a "rule" of Flatter's devising that a character newly entering the stage invariably begins a new line of verse). This context damages his *Romeo* suggestion, for the cornerstone of the book, that Folio punctuation and versification accurately reflect authorial intent, is dubious. As Fredson Bowers notes, "No one is so foolish any more to argue that the punctuation—now demonstrated to be mainly compositorial—is Shakespeare's own or that it represents in any way the authority of the playhouse" ("Today's Shakespeare Texts, and Tomorrow's," *SB,* 19 [1966], 65). Bowers reflects a consensus of responsible textual bibliography today. Thus, Flatter's book is pushed into a stagnant backwater, generally neglected in subsequent textual criticism. Though Flatter's methods and the assumptions they draw upon are naïve distortions, some of his judgments deserve reassessment. In effect, this paper, devoid of the offensive assumption in Flatter, through a fuller, textually responsible treatment, seeks to confirm one of his suggestions. Because in his view it lacks the technique of broken line, Flatter finds the *Romeo* instance of simultaneity the one with Shakespeare's "intention less clearly" expressed. Flatter has not, however, pursued the abundance of relevant textual evidence considered in this article.

3. Most modern editions offer no gloss, and those which do (for example, Hardin Craig's gloss of "confusion" as "destruction, overthrow, ruin; mental agitation") do not fit the imperative, the context of the word. The one edition with an appropriate glossary entry, "(plur.) disorderly behavior, lamenting commotions," Dover Wilson's, makes no mention of even the existence of the Q1 stage direction, so that the rightness of the Friar's reference in relationship to the staging mode is impossible for the reader of the *New Cambridge*. Since glossing is part of the usual editorial treatment, a gloss on "these confusions" would be a very suitable place for editorial clarification of simultaneity.
4. But, as James Thorpe, in *Principles of Textual Criticism* (San Marino, Calif.: Huntington Library, 1972) notes, "My experience as a textual editor has been that there is usually no bibliographical evidence to use in trying to solve the most troublesome problems that I have encountered" (pp. 96–97); Thorpe insists that an editor's responsibilities go beyond the strictly bibliographical realm of transmission and hypothesis reconstructing the archetypal text.
5. Warren Smith, "The Third Type of Aside in Shakespeare," *MLN*, 64 (Dec. 1949), 510–513; Bernard Beckerman, *Shakespeare at the Globe, 1599–1609* (New York: Macmillan, 1962), pp. 186–88; my "Separated Stage Groupings: Instances with Editorial Gain," *Renaissance Papers 1970* (Durham, N.C.: Southeastern Renaissance Conference, 1971), 55–72. Relevant here is the assumption that Shakespeare, as a working member of the permanent acting company for which he wrote, had immediate and continuous potential for "directorial" clarification beyond those stage directions in the manuscript. This assumption is used fruitfully in such recent works as Beckerman, op. cit., and E. A. J. Honigmann, *The Stability of Shakespeare's Text* (Lincoln: Univ. of Nebraska Press, 1965). Arthur Gerstner-Hirzel, *The Economy of Action and Word in Shakespeare's Plays* (Bern: Franche, 1957) explores the problem of deictic gestures: here (less concretely than with the conversational aside) the text demonstrates the existence of some performance feature but leaves its exact form, if a single form of Shakespeare's design existed in Globe production, unrecoverable.
6. Q2 does not provide Paris with a single sustained speech: two lines from Paris, six from Lady Capulet (*Mo.*), six from the Nurse, four from Paris again, and six from Capulet (*Fat.*). Paris' first line in his second speech, unlike his earlier pair of lines, is a series of synonyms, comparable to the first lines of laments of Lady Capulet, Nurse, and Capulet. Thus Paris' role in the simultaneous delivery might be briefer, merely the four lines, a single exception to the symmetry. On the other hand, the division of Paris' contribution could be an attempt, imperfectly (since Capulet's speech is after Paris' second), to provide in the printed text a kind of "framing device" suggestive of simultaneity of delivery. Choice between the two alternatives is beyond proving, but it is not essential

to the case for the appropriateness of the Q1 stage direction to the Q2 dialogue. (I have preferred the latter alternative.)

7. Harry Hoppe, *The Bad Quarto of "Romeo and Juliet"* (Ithaca, N.Y.: Cornell Univ. Press, 1948). Hoppe's view (excluding his specific identification of reporters) is currently accepted generally. Memorial reconstruction is now the preeminent method of explaining the characteristics of bad quartos. Recently, Robert Burkhart in a University of Cincinnati dissertation ("Shakespeare's Bad Quartos: Deliberate Abridgments Designed for Performance by a Reduced Cast," 1967) takes issue with memorial reconstruction by stressing that cuts found in bad quartos eliminate characters deliberately to facilitate acting by a smaller company. This view does not account for verbal anticipations and recollections, for example, but as far as it goes it is compatible with the view of Hoppe, who found in *Romeo* Q1 memorial reconstruction of an abbreviated script. For the present discussion, what is essential is common to Hoppe and Burkhart, namely, (1) that Q2 is more or less a reliable text, vastly superior to Q1 and (2) that Q1 reflects Elizabethan public theater performance. These two judgments are also common to the various attempts to explain the thorny problems of apparent Q2 dependence on Q1 occasionally, so that solving the issue of the Q2 copy-text—how manuscript and occasionally Q1 were used—is not prerequisite or even relevant to the present discussion.
8. Richard Hosley, "The Corrupting Influence of the Bad Quarto on the Received Text of *Romeo and Juliet*," *SQ*, 4 (Jan. 1953), 21.
9. William Shakespeare, *The Most Excellent and Lamentable Tragedie of Romeo and Juliet: A Critical Edition*, ed. G. W. Williams (Durham, N.C.: Duke Univ. Press, 1964), p. xiii.
10. W. W. Greg, *The Editorial Problem in Shakespeare* (Oxford: Clarendon Press, 1954), p. 164.
11. Editions I have checked have included Hosley (rev. Yale), Hankins (Pelican), Hoppe (Crofts Classics), Hardin Craig, Neilson-Hill, Dover Wilson, G. B. Harrison, Peter Alexander, Sisson, G. W. Williams (Critical Ed., Duke), Robert Turner, Jr.-George Walton Williams (Scott, Foresman, Elizabethan Spelling). All modern editions examined included some stage directions unique to Q1, so that no editorial principle prohibits the addition of the Q1 stage direction in IV.v. It is found most rarely of the sixteen unique Q1 stage directions Greg lists, present only in Hosley's new Yale and the Scott, Foresman. Neither of these, however, offers any clarification (even of "*at once*"), and both use (indiscriminately?) *all* the stage directions unique to Q1. Readers of even these editions will likely remain unaware that this stage direction fits what Hoppe identifies as the typical bad-quarto stage direction, one "describing the actors' obvious business," thus unaware of the mode of presentation of the IV.v. laments. An editor's task is more than choice.
12. Hoppe, "The First Quarto Version of 'Romeo and Juliet,' II.vi and IV.v.43 ff," *RES*, 14 (July 1938), 280–81. Although abbreviated, Hoppe's view remains unchanged in *Bad Quarto*, from which "reporter's patchwork" is quoted, p. 187.
13. Hoppe, *Bad Quarto*, p. 194. Hoppe's criterion is practical for working through an entire play as well as generally sound in contrasting scenes reported well and ones reported poorly.

14.	lines 1–16	Nur.	—	12%
	17–23	Nurse, Lady C.	—	0%
	24–35	Nur, Lady C, Cap.	—	9%
	36–98	Nur, Lady C, Cap., Lawr, Par.	—	8%
	98–end	Nur, Peter, Musicians	—	11%

A portion of Table V, "Quality of Reporting: Statistical Analysis," Hoppe, *Bad Quarto*, p. 212. Hoppe's major concern is to establish that *Romeo* Q1 is the product of memorial reconstruction, but his final chapter attempts to identify the reporter(s), suggesting the actors with the Romeo and Paris roles. Thus IV.v offers some embarrassment, with very inadequate reporting yet with Paris on stage through most of the scene. From a hypothesis of Paris as a reporter (whether the scene was cut or performed in the particular production being reported), the Nurse's speech should be of poorer quality than Paris' own lament. It will become apparent that the explanation of the contrasts in the quality of reporting offered here fits more comfortably with Hoppe's tentative identification of reporters than does his own treatment of IV.v.

15. Q1 "I must wake you indeed" parallels the redundant pair in Q2, "I needs must wake her: Madam, Madam, Madam" and "I must needs wake you, Lady, Lady, Lady." And Q1 represents Q2 "Oh wereaday that ever I was borne" in a subsequent lament passage assigned to Lady Capulet (*Moth.*), "Alacke the time that euer I was borne . . . alacke and welladay." Thus the substance of eleven Q2 lines is approximated in Q1 (hence the 68%). What remains in the Q2 speech is repetition, characteristic of the Nurse throughout the play (e.g., Q1 "What Juliet?"; Q2 "Mistris, what mistris, Juliet"), and the Nurse's mannerism of apology after an off-color remark (e.g., "God forgive me. Marrie and Amen"). Admittedly, some very slight substance might be found in several Q2 constructions without Q1 equivalents: "fie you sluggabed," "Heel fright you up yfaith: will it not be?" and "What not a word?"

16. If instances in which Q1 approximates Q2 (e.g., Q1 "What lambe"; Q2 "Why lambe") were included, the ratio of this accuracy would become 53%.

17. *Accurst, alack, cruel, day, dead, death, distresst, ever, face, joy, life, miserable, morning's, see, thought, time, unhappy, woe, wretched.*

18. See, for example, Hoppe's section on "Recollections" characteristic of memorial reconstruction, *Bad Quarto*, pp. 150–59.

19. As demonstrated, the Nurse's initial speech contains the essential substance, using about half the vocabulary of Q2 in syntactic sequence. The reporter fails, quite understandably from probable rapidity of delivery, with the stichomythia after the Nurse's cry, 'Some Acquavitae ho, my Lord my Lady."

Q2: *Mo.* What noise is here?
Nur. O lamentable day.
Mo. What is the matter?
Nur. Looke, looke, oh heauie day.
Mo. O me, O me, my child, my onely life.
Reuiue, looke vp, or I will die with thee:
Helpe, helpe, call helpe.

Q1: *Moth*: How now whats the matter?
Nur: Alack the day, shees dead, shees dead, shees dead.
Moth: Accurst, vnhappy, miserable time.

Yet the abbreviated exchange prior to the laments and the abbreviated speech from the Friar after the laments are, in terms of substantive vocabulary in syntactic sequence, 40% accurate in reflecting comparable portions of Q2. The Friar's speech in Q1 is seven lines (compared with nineteen in Q2) and does not contain "these confusions."

20. Paris as reporter would explain the oddity that the single Q1 line faithfully reproducing the text found in Q2 is Paris' opening line, just as the simultaneity explains the apparent paradox of a scene poorly reported (even by the standards of the last half of the play, generally poorer than the first) containing one of Hoppe's presumed reporters.
21. Harley Granville-Barker, *Prefaces to Shakespeare* (Princeton: Princeton Univ. Press, 1946), II, 319.
22. Flatter, p. 69; Levin, "Form and Formality in *Romeo and Juliet*," *SQ*, 11 (Winter 1960), 10.
23. S. L. Bethell, *Shakespeare and the Popular Dramatic Tradition* (London: King & Staples, 1944), p. 111. Although he fails to recognize both the assurance of Juliet's survival provided by the laments and their simultaneity of delivery, Bethell appreciates their tonal relationship to the last act: "this *Romeo and Juliet* passage is anything but subtle. Its blatancy is necessary to overcome the audience's natural tendency to join the Capulets in their mourning. And the audience must not do this, because their tears are to be reserved for the last scene" (p. 110). Recognition of the humor in this passage came as early as 1854, albeit with too narrowly topical an explanation to serve the play as a whole: "In this speech of mock heroic woe [Nurse's, beginning 'O woe!'], and perhaps in the two that follow, Sh. seems to have ridiculed, as he has done elsewhere, the translation of Seneca's Tragedies, published in 1581" (Richard Grant White, *Shakespeare's Scholar*, quoted in *'Romeo and Juliet': A New Variorum Edition*, ed. H. H. Furness [New York: J. B. Lippincott, 1871], p. 244.) Readings I have supervised have invariably provoked laughter; such response to the simultaneous wailing is, I believe, inevitable.
24. Granville-Barker, for example, has noted this function of the Peter-musicians episode: "the farce of the ending—which helps to remind us that, after all, Juliet is not dead." He properly characterizes the tone of this exchange as "the traditional riddle-me-ree business done . . . Will Kempe having 'brought off an exit' amid cheers," II, 319.
25. Ibid.
26. Flatter, p. 71.
27. Evans, *The Osier Cage: Rhetorical Devices in Romeo and Juliet* (Lexington: Univ. of Kentucky Press, 1966), p. 64.
28. Ibid., p. 63.
29. Calderwood, *Shakespearean Metadrama* (Minneapolis: Univ. of Minnesota Press, 1971), p. 94.
30. If represented thus, the note must explain the original state of Paris' speeches.

A printing format for conveying simultaneity occurs in the Folio text of Jonson's *The Alchemist,* IV.v, where the final portion of the monologue of Dol *"In her fit of talking"* and the competing dialogue from Face and Mammon are presented in two parallel columns of reduced size type, prefaced by the stage direction *"They speake together."*

Dion, Alexander, and Demetrius—Plutarch's Forgotten *Parallel Lives*—as Mirrors for Shakespeare's *Julius Caesar*

SIDNEY HOMAN

In a recent edition of *Julius Caesar,* Maurice Charney makes the timely observation that "Critics have tended to neglect the comparisons between Grecians and Romans that follow each set of parallel lives" in Plutarch.[1] Not only have the comparisons been neglected but the parallel lives as well, those of Dion (coupled with Brutus), Alexander (with Caesar), and Demetrius (with Antony). In his excellent study of Shakespeare's sources Geoffrey Bullough reminds us that Plutarch "paired off men of similar character or men in like situations or at similar periods of national history"; still, his discussion of Plutarch is confined to the trinity of Romans, with a glance at the "Life of Cicero."[2] There is also no mention of the Greek lives in Kenneth Muir's *Shakespeare's Sources,*[3] and the best-known anthologies of Plutarch—those of Skeat (1875), Tucker-Brooke (1909), and T. J. B. Spencer (1964)—omit both the parallel lives and the comparisons, though the latter are so brief as to present little added printing expense.

This omission, both in editions and in the commentary on Shakespeare's use of North's Plutarch, is understandable. Quite possibly Shakespeare himself read no further than the lives of Brutus, Caesar, and Antony. Reading even these lives is a difficult task. Plutarch's purpose, as he tells us in the introduction to "The Life of Alexander" (V, 164), is "not to write histories, but only lives"; yet often these lives are merely a series of amusing digressions, compilations of anecdotes which are anything but dramatic, and—with military leaders such as Alexander and Caesar—endless accounts of peoples and territories conquered. Then, too, Shakespeare's indebtedness to the three Roman lives is so striking, so pervasive—though even this has been disputed[4]—that the three Roman lives seem to provide a broad enough field for scholarly investigation. The irony is that whereas scholars of the play have gone beyond Plutarch in their considerations of possible sources—the list of these has included Appian's *Civil Wars,* Elyot's *The Governour,* Lucan's *Pharsalia,* Ovid's *Metamorphoses,* Virgil's *Georgics,* Dekker's *Canaans Calamitie,* Nashe's *Fall of Jerusalem,* Cicero's *De Claris Oratoribus* and *De Officiis,* the *Mirror for Magistrates,* Tacitus' *Annals,* Sallust's *Histories,* Daniel's *Civil Wars,* Seneca's *De Beneficiis,* along with five earlier Caesar plays—they have not always been so willing to plunge deeper into Plutarch, whose 1579 (or 1595) translation we can be absolutely sure—as we can with no other suggested source—was on Shakespeare's desk in 1599 when he wrote *Julius Caesar.*

I think it important for several reasons that we reconsider the lives of Dion, Alexander, and Demetrius, and the comparisons in two cases. (A comparison between Alexander and Caesar—the one planned by Plutarch has been lost—was supplied in the 1603 edition by one "S. G. S." [Simon Goulard Senlisien], who also did the comparison for Hannibal and Scipio.) The parallels and comparisons were, quite simply, part of Plutarch's design; if one is to speak authoritatively about Shakespeare's major, indeed, almost exclusive source here, he should recognize that design. "The Life of Brutus" is not an entity in itself but forms, at very least, a sequel to "The Life of Dion." Without the latter the former is incomplete; the context for Plutarch's judgment of Brutus—a judgment which at various times Shakespeare accepted, rejected, or qualified—is missing. Clearly the source of *As You Like It* is Lodge's *Rosalynde,* and that romance is complete in itself. Yet in studying the sources of the comedy, we might want to become familiar with other pieces by Lodge and, in a more general fashion, with the genre itself. Shakespeare uses such romances early and late; a generation later Greene's *Pandosto* would supply the source for *The Winter's Tale.* The integrity of each pair of parallel lives is surely as great as that of *Rosalynde.*

Shakespeare, we will also probably admit, read "The Life of Brutus" with a purpose different from that of a critic. He had no ax to grind; Brutus would be what he wanted him to be, or what Brutus had to be within the larger design of the play. In a way, Shakespeare was a more disinterested reader of Plutarch than we can hope to be, for whereas we often turn to *The Parallel Lives* not for themselves but for the light we think they shed on the play, Shakespeare had no such illusions about using Plutarch to explain his characterization of Brutus or Caesar. And even when critics do turn to Plutarch, they do not always agree. Romantic critics, who saw Brutus as the flawless hero of the play, argue that Shakespeare champions Brutus as did Plutarch. But to what degree does Plutarch champion Brutus, and therefore to what degree does Shakespeare merely copy him? Plutarch does not fail to mention how Brutus allowed his soldiers to sack Lacedaemon and Thessalonica, or the disease that attacked him at Dyrrachium, a "cormorant and unsatiable appetite" (VII, 133)—details which Shakespeare omits. Conversely, Shakespeare omits Plutarch's reference to Brutus' stoic courage when, on the eve of the conspiracy, he was brought news of Portia's illness but refused to abandon his plans. While Brutus is indeed Plutarch's darling, he is not a darling without qualifications. And while Shakespeare's view of Caesar seems less critical than that in Plutarch, Plutarch does not put as much stress on Caesar's physical ailments.

My point here is that it may be a bit dangerous to use the three Roman lives as boundaries for our survey of the sources of *Julius Caesar* since the "certainty" offered by those lives may be questioned. In that splendid edition for the New Cambridge Shakespeare, composed in the aftermath of a war, John Dover Wilson quotes extensively from Plutarch, prefacing the notes for each scene with passages from North—all for the purpose of proving that Shakespeare meant us to respond to Caesar as a precursor of the *Führer*, and to Brutus as the liberator. His interpretation was similar to that in Orson Welles's 1937 production of the play. But in the New Arden edition, Mr. Dorsch, impressed by Dover Wilson's work and yet taken aback by his reading of the play as propaganda, also quotes extensively from Plutarch; yet he concludes that Caesar, while not blameless, is an awesome figure, just what we might expect from a capable and successful world leader. If Shakespeare truly understands Plutarch, if he absorbs his mind in the way T. J. B. Spencer suggests in contrasting Shakespeare's classicism with the more striking but superficial learning of Jonson,[5] perhaps our obligation is to understand Plutarch more on his own terms, in a broader fashion—in a word, by looking at six lives rather than three.

There may also be more direct evidence that Shakespeare read beyond the three Roman lives. We may be fairly certain that he was familiar with "The Life of Cicero." Scholars have at various times argued that he knew the lives of Alcibiades, Pompey, Cato the Younger, and Cato the Elder. There are references to the "other" characters of *The Parallel Lives* in *Love's Labor's Lost* (Nathaniel's "Alisander" at V.ii.567), *A Midsummer Night's Dream* (in the account of Theseus' amours at II.i.79–80), *Merchant of Venice* (a reference to Brutus' Portia at I.ii.166), and *Henry V* (IV.vii.24–52). In the latter play Fluellen seems to parody the method of Plutarch as he makes a comparison for Gower between the general born in Macedon and Henry V born in Monmouth:

> I tell you, captain, if you look in the maps of the 'orld, I warrant you sall find, in the comparisons between Macedon and Monmouth, that the situations, look you, is both alike. There is a river in Macedon; and there is also moreover a river at Monmouth. It is call'd Wye at Monmouth; but is it out of my prains what is the name of the other river; but 'tis all one, 'tis alike as my fingers is to my fingers, and there is salmons in both. If you mark Alexander's life well, Harry of Monmouth's life is come after it indifferent well; for there is figures in all things. Alexander, God knows, and you know, in his rages, and his furies, and his wraths, and his cholers, and his moods, and his displeasures, and his indignations, and also being a little intoxicates in his prains, did, in his ales and his angers, look you, kill his best friend, Cleitus.

When Gower protests that Harry, unlike Alexander, never killed any of his friends, Fluellen qualifies his statements in a manner that recalls Plutarch's method of suggesting surface parallels which, on closer inspection, lead to significant personality differences:

> I speak but in the figures and comparisons of it. As Alexander kill'd his friend Cleitus, being in his ales and his cups; so also Harry Monmouth, being in his right wits and his good judgments, turn'd away the fat knight with the great belly doublet. He was full of jests, and gripes, and knaveries, and mocks; I have forgot his name.[6]

There is also one suggestion for the characterization of Cassius, otherwise treated sparsely in "The Life of Brutus," in the opening paragraphs of "The Life of Dion":

> For, he [Dion] had no cohelper to bring him unto that greatnesse, as *Brutus* had of *Cassius*: who doubtlesse was not comparable unto *Brutus*, for vertue & respect of honor, though otherwise in matters of warre, he was no lesse wise & valliant then he. For many doe impute unto *Cassius*, the first beginning & originall of all the warre & enterprise: and sayd it was he that did encourage *Brutus*, to conspire Caesars death.
>
> *(VII, 168)*

That this long association with North proves Shakespeare "became a confirmed student of Plutarch" is another thing.[7] And yet we may ask: in reading the lives of Brutus and Anthony would Shakespeare not have glanced, at very least, at the comparisons between Dion and Brutus, and between Demetrius and Antony, as he began to design these contrasting figures, the high-minded idealist and the practical, sensual man of the world?

When we do look at the parallel lives and the comparisons, I think that our response to Brutus, Caesar, and Antony is more complex than that response we have when narrowing our study of the sources. A more extensive reading gives a divided response toward all three figures, as men both praiseworthy and blameworthy, with a mingling of vices and virtues, similar to that divided response so prevalent in twentieth-century criticisms of the play. Indeed, in our age there has been a reaction against the extreme veiws of romantic or colonial spokesmen; I think here especially of a book like Ernest Schanzer's *The Problem Plays of Shakespeare: A Study of "Julius Caesar," "Measure for Measure," and "Antony and Cleopatra."*[8] I would like now to look at the three major characters—Brutus, Caesar, and Antony—both in terms of contemporary criticism and in terms of this larger concept of Shakespeare's source.

I

Among modern writers Gordon Ross Smith has offered one of the most severe indictments of Brutus.[9] Citing such judgmental words as "fault" and "blame" in Brutus' vocabulary, Mr. Smith contends that Brutus' "philosophy" is nothing more than "a specious structure of rationalizations for the various impulses of his character," that Brutus epitomizes all "impractical and ineffectual reformers, do-gooders," that in him "we see the effects of a tyrannical superego in its struggle against both id and ego." And thus Brutus' line "Judge me, you gods; wrong I mine enemies?" (IV.ii.38), in response to Cassius' charge that Brutus has done wrong to him, is for Mr. Smith a reply dripping with "injured innocence and unconscious hypocrisy."

While extreme, this qualification of Brutus' integrity is very much in the mainstream of recent criticism. One commentator finds that it is his "assumption of divine retribution" which ruins Brutus.[10] For Harold Wilson, Brutus, albeit nobler than any other conspirator, is "nevertheless blind to his own limitations and the guiding motives of other men."[11] Other critics would dismiss him as a true intellectual,[12] or brand him as one of those "dogmatic moralists."[13] Virgil Whitaker points to the logical fallacies in the orchard soliloquy;[14] for David Daiches, Brutus is "the liberal intellectual in a world of *Realpolitik*."[15] In his well-known essay " 'Or Else This Were a Savage Spectacle,' " Brents Stirling comments on Brutus' attempt to elevate butchery to the level of ritual and calls attention to the corresponding satire of that attempt.[16]

We have moved here far from earlier assessments of Brutus, the assumed Plutarch-Shakespeare-Brutus, the ideal republican thought of as a man of "nobility without harshness, full of generosity, of goodness, of gentleness."[17] The republican argument is eloguently voiced by Schelling when he sees in Brutus the "dignity and restraint which we habitually associate with the republic of ancient Rome."[18] An early psychological critic saw in Brutus "no murderer, no conspirator, no narrow republican fanatic, but simple gentle Shakespeare discovering to us his own sad heart and the sweetness which suffering had called forth in him."[19] There are, of course, qualifications to Brutus' character in Plutarch, qualifications not always adopted by Shakespeare. Still, holding up the source and the play, Virgil Whitaker reasonably concludes that in the play Brutus emerges "shorn of the perfection which Plutarch gave him."[20]

Now without limiting Shakespeare's own inventiveness, we find, I believe, much these same flaws—the cloying sense of moral rightness, the inflexibility, the unattractive harshness of his moral code, the aristocratic superiority which in some measure inhibits Brutus' function as a leader of men—in the portrait of his parallel Greek, Dion. Plutarch tells us that Dion "gave him self to no sport nor pleasure," with the result that other men, envying him and yet oppressed by his sense of superiority, accused him so that his virtues seemed vices: "As in calling his gravetie, pride: his plainnes and boldness in his Oration, obstancie." It was "because he would not make one in their fonde pastimes: that therefore he despised them." Plutarch admits that "his manners by nature had a certain hawtinesse of minde and severitie, and he was a sower man to be acquainted with: whereby his companie was not onely troublesome, but also unpleasant." While some commended his plain manner of speaking and his noble mind, "they did yet reprove his sternenes, and austere conversation with men. For it seemed unto them, that he spake too roughlie, and delt overhardlie with them that had to doe with him, and more then became a civill or curteous man." Plato himself warned Dion to beware of "obstancie, the companion of solitarinesse, that bringeth a man in the ende to be forsaken of everie one" (VII, 49–50).

Indeed, what this portrait suggests is Shakespeare's Caesear as well, in particular that same sense of superiority which at once elevates and divorces him from other men. Part of the "renaissance" of Cassius in this century, both in the criticism and in the performances of the play, has been the recognition of his "humanness," particularly in the quarrel scene. A creature driven by envy, by hatred of anyone above him, he is also, like Antony, a fast, passionate friend. He loves openly, and when that love is denied—his opening lines to Brutus concern a loss of affection—he is driven to despair. The opposite trait, this coldness in Brutus, Dion, and Caesar, is defined in *The Governour*, when in discussing "Affability" Elyot comments how Caesar, obsessed with himself and his position, gradually "withdrew from men his accustomed gentilnesse, becomyng more sturdy in langage, and straunge in countenance than ever before had ben his usage."[21] Perhaps we might want to see Brutus, in slaying his former friend Caesar, as destroying the extreme image of himself. Shakespeare makes no mention of the rumor that Brutus was Caesar's bastard son; the symbolic connection between the two men may surface more subtly in the play.

The parallels between Dion and Brutus are among the closest in all the lives, one of the most obvious being that both are given to the study of philosophy, Brutus to Stoicism, Dion to the philosophy of Plato. In fact, one of Dion's schemes to reform Dionysius, to modulate his tyranny, was to keep him under Plato's instruction. Shakespeare goes to considerable lengths to stress Brutus' academic affiliations. In Plutarch Volumnius is a philosopher who has been with Brutus from the beginning of the conspiracy, but in a revealing addition Shakespeare makes him an old school-friend as well: "Good Volumnius, / Thou know'st that we two went to school together (V.v.25–26). Dion and

Brutus, both liberators, both idealists, both slayers of their best friend, both given to philosophy, both with time spent at studies, both engaged with tragic results in rebellion against the established monarch—the parallel here qualifies as that between "men of similar character," the closest of the three general parallels that Mr. Bullough cites in Plutarch.

"The Life of Dion" may also cast some light on the nature of Brutus' political principles. This is a thorny matter in the play. In the orchard soliloquy Brutus' motive is not primarily to replace tyranny with a republican government. Cassius, whatever his other motives, is more the orthodox republican. Rather, Brutus will murder Caesar to prevent him from becoming an absolute tyrant, a man who, in the Renaissance sense of the word, has lost the ability to feel "remorse." Brutus has no real complaint against Caesar at present. Nor does the play seem to be an argument for absolutism. Shakespeare's age seems to have preferred a limited monarchy, a government in which the rulers would be constrained "to make use not of their own licentious wills in judgment, but of that right or privilege which the People had conferred upon them" (Buchanan in *De iure regni apud Scotos*, 1689). James Emerson Phillips in his *The State in Shakespeare's Greek and Roman Plays* observes that "under the sovereign authority of Caesar the political society of Rome was brought into conformity with that pattern of civil organization which the Renaissance considered ordained by universal law."[22] Clearly the Elizabethans were not republicans. That the play is propaganda for monarchy, limited or otherwise, as MacCallum in his *Shakespeare's Roman Plays* or as Phillips contends, may be a moot point; that the ultimate function of Shakespeare's theater is political is questionable.

We are left with Brutus' muddy politics: is he or is he not a republican; and if he is, is it essentially political principles which drive him into the conspiracy? Ernest Schanzer makes the astute observation that "Had he [Brutus] been a doctrinaire republican and murdered Caesar to save the republic from kingship he would have been safe, if not from inner conflicts, at least from tragic disillusion."[23] Granting its uncertain politics, or at least the uncertain politics of the lead conspirator, Schanzer sees the issues in the play as moral, not political.

We find the same political ambiguity in Dion and the same moral issues overshadowing the political. Dion was not a republican; he wanted to abolish "Democratia" and establish the Laconian or Cretan commonwealth as a blend of Princely and popular government (VII, 99). In wealth and power he was like a tyrant. Plutarch takes great pains to remind us that as long as he remained Dionysius' friend, Dion was content to support his tyranny. It was a violation of friendship, stemming from Dionysius' marrying Areta, Dion's wife, to another man, which led to the opposition between ruler and subject. With political overtones—like Brutus, Dion professes republican sentiments, casting himself as the champion of personal liberties—the story shows rebellion springing essentially from a moral violation. This is the very blend of politics and morality in Brutus' vision of Caesar at the top of ambition's ladder, forgetting his obligations to those below him who were once his supporters.

In stressing the issue of friendship we have come full-circle to that question of affability central to the portraits of Dion, Caesar, and the Brutus of Shakespeare's play. Male friendship is the major theme on which G. Wilson Knight focuses in his influential essay on "The Eroticism of *Julius Caesar*."[25] There he sees Brutus moving from the certain sphere of male love to the illusive, tragically deceptive world of politics. Brutus, in effect, substitutes honor for love, here male love complementing the heterosexual love celebrated in *Antony and Cleopatra*. By denying such love he opens up a division in his soul. In this regard it is perhaps significant that Archbishop Trench in his study of Plutarch criticizes the author for an immature political grasp of history, for understanding men better than their political institutions.[25] We may want to see "The Life of Dion," the bulk of which concentrates not just on Dion but on Dion in the company of Plato and Dionysius, as an essay on friendship. Similarly, *Julius Caesar* begins with a subordination of friendship to politics, focuses in Acts II and III on Caesar encompassed by hypocritical friends and on Antony vowing revenge for the murder of his friend, and ends with Brutus attended by friends, holding that certain joy above the public honor which he has sought and lost. In Mr. Knight's reading, only when Brutus is forced out of the public sphere does he find peace, for then "the long torment of division in Brutus' soul is closed, the wounding dualism healed in death, an easy 'rest'; and in thoughts of his friends' faith."[26]

The deaths of Dion and the Brutus of the play also offer an interesting similarity. Just before his death "a great and monstrous ghost or spirit," a "monstrous great woman" sweeping the house with a broom, appeared to Dion (VII, 101). Dion's situation here is similar to that of Brutus on the battlefield: alone, at night, in deep thought (Brutus is reading a book in the play). The essential fact is that Dion sees an external spirit, not a manifestation of a guilty conscience. We also learn in the opening of "The Life of Dion" that one thing common to Dion and Brutus is that a "wicked spirit" foreshadowed the death of each (VII, 43). However, in "The Life of Brutus" the "evil spirit" belongs to Brutus himself (VII, 47), and in "The Life of Caesar" it is Brutus' own "ill angell" (V, 349).

The discussion so far has centered on whatever light the actual "Life of Dion" casts on the Brutus of Shakespeare's play. The brief "Comparison" presents a far more qualified portrait of Brutus, a portrait closer to the play than to "The Life of Brutus." Plutarch distinguishes between Dion, who warred only for liberty, and Brutus, who won his position by war—initially siding with Pompey, he changed to Caesar's side just before Pompey's defeat—and who was later forced by necessity to battle Octavius and Antony. The "Comparison" suggests that in action, in battle, Brutus lost that philosophical stance which otherwise made him Dion's equal. We need only think of the difference between the Brutus of Acts IV and V and the Brutus earlier in the play to grasp Plutarch's distinction between Dion and Brutus as warriors. By the end of *Julius Caesar* we see Brutus world-weary, quarreling ignobly with Cassius, caught up in the mechanics of war, making several serious military errors. Earlier, however, he has been the intellectual suffering to the point of sleeplessness over the moral issues raised by the assassination (in Plutarch his sleeplessness results only from anxiety over the success of the conspiracy), a noble, though perhaps arrogant leader of smaller men.

Even more important is the distinction Plutarch makes in the "Comparison" between the men opposed by Dion and Brutus. He reminds us that Dionysius was clearly a tyrant, whereas Caesar cannot be so easily labeled:

> For *Dionysius* denyed not, that he was not a tyranne, having filled SICILIE with suche miserie & calamitie. Howbeit *Caesars* power and government when it came to be established, did in deed much hurt at his first entrie and beginning unto those that did resist him: but afterwardes, unto them that being overcome had received his government, it seemed he rather had the name and opinion onely of a tyranne, then otherwise that he was so in deede. For there never followed any tyrannicall nor cruell act, but contrarilie, it seemed that he was a merciful Phisition, whom God had ordeyned of speciall grace to be Governor of the Empire of Rome, and to set all thinges againe at quiet stay, the which required the counsell and authoritie of an absolute Prince.
>
> (*VII, 169*)

Caesar is an absolute ruler, to be sure, hardly a paragon of virtue; still, the "Comparison" introduces serious questions about the "propriety" of the assassination, questions which have no parallels in Plutarch's story of Dion and Dionysius. Only Plato tries to dissuade Dion from opposing Dionysius: "both for the respect of *Dionysius* good entertainment he had geven him, as also for that *Dion* was of great yeares" (VII, 63). Plutarch also comments that whereas Brutus always referred friendship to matters of justice and equality, he nevertheless slew the man who had saved his life (VII, 171). This paradox in the "Comparison," a paradox also sustained by the play when we consider Brutus' anguished reaction to Caesar's ghost, is raised by classical, medieval, and Renaissance commentators who, while admiring Brutus for his virtue, also detested his role in the conspiracy, a role he chose because of his principles. One might think of Brutus dangling from Satan's black face in *The Inferno*, or of Suetonius, who in his *Historie of Twelve Caesars* reminds us that Brutus and his fellow conspirators "stood condemned: and by one mishap or other perished."[27] Appian speculates that Brutus acted "either as an ingrate man, or ignorant of his mothers faulte, or distrustfull, or ashamed, or very desirous of his countrys libertie."[28]

Perhaps William Fulbecke writing in 1586 best summarizes the questions surrounding Brutus, questions very similar to those found in the "Comparison":

> M. Brutus, the chiefe actor in Caesars tragedie, was in counsel deepe, in wit profound, in plot politicke, and one that hated the principality whereof he devested Caesar. But did Brutus looke for peace by bloudshed? did he thinke to avoyd trannie by tumult? was there no way to wound Caesar, but by stabbing his own conscience? & no way to make Caesar odious, but by incurring the same obloquie?[29]

In effect, the "Comparison" and, I believe, the play are more in the tradition of that divided response towards Brutus and the assassination than is "The Life of Brutus" itself.

It is revealing that in the "Comparison" Plutarch prefers Brutus before Dion on the matter of friendship. Whereas Brutus was wise in choosing his friends, Dion "either from the beginning made no wise choyse in trusting of evill men, or else bicause he could not tell how to use them he had chosen: of good men he made them become evill, so that neither the one nor the other coulde be the parte of a wise man" (VII, 172). Such a distinction, I would think, adds a new emphasis to that moment in the play (II.ii) when Caesar bids Brutus and the other conspirators as "Good friends" to "go in, and taste some wine with [him]." To this offer Brutus' pregnant aside is: "That every like is not the same, O Caesar! / The heart of Brutus earns to think upon" (II.ii.126–29). Brutus' last line in Caesar's presence, before the actual assassination, concerns friendship; and here Caesar, like Dion, has misjudged his friends, failing to distinguish, as Brutus can do, between true friendship and being "like" a friend but in reality an enemy.

The "Comparison" ends with an anecdote embodying a paradox not to be found, I would contend, in "The Life of Brutus." Coming upon a statue of Brutus, Octavius charges that those who erected it "were his enemies, and traitors unto him, bicause they kept an enemie of his among them." The citizens and their leaders are frightened by his remarks, and by his "bending his browes," but then "*Caesar* laughing, and commending the GAULES for their faithfulness to their friendes, even in their adversitie," reassured them "he was contented *Brutus* image should stand still as it did" (VII, 173).

II

Again, the comparison for Alexander and Caesar has been lost, but reading "The Life of Alexander" itself provides a larger context for "The Life of Caesar" and, by extension, the play. While Plutarch does not slight any of Caesar's accomplishments (particularly his military victories), he does remind us that his covetous desire to be called king influenced, indeed perverted, almost every action of his career. Plutarch's judgment of Caesar is a harsh moral one; implicit in "The Life of Caesar" is the contrastive "Life of Brutus." In "The Life of Alexander," however, we are reminded of the good qualities found in these two militarists. Both battled, Plutarch tells us, not for some personal wrong but for a principle, even if that principle included nothing beyond personal honor. Alexander did not "fight with *Darius*, but for his kingdom only" (V, 191), Darius being "Caesar's Pompey" to Alexander. Both men "never eschewed any bodily daunger" (V, 227); we may think of the vastly different picture Cassius paints in that opening conversation with Brutus. Furthermore, both were temperate in their eating, though Alexander's drinking was, to be sure, another matter.

In some ways Alexander is to be preferred. Most probably he was divinely descended, and thus Caesar's claims for the godship of a king stand out in sorry contrast. (S. G. S. in the "Comparison" points out how Caesar struggled from obscure, penniless origins.) Alexander was more of the philosopher, Aristotle being his companion just as Plato was the companion of Dion. Diogenes himself envied Alexander. Such facts may place in a new perspective Caesar's wish to have fat, basically unthinking lackies about him rather than lean, introspective men. In Plutarch Brutus is included in Caesar's strictures against those men who with "lean and hungry look" think too much (I.ii.191–92).

It is, however, the account of Alexander's vices which lends a new dimension to Caesar's character, a dimension not always clear in "The Life of Caesar," and yet one which shows a divided response towards Caesar that some have argued the play itself elicits. Plutarch makes no excuses for Alexander's alcoholism and his choler, the end product of his intemperance. After reading the several accounts of his drinking in "The Life of Alexander," we may admit more irony to Hamlet's vision in the graveyard of Alexander turned to dust and clay, the world conqueror reduced to stopping the bunghole of—appropriately—a beer barrel. And it is during that fateful meeting between Hamlet and his father that Claudius' drinking, which has "traduced" the name of Denmark among other nations, is underscored by the kettledrum and trumpet that "bray out" each of his pledges (I.iv.11–20). It was Alexander's drinking, Fluellen tells Gower, which led to the murder to his friend Clitus.

Plutarch's Caesar, in contrast, is temperate in both food and drink, and it is this moderation, this consistency, if you will, in both small and large matters, which distinguished him from his Greek protoype. Constant "as the northern star," a man holding "his rank, / Unshak'd of motion" while other men are wavering and inconstant (III.ii.58–70)—these very traits which confirm for some critics the judgment of Caesar as a creature full of pride are, within the context of "The Life of Alexander," more like virtues. In *Antony and Cleopatra,* Octavius Caesar is the most moderate drinker, while it is Lepidus, a member of the triumvirate in name only, who is carried out drunk from the conference. For Antony, who even in *Julius Caesar* is branded as a drinker, reveling becomes a symbol of his intoxication with Cleopatra, a synthesis of the flesh, heady drinking, and other soft pleasures of the East. Caesar's request that the conspirators have a glass of wine with him strikes a tone of moderation like that of a Last Supper, the eve of a betrayal. At such a moment he is the very antithesis of Alexander.

Near his time of death Alexander grew so superstitious that "no strange thinge happened unto him . . . but he tooke it straight for a signe and prediction from the godds" (V, 263). For Plutarch, such fear was a defect in character as serious as Alexander's intemperance. Upon the revelation of Calpurnia's dream Plutarch comments that Caesar "did feare and suspect somewhat" (V, 342), but he is clearly not the superstitious soul that we see in Alexander. Shakespeare, I believe, makes Caesar more admirable in this respect. In II.ii Caesar asks the priests to make a sacrifice and to bring him "their opinion of success" (l. 6), but he is only responding to the portents that have troubled everyone. He at first refuses to go to the Senate, not out of fear—unless we choose to see him hiding behind Calpurnia's fears—but out of concern for his wife: while it would not trouble him, going out would surely trouble Calpurnia. Caesar then makes a careful distinction between not being able to go ("cannot") and not wishing to go ("will not"), the latter being relevant in his case. If we recall Caesar's dislike of the Senate—Shakespeare would have known this from reading Plutarch, though he does not make direct reference to it in the play—Caesar is distinguishing between personal weaknesses, which might inhibit his going, and the arbitrary will of a man who does not feel constrained to give reasons to an inferior body of men. He finally decides to go to the

Senate, not from a change in convictions, not because Decius' interpretation of the dream convinces him not to fear but because such a "well expounded" interpretation should allay Calpurnia's fears, thereby allowing him to get on with his normal business. If he seems arrogant, is he not also the thoughtful husband?

There is one more detail in "The Life of Alexander" which may be of some value here. We will recall the line in which Caesar bids Antony to "Come on my right hand, for this ear is deaf" (I.ii.210). Dover Wilson, among others, finds in this an ironic comment on Caesar's reaching for godlike status; the man claiming divinity is woefully mortal, flawed with a partial hearing loss.[30] Douglas Peterson goes one step further and sees this reference to deafness as symbolic: unless one gets on the right side of Caesar, he will be inattentive to pleas. Caesar is deaf to anything he does not wish to hear; the line is thus evidence of that indifference to others which leads to tragedy.[31] There is, however, an interesting comment about the left and right ears in "The Life of Alexander" where North, or his printer, attracts our attention with a marginal heading: "Alexander kept one eare for the condemned person" (V, 223). Plutarch comments at length on Alexander's habit of closing with his hand one of his ears while listening to rumor or accusations of any sort. The suspected party could then deliver his confession or rebuttal to the other ear, which, when uncovered, might hear the truth and not be prejudiced by earlier testimony. Caesar has a similar concern in bringing Antony to his right side, to his good ear, so that he can tell him "truly" what he thinks of Cassius. Charges have been made against Cassius; Caesar has based his suspicions on certain physical qualities, certain predispositions in the man: he loves no plays, hears no music, seldom smiles, or "smiles in such a sort / As if he mock'd himself and scorn'd his spirit" (195–207). Literally, Caesar himself has been the accuser or slanderer, introducing some circumstantial evidence, though it is evidence we know to be significant since as audience we have just heard Cassius raise with Brutus the possibility of assassination. Caesar now wants an opinion other than his own; for this reason the right ear is to be "uncovered." There is no mention of Caesar's deafness in Plutarch, though some criticis point out that epilepsy (Plutarch's "falling sickness") often impairs the hearing on the left side. In any case, the reference to Alexander's use of his ears adds a new meaning to a line in the play which has already been challenged as being merely literal.

III

Antony as a character may not blossom as fully in *Julius Caesar* as does Brutus or Caesar, and for this reason our study of the lives of Demetrius and Antony, and the "Comparison," though not without profit, comes last. We may prefer to think of Antony as nothing more than a jaded sensualist or as the practical, ruthless revenger of Act IV. Recent critics, however, have taken a less extreme view. Mr. Knight, in the essay mentioned earlier, suggests that Antony epitomizes the loyal friend, that his love for Caesar directs his every action, no matter how vile. In our time we have witnessed something of a divided critical response to Antony: loyal but maniacal, a man flexible in a way that makes him superior to Brutus and yet also a creature of the moment, shallow, cruel in the name of love, a man in whom all the emotions exist in the extreme.

The "Comparison of Demetrius and Antony" suggests this same complex character, for Plutarch sees both men as at once "valiant and liberal" and yet dissolute (VI, 228). He distinguishes between Demetrius, whose lust did harm to others (as when he defiled the Temple of Minerva), and Antony, who did harm only to himself. Furthermore, Demetrius' death was "more reproachefull" in that he attempted to compromise with his enemies during his three-year captivity; Antony's death was "cowardly" but "yet was it before his bodie came into his enemies hands" (VI, 405). The "Comparison" may also give some hints for the characterization of Antony in *Antony and Cleopatra*, for Plutarch, while praising Demetrius, points out that Demetrius gave himself to sensual pleasures only when he had nothing else to do. For Antony pleasure became a way of life.

There are also some interesting commentaries on Demetrius as an actor, commentaries which place in context the highly theatrical nature of Antony in the play. We may think of his hypocritical pose when he comes on stage after the assassination and professes his friendship for the conspirators; surely this is a moment of conscious and consummate acting. There is also his "performance" in the funeral oration. Antony as an actor, a brilliant dissimulator, a manipulator of an audience—of this there is little hint in "The Life of Antony." Mr. Schanzer has suggested that Shakespeare's model for the funeral oration comes from Appian.[32] But "The Life of Demetrius" also places great stress on Demetrius' essential theatricalism, as well as that of his father. When they were first called kings, "they grewe more prowd and stately, then ever they were before: like unto common players of tragedies, who apparelling them selves to playe their partes upon the stage, doe chaunge their gate, their countenaunce, their voyce, their manner of sitting at the table, and their talke also" (VI, 247). Lacking true nobility, Demetrius often resorted to counterfeiting a princely countenance "like players upon a stage that would counterfeate his countenaunce and gesture" (p. 280). Near his death he went into his tent, cast a black cloak about his face, instead of the rich and stately cloak he normally wore, and appeared "not like unto a king, but like a common player when the play is done, and then secretly stale away" (p. 285). For the most part, however, Plutarch finds the same extremes of personality in men such as Demetrius and Antony; and the parallel Greek life, while it sustains the divided response evoked by a reading of "The Life of Antony," does not enlarge or refine our knowledge of Antony, in Plutarch or in the play.

My purpose here is not to "prove" that Shakespeare read these three parallel lives of Dion, Alexander, and Demetrius, nor even the two brief comparisons. I do think, of course, that we should raise this possibility. But surely we would want to know of the larger context of his more immediate sources in the three Roman lives. That this more extensive reading of the source parallels the complex response to the play urged by recent criticism is important. Shakespeare's Brutus is not identical with the character in "The Life of Brutus." And Plutarch's thoughts on Brutus, I would argue, are not confined to the actual life but are also to be found in the portrait of Dion, as well as in the "Comparison." This same argument holds for Caesar and Antony. We also would admit that Shakespeare's general attitude toward Brutus, even before he picked up his copy of North's Plutarch, was conditioned by the thoughts of his age toward Caesar's rule and the assassination; and it is for this reason that a study like J. Leeds Barroll's "Shakespeare and Roman History" is indispensable.[33] In our search for sources, then, we might want to reconsider the work, or works, we know for sure Shakespeare had. Did he not do a bit more leafing through the North translation than we have previously thought?

Notes:

1. The Bobbs-Merrill Shakespeare series (New York: Bobbs-Merrill, 1969), p. 161. I would also want to call attention here to Mr. Charney's important study of the play in his *Shakespeare's Roman Plays: The Function of Imagery in the Drama* (Cambridge, Mass.: Harvard Univ. Press, 1961). The text for North's Plutarch is *The Lives of the Noble Grecians and Romans,* 8 vols. (Oxford: Shakespeare Head Press, 1928). The text for *Julius Caesar* is that of T. S. Dorsch, New Arden ed. (London: Methuen, 1955). For convenience of reference among Shakespeare's other plays I use the New Cambridge Shakespeare, ed. W. A. Neilson and C. J. Hill (Cambridge, Mass.: Houghton Mifflin, 1942).
2. *Narrative and Dramatic Sources of Shakespeare* (New York: Columbia Univ. Press, 1964), V, 13.
3. *Shakespeare's Sources* (London: Methuen, 1957), I.
4. M. W. MacCallum distinguishes between Plutarch, a moralist, and Shakespeare, the inspired tragedian, and argues that there is no sense of discrimination or arrangement in Plutarch, in *Shakespeare's Roman Plays and Their Background* (London: Macmillan, 1910), p. 164 ff.
5. "Shakespeare and the Elizabethan Romans," *ShS,* 10 (1957), 35.

6. See the discussion of Martha Hale Shackford, *Plutarch in Renaissance England with Special Reference to Shakespeare* (Folcroft, Pa.: Folcroft Press, 1929), p. 36.
7. C. J. Gianakaris, *Plutarch* (New York: Twayne, 1970), p. 140.
8. *The Problem Plays of Shakespeare: A Study of "Julius Caesar," "Measure for Measure," and "Antony and Cleopatra"* (New York: Schocken Books, 1963).
9. "Brutus, Virtue, and Will," *SQ*, 10 (Summer 1959), 367–79.
10. Anne Paolucci, "The Tragic Hero in *Julius Caesar*," *SQ*, 77 (Summer 1960), 333.
11. *On the Design of Shakespearian Tragedy* (Toronto: Univ. of Toronto Press, 1957), p. 85–97.
12. William Bowden, "The Mind of Brutus," *SQ*, 17 (Winter 1966), 57–67.
13. H. M. Richmond, *Shakespeare's Political Plays* (New York: Random House, 1967), p. 215.
14. "Brutus and the Tragedy of Moral Choice," in *Shakespeare's Use of Learning* (San Marino, Calif.: Huntington Library, 1953), pp. 242–43.
15. *Literary Essays* (Edinburgh: Oliver and Bowd, 1956), p. 3.
16. *Unity in Shakespearian Tragedy* (New York: Columbia Univ. Press, 1956), pp. 40–54.
17. Hugo Von Hofmannsthal, in *Selected Prose,* trans. Mary Hottinger and Tania and James Stein, Bolligen Series, 33 (New York: Pantheon Books, 1952), pp. 247–67.
18. *Elizabethan Drama, 1558–1642* (Boston: Houghton Mifflin, 1908), II.
19. Frank Harris, *The Man Shakespeare and His Tragic Life-Story* (New York: Kennerley, 1909), quoted by Arthur Eastman, *A Short History of Shakespeare Criticism* (New York: Random House, 1968), p. 222.
20. *Use of Learning,* p. 236.
21. Reprinted in Bullough, V, 166–68.
22. *The State in Shakespeare's Greek and Roman Plays* (New York: Columbia Univ. Press, 1940), p. 183 (Buchanan quoted), p. 175 (Phillips).
23. "The Tragedy of Shakespeare's Brutus," *ELH*, 22 (March 1955), 1–15.
24. *The Imperial Theme* (London: Methuen, 1951).
25. *Plutarch: His Life, His Parallel Lives, and His Morals,* 2nd ed. (London: Macmillan, 1874).
26. Knight, p. 79.
27. Reprinted in Bullough, V, 147–56.
28. Reprinted in Bullough, V, 14.
29. *An Historical Collection of the Continuall Factions, Tumults, and Massacres of the Romans and Italians during the space of one hundred and twentie yeares before the peaceable Empire of August Caesar* (London, 1601), sig. Z1^{v}.
30. *The New Shakespeare* (Cambridge: Cambridge Univ. Press, 1949), p. 113.
31. " 'Wisdom Consumed in Confidence': An Examination of Shakespeare's *Julius Caesar*," *SQ*, 16 (Winter 1965), 19–28.
32. *Shakespeare's Appian* (Liverpool: Liverpool Univ. Press, 1956).
33. *MLR*, 53 (July 1958), 327–43.

The Love-Death Nexus in English Renaissance Tragedy

CHARLES R. FORKER

Do I delight to die, or life desire?
But now I liv'd, and life was death's annoy;
But now I died, and death was lively joy.

O, thou didst kill me! Kill me once again!

(*Ven.*, *ll.* 496–99)

What will it be
When that the wat'ry palates taste indeed
Love's thrice-repured nectar? Death, I fear me;
Sounding destruction; or some joy too fine,
Too subtile-potent, tun'd too sharp in sweetness
For the capacity of my ruder powers.

(*Tro.*, *III.ii.21–26*)[1]

"Love is as strong as death," wrote the poet of the *Song of Songs*, and the paradox that identifies the vital with the lethal, Eros with Thanatos, *l'amour* with *la mort* (as the punsters of medieval Provence might have it[2]), continues now, as then, to work its baffling fascinations, both mystical and horrific, upon our psyches. But the theme seems to have had a special force for Shakespeare and his fellow dramatists. Indeed, it became the basis for that entire genre which we call love tragedy, experimental and ill-defined though this was even in Elizabethan times.

In Kyd's *Soliman and Perseda* allegorical personifications of Love and Death preside with Fortune over the tragic action of the play, inviting the theater audience to judge for itself which of the three forces shall ultimately prove "greatest" (I.vi.38),[3] but the debate remains mysteriously unsettled. After a double climax in which Soliman, the rival lover, separates Perseda from her beloved Erastus and has him executed, only to become unwittingly both the agent of the lady's suicide and the victim of her revenge through a poisoned kiss, Love exits from the stage asserting defiantly that he "shall neuer yeeld to *Death*" (V.v.30). As is proper to tragedy, Kyd assigns the final speech to the gloomiest member of his choric trinity, but he does not permit Death to contradict the doctrine, at least twice reiterated, that "*Loues* workes are more then of a mortall temper . . ." (I.vi.11). Similarly, Marlowe in *Dido, Queen of Carthage*, a play that ends with three romantically induced suicides, allows his heroine, in words that anticipate Cleopatra's, to exclaim of Aeneas, "I never die, / For in his looks I see eternity . . ." (IV.iv.121–22).[4] As Kyd and Marlowe, among others, suggest, Love and Death are not only the cruelest of antagonists; they are also in some sense allies. Romances such as those of Pyramus and Romeo and Guilford Dudley[5] are "death-marked" from their inception. Juliet half-perceives this truth when she predicts after first meeting Romeo that "My grave is like to be my weddingbed" (I.v.137), and her lover confirms it by his allusion to "love-devouring death" (II.vi.7) and later to "the lean abhorred monster" of the tomb who is finally as "amorous" of his wife as he himself (V.iii.103–5). One of Ben Jonson's shepherds sums up the mysterious conjunction with lyric elegance:

> Though I am young, and cannot tell,
> Either what Death, or Love is well,
> Yet I have heard, they both beare darts,
> And both doe ayme at humane hearts:
> And then againe, I have been told
> Love wounds with heat, as Death with cold;
> So that I feare, they doe but bring
> Extreames to touch, and meane one thing.
> (*The Sad Shepherd, I.v.65–72*)[6]

My purpose in this essay is to explore some implications of the love-death nexus in Renaissance tragedy—to suggest several functions which it fulfilled in differing contexts and to illustrate the variety of attitudes and values of which it could be made the dramatic vehicle. I shall begin with Shakespeare and, after some associative excursions into the work of his contemporaries and successors, return to him at the end, hoping (with Polonius) by indirection to find directions out.

II

The religious idealism of courtly love, embodied archetypally (as de Rougemont has pointed out) in the myth of Tristan and Iseult,[7] endowed erotic love with mystical transcendence. Death became the ultimate test of love's purity and intensity, for trammeled by merely earthly imperfections and hostilities, it could free itself from anticlimax and fulfill its yearning for perfection only through union with the absolute. Such is the love which is not Time's fool, though rosy lips and cheeks within his bending sickle's compass come—the love which Shakespeare inherited from Neoplatonism and the conventions of Petrarchan rhetoric. *Romeo and Juliet* is, of course, the classic expression of this pattern in Elizabethan drama, and it stands as perhaps the most powerful refutation we could summon to the comic astringency of Rosalind's lesson that men have died from time to time, and worms have eaten them, but not for love. In debased, almost parodic, form, the pattern persists even into such domestic tragedies as *Arden of Feversham,* where Arden's servant Michael, by assisting his master's assassins, risks everything for his beloved's sake and exclaims in the final scene when both he and she are condemned, "Faith, I care not, seeing I die with Susan" (xviii.37).[8]

Yet to consider the erotic components of Renaissance tragedy in anything like their full range is instantly to overflow the confining singleness of the *Liebestod,* however richly Shakespeare orchestrated it in his play of star-crossed love. The involvement of eros with violence, terror, and revenge in the great majority of the plays, its corrupting entanglements with *Realpolitik,* ambition, lust, and murder, remind us that the self-destructive and tyrannical power of love was more variously usable by most tragedians, including Shakespeare, than its more idealized counterpart. When Burton speaks of erotic passion as a "*rabies insana,*" a raging madness which "subverts kingdoms, overthrows cities, towns, families, mars, corrupts, and makes a massacre of men,"[9] we have no difficulty supplying illustrative titles from the repertory of the Globe and its rivals.

No doubt one could argue—on the authority of Burton as well as Freud—that nearly all tragic subjects are erotic *in posse* if not *in esse,* that most actions and emotions, pushed to their limit, imply their increment of passion. Yet it is difficult to regard the persistent association of the erotic with the violent in Shakespeare and his successors as unconscious. Richard III takes the Lady Anne into a marriage bed that becomes successively both rack and bier by trapping her in the cul-de-sac of her own hyperbole and thus converting her hatred into a kind of lust. Hamlet, joking bitterly about the fearful economy of a Denmark where death nourishes sensuality, where funeral baked meats coldly furnish forth marriage tables, reduces innocent and incestuous lovers alike to the moral democracy of the grave. Lady Macbeth tries by diabolic prayer to unsex herself even as she enjoins her husband to "screw [his] courage to the sticking place" (I.vii.60)[10]—in fact to prove his manhood by sexualizing murder—and as he moves toward Duncan's chamber, he goes "with Tarquin's ravishing strides" (II.i.55). Rape and regicide become metaphorically one. The ingratitude of unnatural daughters maddens Lear to confront the paradox of his having engendered monsters, and the Machiavel for whom both monsters lustfully compete pronounces their common epitaph: "All three / Now marry in an instant" (V.iii.228–29). Such unions are part of an ironic pattern in the tragedies: Othello sacrificing his wife in her wedding sheets only to join her minutes later in "the tragic loading of [their] bed" (V.ii.363); Antony and Cleopatra made one through a sword which he rushes upon "As to a lover's bed" (IV.xiv.101) and a "pretty worm of Nilus" (V.ii.243) that sucks its nurse asleep; Bianca and the Duke of *Women Beware Women* celebrating their nuptials by "Tasting the same death in a cup of love" (V.ii.219);[11] Giovanni in *'Tis Pity She's a Whore* grotesquely literalizing a Petrarchan metaphor by possessing Annabella's heart upon his dagger before himself "embracing" the death which he calls "a guest long look'd for" (V.vi.105).[12] One could multiply instances.

For the tragic dramatist, then, the subject of love or infatuation shadowed by death had its obvious utility. It could be the means of showing the isolation or vulnerability of happiness, "brief as the lightning in the collied sky." It could function to bring incompatible systems of value into poignant or devastating collision, at the same time embodying interior, psychic conflicts of almost every stripe. In homiletic tragedies such as *A Woman Killed with Kindness* it could be the occasion for dramatizing a pattern of sin, self-sacrificial suffering, and atonement, a way of reaffirming the supremacy of Christian *agape.* On the other hand, in a chronicle play such as *Edward II,* Marlowe could make the king's homosexual love for Gaveston (a form of attraction which Burton calls "an inordinate passion even to death"[13]) the focus of an almost nihilistic tussle between private desire and public power as well as a way of rendering intelligible the pathetic psychology of a royal figure in whom tenacity of will and emotional dependence were complementary elements. The climactic scene of Edward's degradation and murder recapitulates with uncompromising irony the contrarieties of politics and personality shown earlier for the obscene manner of the monarch's death—pressing under the weight of a table and rectal penetration with a fiery spit (the "braver way" [V.iv.37][14] that must have suggested Lightborn's ironic name to the author)—unites the antitheses of cruelty and sexual passiveness, of retributive force and the need for love, that define both the central character and the action of which he is cause and victim. Here is a love-death physically and psychologically horrible enough to call in question our traditional definitions of natural order. The weakling hero, unnatural both as king and as man, becomes in death a pitiable symbol of royalty desecrated and humanity violated, of helplessness savaged by the machine-like force of a nearly incomprehensible brutality.

Stories of disastrous love could explore the ambivalent relations between attraction and repulsion, commitment and doubt, freedom and bondage, elation and despair; they could address the contradictory needs for intimacy and separateness, for self-discovery and self-annihilation. No motive is so universal in Elizabethan tragedy as love or its frustration. Perceiving that romantic passion radically alters those whom it invades, playwrights could naturally locate the source of a character's energy at the place where joy and misery converge. They saw that love creates its own structures of order than which nothing is more frail or illusory, that where everything is invested everything may be lost. We think of Troilus and, more terribly, Othello:

> Excellent wretch! Perdition catch my soul
> But I do love thee! and when I love thee not,
> Chaos is come again.
>
> (*III.iii.90–92*)

III

In a large group of plays, especially the tragedies of revenge, love is either ranged against violence and death or else perverted into becoming their instrument. The prevalence of this pattern and the grotesque ironies which it is so often made to enforce suggest a more than casual interest in what a modern clinician might term psychosexual fear. We need look for no Freudian perversity in the threat of death that tears Romeo from his nuptial bed at dawn or the street brawls that twice shatter Othello's nocturnal privacy with Desdemona. Apart from special cases such as *Hamlet,* Shakespeare's treatment of sexuality is refreshingly wholesome. But violent intrusions upon the pleasures of romance recur in Renaissance tragedy—with increasing frequency and prurience in the Jacobean period—and it is worth noticing that the two dramas which frame the historical limits of the revenge play both make sensational use of it. In Kyd's *Spanish Tragedy* the arbor where Horatio and Belimperia make love is converted before our eyes into a gallows; the two have been analogizing love and war in a playful duet of Petrarchan rhetoric, and the assassins enter with appropriate irony just as their victim puts the concluding flourish upon his amorous paradox:

> O stay awhile and I will die with thee,
> So shalt thou yield and yet have conquer'd me.
>
> (*II.iv.48–49*)[15]

In Shirley's *Cardinal* the rejected suitor murders his rival on his wedding night, threatening to "cut" whatever lover Rosaura should dare to take next from her "warm embrace, and throw his heart to Ravens" (IV.ii.72–73).[16] Consummations devoutly to be wished are forever being disturbed in scenes that range from the satiric to the shocking: Guiszard of *Tancred and Gismund* discovered naked in his lady's arms by her jealous father, who then hales the young earl off to strangulation and presents the eviscerated heart to his daughter in a golden cup; Bassianus and Lavinia, the newlyweds of *Titus Andronicus*, intercepted in a forest by Aaron and Tamora, whose sons then stab the bridegroom that "his dead trunk" may serve as "pillow" for their rape of his wife (II.iii.130); Ferneze in *The Malcontent* surprised between the sheets with the Duchess and impaled upon a sword as he flees in his nightshirt across the stage; Massinissa prevented from entering his own wedding bed in *Sophonisba* by the sudden entrance of a bleeding senator who summons him to battle; the defeated hero of *Caesar and Pompey* interrupted in a touching reunion with his wife Cornelia by political enemies who mercilessly cut him down with swords; Diaphanta in *The Changeling* literally fired from Alsemero's embraces and then shot.

Webster makes such an incident the very paradigm of his love-death psychology in the tense scene where Ferdinand surprises the Duchess of Malfi in her private apartments as she and her husband prepare for bed. By presenting his naked poniard with the words, "Die then, quickly!" (III.ii.71;[17] the erotic pun is but one of many such in the play), the Duke instantly converts his sister's world of sexual happiness and imagined safety into one of freezing terror. The place of the Duchess's "private nuptial bed," what Bosola refers to ironically as her "humble and fair seminary of peace" (III.ii.281–82), changes in a trice to a torture chamber. Positioned at the very center of the tragedy, this episode is pivotal, for it is full of echoes from the betrothal scene which also contains foreshadowings of death (she is making her will, for instance), and it anticipates the scenes of torture and execution which comprise a ghoulish parody of courtship, marriage, and sexual union (her taking Antonio's hand in marriage, for instance, is grotesquely repeated in Ferdinand's presentation of the severed hand).

Webster seems to be dramatizing more than sadism here, though the Duchess's brothers embody all too powerfully those savage irrationalities that love in its fragile insecurity must steel itself to confront. The scene shows chaos wrecking man's feeble attempts at order, but, perhaps more tragically, it shows that order half-betrayed from within. The Duchess can live and die like a prince, but when she invites Antonio into her heart, she also invites her incestuous brother with his deadly key and even deadlier dagger. From the beginning she instinctively senses the ruinous consequences of her decision, for she confides to Cariola, "I am going into a wilderness, / Where I shall find nor path, nor friendly clew / To be my guide" (I.i.359–61). In Webster's dark universe exposure to death is a condition of love, nor must we forget that the Duchess and her destroyer are twins.[18]

The more sensationally morbid and grotesque ironies of the love-death nexus—what textbooks used to call the decadence of Jacobean drama—appear to be rooted, perhaps half-consciously, in the conflict of repression with desire.[19] The strong infusions of horror that subtend sexuality in the tragedies of Marston, Tourneur, Fletcher, Middleton, and Ford suggest an overwhelming burden of guilt coupled with the gloomiest of metaphysics. We can hear the *Dies Irae* reverberating through these plays. But the lesson that punishment is inescapable, that sin unwittingly hungers for the retribution that will devour it, takes on egotistical energy and relish. As love slides into lust, humanism gives way to satire. The deterministic theology of Marlowe's Faustus spreads and darkens like a stain to teach man that the Helen he hopes will make him immortal with a kiss is in truth a succubus who will suck forth his soul. Misogyny becomes a fashionable dogma in the visual arts as in the literary, and a painter such as Abraham Bloemaert (1564–1651) can depict woman emblematically as the gateway to death. One of his better known pictures shows a beplumed gallant reaching under the skirts of a fashionable lady only to encounter the chill of the skeleton where he had expected voluptuous flesh.[20] A medieval emphasis on chastity is revived so that one of the typical dramatic heroines of the period can describe her temptation to yield to a seducer as a desire to "run thus violently / into the armes of death, and kisse distruction."[21] Calvinistic horror of the body unites opportunely with the vogue for anti-feminine satire, *contemptus mundi*, *memento mori*, and the *danse macabre*.

The symbolism of *The Revenger's Tragedy* underscores such attitudes with bizarre clarity. A lecherous duke, having murdered a virgin because of her chaste resistance to him, is himself murdered through the act of re-seducing her. The poisoned lips of Gloriana's skull repay him for his sexual crimes with gruesome exactitude, thus uniting polar opposites in a ghastly embrace. Victim and criminal, chastity and lust, frustration and desire, appearance and reality, love and death fuse in a *seductio ad absurdum*. Nor should we forget that the revenger who sets up this mortal tryst is himself a thwarted lover, a monster of egocentricity whose fanatic rediversions of love into loathing recoil to ensure his own extinction.

Seventeenth-century dramatists were not slow to seize upon the titillating possibilities of necrophilia in their eagerness to equate both depraved and idealistic love with death. Nor was the taste for baroque horror limited to the drama. A fictional account of the lecherous Queen Veneria, as told in an anonymous collection of related tales under the general title of *The Famous and Renowned History of Morindos* (1609), concludes with a didactic morbidity that is curiously parallel to Tourneur's celebrated *coup de théatre*. The author of the prose tale relates how Veneria, having seduced a scullion from the palace kitchen, is taken unawares by her cuckolded husband, the King of Bohemia, as she lies asleep in the servant's arms. After sheathing "a short scimitar . . . in the breast of his wife's minion, whose blood with such fury gushed from his polluted bosom as it wakened the sin-stained queen," the enraged king

> caused a large coffin to be brought, wherein he put the murdered body of the scullion; then to the same dead body, beginning now to putrefy and stink, he tied the live body of his queen, so in the coffin closed them up both together, that as she enjoyed his fellowship in life, so might she consume with him being dead, by which means the very worms that bred upon the dead carcass in a manner devoured up her live body. And thus were the sins of lust and adultery scourged with a plague but seldom heard of.[22]

The juicier forms of perversity were clearly becoming a literary vogue.

Marston in the opening lines of *Antonio's Revenge*, a play which antedates both *The Revenger's Tragedy* and *Morindos*, has his depraved duke, Piero Sforza, command an accomplice to bind Feliche's freshly stabbed body "Unto the panting side of Mellida" (I.i.2).[23] The heroine of the anonymous *Second Maiden's Tragedy* commits suicide to preserve her chastity, whereupon her lustful oppressor embalms the cadaver and dies making love to its poisoned lips; Massinger imitates this corpse-kissing scene in his *Duke of Milan* (V.ii.) to similar effect, as does Shirley in *The Traitor* (V.iii). In the more Platonic and courtly vein of Ford's *Broken Heart*, Calantha weds the "*lifeless trunk*" (V.iii.100) of Ithocles before expiring of grief to the accompaniment of a song which she has expressly composed for the purpose:

> Love only reigns in death, though art
> Can find no comfort for a broken heart.
>
> (*V.iii.93–94*)[24]

The want of necro-erotic action is sometimes supplied by imagery, and we find appropriate examples in the plays of Marston, Webster, and Jonson, among others. Marston appears to have been especially attracted to such grotesqueries and should perhaps be credited with popularizing them with his theatrical rivals and imitators. In addition to the offstage incident in *Antonio's Revenge* already mentioned, he resorts to necrophilic ideas in two later plays: Herod Frappatore in *The Fawn* alludes to the tyranny of Mezentius, who bound "the living and the dead bodies together, and forced them so to pine and rot" (I.ii.198–99);[25] in *Sophonisba*, Syphax threatens to "use, / With highest lust" the "senseless flesh" of the heroine, should she kill herself to fend off rape,

"And even then thy vexèd soul shall see, / Without resistance, thy trunk prostitute / Unto our appetite" (IV.i.58–62).[26] Jonson in *Volpone* has Corvino threaten Celia in similar terms: "Death! I will buy some slave / Whom I will kill, and bind thee to him, alive" (III.vii.100–01);[27] and he repeats the idea even more repellently in *The Sad Shepherd,* where Aeglamour imagines himself embracing the drowned body of Earine:

> I will love it still,
> For all that they can doe, and make 'hem mad,
> To see how I will hugge it in mine armes!
> And hang upon the lookes, dwell on her eyes:
> Feed round about her lips, and eate her kisses!
> Suck of her drowned flesh!
>
> (*I.iii.67–72*)

Webster also employs such imagery, as for instance in *The White Devil,* where Francisco curses Vittoria and Bracciano ("Let him cleave to her and both rot together" [II.i.398][28]) and in *The Duchess of Malfi,* where the heroine desires that her persecutors "would bind me to that lifeless trunk [of Antonio], / And let me freeze to death" (IV.i.68–69).[29]

The transmutation of sexual attraction into violence and death receives one of its most powerful explorations in *The Changeling,* where Middleton shows us the indissolubility of murder and lust in the fatal congress of Beatrice with De Flores. Regretting the rashness of her betrothal to one man in her infatuation with a second, Beatrice employs a third to liquidate the inconvenient fiancé only to discover that the price of her murderous naïveté is sexual union and death in the arms of the figure whom she thought she loathed most. Middleton employs this plot to search the ironies of moral self-recognition: an overplus of disgust masks desire, repulsiveness is shown to be magnetic, and the servant becomes the master. Beauty is drawn into coalescence with the beast as a means of dramatizing to a shallow girl what beastliness she has already embraced. To be "the deed's creature" is also to be De Flores' paramour and, in fact, to have lusted for one's own death. Middleton's persistent punning on the word *blood* makes the ethical and psychological burden of the love-death pattern inescapable, as do the phallic symbolism of Piraquo's severed finger which De Flores presents to his mistress and the double connotation of the seducer's name.

Beaumont and Fletcher exploit such sadomasochistic ideas less intensely but not less theatrically. *The Maid's Tragedy* contains a scene in which the lustful king, awakening to find that his mistress has tied him to his bed, believes this prelude to his own assassination to be some "prettie new device" (V.i.46)[30] to enhance sexual pleasure. This pornographic murder is neatly contrasted with an almost equally sexual suicide: the chaste but rejected Aspatia fulfills her amorous desire by pretending to be her own brother and so provoking her wished-for lover into running her through with his rapier. Lubricity and spotless frustration both invite the unsheathed blade.

Love Lies a-Bleeding, the suggestive subtitle of *Philaster,* provides still another example of the masochistic principle in operation. Fletcher and his collaborator so pattern the amorous relationships of this play as to contrast two feminine idealizations of virtuous love—one overt and passionate (the much calumniated Arethusa) and the other covert and Platonic (the selfless Euphrasia, disguised until her final speeches as the page Bellario). Both ladies are loyally devoted to the play's hero Philaster, and both, as an additional intricacy, are believed at the crisis to be libidinously involved with each other. The tragicomic mode of the drama offers us merely dangers, not deaths; but, significantly, all three principals of the romantic triangle sustain physical wounds, a fact that is symptomatic of a sophisticated taste for artful pathos and what might almost be called the luxury of suffering. When Philaster first threatens Bellario with his sword, the page offers to "love those pieces you have cut away, / Better then those that grow: and kisse those limbes, / Because you made um so"; and she can describe the death for which she begs as "A thing we all persue," the "giving over of a game, / That must be lost" (III.i.246–58).[31] The succeeding act reverses this situation with balletic symmetry to present Philaster offering the same sword to both ladies whom he now invites jointly to kill him. Of course they refuse, just as he had earlier refused to kill Bellario. Then, after the page has been dismissed, Arethusa reverses matters once more and persuades her aggrieved lover to give her "peace in death" (IV.v.65). He now stabs her only to be interrupted by a rustic who is horrified to see a man strike a woman, but this invasion of intimacy by a bumpkin so unschooled in emotional subtlety only elicits Arethusa's cry, "What ill-bred man art thou, to intrude thy selfe / Upon our private sports, our recreations?" (IV.v.89–90). Philaster himself is hurt in the ensuing struggle, and, in an effort to throw off his pursuers, he in turn wounds the sleeping Bellario whom he hopes they will take for Arethusa's assailant. In this highly contrived and experimental play the less than fatal stab-wound becomes almost a metaphor for unrequited or unrecognized affection, a physical conceit for the displacement of psychic pain. As such, its recurrence serves as a kind of *Leitmotiv* to exploit the ambivalences of creative and destructive love and to arouse complicated questions about the nature of selfhood. Nor is it accidental that Beaumont and Fletcher gain their elaborate and glossy effects in part by drawing upon the pastoral traditions of

Sidney, Tasso, Montemayor, and others who had already treated romantic love in such a way as to suggest the interdependence of suffering and fulfillment.

IV

As a form, romantic tragedy seems to have offered unique opportunities for probing the very paradoxes of identity that plays such as *Philaster* touch upon so tantalizingly. Questions of identity, of course, are central to a great variety of Renaissance tragedies, as Shakespeare's Northumberland reminds us when he observes of Richard II that "The King is not himself" (II.i.241), or Webster's Ferdinand when he remarks to Bosola that the latter's "pity is nothing of kin" (IV.i.138) to the henchman he thought he knew. Yet romantic involvements under conditions of extreme pressure seem peculiarly apt to tease us out of thought. Do lovers win their precarious individualities *through* a great passion or merge into some higher synthesis? Do assertiveness or abnegation, aggression or surrender, selfishness or altruism lie at the roots of ardor? Donne, perennially fascinated by the mystical mathematics of love, could repeatedly argue that one plus one equals one, that two souls "endure not yet / A breach but an expansion," and that, like the Phoenix, they "die and rise the same, and prove / Mysterious"[32] by love. But Marvell could write with equal force of a love "begotten by Despair / Upon Impossibility," a love whose limits were defined by the grave—"a fine and private place," no doubt, "But none, I think, do there embrace."[33] Dramatists who sought to portray tragic love inevitably involved themselves in this dualism, and the greatest plays explore the unremitting tensions between oneness and otherness, transcendence and finitude, sacrifice and defiance, hope and nihilism. By way of example, let me now suggest briefly two extreme cases—one from Shakespeare and one from Webster—and then conclude with two tragedies, both Shakespearean, that in their different ways might be seen as intermediate.

Romeo and Juliet with its breathless idealization of romance seems to lie near the conservative, more medieval, end of a historic spectrum. Although much is made of hostile destiny and feuding families, the love itself is free of all interior obstacles. The principals never quarrel or doubt each other, their union is sacramentally ratified, and they define their existences totally in relation to each other. In such circumstances a mutual suicide which tenderly, if ironically, re-enacts their sexual consummation,[34] a "dateless bargain to engrossing death" (V.iii.115), is the ineluctable climax of the play's ecstatic teleology. Juliet repeatedly refers to her lover's death at earlier points: in the orchard as Romeo descends from her window she observes, "Methinks I see thee, now thou art below, / As one dead in the bottom of a tomb" (III.v.55–56), and then to her mother (with a *double entendre*), "Indeed I never shall be satisfied / With Romeo till I behold him—dead" (III.v.93–94). Only in Capulet's vault, where Tybalt lies in his bloody sheet and where Paris now keeps him company, can this couple fully satisfy the intensity of their need to be one, and Romeo unconsciously betrays his conception of death as at once end and beginning by referring to the charnel house in a single line as "detestable maw" and "womb" (V.iii.45).

At the other and more modern extreme from *Romeo and Juliet* we might adduce Webster's *White Devil.* Vittoria and Bracciano build their relationship upon open defiance of the savage world that closes upon them, tearing their pleasures with rough strife from the very jaws of death rather than making love to the "lean, abhorred monster" who is the paramour of Shakespeare's couple. Participating almost heedlessly in the treachery and evil of their persecutors, Webster's characters seem to fuel their passion for each other through acts of physical and verbal aggression. Though both seem "lost"[35] in and to each other, though both describe their doomed commitment in terms of immolation and sacrifice,[36] Webster stresses the courageous inviolability of their separate identities. Vittoria, for instance, can insult her lover with a grotesque metaphor that asserts her willingness to be rid of him even as it reveals how much he has already become a part of her:

> Go, go brag
> How many ladies you have undone, like me.
> Fare you well sir; let me hear no more of you.
> I had a limb corrupted to an ulcer,
> But I have cut it off: and now I'll go
> Weeping to heaven on crutches.
>
> (*IV.ii.118–23*)

We rarely see them together, and when we do, it is in situations of extreme duress or alienation—an oblique consideration of the impending murder of their tedious spouses, a trial, a jealous quarrel, an excruciating death by poison and strangling. A significant interval separates their deaths, and the imagery of fatal eroticism (the mention, for instance, of the strangling noose as "a true-love knot" [V.iii.174]) is used to invoke the terrors of annihilation and despair, not supernatural reunion.[37] Vittoria uses every trick and wile, every resource of her explosive energy, to evade death, and when doom is not to be cheated, she scorns her assassins and speaks of the "black storm" (V.vi.248) that lies beyond.

Although Bracciano and his lady are criminals in a world which she aptly equates with hell, their love possesses dignity, even grandeur, and Webster presents it as the one existential experience through which two strong and lonely personalities may locate and preserve their integrities. The stoic postures and bitterly egotistic denigrations which give Websterian verse its diamond brilliance are symptomatic of how far we have come from the Petrarchan formalism and Elizabethan exuberance of Shakespeare's early success. Death is the price of both loves, but if Romeo and Juliet may be said in some sense to die into life, Vittoria and Bracciano only die out of it.

Othello and *Antony and Cleopatra,* Shakespeare's mature tragedies of love, fall somewhere between these two extremes. The noble Moor and his chaste bride take each other in what they conceive to be a marriage of true minds, a high and somewhat cloudy romance in which the sensual element is to be minimized. But since Othello confuses his wife, a girl of some obvious independence, with the projection of his own ideal, he is more susceptible than a less inexperienced man would be to Iago's masterful infusions of distrust. Othello's idea of marriage is a romantic union with perfection, an alliance with a "young and rose-lipp'd cherubin" (IV.ii.63),[38] and if a lower reality supervenes, his relief must be to loathe it. His image of the place where he has garnered up his heart, "Where either I must live or bear no life, / The fountain from the which my current runs / Or else dries up," changes with terrible completeness into "a cistern for foul toads / To knot and gender in" (IV.ii.58–62). Consequently he sets about his appalling ritual of justice in a demented attempt to change the "cunning'st pattern of excelling nature" into the "monumental alabaster" (V.ii.5–11) of his own visionary rhetoric. We recall his premonition upon rejoining Desdemona at Cyprus:

O my soul's joy!
If after every tempest come such calms,
May the winds blow till they have waken'd death!
And let the labouring bark climb hills of seas
Olympus-high, and duck again as low
As hell's from heaven! If it were now to die,
'Twere now to be most happy; for I fear
My soul hath her content so absolute
That not another comfort like to this
Succeeds in unknown fate.

(*II.i.186–94*)

When Desdemona tries to pacify rages in her jealous husband that she cannot comprehend, she tragically invites the death that is the psychological corollary of her husband's absolutism. She grants human imperfection in her spouse ("Nay, we must think men are not gods" [III.iv.148]), and her ill-timed intercessions on behalf of a man whose failure of duty she is eager to excuse only feed the rage of her husband's resentment for sublimity disfigured. *Othello* is the tragedy of an idealistic, potentially transcendental love in which the lovers fatally misconceive each other. Ultimately each comes to a higher truth, a deeper self-realization through involvement with the other—she through self-sacrifice and he through the recognition of his terrible error, but, though their bodies are united upon the same bed of death, their souls transpire, Shakespeare suggests, to separate eternities.

Antony and Cleopatra, as everyone knows, is the most complex and profound portrayal of tragic love in English, for in the developing relation between its hero and heroine and through the incandescence of his poetry, Shakespeare somehow fused the comic with the heroic, the mundane with the exalted, the dung with the fire and air, in an amalgam so rich and various as to elude analysis. As many readers have been constrained to grant, the tone of the play, particularly in its final act, flies in the face of conventional expectations and will admit of no narrow moralism. One is led to speculate that Shakespeare may even have deliberately chosen—though in a fully qualified and deliberately paradoxical way—to invert the traditional hegemony of reason over passion and to explore the possibilities of a new kind of triumph. The triple pillar of the world and his Egyptian queen throw away greater earthly power than Vittoria and Bracciano ever possess, but the world which they purchase in exchange participates in none of Webster's Medician bitterness and depravity. Its richness redeems its corruption; its decay ministers to its ripeness and fertility; creativity springs from its disgrace. The affair between Antony and his regal courtesan involves mutual distrust and betrayal, and their crossings of each other—his Roman marriage, her flight at Actium, for instance—only serve to illustrate the principle that opposites attract. Selfishness mingles with generosity, the pettiest of weaknesses with the spirit of Renaissance magnanimity. Pride of self is the rock from which the oceans of emotional spending flow, and the lovers might say to each other as Juliet says to Romeo, "My bounty is as boundless as the sea, / My love as deep; the more I give to thee, / The more I have, for both are infinite" (II.ii.133–35).

The sexual imagery which suffuses the play suggests a union which is at once fatally weakening and spiritually fortifying, a relationship that subsists upon a struggle of wills but in which resistance is the source that keeps appetite perpetually uncloyed, an interpenetration of personalities that, like the act of love which is its regnant metaphor, exhausts itself in the very process of creation. The truth of Madame de Stael's definition of love as "*égoisme à deux*" applies here, as perhaps also does Havelock Ellis's more clinical formula that love is "lust plus friendship."[39] Shakespeare patterns the physical separations so as to express the drama's psychic polarity more grandly—in order to endow the dynamics of the romance, its inherent conflict between dominance and submission, independence and union, with geographical extension. Yet, as physical as the attachment clearly is, it triumphs over distance, and the Herculean hero can reply to Cleopatra's protest, "O, my oblivion is a very Antony, / And I am all forgotten," with the paradoxical comfort that

> Our separation so abides and flies
> That thou, residing here, go'st yet with me,
> And I, hence fleeting, here remain with thee.
>
> (*I.iii.90–104*)

The insights into each other which the lovers progressively acquire, and acquire fully only through death, reinforce their own solipsism; yet they continually become more like each other. Their growth toward a third identity is comically implied in the delightful symbolism of their exchanging clothes in a moment of alcoholic abandon:

> O times!
> I laugh'd him out of patience; and that night
> I laugh'd him into patience; and next morn
> Ere the ninth hour I drunk him to his bed,
> Then put my tires and mantles on him, whilst
> I wore his sword Philippan.
>
> (*II.v.18–23*)

Antony and Cleopatra sets out to define the limits of hedonism only to transcend these limits, to rise to a mystical love-death which "shackles accidents and bolts up change" (V.ii.6). Traditional discriminations between love and lust, subject and object, union and duality, dissolve in the great climax of Cleopatra's luxurious suicide—a death as fully dignified and numinous as it is sexual and hedonistic. The gorgeous ritualism of "Give me my robe, put on my crown. I have / Immortal longings in me" melts into the sensual ecstasy of "Husband, I come . . . I am fire and air . . . As sweet as balm, as soft as air, as gentle—O Antony!" (V.ii.283–315).

Shakespeare's most ardent love tragedy, the tragedy whose hero Agrippa calls "thou Arabian bird" (III.ii.12) in his parody of Lepidus's deference, returns then to the paradox of self-annihilation and self-fulfillment that the dramatist had so cryptically and abstractly addressed in *The Phoenix and the Turtle:*

So they lov'd as love in twain
Had the essence but in one;
Two distincts, division none:
Number there in love was slain.

. . . . .

Property was thus appalled,
That the self was not the same;
Single nature's double name
Neither two nor one was called.

(*ll.25–40*)

Antony and Cleopatra synthesizes the very principles of individuation and totality in an emotional fusion beyond the reach of reason, a fusion in which loss and gain are felt to be but aspects of the same truth. Iras expresses the heavy side of this insight when she laments that "The bright day is done, / And we are for the dark" (V.ii.193–94), but the lover's pinch that hurts and is desired annuls our rational categories. Distinctions between mirth in funeral and dirge in marriage, between immortal longings and oblivion, are assimilated into the mystery of art.

V

The conjunction of love and death has always been a powerfully charged idea in western civilization, but its force has lain essentially (as Shakespeare profoundly knew) in the kinetic ambiguities that radiate from its core. For to raise the topic at all is instantly to be concerned with fundamental questions about the nature and limits of human kind and hence to approach that murky territory where psychology, ethics, metaphysics, and religion shade imperceptibly into each other. It is therefore not surprising that tragic dramatists of the sixteenth and seventeenth centuries should have been attracted to such a subject and have tried to exploit its rich possibilities in language, character, and action. How better to evoke pity and terror for that continuing struggle between order and chaos that is one definition of the human lot? It is love that brings Bracciano to the torture and yet makes him fight fiercely for life:

O thou strong heart!
There's such a covenant 'tween the world and it,
They're loth to break

. . . . .

Where's this good woman? had I infinite worlds
They were too little for thee. Must I leave thee?
. . . . .
Oh pain of death, let no man name death to me,
It is a word infinitely terrible,—

(*V.iii.13–40*)

But love is also the power that drives the dagger so eagerly into Juliet's breast and applies the asp so luxuriously to Cleopatra's. Such mysteries were not lost upon Shakespeare or even the lesser dramatists of his age. How, indeed, could they be missed by playwrights who remembered Anne Boleyn or Catherine Howard or Mary of Scotland or Lady Arabella Stuart or the murderous Countess of Somerset? Clearly these poets sensed that to bring love into meaningful contact with death was an effective way of rendering on the stage that "fierce dispute," as Keats was to call it, "Betwixt damnation and impassioned clay."

Notes:

1. All references to Shakespeare are from G. L. Kittredge, ed., *The Complete Works* (Boston: Ginn, 1936).
2. In Provençal the word for love was spelled *l'amor* and to the ear was indistinguishable from *la mort.* A play on the two words also appears in the prose *Tristan* where Brengain says after the lovers have drunk the love potion, "*dans la coupe maudite, vous avez bu l'amour et la mort*" (see Joseph Bédier, *Le Roman de Tristan et Iseut* [Paris: H. Piazza, 1962], p. 50).
3. Frederick S. Boas, ed., *The Tragedie of Soliman and Perseda* in *The Works of Thomas Kyd,* 2nd ed. (Oxford: Clarendon Press, 1955).
4. Christopher Marlowe, "*Dido Queen of Carthage*" and "*The Massacre at Paris,*" ed. H. J. Oliver (London: Methuen, 1968); cf. Shakespeare's *Antony and Cleopatra*: "Eternity was in our lips and eyes, / Bliss in our brows' bent . . ." (I.iii.35–36).
5. Lord Guilford Dudley and Lady Jane Grey are the youthful lovers of Dekker and Webster's *Sir Thomas Wyatt* (1607), tragically victimized by the political ambitions of their fathers. In the first scene in which the newly married couple appear Jane likens their ascent together into "chaires of State" to "funerall Coffins . . . Descending to their graues" (I.ii.64–66), and in the pathetic execution scene that inevitably follows, Jane kisses her husband but moments before she "must kisse the blocke" (V.ii.97); see Fredson Bowers, ed., *The Dramatic Works of Thomas Dekker,* I (Cambridge: Cambridge Univ. Press, 1953). The Pyramus and Thisbe story, an analogue to *Romeo and Juliet,* is best known to students of the drama through Shakespeare's parody in *A Midsummer Night's Dream,* but an English company is known to have performed a play of this title

at Nördlingen in 1604; see A. Harbage, *Annals of English Drama,* rev. S. Schoenbaum (London: Methuen, 1964), p. 206.

6. C. H. Herford and P. Simpson, eds., *Ben Jonson,* VII (Oxford: Clarendon Press, 1941).
7. Denis de Rougemont, *Love in the Western World,* trans. Montgomery Belgion, 2nd ed. (Garden City, N.Y.: Doubleday, 1957).
8. In A. H. Nethercot, C. R. Baskervill, and V. B. Heltzel, eds., *Elizabethan Plays,* rev. A. H. Nethercot (New York: Holt, Rinehart and Winston, 1971).
9. Robert Burton, *The Anatomy of Melancholy,* ed. Holbrook Jackson (London: Dent, 1964), III, 49.
10. The word "courage" in Renaissance English was often used to denote "sexual vigour and inclination, lust" (see *OED*).
11. Thomas Middleton, *Women Beware Women,* ed. Roma Gill (New York: Hill & Wang, 1968).
12. John Ford, *'Tis Pity She's a Whore,* ed. N. W. Bawcutt (Lincoln: Univ. of Nebraska Press, 1966).
13. *"Nihil usitatius apud monachos, cardinales, sacrificulos, etiam furor hic ad mortem, ad insanum"* (*Anatomy of Melancholy,* III, 51).
14. Christopher Marlowe, *Edward II,* ed. W. Moelwyn Merchant (London: Ernest Benn, 1967).
15. Thomas Kyd, *The Spanish Tragedy,* ed. Philip Edwards (London: Methuen. 1959).
16. James Shirley, *The Cardinal,* ed. C. R. Forker (Bloomington: Indiana Univ. Press, 1964).
17. John Webster, *The Duchess of Malfi,* ed. J. R. Brown (London: Methuen, 1964).
18. For a more detailed explication of this pattern in *The Duchess of Malfi,* see my "Love, Death, and Fame: The Grotesque Tragedy of John Webster," in *Anglia,* 91 (1973), 194–218.
19. Even a very early play such as the Inner Temple *Gismond of Salerne* (1566), revised by Robert Wilmot as *Tancred and Gismund* (1591), provides a classic example. That the couple in this drama have to meet in a secret cave located beneath Gismund's bedchamber serves to emphasize the tyrannical suppression of emotional and sexual fulfillment that is a *donnée* of the action. The moment the lovers emerge above ground, they court their destruction in the form of a hostile father and can realize their commitment to each other only through dying. Looked at symbolically, the entire action could be read as a conflict between libido and guilt—irreconcilable in life but capable of being sublimated (and therefore resolved) in death.
20. See Bloemaert's allegorical "Vanity" now in the Courtauld Institute of Art, London, and reproduced in *Life,* 71 (13 August 1971), 43.
21. Anon., *The Second Maiden's Tragedy* (I.ii.535–36), ed. W. W. Greg, Malone Society Reprints (Oxford: Oxford Univ. Press, 1909).
22. Charles C. Mish, ed., *Short Fiction of the Seventeenth Century* (New York: New York Univ. Press, 1963), pp. 38–39.
23. John Marston, *Antonio's Revenge,* ed. G. K. Hunter (Lincoln: Univ. of Nebraska Press, 1965).

24. John Ford, *The Broken Heart*, ed. Donald K. Anderson, Jr. (Lincoln: Univ. of Nebraska Press, 1968).
25. John Marston, *The Fawn*, ed. Gerald A. Smith (Lincoln: Univ. of Nebraska Press, 1965).
26. *The Wonder of Women, or The Tragedy of Sophonisba* in A. H. Bullen, ed., *The Works of John Marston* (London: John C. Nimmo, 1887), II, 289.
27. Ben Jonson, *Volpone*, ed. Alvin B. Kernan (New Haven: Yale Univ. Press, 1962).
28. John Webster, *The White Devil*, ed. J. R. Brown (London: Methuen, 1960).
29. The punishment of binding live bodies to dead ones derives from Virgil's *Aeneid*, VIII, 485–88 (the passage to which Marston alludes in *The Fawn*), but it became a familiar emblem of unhappy marriage (see R. D. Dent, *John Webster's Borrowing* [Berkeley: Univ. of California Press, 1960], p. 231). Not surprisingly, Milton refers to it in *The Doctrine and Discipline of Divorce* (Frank A. Patterson, ed., *The Works of John Milton*, III [New York: Columbia Univ. Press, 1931], 478). Burton in a passage listing sexual enormities mentions certain Egyptians "who lie with beautiful cadavers" ("*qui cum formosarum cadaveribus concumbunt*"; *Anatomy of Melancholy*, III, 51).
30. Fredson Bowers, ed., *The Dramatic Works in The Beaumont and Fletcher Canon*, II (Cambridge: Cambridge Univ. Press, 1970).
31. Bowers, *The Beaumont and Fletcher Canon*, I (1966).
32. John Donne, "A Valediction: Forbidding Mourning" (ll. 22–23) and "The Canonization" (ll. 26–27).
33. Andrew Marvell, "The Definition of Love" (ll. 3–4) and "To His Coy Mistress" (ll. 31–32).
34. Both lovers expire on lines which utilize the same familiar pun: cf. Romeo's "Thus with a kiss I die" (V.iii.120) and Juliet's "O happy dagger! / This is thy sheath; there rest and let me die" (V.iii.169–70). The concept of love here dramatized is well expressed by the eighteenth-century German mystic Novalis, who wrote: "A union formed even unto death is a marriage bestowing on each a companion for Night. It is in death that love is sweetest. Death appears to one still alive as a nuptial night, the heart of sweet mysteries" (translated by M. C. D'Arcy in his *The Mind and Heart of Love* [New York: Meridian, 1956], p. 45).
35. Cf. Bracciano's "Quite lost Flamineo" (I.ii.3) and "Loose me not madam, for if you forego me / I am lost eternally" (I.ii.207–8); also Vittoria's "I am lost forever" (V.iii.35).
36. Cf. Bracciano's "Thou hast led me, like an heathen sacrifice / With music, and with fatal yokes of flowers / To my eternal ruin" (IV.ii.89–91); also Vittoria's "Behold Bracciano, I that while you liv'd / Did make a flaming altar of my heart / To sacrifice unto you; now am ready / To sacrifice heart and all" (V.vi. 83–86).
37. Frank Dunlop in his 1969 production of *The White Devil* at the National Theatre, London, stressed the connection between murder and sexuality by having Count Lodovico stab Vittoria in the vagina.
38. Othello uses this phrase insultingly in one of his most brutal attacks upon his wife, but it nevertheless seems to embody his earlier conception of her purity—the conception which Iago has now so fatally shattered. The precise meaning

is admittedly problematic since the syntax of the entire passage in which the quoted words appear is a much debated textual crux. Interpretation depends upon several factors, chiefly upon a choice of various ways of punctuating the passage as well as upon a choice between quarto and folio readings (see M. R. Ridley's New Arden ed. [London: Methuen, 1958], pp. 153–54, for a full discussion of the particulars). I follow Ridley in supposing that "cherubin" is a sarcastic epithet for Desdemona and "not an address to a personified virtue" (Patience).

39. See Paul Robert, *Dictionaire alphabétique et analogique de la Langue Française* (Paris: Société du nouveau Littré, 1953–64), II, 1485; also John Bayley, *The Characters of Love* (New York: Basic Books, 1960), p. 4.

Cressida and the World of the Play

GRANT L. VOTH AND OLIVER H. EVANS

Despite the range and diversity of critical approaches to and estimates of Shakespeare's *Troilus and Cressida*, one judgment has remained constant: Cressida is a mere prostitute, a cold and calculating woman; she is Falsehood in Love.[1] Even her defenders (and she has had a few) have qualified their admiration of her wit, beauty, and charm by finding her too frail to fulfill Troilus's idealization of her or to answer his love in kind.[2] Whatever else critics have disagreed about in reading the play, such estimates of Cressida's character have seldom been called into question.

One of the reasons for her dismissal by the critics has been their desire to talk about Troilus. His role and character, unlike Cressida's, have been fully discussed, and responses to him have ranged from unqualified admiration to disdain.[3] Such exclusive attention to Troilus, however helpful it has been in illuminating his part in the play, has not been entirely fair to Cressida. Her character is not as static as critics have described it, nor is her behavior as vicious as it has been judged; she does change during the course of the play, and, in context, her decisions are both more difficult and better motivated than has been assumed.

Cressida's movement in the play is from awareness to self-deception and back to awareness again, a counterpoint to Troilus's movement, whether it be from innocence to awareness or from ignorance to animal rage. Cressida begins her career as one totally at home in the world of the play. A realist and a cynic, she knows what men value in women in spite of what they sometimes say they admire. But in the course of her affair with Troilus, she is seduced by him from her initial position and persuaded to believe in his inadequate "ideal" vision. Finally, back in the real world of the Greek generals and Diomedes, she reluctantly returns to her initial and more accurate, if less attractive, understanding of the way things go in the world. There is thus a complexity in Cressida's character and role which has not very often been recognized, and which deserves more attention than it has received.

To understand this complexity, however, it is necessary to understand the nature of the world assumed by *Troilus and Cressida*. It is, to begin with, a world stripped of metaphysical and temporal dimensions; and it is thus a world in which there is no absolute universal order, as there is in both Shakespearean comedy and tragedy, with which man can harmonize or against which he can struggle. The top of the chain of being is omitted in the play, and its omission, coupled with the absence of temporal dimensions, severely limits the scope and significance of the action.[4] In this play there is no possibility of a universal order reasserting its claim, and it can end, therefore, only in what Dryden describes as "a confusion of drums and trumpets, excursions and alarms."[5]

A consequence of this single-dimension reality is the loss of the multiple perspectives which characterize Shakespeare's other plays. In the comedies, for example, love is seen both realistically and idealistically, and we are made to recognize the claims of both.[6] But in the confined world of *Troilus and Cressida*, there is only one perspective: the entire world of the play is hopelessly corrupt, and the knight whose sumptuous armor covers a "most putrified core" (V.-viii.1)[7] is a symbol for that world.[8]

Since there is no higher reality to offer hope of redemption, the juxtaposition of the armor and the putrified core presents us not with the tension of two perspectives but with an ironic contrast between appearance and reality. The contrast is already presented in the Prologue, in which the magnificent walls of Troy, with their "massy staples / And corresponsive and fulfilling bolts" (Prologue, ll. 17–18) are shown to contain nothing more than the truth that "ravish'd Helen, Menalaus' queen, / With wanton Paris sleeps" (Prologue, ll. 9–10); and we discover very quickly that the "brave pavillions" (Prologue, l. 15) of the Greeks hide the reality of Achilles, Patroclus, Ajax, and Thersites. Such contrasts, which run throughout the play, can be seen at their most extreme in Pandarus' "complimental assault" (III.i.43) upon Paris, Helen, and their court:

> Fair be to you, my lord, and to all this fair company! Fair desires, in all fair measure, fairly guide them, especially to you, fair queen! Fair thoughts be your fair pillow!
>
> (*III.i.46–49*)

Here, in the corruption which lies at the center of the entire play, the excessive language, like the knight's sumptuous armor, only contrasts more markedly with the decay it attempts to hide.

Such irony is available, of course, only to the reader, not to the characters in the play. For them, the eloquent and rhetorical language is an attempt to establish values in their world, to cloak reality in a "fair" cover, to make things more glorious by calling them by different names. Their language, strained and hyperbolic, becomes the sumptuous armor with which the citizens of Troy and of the Greek camp attempt to cover over the putrified core. In spite of their efforts, however, the hollow and botchy core within, like the disconcerting truth that the whole war is being fought over a "placket" (II.iii.21), keeps reasserting itself; like everything else in the play, the language carries within its sumptuous armor a "most putrified core."

While this is true of most of the language in the play, it is particularly true of Troilus' language, and his idealism should, therefore, be viewed with some suspicion. His verbal projections onto the world of the play, ideal as they may seem, are undermined by the same imagery of disease, mercantilism, and decay present in all the language of the play.[9] He sees himself, for example, as a courtly lover, but his conceit of the festering wound love has given him undercuts his expression of that sentiment and links his attitude to his corrupt world (I.i.51–64); his deliberately poetic description of Cressida as a pearl, Pandarus as a ship, and himself as the merchant (I.i.103–7) reduces Cressida to an object, whose possession is his aim; and his well-known anticipation speech (III.ii.19–30), with its insistent undercurrent of such sense-words as *taste, palate, ruder powers,* and *love's thrice repured nectar,* belies the ideal aspirations which it professes and indicates that the source of Troilus' vision, in spite of his own disclaimers, is the desire to "wallow" in Cressida's "lily beds" (III.ii.13).

Troilus' attempts to project an ideal vision upon the sordid business of the war are likewise unsuccessful, for once again his imagery shows the extent to which his own projections participate in the decaying world he is trying to make "fair without." In the Trojan council scene, Helen becomes for Troilus the pearl (II.ii.81–82), the silk cloth, and the exotic food (II.ii.69–72) which traders bring back from their voyages; and the Trojan nation becomes a pack of thieves who, having stolen the pearl of great price, have now become too cowardly to keep it (II.ii.94–96). The adaptation of Marlowe's line ironically indicates the baseness of all of Troilus' vision, for it is Helen's "price," not her "face," which has launched the thousand ships, and the net result has been that crowned kings have become "merchants" (II.ii.83).

Thus while Troilus spends most of the play projecting on the world his own valuation of it—"What's aught, but as 'tis valued?" (II.ii.53)—his imagery consistently reveals that the core of his vision is as corrupt as the real world of the play. That world is the one in which, as Thersites notes, Menalaus and Paris are simply "cuckold and cuckold maker" (V.viii.9), in which the argument of the war is "a cuckold and a whore" (II.iii.78), and in which "nothing else holds fashion" except "lechery, lechery, still wars and lechery" (V.ii.196–97).[10] No verbal projection of Troilus' own devising can make that world less sordid; in such a world, in fact, the best Troilus' idealism can do is to bring upon himself a catastrophic disillusionment and to lead Hector, indirectly, to his death.

It is in this world, and in contrast to this Troilus, that we must see Cressida.

At home in the world of the play, she has no illusions about the "enterprise" (I.ii.309) of love. She knows that once men have achieved their end, they no longer "beseech," but "command" (I.ii.319); she knows that

> Things won are done, joy's soul lies in the doing:
> That she belov'd knows nought that knows not this:
> Men prize the thing ungain'd, more than it is.
>
> (*I.ii.313–15*)

Unattractive and calculating as this may appear to us, given the world of the play, it is a more legitimate approach to love than is Troilus' corrupt idealism.

But there is more to Cressida's calculating posture than a simple desire to delay gratification and thereby to retain control of the situation, for in her wiliness there is also an element of self-defense. During her scene with Pandarus, while he tries to convince her of Troilus' worth, Cressida deliberately misunderstands him, confusing his metaphors for literal truth and his literal truth for metaphors (I.ii.68–191). Unlike Troilus, who wishes to remind himself of his love and to dress it in as fine a language as possible, Cressida uses language to keep herself from remembering how much she loves Troilus and from revealing too much of that love. This becomes clear when Pandarus, in exasperation, makes explicit the defensive tactic she is using by saying, "You are such another woman, one knows not at what ward you lie" (I.ii.282–83). Cressida responds with what, at the outset of the play, has to be her stance in her situation:

> Upon my back, to defend my belly; upon my wit, to defend my wiles; upon my secrecy, to defend mine honesty; my mask to defend my beauty, and you to defend all these: and at all these wards I lie, at a thousand watches.
>
> (*I.ii.285–88*)

Her wit is her chief defense, and when it deserts her, she becomes another victim (like Hector) of Troilus' hyperbole and naïveté. In her first confrontation with Troilus, Cressida reveals once more her knowledge of the way things go in the world of the play when she fears that there are "more dregs than water" in the fountain of love (III.ii.72). When Troilus confidently asserts that the only "monstrosity" in love is "that the will is infinite, and the execution confined, that the desire is boundless, and the act a slave to limit" (III.ii.87–90), Cressida more accurately replies that "all lovers swear more performance than they are able, and yet reserve an ability that they never perform, vowing more than the perfection of ten, and discharging less than the tenth part of one" (III.ii.91–95).

Ultimately, Cressida yields and confesses to Troilus that she has been "won" all along (III.ii.125). In comedy, in a situation like that of Beatrice and Benedick, such a confession would signal the destruction of barriers that stand in the way of creating a new social and individual identity; in this play, however, Cressida's speech marks a betrayal of herself and of her knowledge of what her world is like: "Where is my wit? / I would be gone. I speak I know not what" (III.ii.157–58).

Throughout the trysting scene, part of the drama lies in the conflict between Troilus' attempt to seduce Cressida to his idealistic vision and Cressida's attempt to act on the basis of what she knows the world to be like. All her attempts to point out the truth to Troilus fail. When she asks him to make her stop talking, Troilus, not understanding, thinks that she is angling for a kiss (III.ii.141–45). When she tries to deflect Troilus' hyperbolic protestations of purity and eternal faithfulness with "In that I'll war with you" (III.ii.179), Troilus again misunderstands. His response is to offer his name as a title for faithful love, and at that point Cressida gives over her position, offering her own name as a type of unfaithfulness (III.ii.191–203). Against what she knows to be the reality of the world of the play, she takes on the sumptuous armor of Troilus' hyperbole and speaks "the thing [she] shall repent" (III.ii.131). Full of false hope and true regret, she tells Troilus, "Prophet may you be" (III.ii.-190), closes her eyes to the grim reality of her world, and yields to her lover.

Critics who have insisted that Cressida is nothing more than a wanton have had to do so by ignoring or misunderstanding her speech when she is informed that she must leave Troy (IV.ii.102–11). When she says that she has forgotten her father, she is indicating that, having once committed herself to Troilus, she will now attempt to maintain that commitment in the face of an uncle whose chief interest can be summed up in his question, "How go maidenheads?" (IV.ii.24), and of a world in which there is a price on everything from loyalty (Calchas) to honor (Achilles) to love (Paris). Cressida, of course, has never really escaped from that world any more than Troilus has by calling it by another name; but insofar as she, like Troilus, thinks that she has escaped, she has lost touch with her earlier, more accurate vision. The fullest indication of the extent to which Cressida is taken in by Troilus' vision is the repetition, in the farewell scene, of her vow to have her name stand for faithlessness if she prove false:

> O you gods divine,
> Make Cressid's name the very crown of falsehood,
> If ever she leave Troilus!
>
> *(IV.ii.105–7)*

The directness and simplicity of these words, in contrast with Troilus' (and her own) earlier hyperbole, is another indication of the sincerity of her resolve.

At once, however, Cressida finds herself back in the real world of the play, a world in which beauty pleads little more than "fair usage" (IV.iv.126). In the Greek camp, for reasons which are not entirely clear, Ulysses initiates the kissing scene and then, believing that he has read "the tables of her thoughts" (IV.v.60), he dismisses Cressida as a mere "daugher of the game" (IV.v.62–64).[11] In so doing, he once again throws Cressida back upon her "watch." She manages, with her wit, to keep most of the Greeks, including Ulysses, at arm's length for the entire scene; but her tactic here (the same one she used earlier in her talk with Pandarus) is Cressida's admission that she has returned once more to the real world of the play. Once more language must serve as her defense against a sordid and corrupt environment.

For the rest of the play, then, Cressida's "wit" is the "ward" at which she lies. Such a defense, however, is of no avail when she must deal with Diomedes. For Diomedes has no use for the "fooling" of wit, and his hardheaded, realistic appraisal of Helen as a "flat tamed piece," out of whose "whorish loins" Paris is content to breed his heirs (IV.i.62–64) establishes his position as one poles away from that of Troilus.[12] Thus in his meeting with Cressida, Diomedes' function is almost as much symbolic as it is literal: he, as representative of the real world of the play, comes to reclaim Cressida.

But it is important to see the reluctance with which Cressida finally submits to that real world. The sleeve is the symbol of her brief stay in the vision of Troilus; holding it, she says:

> O all you gods! O pretty, pretty pledge;
> Thy master now lies thinking in his bed
> Of thee and me, and sighs, and takes my glove,
> And gives memorial dainty kisses to it. . . .
>
> (*V.ii.77–80*)

We know, of course, that he is doing nothing of the sort; but it is the kind of thing Troilus himself might well have said earlier in the play; it is at least consistent with the vision of the world he has seduced Cressida into believing in. There is a definite touch of regret, perhaps even of pathos, in Cressida's final lines as she returns for once and all to the real world of the play:

> Troilus, farewell! one eye yet looks on thee;
> But with my heart the other eye doth see.
>
> (*V.ii.107–8*)

Cressida's career in the play is, then, neither as simple nor as corrupt as critics have judged it. Derek Traversi has said that "any attempt to subject Cressida's inconsistency to a moral judgment . . . is out of place because the spirit in which Shakespeare created her made it impossible for her to be shown as really responsible for her actions. . . ."[13] Insofar as her actions are determined by the world of the play, a world which makes human attempts at ideals nothing more than attempts to give "fair" covering to sordidness and corruption, Cressida is not responsible. She is responsible, as we have shown, for the "folly" (III.ii.110) of ignoring her knowledge of the world of the play and of giving herself to Troilus's "ideal" vision. It is, however, a folly which we feel has won for her a disproportionate amount of blame.

Notes:

1. Thomas Marc Parrott, *Shakespearian Comedy*, 2nd ed. (New York: Russell & Russell, 1962), p. 53, refers to Cressida as a "wanton"; William Empson, *Seven Types of Ambiguity* (London: Chatto & Windus, 1930), p. 178, calls her "conscious and calculating"; for W. W. Lawrence, *Shakespeare's Problem Comedies*, 2nd ed. (New York: Frederick Ungar, 1960), pp. 140–42, Cressida's passion is "sensual and calculating," and Cressida herself "a false and shallow woman"; Una Ellis-Fermor, *The Frontiers of Drama*, 2nd ed. (London: Methuen, 1964), p. 59, describes her as "a light woman"; E. M. W. Tillyard, *Shakespeare's Problem Plays* (Toronto: Univ. of Toronto Press, 1950), p. 49, finds that she becomes "Falsehood in Love"; and George Wilbur Meyer, "Order Out of Chaos in Shakespeare's *Troilus and Cressida*," *Tulane Studies in English*, 4 (1954), 53, is content to call her a "whore."
2. E. K. Chambers, *Shakespeare: A Survey* (London: Sidgewick & Jackson, 1925), p. 196, says that although her vows are sincere when she makes them, Cressida "is not made of the stuff of heroines"; Hamill Kenny, "Shakespeare's Cressida," *Anglia*, 61 (1937), 176, qualifies his defense by finding Cressida tainted with "selfishness, inconstancy, frailty, small self-knowledge, and a tendency to be easily enamored"; and Robert Ornstein, *The Moral Vision of Jacobean Tragedy* (Madison: Univ. of Wisconsin Press, 1960), p. 45, while admitting that she is "a daughter of the game which men would have her play and for which they despise her," and while finding that she is "more realist than sensualist, more wary and weary than wanton," still pronounces her a "slut." For similar qualified apologies, see G. I. Duthie, *Shakespeare* (London: Hutchinson's Univ. Library, 1950), pp. 110–11, and A. P. Rossiter, *Angel with Horns* (London: Longmans, Green, 1961), pp. 132–33.
3. The extreme positions can be represented by Winifred M. T. Nowottny, " 'Opinion' and 'Value' in *Troilus and Cressida*," *EIC*, 4 (July 1954), 294, and by Alice Shalvi, " 'Honor' in *Troilus and Cressida*," *SEL*, 5 (Spring 1965), 294–96. Miss Nowottny feels that while Troilus learns what Cressida truly is, his refusal to "deny the values by which he has lived" makes him noble. Miss Shalvi, on the

other hand, feels that Troilus suffers throughout from "impaired judgment" and that Cressida's betrayal brings him no true enlightenment: "the change he undergoes is not a change for the better."

4. Tillyard, p. 84, notes the omission in Ulysses' speech on degree of "the angelic end of the chain of being" and its consequent limiting effect; John Bayley, "Shakespeare's Only Play," *Stratford Papers on Shakespeare* (1963), 58–83, discusses the absence of the dimension of time in the play; and W. R. Elton, "Shakespeare's Ulysses and the Problem of Value," *ShakS,* 2 (1966), 95–111, has shown that the order speech itself does not necessarily provide an absolute against which the actions of the play should be judged; it may, in its context, be seen ironically.
5. "Preface" to *Troilus and Cressida, John Dryden's Works,* ed. Sir Walter Scott, rev. George Saintsbury (Edinburgh: William Paterson, 1882), VI, 225.
6. George C. Taylor, "Shakespeare's Attitude toward Love and Honor in *Troilus and Cressida,*" *PMLA,* 45 (Sept. 1930), 784–86, discusses the balance between the ideal and the real in Shakespeare's comedies and then notes that in *Troilus and Cressida* "Shakespeare bears down much more heavily than in any other play on that side which reduces love and honor to laughter and scorn"; he thus fails to preserve "that more exact and even balance . . . which elsewhere he kept."
7. All quotations are from the New Cambridge edition, ed. W. A. Neilson and C. J. Hill (New York: Houghton Mifflin, 1942).
8. A number of critics have seen the world of the play as corrupt: e.g., Bertrand Evans, *Shakespeare's Comedies* (Oxford: Clarendon Press, 1959), p. 167; and Barbara Heliodora C. M. F. de Almeida, "*Troilus and Cressida*: Romantic Love Revisited," *SQ,* 15 (Autumn 1964), 327–32. Our reading of the "one in sumptuous armour" follows that of S. L. Bethell, *Shakespeare and the Popular Dramatic Tradition* (Durham: Univ. of North Carolina Press, 1944), p. 127.
9. For a discussion of the various ways in which characters are undermined by their language, see T. McAlindon, "Language, Style, and Meaning in *Troilus and Cressida,*" *PMLA,* 94 (Jan. 1969), 38–39. Particularly relevant is McAlindon's discussion of "unconscious tapinosis," whose "effect is to introduce images and ideas which work counter to the speaker's usually panegyric intention. . . ." While the device, as McAlindon says, "tends . . . to reveal disorder in the individual rather than in society," Troilus' particular images link his inner corruption to that of his world; McAlindon's position that Shakespeare and other sixteenth-century poets employed this device as "an apt instrument for expressing their double consciousness of the splendor and folly of passion" is no doubt correct and would be true of *Troilus and Cressida* were it not for the lack of balanced perspectives discussed above.
10. See Derick R. C. Marsh, "Interpretation and Misinterpretation: the Problem of *Troilus and Cressida,*" *ShakS,* 1 (1965), 196. Marsh correctly concludes that since the play shows a world "devoid of genuine honour, love and integrity of any kind," the judgments of Thersites must be accepted. Marsh goes on to qualify this by saying that "the very violence of [Thersites'] abuse . . . generates an opposite sort of reaction, strengthening in the reader the feeling that . . .

all love need not be lechery, all honour vanity nor all action stupid, brutal and futile." The point, however, is that the accuracy of Thersites' judgments must be measured not against *all* love, honor, and action, but against the love, honor, and action presented within this play.

11. There is no entirely satisfactory way of accounting for Ulysses' behavior here, and critics interested in establishing Cressida's wantonness have generally shifted the discussion to *function* instead of *motive*. Thus James Oscar Campbell, *Comicall Satyre and Shakespeare's Troilus and Cressida* (San Marino, Calif.: Huntington Library, 1938), p. 215, says that "Cressida goes directly to the Greek camp, and kisses all the men, with an abandon much greater than the liberal customs of Elizabethan salutation prescribed. Ulysses . . . is conveniently at hand to keep the audience clear on that point." Ulysses is, however, a somewhat unreliable commentator: a good deal of the action in the first half of the play is given over to his elaborate and highly unsuccessful attempt, based on his misunderstanding of the world of the play, to get Achilles back into the war; and his introduction (albeit second-hand) of Troilus as one who speaks "in deeds, and deedless in his tongue" (IV.v.98) should make us even less willing to accept without question his understanding of Cressida's "game."

12. Ulysses once again illustrates his unreliability as a commentator by describing this same Diomedes as one whose spirit "in aspiration lifts him from the earth" (IV.v.15–16).

13. *An Approach to Shakespeare*, 3rd ed. (New York: Doubleday, 1969), pp. 329–30.

Shakespeare's Hand in *Sir Thomas More*: Some Aspects of the Paleographic Argument

Michael L. Hays

The manuscript of *The Booke of Sir Thomas Moore* (Harley MS. 7368) is replete with so many and such various puzzles that they alone will continue to win the attention of scholars so long as they remain unsolved. However esoteric some of the research may be, the attention is deserved, not only because the puzzles are inherently interesting but also because their solution would reveal much about the processes of authorial collaboration, relations between writers and dramatic companies, the practices of playhouse scribes, and the relations between dramatic companies and the office of the Master of Revels. Moreover, if Shakespeare's hand could be established beyond question, and if the manuscript could be dated with some accuracy,[1] much would be learned about his early career as a writer, especially his relations with several other dramatists.

The question of Shakespeare's hand in *Sir Thomas More* was first raised a little over a hundred years ago.[2] It has, of course, been much discussed ever after.[3] Since the question was most vigorously discussed in the decade after World War I, there has been a decided shift of opinion toward an increasingly skeptical acceptance of the attribution. One reason for this drift is that greater knowledge about Elizabethan manuscripts and documents, scribal practices, and handwriting has somewhat undermined the early confident claims for attribution.

Those claims have variously emphasized paleographic and literary considerations. Originally, Richard Simpson focused his attention on critical and historical matters in offering Shakespeare as the author of certain portions of the play. He found that "there is nothing whatever in the character of the handwriting [of those portions] to militate against this supposition."[4] Simpson, however, did not feel that the paleographic data provided a sufficient basis for a conjecture pointing to Shakespeare's authorship of these portions.[5] But apparently because some portions identified by Simpson on literary grounds as Shakespeare's no longer were accepted as his and because paleography appeared to offer a certain and scientific basis for an argument for attribution, subsequent efforts by Thompson and Greg emphasized this possibility. Later, others offered corroborative arguments based on similarities of imagery and ideas.[6] In the past thirty years, reviews of the problem have offered balanced summaries of both paleographic and literary considerations, generally implying that the weaknesses of the one are remedied by the strengths of the other. The collaborative *Shakespeare's Hand in "The Play of Sir Thomas More"* is an early example of this procedure. This strategy is, however, somewhat disingenuous. First of all, nonpaleographic arguments may reach the same conclusion as paleographic ones, but they cannot strengthen the paleographic arguments themselves. Second, historically, nonpaleographic arguments, except Simpson's, have been adduced to confirm a preexisting conclusion. In addition, other attributions have been based on solely paleographic grounds. The paleographic argument, then, is central to any attribution of Addition IIc in hand D to Shakespeare.[7] It is this argument to which I wish to give my attention.

The most recent consideration of the paleographic argument alone—and a careful and exhaustive one it is—comes from R. A. Huber. Like others, Huber insists upon a scientific approach to the paleographic argument. His brief but lucid summary of Thompson's and Greg's arguments prepares for a detailed examination of the data presented by the handwriting in Addition IIc and the six Shakespeare signatures. Attaching more significance to the differences than to the similarities of the two hands, Huber concludes that "the evidence is *not* sufficiently strong to justify a positive identification of the poet" (his italics).[8] It is my purpose to submit the paleographic argument to a more general scrutiny, asking whether the data on which it is founded is sufficient or reliable for comparison. I shall also raise a question too seldom asked, whether all of the signatures or none or few are, in fact, Shakespeare's. As the case stands, the problems are presently insoluble and, until resolved, make even the sort of endeavor Huber so well undertakes a parlous one.

II

At the very least, a paleographic argument for identification must establish a greater similarity between a known and an unknown hand than that between another known hand and the unknown hand. But an argument meeting this minimal condition does no more than state a hypothesis requiring further research. What distinguishes an argument satisfying minimal requirements from a conclusive one is the latter's exhaustive application of all research procedures to the complete body of possible data. Of course, such absolute conclusiveness is almost never obtained, but for practical, not theoretical, reasons. Still, we can establish an argument as conclusive in a reasonable sense. We can apply the research procedures exhaustively to all possible data at hand. And on the basis of that data and other information, we can establish that the possibility of or the proportion of pertinent data not at hand is or is not likely to be significant. These commonplaces are those underlying not merely paleographic arguments for identification but all scientific enterprises. The "general impression" or the "personal impression" to which paleographers and their adherents too frequently appeal runs counter to their claim that paleography is a science.[9] An "impression" is a hypothesis waiting to be tested, not evidence for that hypothesis.

If the principles of scientific methodology may usefully serve as a model for appraising a paleographic argument, we should turn next to the questions that arise immediately: how much data is at hand, and is the data sufficient for comparison? The answers to these questions are relatively straightforward. In Shakespeare's hand are fourteen words in nine different orthographic representations. These words comprise eleven lower case and three upper case letters.[10] In hand D are over 1,200 words in over 525 different orthographic representations. These words comprise twenty-four lower case and twelve upper case letters.[11] These figures suggest rather forcefully that any attempt at attribution other than a conjectural one must overcome the paucity of data by which to establish Shakespeare's hand as a reliable control. Such a control is indispensable to ascertaining the identity of an unknown hand. But these merely quantitative considerations are not more unpromising than qualitative ones.

The effort to identify an unknown hand depends largely upon the reliability of the control. If we can arrive at a generally accurate, if not altogether precise, account of Shakespeare's hand, then we can go a long way toward establishing a control by which to ascertain whether Addition IIc is his. Such an account must encompass a description of the character of the control as well as the possible sources of distortion. In particular, the character of the control includes the nature of the composition (literary or nonliterary), the kind of composition (personal, business, legal), the specific style (Italian or English or subvarieties),[12] and the state of the manuscript (foul papers or fair copy), as well as individual paleographic features of a distinctive sort. It goes without saying that legibility and certainty of attribution are mandatory. At its best, the control will match each of these factors with those of the unknown hand or account for differences between the two hands.

What can be said, then, of Shakespeare's signatures as a reliable control for attributing Addition IIc to him? The answer is, very little. All six specimens of Shakespeare's hand are signatures affixed to nonliterary, legal documents. The hand is the common secretary hand in which occurs an occasional Italian *s* and *h*.[13] The documents are all official ones not to be recopied for signing. Signatures 1, 2, and 6 are generally clearly legible; signatures 3, 4, and 5 are to varying degrees not so. Variations among these six signatures raise problems for establishing a reliable control, a point to which I shall return.

Addition IIc differs qualitatively from the control provided by the six Shakespeare signatures. Folios 8 and 9 are literary in nature.[14] The writing is a common secretary hand with only two clearly Italian letters, *S* and *r* in the marginal speech heading "Seriant" (l. 139).[15] The writing on the three pages is unclear but tolerably determinate. The corrections in hand D are few and insignificant. Except for subsequent deterioration of folio 8, Addition IIc presents as legible and neat an appearance as any other portion of the manuscript. Despite the few alterations in another hand, it is not unreasonable to conclude that the addition is fair copy. If Addition IIc is not fair copy, it differs the more markedly from the six Shakespeare signatures, for the writing would presumably be less governed by considerations of legibility than it would be on legal documents. Thus, only in respect of the general sort of hand is a similarity between the control and the unknown hand established. This is not an insignificant fact, but it is one whose significance is diminished by the commonness of the secretary hand.

Having compared the character of the control to that of the unknown hand, we must now consider some of those elements of distortion that may affect the control. The possibilities are legion. The interaction of different papers, inks, and pens can be very important. For instance, blots in S1 and S2 may result from overly inked pens; the paper of S3 seems not to have taken the ink very well, with the result that discontinuities make it difficult to know the shape of the letters. Moreover, chemical reactions over long periods of time may introduce distortions of various sorts, making precise determinations of the methods by which the letters were formed impossible. Simple physical changes introduce some difficulties in reading S4 and S5, where wrinkles produce apparent discontinuities. Of great interest and importance is the condition of the writer, a consideration which has occupied a very prominent part in arguments for attributing Addition IIc to Shakespeare.

In some ways, a man's signature reflects his immediate circumstances, his mood, his health, and—some would go so far as to say—his personality. These matters bulk large in Thompson's argument and are set forth fully in *Shakespeare's Handwriting* and subsequent discussions.[16] His explanations of the particular characteristics of each signature depend upon his accounts of Shakespeare's circumstances, mood, and health on each occasion—for which there is only very slight evidence, and that impeachable. That Shakespeare was discomfited by the circumstances surrounding his signing legal documents and wrote in an irregular manner or resorted to an earlier style of writing is not much less problematic than any other speculation about him on those occasions. The circumstances attending his will and its signing are far from clear; something so apparently simple as the order in which the three sheets were signed is still moot.[17] But the issue has been central to the contentions that Shakespeare was very ill at the signing and, consequently, that variations in the signatures on his will reflect his illness. If the arguments are largely unsubstantiated at best, they are sophistical at worst. Not only do they explain one uncertainty by reference to another, but they are constructed to forestall criticism.

Thompson's arguments pursue two lines. One argument concerns problems with the differences among the signatures in the will. To account for these differences, an order of signing its three pages is developed whereby the very legible words "By me William" precede the surname in S6 and signatures S4 and S5. This order makes possible the conjecture that Shakespeare was ill at the time of signing, began well, but finished badly the signatures required on the three pages. If the introductory words be regarded as illegible or if the order of signing follow the order of pagination, that conjecture and the entire description of Shakespeare's hand would have to be altered. The other argument concerns problems between the signatures and Addition IIc. If the letters are identical or similar, their correspondence supports Thompson's attribution; if they differ, then allowance must be made for the writer's ill health, arrived at by the character of the hand itself. A study of one letter in Thompson's argument will illustrate this point.

Thompson's views change remarkably on the question of the uppercase *B* of S6. In *Shakespeare's Handwriting*, he says, "The firmness and legibility of the first three words, 'By me William,' as compared with the weakness and malformation of the surname and of both the other two signatures, are very striking." Three years later, in a letter to the *Times Literary Supplement*, he characterizes the same *B* quite differently. In rebuttal to an argument against identifying the uppercase *B*'s of Addition IIc and S6, he says,

> I see no reason to doubt that the principle of its construction is the same as that of the "B" of the addition. But remember that, at the time of the execution of his will, Shakespeare was a dying man, and, moreover, was apparently suffering from some nervous affection (writer's cramp, perhaps) which prevented his writing legibly and, in fact, on this occasion caused his signature to break down deplorably. We must not, therefore, be surprised to find the "B" in question imperfectly written, patched up, and the lines distorted and entangled.

We cannot explain away this discrepancy by reference to a change of mind during the three intervening years; the discrepancy is more satisfactorily explained by reference to the different tactical uses to which one argument or the other is used. For four years later both views in different contexts appear in Thompson's contribution to Pollard's *Shakespeare's Hand in "Sir Thomas More."*

> This failure to accomplish the signature [S6] successfully after beginning so well may primarily be attributed to Shakespeare's physical condition. . . . by a supreme effort he braced himself to the task, and, with the sense of the formality of the occasion strong upon him, he began to write very fairly well, in scrivener style, with the formal words 'By me.' Again under the same influence of formality, he even introduced among his letters certain ornamental preliminary up-strokes . . . and thus he succeeded in writing his Christian name. But then he came to an obstacle; his failing hand was evidently too weak to form correctly the difficult English *S* of his surname; his effort was exhausted, and the rest of the signature was finished with painful effort.

Later he says of this uppercase *B*, "The capital B written by Shakespeare at the head of the words 'By me' prefixed to Signature No. 6 is constructed on the same lines as the letter in the Addition just described; but, owing to his infirmity, it is malformed, and the base-line rises too high."[18] This having it both ways makes disproof impossible. Unfortunately, a theory which cannot be disproved also cannot be proved.

Everyone has pointed out the problems inherent in identifying two hands separated by about twenty years.[19] To bridge the gap of differing circumstances, mood, and health, what is needed are precise, empirically-founded principles that account for each possible distortion, both in general and particular, and for the interaction of each with all others. But such principles do not and may never exist. To put the matter bluntly, it is a little too much to ask of one considering a paleographic argument that he contract for a medical history as well.

Distortions in folios 8 and 9 of *Sir Thomas More* are not of a sort to impede its identification with a reliable control, if there were one. Both recto and verso of folio 8 are marred by a few small holes in the sheet and by blurring and fading apparently caused by a tissue overlay and the dispersion of the ink in the paper. Even so, a large proportion of the writing is tolerably legible to the eye and bears up to scrutiny under magnification. Folio 9 is in fine condition and is clear throughout. Thompson notices a change in writing as the text progresses. According to him, in the lighter, earlier part of Addition IIc, the style is rapid and fanciful, as the length and fineness of descenders indicate. But as the comic action approaches the more serious business of dealing with the unruly mob, the writing, especially in More's speech, becomes slower and more deliberate, again as the shortness and thickness of the descenders indicate.[20] In a general way, such a distinction may be made, but its meaning is not so clear as Thompson argues. For instance, the *p*'s of "peace peace" (l. 173) are taken as being of a variety not found elsewhere and of a deliberate, three-step construction. "The p is a short, truncated letter, not unlike an ordinary printer's Roman lower-case p, having a short vertical stem commencing with a small hook or serif on the left, then a short horizontal cross-bar is drawn to form the base of the head-loop, which is completed by the addition of the necessary curve."[21] Greg is dubious, for the construction of this letter is not different from that of a common variety found throughout Addition IIc.[22] It is as easy to account for whatever change exists by reference to a progressive settling into the task or an increasing weariness with writing as it is to account for it by appeal to some assumed paleographic-aesthetic correspondence, which needs more than assertion for substantiation. And if Addition IIc is fair copy, paleographic distinctions reflecting changes in the creative process evaporate.

The conclusion which attributes Addition IIc of *Sir Thomas More* to Shakespeare continues to be repeated despite intermittent objections on various points both general and particular. An undercurrent of dissatisfaction is surprisingly evident in Greg's appraisal. "To this conviction on the part of an experienced paleographer at the end of an exhaustive investigation I cannot but attach great weight. But nothing is more difficult than to convey to others the grounds, however valid, upon which such a conviction is based."[23] But the application of the standards of scientific methodology, standards to which paleographers themselves appeal, refuses such an indulgence. What is not readily verifiable by others is not scientific, for there is no "conviction" scientifically arrived at and thereby "valid" unless others employing the same methods on the same materials can achieve the same conclusions. The recognition of similarities (or differences) and the weight attached to them ought to be demonstrable on the one hand and justifiable on the other.

It would seem fitting to conclude with at least a cursory review of the paleographic features of both the six signatures attributed to Shakespeare and Addition IIc of *Sir Thomas More*. But any effort either way—that is, any effort to argue the similarity or dissimilarity of the hands involved—must be inconclusive because the evidence is insufficient. Moreover, those letters and features that have received particular attention are remarkably unproductive. The letters most frequently discussed are lower-case *a*, *h*, *k*, and *p*, and upper-case *B*, *S*, and *W*. The features most often discussed are the *h-a* link, the fine introductory upstrokes, and the looped "per" symbol. Emphasis has also been placed upon the fact that a variety of forms for several different letters appear in both the group of signatures and Addition IIc.[24] However, most Elizabethan writers used a variety of forms for different letters.[25] Because of the differences among the signatures, such overlapping is the less surprising. As a glance at elementary surveys of handwriting suggests, few of the letters are themselves distinctive.[26] The "spurred *a*" is probably the most-discussed letter in this controversy. But the lone instance in S1 does not establish a probability for its occurrence in the control; nor does it establish whether the letter is distinctive, as is usually claimed, or accidental. The *a* in "that" (l. 228), the lone instance offered as strictly identical to that in S1, is more likely to be an accidental, rather than a distinctive, form; it is but one of seventy-one spurred *a*'s in an *h*-*a* environment. Another much-discussed letter is the upper-case *W*. None of the six *W*'s of the control approximates in either formation or proportion that in "Wisedom" (l. 157). There are, of course, some forms in Addition IIc that do not occur in the control. I list a few that, to the best of my knowledge, have not been recorded in the literature on this vexed question, only to cast some doubt on the claims for exhaustiveness by some earlier studies: an *h* shaped somewhat like the abbreviation for "per" in "him" (l. 126) and "have" (l. 135), a cross-looped *h* in "him" (l. 144), an *h* shaped like a reversed *s* in "him" (l. 165), a spurred *o* in "sounde" (l. 240) and "so" (l. 270), and a spurred *e* in "seek" (l. 270).[27] The significance of these forms, however, is no greater than that of any other unusual forms, shared or not. For the scientific foundations for this paleographic argument are currently so insubstantial that no adducing of such forms can be used to construct or demolish a serious argument identifying hand D as Shakespeare's.

III

Thus far, this account of the paleographic argument for attribution has rested on an assumption unchallenged by Thompson, Greg, or any other writer on this particular subject: that the six signatures affixed to four different legal documents are Shakespeare's. Either overlooked or ignored is the caveat issued by Hilary Jenkinson, an expert on Elizabethan manuscripts, handwriting, and scribal practices, especially official and legal documents. As he points out, a signature of a man's name is not proof of his signing. After saying that clerks copying depositions might sign for the deponent, he goes on to caution that "Attribution, therefore, must clearly be a matter for considerable caution and for careful scrutiny of evidence other than that offered by the writing itself; especially when we are concerned with the hands of persons who have left us very little on which to base our judgements. . . . I think it is not unfair to say that in the past even great authorities have been sometimes very casual in this matter."[28] A corollary is that a testator's name may represent the signature of another in his stead.[29] The large number of witnesses to Shakespeare's will may indeed reflect a concern of both friends and beneficiaries to validate a will that Shakespeare did not sign. A casual examination of the six signatures reveals that the differences among them are at least as evident as their similarities.

Recognizing the differences among the signatures, Thompson acknowledges the problems they present for establishing a distinctive and reliable control: "In addition to the ordinary character of Shakespeare's handwriting, the inequality of the several signatures among themselves is also a source of perplexity in the attempt to gauge its standard."[30] The contradiction between his certainty about the "ordinary character of Shakespeare's handwriting" and his "perplexity" about "its standard" needs only be mentioned to indicate the central problem with Thompson's position. Nevertheless, Greg maintains the same position in concluding his general defense of Thompsons' attribution. "On purely paleographic grounds there is less reason to suppose that all six signatures were written by the same hand than there is, granting this identity, to suppose that the hand of the signatures also wrote the addition to *More*."[31] Unwittingly, Greg counters his own case, for he both reduces the likelihood that all the signatures are Shakespeare's and undermines the reliability of each. If we have difficulties with the control provided by Shakespeare's six signatures even when we assume their reliability, we are put in an impossible situation for attributing Addition IIc to Shakespeare if we cannot assume their reliability. Until someone comes forward with highly probable arguments to establish it, no argument for attribution on paleographic grounds is possible.

IV

If one result of my review is to disabuse us of a perdurable but mistaken belief in the soundness of the paleographic argument for attribution, it will have served some useful purpose. But another result is to suggest, not for the first time nor in a new way, some of the demanding requirements of the paleographic enterprise. If no answers to the questions of Shakespeare's hand in the manuscript of *Sir Thomas More* may be expected from paleography in the near future, at least until some systematic method of establishing the character of individual handwriting is achieved, we might look to the larger field of descriptive bibliography for results. For example, the watermarks in the manuscript are of two different kinds, and one kind occurs only in the pages attributed to hand S while the other kind occurs only in the pages attributed to hands A, B, C, D, and E.[32] The distribution of these watermarks, together with the varying character of the chainlines, is one basis for collating the additions, hypothesizing their transmission, and reconsidering one distinction of hands in the manuscript.[33] Perhaps to say that no results may be expected from a paleographic examination of *Sir Thomas More* is a little extreme. Because the manuscript itself provides sufficient data for all these hands distinguished by Greg, except perhaps hand E, his distinction between hands C and D might profitably be reappraised. Greg based the distinction, now generally accepted but not early recognized, on a slight difference in the tendency to form a single letter one way rather than another. If the distinctions are valid, many of the problems of provenience, transmission, and authorship remain; if some distinctions are invalidated, some of these problems may be resolved or at least clarified through reformulation. A new critical edition of the play may well be in order.[34]

Any future efforts to attribute Addition IIc to Shakespeare will have to meet, not merely invoke, stringent standards. A paleographic investigation is an arduous affair, requiring, in addition to painfully slow and minute work, the habitual and willing suspension of belief. For if the obstacles and frustrations are great, the temptations to arrive at premature conclusions are greater. Shakespeare knew as much. He tells us quite plainly that sometimes "on a forgotten matter" even different writers could "hardly make distinction of . . . hands." If writers themselves have difficulties—and they might be expected to recognize their own hands—it is not surprising that paleographers should be misled, if not self-deceived. Certainly, no paleographer who wishes to identify the hand of Addition IIc as Shakespeare's is any more eager to establish a case in accord with his desires than is Malvolio to establish his. Hopefully, he will not declare that "it is, in contempt of question," Shakespeare's.[35]

Notes:

1. Proposed dates for the manuscript range from 1589 to the later years of Elizabeth's reign. Generally, they fall between 1590 and 1596. Since I. A. Shapiro, "The Significance of a Date," *ShS*, 8 (1955), 100–105, the tendency has been to view the date as earlier rather than later within the period. The date 1590 is now established as that on the manuscript of *John a Kent and John a Cumber*. However, it is not yet clear when that date was written or how it bears upon the date of *Sir Thomas More*, with which that play is bound.
2. Richard Simpson, "Are There Any Extant MSS. in Shakespeare's Handwriting," *N&Q*, 4th Ser., 8 (1 July 1871), 1–3.
3. The following references are but some of the more important contributions to the discussion. I have listed them in roughly chronological order. James Spedding, "Shakespeare's Handwriting," *N&Q*, 4th Ser., 10 (21 September 1872), 227–28. W. W. Greg, ed., *The Book of Sir Thomas More*, Malone Society Reprints (1911; rpt. London: Oxford Univ. Press, 1961), with a supplement to the introduction by Harold Jenkins; E. Maunde Thompson, *Shakespeare's Handwriting: A Study* (Oxford: Oxford Univ. Press, 1916); and "Correspondence," *TLS* (12 June 1919), p. 325, and *TLS* (4 August 1921), pp. 499–500. George Greenwood, *Shakespeare's Handwriting* (London: Bodley Head, 1920); "Correspondence," *TLS* (10 June 1920), p. 368; *TLS* (8 July 1920), p. 441; *TLS* (7 July 1921), pp. 436–37. M. A. Bayfield, "Correspondence," *TLS* (30 June 1921), p. 418; *TLS* (18 August 1921), p. 533. A. W. Pollard and J. Dover Wilson, eds.,

Shakespeare's Hand in "The Play of Sir Thomas More" (Cambridge: Cambridge Univ. Press, 1923). E. Maunde Thompson, "The Handwriting of the Three Pages Attributed to Shakespeare Compared with His Signatures" in Pollard and Wilson, pp. 57–112. R. B. McKerrow, review of *Shakespeare's Hand in the Play of "Sir Thomas More,"* ed. Alfred Pollard, *The Library*, NS, 4 (1923), 238–42. George Greenwood, *The Shakespeare Signatures and "Sir Thomas More"* (London: Cecil Palmer, 1924); "Correspondence," *TLS* (6 November 1924), p. 710; *TLS* (15 January 1925), p. 40. Samuel A. Tannenbaum, "Shakespere's Unquestioned Autographs and the Addition to *Sir Thomas More*," *SP*, 22 (April 1925), 133–60; *"The Booke of Sir Thomas Moore" (A Bibliotic Study)* (New York: Tenny Press, 1927); *Problems in Shakespere's Penmanship: Including a Study of the Poet's Will* (New York: Century, 1927). W. W. Greg, review of *Problems in Shakespere's Penmanship, Including a Study of the Poet's Will* and *"The Booke of Sir Thomas Moore" (A Bibliotic Study)*, by Samuel A. Tannenbaum, *TLS* (24 November 1927), p. 871; *TLS* (1 December 1927), p. 908. R. C. Bald, "*The Book of Sir Thomas Moore* and Its Problems," *ShS*, 2 (1949), 44–61. R. A. Huber, "On Looking Over Shakespeare's 'Secretarie,' " *Stratford Papers on Shakespeare 1960*, ed. B. A. W. Jackson (Toronto: W. J. Gage, 1961), pp. 51–70. Thomas Clayton, *The "Shakespearean" Addition in "The Booke of Sir Thomas Moore": Some Aids to Scholarly and Critical Studies* (Dubuque, Ia.: Wm. C. Brown, 1969). Clayton's use of quotation marks reveals as graphically as I could desire the present climate of uncertainty regarding the attribution.

4. Simpson, p. 3.
5. One of the signatures which Simpson accepted as Shakespeare's is no longer so regarded. Because the signature on the Bellott-Mountjoy deposition was not discovered until 1910, he cannot be referring to it. Probably he was referring to the signature, now generally regarded as a forgery, in a copy of Florio's translation of Montaigne's *Essays*.
6. R. W. Chambers, "The Expression of Ideas—Particularly Political Ideas—in the Three Pages and in Shakespeare," in Pollard and Wilson, pp. 142–87; "Some Sequences of Thought in Shakespeare and in the 147 Lines of 'Sir Thomas More,' " *MLR*, 26 (July 1931), 251–80. Caroline F. E. Spurgeon, "Imagery in the *Sir Thomas More* Fragment," *RES*, 6 (July 1930), 257–70.
7. Greg, in preparing the first and only critical edition of the play, identified seven hands in the text, designating them as hands T, S, A, B, C, D, and E. He also distinguished six additions to the original text, of which he divided the second into three parts later given the designations IIa, IIb, IIc to reflect three different hands in it. Addition IIc is the one attributed to Shakespeare. Jenkins, p. xxxiv, summarizes the various attributions now accepted with "varying degrees of confidence": T (Tilney), S (Munday), A (Chettle), B (Heywood), C (a playhouse book-keeper), D (Shakespeare), and E (Dekker). I have used Greg's line numbering throughout; Thompson numbers the lines of Addition IIc only, from 1 to 147.
8. Huber, p. 66.
9. See Pollard and Wilson, p. 13; Percy Simpson, "The Play of 'Sir Thomas More' and Shakespeare's Hand in It," *The Library*, 3rd Ser., 8 (1917), 86.

10. My figures are based on Thompson's transcriptions in *Shakespeare's Handwriting*, pp. 4–5, as are my designations of the six signatures claimed as Shakespeare's. The abbreviations S1 through S6 represent the signatures on the Bellott-Mountjoy deposition (1612), the Blackfriars conveyance (1613), the Blackfriars mortgage deed (1613), and the three pages, 1 to 3, of the will (1616).
11. My figures are based on Clayton's orthographical index to Addition IIc, pp. 22–38.
12. For a valuable historical and taxonomic discussion of Elizabethan hands, see Hilary Jenkinson, "Elizabethan Handwritings: A Preliminary Sketch," *The Library*, 4th Ser., 3 (1922), 1–34.
13. Huber, pp. 61–62.
14. Peter W. M. Blayney, "*The Booke of Sir Thomas Moore* Re-Examined," *SP*, 69 (April 1972), 167–91, has announced the existence of writing in hand D on folio 9^v, heretofore "described as blank by every commentator since Dyce" (p. 168).
15. Huber points out that differences in the frequencies of these forms between Addition IIc and the six signatures "modifies the significance of a similarity" (p. 61).
16. Thompson, *Shakespeare's Handwriting*, pp. 4–19, 27–29; "Correspondence"; "Handwriting," pp. 58–67.
17. Thompson indicates his position in *Shakespeare's Handwriting*, pp. 12–13, and in "Handwriting," pp. 61–62. Greenwood's position is outlined in "Correspondence."
18. Thompson's statements may be found in *Shakespeare's Handwriting*, pp. 12–13; "Correspondence," *TLS* (12 June 1919), p. 325; "Handwriting," pp. 61–62, 105, respectively. A similar argument may be advanced against Thompson's account of S2 and S3.
19. Richard D. Altick, *The Scholar Adventurers* (New York: Free Press, 1966), p. 157, states that "It is axiomatic in handwriting analysis that a scientific comparison of handwriting must use as 'control' a genuine specimen written at the same time as the suspected document." It is an axiom more honored in the breach than in the observance.
20. Thompson, *Shakespeare's Handwriting*, pp. 41–44; "Handwriting," pp. 68–69.
21. Thompson, "Handwriting," pp. 73–74.
22. Greg, review, p. 908.
23. Ibid.
24. E. K. Chambers, *William Shakespeare: A Study of Facts and Problems*, I (Oxford: Clarendon Press, 1930), 508. Huber's discussion pays particular attention to these features. See note 15.
25. Ibid. Jenkinson, pp. 13–14, makes the same point and illustrates it on plates VIII, X, and XI.
26. See Ronald B. McKerrow, *An Introduction to Bibliography for Literary Students* (Oxford: Oxford Univ. Press, 1927), pp. 341–50; Muriel St. Clare Byrne, "Elizabethan Handwriting for Beginners," *RES*, 1 (1925), 198–209.
27. I have been unable to examine the manuscript itself. Instead, I have had to resort to John S. Farmer, ed., *The Book of Sir Thomas Moore* [Harleian MS. 7368, c. 1590–96] Tudor Facsimile Texts (Folio Series), 1910; (rpt. 1970).

28. Jenkinson, pp. 31–32.
29. Tannenbaum, *Problems*, p. 85.
30. Thompson, *Shakespeare's Handwriting*, p. 27.
31. Greg, review, p. 308. Greg's point is a logical howler. First, it supports Thompson's conclusion by begging the question, by assuming the identity of the six signatures as Shakespeare's. Second, it may be refuted by reduction to absurdity. For if as many as six different writers wrote Shakespeare's name and the variety of resulting paleographic forms produced a high degree of overlap with the forms in Addition IIc, then more writers would write his name in an even greater variety of forms and produce an even higher degree of overlap. In short, the larger the number of writers, the greater the variety of forms, and the greater the overlap: hardly a persuasive argument for attribution.
32. The discrepancy between Greg, ed., *The Book of Sir Thomas More*, p. v, and Thompson, *Shakespeare's Handwriting*, p. 62, on the matter of their existence called my attention to the possibility of their importance. At my request, Professor William Ingram inspected the manuscript to resolve the discrepancy and kindly made his notes available to me.
33. I have discussed these matters in "Watermarks in the Manuscript of *Sir Thomas More* and a Possible Collation," *SQ* (forthcoming). Blayney argues for two stages of revision separated by some several months, the first falling during the period August-November, 1592, the second falling during the period February and after, until April, 1593. According to him, folio 7 was revised during the earlier period, folio 16 during the later period. Since my paper gives the reasons for thinking folios 7 and 16 originally conjugate, however, Blayney's hypothesis must be reformulated, if not abandoned.
34. In a letter to me, Blayney reports that he is preparing a text for Richard Proudfoot's forthcoming edition of *Shakespeare Apochrypha* (Oxford: Clarendon Press).
35. I wish to express my gratitude to Professor William Ingram and Professor Edmund Creeth, who have offered valuable counsel in this undertaking, to Harriet C. Jameson, Head of the Department of Rare Books and Special Collections at the University of Michigan Library, and to her assistants, Marjorie H. Drake and Beverly J. Schultz, for their cheerful assistance.

Sexuality, Witchcraft, and Violence in *Macbeth*

Dennis Biggins

The consensus of critical opinion appears to be that sexuality has little structural or thematic importance in *Macbeth*. Thus, for example, a recent critic can refer to the play as "the purest of Shakespeare's tragedies," in which the Porter's remarks about drink and sex might easily seem incongruous.[1] Some later writers, however, have drawn attention to a sexual element in the exchanges between Macbeth and his wife. Jan Kott remarks that Lady Macbeth "demands murder from Macbeth as a confirmation of his manhood, almost as an act of love," and that the "two are sexually obsessed with each other." Ian Robinson sees a perverse passion as the source of Lady Macbeth's influence over her husband in the murders of Duncan and Banquo: "the scene in which Banquo's murder is envisaged is a kind of love-passage between the Macbeths of which the natural consummation is the murder." D. F. Rauber comments on Lady Macbeth's strategy of questioning Macbeth's manliness in I.vii: "Her attack is saturated with sexuality, and her main weapon is clearly a kind of sexual blackmail: 'From this time / Such I account thy love' (I.vii.38–39)."[2] These are valuable perceptions, but they are mostly isolated and incidental to the critics' main purposes. It is my chief contention in this paper that there are important structural and thematic links between sexuality and the various manifestations of violence in *Macbeth*; moreover, that these in turn are associated significantly with Shakespeare's dramatized treatment of witchcraft.

The atmosphere of upheaval peculiar to the *Macbeth* world is partly created by Shakespeare's evoking violence in terms of sexual behavior and of the supernatural, both seen as perverted and disordered. This evocation is poetically appropriate: if Duncan (and, more equivocally, Banquo) represents the good with its potential for beneficent increase in a divinely sanctioned world-order, then Macbeth and his wife, who reject that order, are fittingly characterized in terms of the sexually aberrant and unfruitful.

In the first place, there are some passages in the Weird Sisters' speeches whose full purport has not been grasped. Everybody agrees that the Weird Sisters are something other, or at any rate something more, than the malevolent old women of Jacobean witch superstition—they are Lamb's "foul anomalies"—yet many of their characteristics are those traditionally associated with European witchcraft. They are not simply common- or garden-variety witches of the kind described by contemporary witch lore, as Thomas Alfred Spalding alleged (although he rightfully rejected the view that they are Norns). There is a demonic aspect of the Weird Sisters, but their powers are too limited for them to be seen in Walter Clyde Curry's terms as full-fledged demons or devils.[3] They occupy a kind of twilight territory between human and supernatural evildoing. Arthur R. McGee observes that there is much evidence that to Shakespeare's contemporaries "witches, Furies, devils and fairies were virtually synonymous."[4] Nevertheless Shakespeare carefully avoids portraying a Macbeth helplessly caught in the grip of irresistible demonic forces; the Weird Sisters' malice is evident in all their traffickings with him, yet nowhere are we shown invincible proof of their power over him. As Robert H. West puts it:

> The almost self-evident truth is that we simply cannot be *sure* of much about the Weird Sisters, though beyond a reasonable doubt they are representations of some genuinely superhuman evil. . . .
>
> [Shakespeare] treat[s] both Macbeth's fall and the Weird Sisters' part in it as awesome mysteries to the ignorant and the learned alike—mysteries that we may all feel and in part observe, but for which not even the most knowledgeable have a sufficient formula.[5]

Although the Weird Sisters may wear their witchcraft with a difference, they nonetheless exhibit many of its trappings. What has not hitherto been noticed is their claims to participation in those sexual malpractices which are standard evidences of witchcraft with the demonologists. In I.iii the First Witch (I use this label for convenience) announces her enmity toward a sailor's wife who had refused her chestnuts. The Witch refers to this woman as a "rumpe-fed Ronyon" (l. 6).[6] These abusive terms have been variously explained, but they may be used here to express, among other things, sexual antagonism. As Nares suggested, *rumpe-fed* "means, probably, nothing more than *fed*, or fattened in the *rump*,"[7] or full-buttocked. The usual gloss of *ronyon* is "a mangy, scabby creature" (Muir, New Arden ed., p. 12), although the other Shakespearean instance (*Wiv.*, IV.ii.163) couples the word with *witch*, *hag*,[8] *baggage*, and *polecat*, the first two of which are interesting in relation to *Macbeth*, and the last two of which have marked sexual meanings in Elizabethan-Jacobean English, including Shakespeare's.[9] The Witch derisively sees her enemy as a sexual object whose role she intends to usurp, as her later remarks confirm. She states that in retaliation for the slight offered her by the sailor's wife, she will follow the latter's husband to Aleppo.

> And like a Rat without a tayle,
> Ile doe, Ile doe, and Ile doe.
> . . . . .

Ile dreyne him drie as Hay:
Sleepe shall neyther Night nor Day
Hang vpon his Pent-house Lid:
He shall liue a man forbid:
Wearie Seu'nights, nine times nine,
Shall he dwindle, peake, and pine:
Though his Barke cannot be lost,
Yet it shall be Tempest-tost.

(9–10, 18–25)

There are a number of single or double meanings here that contain sexual components referring specifically to witchcraft or demonic practices. The more or less generally accepted interpretation of these lines is as follows: The Witch will assume rat form in order to creep unobserved aboard the *Tiger*, where she will work evil spells on the ship and its master; she will harass him and waste him away by means of her magic, although she cannot destroy either his vessel or himself. I should not wish to deny that the passage has some such meaning, but this coexists with or is subordinate to meanings heralded by the First Witch's announcement of her quarrel with the sailor's wife. Her threats are peculiarly specific in comparison with the Second Witch's generalized maleficence in killing swine. The key statement here is "Ile dreyne him drie as Hay" (l. 18), which most editors leave unexplained, assuming, apparently, that its meaning is self-evident. Furness, in the New Variorum, quotes Hunter (1853): "This, it was believed, it was in the power of witches to do, as may be seen in any of the narratives of the cases of witchcraft" (p. 35). This is hardly an enlightening comment, possibly owing to the writer's excessive reticence, although it is unclear whether or not he really understands the line. Dover Wilson, in the New Cambridge edition (p. 101), supposes that the reference is to the Witch's imposing thirst upon the sailor. This may be its surface meaning. But the line also undoubtedly refers to her intention of draining the unfortunate man of his semen, through her grossly inordinate exploitation of him as a succubus.

The belief that witches and the demons they served and were served by could experience sexual relations with one another or with ordinary mortals of both sexes was an old one. St. Augustine mentions "Silvanos et Panes, quos vulgo incubos vocant . . . et quosdam daemones, quos Dusios Galli nuncupant," as having sexual intercourse with women.[10] St. Thomas Aquinas explains how offspring may result from the unions of demons with humans:

> Si tamen ex coitu daemonum aliqui interdum nascuntur, hoc non est per semen ab eis decisum, aut a corporibus assumptis, sed per semen alicujus

> hominis ad hoc acceptum, utpote quod idem daemon qui est succubus ad virum fiat incubus ad mulierem. . . .[11]

Demons, being sexless like angels, could assume either the male or the female role in sexual intercourse with humans, as St. Thomas states, and thus collect as succubi semen from men for later implanting as incubi in women.

Later writers on witchcraft and demonology develop these ideas. In a work commonly known as the *Formicarius* (c. 1435), the German friar Johannes Nider expatiates learnedly on the existence and nature of incubi and succubi. His argument is conducted in the form of a dialogue between Piger and Theologus. The latter explains that the demons who act as incubi and succubi do so out of their malicious joy in harming man's body and soul.

> Causa autem quare Daemones se incubos faciunt vel succubos, haec esse videtur, ut per luxuriae vitium hominis utriusque naturam laedant, corporis videlicet, & animae, quae in laesione praecipuè delectari videntur.[12]

The formidable Sprenger and Kramer, who jointly compiled one of the most influential of all European witchcraft treatises, the *Malleus Maleficarum* (c. 1486), see insatiable lust as the driving force in witches' coitus with demons.

> Omnia per carnalem concupiscentiam, quae . . . in eis est insatiabilis. Prouerb. penultimo, Tria sunt insatiabilia, &c. & quartum quod nunquam dicit, Sufficit, scilicet os vuluae. Vnde & cum Daemonibus, causa explendae libidinis, se agitant.[13]

The Weird Sisters have characteristics of both witches and demons, so that there is nothing incongruous in the First Witch's avowed intention of acting as succubus to the sailor, although the treatises on demonology mostly discuss this practice as the work of devils.[14] In the colloquy between the Sisters in I.iii there is a mingling of the motifs of unnatural evildoing and of lust that are to recur later in the play with reference to Macbeth and his wife. That "Ile dreyne him drie as Hay" refers to sexual impotence is confirmed by a parallel use of the simile in Spenser's *Faerie Queene*. In Book III, canto ix, stanza 5, the narrator comments on the deficiency in the old miser Malbecco that makes him keep a jealous eye on his lovely young wife.

> But he is old, and *withered like hay*,
> Vnfit faire Ladies seruice to supply;
> The priuie guilt whereof makes him alway

> Suspect her truth, and keepe continuall spy
> Vpon her with his other blincked eye;
> Ne suffreth he resort of liuing wight
> Approch to her, ne keepe her company,
> But in close bowre her mewes from all mens sight,
> Depriu'd of kindly ioy and naturall delight.[15]

The First Witch seeks to render the master of the *Tiger* impotent by sexual exhaustion, so that his wife, too, may be "Depriu'd of kindly ioy and naturall delight." The Witch's motives are purely those of revengefulness and malice. Nider's Theologus cites the opinion of "Gvilelmus" as to the maleficence prompting incubi and succubi to seek human partners: "quod verisimiliter nec succubi, nec incubi, amore concubitus, nec desiderio voluptatis, talia viris & mulieribus faciant, sed potius malignitatis studio, videlicet ut utrimque polluant eos & eas spurcitia" (p. 626). Like the Porter's demon drink, the succubus plays havoc with a man's sexuality: it "equiuocates him in a sleepe, and giuing him the Lye, leaues him" (II.iii.39–40).

The Weird Sisters' proposed vengeance on the sailor's wife embraces another maleficent activity that witches were alleged to practice. This is the prevention of lawful sexual relations between man and wife, technically labeled ligature or, more picturesquely in English witchlore, "tying the points." The authorities have elaborate accounts of this variously manifested process. Nider's Theologus remarks it as one of the seven principal ways in which *maleficiati* work harm, "ne vi generativa uti valeant ad feminam, vel viceversa femellae ad virum. . . ." Piger later comments on the same topic:

> inter sexum utrumque, matrimonii sacramento conjunctum, nonnunquam experti sumus *odia* talia suscitari per maleficia, & similiter infrigidationes generativae potentiae, ut nec redditio, nec exactio debiti matrimonialis locum pro prole valerent habere.[16]

Theologus explains that although God does not allow the Devil to work directly on the human understanding or will, he does permit him to act on the bodily senses and powers, whether internal or external (p. 564). He describes, after "Petrus de Palude," the various ways in which the Devil can act on the powers of imagination, fancy, and generation in order to prevent coition:

> . . . *Secundo* modo, hominem potest inflammare ad actum illum, vel refrigerare ab actu illo, ahibendo occultas virtutes rerum, quas optime novit ad hoc validas. . . . *Quarto*, reprimendo directe vigorem membri, fructifica-

> tioni accommodi, sicut & motum localem cujuscunque organi. *Quinto*, prohibendo missionem spirituum ad membra, in quibus est virtus motiva, quasi intercludendo vias seminis, ne ad vasa generationis descendat, vel ne ab eis recedat, vel ne excitetur vel emittatur, vel multis aliis modis.[17]

The First Witch's intended course of action against the sailor and his wife economically combines the *maleficia* of the succubus with that of the devilish practitioner of ligature. As Daneau remarks, witches practice ligature "to thintent they may sow discorde and contencion betweene them, betweene whom ought to be sounde and great agreement" (sig. E.viii$^{r\&v}$). Boguet observes that besides its offense to God, a further consequence of copulation between a succubus and a man is that

> par ce moyen la semence naturelle de l'homme se pert, d'où vient que l'amitié, qui est entre l'homme & la femme se conuertit le plus souuent en vne haine, qui est le plus grand malheur, qui pourroit arriuer au mariage.[18]

The Weird Sisters' proposed sowing of discord between the spouses looks forward both to Macbeth's murderous acts of disorder and to their ultimate issue in barrenness and estrangement between his wife and himself. The Witch's course of revengeful action for a trivial gesture of exclusion—the sailor's wife's refusal of her chestnuts—is a parodic anticipation of Macbeth's murderous wresting of the crown from the Duncan who had named as his heir not Macbeth but Malcolm. Here, too, the witchcraft theme coalesces with the themes of fruitfulness and offspring, which are associated particularly with Duncan and Banquo, and of unfulfillment, sterility, and the destruction of progeny, associated with Macbeth and Lady Macbeth. The latter, in her disillusioned fretting after the attainment of her goal, voices her baffled sense of failure to achieve fulfillment through destruction. Her language is markedly sexual.

> Nought's had, all's spent,
> Where our desire is got without content:
> 'Tis safer, to be that which we destroy,
> Then by destruction dwell in doubtfull ioy.
>
> (*III.ii.4–7*)

Rauber comments: "the 'all's spent' operates both on the levels of failure to accomplish purpose and of sexual impotence" (*Criticism*, 11 [1969–70] 62). But there is more to the passage than this; "had" includes the idea of satisfying carnal possession, "all's spent" suggests a useless discharge of sexual energy (literally, of semen), and "our desire is got without content" further implies failure to achieve sexual satisfaction. As I shall try to demonstrate later, "destruction"—the murder of Duncan—has earlier in the play been envisaged with growing emphasis as a quasi-sexual act (compare also Kott and Robinson, quoted above). Baffled desire is a recurring motif of *Macbeth*. In the powers of witches "hominem inflammare ad actum illum, vel refrigerare ab actu illo," there is another parallel with the Porter's drink: "Lecherie, Sir, it prouokes and vnprouokes: it prouokes the desire, but it takes away the performance. Therefore much Drinke may be said to be an Equiuocator with Lecherie: it makes him, and it marres him; it sets him on, and it takes him off; it perswades him, and dis-heartens him; makes him stand too, and not stand too. . . ." (II.iii. 32–39).

The reference to sexual *maleficia* is strengthened by other sexual meanings in the Witch's lines. In *Witchcraft in Old and New England* (Cambridge, Mass.: Harvard Univ. Press, 1929) G. L. Kittredge explains "like a Rat without a tayle, / Ile doe, Ile doe, and Ile doe" merely as the Witch's intending to assume rat shape in order to slip on board the *Tiger* unnoticed, then to bewitch the craft and lay a spell upon the captain (p. 13). Muir cites this explanation in his note, adding that it "is doubtless correct" (New Arden ed., p. 12). But the demonologists held that demons could assume animal shapes for the purpose, *inter alia*, of copulation with humans as incubi or succubi. In English witch lore the domestic animal familiar is a common phenomenon. "We find that animals of all kinds were regarded as familiars: dogs, cats, ferrets, weasels, toads, rats, mice, birds, hedgehogs, hares, even wasps, moths, bees and flies" (Summers, p. 101). The power of witches to assume animal shapes is frequently asserted by the authorities—for example, by Bodin and Boguet. These metamorphoses were often undergone by incubi and succubi. Boguet writes of a witch's copulation with the Devil: "Françoise Secretain a confessé qu'il auoit esté accouplé auec elle quatre ou cinq fois, & que pour lors il estoit tantost en forme de chien, tantost en forme de chat, & tantost en forme de poule" (p. 19). The familiars addressed by the Witches in the opening scene of the play, "*Gray-Malkin*" and "*Padock*" (ll. 8, 9), may be incubi as well as attendant spirits. From the beginning, the connection between inverted sexuality and the turning upside-down of moral categories is established.

Nicolas Remy points out that whatever guise the devils assume, some defect invariably gives them away: "insolita, atque insigni aliqua nota, quae naturae immanitatem prodat, conspicuos se ostendunt."[19] Thus the rat's lack of a tail will denote its demonic origin. There may be a further significance in this deficiency. Discussing the various metamorphoses of witches, Boguet mentions cases of the appearance of wolves without tails (pp. 139, 149). Summers comments: "The sexual power of a wolf was popularly supposed to lie in his tail. . . . A wolf without a tail was sexually considered exceptionally unlucky and malign."[20] It is possible that Shakespeare's tailless rat is intended to suggest similar sexual malignity in the succubus-incubus exchange of roles.

Certainly the thrice-repeated verb *doe* has sexual meaning, besides denoting more general maleficence. *Do* in the sense of "copulate with" is a common Shakespearean usage, mostly in transitive constructions, to be sure: "Villain, I have done thy mother (*Tit.*, IV.ii.76); ". . . what has he done?—A woman" (*MM*, I.ii.83–84); "Do't in your parents' eyes" (*Tim.*, IV.i.8). But *do* is sometimes used intransitively in this sense: "Isbel the woman and I will do as we may" (*AWW*, I.iii.19–20); "You bring me to do, and then you flout me too" (*Tro.*, IV.ii.26). The last instance, in which a woman (Cressida) uses *do* in its sexual sense, parallels the First Witch's employment of the verb.[21]

The sailor will be subjected to the Witch-succubus' unremitting coital exactions day and night for a year and a half; he is to "liue a man forbid." While *forbid* doubtless has as its primary meaning "under a curse," as Theobald glossed it, the secondary sense of "*forbidden* [to have conjugal relations with his wife]" seems also to be present. Muir suggests, after earlier editors, that "dwindle, peake, and pine" refers to the Witch's use of a waxen image to make the sailor waste away; more probably it alludes to the debilitating effects of the prolonged sexual assault she plans for him. The "Barke" seems to be both literal and figurative; at the figurative level its significance is plural. In general terms of supernatural maleficence it indicates the Weird Sisters' limited powers: the Witch cannot destroy either the body or the soul of the master of the *Tiger*, but she will give him a rough time. As critics have noted, there is here a proleptic parallel, and contrast, with Macbeth, whose bark *will* be lost. The particular significance of the tempest-tossed ship draws a further parallel, and implies an added contrast. When the Witch says that the sailor's "Barke cannot be lost," she is also expressing the demonologists' contention that while witches could successfully practice ligature upon married couples, they could not undo the sacrament of marriage. This notion is stated by Hecate in Thomas Middleton's *The Witch*, a play that seems to have been influenced in its witch scenes by Scot's *Discoverie of Witchcraft*, and very possibly by *Macbeth* also.

> we cannot disjoin wedlock;
> 'Tis of heaven's fastening. Well may we raise jars,
> Jealousies, strifes, and heart-burning disagreements,
> Like a thick scurf o'er life, as did our master
> Upon that patient miracle; but the work itself
> Our power cannot disjoint.[22]

Similarly, the First Witch in *Macbeth* cannot destroy the sacramental bond between the sailor and his wife, whereas the crimes of Macbeth and his lady eventually result in an isolation of one from the other that mutely points to the self-destruction of their relationship.

Addressing the Weird Sisters, Banquo says "you should be Women, / And yet your Beards forbid me to interprete / That you are so" (I.iii.45–47). In Elizabethan-Jacobean folklore a woman's possessing a beard betokened a witch.[23] In *Macbeth* this physical anomaly perhaps also emphasizes, in the light of the Weird Sisters' plans for the sailor, their demonic bisexuality.

It is interesting to note that elsewhere in Shakespeare, witchcraft is associated with sexual domination and unnatural sexual infatuation. In *1 Henry VI* Talbot refers several times (and Burgundy once) to Joan La Pucelle as a witch and sorceress, and in V.iii. she confirms their descriptions by summoning her demon familiars. After she has beaten him in fight on their first encounter, Charles the Dauphin is smitten with passion for her. When Joan asserts that "Christ's Mother" has helped her to overcome him, Charles replies, "Who'er helps thee, 'tis thou that must help me. / Impatiently I burn with thy desire; / My heart and hands thou hast at once subdu'd" (I.ii.106–9). In "Who'er helps thee" there is an implied suggestion as to the real origin of Joan's power. The ghost of Hamlet's father sees Claudius' conquest of Gertrude as a kind of bewitching:

> . . . that incestuous, that adulterate beast,
> With witchcraft of his wits, . . .
> . . . won to his shameful lust
> The will of my most seeming virtuous queen.
> (*Ham.*, *I.v.42–46*)

Brabantio likewise claims that Othello has won Desdemona by enchantment: "For nature so preposterously to err, / Being not deficient, blind, or lame of sense, / Sans witchcraft could not" (*Oth.*, I.iii.62–64).[24]

The parallel between the Weird Sisters' program of harassment for the sailor and Macbeth's subsequent course after he meets them has often been noted. This parallel extends to the sexual aspect of the Witches' maleficence. Their spiritual seduction of Macbeth will deprive him of true manhood. His violence against Duncan is a more extreme form of the Witches' violence against the master of the *Tiger*. The "terrible Dreames" (III.ii.18) that afflict Macbeth after the murder of Duncan correspond to the Witch's oppression of the sailor, for nightmares were thought to be caused by the assaults of incubi and succubi.[25]

The unnatural reversal of sexual roles characterized by the Witch's treatment of the sailor is echoed in the scenes where Lady Macbeth rouses herself and her husband to commit the act of regicide. As the critics I quoted at the beginning of this paper remark, Lady Macbeth's murderous appeal to Macbeth is couched in sexual terms. She goads him into action by scornfully questioning his manhood, which she evokes equivocally as both virility and valor. Macbeth fails to realize that it is not merely the "Iugling Fiends" who "palter with vs in a double sence" (V.viii.19, 20). The slaying of Duncan is, indeed, to be the proof of Macbeth's manliness in this particular double sense, of sexual potency and courage. At first it appears that Lady Macbeth will herself take the initiative in the crime, with Macbeth functioning as a mere agent of her murderous will (as the assassins of Banquo in turn later function on behalf of Macbeth). In her invocation of the powers of darkness (I.v) she begs to be sexually transformed, dewomanized into an inhuman (yet somehow masculine) destroyer. She entreats the demons to usurp her body, transforming its natural life-giving powers to unnatural purposes, as the succubi-incubi exploit and abuse their victims.[26] When she exclaims, "Come to my Womans Brests, / And take my Milke for Gall, you murth'ring Ministers" (I.v.48–49), the invitation does not merely announce her desire to free herself from natural bonds of mutuality, tenderness, nurture, and all the other life-enhancing associations that the image of breast-feeding carries with it, although this is a major aspect of the lines. As W. Moelwyn Merchant has shown, "take my Milke for Gall" means " 'bewitch my milk for gall, possess it and complete the invasion of my body at its source of compassion.' "[27] But this is not the only meaning of these words. There is at the same time an evocation of a hideously perverted sexual relationship; as the succubus receives a man's seed to use it for evil purposes, as the First Witch will drain the sailor dry, so the demons, at once lovers and sucklings, are invoked by Lady Macbeth to take her milk and leave gall in its place, or perhaps, to take it away for conversion into gall.[28] The monstrous birth produced by this unholy union is the murder, the "Nights great Businesse" (I.v.69), which is finally accomplished by Macbeth—but only after she has aroused him to it as to an act of ghastly love.

It may be asked where Shakespeare acquired his knowledge of the sexual aspects of witchcraft. There are dangers on both sides in evaluating the extent of his reading, although the unlearned Shakespeare is less heard of nowadays than formerly. For a mind as quick and an imagination as fertile as his, Scot and King James's *Daemonologie* provide all he needed to know; yet he may well have had access to other writers, including some of the continental authorities.[29]

It is not only in Lady Macbeth's soliloquy that the murder of Duncan is pictured as a deed of quasi-sexual violence. Very early in the play the imagery establishes a link between sexuality and the physical violence of rebellion. The Captain evokes Macdonwald's rebellious nature in the first of the play's many images of fruitfulness and increase (here it is the spawning of evil that is expressed): Macdonwald is "Worthie to be a Rebell, for to that / The multiplying Villanies of Nature / Doe swarme vpon him" (I.ii.10–12). Of this man, fecund in evil qualities, the Captain further remarks, "And Fortune on his damned Quarry[30] smiling, / Shew'd like a Rebells Whore" (ll. 14–15). Macdonwald's paramour, the strumpet Fortune, ultimately betrays her lover. A few lines later we are told that Macbeth "(Like Valours Minion) caru'd out his passage" (l. 19). The usual gloss of *Minion* here is "favorite," and this is certainly a frequent meaning of the word in Shakespeare. But it often has a sexual implication, mostly with feminine but sometimes with masculine referents: "Mars's hot minion" (of Venus: *Tmp.*, IV.i.198); "You minion, you, are these your customers?" (to Adriana: *Err.*, IV.iv.57); "minion, your dear lies dead" (to Desdemona: *Oth.*, V.i.33); "this your minion, whom I know you love" (to Olivia, of "Cesario": *TN*, V.i.118); "O thou minion of her pleasure!" (to the Friend: Sonnet 126, l. 9). So, too, "Valours Minion" carries sexual overtones: Macbeth disdains meretricious Fortune in his triumphant slaughtering of the rebels, for he is the chosen lover of Valor.

This linking of martial violence and savage bloodshed with sexuality and love is extended in Rosse's later description of Macbeth as "*Bellona*'s Bridegroome" (l. 54). In his role as newly wedded mate of the war goddess, Macbeth is said to have subdued the Thane of Cawdor, another traitorous rebel (and so perhaps, like Macdonwald, another paramour of Fortune), "Curbing his lauish spirit" (I.ii.57). The usual gloss for *lauish* here is "insolent," but at least one other Shakespearean occurrence of the word (*2H4*, IV.iv.64) is in a context that supports the meaning "licentious, lascivious." Since *spirit* is used to mean "semen" in the opening line of Sonnet 129 (see Partridge, s.v.), it is at least possible that Rosse's phrase includes a sexual implication: as one wedded to Bellona, Macbeth outperforms Cawdor and terminates his liaison with Fortune. Lady Macbeth's "High thee hither, / That I may powre my Spirits in thine Eare" (I.v.26–27) employs the same kind of pun: in her mood of masculine aggressiveness she sees herself as impregnating Macbeth's consciousness with her own ruthless ambition for sovereignty.[31]

There is a similar metaphor of fertilizing through the ear in Cleopatra's "Ram thou thy fruitful tidings in mine ears, / That long time have been barren" (*Ant.*, II.v.24–25). A submerged instance of this metaphor may be present in Banquo's "That trusted home, / Might yet enkindle you vnto the Crowne" (I.iii.120–21). In *Shakespeare's Wordplay* (London: Methuen, 1957), Professor M. M. Mahood support's Coleridge's interpretation of *enkindle* here: "The modern editors gloss *enkindle* as 'incite,' a figurative use of the sense 'to set on fire'; but Coleridge thought the image was taken from the kindling, or breeding, of rabbits. Coming from Banquo, the words gain strong irony from this connotation, which fits well into the play's pattern of sterility-fertility images" (p. 139, note 2). Further support for this reading may perhaps lie in its extending the metaphoric use of the idea of fructification through what is heard: the Weird Sisters have, in effect, poured *their* spirits into Macbeth's ear.

The exchanges between Macbeth and his wife that lead up to Duncan's murder, tensioned as they are by an eroticism that is sometimes submerged, sometimes overt, but continuously present, culminate in the decisive act of violence, which is envisaged as a kind of rape. In one of the play's moments of charged proleptic irony, the saintly Duncan himself provides a bridge between the opening scenes' association of violence with sexuality and that of the later scenes presenting Macbeth's transformation into a murderer. He says to his welcoming hostess, of Macbeth: "his great Loue (sharpe as his Spurre) hath holp him / To his home before vs" (I.vi.23–24). Duncan is praising both Macbeth's loyal service and his marital devotion—his love for him and for Lady Macbeth—but there is a deeper significance in his words. They not only are unconsciously ironical (since we know that Macbeth has another motive for swiftness besides the ones Duncan gives him) but they also serve to develop the thematic link between sexuality and crime. Macbeth's "black and deepe desires" (I.iv.51) include murderous impulses that are "sharpe as his Spurre." The latter phrase is an image of sexual passion, as well as of ambition (as in "I haue no Spurre / To pricke the sides of my intent, but onely / Vaulting Ambition": I.vii.25–27).[32] Macbeth has hastened home under a stimulus that is both keenly erotic and deadly.

When Macbeth balks at the consummation of his criminal desires, his wife seeks to urge it by an appeal in terms of the same violent eroticism:

> Was the hope drunke,
> Wherein you drest your self? Hath it slept since?
> And wakes it now to look so greene, and pale,
> At what it did so freely? From this time,
> Such I account thy loue. Art thou affear'd
> To be the same in thine owne Act, and Valour,
> As thou art in desire?
>
> (*I.vii.35–41*)

Here Lady Macbeth explicitly parallels sexual action with murderous action. She appeals to Macbeth's sense of his own virility, in sexual terms. The metaphorical complexity of the passage leaves the reference of line 38 ambiguous:

what is partly the contemplated murder, but partly also an intoxicated act of sexual passion, shamefacedly repented on the "morning after." Dover Wilson quotes the Oxford editors' gloss on *such* (l. 39): " 'so great in promise, so poor in performance' " (New Camb. ed., p. 115). Lady Macbeth scornfully equates Macbeth's quailing from regicide with sexual nonperformance. The drunkenness and hangover images connect this speech with the Porter scene, where drunkenness is linked with lechery and with the impotence paradoxically accompanying the impetus one gives to the other. Macbeth's reply to his wife's sneer is "I dare do all that may become a man, / Who dares no[33] more, is none." She retorts:

> What Beast was't then
> That made you breake this enterprize to me?
> When you durst do it, then you were a man:
> And to be more then what you were, you would
> Be so much more the man. Nor time, nor place
> Did then adhere, and yet you would make both:
> They haue made themselves, and that their fitnesse now
> Do's vnmake you. . . .
>
> (*I.vii.47–54*)

At one level of meaning Macbeth's claim refers to his injured sense of honor and noble manhood: "*is none* i.e. must be superhuman or devilish, which it suits Lady M. to interpret as subhuman" (Dover Wilson, New Camb. ed., p. 115). But at the same time there is a continuing undersuggestion of sexual potency and the proper natural expression of it. Murder is like an unnatural, or nonhuman, sexual act, as Lady Macbeth's further taunt also implies.[34] Her *do it* (l. 49) includes the notion of coitus, although its primary reference is to Duncan's murder; *vnmake* (l. 54) likewise plays upon the double meanings "undo, unnerve" and "render sexually impotent."[35] Building on her earlier soliloquy of erotic self-abandonment to the forces of evil, Lady Macbeth's sexual innuendoes invoking virility as a token of manliness now lead her into an appeal to her mate through horrifyingly violent images of a depraved rejection of womanly ties:

> I have giuen Sucke, and know
> How tender 'tis to loue the Babe that milkes me,
> I would, while it was smyling in my Face,
> Haue pluckt my Nipple from his Boneless Gummes,
> And dasht the Braines out, had I so sworne
> As you haue done to this. (*54–59*)

Macbeth's resounding acceptance of her challenge is appropriately ironical in its language of natural increase, motherhood, and virility: "Bring forth Men-Children onely: / For thy vndaunted Mettle should compose / Nothing but Males" (ll. 72–74). His infatuation with her sees nothing strange in thus acclaiming such a tainted source of manly offspring.

All these associated themes of sexuality, witchcraft, and violence are brought together in Macbeth's final soliloquy immediately prior to the murder of Duncan. One would not wish to press unduly the air-drawn dagger as a phallic symbol, although, as I hope to show, Macbeth's regicide has overtones of an act of sexual ravishment. He himself (unconsciously, one presumes) speaks of the murder in this light after it has been discovered. Whereas Macduff announces the crime in religious terms—"Most sacrilegious Murther hath broke ope / The Lords anoynted Temple, and stole thence / The Life o'th' Building" (II.iii.72–74)—Macbeth reveals it to Duncan's sons in the language of procreation: "The Spring, the Head, the Fountaine of your Blood / Is stopt, the very Source of it is stopt" (ll. 103–4). He seeks to justify his murder of the king's chamberlains in words that suggest another act of uncontrolled sexual passion: "Th'expedition of my violent Loue / Out-run the pawser, Reason" (ll. 116–17). Most strikingly of all, Macbeth transfers his act of ravishment to the slain innocents in an image much criticized by commentators, ancient and modern: "their Daggers / Vnmannerly breech'd with gore" (ll. 121–22). One may or may not agree with Dover Wilson's adverse criticism in his note on "Vnmannerly breech'd": "indecently clothed. With this oxymoron Macb.'s hyperbole topples to absurdity. Cf. *TN* III.iv.251, 'strip your sword stark naked' " (New Camb. ed., p. 129). At any rate, the indecorous metaphor is exactly right as an involuntary indication of Macbeth's own feeling about his crime: it implicitly likens the daggers to phalluses whose nakedness is clothed, most improperly, with the royal blood. Dover Wilson appositely cites the *Twelfth Night* passage, for it contains an allusive quibble on *sword* meaning "penis."[36]

After the lines on the hallucinatory dagger, Macbeth's soliloquy in II.i continues:

Now o're the one halfe World
Nature seemes dead, and wicked Dreames abuse
The Curtain'd sleepe: Witchcraft celebrates
Pale *Heccats* Offrings: and wither'd Murther,
Alarum'd by his Centinell, the Wolfe,
Whose howle's his Watch, thus with his stealthy pace,
With *Tarquins* rauishing sides,[37] towards his designe
Moues like a Ghost.

(*49–56*)

The death of Nature, a suspension of all natural vital and moral processes (for *Nature* here surely means more than merely the natural world; it includes what Banquo means by *Nature* in his lines at the beginning of the scene—human nature and its natural moral discriminations), is an essential preliminary to the unnatural assaults contemplated by the Weird Sisters, by Lady Macbeth, and now by Macbeth himself. The wicked dreams that "abuse / The Curtain'd sleepe" are due, inter alia, to the visitations of the nightmare, of incubi and succubi (*abuse* can have sexual meaning in Shakespeare: see Partridge, s.v.). Hence the transition in thought to the rites of witchcraft, which also hark back to the earlier Weird Sister scenes and their implications of demonic sexual possession. The word *wither'd* also recalls the Weird Sisters, as described by Banquo (I.iii.40); at the same time, this peculiarly suggestive epithet, coupled with the personification, conjures up a vision of the murderer as an elderly psychopath, a sort of Jack the Ripper. This impression is strengthened by the Tarquin allusion, which clinches the suggestions built up, not only in this soliloquy but also through the earlier structural coupling of sexuality with violence, that murder approximates to rape. Indeed, Shakespeare's presentation of Macbeth's plunge into violent criminality might have for its motto the words of Pericles: "Murther's as near to lust as flame to smoke" (*Per.*, I.i.138).[38] There is at any rate poetic justification for Malcolm's applying the epithet *Luxurious* (i.e., "lustful": IV.iii.58) to Macbeth.

Yet while Shakespeare sees analogies between lust and its most brutal form of gratification, on the one hand, and murder, on the other, his perceptions are characteristically subtle and fresh. Although Macbeth's act of regicide originates in an atmosphere of disordered sexuality, we are not to see him as simply moving from lust to murder in a chain of violent passions (there is a contrast here with Shakespeare's portrayal of Claudius, whose regicide is motivated by adulterous sexual appetite linked with unlawful hunger for the crown). Shakespeare carefully avoids the glib moralizing of his contemporaries, whose diatribes against the evils bred by lust are cited by Dickey. In the world of *Macbeth*, disordered sexuality is a function of a deeper moral disorder. There is no assertion in the play of a simple connection between lust and crime, as in, for example, Marston's *The Insatiate Countess*, which hammers home the apothegm "Insatiate lust is sire still to murther."[39] Pericles's comment on the kinship of lust and murder belongs to the same uncomplex ethical framework: having observed the incestuous passion of Antiochus, he reflects that "One sin . . . another doth provoke" (I.i.137), lust will lead to murder, and his life is in danger unless he flees from Antioch. What we have in Macbeth's criminal career is much less straightforward: a richly suggestive evocation of the complexity of evil, of the close interdependence between seemingly opposed natural impulses. We are shown a world of human action in which the barriers between creation and destruction are less sharply defined than we habitually suppose and the borderland between what is natural and what seems unnatural is shadowy. It is a world where violence is taken for granted, alongside the piety and the respect for hierarchical social forms that are reflected in the graciousness of Duncan's court. In such a milieu of mingled barbarism and civility moral sanctions may well appear fragilely based. At the same time, the barely resistible quality of Macbeth's impulse to murder is very powerfully suggested by Shakespeare's metaphorical identification of it with warped sexual passion.[40]

The thematic and structural associations of sexuality, witchcraft, and criminal violence are used chiefly in the shaping of the action up to and shortly after the murder of Duncan. In the Porter scene that immediately follows the murder scene, sexuality is further linked with crime (and in this context its punishment): " 'Faith, here's an English Taylor come hither, for stealing out of a French Hose: Come in Taylor, here you may rost your Goose" (II.iii.16–18). There are a number of double-entendres here that establish the link: *Taylor* may be a euphemism for "penis"; *stealing* includes the ideas of "urinating" and, possibly, "whoring"; *rost your Goose* has among its meanings "treat your venereal infection."[41]

Some later passages continue the sexuality-witchcraft-crime associations. One of these appears in the first of the Hecate scenes, which are generally held to be spurious. Hecate chides the Weird Sisters for their trafficking with Macbeth without calling her in:

> And which is worse, all you haue done
> Hath bene but for a wayward Sonne,
> Spightfull, and wrathfull, who (as others do)
> Loues for his owne ends, not for you.
>
> (*III.v.10–13*)

Dover Wilson's note on this passage states: "No relevance to Macb.; but seems to echo jealous speeches by Hecate in I.ii of Middleton's *Witch*" (New Camb. ed., p. 144). The indebtedness of the Hecate scenes in *Macbeth* to *The Witch* is a moot point; the debt may be Middleton's. The apparently meaningless reference to Macbeth as one who "Loues for his owne ends, not for you" perhaps suggests that Macbeth's relationship with the Weird Sisters is not the sort to be expected of a mortal and his succubus; more immediately, that Macbeth does not love the black arts and the Devil who commands them per se, as the *maleficiati* were believed to do, but only as means to his personal goals. If the scene is spurious, its author has at any rate perceived the sexual component in Shakespeare's presentation of both the Weird Sisters and Macbeth.[42]

Several of the ingredients in the Witches' cauldron have connotations of lustfulness, violence, and the unnatural termination of increase—an appropriate complement to Macbeth's wild desire to know "By the worst meanes, the worst" (III.iv.135), "Though the treasure / Of Natures Germaine,[43] tumble altogether, / Euen till destruction sicken" (IV.i.58–60). The cauldron scene begins with references to familiars (incubi, possibly). Included in the materials for the charm are

> Liuer of blaspheming Jew,
> Gall of Goate, . . .
> . . . . .
> Nose of Turke, and Tartars lips:
> Finger of Birth-strangled Babe,
> Ditch-deliuer'd by a Drab. . . .
>
> (*IV.i.26–27, 29–31*)

The Weird Sisters further strengthen the mixture: "Coole it with a Baboones blood"; "Powre in Sowes blood, that hath eaten / Her nine Farrow" (ll. 37, 64–65). The liver was regarded as the seat of sexual passion (this is surely too well known to need documentation); the Jew is perhaps mentioned not only because he was unchristened, like the Turk, Tartar, and birth-strangled babe, and so useful to witches, but also because of the Jews' reputation, in anti-Semitic tradition, for obscene rites with (and the murder of) Christian children. The goat, like the baboon, was believed to be a particularly lustful animal. Turks and Tartars were celebrated exponents of inordinate lustfulness and heartless cruelty. The drab exemplifies degraded sexuality; both she and the sow have killed their young (*Birth-strangled* being taken to mean "strangled at birth") in a gross denial of natural affection. These last are the most sordid of the various instances in the play of what we might call the "destroyed progeny" theme, which so frequently characterizes the world of the Weird Sisters, Macbeth, and Lady Macbeth, and is set against the fertility theme, which likewise occurs repeatedly, as in Banquo's often-quoted speech, "This guest of summer . . ." (I.vi.3 ff.).

There is a sense in which "How many children had Lady Macbeth?" is a pertinent question. For an overriding impression, built up by the various associations throughout the play between witchcraft, sexuality, and violence, is that sexuality perverted by malice, human or superhuman, issues in an ultimate, life-denying barrenness. Macbeth has, and can have, no children: Rosse's comment on Duncan's supposed murderers, Malcolm and Donalbain, is a profoundly apt description of the self-consuming sterility that is the fate of the real ones: "Thriftlesse Ambition, that will rauen vp / Thine owne liues meanes" (II.iv.28–29). As if to stifle his own awareness of this truth, Macbeth plunges into an orgy of destruction of all who may take his stolen crown away from him. Not only Banquo but Fleance, too, must die; Malcolm must be trapped: "Diuellish *Macbeth*, / . . . hath sought to win me /Into his power" (IV.iii.117–19); and when Macduff escapes him, Macbeth resolves that "From this moment, / The very firstlings of my heart shall be / The firstlings of my hand"; whereupon he orders the destruction of "His Wife, his Babes, and all vnfortunate Soules / That trace him in his Line" (IV.i.146–48, 152–53).[44] This apparently pointless slaughter has a savage logic about it, from Macbeth's point of view: it cuts off a possible source of future retribution. It is strictly relevant to Macbeth's preoccupation with the menace posed by others' offspring that the murderer of Macduff's son should address the boy as "you *Egge*? / Yong *fry* of Treachery?" (IV.ii.84–85; italics mine). Yet for all of Macbeth's efforts to make assurance double sure and destruction sicken, his comment upon the Weird Sisters' prophecy proves to be exactly correct: "Vpon my Head they plac'd a fruitlesse Crowne, / And put a barren Scepter in my Gripe" (III.i.61–62). By a consummate paradox it is Macduff, the "*Bloody Childe*" of IV.i, who finally ends Macbeth's vain hopes of succession along with his usurped rule, for "*Macduff* was from his Mothers womb / Vntimely ript" (V.viii.15–16). The man who gained "the Ornament of Life" (I.vii.42) through an act of life-destroying, quasi-sexual violence, loses it at the hands of an antagonist whose entrance into the world was effected through another act of sexually related violence, but in this instance a life-rendering one.

Violence is an integral aspect of nobility in the society with which the play begins and ends. Properly channeled and directed, by cohesive social forces involving service and selfless courage, it preserves order, upholds just rule, and is a power for good. When released by the individual with the headlong force of overmastering sexual passion and at the urging of evil forces from within and without, violence brings destruction, social disintegration, and personal damnation. Sonnet 129, to which I have already alluded, is surely remarkably apt as an evocation of Macbeth's homicidal career, which, like lust,

> Is perjur'd, murd'rous, bloody, full of blame,
> Savage, extreme, rude, cruel, not to trust;
> Enjoy'd no sooner but despised straight;
> Past reason hunted, and no sooner had,
> Past reason hated, as a swallowed bait,
> On purpose laid to make the taker mad—
> Mad in pursuit, and in possession so;
> Had, having, and in quest to have, extreme;

A bliss in proof, and prov'd, a very woe;
Before, a joy propos'd; behind, a dream.

(3–12)

The one jarring phrase here is "A bliss in proof"—Macbeth has no joy in his crimes, and it is part of his tragedy that he realizes this before, while, and after he commits them. That aside, it is fair to say that *Macbeth* gains a major part of its power through its continued suggestion that "Murther's as near to lust as flame to smoke."

Notes:

1. John B. Harcourt, " 'I Pray You, Remember the Porter,' " *SQ*, 12 (Autumn 1961), 397. Cf. also Eric Partridge: "*Macbeth* is the 'purest' of the Tragedies, and, except for the Porter Scene, pure by any criterion" (*Shakespeare's Bawdy*, rev. and enl. ed. [London: Routledge & Kegan Paul, 1969], p. 46). I realize that these comments refer principally to a felt absence of bawdry, but their implication is that allusions to sexual matters in general are few.
2. Jan Kott, *Shakespeare Our Contemporary*, trans. Boleslaw Taborski, 2nd ed., rev. (London: Methuen, 1967), pp. 71, 72; Ian Robinson, "The Witches and Macbeth," *The Critical Review*, 11 (1968), 104; D. F. Rauber, "Macbeth, Macbeth, Macbeth," *Criticism*, 11 (Winter 1969–70), 61. Since this article was accepted for publication I have seen Roger L. Cox's *Between Earth and Heaven: Shakespeare, Dostoevsky, and the Meaning of Christian Tragedy* (New York: Holt, Rinehart and Winston, 1969). In his chapter on *Macbeth*, Cox draws attention to various hitherto unnoticed sexual meanings in the play. A number of these coincide with my own readings, and I am reassured to find an independent confirmation of them. Cox does not, however, link sexuality in *Macbeth* with witchcraft and violence, as I seek to do; he is, rather, concerned to make biblical connections.
3. Thomas Alfred Spalding, *Elizabethan Demonology* (London: Chatto & Windus, 1880), p. 86 ff.; Walter Clyde Curry, *Shakespeare's Philosophical Patterns*, 2nd ed. (Baton Rouge: Louisiana State Univ. Press, 1959), p. 60.
4. " 'Macbeth' and the Furies," *ShS*, 19 (1966), 57. Cf. also Willard Farnham, *Shakespeare's Tragic Frontier* (Berkeley: Univ. of California Press, 1950), pp. 82 ff.
5. *Shakespeare and the Outer Mystery* (Lexington: Univ. of Kentucky Press, 1968), pp. 76, 78. (These passages are from a revised version of the author's "Night's Black Agents in *Macbeth*," *RenP*, 1956, p. 24.) Cf. also Ch. X, "Supernature and Demonism in Elizabethan Thought," in Wilbur Sanders' *The Dramatist and the Received Idea: Studies in the Plays of Marlowe and Shakespeare* (Cambridge: Cambridge Univ. Press, 1968).
6. *Macbeth* quotations are from the First Folio, as printed in *The First Folio of Shakespeare: The Norton Facsimile*, prepared by Charlton Hinman (New York:

Norton, 1968). Long *s* has been modernized. Act, scene, and line numbers are those of the Globe edition. Reference is sometimes made also to the New Cambridge edition of John Dover Wilson (Cambridge: Cambridge Univ. Press, 1947), and the New Arden edition of Kenneth Muir, 9th rev. ed. (London: Methuen, 1962). Other Shakespeare citations are to Peter Alexander's edition of the *Complete Works* (London: Collins, 1951).

7. Quoted from the note on I.iii.9 in the New Variorum *Macbeth*, ed. H. H. Furness (Philadelphia: Lippincott, 1873), p. 32. None of the commentators remarks on the significance of chestnuts in this context, though the New Variorum edition quotes Dyce's friend's speculation that *rump-fed* may mean "nut-fed," citing Kilian's Dictionary for *Rompe* meaning "empty nut" (ibid.). I have nothing in the way of explanation to offer, but there may well be some special point in the reference to chestnuts.

8. The F reading is *Ragge*. This makes sense ("worthless person"), but "you Witch, you Hagge" occurs a few lines earlier. Dover Wilson in the New Cambridge edition and H. J. Oliver in the New Arden edition retain the F reading.

9. As, for instance, in "The poor Transylvanian is dead that lay with the little baggage" (*Per.*, IV.ii.21–22); "The fitchew nor the soiled horse goes to't / With a more riotous appetite" (*Lr.*, IV.vi.122–23). *Ronyon* is an obscure word. The only *OED* citations of it are the two Shakespearean instances and the form *Runnyon*, from a 1655 imitation of Chaucer, where it means "penis." In Chaucer *ronyon/ronyan* may have ribald connotations: see the note on *Seint Ronyan*, *CT*, VI, 310, and the references there given, in *The Works of Geoffrey Chaucer*, ed. F. N. Robinson, 2nd ed. (Boston: Houghton Mifflin, 1957), p. 728.

10. *The City of God against the Pagans*, XV.xxiii, Loeb Classical Library, IV (Cambridge, Mass.: Harvard Univ. Press, 1966), 548.

11. *St. Thomas Aquinas: Summa Theologiae . . .*, IX, ed. Kenelm Foster O.P. (New York: McGraw-Hill, 1968), Prima Pars, 1 a., Quæstio 51, art. 3, p. 42.

12. Johannis Nideri, . . . *de Visionibus ac revelationibus opus rarissimum . . .* recensente Hermanno von der Hardt (Helmstädt, 1692), pp. 616–17.

13. *Mallevs Maleficarvm . . .*, I (Lyons, 1615), Pars Prima, Quaestio vi, 70. Contractions are expanded in this quotation and in all subsequent ones from older writers, with other slight modernizing. Accounts of incubi and succubi, their sexual relations with witches and other humans, their motives in the practice, and their methods of obtaining and using human semen appear in the following representative writers on witchcraft, besides those already mentioned: St. Bonaventura, *Sententiarum*, Liber II, d.viii, Pars Prima, a. 3, q. 1 (quoted by Montague Summers in *The History of Witchcraft and Demonology* [London: Kegan Paul, 1926], n. 34, p. 105); Ulrich Molitor, *Tractatus de Lamiis et Pythonicis* [1489] (Paris, 1561); Reginald Scot, *The Discoverie of Witchcraft* (London, 1584); Jean Bodin, *De la Demonomanie des Sorciers*, rev. ed. (Anvers, 1593); King James VI, *Daemonologie* (Edinburgh, 1597); Henri Boguet, *Discovrs des Sorciers* (Lyons, 1602); Peter Binsfeld, *Tractatus de Confessionibus Maleficorum et Sagarum*, 2nd rev. and aug. ed. (Trèves, 1605); Francesco Maria Guazzo, *Compendium Maleficarum* [1608, 1626], ed. Montague Summers, trans. E. A. Ashwin (London: John Rodker, 1929); Thomas Cooper, *The Mystery of the Witch-Craft*

(London, 1617); Martin Del-Rio, *Disquisitionum Magicarum Libri Sex* (Cologne, 1633); Lodovico Maria Sinistrari, *De Daemonalitate et Incubis et Succubis* [c. 1670], ed. and trans. Isidore Lisieux (Paris, 1875: English trans., 1879). See also Russell Hope Robbins, *The Encyclopedia of Witchcraft and Demonology* (London: Spring Books, 1959), s.v. *Incubus, Succubus.*

14. Sinistrari observes that the Devil has sexual relations not only with witches but also with ordinary men and women: "Prout autem apud diversos Auctores legitur, et pluribus experimentis comprobatur, duplici modo Dæmon hominibus carnaliter copulatur: uno modo quo Maleficis et Sagis jungitur, alio modo quo aliis hominibus minime maleficis miscetur." (Lisieux, 1879 ed., p. 21). See also Section 25, p. 30.
15. *The Poetical Works of Edmund Spenser*, ed. J. C. Smith and E. de Selincourt (London: Oxford Univ. Press, 1912), p. 189. Italics mine.
16. *De Visionibus ac revelationibus*, pp. 542, 564.
17. Pp. 567–68. Discussions of ligature also appear in *Malleus*, Molitor, Lambert Daneau (*A Dialogue of Witches* . . . [London, 1575]), Scot, James VI, Boguet, Binsfeld, Guazzo, Cooper, and Del-Rio. Guazzo and Del-Rio both list as witches' means of achieving ligature the enforced separation of spouses and the drying up of the husband's semen. The First Witch plans to practice both these evils.
18. *Discovrs des Sorciers*, p. 29.
19. Nicolai Remigii, . . . *Daemonolatreiae libri tres* . . . (Lyons, 1595), Liber 1, Cap. vii, p. 77.
20. *An Examen of Witches* . . . , by Henry Boguet, trans. E. A. Ashwin, ed. Montague Summers ([London: John Rodker,] 1929), note, pp. 311–12.
21. See further Partridge, *Shakespeare's Bawdy*, p. 95. In *Our Naked Frailties: Sensational Art and Meaning in "Macbeth"* (Berkeley: Univ. of California Press, 1971), which I read after having completed this article, Paul A. Jorgensen points out (without illustration) the bawdy sense of *doe* (p. 120).
22. I.ii.171–76: *The Works of Thomas Middleton*, ed. A. H. Bullen, V (London: Bullen, 1885), 375.
23. Cf., e.g., *The Honest Whore*, Part 1, IV.i.184–86 (*The Dramatic Works of Thomas Dekker*, ed. Fredson Bowers, II [Cambridge: Cambridge Univ. Press, 1955], 77); *The Honest Man's Fortune*, II.i (*The Works of Francis Beaumont and John Fletcher*, ed. A. Glover and A. R. Waller, X [Cambridge: Cambridge Univ. Press, 1912], 221); *Wiv.*, IV.ii.169–72.
24. Cf. also *Ant.*, II.i.22, IV.xii.47, and further Daniel Stempel, "The Transmigration of the Crocodile," *SQ*, 7 (Winter 1956), 67–68. In an interesting article, David Kaula notes various Shakespearean instances of the association of love with witchcraft ("Othello Possessed: Notes on Shakespeare's Use of Magic and Witchcraft," *ShakS*, 2 [1966], 115).
25. Cf. *Lr.*, III.iv.118–22:

> Swithold footed thrice the 'old;
> He met the *nightmare* and her ninefold;
>
> . . . . .
>
> And aroint thee, *witch*, aroint thee!

In Middleton's *The Witch* there are references to incubus and succubus activities by Hecate and the witch Stadlin, and Hecate's son Firestone seeks permission "to ramble abroad tonight with the *Nightmare*, for I have a great mind to overlay a fat parson's daughter" (I.ii.90–92: ed. cit., V, 371). Italics mine. See also Robbins, *The Encyclopedia of Witchcraft and Demonology*, s.v. *Nightmare*.

26. Marion Bodwell Smith comments on Lady Macbeth's reversal of sexual roles in *Dualities in Shakespeare* (Toronto: Toronto Univ. Press, 1962), pp. 172 ff. In *The Dramatist and the Received Idea*, Wilbur Sanders analyzes the "Come you Spirits" speech (I.v.41 ff.) in terms of its sexual undertones: Lady Macbeth offers herself to erotic invasion by her demonic lovers; she sees the deed of darkness as an act of sexual fulfillment (p. 268). Dover Wilson had earlier remarked that Lady Macbeth is "invoking the Powers of Hell to take possession of her body, to suck her breasts as demons sucked those of witches" (Introd., New Camb. ed., pp. lvi–lvii).
27. " 'His Fiend-Like Queen,' " *ShS*, 19 (1966), 76.
28. Daneau, discussing the various means by which "Sorcerers can cast their poysons" (Ch. III), remarks, "I haue seene them, who with onely laying their handes vpon a nurses breastes, haue drawne foorth all the milke, and dryed them vp" (*A Dialogue of Witches*, sig. E.iiij.^{v}).
29. It seems clearly wrong to say, as K. M. Briggs says, that "The alleged sexual perversions of the witches did not lodge in Shakespeare's mind" (*Pale Hecate's Team* [London: Routledge & Kegan Paul, 1962], p. 82).
30. Hanmer's emendation, *quarrel*, is practically certain.
31. Kaula (*ShakS*, 2 [1966], 118), remarking that Shakespeare "provides several indications that Iago's hatred for Othello is in fact an inverted love and his campaign against him a kind of sadistic sexual assault," cites as one of these, "I'll pour this pestilence into his ear" (II.iii.345). In a note on the latter passage Kaula states: "That Iago's pouring of poison in Othello's ear represents a kind of impregnation is borne out by the symbolic identification of poison with semen, an identification recognized not only by the modern psychoanalyst . . . but also by Shakespeare's contemporary, Dr. Jorden." Kaula quotes in this connection from Jorden's *Discourse of the Mother*. In Iago's metaphor we have a blend of the actual poisoning through the ear, perpetrated on King Hamlet by Claudius, and the fertilization images cited in this paper.
32. *Vaulting* can likewise be a sexual metaphor: cf., e.g., "vaulting variable ramps" (*Cym.*, I.vi.133).
33. Rowe's emendation, *do*, is necessary here for the antithesis; the assertion as it stands is meaningless.
34. The Shakespearean association of depraved sexuality with beasts is too common to need much illustration, but cf., e.g., "that incestuous, that adulterate beast" (*Ham.*, I.v.42); "O you beast! / . . . Wilt thou be made a man out of my vice?" (*MM*, III.i.137,139); "the beast with two backs" (*Oth.*, I.i.118).
35. Cf. again the Porter on drink and lechery: "it *makes* him, and it *marres* him" (II.iii.36: italics mine).
36. Cf. Partridge, p. 196, s.v. *sword*. Lady Macbeth's *Knife* (I.v.53) is likewise phallic, as Wilbur Sanders points out: ". . . she will do the deed of darkness, in her sexually inverted state, with her 'keene Knife', under the 'Blanket of the

darke'; and there is to be no interfering moralistic heaven to bring about *coitus interruptus*—she will have her fulfilment" (p. 268).

37. Pope's emendation, *strides*, is as certain as these things can be: *sides* is nonsense.

38. In Appendix D of his New Arden edition, Muir notes various parallels between *Mac.* and *Luc.* and comments: "These parallels may possibly be explained by Shakespeare's belief that 'murder's akin to lust as fire to smoke [*sic*]' " (p. 195). On the prevalence of this idea in Renaissance literature see Franklin M. Dickey, *Not Wisely but Too Well: Shakespeare's Love Tragedies* (1957; rpt. San Marino, Calif.: Huntington Library, 1966), pp. 40 ff.

39. IV.ii.78: *John Marston: The Works*, ed. A. H. Bullen (1887; rpt. Hildesheim: Georg Ulms Verlag, 1970), III, 209.

40. My colleague R. P. Laidlaw has suggested that there may be further ramifications of the succubus–incubus–violence association in Duncan's murder and related events. He writes: "Developing from your interpretation of 'dreyne him drie as Hay' (I.iii.18) it seems possible to see significance in Lady Macbeth offering drink to the attendants, turning them into 'spungie Officers' (I.vii.71), since there is a strong emphasis on the draining of Duncan's blood—'who would haue thought the olde man to haue had so much blood in him' (V.i.44–45)—and upon drought imagery after the discovery of the murder—'the Wine of Life is drawne, and the meere Lees / Is left this Vault, to brag of' (II.iii.100–101) and 'The Spring, the Head, the Fountaine of your Blood / Is stopt' (103–4). The link between drinking wine and shedding blood is made explicit in the first of these two latter quotations. If the attendants can be seen as sham succubi (and at the least they share Duncan's bed) as well as sham murderers, Macbeth's act of killing them takes on a double significance, since he is not only severing himself from his guilt but also from the powers which led him on. Your own interpretation of the bloody daggers in phallic terms and a further link with the Witch's speech ('Sleepe shall neyther Night nor Day / Hang vpon his Pent-house Lid': I.iii.19–20), 'Sleep no more: / *Macbeth* does murther Sleepe' (II.ii.35–36), may suggest that Macbeth himself takes on the dual role."

41. See further Harcourt, *SQ*, 12 (Autumn 1961), 398–99 and the references there given. *Steal* and *stale* were homophonic in Shakespeare's English (see Helge Kökeritz, *Shakespeare's Pronunciation* [New Haven: Yale Univ. Press, 1953], pp. 148, 175, 198); *stale* (v.) meant "urinate" but possibly also "whore": Shakespeare certainly uses the noun *stale* to mean "harlot, trollop" (see Partridge, s.v.). On *tailor* meaning "penis" see also Hilda M. Hulme, *Explorations in Shakespeare's Language* (London: Longmans, 1962), pp. 99 ff.

42. Cf. Merchant: ". . . Hecate broods over this play, whatever the status of the 'interpolated scenes' " (*ShS*, 19 [1966], 81).

43. The Globe editors' emendation, *germens*, and the deletion of the comma are obviously correct (the Q. and the F. texts of *Lr.*, III.ii.8 have *Germains* and *germaines* respectively).

44. Miss Mahood comments: "*Firstlings* can mean 'firstborn young' as well as 'the first results of anything, or first-fruits.' Macbeth has no children but acts of violence against the children of others" (*Shakespeare's Wordplay*, p. 135). Paul A. Jorgensen also remarks on the sterility of the relationship between Macbeth and his wife (*Our Naked Frailties*, pp. 153–54).

The Divine Comedy of *The Tempest*

HARRY EPSTEIN

Literary theory tries to explain unique aesthetic experiences by reference to generic literary categories. Using two recent contributions to the theory of comedy, we may analyze the unique experience of *The Tempest;* this generic analysis will reveal the comic structure of the plot and the way the comedy incorporates pathetic and melancholy responses.

I

In *The Theory of Comedy,* Elder Olson founds his understanding of the comic on an analysis of the ridiculous: ". . . when we see something as ridiculous after having taken it seriously, we learn not merely that we were mistaken in taking it seriously, that there was inadequate ground for doing so; we are also impelled to take the contrary view of it, because of a *manifest absurdity.*" For Olson, the heart of comedy is the representation of the ridiculous, and all actions which are not represented as ridiculous cease to be comic. Since the action of *The Tempest* is clearly not ridiculous, Olson discounts it as comedy: "I should thus eliminate . . . *The Tempest,* and *The Winter's Tale,* from the roster of the fourteen so-called comedies in the Shakespeare canon."[1]

Sheldon Sacks, in *Fiction and the Shape of Belief,* develops a different explanation of the comic experience. He begins by defining "represented actions" in which "characters about whose fates we are made to care are introduced in unstable relationships which are then further complicated until the complications are finally resolved by the complete removal of the represented instability." According to Sacks, a represented action is comic when,

> in order to satisfy expectations aroused in the work, the final stabilization of relationships [has] to ensure for each character a fate that [is] commensurate with his moral desert. . . . In such works—which I shall simply call "comic" from now on—all the techniques of representation from beginning to end lead us to expect that all the "good guys" and the "bad guys" will receive their ethical deserts.[2]

We can find common ground in these two views if we consider how our expectations affect our responses to the struggle by which the instability is removed. This struggle is the core of any comic action. When all the techniques of representation lead us to expect that the characters will receive their ethical deserts, we cannot take the antagonist seriously. Although representation of the antagonist as ridiculous often arouses expectations of a happy ending, the process can be reversed; we sometimes judge the antagonist to be ridiculous because we expect a happy ending. In *The Rope,* Plautus represents the villain, Labrax, as capable of carrying out his evil intentions; he is an inherently serious threat to the protagonists. But Plautus assures us that the gods are against Labrax by opening the play with Arcturus' prologue. In this case, our expectations of Labrax's inevitable bafflement make him ridiculous; his ridiculousness does not establish our expectations of the protagonists' success. Artists can also mix the two methods as Jane Austen does in *Pride and Prejudice.* We do not consider the Rev. William Collins a serious threat to Elizabeth because he is represented as inherently ridiculous. But his marriage to Charlotte Lucas casts light on Elizabeth's position, forcing us to recognize that the threat Collins suggests, a marriage of convenience, is in fact serious. Recognizing this serious threat affects our response to the final comic resolution; our joy is increased by our awareness of the danger from which Elizabeth has been saved. Moreover, this final resolution is achieved in spite of obstacles, Elizabeth's prejudice and Darcy's pride, which are ridiculous not inherently but only in light of our expectations. Since we perceive that Elizabeth and Darcy have overcome serious obstacles in achieving their final union, they are more admirable in our eyes, deserving the full felicity they achieve. This rich mixture of inherently ridiculous, contextually ridiculous, and serious material is molded into a comic whole by the overarching structure of expectations and desires.

This example suggests that the quality of our experience varies depending on the nature and function of the serious material we encounter. Nevertheless, the basic form and power of our experience remains comic so long as we expect for each character a fate commensurate with his moral desert.[3] Thus, by specifying the nature and function of the serious material and by showing how this material is integrated into a plot in which our expectations are related comically to our desires, we can define the quality of a unique literary experience within the comic genre.

Olson himself recognizes the possibility of such modulations of the comic and sees a greater end for comedy than evoking laughter through the representation of the ridiculous. He even sees a way in which *The Tempest* is comic:

> Perhaps these are rather matters for the psychologist and the social scientist; they are relevant here, however, as further indications that—while it would be a rare comedy that evoked no laughter—the comic function is less one of producing laughter than one of producing a lighthearted-

> ness and gaiety with which laughter is associated. This is something both deeper and more valuable than laughter; and it involves achieving a state of mind in which we can view human frailties with smiling indulgence. Indeed, it may involve a state like that of a saint or a god; *Saint Joan*, it seems to me, is a comedy for a saint (at least the Saint herself sees it as comedy), while *The Tempest* conveys almost a divine view of human action.[4]

Although Olson does not explore the suggestion, I think his description of the experience of *The Tempest* is most apt. We can best understand how this divine view is achieved by analyzing how Shakespeare has created a comic plot capable of assimilating materials of the highest seriousness.

II

The basic action of *The Tempest* is Prospero's regaining the dukedom of Milan and wedding his daughter to the future king of Naples. By Olson's criteria for serious action, this is clearly a serious action. But Shakespeare opens his play with two scenes that establish the inevitability of Prospero's success. He thereby prevents us from considering the obstacles to the desired ending as serious, making Prospero's struggle potentially comic.

The first scene is an apparently serious, indeed a frightful situation—a tempest which threatens to destroy the king of Naples and his followers. But the second scene immediately dispels our dread, revealing the fact which makes it absurd to have taken the threat of the tempest seriously:

> The direful spectacle of the wrack, which touch'd
> The very virtue of compassion in thee,
> I have with such provision in mine art
> So safely ordered that there is no soul—
> No, not so much perdition as an hair
> Betid to any creature in the vessel
> Which thou heardst cry, which thou saw'st sink.[5]

Thus Shakespeare establishes a comic rhythm in which apparently serious circumstances are revealed to be of no consequence. The pattern is repeated in later events, leading us to judge any apparent threat to the expected resolution as an illusion which will turn to naught.

Having established the comic rhythm, Shakespeare proceeds to develop the two lines of action upon which the plot turns. The basic line of action represents Prospero's successful efforts to revenge himself on his enemies and to wed his daughter to the future king of Naples. Both efforts are dramatically static. As David Grene points out,

> The magic has taken all the ordinary tension out of the plot. In *Cymbeline* and *Winter's Tale* we are still to some degree involved with what happens to the characters. . . . But Prospero's power is so certain of success that the mainspring of our interest, the turn of events, is gone. We are not much concerned for his safety, nor his deliverance from villains, nor indeed about his restoration to his rights in Milan. The working out of the love plot of Ferdinand and Miranda is perfunctory.[6]

Our recognition of Prospero's power makes these events dramatically static. Consequently, we focus our attention on Prospero, not as he relates to the characters he manipulates, but as he relates to the power by which he performs his manipulations. As the play progresses, we look behind the first line of action to discover a dramatically tense second line of action in the psychological process which culminates with Prospero's rejection of his magic—the only event in the play not dominated by Prospero's magic powers. Gradually it becomes apparent that the comic resolution cannot be achieved until Prospero rejects the magical powers which have served him as both friend and foe.

Shakespeare reveals the ambiguity of Prospero's magic early in the play. Although this magic gives him remarkable powers, it has made him remarkably weak and vulnerable in the past:

> The government I cast upon my brother
> And to my state grew stranger, being transported
> And rapt in secret studies—
>
> (*I.ii.75–77*)

Prospero lost his dukedom because he preferred occult studies to his duties as a ruler. This interest tempted him to give the power to his brother, who then used that power to banish him. Thus Prospero has been his own worst enemy and his fascination with "secret studies" has been as much a source of weakness as it now appears to be a source of strength.

Through Prospero's exposition of his history, Shakespeare suggests an analogy between Prospero's behavior as duke and his behavior on the island. As duke, Prospero trusted the love of others for his protection; on the island he trusts his own power and delights in manipulating events, playing the unseen providence in people's lives. Immediately after Prospero's exposition of his past, Shakespeare makes the point through Prospero's management of Miranda and Ferdinand. Prospero is not content with bringing the two together and allowing nature to take her course; like the fathers in *The Fantasticks*, he must make their courtship into a little play, complete with its own "unstable relationships which are then further complicated until the complications are finally resolved by the complete removal of the represented instability." His magic gives Prospero the power to control the individual destinies of men, but this is the power to play God, and Prospero's delight in it is a manifestation of his pride, the same pride which, as duke, had made him trust to the fidelity of others.

In both cases, Prospero's genuine excellence seems almost to justify his trust and hence his pride. The care Antonio had to take to prevent the Milanese from suspecting his usurpation suggests how much, in fact, Prospero was loved. Similarly, Prospero's skill in magic (as evidenced in his control of the tempest, of the king's party, and of Ferdinand and Miranda) suggests how well he can contrive men's lives. But in both instances, though Prospero approximates his ideal of himself, the real distance which separates him from it is absolute and unbridgeable. His fate in Milan is evidence for this judgment: no man is ever so loved that he can lay temptation in front of others and expect everyone to restrain himself for love. Just as the power of the love we inspire in others can never be absolute, so the power of magic is not absolute, and the pride which leads Prospero to trust in the latter will prove as mistaken as when it led him to trust in the former.

If Prospero is wholly the protagonist whose magic enables him to triumph in the first line of action, it is otherwise in the second line. There Prospero is both protagonist and antagonist; his magic is the tool of the antagonist, seducing Prospero away from the humanly happy ending that awaits him and threatening that ending by making Prospero blindly trust in his skill.

The magic, which in the external events of the play acts as the guiding providence, is the threat in the psychological struggle; therefore Shakespeare must introduce another providence to which Prospero is subject and relative to which we can perceive that the threat Prospero's magic poses to Prospero is comic. Shakespeare does this by having Prospero himself refer to a providence beyond the providence of his magic.

> By accident most strange, bountiful Fortune
> (Now my dear lady) hath mine enemies
> Brought to this shore; and by my prescience
> I find my zenith doth depend upon
> A most auspicious star, whose influence

> If now I court not, but omit, my fortunes
> Will ever after droop.
>
> (*I.ii.178–84*)

Thus Prospero recognizes a providence beyond his control which limits his powers. His powers enable him to know and to communicate to us that this providence has now turned its favour on him and will enable him to overcome his enemies and regain his rightful place. What gradually reveals itself is that Prospero is himself one of these enemies. However, we now know that here, too, where his magic not only leaves him defenseless but threatens him, there is a transcendent providence which assures his well being.

By creating a dual perspective, Shakespeare establishes Prospero as formally ridiculous while preventing the ridiculousness from evoking out and out laughter. Instead, we appraise Prospero's actions with that "state of mind in which we can view human frailties with smiling indulgence." For viewed from the purely human perspective, Prospero's stature is immense and we must regard him as a serious agent; that is how we regard Prospero in the aspect of protagonist. But the moment we take into account his pretensions (in his manipulation of others), it becomes impossible to take him seriously. The pretensions of the antagonist Prospero to a divine power over the destinies of those around him are implicitly contrasted with the truly transcendent providence introduced in the second scene.[7] The contrast forces us to cease to view Prospero's pretensions from the human perspective and to view them from the transcendent perspective. From that point of view, Prospero's pretensions are patently absurd despite his obvious greatness: no man is ever so loved as Prospero thought himself, nor is he ever so powerful as Prospero still thinks himself.

There are two senses in which the pretensions of Prospero must be recognized as ridiculous. First, the audience must perceive the absolute distance which separates Prospero from his ideal; otherwise, his failure to realize this ideal may appear as a tragic failure. Shakespeare assures this perception by making the transcendent providence so clearly evident that Prospero's limitation is fully perceived. But second, we must also recognize that the threat to Prospero from his pretensions is comic. Initially, this ridiculousness is guaranteed by the operation of providence together with the comic rhythm established in the opening scenes. But unlike the comic assurance operating in *The Rope*, in *The Tempest* these guarantees are inadequate by themselves. Labrax is wholly base and therefore we can delight in his frustration, but Prospero is noble. Consequently, the pain he suffers through the frustration of his pretensions will generate a genuine pathos that has no counterpart in the Roman comedy. The frustration of Prospero's pretensions comes when he realizes that they are a threat, when they produce a dangerous situation. But if the danger is serious, the comedy will be compromised. The seriousness of the danger would overbalance the comic assurances of the opening, making the action melodramatic.[8] Hence the pathos must be generated by the frustration of Prospero's pretensions through a natural danger which it is absurd to take seriously. Prospero remains comic only if we recognize that, although he cannot succeed in his pretensions, he cannot fail in his goals. Hence the comedy requires a ridiculous set of antagonists who reveal the danger to which Prospero's pretensions expose him. Since Prospero's danger is that his pride blinds him to his own weakness, providence creates a danger that confronts him with his human limitations. The ridiculous antagonists who deflate his pride are Caliban, Stephano, and Trinculo.

As contrasted to Prospero, their ridiculousness provokes unrestrained laughter. Yet Caliban also evokes the most delicate pathos. In his speech on the pleasures of the island, especially the music, Caliban suddenly reveals a touch of sublimity which is wholly unexpected; we glimpse in him a soul not wholly bare of divine influence. The pathos he generates is the complement to the pathos generated by Prospero. We find Prospero pathetic at the moment he recognizes the foolishness of his pretensions to exercising a divine providence, and we find Caliban pathetic at the moment we see through his baseness to a touch of the divine. It is inherently fit that this beast, who yet has the divine spark, should teach Prospero the limitations of his divine pretensions.

Thus Caliban is ridiculous, yet possessed of a character which makes him appropriate to his function. Finally, the kind of threat he poses is suited to the weakness created by Prospero's pretensions without being serious in any way. Prospero is master enough to have all the serious dangers well in hand. But Prospero's natural human weakness can reveal itself in his inability to master the details which have no effect on his destiny. Caliban's plot is such a detail, and by slipping his mind it reminds him of his ultimate humanity. Caliban's plot has no external effect; its effect is wholly confined to the internal psychological struggle. And here its effect is decisive, opening Prospero's eyes once and for all to his human nature and leading him directly to the abandonment of his magical art and his reincorporation into human society. The acknowledgment of his human weakness is the final act in the growth of his strength and power from that of the magic master of a desert island to that of a sovereign of a human community.

Throughout Prospero's manipulation of Miranda and Ferdinand, he has been aiming toward the final crowning effect of the little play he wants to give, the masque scene of IV.i. It is meant as the capstone of a perfect pastoral romance, the betrothal entertainments of a fond father for the dear daughter and the

Prince Charming he has conjured up for her. He begins the final act of this little play of his by majestically giving his daughter to the prince whose feats have earned her:

> If I have too austerely punish'd you,
> Your compensation makes amends; for I
> Have given you here a third of mine own life,
> Or that for which I live; who once again
> I tender to thy hand. All thy vexations
> Were but my trials of thy love, and thou
> Hast strangely stood the test. Here, afore heaven,
> I ratify this my rich gift.
>
> (*IV.i.1–8*)

The father then gives to the prince a final warning to be honorable in his dealings with his daughter. When the prince, in the most certain terms, has affirmed his honor, Prospero turns and, once more behind their backs, begins to arrange things. Calling to Ariel, he tells him to bring on the play he has prepared for this moment:

> Go bring the rabble,
> O'er whom I give thee pow'r, here to this place.
> Incite them to quick motion; for I must
> Bestow upon the eyes of this young couple
> Some vanity of mine art. It is my promise,
> And they expect it from me.
>
> (*IV.i.37–42*)

We have no better clue to Prospero's state of mind than the poetry Shakespeare has created for him. It bubbles over with the anticipation and delight of a stage manager putting on a production he joys in:

> Dearly, my delicate Ariel. Do not approach
> Till thou dost hear me call.
>
> (*IV.i.49–50*)

> Now come, my Ariel! Bring a corollary
> Rather than want a spirit. Appear, and pertly!
> No tongue! All eyes! Be silent.
>
> (*IV.i.57–59*)

The explosion of exclamations is the perfect indication of the joy Prospero feels in the ideal moment he has created.

His production begins. His actors appear and in stately couplets commence a pastoral masque with which

> A contract of true love to celebrate
> And some donation freely to estate
> On the bless'd lovers.
>
> (*IV.i.84–86*)

Amidst the splendor of his entertainment, an enraptured spectator turns to the father, impresario, and host to praise it:

> This is a most majestic vision, and
> Harmonious charmingly. May I be bold
> To think these spirits?
>
> (*IV.i.118–20*)

To which Prospero replies with one of the most elegant and well turned pieces of nonchalant self-flattery in the English language:

> Spirits, which by mine art
> I have from their confines call'd to enact
> My present fancies.
>
> (*IV.i.120–22*)

It is the gracious but self-assured host modestly praising his own Chambertin Clos de Bèze, 1949.

As the masque progresses, Prospero cannot resist pointing out to his spectators the choice parts, cautioning them to be silent so that they will not miss anything:

> Sweet now, silence!
> Juno and Ceres whisper seriously.
> There's something else to do.
>
> (*IV.i.124–26*)

This is Prospero's most expansive moment; he is unfolding the character of gracious lord and host which he had to stifle for twelve years. But this is also Prospero's most pompous moment. He sits, pulling the strings on both sides of the stage (he has, after all, been controlling Ferdinand and Miranda as well as the spirit-actors), and being applauded for his efforts. And like all comic antagonists at the height of their power, Prospero is about to slip on the banana peel; he is about to be deflated from demigod to mere human. For amidst the splendor of his production, Prospero remembers that which he had forgotten:

> [*aside*] I had forgot that foul conspiracy
> Of the beast Caliban and his confederates
> Against my life. The minute of their plot
> Is almost come.—[*To the Spirits*] Well done! Avoid! No more!
> (*IV.i.139–42*)

The spirits disappear and Prospero stands trembling in anger before the naked stage:

> Fer. This is strange. Your father's in some passion
> That works him strongly.
> Mir. Never till this day
> Saw I him touch'd with anger so distemper'd.
> (*IV.i.143–45*)

It is a moment in which the extremities of pathos and comedy are blended together. A truly remarkable man, an accomplished prince and scholar who has suffered grievous wrongs, has, at a moment of comparatively innocent joy and pride—the betrothal of his daughter to the future king of Naples—been rudely upset by the scheming of three incompetent drunkards who can do him no harm and who would not even be interrupting him were it not for his own failure to remember them earlier.

The pathos lies in Prospero's recognition of the truth of his position. It has all been false:

> Our revels now are ended. These our actors,
> As I foretold you, were all spirits and
> Are melted into air, into thin air;
> (*IV.i.148–50*)

We can only feel the full effect of Prospero's speech if we recognize that throughout this scene he has been aping the part which he would be fulfilling in Milan had he not abdicated his responsibilities as duke for the pleasures of occult studies. At their best, then, these studies only make possible an imitation of the reality which Prospero had abandoned. The first effect of the intrusion of Caliban and his confederates is to shatter the illusion of the magic, revealing the fragility of the imitation. They are the representatives of the human reality which continually threatens any such world of make believe. But the recognition of the incapacity of his art to achieve more than a fragile imitation of the reality he has once forsaken carries Prospero on to another recognition. As Kenneth J. Semon points out, "The delight he usually feels in his art is disrupted by thoughts of the mutability, not only of his device, but of all material things. For a moment the realization that all is not within his power stuns both himself and the audience. It is a melancholy moment."[9]

> And, like the baseless fabric of this vision,
> The cloud-capp'd towers, the gorgeous palaces,
> The solemn temples, the great globe itself,
> Yea, all which it inherit, shall dissolve,
> And, like this insubstantial pageant faded,
> Leave not a rack behind. We are such stuff
> As dreams are made on, and our little life
> Is rounded with a sleep.
>
> (*IV.i.151–58*)

But we must remember that his delight in his art has been disrupted in a way which reveals that his art is not even worth the reality he had sacrificed for it. Thus the perception of the mutability of all things heightens the value of reality by making it all the more precious; each moment spent toying with his power and not attending to reality is a moment lost forever. The melancholy that is felt at the recognition of his humanity also guarantees the value of the reality Prospero is about to repossess. Later, when Prospero tells us that after his return to Milan "every third thought shall be my grave" (V.i.311), he is not despairing. It is a *memento mori*, but its purpose is positive, to teach Prospero how to live by reminding him that he must die. Every third thought reminds Prospero of the superiority of the world he is repossessing over the world of magic whose lure depended on his refusal to acknowledge his humanity.[10]

The smallness of the detail which trips Prospero makes the psychological pain that much more severe. On the other hand, the triviality of his oversight makes the moment comic. There is in fact no danger to Prospero, except of course from himself and his own pretensions. Since "there is a special providence in the fall of a sparrow," it is precisely the insignificance of the oversight which shows the absurdity of Prospero's pretensions: only providence can attend to all the details. Prospero is great and fortunate in that he overlooks sparrows rather than hawks. As an over-proud magician, Prospero hinders Prospero the wise duke from exercising his happy and beneficent sway over Milan. Caliban and his drunken companions humiliate and defeat this comic antagonist, thus liberating the comic protagonist.

In Act V we watch the triumph of the comic protagonist as he overcomes the impulses of his antagonist self. Prospero's humiliation reminds him of the humanity to which his magic had almost blinded him. The recognition is made explicit and its first result revealed in his behavior towards the King of Naples and his party. Prospero has been playing the part of a stern and revengeful providence towards them. Recognizing his humanity leads Prospero to abandon this pose:

> Ari. Your charm so strongly works 'em,
> That if you now beheld them, your affections
> Would become tender.
> Pros. Dost thou think so, spirit?
> Ari. Mine would, sir, were I human.
> Pros. And mine shall.
> Hast thou, which art but air, a touch, a feeling
> Of their afflictions, and shall not myself,
> One of their kind, that relish all as sharply
> Passion as they, be kindlier mov'd than thou art?
>
> (*V.i.17–24*)

The by-play on the difference between Ariel's spiritual and Prospero's human nature makes the issue clear: Prospero's behavior depends on his recognizing that he is "one of their kind." Recognizing this, Prospero can leave justice to God:

> Though with their high wrongs I am struck to th' quick,
> Yet with my nobler reason 'gainst my fury
> Do I take part. The rarer action is
> In virtue than in vengeance.
>
> (*V.i.25–28*)

Renouncing the role of providence is the first step in Prospero's reintegration into the human community, but it must be followed by a second and more wrenching renunciation. Prospero has been addicted to magic, and the addiction has cost him severely: it has cost him twelve years of his life, it has cost him an absurd humiliation at a precious moment. To be free and able to fulfill his destiny as duke, he must break the addiction, an act he can only do because he has finally confronted the ultimate weakness of his magic:

> Ye elves of hills, brooks, standing lakes, and groves,
> And ye that on the sands with printless foot
> Do chase the ebbing Neptune, and do fly him
> When he comes back; you demi-puppets that
> By moonshine do the green sour ringlets make,
> Whereof the ewe not bites; and you whose pastime
> Is to make midnight mushrumps, that rejoice
> To hear the solemn curfew; by whose aid
> (Weak masters though ye be) I have bedimm'd
> The noontide sun, call'd forth the mutinous winds,
> And 'twixt the green sea and the azur'd vault
> Set roaring war; to the dread rattling thunder
> Have I given fire and rifted Jove's stout oak
> With his own bolt; the strong-bas'd promontory
> Have I made shake and by the spurs pluck'd up
> The pine and cedar; graves at my command
> Have wak'd their sleepers, op'd and let 'em forth
> By my so potent art. But this rough magic
> I here abjure; and when I have requir'd
> Some heavenly music (which even now I do)
> To work mine end upon their senses that
> This airy charm is for, I'll break my staff,
> Bury it certain fadoms in the earth.
>
> (*V.i.33–55*)

It is a painful and wrenching farewell; Prospero cannot give up his magic without once more recalling the power it has given him. The rehearsal once more tantalizes him, and he can only tear himself away from his "so potent art" by reminding himself that it is after all only a "rough magic." Finally, to save himself from the temptation of his magic, Prospero must, like many another addict, put his vice beyond reach.

> And deeper than did ever plummet sound
> I'll drown my book.
>
> (*V.i.56–57*)

The richness of the effect Shakespeare achieves resides in his having located the antagonist and protagonist in the same character. We cannot react to them separately; because of the divine perspective Shakespeare has provided, we experience Prospero's freeing himself from his magic as a triumph and a liberation, yet see it as a liberation from a part of himself. Prospero must feel the pain he is causing himself in subduing his antagonist self. Our experience of the comic joy in Prospero's triumph has as a necessary condition our experience of the pain and pathos involved in his suffering. Shakespeare has here resolved a problem which he had confronted less successfully in an earlier play. In *The Merchant of Venice*, Shakespeare created a comic antagonist, Shylock, whose suffering in his defeat injected an element of pathos which could not be integrated into the comic form of the action. In *The Tempest*, the identity of the protagonist and antagonist leads to a reabsorption of the pathos at the antagonist's suffering into the joy at the protagonist's triumph, creating an experience unique to the comic form.

The psychological strain has been immense, and Prospero is weary throughout the rest of the play. Professor Grene thinks this weariness is an ultimate exhaustion and reads Prospero's remark that "every third thought shall be my grave" as the admission of near despair: "What is left is the weariness of an old man who has no longer any passionate concern even with what is good and right in the new pattern of events to which he has lent his help." He founds this reading on the judgment that the island and its world are better than the reality for which Prospero is abandoning the island:

> The task of revenge for the wrongs committed in Milan has disguised from us (and perhaps we are meant to think from Prosperc too) the truth that the exercise of the magic is more exciting than the ends for which it is exercised.
>
> The island has been Prospero's as Milan never was and never will be.

Professor Grene justifies this judgment by equating the island with the imaginative process:

> The island is not the theater. It is the dimension in which is expressed the playwright's reality when he has created it—and in this play largely *while* he is creating it, while it is emerging from him only partly sprung of his conscious intention and craftsmanship. . . . The life on the island and the happenings there express the process of creation for the writer.[11]

This argument rests on the fact that it is more pleasant to day dream than to live and that the world of our daydreams is always much more our world than the world in which we must act. Thus Professor Grene's reading depends on a preference for the world of imagination over the world of political reality. But this ignores the evidence of the masque scene, which suggests that at best Prospero's magic can only provide a fragile imitation of the reality of being Duke of Milan. Moreover, I do not think it is reasonable to assume that either Shakespeare or his audience would have shared Professor Grene's devaluation of the realm of political action.[12] Thus Prospero's weariness does not reflect an ultimate exhaustion and disillusionment with the dukedom he has regained; rather, it is the justified weariness of a man who has wrenched his freedom from a lifelong crutch in order to stand in his rightful place among men. Gonzalo emphasizes the point:

> Was Milan thrust from Milan that his issue
> Should become kings of Naples? O, rejoice
> Beyond a common joy, and set it down
> With gold on lasting pillars: In one voyage
> Did Claribel her husband find at Tunis,
> And Ferdinand her brother found a wife
> Where he himself was lost; Prospero his dukedom
> In a poor isle; and all of us ourselves
> When no man was his own.
>
> (*V.i.205–13*)

The speech has a powerful impact because of the extraordinary care with which Shakespeare has assured the audience of the reliability of Gonzalo's preception. In the very first scene we find Gonzalo prophesying, in the face of overwhelming odds, that the boatswain will not drown:

> I'll warrant him for drowning, though the ship were no stronger than a nutshell and as leaky as an unstanched wench.
>
> (*I.i.49–51*)

> He'll be hang'd yet,
> Though every drop of water swear against it
> And gape at wid'st to glut him.
>
> (*I.i.61–63*)

Immediately after the "Beyond a common joy" speech, we are reminded, lest we have forgotten, of the truth of Gonzalo's prophecy:

> *Enter* Ariel, *with the* Master *and*
> Boatswain *amazedly following.*

O, look, sir; look, sir! Here is more of us!
I prophesied, if a gallows were on land,
This fellow could not drown.

(*V.i.216–18*)

In Act II, scene i, we have numerous clashes between Gonzalo and Sebastian and Antonio. Though the latter two seem to have more wit, Shakespeare carefully establishes that Gonzalo has truth on his side. He is correct about the beauty of the island, about the supposed location of Carthage, and about the fact that Dido was a widow. More startlingly, he is correct about the condition of their clothes:

Gon. That our garments, being, as they were, drench'd in the sea, hold, notwithstanding, their freshness and gloss, being rather new-dy'd than stain'd with salt water.
Ant. If but one of his pockets could speak, would it not say he lies?
Seb. Ay, or very falsely pocket up his report.
Gon. Methinks our garments are now as fresh as when we put them on first in Afric.

(*II.i.61–69*)

In the preceding scene Shakespeare has drawn our especial attention to the question of the condition of the castaways' garments and given us unimpeachable authority for crediting Gonzalo's observation:

Pros. But are they, Ariel, safe?
Ari. Not a hair perish'd.
On their sustaining garments not a blemish,
But fresher than before.

(*I.ii.217–19*)

Again as with his prophecy in Act I, scene i, Gonzalo is correct even though what he perceives seems contrary to the common sense inference.

In so calling our attention to Gonzalo's correct perception in the face of common sense reasoning, Shakespeare's intention can only be to establish Gonzalo's reliability as a witness capable of perceiving truths which escape more cynical and worldly wise observers. Thus when he asserts that "all of us" have found ourselves "when no man was his own," we recognize that this includes Prospero, who was, until he freed himself and became his own master, the subject of his magic. The return to Milan and the exercise of his role as duke constitute the just moral desert for both the comic protagonist and the comic antagonist: it rewards the virtues of the one and punishes the vices of the other by bestowing the rights of a lord and the duties of a governor.

We see that the form of the play is comic: all the techniques of representation lead us to expect that the characters will receive their ethical deserts. But within the framework of this comic structure, Shakespeare has created a situation in which the choices his protagonist makes as he moves towards the final comic resolution bring him into the most stark confrontation with the meaning of human limitation. Out of this confrontation grows a rich pathos. Yet Shakespeare has created a perspective, supported by appropriate characters and incidents, from which even this most painful confrontation must be viewed as a part of the comic process by which each character is brought to his just fate. Thus the pathos and melancholy generated by the play's confrontation with human mortality cease to be absolute experiences. Instead they become components of the comic joy. But our comic joy is changed by absorbing this pathos; it is made larger and richer. It is also made more serious and self-reflective: at the moment we become aware that we are experiencing a joy compounded of pathos, we also become aware that we are looking at life from that divine plane from which all life earns its just deserts.

Notes:

1. Elder Olson, *The Theory of Comedy* (Bloomington: Indiana Univ. Press, 1968), pp. 14, 88–89.
2. Sheldon Sacks, *Fiction and the Shape of Belief: A Study of Henry Fielding with Glances at Swift, Johnson and Richardson* (Berkeley: Univ. of California Press, 1967), pp. 15, 20–21.
3. Cf. Sheldon Sacks, "The Psychological Implications of Generic Distinctions," *Genre*, I (Spring 1968), pp. 106–15, for an illuminating discussion of the possibilities of realizing different varieties of comic experience and the conditions which control such possibilities.
4. Olson, p. 40.
5. *The Complete Works of Shakespeare*, ed. by George Lyman Kittredge (Boston: Ginn, 1936), I.ii.26–31. Subsequent references to this edition are in the text.
6. David Grene, *Reality and the Heroic Pattern: Last Plays of Ibsen, Shakespeare, and Sophocles* (Chicago: Univ. of Chicago Press, 1967), pp. 88–89. Although I have strong disagreements with Professor Grene, the basic insight that the struggle in *The Tempest* is the psychological conflict in Prospero owes much to him.
7. Shakespeare uses the byplay about Claribel's wedding in II.i.66–135 to emphasize the unusualness of the event which brought Prospero's enemies into his sphere of influence (cf. especially ll. 124–27). By emphasizing the unusualness

of the event, Shakespeare draws the audience's attention to the guiding providence which ordained that Prospero might be given his opportunity. The reference appears again in V.i.209.

8. Cf. Sacks, "The Psychological Implications," pp. 109ff, for further discussion of the differences between the melodramatic and the comic.
9. Kenneth J. Semon, "Shakespeare's *The Tempest:* Beyond a Common Joy," *ELH*, 40 (Spring 1973), p. 39.
10. I think the same principle is at work in Prospero's acknowledgement that Caliban is his "This thing of Darkness I / Acknowledge mine" (V.i.275–76). It has been Caliban who has awakened Prospero from the dream of omnipotence to the reality of human mortality. He is thus the concrete symbol of the humanity Prospero has denied. Through the pathos he has aroused, Caliban also proves that he is in fact of the same kind as Prospero and, though they occupy the opposite extremes of mankind, that they are both men. Caliban is thus Prospero's because he fully reveals the human limitation which Prospero shares.
11. Grene, pp. 100, 102, 103.
12. On the importance of such ethical judgments in determining our response to literary works, cf. Elder Olson, *Tragedy and the Theory of Drama* (Detroit: Wayne State Univ. Press, 1961), pp. 129–32, 149–60.

Henry VIII and the Crisis of the English History Play

Frederick O. Waage, Jr.

With regard to Shakespeare's *Henry VIII*, there is no doubt that the "fraction of commentary on the play not worried by the academic question of who wrote it is mostly patronizing and wholly disappointing. Both its foes and its few champions present . . . not the play as we have it, but some preconception of what the play should be."[1] Unfortunately, many of the reformers of this condition seem to labor under a similar preconception, namely that the play is "mythical," and must be considered a companion of *Cymbeline, The Winter's Tale,* and *The Tempest*. In this view Anne Boleyn becomes a *venus genetrix*,[2] and Shakespeare creates a mythical history "of a Tudor golden age emerging under the watchful eye of God from a long ordeal of tyranny and dissension."[3] The latter view, of course, has a place in the earliest Tudor chroniclers; the former assumes what I deny, that the last scene of the last act, predicting the glory of Anne's offspring, is an organic growth from the body of the play and not an artificial appendage tacked on at the end to redeem the somber vision of the play as a whole. Another contention of the mythologists is that Wolsey, Buckingham, and Katherine, defeated in life, attain Lear-like spiritual victory and self-fulfillment in death; such personal triumphs mitigate "the sour dichotomy between moral and political distinction"[4] in Shakespeare's earlier histories. I would contend, on the contrary, that this distinction is at its sourest in *Henry VIII*, and that the assertions of mythical historical continuity and of personal spiritual regeneration through death are contradictory. In *Henry VIII* those personal qualities in the principals which would allow them to insure the tranquil continuity of their state emerge only when death is denying them the power to insure that continuity. This paper will suggest that Shakespeare's *inability* to mythologize history in *Henry VIII*, a function of his reaction to the death of Prince Henry in 1612, can help us to understand why it signalled the virtual end of the reign of the English history play on the Stuart stage.

Shakespeare's Katherine is the character most torn between a "moral" and a "politico-religious" identity. In 1613, the year when Shakespeare's *Famous History of the Life of King Henry the Eight* was indubitably first performed,[5] two interesting books were published for the first time. The first (judging from the entry in the Stationers' Register) was Barnabe Rich's *The Excellency of Good Women*, and the second, Thomas Williamson's *The Sword of the spirit to smite in pieces that Antichristian Goliah* . . . (i.e., the Church of Rome). Rich mainly expounds the Solomonic ideal of a good wife and attacks the female abuses (such as excessive cosmetics) of his time, but he is very clear about the perfection of the truly good woman. Women are more "superexcellent" in 1613 than they ever have been before, and the marks of a good woman are clear to see: "modesty, bashfulness, silence, abstinence, sobrietie," obedience to her husband, wariness but wisdom of speech, carefulness of her household, abhorrence of idleness.[6] Williamson's treatise[7] is really just one of many contributions to the controversial literature surrounding King James's anti-Catholic writings but is particularly interesting because of the forcefulness of its anti-Papal assertions. Most notable are the final chapter, denying the title of martyr to one who dies for the Catholic faith, and the chapter discussing the "preheminent authority and office of kings," which dates (by implication) this preeminence from the "reformation began by King Henry 8. of famous memory" in 1534, "perfected by our late souereigne Queene Elizabeth," and continued "by our now reigning King and dread souereigne IAMES."[8]

In Shakespeare's *Henry VIII*, Katherine of Aragon is clearly a good woman, in Barnabe Rich's terms and in terms of conventional values;[9] but she is also, in common knowledge, one of Williamson's unreformed Catholics. She obeys her husband as her spouse, but not as her king; Shakespeare has her acknowledge only the Pope as her judge (II.iv.117). Her divorce, if not its cause, was considered at least a great step forward in the glorious reformation of the Tudors lauded by Williamson.[10] How disingenuous is Shakespeare in presenting the most sympathetic figure in his play as so dangerously self-contradictory: perfect according to the Christian ideal of woman, but in Christian reformed doctrine a disciple of Antichrist?[11] How could Shakespeare at the time have dared to elaborate the character of such a dubious heroine, particularly since his play was, quite certainly,[12] intended to a great degree to celebrate the wedding of Princess Elizabeth and Prince Frederick, a union believed to herald a Protestant victory over the arms and faith of Catholicism in Europe?

To approach Shakespeare's curious treatment of Katherine, we must also consider what R. A. Foakes noted,[13] that many historical plays dealing with the Tudor and immediately pre-Tudor periods were reprinted in 1613 (and doubtless revived on stage) as tributes to the above mentioned millenial wedding. Of the four Renaissance English dramas devoted to Henry VIII's reign—*The Book of Sir Thomas More*, *Thomas Lord Cromwell*, Rowley's *When You See Me, You Know Me*, and *The Famous History of Henry VIII*—the last three were printed in 1613. Not enough attention has been given to the different ways in which these plays handle the reign and to the significance of their simultaneous appearance in 1613.

Naturally, of course, the death of Prince Henry meant that the glories of his namesake's kingdom would not be renewed.[14] Despite the rhetoric, Elizabeth's marriage was insufficient recompense for this loss, and the fashionable belief that Anne Boleyn's marriage and the birth of the earlier Elizabeth at the end of *Henry VIII* celebrate the 1613 marriage[15] does not exhaust the wealth of contemporary allusion in the play. In fact, I believe that the great difference in approach between Shakespeare's play and the others treating the same reign is due to his sense of historical discontinuity, experienced in 1613 and projected onto a past whose outlines were, to Rowley, to the author of *Thomas Lord Cromwell*, and to the chroniclers, much simpler. *Henry VIII*, as the penultimate significant English history play written before 1642,[16] demonstrates by its richness and its confusions the extent to which history had become by 1613 unapprehendable within the formal limits of a three-hour drama. In this period "men turned from an examination of the state [in drama] to an examination of themselves,"[17] but this does not mean simply that, as F. J. Levy suggests, the English state as history was too well known by the populace to provide dramatic interest. Henry Kelley's conclusion that Shakespeare *consistently* in his histories "de-Providentialized" dynastic succession, reducing history to "the realities of human passion and action,"[18] is also valid, but the pointed omission of *Henry VIII* from discussion in his book is significant. In *Henry VIII*, even when the providential millenial view of the reign is discounted, the parallels with 1613 allow a contradiction to emerge, most pointedly in the case of Katherine, between "the realities of human passion and action" and a non-providential, secular, conventional view of Henry VIII as a founder of the Reformation and Tudor glory. We must recognize, as an example of the contradiction, the dramatic incongruity of Cranmer's victimization and political impotence in V.ii preceding his prophecy of Queen Elizabeth and King James in V.iv. Cranmer's prophecy is not a historically or dramatically appropriate conclusion. In speaking it, he has ceased to exist as a person and become an obligatory, ceremonial, disembodied voice. The real content of *Henry VIII* precedes the last scene and is filled with the consciousness of the meaning of Prince Henry's death.

King James, not his first son, claimed to be the mirror of Henry VIII as reformer, particularly following his anti-Papal treatises. As Joseph Hall said in a 1613 accession day sermon, "all Christian Churches, in their prayers and acclamations, stile him, in double right, *Defender of the Faith*. . . ."[19] The insincere conventionality of Cranmer's tribute to James as the "mountain cedar" is shown by its many echoes in the epithalamic literature of the time.[20] If Shakespeare's Henry is meant to have any noble qualities attributable to James, they are not evident; for it is a fact that he is presented (particularly because of

Shakespeare's extensive and detailed use of chronicle sources) warts and all. With no strength of mind or ability to see through the plots of Wolsey and Gardiner, unless they are presented to his eyes overtly, he becomes decisive and regal only in the last scenes, where at the same time he ceases to be lifelike and the famous "Ha" is stilled. Nor is any of Henry's speech a proclamation of Protestant principle befitting the founder of reformation. The plotters against Cranmer are rebuked, not for attempting to overthrow Cranmer's religious reform but for their personal "malice" towards him. Cranmer himself is less an archbishop than a politic counsellor. Nowhere is there a scene like the one in *When You See Me*,[21] where Cranmer teaches Prince Edward, who sees his land wavering "betwixt the Protestants and the Papists," what true Protestant doctrine is. And this at a time (1613) when an Anglican minister, in his wedding sermon on Elizabeth and Frederick, could use such language as "Why do seduced and seducing Soules who are bewitched with the Circean dregs of the Babylonish Roman strumpet, so much glorie in the outward pompe and glorye of their Bastard Church?"[22] while praising Elizabeth as a personification of true (inward) Protestant religion. We remember that in Shakespeare's play Katherine, who never abjures nor is shown as strumpetlike in her devotion to this bastard church, is the one who as a "good" obedient wife first arouses in Henry (who is completely taken in by the "plot" of Wolsey to discredit Buckingham) a "moral" awareness of the state of his own subjects, driven almost to rebellion by Wolsey's taxations (I.ii).[23] Again, Robert Allyne in 1613 calls the wedding of Elizabeth and Frederick "A light, a starre, a fire, that shall consume, / And dim th'adulterate light of *Spanish Rome*."[24] Shakespeare's Katherine, the noble yet pathetic victim of Wolsey's plotting, does not disguise at her trial (II.iv) her Spanish ancestry and loyalty. In fact, by implication, she equates her Catholic father with Henry VII in their mutual judgment and accord (this is particularly striking since Henry VII's wife, the first Elizabeth, type of James's daughter, was the uniter of Lancaster and York who made James's Protestant kingdom possible):[25]

> The king your father was reputed for
> A prince most prudent, of an excellent
> And unmatch'd wit and judgment: Ferdinand
> My father, King of Spain, was reckon'd one
> The wisest prince that there had reign'd by many
> A year before.
>
> (*II.iv.43–48*)

And they both in concert deemed Katherine's marriage lawful. Katherine goes on to plead for time so that she can be advised by "her friends in Spain" in conducting her defense—but without any of the sinister connotations that such a reference would bear in a play like Heywood's *If you Know Not Me . . .* (also republished in 1613), where Philip II's comment "This shalbe Spanish England, our English Spain"[26] sends chills down any patriotic back. In *Henry VIII*, Shakespeare is avoiding, until the last moment, giving any of the obvious and universally acceptable contemporary connotations to the reign, and avoiding (*except at the end*) any transformations of history that could flatter the king or the king's cause.

To see more clearly into Shakespeare's ambiguous intentions, we must look at two other factors: what the death of Prince Henry, which I see as the decisive underlying factor in the play, meant at the time and how Shakespeare has veered from the course set by earlier dramatizations of Henry VIII's reign.

Among all the eulogies of Prince Henry, which have been much discussed, let us take as a sample those written by Shakespeare's fellow dramatists, those eulogies with which he might most likely have been acquainted. The most interesting volume in this respect is *A Griefe on the Death of Prince Henrie*, containing elegies by Cyril Tourneur, John Webster, and Thomas Heywood. Heywood, of course, also provided *A Marriage Triumphe* on the sequent event, in which he felt he could begin, "Now the wet winter of our teares is past, / And see, the cheerefull Spring appeares at last . . . ,"[27] and consign the Prince to the peace of his grave. However, in the nuptial hymn concluding this poem, Heywood made the interesting decision to rhyme "Elizabeth" and "death" in the last couplet of each stanza, suggesting an obsession with what shall conquer even the hopeful young couple.[28] Henry was, of course, a martial prince, properly considered the mirror of the Black Prince,[29] and we can suspect that his chivalric bearing was contrasted in many minds with his father's physical weakness, despite James's addiction to horsemanship. It certainly recalled Henry VIII's military campaigns and imperial ventures, so similar to those of the Black Prince (e.g., the obsession with Bordeaux). *When You See Me* glorifies this aspect of Henry VIII's reign. Rowley ostentatiously never resolves the contradiction between Henry's ambitions in France, his alliance with Charles V in a pan-Christian crusade against the Turks, and his violent anti-Catholicism (expressed particularly through the jokes of Will Summers). On the contrary, Shakespeare's Henry VIII is a sedentary monarch; the Field of the Cloth of Gold is soon revealed as a glittering sham, a humiliation to British imperial policy.

Virtue, in its Spenserian sense, is the quality most praised in Prince Henry—and, most interestingly, virtue in direct contrast to the false light in "gaudy show of ceremonies" and "court Sport,"[30] virtue active on the *stage* of the world. Says Heywood,

This Vniuerse imagine a Theater,
Nations spectators, and this land a stage.
Was euer Actor, made by the Creator,
That better scean'd his part unto his age . . .
So grauely yong, and so vnmellowed sage. . . .[31]

Says Webster,

Wee stood as in some spacious Theater
Musing what would become of him; his flight,
Reacht such a noble pitch aboue our sight. . . .[32]

Prince Henry is on the world's stage most like Henry V, "this star of England" within "this wooden O" of the world. He incarnates all the qualities lacked by the characters in Shakespeare's *Henry VIII* except when they are already in the grip of death. *Henry VIII* ends with virtue only in potential, only hoped for; Edward VI is unembarrassedly actualized virtue in *When You See Me*, as Cromwell is (particularly in the significant and often critically neglected scenes from his private life) in *Thomas Lord Cromwell*. Prince Henry is popularly believed to be virtue actualized, young but sage, to such an extent that he is imaged as an actor on a world-stage, like the young Sidney, both more real than other mortals and at the same time more distant, removed from the human audience (fallible) because of his supreme perfection. Ironically, this vision of Prince Henry as Virtue personified makes his death much more the epitome of all men's deaths (and thereby the death of the moral order by which society maintains its coherence) than the deaths of other great men. Cyril Tourneur expresses well this mood of the death of the supernal:

His youths great broken promise wee complaine.
Yet none was greater. And are ours lesse vaine?
Mistake not. As Humanitie now goes;
Hee liu'd a *Man* as long as any does.
For (onelie) in those Minutes that wee giue
To *Vertue*, wee are *Trulie* said to liue
Men, and no longer.[33]

Tourneur goes on to declare that Henry's death ended any hope that ours could be as glorious an age as the ancients'. The expressions suggest that the events of Shakespeare's *Henry VIII* ensue as a function of his sense that there is "now" no man who is truly a "man" in Tourneur's sense, in being at one with virtue. Similarly, history, even conceived in a purely non-providential light, cannot any longer be comprehended by its actors' deviations from a moral idea embedded in man. As the Elizabeth-Frederick marriage is a "court sport," a glittering ceremony covering up an empty pit of loss, so is the Field of the Cloth of Gold a glittering "garment" (I.i.93) easily broken by the tempest of war. Or, to take another random example, when the gentlemen meet in IV.i.2–7, they say,

> *I Gent.* You come to take your stand here, and behold
> The Lady Anne pass from her coronation?
> *II Gent.* 'Tis all my business. At our last encounter
> The Duke of Buckingham came from his trial.
> *I Gent.* 'Tis very true. But that time offer'd sorrow,
> This general joy.

The allusion to the events of 1612–13 is obvious here. This neat symmetry of coronation and conviction, joy and sorrow, is unbalanced by the audience's memory of the recent heroism of the displaced queen (III.i). Anne's coronation, as presented, obviously implies her acquiescence to the unsavory, virtueless views of a queen's estate held by the Old Lady (II.iii), since, before we leave that scene, Anne has moved from a refusal on moral grounds to accept the crown, to a wavering hesitation ("This is strange to me," II.iii.88). Again, immediately following the Third Gentleman's idealized description of the coronation of "saintlike" Anne, he mentions the procession's return to "York-place":

> *I Gent.* You must no more call it York-place, Sir, that's past;
> For since the cardinal fell, that title's lost,
> 'Tis now the king's, call'd Whitehall.
> *III Gent.* I know it.
> But 'tis so lately alter'd that the old name
> Is fresh about me.
>
> (*IV.i.94–99*)

As Foakes says, this is "a device to enable the dramatist to refer to Wolsey," but in this seeming irrelevance he refers to Wolsey for a purpose: to bring to mind the instability of buildings, names, men, and, of course, ceremonies like the one just described—an instability that the future execution of the "saint," of which none could have been ignorant, substantiates.

In all these examples, the ceremony and pageantry to which everyone points as providing the basic texture of *Henry VIII* has its validity undercut by event and allusion. It is good at this point to refer to another eulogy of Prince Henry: ". . . in Him, a *glimmering light* of the Golden times appeared, all *lines* of expectation met in this Center, all spirits of vertue, scattered into others were extracted into him. . . . His *Magnetique* vertue drewe all the *eies*, and *hearts*, of the *Protestant* world, vpon him . . . he stood like a *Center*, vnmoved, the *circumference* of his estate, being drawne aboue, beneath, about him. . . ."[34] This Jonsonian idea of Henry as the magnetic center of a socioreligious model of the cosmos reflects the deep anxiety that his death aroused, transcending the kingdom or succession or other temporal questions. As Henry symbolized order, so his death symbolized chaos, or social death. Accordingly, the dramatic and empathetic center of *Henry VIII* is not Henry or Anne or Will Summers (as in Rowley) but a series of the great, images of Prince Henry, moving towards death. In particular, it is Katherine, whose faith is a spiritual death in terms of the rhetoric surrounding the 1613 marriage, who gathers our sympathy, who dominates the play by her noble refusal to play the world's game, whose last words (IV.ii), "unqueen'd, yet like a queen," mock the queening (IV.i) of Anne. We are allowed into the intimacy of Katherine's chamber, but must hear of Anne's coronation at second hand—as words, not action. We *see* the heavenly (and in its imagery extraordinarily papistical) coronation of Katherine, her Vision (IV.ii) which even Griffith is too dull to see. We know it is more "real" than Anne's worldly coronation; yet we know the latter stands for the future hopes of Princess Elizabeth and Prince Frederick, and if we accept that Shakespeare was no secret Catholic, we are driven to the conclusion that Death, even if glorious and nobly faced, is more real than the life-asserting posterity of James's "mountain cedar." A rather hack verse of 1613 expresses Shakespeare's theme here very well:

> There is great strife twixt death and love,
> Which of them is the stronger,
> And which of them can strike the stroake,
> Whose wound endures the longer.
> *Henry Frederick* sayd they both,
>   Shall be our marke to trie;
> Which of us twaine can do the deede,
>   To get the victorie:
> Death *Henry* strikes, God *Cupid* strikes,
>   Faire *Fredericks* strength to prove.
> So *Henry* dyes a sodaine death,
>   So *Frederick* is in loue.
> We know love is as strong as Death,
>   But Death to Loue must yeeld;

For Death is past, Loue still remaines,
God Cupid wins the field.[35]

"Love" is more extensive than the particular love between Frederick and Elizabeth which the pamphleteer is ostensibly celebrating. It is the force, born at the Creation, that binds men to God on one hand and in the created universe creates history through the conjunction and generation of men and women ("our children's children shall see this, and bless heaven," *Henry VIII*, V.iv.54–55). The playful yet moving scene between Henry V and Katherine at the end of *Henry V* is Shakespeare's joyous expression of this love ("man and wife, being two, are one in love," V.ii.379), and so are their respective kingdoms. *Except for Cranmer's prophecy*, there is no such love to counteract death in *Henry VIII*. In the great strife death wins: Buckingham dies, Katherine's loving concern for her husband's kingdom is cast aside. No loving charity, such as that of Cromwell or Friskiball in *Thomas Lord Cromwell*, governs any one of the characters. There is no loving reconciliation of nations (however historically manipulated) as in Henry's meeting with Charles V in *When You See Me*. Only at Wolsey's party (I.iv) do Henry and Anne, whose dramatized love *could have* counterpointed the machinations of other protagonists, even appear on stage together.

At this point we must contrast the three plays on Henry VIII published in 1613 in terms of their treatment of Henry VIII himself in order to see the point which the historical genre had reached by that time. To assert the manifest destiny of the Tudor regime while describing the events which filled it was always a ticklish business under that regime or its legitimate successor. Heywood's two-part history of Elizabeth's reign, like other similar pieces (except for the interesting *Sir Thomas Wyat*), is extremely selective, leaping from the oppressions of the evil Catholic Queen Mary, wrought against the innocent Elizabeth, through many scattered episodes to the Armada victory. And the rest is silence.

Thomas Lord Cromwell, first published in 1599, solves the problem of reconciling literal and emotional history concerning Henry VIII's reign by omitting the king entirely from the stage and allowing a fictitious last-minute royal reprieve to arrive just too late to prevent the evil Gardiner (archvillain of all these plays, showing their inheritance from Foxe) from executing Cromwell. But it is basically a Mirror for Magistrates tale, applied to more recent politics. Its structure is linear and assumes in its audience the acceptance of an archetypal reality to which human fate conforms. It also emphasizes the continuity between Cromwell's public and private, or political and moral, lives. As one citizen says, " 'Tis pitty that this noble man should fall, / He did so many charitable deeds."[36] The actual events of Henry's reign are less important than the career of the hero, including his charity to noble (Duke of Bedford), bourgeois (Banister), and peasant (Seely and Joan). Cromwell personifies the ideal Englishman, but there is nothing paradoxical about the destruction of such virtue because it can be explained by universal fatality or by human malice. And there are no strange implications in Henry's uninvolvement in all events of the play, because his absence is an attribute of regal grandeur and he is the victim of evil advisers.

Rowley's play is a different matter; it idealizes Henry by giving him some of Cromwell's attributes in the earlier play. Perhaps most striking is the use of Edward, rather than Elizabeth, as the hope of the future (avoiding the embarrassments of Anne Boleyn's life) and the corollary of presenting Henry as torn between the necessity of diplomatic business (dealing with the Pope) and of deciding the fate of his beloved Jane Seymour—whether she or her son shall live. Given the fantasy involved in having to make such a decision (an incredibly philosophical approach to obstetrics), his choice of Jane is a victory of love over self-interest, of personal over public good. It emphasizes Henry's ethical, at the expense of his political, identity. Similarly, the elaborate use of the proverbial Will Summers[37] and Henry's escapade with the brigand Black Will and the Counter prison should be remarked, not as is conventionally done for their dramatic vulgarity,[38] but as attempts to assert an ideal of kingship founded in royal self-awareness. Rowley's Henry always *knows* he is *ultimately* no different from other men, even brigands or felons. The audience loves him for being a "true" man in Tourneur's sense, identified with virtues. Rowley's conclusion, with the aged Henry married to Catherine Parr yet receiving the Emperor on English soil, is a distortion of historical fact but not of "reality," because the event expresses a truth about Henry and his reign more abstract, yet more emotionally powered, than pure historical fact—an *ideal* truth.

Rowley's Henry VIII, like Prince Hal, is unsobered by kingship. In *Henry IV*, Shakespeare was already aware how problematic was the dramatization of "true" English history—much more so than Rowley's mind could imagine. But in 1613, Shakespeare found that the problem of the history play was not just one of giving historical characters passions without violating their historical identities as preserved in the chroniclers' facts. Rather, the very existence of such passions (as in Katherine) tended to subvert a conventional progressivist view of history. Shakespeare and his contemporaries had so much emotion invested in Prince Henry, saw him so much in terms of historical millenarianism (as they also saw Henry VIII) that, fully conscious of James's and Charles's personal characteristics, they felt Henry's death somehow deprived centuries of previous history of its meaning. Shakespeare, subtly and darkly, expresses this sense of despair in a positive way by creating in Katherine a single light in darkness (we remember that Wolsey and Buckingham are noble only at death), who is ostentatiously and persistently a *Spanish Catholic*:

> my friends,
> They that must weigh out my afflictions,
> They that my trust must grow to, live not here;
> They are, as all my other comforts) far hence,
> In my own country, lords.
>
> (*III.i.87–91*)

Perhaps the cul-de-sac of *Henry VIII* is a foreshadowing of a sense of inner division in a country imperceptibly breaking apart as revolution approaches. Such cultural alienation would make any appeal to a common history distasteful to an audience large enough to make plays dealing with a common history unprofitable. Katherine may please favorers of King James's Spanish policy, but she alienates favorers of his intervention for Frederick in the Thirty Years' War. What man impassioned about domestic issues, like the primacy of common law versus that of royal prerogative, wants to joy in the famous victories of Henry V? What royalist wants to watch Richard II give up his crown, when such an act has vivid contemporary, not just historical, relevance? The topicality of *Henry VIII* gives it vigor but also denies it successors.

When John Ford wrote *Perkin Warbeck*, he was aware of what dangerous material he was choosing. Perhaps he purposely selected an incident whose historical outlines were relatively simple. Henry VII's conclusion that

> public states
> As our particular bodies, taste most good,
> In health, when purged of corrupted blood,[39]

shows clearly what side Ford was on. Yet his epilogue, referring to "theatres of greatness," hopes of an empire, change of fortune, clearly shows his nostalgia for a time when such histories could serve merely to raise and inspire the soul and did not have to be considered the voices of faction. But Shakespeare's Katherine had anticipated him; as good woman and bad Catholic, her impossibility had shown the impossibility in coming years of a "universal" English historical drama which could appeal to a concert of hearts and minds.

Notes:

1. Howard Felperin, "Shakespeare's *Henry VIII*: History as Myth," *SEL*, 6 (Spring 1966), 225. Felperin praises the Arden edition of *Henry VIII*, ed. R. A. Foakes

(London: Methuen, 1954). I concur, and all quotations from *Henry VIII* which follow are from that edition.

2. Ronald Berman, "*King Henry the Eighth*: History as Romance," *ES*, 48 (April 1967), 119.
3. Felperin, p. 245.
4. H. M. Richmond, "Shakespeare's *Henry VIII*: Romance Redeemed by History," *ShakS*, 4 (1968), 348.
5. See Foakes, pp. xxvi ff.
6. Barnabe Rich, *The Excellency of Good Women* (London, 1613), sig. E4r.
7. See the woodcut of the aged author as "gentleman" on verso of title page; he is clearly the average, wise Protestant Londoner.
8. Thomas Williamson, *The Sword of the Spirit* . . . (London, 1613), sig. G2r–v.
9. She is modest in addressing Henry, is tormented at being forced to obey him, has a loyal and close household, and is busy at work with her ladies even at exile from court and in despair.
10. See, for example, John Stow's *Annales of England* (London, 1605), sig. Nnn8r ff. Qqq2r, Qqq8r ff. I do not deny the extent to which Shakespeare's play is a paraphrase of chronicle histories; what is interesting is his arrangement of these materials.
11. See Bernard Harris, " 'What's Past is Prologue': *Cymbeline* and *Henry VIII*," *Stratford-upon-Avon Studies*, 8 (1966), 233, for the relationship between *Henry VIII* and James's Spanish policy.
12. Foakes, pp. xxviii ff.
13. Ibid., p. xliii.
14. See E. C. Wilson, *Prince Henry and English Literature* (Ithaca: Cornell Univ. Press, 1946), Part 3.
15. Foakes, p. xxx. Foakes assumes (pp. xxix–xxx) that *Henry VIII* is anti-Catholic.
16. Cf. the comments on Ford's *Perkin Warbeck*, p. 15 below.
17. F. J. Levy, *Tudor Historical Thought* (San Marino, Calif.: Huntington Library, 1967), 233–34.
18. Henry A. Kelley, *Divine Providence in the England of Shakespeare's Histories* (Cambridge: Harvard Univ. Press, 1970), 304–6.
19. Joseph Hall, *Workes* (London, 1625), sig. T4r.
20. E.g., Jacobus Aretius, *Primula Veris Seu Panegyrica; Ad Excellentiss. Principem Palatinum* (London, 1613), sig. C4r:

> How well doth he become the royall *side*,
> Of that erected and broad-spreading tree
> Under whose shade may *Britaine* ever be.
> And from this branch may thousand branches more
> Shoote ore the Maine, and knit with every shore
> In bonds of Marriage, Kindred, and Increase . . .

21. Samuel Rowley, *When You See Me, You Know Me*, ed. F. P. Wilson, Malone Society (Oxford: Oxford Univ. Press, 1952), sig. G3r.
22. George Webbe, *The Bride Royall* (London, 1613), sig. D2v.

23. As Foakes notes, this scene and the rebellion itself are the author's invention or exaggeration.
24. Robert Allyne, *Teares of Joy* . . . (London, 1613), sig. A4^r.
25. As Webbe points out, sig. F6^r.
26. Thomas Heywood, *If You Know Not Me, You Know Nobody*, ed. Madeleine Doran, Malone Society (Oxford: Oxford Univ. Press, 1934), sig. B3^r.
27. In *Percy Society*, III (London: T. Richards, 1841), 3.
28. Ibid., pp. 25–29.
29. Webster makes the comparison in *Three Elegies on the most lamented Death of Prince Henrie* (London, 1613), sig. B1^r. Also in John Taylor, *Great Britain All in Black* (London, 1613), sig. B3^r.
30. *Three Elegies*, sig. B1^v.
31. Ibid., sig. B1^r.
32. Ibid. The elegies are separately paginated.
33. Ibid., sig. B4^r.
34. Daniel Price, *Prince Henry His First Anniversary* (Oxford, 1613), sig. A2^r.
35. Joannis Marie de Franchis, *Of the Most Auspicious Marriage betwixt . . . Frederick and Elizabeth* (London, 1613), sig. L3^r.
36. *Thomas Lord Cromwell* (London, 1602), sig. F4^v.
37. Cf. Thomas Deloney's similar glorification of Summers.
38. Harris, p. 229.
39. John Ford, *Perkin Warbeck*, ed. Peter Ure (London: Methuen, 1968), p. 140.

Shakespeare's *The Phoenix and the Turtle* and the Defunctive Music of Ecstasy

Vincent F. Petronella

Let the bird of loudest lay
On the sole Arabian tree
Herald sad and trumpet be,
To whose sound chaste wings obey.

But thou shrieking harbinger,
Foul precurrer of the fiend,
Augur of the fever's end,
To this troop come thou not near.

From this session interdict
Every fowl of tyrant wing,
Save the eagle, feather'd king;
Keep the obsequy so strict.

Let the priest in surplice white,
That defunctive music can,
Be the death-divining swan,
Lest the requiem lack his right.

And thou treble-dated crow,
That thy sable gender mak'st
With the breath thou giv'st and tak'st,
'Mongst our mourners shalt thou go.

Here the anthem doth commence:
Love and constancy is dead;
Phoenix and the Turtle fled
In a mutual flame from hence.

So they lov'd, as love in twain
Had the essence but in one:
Two distincts, division none;
Number there in love was slain.

Hearts remote, yet not asunder;
Distance and no space was seen
'Twixt this Turtle and his queen:
But in them it were a wonder.

So between them love did shine
That the Turtle saw his right
Flaming in the Phonenix' sight;
Either was the other's mine.

Property was thus appalled
That the self was not the same:
Single nature's double name
Neither two nor one was called.

Reason, in itself confounded,
Saw division grow together,
To themselves yet either neither,
Simple were so well compounded:

That it cried, How true a twain
Seemeth this concordant one!
Love hath reason, reason none,
If what parts, can so remain.

Whereupon it made this Threne
To the Phoenix and the Dove,
Co-supremes and stars of love,
As Chorus to their tragic scene.

THRENOS

Beauty, truth and rarity,
Grace in all simplicity,
Here enclos'd, in cinders lie.

Death is now the Phoenix' nest,
And the Turtle's loyal breast
To eternity doth rest;

Leaving no posterity:
'Twas not their infirmity,
It was married chastity.

Truth may seem, but cannot be;
Beauty brag, but 'tis not she;
Truth and beauty buried be.

To this urn let those repair
That are either true or fair:
For these dead birds sigh a prayer.

(Above text of *The Phoenix and the Turtle* is taken from *The Arden Shakespeare: The Poems*, ed. F. T. Prince [Cambridge, Mass.: Harvard Univ. Press, 1960])

Twenty years after G. Wilson Knight declared that *The Phoenix and the Turtle* had been "unjustly" and "too long" neglected, Muriel Bradbrook observed that "very little has been written upon this poem."[1] Another twenty years passed. During that interim a different note was sounded when Robert Ellrodt announced that *The Phoenix and the Turtle* would have become smothered in "the dust of scholarly debate" if it were not for the clarifying commentary of scholars like Heinrich Straumann, A. Alvarez, G. Wilson Knight, F. T. Prince, and C. S. Lewis.[2] Although the poem has escaped suffocation (as if any great piece of literature can ever be deprived of life in this way) and has been elucidated in different ways, a critical debate still goes on as to what the poem means and, specifically, as to what the significance of the dead Phoenix is.

Several readings of the poem hinge on the way the Phoenix's role is interpreted. In order to simplify a discussion of the diverse commentary, we can label "orthodox" those critics who believe that Shakespeare is asking us to respond traditionally to the legendary Arabian bird and hence to see a revived Phoenix in the poem. The "unorthodox," on the other hand, are not ready to accept this characteristic of the Phoenix tradition given the context of Shakespeare's poem.

One of the orthodox critics is William Empson, who explains that although the poem "expresses the despair felt by the spectators (the 'chaste' or non-predatory birds who are the voice of Reason) . . . at last the magic works and a new Phoenix rises from the ashes"; another is J. V. Cunningham, who goes even further by claiming that "[Phoenix and Turtle-Dove] become one and yet neither is annihilated . . . they have only passed into the real life of Ideas from the unreal life of materiality."[3] For I. A. Richards, the Turtle-Dove "is consumed, burnt up on the pyre, in the flames of her [the Phoenix's] regeneration"; and for Sister Mary Bonaventure, the Phoenix and the Turtle are "united—fused—by one mutual flame which transforms them, raises them to a new level of being . . . "—a process that is suggestive of the grace through which "man is reborn to a new life."[4] All of the orthodox readings are not so obviously "Christian" as this last one, nor are they all necessarily explicit about the regeneration of the Phoenix. Alvarez, for example, speaks of the theme of *The Phoenix and the Turtle* in terms of the "transcendence of Reason by Love"; but he goes on to say that "the very difficulty of the anthem is that it will not rest in the power of faith to transcend Reason (and this makes me suspicious of a purely Christian interpretation)."[5] Behind many of the orthodox approaches is the seminal criticism of G. Wilson Knight. In *The Mutual Flame* he reasserts a point he had made in *The Shakespearian Tempest*: ". . . the very death of truth and beauty [Turtle-Dove and Phoenix] creates . . . immortality"; the "new Phoenix," therefore, is present in Shakespeare's poem.[6]

Antithetical to the orthodox view of the Phoenix image is that represented by critics like Robert Ellrodt, who are not at all convinced that Shakespeare's *The Phoenix and the Turtle* is a poem dealing with a revived Arabian bird. Shakespeare's "very subject," writes Ellrodt, "was a modification of the Phoenix myth which implied disbelief in, or at least disregard for, the time-honoured legend . . . Beauty, truth and rarity here enclosed in cinders lie, and any assurance, any hint of survival in a world beyond, is withheld. The rest is silence."[7] Murray Copland puts this even more strongly: "Shakespeare's most original and imaginative stroke in *The Phoenix and Turtle* is to assert that the unique, peerlessly beautiful bird is fully and finally *dead* . . . the Phoenix is . . . laid asleep for ever. Its bed is, simply and baldly, the final bed of death."[8] And Muriel Bradbrook, in a refutation of certain ornithological points made by Ronald Bates in his analysis of the poem, says nothing about a revived Phoenix, so that at least in this regard she apparently concurs with Bates, who, like Copland, does not accept the idea that a renewed Phoenix is part of the poem.[9] Daniel Seltzer, who in turn takes issue with Miss Bradbrook's literal understanding of the "married-chastity" stanza (ll. 59–61), makes helpful connections between *The Phoenix and the Turtle* and Shakespeare's tragedies by demonstrating how the absence of a revived Phoenix creates the "tragic scene" of the poem.[10] Similarly, Elias Schwartz discusses the relationship between poem and tragic drama; he notes that in the Threnos, Reason laments the "total extinction" of Phoenix and Turtle—the emphasis being "not on the immortality of the Phoenix . . . but on its death."[11] As do the orthodox critics, the unorthodox echo over the years an earlier study of the poem; if the orthodox have G. Wilson Knight, the unorthodox have A. H. R. Fairchild, who in 1904 wrote the following about the Threnos: "Since the death of the phoenix and turtle, absolute beauty, real truth, the world-rarity of their union, and grace, which were their unique characteristics, have passed away . . . real beauty and true wisdom are lost . . . the hope of restoration rests entirely in those 'that are either true or fair' . . ."[12]

As if one major controversy were not enough in critical analyses of so relatively brief a work by Shakespeare, a second area of contention has expanded along with the problem of the Phoenix image: the question whether Shakespeare's *The Phoenix and the Turtle* is a metaphysical poem in the technical, literary sense. If the first controversy compels us to grapple with the interpretation of a provocative symbol, the second one forces us to question the style of the poem, especially its tone of poetic voice. "Nothing could in fact be further from the methods of Donne's love-poetry than the method of this poem," writes F. T. Prince in the New Arden edition of *The Poems.*[13] Agreeing with this judgment are Alvarez, who tells us that Shakespeare in *The Phoenix and the Turtle* is "not at all the Metaphysical poet," and C. S. Lewis, who states that Shakespeare here "is not writing 'metaphysical poetry' in the technical sense critics give to that term, but he is writing in the true sense, a metaphysical poem."[14] Generally these are negative reactions to Cleanth Brooks's well-known essay dealing with Donne's *Canonization* and the language of paradox that links the great metaphysical poet with the style of *The Phoenix and the Turtle.*[15] Brooks does not tell us explicitly that Shakespeare's poem anticipates the metaphysicals; nevertheless, the implication is clear. Helen Gardner, although she does not include a reference to Brooks's essay in the select bibliography of her edition of *The Metaphysical Poets,* follows the lead of those who believe, as Brooks does, that *The Phoenix and the Turtle* is part of the metaphysical tradition.[16] Some scholars, in fact, go so far as to describe Shakespeare as either one who "might have been the greatest of the metaphysical poets" had he concentrated primarily on nondramatic poetry around 1600 or one who wrote at least one poem that is a metaphysical work par excellence.[17]

In addition to considering the problems of symbol and style, any serious student of *The Phoenix and the Turtle* must eventually address himself to the question of the poem's literary genetics. What are the relevant sources and analogues of this poem? In the words of at least one scholar, a thorough response to this kind of question would assume the dimensions of a study "as extensive and multifarious as *The Golden Bough,* so full is [*The Phoenix and the Turtle*] of esoteric classical and post-classical lore."[18] Indeed a thorough commentary on the symbolism, style, and genetics of any complex piece of literature implies the massing of volumes of scholarly and critical materials. The scope of my analysis does not permit this kind of extensive consideration of *The Phoenix and the Turtle,* fascinating as such an undertaking might be. And yet it is my purpose to explore the poem's literary genesis as well as its symbolic and stylistic elements in order to understand better what forces are at work beneath the marmoreal surface of Shakespeare's enigmatic elegy.[19] At the same time, I should make it clear at the outset that I believe this poem is not to be restricted to any one explanation. Its highly suggestive imagery and its sometimes intriguing genesis do not allow for rigid critiques of origin, meaning, and structure. Straumann's emphasis upon the principle of *Mehrdeutigkeit,* or "layers of meaning," as it concerns *The Phoenix and the Turtle* is a perfectly sound one, as is Muriel Bradbrook's reminder that "negative capability, or the power to refrain from specific associations is not out of place in the reading of poetry."[20] At the outset, then, I can say that my study of *The*

Phoenix and the Turtle will be a critical conflation—hopefully, one that leads to a greater awareness and comprehension of the intricacies of the poem at hand—rather than strictly a refutation of what has already been said by others.

If we look first at Shakespeare's image of the unrevived Phoenix, we see before us a symbol of death—a symbol of a supposedly immortal force rendered mortal. The call is out for "defunctive music" for a defunctive pair of birds, one of which has in some mysterious way lost the legendary function of self-regeneration. This depiction of the Phoenix should not be loosely referred to as an original detail, for it is unlikely that the dead, unrevived Phoenix in Shakespeare's poem would have come as a shock to the well-read Renaissance Englishman, primarily because prior to the composition of *The Phoenix and the Turtle* three important writers had already dealt with the same idea. Petrarch, Marot, and Spenser are names that do not crop up often enough in discussions of sources and analogues for *The Phoenix and the Turtle*, and one wonders why this is so, for in Petrarch's *Canzoniere* 323 (*Standomi un giorno solo a la fenestra*) lurks the unrevived Phoenix that remains just as unrevived in Marot's *Des Visions de Petrarque* and Spenser's *Visions of Petrarch*.[21] Specifically, Petrarch tells us of a "strania fenice" that

Volse in se stessa il becco,
Quasi sdegnando, e 'n un punto disparse:
Onde 'l cor di pietate, e d'amor m'arse.

(*58–60*)[22]

"A solitary Phoenix," writes Petrarch, "turns its beak upon herself in disdain and vanishes aloft, causing the heart to burn with pity and love." In Marot's

Comme en desdaing, de son bec s'est feru,
Et des humains sur l'heure disparu:
Dont de pitié et d'amour mon cueur ard.[23]

Spenser has two versions of the lyric from which the above comes, the earlier one appearing in *A Theatre for Worldings* (1569) as "Epigrams": the Phoenix alone in a wood strikes himself

with his beake, as in disdaine,
And so forthwith in great despite he dide.
For pitie and loue my heart yet burnes in paine.

(*62–64*)[24]

The later version occurs in *Complaints* (1591) as *The Visions of Petrarch.* Here Spenser expands his own earlier translation and produces a long lyric made up of seven fourteen-line sonnets, the fifth one of which is in the "Shakespearean" form:

> I saw a Phoenix in the wood alone,
> With purple wings, and crest of golden hewe;
> Strange bird he was, whereby I thought anone,
> That of some heauenly wight I had the vewe;
> Vntill he came vnto the broken tree,
> And to the spring, that late deuoured was.
> What say I more? each thing at last we see
> Doth passe away: the Phoenix there alas
> Spying the tree destroid, the water dride,
> Himselfe smote with his beake, as in disdaine,
> And so foorthwith in great despight he dide:
> That yet my heart burnes in exceeding paine,
> For ruth and pitie of so haples plight.
> O let mine eyes no more see such a sight.
>
> (57–70)[25]

By adding two lines to the original twelve-line Petrarchan stanza, Spenser underscores the shock of seeing the Phoenix die by what becomes essentially an act of suicide. No miraculous resurrection follows the self-immolation. Spenser emphasizes a thematic line similar to that of Shakespeare's *The Phoenix and the Turtle.* This is, of course, not in any way absolute proof that Shakespeare knew either the original material of Petrarch or the versions of Marot and Spenser, but there is no question about the possibility of Shakespeare's having been familiar with one or all of the above. Clearly the idea of an unrevived Phoenix is not new with Shakespeare, nor is the idea of a female Phoenix, which appears in Chester's *Loves Martyr* as well as in Matthew Roydon's elegy on Sir Philip Sidney in *The Phoenix Nest* (1593).[26]

Shakespeare in *The Phoenix and the Turtle* uses not only the image of the unrevived Phoenix but also another ingredient found in the Petrarch-Marot-Spenser poems and referred to in Marot's and Spenser's titles: the wondrous visionary experience. To see the Phoenix is marvelous enough, but to see the Phoenix die and fail to regain its own life is a nightmare vision almost beyond words. Shakespeare's *The Phoenix and the Turtle* is similarly a vision of an overwhelming disaster—the destruction of those values linked with the Phoenix and the Turtle-Dove. Love—spiritual and erotic—is central to Shakespeare's poem but is dealt with as part of a mystical or magical perception of the obliteration of love and truth symbolized by the Turtle-Dove and the Phoenix. The poem is apocalyptic. It is a "Jacobean" insight into what could and what might indeed happen in the lives of individual men or in the world in general. What makes the poem's vision powerful is the pulsation of *energia* and *enargia* generated by an intense, ecstatic music. Or, to put it another way, *The Phoenix and the Turtle* is a work dealing with the music of ecstasy. But the ecstasy does not succeed in doing what it is traditionally supposed to do, although the poetry achieves a power of expression that compels our sensory faculties to respond fully. To put it still another way, we may say that the music and the ecstasy are "defunctive"—that is, no longer capable of functioning to bring about a hopeful and enduring vision of truth and love. In brief, *The Phoenix and the Turtle* is about "defunctive" ecstasy, mystical ecstasy that does not work[27]

To understand why mystical ecstasy is ineffectual in *The Phoenix and the Turtle,* we should review briefly the tradition of ecstasy and the very close association between music and spiritual rapture, always bearing in mind that ecstasy and music are present in Shakespeare's poem not only as subjects but also as principles governing the poem's style. In recent years the nature of spiritual ecstasy has captured the interest of literary critics by way of John Donne's poetic analysis of the experience in *The Extasie.* Scholarly and critical emphasis upon *The Extasie* and related literary materials (English or otherwise) has not run its course. One of the reasons for this is that no one discussion of either the religious ecstasy itself or its incorporation into a literary setting solves the mystery of its supranatural qualities in the strictly religious context or its potency as an aesthetic value in a work of art. This is not the place to discuss at length Donne's poetry or the scholarship dealing with Donne and his contemporaries outside of Shakespeare. But we can at least take advantage of the time and effort contributed by others in establishing here a working definition of the ecstatic experience.

"Mystic ecstasy in the Christian sense," says the *Oxford Dictionary of the Christian Church,* "is one of the normal stages of the mystic life. . . . The chief characteristic of the ecstatic state is the alienation of the senses, caused by the violence of the Divine action on the soul." In his edition of Donne's poetry, John T. Shawcross tells us that Christian mystics used the term "ecstasy" to describe "a state of extreme and abnormal awareness"—an awareness "derived from the detachment of the soul from the body, the soul standing outside the body contemplating their [i.e., body's and soul's] unity and relationship." To these statements we may add Theodore Redpath's explanation that "ecstasy" is the "mystical state in which a soul, liberated from the body, contemplates divine truths."[28] If we let the one word *ecstasy* stand for a cluster of related words, Robert Petersson advises us, it refers to "the state in which man is farthest removed from his normal human condition, the state in which prayer perfectly attains its ideals"; it is a term inseparable from closely related experiences such as vision, trance, transport, rapture, and union itself.[29] Such is the nature of spiritual ecstasy. But what of sensual ecstasy? A commonplace similarity exists between spiritual ecstasy and sensual ecstasy despite the emphasis that the first places on the soul and the second on the body. It is not necessary to argue here about the similarity. Only the naïve or the strictly puritanical would fail to respond to the erotic element in St. Teresa's spiritual ecstasy and the spiritual power of the earthly lovers' experience in *The Extasie* of Donne. Love theorists from Plato through Ficino, Bruno and Leone Ebreo have said much about the role of "divine madness" (i.e., "frenzy," "furor," "enthusiasm," or "ecstasy") in the life of the lover.[30] In his *Commentary on Plato's "Symposium,"* Ficino writes: ". . . there are four kinds of divine madness. The first is the poetic madness, the second is that of the mysteries, the third is that of prophecy, and the fourth is that of love."[31] Ecstasy, we are to understand, occurs over a wide range of categories; it is not limited solely to a world of disembodied creatures.

The Phoenix and the Turtle reflects the Ficinian analysis of the *furores*, but whether Shakespeare was consciously using Ficino's work or that of any other Renaissance writer in composing this poem is impossible to determine finally. Standing within a rich intellectual tradition as it does, Shakespeare's poem is a reflector of developments in the history of thought. And the relationship between poetic text and the intellectual tradition strikes me as shedding more light on this poem than any theory of biographical or political associations. What I am suggesting is that the Neoplatonic discussions of "divine madness" (or what Shakespeare calls "fine frenzy" in *A Midsummer Night's Dream* [V.i.12]), with the religious mystical vestiges that the term carries, are deeply involved in the thematic and stylistic constitution of *The Phoenix and the Turtle.*

Consider first "poetic madness": this is heard and felt by virtue of the poem's heightened incantatory quality. The poetry is intense, marked sometimes by what apparently is a sense of total abandon. Its lyrical intensity is achieved by a hard-driving, basically trochaic, meter that energetically presses all sixty-seven lines of the poem to get somewhere without hesitation. No caesural rest-stops here—Shakespeare's libretto affords no timeless fermatas. To complement this rhythmical urgency, the poem is structured so that prior to the Threnos, several stanzas, although rhyming *abba*, very often become four lines ending not only in rhymed words but also in words related through assonance:

Let the bird of loudest lay,
. . . tree,
. . . be,
. . . obey.
(1–4)[32]

Here the anthem doth commence;
. . . dead;
. . . fled
. . . hence.
(21–24)

So between them love did shine
. . . right
. . . sight:
. . . mine.
(33–36)

Or the line endings may be related through consonance—assisted by one instance of a partial repetition of end words (stanzas 9 and 12):

So they lov'd, as love in twain
. . . one;
. . . none:
. . . slain.
(25–28)

Hearts remote, yet not asunder;
. . . seen
. . . queen;
. . . wonder.
(29–32)

That it cried, How true a twain
. . . one!
. . . none,
. . . remain.
(45–48)

And at least one stanza has a touch of both assonance and consonance:

But thou shrieking harbinger,
. . . fiend,
. . . end,
. . . near.
(5–8)

This handling of the line endings, together with the rhymed triplets of the Threnos and the quick-paced rhythm of the lines throughout the poem, creates a lyrical intensity that flickers occasionally to permit, as it were, an almost Skeltonic flippancy to flash through. But Shakespeare is not writing meaningless doggerel or a *jeu d'esprit.* The intense lyricism he develops is an attempt to capture a poetic ecstasy commensurate with the vision that the poem offers us. This is done neither with grim solemnity nor tongue-in-check; on the contrary, Shakespeare executes it with a metaphysical mixture of levity and seriousness.

Never mellifluous, yet melodic (even to a frenetic degree), the lyricism of *The Phoenix and the Turtle* is bolstered by several musical-aural images: "loudest lay," "trumpet," "sound," "shrieking," "defunctive music," "requiem," "anthem," "Threne," "Chorus." Several of the words in the poem have a double function, one of which is submerged musical metaphor: "treble," "division" (occurring twice, once at line 27 and again at line 42), "number," "concordant," "parts," and perhaps "confounded" (l. 41). In addition to the individual words and phrases with musical-aural values, the poem has as its conclusion a funeral song. That the poem becomes a piece of music is a result of the sound it makes combined with its many musical-aural references. In this way *The Phoenix and the Turtle* is poetic and musical at the same time that it speaks about poetry and music; and as the style is in keeping with the idea of "defunctive music," so the subject matter is defunction—the lack of function and the lack of effective power to prevent defunction. G. Wilson Knight maintains that in *The Phoenix and the Turtle* tempest (usually associated with tragedy) becomes music (symbolically linked with love and union in Shakespeare) and that "the tempest-music distinction is resolved."[33]

It is true that love and union do occur in *The Phoenix and the Turtle,* but what does not occur is the regeneration of love and union. The magic does not work. The music here would not succeed in reviving a broken Coriolanus. If the music of *The Phoenix and the Turtle* can in any way be thought of as a kind of Orphic incantation, with its traditionally magic power to influence the astrological powers above in order to achieve a revival of spirit, the incantation fails.[34]

Incantation, magic-song, ecstasy, furor are all terms that apply to the style and subject matter of *The Phoenix and the Turtle.* But if ecstasy is supposed to be the state in which a literal separation of soul from body takes place, then why talk of union of Phoenix (soul) and Turtle-Dove (body), as if this were the end toward which the poem's central characters are supposed ultimately to be headed?[35] Ideally the ecstatic state would find soul released from body. But in *The Phoenix and the Turtle* the ecstasy is never brought off, and this is the reason why Shakespeare speaks of "division none" and the "mutual flame" of death. The problem here is that body and soul are consumed together, mutually. Never does the soul become separated in order to enjoy observing the body from a distance as it would do if true spiritual ecstasy took place. If any separation were to occur (either explicitly or implicitly) in Shakespeare's poem, it would become the kind of separation of body and soul that is in fact death. But rather than dramatizing the soul's standing off from the body, the poem confronts us with the death of both body and soul. Immortality, then, is out of the picture, no less than ecstatic fulfillment. Tragic tempest does not become comic or unifying music here, as Knight argues; instead, the enthusiastic music of ecstasy falls on the deaf ears of stony mortality, which in turn means that music gives way to a brewing tempest, the tempest suggestive not of tragedy but of pathetic calamity. One's awareness of what Shakespeare is doing is greatly increased if one understands that the sound of music in *The Phoenix and the Turtle* is also the sound of ominous, far-off thunder.

The monitory and oracular quality of *The Phoenix and the Turtle* links it with those two other *furores* discussed in the Platonic tradition: the madness of prophecy and the madness of mystery (religious rite). The bird imagery of the poem asks us to recall the commonplace use of winged creatures in discerning omens or prophecies. Furthermore, the personification Reason singing the Threnos is symbolically apt in that it suggests the clear-mindedness and hence the clear-sightedness rather than simply the frenzy of prophecy. In this way Shakespeare concludes his poem. Earlier, Reason has been puzzled, stumped—its dilemma reinforcing the "madness" element in the poem:

> Reason, in itself confounded,
> Saw division grow together,
> To themselves yet either neither,
> Simple were so well compounded:
>
> That it cried, How true a twain
> Seemeth this concordant one!
> Love hath reason, reason none,
> If what parts, can so remain.
>
> (*41–48*)

At this point it appears that ecstasy or "enthusiasm" has prevailed, for Reason is at sixes and sevens.[36] But Reason has the last word in *The Phoenix and the Turtle*, and what Reason is talking about to us is death as the finality of being —what is described in *Macbeth* as "the be-all and the end-all—here" (I.vii.5).

Reason makes its recovery in the third section of the poem's tripartite structure. It is this framework that organizes the ritualistic movement, the first notable indication of which is the formal gathering of the different birds who are asked to "keep the obsequy so strict," particularly the swan, who will bring to the requiem his "right" (i.e., "his due" with a pun on "rite"). Prophecy and religious rite are traditionally interconnected, and in Shakespeare's poem the themes of prophecy and mystery-rite, although not presented in any clearly sectarian way, work together to heighten the ecstatic pulse of the poetry. Instead of working toward the level of divine understanding, however, *The Phoenix and the Turtle* takes us in the direction of a rational, rather than a nonrational or "enthusiastic," vision. Shakespeare is using ecstatic style and content for strictly terrestrial ends, as does Ben Jonson in *Ode enthousiastike*, one of his contributions to *Loves Martyr*. Speaking of the Phoenix-Lady in exalted terms, Jonson writes,

> Her breath for sweet exceeding
> The *Phoenix* place of breeding,
> But mixt with sound transcending
> All *Nature* of commending.[37]

Jonson's poem is not the enigmatic song that Shakespeare offers us, and whether he is following Shakespeare's lead or vice versa has not been finally determined; in any event, he attempts to do something similar to what Shakespeare is doing: make use of the ecstatic experience in a secular poem. One major way in which Shakespeare's poem differs from Johnson's, however, is in developing the kind of stylistic and thematic *energia* that recalls the Platonic interest in the divine madnesses of prophecy and religious rite.

All of the *furores* involve emotional intensity and are in this way related to one another, but central to *The Phoenix and the Turtle* is the all-important love-madness, which, as Ficino tells us, turns the head of the charioteeer in man's soul "toward the head of all things."[38] The poem's tripartite structure, a feature recognized by many of the commentators already referred to, acts as a vehicle for the theme of love-madness. Commentary on the poem's structure, however, has not touched upon the similarity between the stylistic mode of *The Phoenix and the Turtle* and that of the Orphic pastoral. A consideration of the similarity is illuminating. Richard Cody, commenting on the *Orfeo* of Poliziano as part of a discussion that eventually focuses on Shakespearean drama, analyzes the basic rhythm of Neoplatonic pastoral in terms of three phases: *Emanatio* (procession), *Raptio* (rapture or ecstasy), and *Remeatio* (return or recession).[39] Poliziano, like Pico della Mirandola and Ficino, envisions the Orpheus myth as an allegory of the death and the new life of the Rational Soul, "lost and found again in the flames of intellectual love"; the *Orfeo*, moreover, portrays the death of Orpheus as a gift of Love (Eros) to the Rational Soul.[40] This is not to say that Shakespeare's poem is about Orpheus or that it is a Neoplatonic pastoral. It does manifest, however, pastoral elements and a handling of the mystery of love-in-death. But *The Phoenix and the Turtle* is more than a quasi-pastoral depiction of birds in a forest or meadow, and it is more than a poem expressing Neoplatonic values. It is, in fact, a richly metaphorical portrait of an attitude, a frame of mind. And I contend that the intellectual attitude is made concrete not only by suggestive symbols but also by structural rhythm. The first twenty lines constitute the *Emanatio* of Shakespeare's poem: in comes a procession made up of "the bird of loudest lay," the "shrieking harbinger" (i.e., screech owl), the eagle, the swan, and the crow. We then move into the anthem and its attempt to analyze the mystery of love-madness and the love-death of Phoenix and Turtle-Dove; this is the poem's *Raptio*, and rapturous it is. Union is spiritual and physical for Phoenix and Turtle-Dove; their mutual consummation, given one of the meanings of dying in Shakespeare's time, is highly erotic as well as hopefully regenerative. But although the erotic ecstasy takes place, the spiritual ecstasy never reaches its special kind of climax. Reason, as I have already indicated, is perplexed at this point: only momentarily do Apollonian values surrender to Dionysian ones. It is as if the *furores* (poetry, prophecy, and religious rite) combine to drive the love-ecstasy into divine clarification, a clarification that hopefully will endure forever. But, alas, with the *Remeatio* (the Threnos in this case) the poem's movement recedes, and Reason leads the way. Phoenix and Turtle-Dove have not attained the divine level through ecstasy; instead, they become the subject of Reason's dirge on the grim fact that truth and beauty have been destroyed beyond the point of revival. If the poem is a frame of mind, it portrays the Jacobean intellectual landscape.

Poetry, ritual, prophecy, and love are the enticing ingredients in an artistic *olla podrida*; they blend and become the overall tone and meaning of *The Phoenix and the Turtle*. To say that the tone of *The Phoenix and the Turtle* is a mixture of seriousness and playfulness is to get closer to what the poem means. With its tripartite structure reflecting the *Emanatio-Raptio-Remeatio* triad of the Neoplatonists, *The Phoenix and the Turtle* to some extent partakes of the Orphic tradition of poetic theology, which always implies *serio ludere*, that is, jesting in earnest, playfulness combined with learned diligence.[41] This helps us to understand why the verse technique discussed earlier has a flippant air about it and why levity works hand in hand with seriousness. The poem exhibits a metaphysical wit as it deals with "serious" metaphysical issues. Seen this way, the poem is simultaneously a metaphysical poem (in the literary sense) and a metaphysical poem (in the philosophical sense).[42] We are asked to take its vision seriously, but we are also permitted to enjoy the wit and the irony of the vision. Ecstasy is ultimately defunctive in the world of *The Phoenix and the Turtle*, but ecstasy also governs the pulse of the poem until the voice of Reason enumerates the ontological details of life and especially those of death.

Notes:

1. See Knight's review of Ranjee G. Shahani's *Towards the Stars: being an appreciation of "The Phoenix and the Turtle"* (Rouen: n.p., 1931) in *The Criterion*, 10 (April 1931), 40; rpt. in Knight's *Shakespeare and Religion* (New York: Simon & Schuster, 1967), pp. 342–45. See also his *The Imperial Theme* (London: Oxford Univ. Press, 1931; 3rd ed. London: Methuen, 1951), p. 349; and *The Christian Renaissance* (New York: Norton, 1963), pp. 235–37. Knight's full reading of *The Phoenix and the Turtle* is found in *The Mutual Flame* (1955; rpt. London: Methuen, 1962), pp. 193–204. Miss Bradbrook's comment occurs in her *Shakespeare and Elizabethan Poetry* (London: Chatto & Windus, 1951), p. 247, n. 26.
2. Ellrodt, "An Anatomy of 'The Phoenix and the Turtle,'" *ShS*, 15 (1962), 99. The works Ellrodt refers to at this point are as follows: Straumann, *Phönix und Taube* (Zurich: Artemis-Verlag, 1953); Alvarez in *Interpretations*, ed. John Wain (London: Routledge & Kegan Paul, 1955); Knight (see above); Prince, *The Poems*, New Arden Shakespeare (Cambridge, Mass.: Harvard Univ. Press, 1960); and Lewis, *English Literature in the Sixteenth Century* (London: Oxford Univ. Press, 1954), pp. 508–9. In *Shakespeare: The Poems* (London: Longmans, Green, 1963), F. T. Prince can say with surety that the poem has arrived critically: ". . . in our time *The Phoenix and Turtle* has become one of the most admired of Shakespeare's poems, benefitting from the change of taste which has brought Metaphysical poetry back into favour" (p. 44).
3. Empson, "The Phoenix and the Turtle," *EIC*, 16 (April 1966), 152. Some of the material in this essay Empson uses in his introduction to *Narrative Poems*, Signet Classic Shakespeare, ed. William Burto (New York: New American Library, 1968), pp. xxxvi–xlvii. Cunningham's statement is found in "'Essence' and *The Phoenix and Turtle*," *ELH*, 19 (Dec. 1952), 272; see also his "Idea as Structure: *The Phoenix and Turtle*" in *Tradition and Poetic Structure* (Denver: Alan Swallow, 1960), pp. 76–89.
4. Richards, "The Sense of Poetry: Shakespeare's 'The Phoenix and the Turtle'" in *Symbolism in Religion and Literature*, ed. Rollo May (New York: Braziller, 1961), p. 206. The statement by Richards also appears in *Daedalus*, 87 (1958), 86–94; and S. M. Bonaventure, "The Phoenix Renewed," *Ball State Univ. Forum*, 5 (Autumn 1964), 75. Cf. W. J. Ong, "Metaphor and the Twinned Vision," *SR*, 63 (Spring 1955), 193–201.
5. Alvarez, p. 8. See also K. T. S. Campbell's "The Phoenix and the Turtle as a Signpost of Shakespeare's Development," *British Journal of Aesthetics*, 10

(April 1970), 169–79. Campbell, who is not concerned with the religious or mystical elements in the poem, does not really come to grips with the Phoenix problem; but he does see Shakespeare's aesthetic in a strong, positive light: Shakespeare avoids the radical resolution of "the destructive crisis of identity" adopted by many of our present-day poets in "their fragmentation and destruction of the poetic symbol itself" (p. 178).

6. Cited above, pp. 200, 195.
7. "An Anatomy of 'The Phoenix and the Turtle,'" *ShS*, 15 (1962), 107–8.
8. "The Dead Phoenix," *EIC*, 15 (July 1965), 285.
9. Bradbrook, "'The Phoenix and the Turtle,'" *SQ*, 6 (Summer 1955), 356–58; Bates, "Shakespeare's 'The Phoenix and Turtle,'" *SQ*, 6 (Winter 1955), 19–30. Shakespeare, writes Bates, "contradicts Chester and the others [in *Loves Martyr*]" as far as the expectation of a new little Phoenix is concerned (p. 29). Monroe K. Spears, in his introduction to *Narrative Poetry*, The Laurel Shakespeare, ed. Charles J. Sisson (New York: Dell, 1968), also subscribes to the unorthodox view that "the unique Phoenix was consumed and not reborn (p. 39). One should consult, in addition, the forthright analysis of the poem by Edward Hubler in his edition of Shakespeare's *Songs and Poems* (New York: McGraw-Hill, 1959). The poem, writes Hubler, is "Shakespeare's allegory of love," in which the Phoenix is clearly not an emblem of Christian immortality (pp. xlvii and 318, gloss on line 23 of the poem).
10. "'Their Tragic Scene': *The Phoenix and Turtle* and Shakespeare's Love Tragedies," *SQ*, 12 (Spring 1961), 96, 99–100. See Bradbrook in her essay, p. 357. Seltzer comments interestingly on the thematic similarities between *The Phoenix and the Turtle*, *Troilus and Cressida*, and *Antony and Cleopatra* in his Signet edition of *Troilus and Cressida* (New York: New American Library, 1963), pp. xxxiv–xxxvi.
11. "Shakespeare's Dead Phoenix," *ELN*, 7 (Sept. 1969), 27–28.
12. "*The Phoenix and Turtle*: A Critical and Historical Interpretation," *Englische Studien*, 33 (1904), 372–73.
13. P. xliv. Reaching the same conclusion after a full study of scholarship on the poem is Richard A. Underwood in "Shakespeare's 'The Phoenix and Turtle,'" *DAI*, 31 (1970), 2357–A.
14. Alvarez, p. 11; and Lewis, p. 509.
15. *The Well-Wrought Urn* (New York: Harcourt, Brace & World, 1947), pp. 3–21, especially 19–21.
16. (Baltimore: Penguin, 1957), pp. 23, 39–42, 316. Miss Gardner explains that Shakespeare created out of the Phoenix myth "a myth of his own" (p. 39, n. 1).
17. F. P. Wilson, *Seventeenth Century Prose*, The Ewing Lectures (Berkeley: Univ. of California Press, 1960), p. 12; and Seltzer, pp. 96–97.
18. James A. K. Thomson, *Shakespeare and the Classics* (London: George Allen & Unwin, 1952), p. 46.
19. It is not my intention to worry the problem of the poem's occasion or its literary relationship to Robert Chester's *Loves Martyr*. Many reliable scholars have already offered us the results of patient searches for useful data in this regard. Essential to a thorough study of sources and analogues are the following: *Robert*

Chester's *"Loves Martyr, or Rosalins Complaint,"* (1601), ed. Alexander B. Grosart, The New Shakespeare Society (London: N. Trübner, 1878); Carleton Brown, *Poems by Sir John Salusbury, Robert Chester, Etc.*, Early English Text Society (London: Oxford Univ. Press, 1913); *The Phoenix Nest* (1593), ed. Hyder Edward Rollins (Cambridge, Mass.: Harvard Univ. Press, 1931); especially the elegy (now usually attributed to Matthew Roydon) on Sir Philip Sidney; G. Bonnard, "Shakespeare's Contribution to R. Chester's *Loves Martyr*: *The Phoenix and the Turtle*," *ES*, 19 (April 1937), 66–69; *The Phoenix and the Turtle*, ed. Bernard H. Newdigate (Oxford: Shakespeare Head Press, 1937), especially pp. xvi–xxiv; *The Poems*, New Variorum Shakespeare, ed. Hyder Edward Rollins (Philadelphia: Lippincott, 1938), pp. 323–31 and 559–83; Thomas W. Baldwin, *On the Literary Genetics of Shakespeare's Poems* (Urbana: Univ. of Illinois Press, 1950; Heinrich Straumann, *Phönix und Taube*; G. Wilson Knight, *The Mutual Flame*, pp. 156–224; *The Poems*, New Arden Shakespeare, ed. F. T. Prince, pp. xxxviii–xlvi, 179–83; J. W. Lever, "The Poems," *ShS*, 15 (1962), pp. 18–30, especially pp. 25–30; William H. Matchett, *"The Phoenix and the Turtle": Shakespeare's Poem and Chester's Loves Martyr* (The Hague: Mouton, 1965); *The Poems*, New Shakespeare, ed. J. C. Maxwell (London: Cambridge Univ. Press, 1966), pp. xxvi–xxxiii; *The Reader's Encyclopedia of Shakespeare*, ed. Oscar J. Campbell and Edward G. Quinn (New York: Crowell, 1966), pp. 476–77, 632–33; *Narrative Poems*, Signet Classic Shakespeare, ed. Burto, intro. Empson; and Richard Allan Underwood, "Shakespeare's 'The Phoenix and Turtle': A Survey of Scholarship." Unfortunately the first volume (*Early Comedies, Poems, "Romeo and Juliet"*) of Geoffrey Bullough's *Narrative and Dramatic Sources of Shakespeare* (New York: Columbia Univ. Press, 1957) does not include a section devoted to *The Phoenix and the Turtle*.

20. Straumann, p. 37; Bradbrook, " 'The Phoenix . . .,' " p. 357. Also instructive with regard to the idea of multiple readings is Helen Gardner's use of the Gestalt-oriented approach to art in her *Religion and Literature* (New York: Oxford Univ. Press, 1971), pp. 34–35, where by means of an illustrative pattern of four linked equal rhomboids the point is made that "there is no 'right way' to read the image."

21. William Matchett, in his study of Shakespeare's poem and Chester's *Loves Martyr*, is one of the few scholars who discusses in some detail the Petrarch-Marot-Spenser material in connection with *The Phoenix and the Turtle* (p. 24). See also Robert Ellrodt's esay in *ShS*, 15, pp. 101, 109 n. 14. Consideration of the earlier treatment of the Phoenix by Petrarch and then by Marot and Spenser in their translations would have made the articles by Murray Copland (especially p. 285) and Elias Schwartz (p. 25 and passim) more convincing. In the Variorum edition of *The Works of Edmund Spenser*, ed. Edwin Greenlaw et al, II (Baltimore: Johns Hopkins Press, 1947), Marot is mentioned in connection with *A Theatre for Worldlings* and then again in commentary on *The Visions of Petrarch*, but not in connection with the Phoenix (pp. 274–76, 611). In R. P. C. Mutter's edtion of *Spenser's Minor Poems: A Selection* (London: Methuen, 1957) an entry is lacking for the Phoenix in the glossary, although *The Visions of Petrarch*, 5, is printed on page 53. References are made to Spenser's *Visions*

in Muriel Bradbrook's *Shakespeare and Elizabethan Poetry*, pp. 24, 29, but never are these made in connection with her comments on *The Phoenix and the Turtle* (pp. 32–34, 145, 247 n. 26). W. B. C. Watkins, in *Shakespeare and Spenser* (Princeton: Princeton Univ. Press, 1950), considers Marot's translation of Petrarch but makes no specific reference to the Phoenix image in general or to *The Phoenix and the Turtle* in particular (p. 225). What is even more unusual, Alfred W. Satterthwaite's useful account of *Spenser, Ronsard, and DuBellay* (Princeton: Princeton Univ. Press, 1960) never mentions the name of Marot. The same thing is true of William Nelson's *The Poetry of Spenser* (New York: Columbia Univ. Press, 1963), see especially pp. 64–83. And in a full-length essay on "The Reputation of Clément Marot in Renaissance England," *SRen*, 18 (1971), pp. 173–202, Anne Lake Prescott presents a much-needed study but does not take note of either Marot's *Des Visions de Petrarque* or Spenser's *Visions of Petrarch.* The Marot–Spenser relationship as it regards the *Visions* does come into discussions by John Hollander, "Spenser and the Mingled Measure," *ELR*, 1 (Autumn 1971), 234–35 n. 13; and by Veselin Kostić, "Spenser's Sources in Italian Poetry," Diss. Univ. of Belgrade 1969, pp. 13–14. Kostić argues that there is a possibility that Petrarch's original *Canzoniere* 323, rather than Marot's version, influenced Spenser in the *Visions* (p. 14). Cf. Pauline M. Smith, *Clément Marot, Poet of the French Renaissance* (London: Athlone Press, 1970).

22. *Petrarch: Sonnets and Songs*, trans. Anna Maria Armi (New York: Pantheon, 1968), pp. 446, 448. The loose translation following the quotation is mine.
23. *Oeuvres Complètes de Clément Marot*, II, ed. B. Saint-Marc (Paris: Garnier, 1879), p. 131.
24. *The Poetical Works of Edmund Spenser*, ed. J. C. Smith and E. De Selincourt (1912; rpt. London: Oxford Univ. Press, 1961), p. 606.
25. Ibid., p. 526.
26. See Matchett, pp. 21–29. In a brief but helpful statement on *The Phoenix and the Turtle*, Richard Wilbur makes one comment that may be misleading: Poets often made "*ad hoc* revisions of mythology or conventional symbolism . . . the phoenix is assigned the feminine gender . . ." (*The Complete Pelican Shakespeare* [Baltimore: Penguin, 1969], p. 1404). Wilbur seems to be implying that Shakespeare was original in assigning the feminine gender to the Phoenix. But as Matchett and others have shown, Shakespeare was not. For the use of a female Phoenix with conventional self-regenerative powers, see William Smith's *Chloris* (1596), Sonnet 23, in *The Poems of William Smith*, ed. Lawrence A. Sasek (Baton Rouge: Louisiana State Univ. Press, 1970), p. 60. Matthew Roydon's elegy with its female Phoenix (along with a Turtle-Dove and other birds, ll. 41–42) was printed along with Spenser's *Astrophel* in 1595. For the view that the elegy beginning "As then, no winde at all there blew" is indeed Roydon's, see Lisle Cecil John, *The Elizabethan Sonnet Sequences* (New York: Columbia Univ. Press, 1938), p. 181; Hallett Smith, *Elizabethan Poetry* (Cambridge, Mass.: Harvard Univ. Press, 1952), p. 58; *A Literary History of England*, ed. Albert C. Baugh, 2nd ed. (New York: Appleton-Century-Crofts, 1967), pp. 384–86; and *The Renaissance in England*, ed. Hyder Edward Rollins and Herschel Baker (Boston: Heath, 1954), p. 231.

27. Several commentators have used terms that are relevant to my discussion of *The Phoenix and the Turtle*, but generally the ecstatic element in the poem is not fully explored. G. Wilson Knight, in *The Mutual Flame*, speaks of the Phoenix symbol in light of "the flaming mysticism of a Crashaw" (p. 153) and calls Marston's contribution to Chester's *Loves Martyr* a poem possessing "lyric ecstasy," making it the "most ecstatic of the contributions" (pp. 194–95). "Music," "ecstasy," and "vision" are considered in Knight's chapter on Shakespeare's poem (pp. 203–4). In his New Arden edition of *The Poems*, F. T. Prince tells us that *The Phoenix and the Turtle* "shows unsurpassed musical imagination" and that Shakespeare creates "a kind of ethereal frenzy" (pp. xliii–xliv). Robert Ellrodt's discussion mentions "the soul rapt in contemplation" (p. 105); and C. S. Lewis states that the "oracular" style is in *The Phoenix and the Turtle* "completely successful" (p. 509). John Masefield, in *William Shakespeare* (London: Williams & Norgate, 1911), begins his brief discussion of *The Phoenix and the Turtle* by stating that "spiritual ecstasy is the only key to work of this kind" (p. 249). Regarding *defunctive*, the *OED* cites Shakespeare's *The Phoenix and the Turtle*, line 14, after indicating that the word pertains to "defunction or dying." *Defunctive* is a term not only for death but also for a state in which function is lost. The "defunctive music" of the swan is funereal music, the music of death, but it is also music bemoaning the loss of function, whether it be the life-function or function in general.
28. *Oxford Dictionary of the Christian Church*, ed. F. L. Cross (London: Oxford Univ. Press, 1958), p. 437; *The Complete Poetry of John Donne*, ed. John T. Shawcross (New York: Doubleday, 1967), pp. 130 and 401; and *The Songs and Sonnets of John Donne*, ed. Theodore Redpath (London: Methuen, 1956), pp. 88–93. See also A. J. Smith, "The Metaphysic of Love," *RES*, NS 9 (Nov. 1958), 362–75; Frank A. Doggett, "Donne's Platonism," *SR*, 42 (July–Sept. 1934), 284–90; E. M. W. Tillyard, *The Metaphysicals and Milton* (London: Methuen, 1960), pp. 79–84; G. R. Potter, "Donne's *Extasie*, Contra Legouis," *PQ*, 15 (July 1936), 247–53; George Williamson, "The Convention of *The Extasie*," in *Seventeenth Century Contexts* (London: Faber & Faber, 1960), pp. 63–77; Louis L. Martz, *The Wit of Love* (Notre Dame, Ind.: Univ. of Notre Dame Press, 1969), pp. 48–50; Helen Gardner, "The Argument about 'The Ecstasy,'" in *Elizabethan and Jacobean Studies: Presented to Frank Percy Wilson*, ed. H. Davis and H. Gardner (Oxford: Clarendon Press, 1959), pp. 279–306; René Graziani, "John Donne's 'The Extasie' and Ecstasy," *RES*, NS 19 (May 1968), 121–36; Charles Mitchell, "Donne's 'The Extasie': Love's Subtle Knot," *SEL*, 8 (Winter 1968), 91–101; John E. Parish, "The Parley in 'The Extasie,'" *XUS*, 4 (1965), 188–92; and Elizabeth T. McLaughlin, "'The Extasie': Deceptive or Authentic?" *BuR*, 18 (1970), 55–78. G. Wilson Knight is fond of referring to Donne's *Extasie* in *The Mutual Flame*, passim.
29. *The Art of Ecstasy: Teresa, Bernini, and Crashaw* (New York: Atheneum, 1970), p. 26. Any full discussion of spiritual ecstasy must eventually make reference to the episode of the seraph and the flaming arrow in St. Teresa's *Vida*. Here the mystery of estatic experience comes alive, as it also does in Bernini's magnificent sculpture at Santa Maria della Vittoria (Rome) and in Crashaw's passionate

poem of *The Flaming Heart*. In connection with the last, see Mario Praz's fine essay in *The Flaming Heart* (New York: Doubleday, 1958), pp. 204–63.

30. Plato's *Phaedrus* deals generally with the four madnesses; in his *Ion* he focuses on poetic "madness" and in the *Symposium* on amatory "madness." Marsilio Ficino acknowledges these Platonic sources in his own analysis of the four madnesses (the *furores*) in *Commentary on Plato's "Symposium,"* trans. Sears R. Jayne, *University of Missouri Studies*, 19 (1944), pp. 231–33. Leone Ebreo's consideration of love-ecstasy occurs in his *Dialoghi d'Amore*, available in the translation by F. Friedberg-Seeley and Jean H. Barnes: *The Philosophy of Love* (London: Soncino Press, 1937), p. 176. Bruno's *De gli eroici furori* has been translated by Paul E. Memmo as *The Heroic Frenzies* (Chapel Hill: Univ. of North Carolina Press, 1964). The third dialogue of Part I of Bruno's work asserts that although there are many species of frenzies, all of these may be reduced to two sorts: ". . . blindness, stupidity, and an irrational impulse which tends to bestial folly" and ". . . a certain divine rapture which makes some become superior to ordinary men" (p. 107). In addition to the very useful translation, Memmo's edition offers a substantial introduction, part of which deals with the business of the *furores* as discussed by Plato, Ficino, and Bruno (pp. 17–20).

31. Jayne's trans., p. 231.

32. All references to *The Phoenix and the Turtle* are drawn from F. T. Prince's New Arden edition. The question whether the title of the poem should include the second "the" before "Turtle" is quite important to Murray Copland (pp. 279–80). Frankly, I believe Copland is attempting to split hairs. For a counter-argument to Copland see Empson's introduction to the Signet Classic Shakespeare edition of *Narrative Poems* (p. xxxvi, note).

33. *The Christian Renaissance* (New York: Norton, 1963), pp. 235–37.

34. Cf. Castiglione's discussion of music, the spirit, and ecstasy in *The Book of the Courtier*, trans. Charles S. Singleton (New York: Doubleday, 1959), pp. 74–76, 104–6, 356. Very helpful studies dealing with music, magic, Orphic incantation, and ecstasy are D. P. Walker, *Spiritual and Demonic Magic from Ficino to Campanella* (London: The Warburg Institute, Univ. of London, 1958), esp. pp. 3–29; Walker, "Orpheus the Theologian and Renaissance Platonists," *JWCI*, 16 (1953), 100–20; F. W. Sternfeld, *Music in Shakespearean Tragedy* (London: Routledge & Kegan Paul, 1963), pp. 79–97; Edward J. Dent, "Music in Shakespeare," in *A Companion to Shakespeare Studies*, ed. H. Granville-Barker and G. B. Harrison (1932; rpt. New York: Doubleday, 1960), pp. 142–43 and 156–60; W. H. Auden, "Music in Shakespeare," in *The Dyer's Hand and Other Essays* (New York: Random House, 1968), pp. 507–11; John Hollander, *The Untuning of the Sky* (Princeton: Princeton Univ. Press, 1961), pp. 111, 199–201, 233–38, 353–54, and passim; Gretchen L. Finney, "Ecstasy and Music in Seventeenth-Century England," *JHI*, 8 (April 1947), 153–86; Finney, "'Organical Musick' and Ecstasy," *JHI*, 8 (1947), 273–92; F. W. Sternfeld, "Shakespeare and Music," in *A New Companion to Shakespeare Studies*, ed. Kenneth Muir and S. Schoenbaum (London: Cambridge Univ. Press, 1971), pp. 157–67; Catherine M. Dunn, "The Function of Music in Shakespeare's Romances," *SQ*, 20 (Autumn 1969), 391–405; Edgar Wind, *Pagan Mysteries in the Renaissance* (1958;

rev. ed., London: Penguin, 1967), passim; and Michael Fixler, "The Orphic Technique of 'L'Allegro' and 'Il Penseroso,'" *ELR*, 1 (Spring 1971), 165–77. Jerome Mazzaro's *Transformations in the Renaissance English Lyric* (Ithaca, N.Y.: Cornell Univ. Press, 1970) considers at length the "shift from music and words to music and self-understanding and words and self-understanding . . ." (p. 185). In his Variorum edition of *The Poems*, Rollins tabulates information on "Musical Settings for the Poems" (pp. 610–21). What is quite surprising is that *The Phoenix and the Turtle* has never been set to music. It would make an excellent text for a choral group accompanied by an orchestra. Inga-Stina Ewbank refers to the poem as "incantation" and "song" in *A New Companion to Shakespeare Studies* (p. 105); and in the earlier *Companion to Shakespeare Studies*. George Rylands writes regarding *The Phoenix and the Turtle*: "Shakespeare's own adventure in the metaphysical style combines at once the quality of a proposition in Euclid and of a piece of music" (p. 111).

35. For the Phoenix as soul and the Turtle-Dove as body, see Knight's *Mutual Flame*, pp. 164–65, 186. I agree with Knight in seeing these associations, although I think of them as only one possible set of associations as far as the two central symbols of the poem are concerned.
36. For the relationship between ecstasy, enthusiasm (the "ravishing of the spirit"), and music, consult Hollander, *The Untuning of the Sky*, pp. 199–201, and Finney, p. 179 and passim.
37. *The Complete Poetry of Ben Jonson*, ed. William B. Hunter, Jr. (New York: Doubleday, 1963), p. 334. For informative notes on Jonson's poems in *Loves Martyr* see also pp. 96–101, 333 of Hunter's edition. In commenting on Jonson's *Ode* in *The Mutual Flame*, G. Wilson Knight says nothing about the significance of the poem's title, but he does call John Marston's pieces in *Loves Martyr* the "most ecstatic" of the contributions (p. 194) and points to the first of these, "A Narration and Description of a Most Exact Wondrous Creature, Arising out of the Phoenix and Turtle-Dove's Ashes," as exhibiting "lyric ecstasy" (p. 195). It is clear that Marston's Phoenix does revive. J. B. Leishman has some pages on *The Phoenix and the Turtle*, Jonson's *Ode*, and Donne's *Extasie* in *The Monarch of Wit* (1951; rpt. New York: Harper, 1965), pp. 177, 225.
38. *Commentary on Plato's "Symposium,"* p. 232.
39. *The Landscape of the Mind* (Oxford: Clarendon Press, 1969), pp. 34–35. Edgar Wind, in *Pagan Mysteries in the Renaissance*, deals quite interestingly with the *Emanatio-Raptio-Remeatio* pattern in his discussion of Pico's closely related *Pulchritudo-Amor-Voluptas* triad (pp. 36–52, esp. 37 and 45–46). Ecstasy is also dealt with here.
40. Cody, p. 29.
41. Ibid., p. 76 and passim.
42. Cf. C. S. Lewis, p. 509 (see note 14 above). Monroe Spears, in his introduction to the Laurel Shakespeare edition of the narrative poetry (cited earlier) calls *The Phoenix and the Turtle* an "ontological" poem that speaks of the impossibility of love (pp. 39, 42).

"The *Ipsissima Verba* in My Diary"? Review Article

John F. Andrews

R. A. Foakes's prolific labors over the past two decades have earned him a distinguished reputation as a reviewer, an editor, a scholar, and a critic.[1] Readers of *Shakespeare Studies* will recognize Professor Foakes (who now teaches at the University of Canterbury) as a frequent and valuable contributor to the review sections of this journal. Students of Elizabethan-Jacobean theatrical conditions know him as the editor (in collaboration with R. T. Rickert) of *Henslowe's Diary* (Cambridge: Cambridge Univ. Press, 1961). Shakespeare specialists are indebted to him for fine editions of a number of the playwright's works, including the New Arden editions of *King Henry VIII* (London: Methuen, 1957) and *A Comedy of Errors* (London: Methuen, 1962), and for such critical studies as *Shakespeare: The Dark Comedies to the Last Plays* (Charlottesville: Univ. Press of Virginia, 1971). To have produced all this and more in so short a span is tribute enough to Professor Foakes's acuity and industry. But the clearest testimony to the breadth of his interests and talents is the fact that he has also published widely on nineteenth-century English literature, with two book-length studies that are well recognized: *The Romantic Assertion* (London: Methuen, 1958) and *Romantic Criticism, 1800–1850* (London: Arnold, 1968). In view of Professor Foakes's long and fruitful association with English literature in both the Renaissance and Romantic periods, there would seem to be something of inevitability in the fact that it was he who recently discovered and sought to meet the need for a new edition of Coleridge's 1811–12 lectures on Shakespeare.

Professor Foakes explained the need for a new edition in 1970 in an article in *Shakespeare Survey*;[2] his new edition appeared in 1971. Entitled *Coleridge on Shakespeare: The Text of the Lectures of 1811–12*, the volume was printed in Great Britain and published there by Routledge and Kegan Paul. In the United States it appeared as No. 3 in the distinguished series of Folger Monographs on Tudor and Stuart Civilization and was published for the Folger Shakespeare Library by the University Press of Virginia.

In the preface to his edition, Professor Foakes says that *Coleridge on Shakespeare* "has the nature of an interim report" and that its material "will eventually appear more fully documented, and in greater detail, in the appropriate volume of the *Collected Coleridge*" (p. ix). Professor Foakes's decision to produce this volume before the other Coleridge volumes to come is one for which we may be grateful, because *Coleridge on Shakespeare* seeks to make available for the first time in printed form what is indubitably the most reliable transcript of Coleridge's lectures on Shakespeare in 1811–12.

Coleridge did not publish his own lectures, or even preserve what few notes he made in preparation for them. Brief digests of some of Coleridge's remarks were written for one of the periodicals of the day by reviewers who attended the lectures, but it was not until 1856 that anything approaching a full account of what Coleridge said was put into print. In that year John Payne Collier published a volume entitled *Seven Lectures on Shakespeare and Milton by the Late S. T. Coleridge.*

Two years earlier, Collier had announced his fortuitous discovery of a set of shorthand notes and diary entries he had made at the time of the lectures—ten "brochures" of "memoranda" that he said he had searched for on several occasions but had hitherto been unable to locate. In the 1854 announcement in *Notes and Queries*, Collier had described his notes as "generally very full, and in the *ipsissima verba* of the author" (quoted by Foakes, p. 11). By the time the full text of the lectures appeared in 1856, Collier felt it prudent to modify his assertions of completeness and accuracy, but he still claimed a good deal. "That these were Coleridge's *ipsissima verba* I cannot, at this distance of time, state; but they are the *ipsissima verba* in my Diary . . ." (*Seven Lectures*, p. xxv). Earlier in his introduction to the 1856 text Collier had said, ". . . I am certain, even at this distance of time, that I did not knowingly register a sentence, that did not come from Coleridge's lips, although doubtless I missed, omitted, and mistook points and passages, which now I should have been most rejoiced to have preserved. In completing my transcripts, however, I have added no word or syllable of my own . . ." (pp. vi, vii).

Collier's protestations of veracity were altogether to the point, for by this time he had already come under suspicion as a forger of literary documents, this suspicion owing primarily to his publication in 1852 of some manuscript notes of questionable antiquity that he said he had come across in a copy of a Second Folio of Shakespeare's plays. It was therefore not surprising that his announcement about the newly recovered text of Coleridge's lectures was greeted with some skepticism. In an 1856 pamphlet written under the pseudonym "A Detective," Andrew Edmund Brae demonstrated that the prospectus of the Coleridge talks, which Collier described in his announcement and said was dated 1812, was actually printed in 1811 and left undated. Five years later Brae carried his insinuations about Collier's literary integrity even further. In a review titled *Collier, Coleridge and Shakespeare*, Brae asserted that the reader of Collier's text would "seek in vain for that vivid and peculiar phraseology" that characterized Coleridge, and he dismissed the whole enterprise as a "literary fraud" (quoted by Foakes, pp. 12, 10). Meanwhile, attacks were mounting against the purported antiquity and authority of the Second Folio emendations (which Collier had boldly republished, with a lengthy introduction defending their authenticity, in 1856 in the same volume with the *Seven Lectures*) and by 1861 it could be proven that Collier had written them himself.[3]

Given these facts, one might have expected the *Seven Lectures* to be condemned to oblivion as a fabrication. Evidence uncovered during the next decade (including portions of Henry Crabb Robinson's diary and correspondence), however, supported Collier's testimony that he had attended some of Coleridge's lectures and provided corroboration for parts of his text. Accordingly, Collier's report of the lectures was gradually admitted into the canon of Coleridge's works and was being reprinted by 1883. In this century it has been republished, virtually unchanged, by T. M. Raysor in his two-volume 1930 edition of *Coleridge's Shakespearean Criticism* (Cambridge, Mass.: Harvard Univ. Press) and, with minor revisions, by the same editor in his 1960 Everyman edition of the same title. Raysor's 1930 edition of the 1811–12 lectures, based on Collier's 1856 text, has been the standard for subsequent reprintings of all or part of Coleridge's remarks, and most modern editors have accepted Raysor's verdict (II, 25) on the reliability of Collier's transcripts of the lectures. "No one will believe that they are accurate in detail; nor does Collier claim that they are so. But that Collier could have manufactured out of whole cloth a body of reports so characteristic of Coleridge in his greatest excellences as well as his faults is to attribute to the great literary forger genius rather than dishonesty."

In the superb introduction to his edition of *Coleridge on Shakespeare*, R. A. Foakes offers a strong second to Raysor's verdict. There can be no doubt, he says, that Collier attended at least seven of the seventeen lectures Coleridge delivered in 1811–12; that he took down shorthand notes at some if not all of them; that he then wrote out in longhand fuller versions of the lectures, drawing closely on his shorthand notes; that usually, if not always, he completed the longhand version of the lectures within a day or two after hearing them, while Coleridge's comments were still fresh in his memory; that his reverential attitude toward Coleridge at this time predisposed him to record the sense of Coleridge's remarks as faithfully as possible, and frequently in the very words that Coleridge employed to phrase his thoughts; and that the 1856 text was an edited version of the longhand transcripts that Collier wrote out in 1811–12.

An *edited* version of the 1811–12 longhand transcripts—the italicized word cannot be emphasized too strongly. Brae was wrong in 1869 when he declared that Collier's 1856 text of the Coleridge lectures was a complete forgery. He was perfectly on target, however, when he said that it was often lacking in Coleridge's "vivid and peculiar phraseology." For Collier made hundreds of small alterations in the language of the 45-year-old notes he claimed to be reproducing word for word.

In the preface to the 1856 edition of *Seven Lectures*, Collier implied that the only way he had altered the early transcripts for printing was in shifting from the narrative third person—"with constant repetitions of 'he said,' 'he remarked,' 'he quoted,' &c."—to the first person—" 'I beg you to observe,' 'it is my opinion,' 'we are struck,' &c."—in which he said he had originally recorded the lectures in shorthand (p. xii). In fact, as Foakes demonstrates by comparing numerous passages in the 1856 edition with the corresponding passages in the 1811–12 transcripts (now in the collection of the Folger Shakespeare Library), Collier "continually rewrote and added a great deal of material of his own. Almost every sentence is changed, most commonly by the addition of words or phrases that contribute little to the basic sense of the passage . . ." (p. 22).

> Often these are phrases qualifying a plain statement or a challenging comment by Coleridge, weakening it by "as it were," "sometimes," "in many cases," "generally," "may be said to," or something of this kind. Collier was also fond of duplicating words so that "attribute" in the brochure becomes "trace and attribute"; "with especial pleasure" is altered to "with peculiar pleasure and satisfaction"; "an age of high moral feeling" becomes "an age of high moral feeling and lofty principle," and "England overflowed" is changed to "England may be said to have then overflowed."
>
> (*p. 23*)

Foakes goes on to observe that

> Collier's alterations in 1856 were not all additions and expansions. He made a number of cuts, removing proper names he did not see as relevant, or references he perhaps could not trace, like "Catalania," "Drummond," "Monk Lewis," and "Fata Morgana." He also left out, for no clear reason, some phrases that help to explain Coleridge's thinking; so, for example, in Lecture 7, Coleridge described Mercutio, according to the brochures, as "a man possessing all the elements of a Poet: high fancy; rapid thoughts; the whole world was, as it were, subject to his law of association." In the 1856 text the words "high fancy; rapid thoughts" were omitted, a phrase which makes Coleridge's meaning more precise.
>
> (*p. 25*)

Occasionally the 1856 text differs slightly by substituting alternate words for those in the 1811–12 text. To avoid repetitions or to "elevate" the style, for instance, Collier did such things as replace "works" with "'productions." Other alterations involve emendations evidently intended to clarify or "improve" the meaning of a passage.

> Some changes of a single word affect the sense radically, as, in Coleridge's description of Ariel, "moral" in the brochures is changed to "mortal" in the 1856 text: in the early text, Shakespeare, it is said, "divests him of all moral character," and in the 1856 text this has become "divests him of all mortal character." Collier's alterations are not neutral; they frequently alter the sense in subtle ways, and sometimes drastically.
>
> (*p. 24*)

These few illustrative instances point toward what a complete collation of the 1811–12 and 1856 texts makes indisputably clear: that the 1856 text that Collier published—with its myriad of omissions, additions, and other departures from the wording of the brochures of 1811–12—is a far cry from "the *ipsissima verba* of my Diary." What R. A. Foakes has attempted in his new edition of *Coleridge on Shakespeare* is what John Payne Collier claimed to be doing in 1856: to provide a printed version of the memoranda preserved in Collier's early diary.

The textual apparatus is in many ways excellent. Foakes begins with a twenty-nine-page introduction, which includes a concise summary of essential biographical information about Collier; a brief sampling from his early diary entries (which reveal him as an impressionable youth whose admiration of Coleridge extended almost to hero worship); photographs of pages in the brochures and in the shorthand notes; a judicious survey of the nineteenth-century controversy over Collier's integrity as an editor; an admirably documented and altogether convincing argument that the 1856 text, though not a forgery, is nevertheless not a completely trustworthy account of what Coleridge said in 1811–12; and a note on the presentation of the text.

The introduction is followed by a chapter reprinting the entries in Collier's diary relating to Coleridge during the months of October and November 1811. Collier had included some excerpts from this portion of his diary in the 1856 edition—as parts of the preface defending the authenticity of his text of Coleridge's lectures—but he had edited the diary entries just as thoroughly as he had edited the transcripts of the lectures. These October–November entries, which were made before Coleridge began delivering his public lectures, record a number of memorable observations both by and about Coleridge, and Foakes renders a good service in publishing them.

The bulk of the remainder of the volume is devoted to a reprinting of the transcripts of Lectures 1, 2, 6, 7, 8, 9, and 12. Lectures 1 and 2 are recorded as parts of larger entries in Collier's diary, and Foakes exercises good editorial judgment by printing most of these entries in their entirety. He also prints other entries, such as that for Wednesday, November 27, 1811, in which Collier records his reading and writing activities for the day and recalls the evening's conversations about Coleridge with such contemporaries as Hazlitt and Lamb. Professor Foakes's rich knowledge of history, biography, and wide ranges of literature is put to good use in this section of *Coleridge on Shakespeare*, which contains numerous footnotes illuminating quotations, allusions, and difficult passages.

The main text is followed by three valuable appendixes. In Appendix A, Professor Foakes reprints from the 1856 preface the quotations that Collier said he was taking directly from his diary entries about Coleridge's conversation. This allows for convenient comparison of the 1811 notes with the 1856 edition of them and shows the extent to which Collier was rewriting and altering the language he claimed to be presenting verbatim. In Appendix B, Foakes provides brief but thorough descriptions of the ten sewn gatherings (what Collier referred to as "brochures"), known as Folger MS. M.a. 219–28, upon which his text of *Coleridge on Shakespeare* is based. In Appendix C, which is the most interesting and useful of the three appendixes, Foakes describes the shorthand alphabet employed by Collier, summarizes the process by which he was able to work out rough translations of the two shorthand notebooks recording Lectures 9 and 12, and compares three versions (shorthand, 1812 transcript, 1856 edition) of a passage from Lecture 9. On the basis of this comparison, Foakes concludes—correctly, in my opinion—that

> the long-hand transcriptions made soon after the lectures were given, and printed for the first time in this volume, are based on the short-hand notes, and represent a polished version of them. Collier seems to have amplified and corrected from memory what he set down in the course of the lecture, and since he did this soon after the lectures were delivered, the text of his early transcriptions may be presumed to be close, usually very close, to what Coleridge actually said.
>
> (*p. 159*)

Foakes notes further:

> It is true that this omits some phrases and sentences of the short-hand notes, probably because Collier himself could not make sense at these points, and there is little reason to suppose that we can now adequately reconstruct what Coleridge was saying. At the same time, the early tran-

> scripts, made, if I am right, when the lectures were fresh in Collier's mind, fill out the short-hand notes with what he recollected, and provide us with the best text available, even if it does not at all points offer the very words Coleridge spoke.
>
> (*pp. 160, 161*)

One reviewer of Professor Foakes's edition of *Coleridge on Shakespeare*, writing anonymously for *The Times Literary Supplement* (27 August 1971, p. 1033), has questioned the need to replace Collier's 1856 text as the definitive version of the 1811–12 lectures. He argues that in Collier's 1811–12 transcripts of his shorthand notes "he dressed up the bare bones of his notes as well as he could by the light of what he could remember and of what he had heard Coleridge say on other occasions" and that in 1856 he did nothing worse than "to convert them from the third to the first person and also to dress them up a little more by the light of what he had since learnt, generally, of life and letters." He further asserts that "not all Professor Foakes' ingenuity can establish a strong case for really wanton interpolations." He concludes his review by saying that ". . . it is greatly to be hoped that Collier's proverbially bad name may not lead to the supersession of his carefully considered version by this rougher product that is also his, in the fond hope that the latter is 'more authoritative.' "

In my own mind there is no doubt that the version of the lectures represented in Collier's 1811–12 transcripts is considerably more authoritative than that represented in his 1856 edition. The 1856 text may read more smoothly in places, but all too frequently its smoothness is purchased very dearly. Collier is seldom if ever guilty of "really wanton interpolations," nor does Professor Foakes accuse him of being so. On the other hand, the wording of Collier's 1856 edition quite often differs markedly from that of his 1811–12 transcripts, and it strikes me as exceedingly unlikely that Collier remembered Coleridge's remarks more accurately forty-five years after they were delivered than he did less than forty-five hours after they were delivered.

I have little doubt, therefore, that future editions of the 1811–12 lectures on Shakespeare will be based on the Folger manuscripts that Foakes has made available for the first time in *Coleridge on Shakespeare.* I do doubt, however, that this 1971 version of the lectures, even when it appears "more fully documented, and in greater detail, in the appropriate volume of the *Collected Coleridge*," will become the definitive published version of that material. We should be thankful for Professor Foakes's promise to follow this "interim report" with a second edition of Coleridge's 1811–12 lectures on Shakespeare, for the significant achievement represented by the present volume is marred by a surprisingly large number of imperfections in the presentation of its text.

I have had the opportunity to examine the Collier transcripts in the Folger

Shakespeare Library and to compare them with Professor Foakes's edition based on them. One relatively minor thing that impressed me early in the process of collation was that the editor apparently failed to apply any policy consistently with regard to the treatment of accidental features of the text.

The usual practice in Professor Foakes's edition is to modernize or standardize spellings. Accordingly, spellings such as *develope, groupe, stye, melancholly, compells, mysery, controul, pourtrayed, axium, prudencial, devining,* and *surprize* are always normalized. With other spellings, however—such as *shew, transitoryness, comprize, leizure, phraze, phrazeology,* and *advertized*—Foakes sometimes normalizes and sometimes reproduces the spelling in the manuscript.

A similar capriciousness is observable in the treatment of capitalization. Rather like Carlyle, Collier tends to capitalize words for special emphasis; for the most part, Foakes's edition preserves this stylistic trait. There are frequent exceptions, however.

p. 37 The word "supper" should be capitalized in the clause "After Dinner Coleridge gave us a few of his definitions as well as after Supper. . . ."

p. 45 The word "sun" should be capitalized in the phrase "like the Sun the Spring or the Showers." (Here and elsewhere I am quoting the text as represented in Collier's MS, including peculiarities of punctuation and abbreviation.)

p. 49 The words "sublime" and "majestic" should be capitalized in the phrase "as well as the epithets, Sublime Majestic, grand, striking picturesque &c." In the following line, "he" should be capitalized following the dash: "He related the following anecdote—He was surveying. . . ."

p. 52 The word "evening" should be capitalized in the clause "This Evening Coleridge delivered his second Lecture. . . ."

p. 59 The word "elements" should be capitalized in the phrase "complaining to the Elements & accusing them of ingratitude. . . ."

p. 63 The line "*W. Hazlitt* as naturally as that an African should be a black." should read "*W. Hazlitt* As naturally as that an African should be a black." Similarly, two lines later, "*C. Lamb* had compared Halliday's translation of Persius and found it better than the original." should read "*C. Lamb.* Had compared Hallidays translation of Persius and found it better than the original."

p. 70 The word "puns" should be capitalized in the clause "they would find not only that conceits but even Puns were very natural."

p. 99 The word "stage" should be capitalized in the clause "Early in the lectures the Greek Stage had been noticed. . . ."

Several other examples of failure to capitalize as in the Collier manuscripts could be cited. Of perhaps more interest are several instances in which Foakes employs uppercase where Collier's manuscripts employ lowercase.

p. 39 "It" should be lowercase in the passage "than which nothing could be worse: it degraded them to a level with brutes. . . ."

p. 57 "Latin" is written in lowercase in Collier's MS in the phrase "a just latin maxim."

p. 70 "Nature" should be printed lowercase in the clause "He could point out Puns in Shakespeare where they seemed as it were the first openings of the mouth of nature. . . ."

p. 103 "Work" should be printed lowercase in the clause "Yesterday afternoon a friend had left for him a work by a German writer. . . ."

p. 110 "Lady" should be lowercase in the clause "The Lecturer knew a young lady of much taste. . . ." Moreover, "Poetry" should be lowercase in the clause "The power of poetry is by a single word. . . ."

Again, other instances could be cited, but these will serve to illustrate how frequently Foakes's text, while appearing to reproduce Collier's peculiar capitalization practice with minute fidelity, actually proves misleading.

Related to this is Professor Foakes's treatment of Collier's abbreviations. As the editor points out in his preface, his normal procedure for contractions such as "w^{ch}" ("which") is to expand to full spellings. Much of the time, Foakes does the same for abbreviations of ordinal numerals. Thus, for instance, Foakes's text reads "third Lecture" on page 44, where the Collier manuscript reads "3^{d}. Lecture." On many occasions, however, Foakes retains the numeral form, but renders it "3rd" instead of "3^{d}" as Collier almost invariably spells it. Foakes generally renders cardinal numbers just as Collier does. Thus, on page 31 we read, "I went into the room where he and many more were at ½ past 8, and before a quarter past 9. . . ." But there are a few places where the numbers are spelled out in Foakes's text. On page 101, for instance, Collier's MS reads "24" twice where Foakes's text reads "twenty-four" in the sentence beginning "The limit allowed by the Greeks was 24 hours. . . ."

Normally in Collier's MS, titles of works are not underscored or placed in quotations. Most of the time, especially in his text of the later lectures, Foakes preserves this peculiarity by printing the titles in roman type without quotation marks. It seldom if ever causes any ambiguity. Often, though, and usually for no apparent reason, Foakes departs from his customary practice and employs italics. Among the instances are the following: "*Samson Agonistes*" (p. 33), "*Arabian Nights Entertainments*" (p. 35), "*Gulliver's Travels*" (p. 53), "*Ham-*

let, King Lear, Macbeth" (p. 57), "*Lear*" and "*Oedipus*" (p. 58), "*Vanity of Human Wishes*" and "*London*" (p. 62).

There are several other occasions when Foakes's text employs roman type for words and phrases italicized in the Collier brochures.

p. 54 The fifth of six italicized clauses presenting Coleridge's definition of poetry is printed incorrectly in roman type: "*The work must be so constructed, . . . pleasure.*"

p. 57 The Latin clause " '*Oportet discentem judicare, edoctum credere*' " should be italicized as in the brochure.

p. 69 The word "spendthriftness" should be italicized in the phrase " 'the pomp and *spendthriftness* of Heaven.' " It is italicized in the brochure and in the 1856 edition, page 41.

Three of the words italicized in Professor Foakes's text are underscored in pencil rather than pen in Collier's MS. It is by no means clear that these words were meant to be italicized, for all three are printed in roman type in the 1856 text.

p. 75 "From thence he passed on to the Love's Labour['s] Lost as the *link* between his character as a Poet and a Dramatist. . . ."

p. 82 "A Skeleton, perhaps the *dryest* image that could be discovered. . . ."

p. 103 "It was not a little wonderful that so many ages had elapsed since the time of Shakespeare and that it should remain for *foreigners* first to feel truly . . . his mighty genius."

It seems possible that Collier underscored these words relatively late, perhaps in the 1850s when he was preparing copy for his printer (one finds numerous other pencil marks in the brochures, such as vertical lines through footnotes that, it turns out, are omitted from the 1856 text), and that the words so marked were, in some cases at least, words whose correctness he queried. Even if he did underscore some of them with the intention of having them italicized in print, we should not accord them the same degree of authority as the underscorings done in ink and, with a few possible exceptions, done while Coleridge's words and emphases were still fresh in Collier's memory. At the very least, we should expect the editor to call attention to these instances of penciled underscorings in a note somewhere in his edition.

There are several other occasions where needed editorial notes have not been supplied in *Coleridge on Shakespeare*. The following may serve as illustrations.

p. 86 The last sentence of a difficult passage reads: "In Shakespeare they were every where introduced with respect & he had acted upon them and had drawn his characters as seriously influenced by them." In the MS, the letters "*Qy.*" are written and circled (in ink) to the left of this sentence, indicating that the statement was apparently obscure enough to Collier that he queried the accuracy of his transcription of Coleridge's words.

p. 102 The word "askance" (spelled "ascance" in MS) is underscored in pencil, apparently to query it, in the phrase "when the glorious beams are shot ascance the mountain."

p. 126 In the line "Great wit to madness, nearly is allied," Collier underscored "*nearly*" and wrote "*qu*" in the margin (both in ink, and apparently while he was transcribing the line for the first time). He probably realized that he (or Coleridge) had recalled Dryden's line inaccurately: "Great Wits are sure to madness near alli'd."

In his "Notes on the presentation of the Text" (p. 28), Professor Foakes says:

> Collier frequently, but not invariably, used contractions for some common words, like the ampersand for "and," and "w^{ch}" for "which"; I have silently expanded all of these. Occasionally he repeated a word, and all such duplications have been omitted. At other times he inadvertently left a word out, or wrote half a word at the end of a line, and omitted to complete it at the beginning of the next. In such cases I have supplied a word, or completed one, but all such additions are enclosed in square brackets.

Inasmuch as Professor Foakes says nothing about any other substantive editorial emendations of the text, the reader naturally infers that if there are any, they are called attention to somewhere in the notes. Collation indicates, however, that the editor has made a large number of silent corrections that do not fall into the categories mentioned in his "Notes on the presentation of the Text." Some of them seem worth pointing out.

p. 38 The Collier MS's "that" has been silently emended to "than" in the phrase "nothing more erroneous that this assertion." (Foakes's text incorrectly reads "erronious.")

p. 61 Collier's "Saml." has been altered to "Sam" in the phrase "to remind Colleridge of D^{r}. Saml. Johnson."

p. 67 The word "others" has been changed to "other" in the phrase "even furnish to others men's minds."

p. 78 The word "have" has been altered to "has" in the clause "but even in the subordinate personages the passion is made instructive (Foakes's text incorrectly reads 'instinctive') at least even if it have not been an individual. . . ."

p. 87 The word "in" has been emended to "and" in the phrase "In Beaumont in Fletcher."

p. 89 Professor Foakes has slightly misrepresented the MS with one of his editorial alterations. The MS reads "Whe- / there is a Universe," and the editor corrects it to read "Whether [there] is" rather than "Whe[ther] there is."

p. 89 The word "the" has been silently altered to "that" in the phrase "the dew that glistens."

p. 110 "Grandos" has been silently emended to "Grandees" in the clause "she saw such and such Grandos. . . ."

What is disturbing about these silent editorial alterations is not so much the fact that the editor has made them (most of the emendations are perfectly justified, even necessary) as the fact that he nowhere gives any indication that many of these kinds of emendations needed to be made. Indeed, by calling attention in footnotes to a number of emendations of obvious manuscript errors (see, for instance, those on pp. 34, 55, 66, 87, 101, 102, 109, 114), many of them no different in kind or degree from those I have listed, Foakes enhances the impression that he has made no silent emendations other than those in the categories listed in the "Notes."

In some instances Professor Foakes's bracketed emendations are left insufficiently explained, as the following examples will illustrate.

p. 43 The reader is left to wonder whether, in the phrase "Of the story of Cain [and] *Abel*," the word "[and]" fills a blank left in the manuscript, is inserted between two words standing side by side in the manuscript, or replaces another word in the manuscript. It would not have been difficult for the editor to note that Collier wrote "Of the story of Cain of *Abel*."

p. 104 In the lines "The [physiognomy] of shades, and give / Them sudden birth, wondering how [oft they live,]" the editor might have pointed out that the word "[physiognomy]" replaces a blank space and that the phrase "[oft they live]" replaces the word "fate."

pp. 104–5 The editor might have noted that the bracketed lines "[Senseless . . . hurl'd]" occur where Collier left several lines blank in the MS (indicating that he was aware of the omission at the time he was transcribing Coleridge's lectures), whereas the bracketed lines "[and, by elaborate play, . . . ourselves:—]" occur where Collier left no blank space to indicate omission (perhaps because Coleridge omitted these lines when delivering his lecture, and Collier was unaware of the omission when transcribing Coleridge's remarks).

If it is somewhat surprising that Foakes's notes on this last passage give no indication of what the bracketed words and lines in his text replace in Collier's

MS, it is well-nigh astonishing that the editor provides no note to say that he has silently emended ten words in the part of the quotation that extends over to page 105. Collier's MS reads:[4]

To raise ~~the~~ our ancient Sovereigns
from their herse
Make Kings & subjects by exchanging
~~of~~ verse
their old trunks that the pre-
sent age
Joys in their joys & trembles in their
rage
Yet so to temper passion that our ears
Take pleasure at their pain & eyes
in tears
Both weep & smile, fearful at plots
so sad
Then laughting at our fear beside
and glad
To be beside affected with that truth
Which we perceive is false pleased
in that ruth
At which we start. ~~This & much more~~
This & much more which cannot be
expressed
But by himself, his tongue & his—
own breast
Was Shakespeare wch his cunning
brain
Improved by favour of the seven fold
train

Foakes's text reads as follows (with my italics indicating his silent emendations):

To raise our ancient Sovereigns from their hearse,
Make Kings *his* subjects; by exchanging verse
[Enlive] their *pale* trunks; that the present age
Joys *at* their *joy*, and trembles *at* their rage:
Yet so to temper passion, that our ears
Take pleasure *in* their pain, and eyes in tears

Both weep and smile; fearful at plots so sad,
Then *laughing* at our fear; *abus'd*, and glad
To be *abus'd*; affected with that truth
Which we perceive is false, pleas'd in that ruth
At which we start, [and, by elaborate play,
Tortur'd and tickl'd; by a crab-like way
Time past made pastime; and in ugly sort
Disgorging up his ravin for our sport:—
—While the plebeian imp, from lofty throne,
Creates and rules a world, and works upon
Mankind by secret engines; now to move
A chilling pity, then a rigorous love;
To strike up and stroke down, both joy and ire
To steer th'affections; and by heavenly fire
Mold us anew, stol'n from ourselves:—]
This, and much more, which cannot be express'd
But by himself, his tongue and his own breast
Was Shakespeare['s freehold;] which his cunning brain
Improv'd by favour of the *nine*-fold train.

The inaccuracy of Collier's transcript of these lines may reflect something either about Coleridge's recollection of the lines he was quoting (if he was quoting from memory) or, as appears much more likely, about Collier's ability to record a speaker's words verbatim by means of the shorthand he employed. It is interesting to observe, for instance, that three of the incorrect words are prepositions and that a fourth is a short article; the most probable explanation is that Collier did not record anything but what he regarded as the important words in his shorthand notes, relying on memory to supply the missing connectives. It is also interesting to observe that Collier twice transcribes *beside* in positions where Coleridge almost surely said *abus'd*. If Professor Foakes is correct in saying that Collier's shorthand alphabet contained only consonants, it is easy to see how symbols for *b s d* could be read *beside* rather than *abus'd*. In any event, such inaccuracy (or accuracy, depending on one's point of view) is certainly a revealing piece of data relative to the question of the reliability of Collier's transcripts of the Coleridge lectures as a whole. It is to be hoped that when Professor Foakes publishes a revised edition of *Coleridge on Shakespeare*, he will print this passage as it appears in Collier's MS and devote some space to a discussion of its possible implications. A passage that offers so many possibilities for close (and, I would argue, necessary) examination of the Collier text should not be passed over lightly.

Nor should one pass over lightly—as it seems to me that Professor Foakes has done—the large number of manuscript deletions, corrections, and interlineations in Collier's brochures. What Foakes says about this feature of Collier's text reveals, I think, a surprising lack of sensitivity to some of the editorial problems that his new edition of the Coleridge lectures inevitably raises.

> Collier also made a number of corrections in the manuscript, and added some interlineations. These are of various kinds. Sometimes he mis-spelt a word, deleted it and started again. He also occasionally made a false start or misinterpreted his short-hand, as in Lecture 9 he wrote "which," then deleted it and substituted "while," clearly the correct word. In a similar way a little later he deleted "predominant" and substituted "prominent," and replaced "intensely" by "intentionally." In all such cases I have simply printed Collier's final version, as I have done also in other instances where he substituted alternative words for those he first wrote. These may represent revisions as he went along, or changes made later, but in any case do not seriously affect the text.
>
> (*p. 28*)

In the sentences that follow, Foakes lists what he considers "the most interesting" of Collier's manuscript revisions. Many of the revisions he lists "do not seriously affect the text," if by this phrase one means only radical alterations in meaning. But very few of the alternative words that Foakes lists are exact synonyms, totally without shades of difference in denotation or connotation. And some of the alternative words do introduce significant changes in meaning. What is true of the alterations listed on page 28 is also true of the relatively small number of alterations noted in footnotes in the main body of the text. It is true as well of the larger number of revisions that are never noted at all, let alone discussed, anywhere in *Coleridge on Shakespeare.* If we assume —as Professor Foakes would have us assume—that the basic rationale for printing Collier's early transcripts is to recover as much as is now possible of exactly what Coleridge said in 1811–12 (preserving as much as is possible Coleridge's own "vivid and peculiar phraseology"), then it is conceivable that many—perhaps most—of Collier's revisions *do* seriously affect the text.

On page 12 of his edition, Professor Foakes quotes with approbation a statement about Collier by G. F. Warner: "None of his statements or quotations can be trusted without verifying, and no volume or document that passed through his hands can be too carefully scrutinised." I would infer from Professor Foakes's silence about many of Collier's manuscript revisions that he intends to postpone careful scrutiny of them until he is able to publish his revised, "more fully documented" edition of the text. Inasmuch as the present edition includes no statement indicating the amount of scrutiny required, however, I shall take the liberty to discuss some of the revisions and the editorial problems they seem to me to indicate. To keep the discussion within manageable limits, I will focus almost entirely on revisions that receive no mention anywhere in *Coleridge on Shakespeare.*

One of the most provocative statements ever attributed to Coleridge occurs in Collier's diary entry for Sunday, October 13, 1811. As it appears in Foakes's text, the assertion is "That Falstaff was no Coward but pretended to be one merely for the sake of trying experiments on mankind!!" (p. 30). In the MS, "trying experiments on" is written above the line and replaces a crossed-out phrase that reads "incurring the contempt of." It seems highly probable that Coleridge actually said "That Falstaff was no Coward but pretended to be one merely for the sake of incurring the contempt of mankind." Apparently Collier, looking back over the passage at a later time, perhaps, and finding the phrasing awkward or unclear, decided to "improve" it.

In the diary entry for Thursday, October 17, Collier replaced "created" by "manufactured" in the sentence (p. 33) "Talent was a manufactured thing; genius was born." Most of us would probably agree with Collier that "manufactured" is preferable here; but is this the word that Coleridge employed? Later in the same entry, Collier added the words "a quarter" above the line in the sentence (p. 34) "He would require more than a Herchellean Telescope of 10 feet diameter for him to see half a quarter as far." Collier printed "half a quarter" when he quoted from this entry in the preface (p. xxvii) to his 1856 edition. My suspicion, nevertheless, is that Coleridge actually said either "half as far" or "a quarter as far" and that when Collier added "a quarter" in his MS, he originally intended to cross out "half." A few paragraphs later in the October 17 entry, Collier altered "the army was filled with the greatest number of blackguards" to "the greater part of the army was composed of such blackguards" (p. 35). Again, the revision makes the passage seem more comprehensible, but does it capture Coleridge's actual statement more accurately?

Collier's transcripts for the lectures themselves contain dozens of revisions that seem worth noting. I shall list and discuss them in order of occurrence.

p. 53 Early in Lecture 2, the clause "but the parties never thought of enquiring what was meant by the words *Poet* w$^{ch.}$ they used as by *Poetry*" is changed to "by the words *Poet* or *Poetry.*" It appears likely that Collier originally wrote "word" and added an *s* when he decided to revise the last words of the sentence.

p. 54 Collier interlined the phrase "in words" to render Coleridge's definition of poetry as follows: "It is an art . . . of representing in words external nature. . . ." A few lines later, Collier interlined "minuteness" to yield the clause "excepting that the latter describe with more truth minuteness and accuracy than is consistent with Poetry."

p. 56 Collier scratched out "softness" and interlined "sweetness" in the quotation from *L'Allegro*, "With many a bout / Of linked sweetness long drawn out"—another revision that seems to illustrate the difficulties Collier encountered in transcribing from a shorthand system that contained no symbols for vowels.

p. 69 Midway through Lecture 6, Collier changed "kind" to "species" in the phrase "might fit them more for one species of Poetry than another." As he was transcribing the next paragraph, Collier crossed out "decently" and went on to write "with dignity" in the sentence "In Italian things might be represented naturally yet with dignity." In the following paragraph, Collier interlined "modern" to produce the clause "But in the English he saw that which was possessed by no other modern language. . . ." In the penultimate paragraph printed on page 69, Collier interlined "nearly" to yield the clause "because they had not as we had two words with nearly the same meaning. . . ." This interpolation, like the one immediately preceding it, involves a qualification that may well have been Collier's rather than Coleridge's.

p. 74 Near the end of the transcript for Lecture 6, Collier crossed out "an" and interlined "the best" to yield the clause "because it gave him the best opportunity of introducing Shakespeare. . . ."

p. 75 Early in his summary of Lecture 7, Collier crossed out "light" and went on to write "dazling [*sic*] light," yielding the phrase "derived from the dazling light which a man of genius throws over every circumstance."

p. 77 Collier interlined "predominant" to produce the phrase "the one predominant passion acting as the leader of the band to the rest."

p. 78 Collier crossed out "of its" and went on to write "in its" in the phrase "having formed a theory and a system in its own nature."

p. 82 Collier crossed out "becomes," wrote "is" above it, and then interlined "on one," so that the original clause "as soon as it becomes understanding" was altered to read "as soon as it is fixed on one it becomes understanding. . . ."

p. 83 Collier added the qualifier "even" to yield the clause "at the time this great Poet lived there was an attempt at and an affectation of quaintness w[ch] emanated even from the Court"—a small alteration but one that significantly affects the meaning of the passage.

p. 84 Collier interlined "of itself" to produce the sentence "It is inevitable to every noble mind whether man or woman to feel itself of itself imperfect and insufficient, not as an animal merely but altogether as a moral being." Just what "of itself" adds to the meaning of this sentence I find difficult to discern. Is it possible that Collier intended to cross out the original "itself" and replace it with "*in* itself"?

p. 85 Collier began a paragraph with the conditional clause "If God has given us all these blessings" and then scratched it out; he thereupon wrote "Providence then has not left us to Prudence only for the power of calculation which prudence impels cannot have existed but in a state which pre-supposes the Marriage State." The following sentence reads "If God has done this shall we suppose that he has given us no moral sense . . ." Here it appears that Collier got ahead of his shorthand notes at the beginning of the paragraph; the second sentence of the final transcript seems to be a completion of the idea initiated in the excised sentence. But the second sentence differs enough from the scratched-out sentence that one cannot help speculating just what was in the shorthand notes at this point.

p. 86 Collier crossed out "beings" and wrote "things" above it in the passage "they were looked upon as hints which Philosophy could not explain: as the terra incognita for future discoveries; the great ocean of unknown things to be afterwards explored."

p. 87 Collier interlined "of" and changed "passion" to "nature" in the clause "Wherever love is described as *of* a serious *nature*, & much more when it is to lead to a tragical end it depends on a law of the mind which Coleridge believed he should make intelligible . . ." (italics mine).

p. 89 Near the beginning of Lecture 8, Collier interlined "particular" to yield the phrase "tho' not the slaves of any particular sectarian opinions." Three paragraphs later, he changed "upon" to "to" in the clause "he sho^{d}. make some demand on the attention of his hearers, to a most important subject. . . ."

p. 90 In the concluding clause of the same sentence, Collier interlined "mainly": ". . . a most important subject upon which mainly depends all the sense of the worthyness or the unworthyness of of our nature. . . ." In the next paragraph, Collier crossed out "persons" and interlined "writers" in the sentence "Certainly that 'Gentleman of Europe' that all-accomplished man and our great Shakespeare were the only writers of that age who pitched their ideas of female perfections according to the best researches of philosophy. . . ."

p. 92 Collier interlined "friendship or a" to yield the clause "name it friendship or a sense of duty. . . ."

p. 93 Collier added "a deadly" to produce the clause "or when a parent was transported at the restoration of a beloved child from a deadly sickness. . . ."

p. 94 Collier crossed out "in our" and then went on to write "perhaps dormant in our" in the phrase "yet unrealized excellences perhaps dormant in our nature." Three paragraphs later, Collier crossed out "secured" and went on to write "& Providence secured" to yield the sentence "The question is how has nature & Providence secured these blessing to us?" This example illustrates, I believe, the extent to which Collier may have been adding clarifying or qualifying phrases to "improve" Coleridge's statements even as he was transcribing his shorthand notes for the first time. It illustrates as well the sort of awkward (and ungrammatical) phrasing that often results from Collier's revisions—something that Professor Foakes would do well to point out in his future edition by means of explanatory notes on such passages.

p. 95 Collier interlined "young" to produce the clause "a new young visitor is introduced to the family. . . ."

p. 98 In the first paragraph of Lecture 9, Collier crossed out "& others" following the phrase "notwithstanding the admiration bestowed upon the ancient paintings of Apelles"—probably because he realized he had misplaced the two words, which occur in the immediately succeeding phrase "by Pliny and others." In the following sentence, Collier deleted "never" and interlined "not" in the clause "had Titian not lived the richness of representation by colour even there could never have existed." The revision in this case was probably determined by Collier's desire to avoid repeating "never."

p. 99 Collier crossed out "sculpture" and went on to write "statuary" in the phrase "compared to painting and statuary." A few lines later, he crossed out "beings" and went on to write "figures" in the clause "which would prevent a great many figures from being combined into the same effects."

p. 101 Collier crossed out "Poet" and went on to write "Dramatist" in the clause "the grandest effort of the Dramatist to be the mirror of life is completely lost." Two paragraphs later, Collier crossed out an entire line, apparently because he noticed he had misplaced a phrase. He first wrote "Coleridge had seen some plays so well acted & so ill understood"; then he crossed out "some" and "so well acted & so ill understood" and concluded with the following sentence: "Coleridge had seen plays some translated and some the growth of our soil so well acted & so ill written that if the auditor could have produced an artificial deafness he would have been much pleased with the performance as a pantomime."

p. 102 Collier crossed out "the" and "of Shakespeare" and wrote "his" above "the" in the phrase "the peculiarities of Shakespeare" to avoid repetition and yield the clause "since Shakespeares time none of our Critics seem [Foakes silently emends to "seems"] to enter into his peculiarities."

p. 103 Collier deleted "all the" and went on to write "every" in the clause "they perhaps exceeded every people of the globe."

p. 105 Collier deleted "predominantly" and went on to write "prominent" in the clause "in which the ideal is more prominent to the mind. . . ."

p. 106 Collier crossed out "one" and went on to write "a" in the phrase "producing a discordant mass of genius." Three paragraphs later, Collier interlined "happy" to produce the clause "A great part of the Genius of Shakespeare consisted of these happy combinations of the highest & lowest. . . ."

p. 109 Collier deleted "reader" and interlined "audience" in the phrase "informing the audience of the story." In the next sentence, Collier crossed out "means" and went on to write "proof" in the phrase "his first & mildest proof of his magical power."

p. 110 Collier added "happy" to yield the phrase "by introducing the simple happy epithet *crying*." In the following paragraph, he added the word "ordinary" in the clause "The fact of Miranda being charmed asleep fits us for what goes beyond our ordinary belief. . . ."

p. 111 In a sentence printed near the top of this page, Collier first wrote "the reader was prepared to exert his imagination for an object so interesting and lovely." He then crossed out the words "and lovely" and went on to write the next sentence: "The Poet made him wish that if supernatural agency were employed it should be used for a being so lovely." Here Collier may have anticipated as he transcribed from his shorthand notes—unless, as also seems plausible, he deleted "and lovely" at a later time when he reread the passage and noticed the repetition of "so lovely" in the next sentence. Two paragraphs later, Collier interlined "the story of" to yield the phrase "as in the story of King Lear." In the following paragraph, Collier first wrote "If ever there could be a doubt that Shakespeare was a great Poet acting by laws arising out of his own nature it would"; he then crossed out "it would" and continued "and not acting without law as had been asserted it would be removed by the character of Ariel." Here again Collier may have anticipated as he transcribed. On the other hand, it seems possible that he decided to insert "and not acting without law as had been asserted" as a transitional clarifying phrase.

p. 112 Collier deleted "to Ariel" from the original phrasing "when Shakespeare contrasts the treatment of Prospero to Ariel with that of Sycorax"—the deletion in this case apparently arising from Collier's sense that the sentence as originally written was slightly awkward. Two paragraphs later, Collier deleted "being" and went on to write "creature" in the phrase "a monstrous unnatural creature."

p. 113 Collier crossed out a phrase that seems to read "by his vices" and went on to write "in two ways" in the passage "he is a sort of creature of the earth, partaking of the qualities of the brute and distinguished from them in two ways 1 By having mere understanding without moral reason 2 By not having the instincts which belong to mere animals."

pp. 113–14 Collier crossed out "blank" and interlined "chasm" in the clause "yet it would leave in Coleridges opinion a complete chasm if it were omitted."

p. 115 In the final paragraph of Lecture 9, Collier first wrote ". . . Shakespeare whom he declared to be the wonder of mankind"; he then deleted "mankind" and completed the phrase so that it reads " . . . Shakespeare whom he declared to be the wonder of the ignorant part of mankind."

p. 116 In the second paragraph of Lecture 12, Collier deleted the first "Henry" from the phrase "under the name of Henry Bolingbroke or Henry 4th"—clearly to avoid a repetition.

p. 117 In a sentence printed near the top of the page, Collier added the interlined phrase "at first sight" to yield the clause "this great man could take two characters which seem to be the same at first sight and yet when minutely examined are totally distinct." Three paragraphs later, Collier crossed out "earliest" and interlined "earnest" in the clause "York is a man of no strong powers of mind but of earnest wishes to do right. . . ." In the last sentence on the page, Collier deleted "the" and went on to write "one of the" to yield the phrase "As one of the great objects of these lectures."

p. 119 Collier crossed out "was" and went on to write "originated" in the clause "by far the greater part of the filth heaped upon Shakespeare originated in this circumstance." In the next sentence he interlined "or a play upon words" in the phrase "and can no more withstand a pun or a play upon words than his Antony could Cleopatra." In the second sentence of the next paragraph, Collier crossed out the first "altogether" in the phrase "are altogether misplaced in a man, and altogether unfit for a King." In the last line on the page, Collier crossed out "It was true" preceding "Dr Johnson"; the next sentence begins, "It was true, Coleridge admitted . . ."

p. 121 Collier crossed out "instance" and wrote "stages" in the clause "of which he was himself unconscious in the first stages."

p. 122 Collier crossed out "it" and interlined "The answer" and a few words later interlined the phrase "tone of the" to yield the sentence "The answer is in unison with the tone of the passion. . . ." In the last paragraph, Collier crossed out "that" and went on to write "to shew that" in the clause "the reason Shakespeare used the personal pronoun 'his' was to shew that altho Bolingbroke was only speaking of the castle his thoughts dwelt on Richard the King."

p. 124 In the second paragraph, Collier interlined "of excellence" and crossed out "admirable" between "the" and "preservation" in the clause "Shakespeare seems to have risen to the summit of excellence in the preservation of character." In the next paragraph, Collier interlined "of the highest kind" and "somewhat," to yield the clause "and many beauties of the highest kind had been neglected, because they were somewhat hidden." The paragraph printed in the middle of the page was revised so thoroughly that it seems best simply to represent it as it appears in Collier's transcript.[5]

The first question was—What did

Shakespeare mean when he drew the character of Ham-

let? Coleridge's belief was that the poet regarded his
before he began to write
stor~~ies~~,^much in the same light that a painter looked[7]
to paint
at his canvas before he began^~~to paint his picture.~~

What was the point to which Shakespeare directed

himself? He meant to pourtray a person in whose
external and objects
view ~~of~~ the^world and all its incidents^were compa-
and
ratively dim, and of no interest in themselves, ~~but~~^which
only when
began to interest [*illeg.*^] they were reflected in the
his
mirror of ~~the~~^mind. ~~of a being of vivid imagination.~~

Hamlet beheld external objects in the same way
of vivid imagination
that a man^ who shuts his eyes, sees what has pre-
an
viously made some^impression upon his ~~sight.~~ organs.

~~of vision.~~

Professor Foakes makes no mention of any of these revisions, either in a footnote or in the brief list of "the most interesting" alterations on page 28 of his edition. Nor does he mention two other revisions in the last paragraph on page 124: the addition of "for his sloth" in the phrase "ceaseless reproaches of himself for his sloth" and the deletion of "as it were" from the phrase "among such as have as it were a world within themselves."

p. 125 In the first paragraph, Collier added "highly wrought" to the clause "the reader is totally divested of the notion that the vision is a figure in the highly wrought imagination." The second paragraph is another that Collier heavily revised and one that seems best represented as it stands in the transcript.[6]

himself
Here Shakespeare adapts^ ~~his language~~
and as it were puts himself into the situation
to the situation so admirably^, that though poetry, ~~it is~~
his is the language
~~the pure~~^language^of ~~na~~ nature: no words, associated
~~properly~~ he
with such feelings, can^occur to us but those which ~~the~~
~~author~~ especially
~~poet~~^has employed^on the highest, the most august &
the most awful subjects that can interest a human
mere fancy
being in this sentient world. That this is no^~~notion~~
undertook to
~~of mine~~ Coleridge ~~could~~^shew from Shakespeare him-
~~among other instances~~
self-. as^~~in Hamlet, after not long after the Players come~~

~~in, where he speaks of a drama "well digested in the~~

~~scenes, & set down with as much modesty as cunning"~~

No character he has drawn could so properly express himself as in the language put into his mouth

Whether Collier had difficulty deciphering his shorthand notes here, or whether he felt that what he could decipher needed editing, is not altogether clear. Nor is it easy to determine how many of the alterations were made at the time he transcribed his first draft and how many were made later. What does seem apparent is that one can by no means be certain that Collier's final version is any closer to what Coleridge said than is the earlier state of this passage. Of special interest, I think, is the long clause about Hamlet that Collier crossed out. It seems evident that Coleridge said something to this effect, for Collier is unlikely to have made up this statement. What is more, the last sentence of the paragraph makes little sense without the deleted clause.

p. 127 Collier crossed out "contended" and interlined "repeated" in the passage "This, Coleridge repeated. . . ."

p. 128 Collier crossed out "adhered to" and interlined "followed" in the clause "but Shakespeare never followed a novel. . . ." In this instance, Collier evidently noticed that he had used the word "adhering" in the immediately preceding clause and revised the sentence to avoid the repetition. The second paragraph printed on page 128 is another that Collier altered extensively and therefore one best represented as it stands in Collier's MS.[7] See plate 1.

Even after the scene with Osrick, we

see Hamlet still indulging in reflection~~s~~, and thinking lit-
new task
tle of the^~~action~~ he has just undertaken: he is all medita-
as far as words are concerned irresolution when called
tion, all resolution^ all hesitation &^~~inaction, so that~~
upon to act; so that infact
^resolving to do every thing he^does nothing. He is full of
that quality of mind wch w^{d} lead him
purpose, but void of ~~disposition~~^at the proper time to carry

his purpose into effect.

There is little question that the final version is fuller and clearer than the earlier, but there is considerable doubt about how much of the revised wording is Coleridge's and how much of it is Collier's. My own view is that the revisions probably take us away from rather than toward the *ipsissima verba* of Coleridge. In the first sentence of the final paragraph, Collier originally wrote "Shakespeare wished to impress upon us the truth that action is the great end of acceptance and purpose"; he then crossed out "acceptance and purpose" and went on to write "existence." In the last sentence, Collier added "to act" to the phrase "called upon to act by every motive."

Before concluding this discussion of Collier's revisions in the 1811–12 brochures, I think it worth calling attention to one of Professor Foakes's footnotes on page 127 of his edition. Alluding to a parenthetical note in the transcript of Lecture 12—"(See Mal. Sh., VII.382)"—Foakes writes as follows: "The

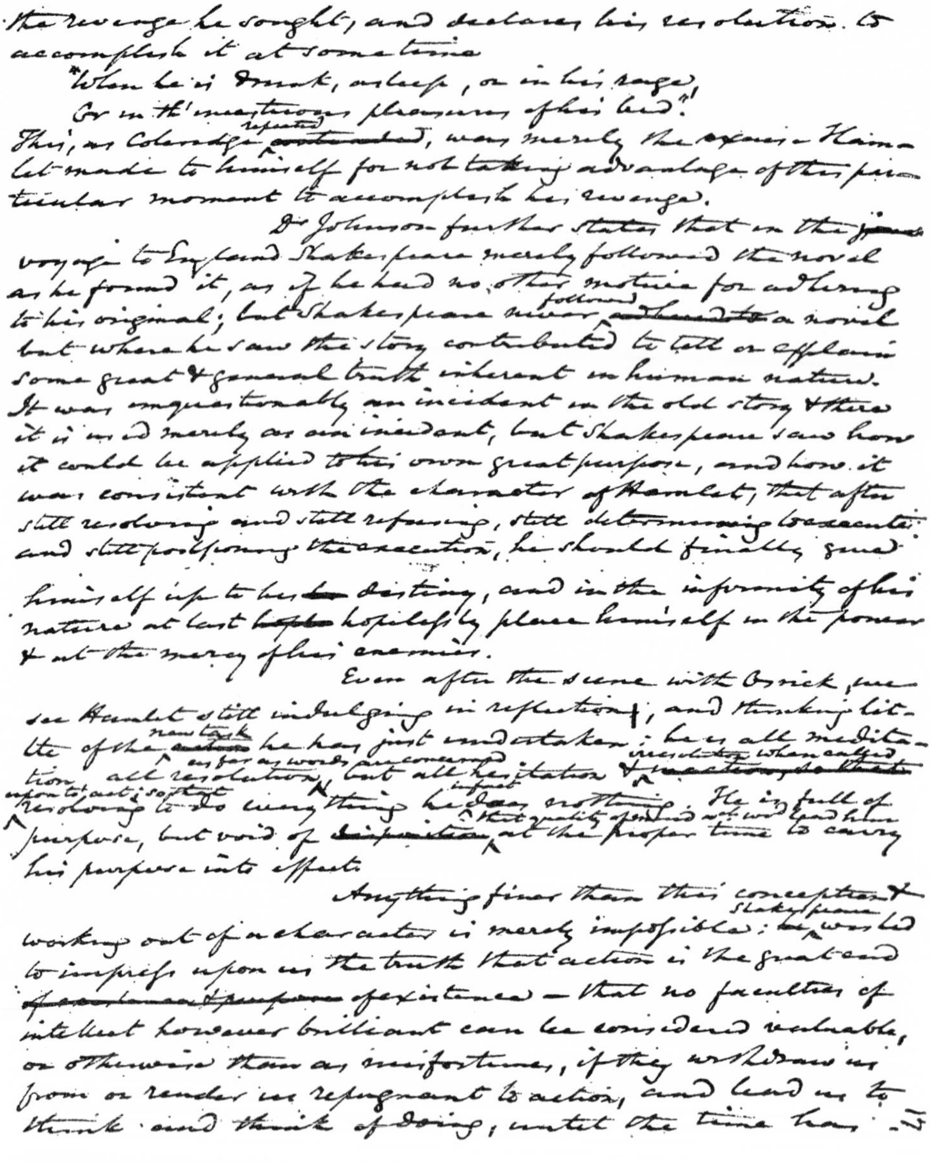
the revenge he sought, and declares his resolution to accomplish it at some time

"When he is drunk, asleep, or in his rage,
Or in th' incestuous pleasures of his bed."

This, as Coleridge repeated, was merely the excuse Hamlet made to himself for not taking advantage of this particular moment to accomplish his revenge.

Dr Johnson further states that in the voyage to England Shakespeare merely followed the novel as he found it, as if he had no other motive for adhering to his original; but Shakespeare never followed a novel but where he saw the story contributed to tell or explain some great & general truth inherent in human nature. It was unquestionably an incident in the old story & there it is used merely as an incident, but Shakespeare saw how it could be applied to his own great purpose, and how it was consistent with the character of Hamlet, that after still resolving and still refusing, still determining to execute and still postponing the execution, he should finally give himself up to his destiny, and in the infirmity of his nature at last hopelessly place himself in the power & at the mercy of his enemies.

Even after the scene with Osrick, we see Hamlet still indulging in reflections, and thinking little of the new task he has just undertaken: he is all meditation, all resolution as far as words are concerned, but all hesitation & irresolution when called upon to act; so that resolving to do every thing he in fact does nothing. He is full of purpose, but void of that quality of mind which would lead him at the proper time to carry his purpose into effect.

Anything finer than this conception & working out of a character is merely impossible: Shakespeare wished to impress upon us the truth that action is the great end of existence — that no faculties of intellect however brilliant can be considered valuable, or otherwise than as misfortunes, if they withdraw us from or render us repugnant to action, and lead us to think and think of doing, until the time has

Plate 1. John Payne Collier's transcription of Coleridge's Lecture 12. Folger MS M.a. 228, pp. 16v, 17 *Courtesy of the Folger Shakespeare Library*

reference in brackets is interlined, and must have been added after 1821, when Malone's edition of Shakespeare in 21 volumes was published. The page reference fits this edition." (The note under discussion may be seen in the lower half of Plate 2.) I have been able to corroborate Professor Foakes's statement that Collier's interlined note fits the seventh volume of Malone's 1821 edition of Shakespeare. I cannot say with certainty that it fits no earlier edition, but I believe that such is the case. If indeed Collier's reference fits only the 1821 edition and if it follows that his note cannot have been written earlier than 1821 (and may have been written at almost any later date, up to 1856), then an editorial problem of some magnitude emerges. For I find it impossible to discern by analysis of Collier's script that this reference was written any later than the rest of the interlined and marginal notes—indeed, any later than the unrevised main body of the transcript of Lecture 12. I would therefore assert that at present it is not definitely known which of Collier's revisions were made in 1811–12 (or whenever the transcript of Lecture 12 was first written out) and which were made later, even many years later. I would suggest, further, that many of the revisions in the texts of the earlier lectures (especially Lecture 9, where revisions are especially numerous) may have been written after 1821—or at least that the possibility should be carefully considered. Professor Foakes, it should be noted, indicates an awareness of the possible implications of the Malone reference. In his introduction (p. 19) he says:

> My guess is that Collier transcribed the bulk of the lectures soon after they were delivered, not necessarily within a day, but certainly while they were fresh in his mind; that he paused in the middle of Lecture 12, and resumed after an interval possibly of weeks or even months; and that some time after all were finished, he went back over them and made a number of corrections and interlineations, like the reference to Malone's Shakespeare.

It surprises me that Professor Foakes can say, on the one hand, that many of Collier's revisions were made "some time" (even many years) after the main transcripts were completed, and, on the other hand, that these revisions "do not seriously affect the text." For it seems highly probable that the process of editing that eventually resulted in the unreliable 1856 text of the 1811–12 lectures had already begun as Collier revised his brochures. Let us hope that when Professor Foakes publishes a more fully documented version of the material in *Coleridge on Shakespeare*, he will give a full account of Collier's revisions, suggest their probable dates, and discuss their textual ramifications.

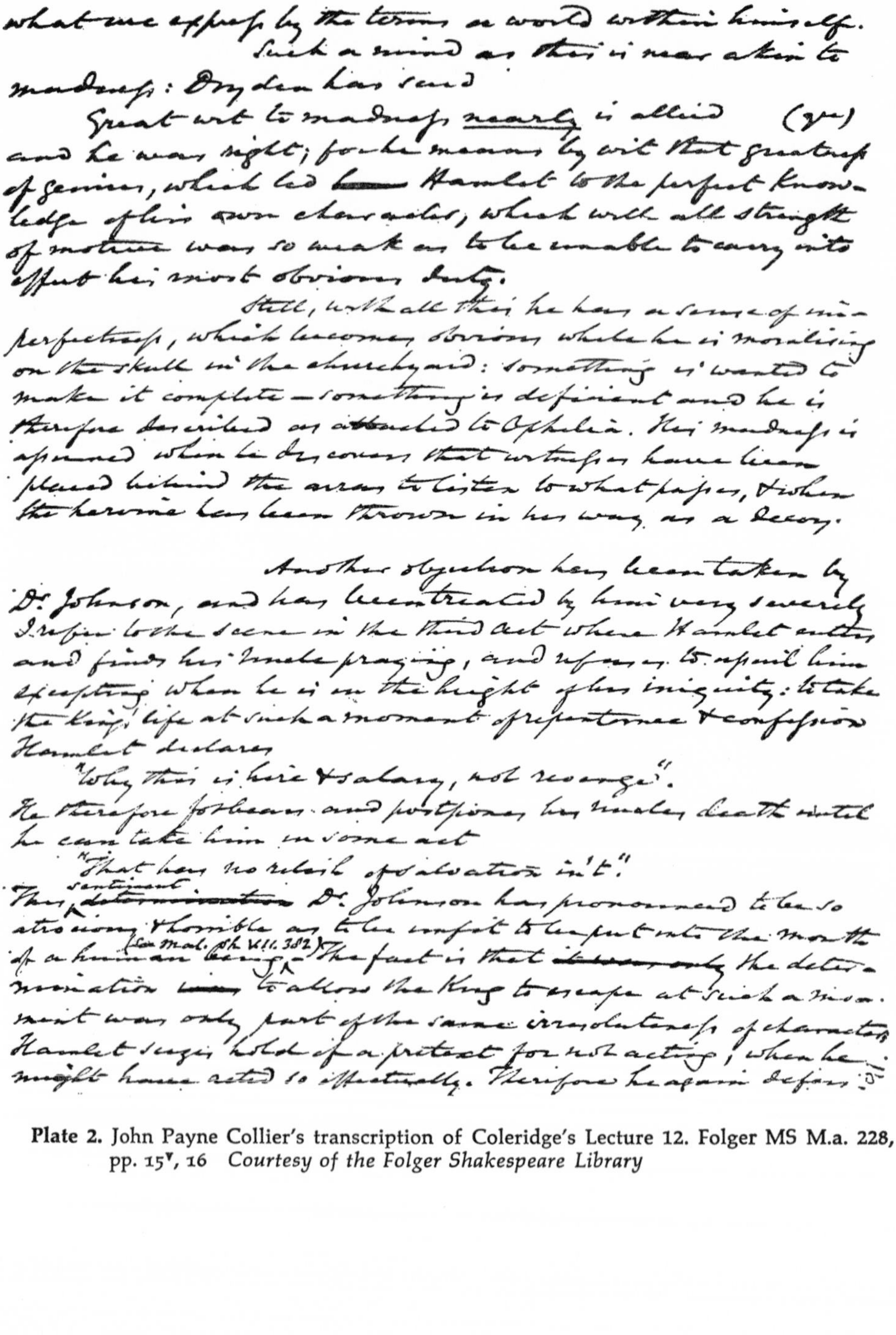

what we express by the terms a world within himself.
Such a mind as this is near akin to
madness: Dryden has said
Great wit to madness nearly is allied (qu.)
and he was right; for he means by wit that greatness
of genius, which led ~~him~~ Hamlet to the perfect knowledge of his own character, which with all strength
of motive was so weak as to be unable to carry into
effect his most obvious duty.
Still, with all this he has a sense of im-
perfectness, which becomes obvious while he is moralizing
on the skull in the churchyard: something is wanted to
make it complete – something is deficient and he is
therefore described as attached to Ophelia. His madness is
assumed when he discovers that witnesses have been
placed behind the arras to listen to what passes, & when
the heroine has been thrown in his way as a decoy.

Another objection has been taken by
Dr Johnson, and has been treated by him very severely
I refer to the scene in the third act where Hamlet enters
and finds his Uncle praying, and refuses to assail him
excepting when he is in the height of his iniquity: to take
the King's life at such a moment of repentance & confession
Hamlet declares
"Why this is hire & salary, not revenge".
He therefore forbears and postpones his uncles death until
he can take him in some act
"That has no relish of salvation in't".
This sentiment ~~determination~~ Dr Johnson has pronounced to be so
atrocious & horrible as to be unfit to be put into the mouth
of a human being. (See Mal. Sh. vii. 382) JPC The fact is that ~~[illegible]~~ the deter-
mination ~~[illegible]~~ to allow the King to escape at such a mo-
ment was only part of the same irresolutenes of character
Hamlet seizes hold of a pretext for not acting, when he
might have acted so effectually. Therefore he again defers: 16

Plate 2. John Payne Collier's transcription of Coleridge's Lecture 12. Folger MS M.a. 228, pp. 15ᵛ, 16 *Courtesy of the Folger Shakespeare Library*

Let us hope, too, that the editor will collate his text more closely with the Collier brochures. My own collation disclosed a large number of discrepancies in phrasing, which I shall list in order of occurrence.

p. 3 Instead of "more meager" the text should read "meaner" in the clause "and yet in many things I do not know any body that I have a meaner opinion of than, of myself."

p. 4 The word "of" should be deleted or placed in brackets in the phrase "and heard nothing particularly worthy notice"; it is not in the MS.

p. 31 Two phrases printed in Foakes's text are crossed out in Collier's diary: "on the tablet of my memory," line 3, and "and the mere substance," line 13.

p. 35 The word "that" should read "this" in the phrase "and this was the the reason," line 11.

p. 40 The word "action" in the top line of the page should read "actions."

p. 47 Foakes's text omits Collier's interlined addition "vigorously" from the phrase "After vigorously censuring personality," line 3.

p. 50 Collier wrote "brilliancy" rather than "brilliance" in the phrase "and in the brilliancy, which was not dazling," line 19.

p. 54 (a) Collier's MS reads "afford" rather than "offer" in the parenthetical phrase "or whatever better term our language may afford," line 4. In this instance, the 1856 text (p. 17) correctly renders "afford" and is thus a more accurate record of Collier's diary than is Foakes's edition.
(b) The editor has altered Collier's "do" to "does" in the clause (penultimate paragraph) "and if the Poet *does* not do that he ceases so far to be a Poet" (italics mine). The 1856 text correctly reads "do" (p. 18).
(c) Collier's MS reads "There" rather than "Here" in the clause "There Metre introduces its claims," six lines from the bottom of the page. Again, the 1856 text (p. 18) reads correctly.

p. 55 In the second paragraph, Foakes's text omits Collier's interlined addition "M^{r}" before "Coleridge added."

p. 60 (a) Collier's MS contains no word "all" between "Bakewells" and "came" in the entry for Tuesday, November 26.
(b) Collier's footnote to the entry for Wednesday, November 27, reads "*not far famed Clio," rather than "*not performed Clio."

p. 61 (a) Collier's MS interlines the clarifier "(H's)" between "his" and "mind" in the second sentence of the fourth paragraph.
(b) Foakes's text omits "yet" from the clause "It was owing to this ignorance that Coleridge had not yet exemplified any of his positions by quoting passages. . . ."

p. 68 Collier's MS reads "effort" rather than "effect" in the clause "but the language in which it was contained possessing such a facility that one would say almost, that it was impossible for it to be thought, unless it were thought as naturally & without effort as Mercutio represented it." Clearly, "effect" does not fit the context here and should have been suspected as an error, particularly in view of the fact that the 1856 text, correctly, reads "effort" (p. 38).

p. 70 Collier's MS reads "warred" rather than "warned" in the clause "but what Coleridge warred against was the notion that whenever a conceit is met with it is unnatural." The 1856 text (p. 42) captures the sense of the MS: "The notion against which I declare war is, that whenever a conceit is met with it is unnatural."

p. 71 Instead of "excellences" (line 3), the Collier MS reads "excellencies." Except for a few isolated instances to the contrary, Foakes's text invariably alters "excellencies" to "excellences" (twice in line 5 of the penultimate paragraph on page 83; once on page 100 at the foot of the page; and once on page 115 near the end of the penultimate paragraph). The same is true of the 1856 text. But the fact that Collier's MS almost always has "excellencies" suggests the strong possibility that this was Coleridge's pronunciation of the word. I see no reason for altering to "excellences."

p. 75 Instead of "afterward" (line 10), the Collier MS reads "afterwards." In every instance of this word that I have noted, Collier's MS and Collier's 1856 text both print "afterwards." Foakes's text, however, invariably prints "afterward." See, for example, page 81 (line 6), page 86 (seven lines from the bottom). Again, I see no reason for the alterations.

p. 78 Foakes's text incorrectly reads "instinctive" rather than "instructive" in the clause "but even in the subordinate personages the passion is made instructive at least even if it have not been an individual and it has made the reader look with a keener eye into human nature than if it had not been pointed out to us." The 1856 text (p. 56) reads ". . . the passion is at least rendered instructive. . . ."

p. 81 The Collier MS has "works" rather than "work" in line 10.

p. 83 Foakes's text omits Collier's "as" from the clause "it came into his mind to do it as one way, and sometimes the best, of replying" (line 4). The 1856 text, in the corresponding passage (p. 66), includes the "as." Here Foakes may have omitted the word because it is slightly obscured by an ink smudge. In the line above "as," Collier had scratched out "eventually" between "it" and "came," accidentally causing a smear on the line below.

p. 84 (a) The Collier MS reads "pretented" rather than "pretended" in the phrase (line 20) "equally free from extravagance and pretented Platonism." Collier printed "pretended" in the 1856 text, and it may well be the correct reading. But since Collier may have been recording Coleridge's pronunciation of the word when he wrote "pretented" in 1812, there should at least be an editorial note calling attention to this spelling.

(b) In the penultimate sentence on the page, Foakes's text omits Collier's "a" from the phrase "exaltation to a higher & *a* nobler state" (italics mine).

p. 91 Foakes's text omits Collier's "and" from the clause "that this mutual transfusion can take place more perfectly & totally, than in any other mode" (line 12).

p. 92 Collier's MS contains "if" before the phrase "he might so say" (four lines from the bottom of the page). The 1856 text preserves the sense of "if he might so say"; it reads (p. 84) "if I may so say."

p. 93 Foakes's text omits three words from the clause "upon which the *whole frame, the* who[le] structure of human society rests . . ." (line 22, italics mine). The omitted words appear in the 1856 text, page 85.

p. 94 Foakes's text omits "cousin" from the phrase "from sister to wife from wife to child, to Uncle, cousin, one of our kin" (line 17). The 1856 text, page 87, contains the omitted word.

p. 97 Collier's MS reads "they" rather than "thus" in the clause "they only see what is good & *they* have no conjecture of his imperfections . . ." (line 1, italics mine). The 1856 text reads "they" in the corresponding passage, pages 92–93.

p. 98 (a) In line 6, Foakes's text reads "bestowed upon the ancient paintings by Apelles by Pliny"; Collier's MS reads "bestowed upon the ancient paintings *of* Apelles by Pliny" (italics mine). (b) Foakes's text omits Collier's "had" from the clause (line 15) "the assertions of those who had maintained that the ancients were wholly ignorant of it."

p. 99 Foakes's text omits four words from the sentence (line 20) "The Shakesperian drama *and the Greek drama* might be compared to painting & statuary" (italics mine). The omitted words are included in the 1856 text, page 96.

p. 102 (a) Foakes's text reads "seems" rather than Collier's "seem" in the clause (line 20) "that since Shakespeares time none of our Critics seem to enter into his peculiarities." This alteration may be a deliberate emendation; if so, I think it an unwarranted one. In the corresponding passage the 1856 text reads ". . . none of them seem to understand even his language, much less the principles upon which he wrote, and the peculiarities which distinguish him from all rivals" (p. 102).

(b) Foakes's text reads "feeling" rather than Collier's "feelings" in the clause "they only exercized the most vulgar of all feelings—that of wonderment" (line 27). In the corresponding passage (p. 102) the 1856 text reads "feelings."

p. 103 (a) Collier's MS reads "on" rather than "of" in the phrase (line 1) "as well might a man pride himself on acting the beast."

(b) Foakes's text adds a superfluous "so" in the clause "that it should remain so for *foreigners* first to feel truly. . . ." The 1856 text, page 103, correctly reads "that it should remain for foreigners first to feel truly. . . ."

(c) Collier's MS reads "nations" rather than "nation" in the clause "The German nations on the other hand, unable to act at all have been driven into speculation" (line 17). The 1856 text, page 103, replaces "The German nations" with "the Germans."

p. 112 (a) Foakes's text omits "from" from the clause "He is introduced discontented from his confinement, and *from* being bound to obey anything that he is commanded" (line 8, italics mine). Collier's pen was overloaded when he wrote "from," and hence its letters are somewhat run together. (b) Foakes's text incorrectly prints in brackets "[is]" five lines from the bottom of the page; "is" is in Collier's MS.

p. 119 Collier's MS reads "a" rather than "the" in the phrase "because it was a play in *the* wrong place" (line 16; italics mine). The 1856 text, page 133, reads "because it is a play upon words in *a* wrong place, and at a wrong time" (italics mine).

p. 120 (a) Collier's MS reads "overwhelms" rather than "overwhelmed" in the clause "It was true, Coleridge admitted, that the first misfortune Rich^{d}. meets with overwhelms him . . ." (line 2).

(b) Collier's MS reads "Snakes" rather than "Shakes" in the line "Snakes in my heart's blood warmed, that sting my heart" (line 21). The 1856 text correctly prints "Snakes," page 135.

p. 122 Collier's MS reads "There" rather than "Here" in the sentence (line 17) "There the play on words is perfectly in character."

p. 124 (a) Collier's MS reads "the poet" rather than "a poet" in the clause (line 18) "that the poet regarded his story. . . ."

(b) Collier's MS reads "much in" rather than "in much" in the clause (line 19) "before he began to write much in the same light that a painter looked at his canvas before he began to paint." The 1856 text, page 141, reads "much in" in this passage.

p. 125 (a) Collier's MS reads "though poetry" rather than "through poetry" in the clause (second paragraph) "and as it were puts himself into the situation, that though poetry, his language is the language of nature. . . ." The 1856 text correctly reads "though poetry," page 143.

(b) Foakes's text omits Collier's "on" from the immediately succeeding clause "no words, associated with such feelings, can occur to us but those which he has employed especially *on* the highest, the most august . . . " (italics mine). The 1856 text includes the "on."

(c) Foakes's text reads "subject" rather than the Collier MS's "subjects" in the phrase "especially on the highest, the most august, and the most awful subjects that can interest a human being in this sentient world." The 1856 text correctly reads "subjects" in this passage, page 143.

p. 128 (a) Collier's MS reads "misfortunes" rather than "misfortune" in the clause "no faculties of intellect however brilliant can be considered valuable, or otherwise than as misfortunes, if they withdraw us from or render us repugnant to action . . ." (line 22). The 1856 text correctly reads "misfortunes," page 148.

(b) Collier's MS reads "has" rather than "had" in the concluding clause of the sentence just quoted: ". . . and lead us to think and think of doing, until the time has escaped when we ought to have acted." The 1856 text reads "until the time elapsed," page 148.

It is alarming to discover such a high frequency of inaccuracies in an edition whose *raison d'être* is to remedy the harm done by inaccurate earlier editions, especially when one discovers so many instances in which the earlier editions are more faithful to the sense of the Collier MS than is the modern edition purporting to present the MS almost verbatim. Well it is that a new edition of *Coleridge on Shakespeare* is forthcoming, because, as should be manifest by now, the 1971 edition as it stands does not serve the purpose for which it was intended.

I shall conclude these remarks with some brief comments on the punctuation of the text in *Coleridge on Shakespeare.* In his "Notes on the presentation of the Text," Professor Foakes says: "Collier's long-hand manuscripts are very lightly pointed, and some passages have no punctuation at all. He often used a dash for a period, and a number of these have been retained. I have added enough punctuation to make the Diary and lecture notes easily readable" (p. 28).

All of what the editor says here is true. First, Collier's manuscripts *are* lightly pointed and need to have punctuation added in order to make many passages more readily comprehensible. I could not help feeling, however, that Professor Foakes has frequently added or otherwise altered punctuation when the MS pointing was perfectly adequate. The result is a text literally sprinkled with commas, far more than modern standards normally prescribe, and a text that often has semicolons substituted for colons (and occasionally vice versa) and periods substituted for colons and semicolons even when such alterations do nothing to clarify Collier's language. Second, Collier *did* use a dash for a period quite often (or a combination of a period and a dash), especially in the early diary entries and lecture transcripts. Occasionally Professor Foakes has retained the dash, but I often find it difficult to determine what principle has led the editor to retain a dash or substitute a period in a given context. In this matter, as in his treatment of spellings and other accidental features of the text, Professor Foakes's editorial behavior seems strangely capricious. Fortunately, it can be said that Foakes's freedom in altering punctuation seldom does any positive harm to the sense of Collier's prose.

There are a few occasions, however, in which his decision to retain Collier's dashes tends to misrepresent the text. The reader who examines the photographs of the brochures opposite pages 6 and 7 in Foakes's edition will observe that Collier has something of a fetish for even margins. It is quite common to find him employing dashes to "justify" lines that do not quite reach the margin on the right (see, for example, line 9 of the left-hand page reproduced in plate 2 of Foakes's edition: "baskets to the derision of his— / Schoolfellows"), and it soon becomes apparent that these dashes serve no function as punctuation. In a few isolated instances, Foakes's text retains these dashes, as in the following clause on pages 67–68: "Meditation looked at every character with interest—only as it contains in it something generally true and such as might be expressed in a philosophical Problem." Here, clearly, the dash obscures the meaning of the passage (compare the 1856 text, p. 37), and one can only speculate about why Professor Foakes chose to retain it.

Enough has now been said, I hope, to indicate my opinion that R. A. Foakes has not satisfactorily confronted all the problems that need to be dealt with in order to produce a definitive new edition of Coleridge's 1811–12 remarks on Shakespeare. He has done us a valuable service in recognizing the need for an edition based on Collier's early notes and transcripts. In the introduction and appendixes to his book, he has lucidly and concisely discussed many of the editorial tasks that are basic to the establishment of a more reliable version of what Coleridge said in 1811–12. But he has not discussed the questions posed by Collier's dozens of textual revisions in the brochures upon which *Coleridge on Shakespeare* is based. Full resolution of these questions may require a monograph or more, and it would be asking too much of Professor Foakes to expect him to solve all the puzzles in the Collier transcripts before publishing a revised edition of *Coleridge on Shakespeare*. But it is not too much to ask, I think, to request of the editor that he at least provide a complete list of all the deletions, additions, and substitutions in Collier's brochures. I believe that it would also be appropriate to request that the revised edition of the brochures provide a more faithful rendering of the accidentals of the manuscripts (Collier's spellings and punctuation wherever possible), an exhaustive account of editorial emendations, and a considerably more accurate reproduction of Collier's exact language.[8]

Notes:

1. The book here reviewed is *Coleridge on Shakespeare: The Text of the Lectures of 1811–12*, ed. R. A. Foakes (Charlottesville: Univ. Press of Virginia for the Folger Shakespeare Library, 1971).
2. "The Text of Coleridge's 1811–12 Shakespeare Lectures," *ShS*, 23 (1970), 101–11.
3. For a fuller account of these matters, see Professor Foakes's excellent introduction, especially pp. 1–9.
4. This quotation, from a poem sometimes attributed to Milton, is printed from Folger M.a. 226, pp. 11–11^v. As Foakes points out in a footnote on p. 104, "The full text, first printed in the Second Folio of Shakespeare's plays (1632), together with an account of the controversy over the authorship of it, may be found in the *Shakespeare Allusion-Book* (1932), I, 364–8."
5. This quotation is printed from Folger M.a. 228, pp. 12–12^v. Here, as in future quotations from the MS, I have represented words I could not decipher by inserting the editorial note [*illeg.*].
6. The passage quoted is printed from Folger M.a. 228, pp. 13^v–14. As I shall point out later, Professor Foakes's text of the revised version of this passage contains three inaccuracies in phrasing.
7. The passage quoted is printed from Folger M.a. 228, p. 17.
8. A truly definitive edition of Coleridge's 1811–12 lectures on Shakespeare would properly be a variorium edition. The MS in the Folger Library would serve as the basic copy-text and would be supplemented (1) by an exhaustive list of all the passages in which it differs substantially from the 1856 edition, (2) by a list of parallel passages to be found elsewhere in Coleridge's writings or recorded statements (such as statements recalled in diaries and letters of his contemporaries), and (3) by the editor's critical commentary about the possible relationships between the variants thus disclosed.

REVIEWS

The Profession of Dramatist in Shakespeare's Time: 1590–1642, by Gerald Eades Bentley. Princeton University Press, 1972. Pp. ix + 329. $10.00.

Reviewer: Jeanne Addison Roberts

The chief merit of this book—and it is considerable—is that it brings together in orderly fashion a large number of facts and quotations previously available only in widely scattered sources. As Professor Bentley points out, he has drawn heavily on *The Elizabethan Stage*, *The Jacobean and Caroline Stage*, Henslowe's *Diary*, *The Dramatic Records of Sir Henry Herbert*, legal documents, and contemporary literature. The resulting study will prove a most useful reference work for students of the period.

As the dates suggest, Bentley's title is somewhat misleading. His book includes twenty-six years after Shakespeare's death and actually deals in more detail with the period from 1616 to 1642 than with the earlier years—probably because of the volume of available materials. His discussion includes Shakespeare but by no means concentrates on him, although his description of the poet reveals him as quite typical of the professional playwright.

Bentley begins by developing a description of the "attached professional" dramatist of the period. Out of "250 or so men who are known to have written plays in England between about 1590 and 1642," he methodically isolates eight who had a close, continuous association with London theaters, who made their living in the theater, and who worked regularly with one troupe for long periods. His attached professionals are Heywood, Fletcher, Dekker, Massinger, Shakespeare, Shirley, Rowley, and Brome. Using these men as the main basis of discussion, Bentley explores questions of the status of the playwright, his relation to his acting company, his pay, his regulation by the censor, and his activities in collaboration and revision. He convincingly establishes that the category of professional playwright did in fact exist and that members of it were characterized by predictable attitudes and behavior. He suggests that these professionals were not at all ill-paid by comparison, for example, with schoolmasters; and he usefully distinguishes between the professionals and the many amateur and unattached playwrights. The most famous of the latter group was Ben Jonson, whose attitudes and behavior separate him, says Bentley, from the strict professionals.

The extraordinary breadth of the author's knowledge and the vast amount of detailed material which he has sifted for us must have made this a difficult book to organize, but the methodology and logical progress are crystal clear. Because of the detailed evidence and extensive quotation, however, it is a difficult book to read through; but the effort is rewarded with a rich sense of the theatrical habits of the time. Like everyone, Bentley must depend heavily—possibly too heavily—on Henslowe and Herbert, but his applications and additional materials are newly illuminating.

Perhaps because he intended his book to be useable as a reference work, the author has frequently repeated: the account of Malone's and Chalmers' transcriptions of Herbert are outlined four times; five lines of identical quotation appear on pages 13 and 38; and repeated descriptions of *The Late Murder of the Son upon the Mother, or Keep the Widow Waking* seem redundant. Such repetitions do make it possible, however, for the separate chapters to stand alone.

Professor Bentley's ordered distillation of stage materials will certainly become an indispensable resource for future students of Elizabethan, Jacobean, and Caroline dramatists.

Hero and Saint: Shakespeare and the Graeco-Roman Heroic Tradition, by Reuben A. Brower. Oxford University Press, 1971. Pp. xv + 424. $10.50.

Reviewer: Philip Rollinson

This is both a simplistic and a very subtle critical reading and appreciation of some of Shakespeare's important works. Its simplicity lies in a twofold limitation of scope and method. Its subtlety lies in the execution of the method.

The "main purpose" of the study, as Brower observes in his Preface, "is to explore probable analogies between the Shakespearian heroic and the Graeco-Roman heroic" (p. ix). Brower's analysis of the Graeco-Roman heroic is limited to Homer, Virgil, Ovid, Seneca and Plutarch (Chapters 1–4). This focus includes significant attention to Renaissance English translations of these classical works. But intentionally avoided are lesser heroic works of antiquity (Statius, Lucan, and the like) as well as the Renaissance epics of Tasso, Ariosto, and others. The second limitation, both the strength and weakness of this work, lies in the tools of description and analysis. Brower works within the realm of stylistics, defining the ethos and pathos of classical and Shakespearean heroism solely in terms of the implications, connotations, and nuances of words, phrases, images, and various figures of speech.

Professor Brower is obviously adept at this sort of critical dissection, which not only sets off from its text hundreds of quotations for the reader's special attention but also includes within the text thousands of quoted words and phrases. Even in Brower's expert hands, this process becomes occasionally tedious. However, Brower's just sense of the significance and complexities of the stylistics of the heroic more than compensates for any tedium. He knows his Virgil and his Shakespeare and reflects this knowledge in a readable work.

The earlier chapters on the classics give way, beginning with *Venus and Adonis* and *The Rape of Lucrece* (Chapter 3), to an increasing attention to Shakespeare in light of the classical and Renaissance context of the heroic. Brower means the saintly as an extension of the heroic, pushed to an extreme of suffering, patience, endurance, and self-knowledge (p. ix and the "Epilogue," pp. 416–20). His "Introduction" (pp. 1–28) briefly illustrates in *Othello* the presence of both extremes of heroic aggressiveness and of saintly suffering in self-recognition. The other chapters on Shakespeare's plays focus on specific questions which the traditional ideas of hero and saint usefully illuminate. *Titus Andronicus* (Chapter 4) is analyzed as a transitional piece in Shakespeare's own developing sense of the heroic. *Julius Caesar* (Chapter 5) is related particularly to North's Plutarch. Critical elaborations follow: the paradoxical nature of *Troilus and Cressida* (Chapter 6); the complexities of Hamlet's character (Chapter 7); Antony's subtle relationships to heroic greatness and heroic love (Chapter 8); how Coriolanus can or should be construed as a tragic figure (Chapter 9); and "the imaginative order" which informs the tragedy of Lear and Cordelia (Chapter 10).

Brower's method is not simply one of source hunting but, as he remarks several times (e.g., page 205), one of defining a particularly important kind of resource available to Shakespeare. Brower attempts thereby to demonstrate how Shakespeare assimilates and modifies this resource to his own particular artistic uses in particular plays. It seems to me that he succeeds admirably. His readings serve to sharpen our critical awareness of what Shakespeare accomplishes in several plays, and this study certainly demonstrates how necessary a thorough acquaintance with the works of classical antiquity is for any proper understanding not just of Shakespeare but of other Renaissance dramatic and literary works dealing with the heroic and the tragic.

Worship and Theology in England: From Cranmer to Hooker, 1534–1603, by Horton Davies. Princeton University Press, 1970. Pp. xix + 482. $17.50.

Reviewer: R. Chris Hassel, Jr.

This fourth volume of a projected five-volume series lives up to the high standards of scholarship, comprehensiveness, and fairness which have marked Davies' earlier efforts. Dealing, as it does, predominantly with the interrelated currents of theology and worship during Shakespeare's lifetime, it is particularly useful to Shakespeareans as a reliable survey of the major Christian assumptions and controversies which Shakespeare's age inherited and debated. Its excellent footnotes will encourage the literary scholar to pursue parallels with the age's literature he might perceive; its well-established reputation will simultaneously provide reliable generalizations concerning Catholic, Anglican, and Puritan worship and theology.

As with the earlier volumes, the framework and scholarly paraphernalia of this work are excellent. A four-part bibliography contains extensive listings of liturgical texts and "Books," but only perfunctory lists of periodicals and sources in English literature. The category "Books," containing five hundred items, might have been more useful had it been subdivided into primary and secondary items. The index is scrupulously divided into three parts: persons, places (including church names), and topics. It is both extensive and accurate and should become a major inducement for scholars to refer to the work. Eleven illustrations are carefully chosen to edify while they decorate. Six portraits (Cranmer, More, Perkins, Jewel, Campion, and Hooker) flesh out our sense of the primary writers Davies cites. Three scenes of martyrdom, persecution, and prejudice illustrate the age's notorious contentiousness. Scenes of holy communion and infant baptism from John Dayes's *A Book of Christian Prayers* enhance our sense of Protestant worship and attitudes towards sacraments.

As in the earlier volumes, Davies provides a systematic, brief introduction which the reader should peruse before he reads particular chapters. After delineating the scope, the methods, and the organization of the work, the introduction mentions most of the issues to be discussed within an overview of their historical and theological contexts. Its organization and its clarity reflect Davies' command of the specific details and the overall patterns of his field. Inevitably Davies omits issues others will consider worth including and deemphasizes and distorts others through his unique nonpartisan and historically isolated perspective. However, considering the size and the complexity of the subject, the book is far more remarkable for what it has been able to include than for what it may have omitted.

Davies states that the aim of the five-volume series, *Worship and Theology in England,* is to study the constantly interrelated worship and theology of English Christians from the Reformation to the present. By worship, Davies refers not merely to rubric but rather broadly to "the corporate offering of thought, emotion, and decision-making, . . . the art of Christian adoration as expressed . . . in prayers and preaching, in sermons as in sacraments, in religious architecture and sacred music, in devotion and in duty" (p. xiii). This present volume focuses on the first of five chronological periods of English worship and theology, 1534–1603, from the English Reformation and the work of Cranmer to the ascension of James I and the work of Hooker.

Part I, entitled "Historical and Theological," stresses "the impassioned partisanship of the period." "Thus the first three chapters demonstrate that it was a continuing struggle to affirm Anglican doctrine against the contentions of the Catholics on the right and those of the Puritans on the left" (p. xvi). The first chapter surveys "Catholics and Puritans in Controversy," reviewing the arguments each side forwarded in its own ecclesiastical defense (the primacy of Prince or Pope, scripture or the primitive church) and the two central doctrinal issues separating them (the nature of sacrament and salvation by faith or works). The second chapter, "Anglicans and Puritans in Controversy," contrasts their theories of human nature, predestination, the sacraments, ethics, and finally eschatology. The final chapter of Part I considers "The Eucharistic Controversy," stressing the Catholic-Anglican split represented by Gardiner disputing with Cranmer. The reviewer sensed here an inadequate treatment of the threefold Anglican-Catholic-Puritan perspective just previously established by Davies. In their official statements of the 1580s and 1590s, the Anglican apologists seem more precariously placed than Davies suggests, refusing to call sacraments "rubbish" and mere "feignings," as was the Puritan wont, but simultaneously unable or unwilling to reinstitute the Catholic mysteries into the "signs," "symbols," and "seals" of their commemorative supper of love. As is elsewhere true, Davies tends to minimize the turmoil and the uncertainty in favor of a hypothetically settled Anglican position.

Part II, entitled "The Liturgical Alternatives," contrasts and compares the formal, verbal worship of Anglicans, Puritans, and Catholics. As in the previous volumes, Davies' fairness to and understanding of each of these perspectives is exemplary if somewhat unspectacular. The study of Catholic worship discusses its progress through Mary's reign, the Counter-Reformation, liturgical reform and the Council of Trent, and the private worship of the recusants late in the century. The discussion of Anglican worship naturally stresses the prayer books and liturgical reform and innovation but also considers the prescribed homilies, biblical interpretation, and representative preachers, sermon styles, topics, and structures. This balance between prayer book and pulpit becomes the fulcrum upon which Davies establishes the centrality of Anglican worship between the extremes of the Catholics' liturgical emphasis and the Puritans' homiletic one. The remainder of Part II considers Puritan and Separatist worship, discussing the primacy of preaching, the use of biblical interpretation, sermon styles and topics, and the Puritan distrust of formal prayer books or sacraments. As this brief summary suggests, Part II presents a panoramic view of Elizabethan worship that is the high point of Davies' work. It is worth the careful study of any scholar who is seriously interested in understanding the sensibility of Shakespeare's audience. Davies' sense of the styles, subjects, structures, and aesthetic qualities of the sermon and the liturgical observance establishes ideological and aesthetic preconceptions which may have carried over from the churchgoer to the theatergoer.

Part III, "Liturgical Arts and Aids," is more encyclopedic than either of the former sections and seems therefore less intense and less interesting. Generally, the chapter on architecture and art has been challenged for chronological inconsistencies. Further, the frequent differences between Anglicans and Puritans are minimized, both in the areas of iconoclastism and formal piety. Hooker, for example, seems far more attached to the aesthetic qualities of worship than Davies' summary would suggest to be characteristic of the Anglican sensibility. The chapter on church music is similarly compressed but, like the previous one, seems to contain at least a reference to most of the important contributors the serious researcher might wish to pursue. Some readers would find the section on religious music and art to be the most disappointing. Both seem peripheral either to Davies' interests or to his immediate expertise; consequently, each is treated more with a concise competence than a sense of their important aesthetic relationship to the experience of worship. The section on music, for example, seems to miss the opportunity to discuss the primacy of Byrd's, Morley's, or Tallis' works in terms of their peculiar Catholic sensibilities. Similarly, the music, like the art, is rather dismissed as a fact of the age than as a reflection of its sensibility or its beliefs. The factual treatment of the composers and their works suggests an encyclopedic survey and evidences an uncertain grasp of their relationship to theology or worship.

The final chapter discusses Catholic, Anglican, and Puritan spirituality by beginning with the debatable assumption that private devotional treatises would have contained the most deeply believed doctrines (p. 406). By discussing the demand for Catholic and royal primers, this chapter seems to revive and confirm the assumption of T. W. Baldwin that most Elizabethans would have studied devotional works in their primers, though not necessarily in Nowell's Catechism per se (p. 411). Incidentally, Davies fails to refer to either of the longer catechisms, Nowell's or Calvin's, an omission which would surprise some readers. Though they were admittedly less influential than homilies or prayer books, the Anglican and Calvinist catechisms surely deserve discussion in such a study.

Another somewhat surprising omission is the lack of a systematic discussion of controversial biblical translations and marginal notes, plus the supplementary confutations which arose from them. The two decades from 1560 through 1580 saw the official Calvinist, Anglican, and Catholic translations of the Holy Bible, or at least the New Testament, into English. Each version contained its own marginal notes, its special translation of controversial passages, and its own apologists, like William Fulke and Gregory Martin. Given this explosion of translations in the middle of the period under discussion and adding the stress placed upon scriptural authority by both Anglicans and Puritans, one might have expected a fuller treatment of this phenomenon in its relationship to the worship and theology of sixteenth century England.

Davies also omits another of the most notorious areas of sixteenth-century English worship, the official pressures for compulsory church attendance and uniformity of observance. These confusing but important phenomena need to be clarified for the student of the period, in part because previous treatments have been so much more partisan than Davies'. How fully enforced were the suspension of legal rights, extended imprisonments, and executions for religious nonconformity, and what effects did that enforcement have upon theology and worship in England? Historians and students of literature would both be interested in these matters and would consider them germane to Davies' study.

Finally, two minor faults of his previous volumes seem again present in this one. Davies' work will never completely satisfy the historian or the comparative theologian who demands a sharper sense of the historical origins of these doctrinal and liturgical currents and of their concurrent European manifestations. Though his personal biases remain, they seem diminished by the distance of the sixteenth century from the present. The bias toward liturgical renewal is lessened by the negative strength of the Puritan distrust of liturgy but comes through both in Davies' extremely general definition of worship and in occasional cracks in his historical persona. The other, toward ecumenism, manifests itself positively in the scrupulous fairness towards all perspectives; but it also may explain his predictable down-playing of religious controversy and intolerance during the period. The characteristics which mark the discussions of worship and theology in the Renaissance are their emotional intensity, their personal abusiveness and scurrility, and their energetic and voluminous refutations and confutations, culminating in the Marprelate Tracts of the 1590s. Davies acknowledges these characteristics abstractly, but his illustrations carefully screen out their tangible reality. Without a concrete sense of the discourtesy, the intolerance, even the apparent mutual hatred of William Fulke, Henry Barrow, or Gregory Martin, we misunderstand the decidedly non-ecumenical nature of Christianity in the English Renaissance. Through this omission Davies may be serving the cause of twentieth-century ecumenism, but he has distorted historical perspective in the process.

These few omissions and distortions are slight, however, in comparison to the consistently high quality of this volume and its series, and in view of the enormous scope of the subject. Davies' grasp of worship and theology among English Catholics, Anglicans, and Puritans remains reliable and comprehensive. His tactful inclusion of just enough details to inform, but too few to overwhelm, neither disappoints nor wearies the reader. The balance between the scholarly and the popular is definitely on the scholarly side, but the work should be clear and useful to any interested reader. In fact, *Worship and Theology in England* may finally become more useful for the Renaissance scholar who is not a specialist in theology; for the specialist, it may be too general. Because the work is so consistently trustworthy on issues, beliefs, and practices, so well documented, easy to consult as a reference work, and not unattractive to read, it richly deserves the plaudits and the careful attention it will certainly receive.

Jonson's Moral Comedy, by Alan C. Dessen. Northwestern University Press, 1971. Pp. x + 256. $7.95.

Reviewer: J. A. Bryant, Jr.

For the past fifteen years or so there has been a significant trend in Jonson criticism toward seeing in the major plays an expression of the author's progressive disillusionment with the manners and morals of Stuart England. Alan Dessen's stimulating study, which focuses our attention on three of the major plays, seeks to support that view with new historical evidence. His book has a double thesis. First, it asserts, with convincing documentation, that *Volpone*, *The Alchemist*, and *Bartholomew Fair* picked up the devices, structural and otherwise, and the tone of the Elizabethan morality and brought that neglected form to its Jacobean culmination. Second, it suggests that these plays of Jonson's go one step beyond the moralities and become "sardonic comedies" which not only condemn the times but remove all hope that the times will ever get any better. These theses are interdependent, as Dessen deals with them, but no harm will be done by separating the two, and they can be examined conveniently in that way.

Dessen's first chapter is in part a protest against the view, still current, that the sixteenth-century morality went into decline around 1560. The Elizabethan morality, as he sees it (and a growing number of scholars will agree with him here), remained a supple form and served a variety of uses right up to the end of the century. Admittedly, only a fraction of all these later moralities survive, and thus generalizations about their influence must be made with caution; but they were clearly popular, and enough of them are extant to give us a fair idea of what moralities were like in the 1590s, when Jonson was acting and writing the apprentice pieces that he later successfully suppressed. One difference between Elizabethan moralities and those of the fifteenth and early sixteenth centuries was the displacement of *humanum genus* at the center by a Vice, who was no longer merely a tempter but a dramatic symbol of whatever the dramatist wished to single out as the basic cause of contemporary evils. Another difference was the dominance in Elizabethan times of the "estates" device as a structural principle: that is, instead of the conventional series of debates or conflicts, a cross-sectional, or panoramic, view of society was made to accommodate a thesis-and-demonstration development of the action. Still another difference was the diminished role of allegory in the late plays. Some or all of these special morality characteristics are found in *Apius and Virginia*, Wapull's *The Tide Tarrieth No Man*, Lupton's *All for Money*, Wilson's *Three Ladies of London* and *The Cobbler's Prophecy*, Lodge and Greene's *A Looking Glass for London and England*, and the anonymous *A Knack to Know a Knave*. Marlowe, Shakespeare, and Jonson undoubtedly knew most of these latter-day moralities and probably a host of others like them, now lost and forgotten. At any rate, Dessen would add to the plays just mentioned Marlowe's *Doctor Faustus* and Shakespeare's *Othello*, both of which have *humanum genus* at the center; the three major comedies by Jonson already referred to; and two of Jonson's late plays, *The Devil Is an Ass* and *The Staple of News*. The last of these alone would give us evidence that Jonson recognized the native tradition, for in that play Mirth, one member of a chorus of gossips, suggests that the old-fashioned devices are still present in Jonson's comedy but "attir'd like men and women o' the time." Citing this familiar passage, Dessen poses his question: Is Jonson announcing something new here, or is he merely spelling out the process by which for some time he has been creating his dramatic personae? Obviously Dessen considers the second possibility more likely; and, given only the two choices, so must we.

There is a third possibility, however, that also needs to be kept in mind: viz., that for at least the first part of his career Jonson was writing in conscious reaction against the popular morality tradition rather than in continuation of it. As an actor Jonson could hardly have avoided knowing about that tradition; and, as has been intimated, he may very well have participated in it. Still, Jonson's earliest surviving work has little formal affinity with any part of that tradition. As Dessen acknowledges, the structure, characterization, and plot of *The Case Is Altered* and *Every Man in His Humor* all come from other fields; and even the three comical satires, for all their use of cross-sectional, or "estates," devices, do not emerge as true moralities. Moreover, the two that come closest, *Every Man Out of His Humor and Cynthia's Revels,* are not strong plays; and Dessen suggests that the second play especially would have profited from having a public Vice in it to give the activity vigor and direction. Perhaps Jonson himself would have agreed—at least in retrospect. Nevertheless, one must keep in mind the possibility that the ambitious and status-minded young classicist had deliberately excluded the Vice and other homely morality figures from works that he hoped might survive their author and his age.

After 1605, Jonson's pattern changes. The Vice or something like him does appear in two highly successful plays, *Volpone* and *The Alchemist*; and Dessen suggests that the author may have hit upon this device in the course of working out his tragedy *Sejanus*, where the historical character of that name performs just such a role and presents an active embodiment of what is wrong with Rome. In any case, Volpone (at least in the most widely held view of that character, which Dessen shares) serves as an embodiment of the gold-worship that infects Venice and proceeds to play the Vice with a representative group of money seekers. Similarly, in Dessen's view *The Alchemist* provides a primary Vice in Face and associate Vices in Subtle and Doll; and there, as in *Volpone,* we see the pattern of "estates" comedy played out in a literal scene. Moreover, at the end Face delivers an epilogue which threatens in good morality fashion to involve the members of the audience as future "ghests" in his sphere of activity. This play, Dessen concludes, is "the culmination of Jonson's moral comedy"; but there is one more great moral comedy to come, *Bartholomew Fair,* which equals *Volpone* and *The Alchemist* in bitterness and satiric force but lacks the clear-cut elements of the morality that distinguished its predecessors. In *The Devil Is an Ass* and *The Staple of News,* Jonson continued his sardonic commentary but relaxed his artistic control, slightly in the first and disastrously for his reputation in the second.

Thus, according to Dessen's survey, the influence of the Elizabethan morality did come to life again in Jonson's major plays and survived with some vigor even in his later, less successful work. One can agree with most of what he says in this part of his study. Jonson did not write morality plays, as Dessen points out more than once. What he did do was to use devices very close to those of the morality in order to solve the problems that were arising in the construction of his own comedies; and it is highly significant that he rediscovered or reinvented those devices for use in some of his best plays. To see that he did so is to uncover still another aspect of Jonson's complex art, and for compelling us to look at that art more closely, we should all be in Dessen's debt. Because of his valuable study, Jonson's work as a whole seems richer than ever and the story of its development, appreciably more interesting.

Even so, one cannot accept the study as a whole without reservations. Moral comedy, as Dessen uses the term, is sardonic comedy, which, as has been noted before, exposes the corruption of the times and then deprives the reader of any lingering hope that the times may improve. Most would agree that this characterizes *Volpone* with fair accuracy, especially Stefan Zweig's truncated version of the play, which until recently was the version one usually encountered on the stage. Some recent scholars, but perhaps not most readers, would agree that it also characterizes *The Alchemist* and *Bartholomew Fair*; and some would include *Epicoene* in the list of sardonic comedies, though Dessen himself does not. His reasons for excluding that play are a bit puzzling. *Epicoene* is a lighthearted exposé, he says, of "various social affectations that are not presented as serious threats to the welfare of society." In response to this, one must ask why, if Sir Epicure Mammon in *The Alchemist* symbolizes a corruption of the order of knighthood, the same is not true of Sir John Daw and Sir Amorous La-Foole. If Corvino violates decorum and morality in attempting to prostitute his wife, what of the moral standards of Lady Haughty and her friends? If Dauphine Eugenie be a "wellborn heir" with "a rightful claim to his intended goal," why should the Bonario of *Volpone* be considered reprehensible for wanting to protect his own expected inheritance? And if the "lighthearted" follies of *Epicoene* are not really dangerous to the body politic, why should one be alarmed at the allowed and well-restricted vanities of Smithfield?

Seeing a reflection of the morality in Jonson's comedies and seeing those comedies from the perspective of the morality are two different things, and only the latter is risky. For example, important as it is that we see from time to time that Volpone is like a Vice in that he embodies Venice's lust for gold, it is more important that we see him most often as a man—gifted, highly ingenious and proud of his ingenuity, and more human than his victims in that he can forget gold when overwhelmed by the human lust for a beautiful woman. Jonson's play is much more about Volpone the superior human being than it is about Venice and the incorrigible corruption there. The play satirizes corruption, to be sure, but like Jonson's other great comedies it also satirizes the two-valued ethic that dominates the morality tradition early and late and was even in 1606 threatening to polarize English society. Taken together, Jonson's four great comedies present a world in which simpleminded notions of right and wrong turn out to be ineffectual. Repeatedly in them he presents a picture of man threatened by his own infinite capacity for error but still capable of finding salvation in the ancient injunction to "love thy neighbor and forgive." In Jonson's scheme of things this is the way out of the maze of self-righteousness and error for characters like Jeremy-Face, who receives forgiveness, and Quarlous, who gives it and urges others to do the same.

This is why Dessen's reading of *Bartholomew Fair* seems, to this reviewer at least, to be headed in a wrong direction. He takes at face value the severe judgments that Waspe, Busy, Overdo, and Quarlous (in the beginning) pass upon the Fair; and thus what he sees in the course of the play is the progressive frustration of their several impulses to rectitude and reform. Waspe loses his self-possession. Busy capitulates; so does Quarlous and calls upon Overdo to do the same. All that remains is the Fair itself, which will go on with its merry and ruthless corruption of decent society. Dessen is not entirely alone in his view of this play (or, for that matter, of *The Alchemist*), but that view is still the minority view. Taken seriously, it forces us to discredit the tone of the Induction and some of the statements there and also the Prologue "To the King's Majesty," which runs as follows:

> Your Majesty is welcome to a Fair;
> Such place, such men, such language, and such ware
> You must expect: with these, the zealous noise
> Of your land's faction, scandalised at toys,
> As babies, hobby-horses, puppet-plays,
> And such-like rage, whereof the petulant ways
> Yourself have known, and have been vext with long,
> These for your sport, without particular wrong,
> Or just complaint of any private man,
> Who of himself, or shall think well, or can,
> The maker doth present: and hopes, to-night
> To give you for a fairing, true delight.

If the attitude expressed here can be the starting point for our reading of Jonson's mature work, we shall find the plays no less "moral comedies"; but they will be comedies that satirize the puritanical morality of the "land's action" and, by implication, the humorless Elizabethan morality tradition that is reflected with gentle irony in various important ways in each of them.

Shakespeare: The Dark Comedies to the Last Plays: From Satire to Celebration, by R. A. Foakes. University Press of Virginia, 1971. Pp. 186. $5.75.

Reviewer: Barbara A. Mowat

Shakespeare's last plays are, like the bones and eyes of the supposedly sea-changed King of Naples, "rich and strange"—and often disturbing. The same adjectives—rich, strange, and disturbing—might well apply to R. A. Foakes's commentary on these plays and their predecessors in *Shakespeare: The Dark Comedies to the Last Plays: from Satire to Celebration*. Rich, certainly; the insights of a critic of Mr. Foakes's stature are always of value, and the introduction to the book, which promises to turn away from thematic analysis and mythic / poetic readings to a concentration on the plays as dramatic structures, to lead us from the problematic middle plays through the satiric tragedies and into a final understanding of the last plays, is beautifully written and offers us an approach to Shakespeare and his development which we all welcome. Again, the introduction (pp. 94–98) to the long section on "Shakespeare's Last Plays" is finely written and exciting.

Yet the book is, in many ways, strange—not as the last plays are strange but as scholarship that has gone awry or is carelessly done is strange. In the first major section, on "The Dark Comedies," for example, in his attempt to direct our attention to characters and scenes often overlooked in thematic or ideological criticism, Mr. Foakes gives us idiosyncratic readings of the plays, especially of *Measure for Measure*. It is good to be taken away from the all-too-standard Christian-theological interpretations of this play, to be reminded that Lucio, Barnardine, and Pompey represent a comic, life-serving force that helps to control our attitude toward the action of the play as a whole. But must one then censure Shakespeare for "weakening the balance" of *Measure for Measure* with his powerful scenes of confrontation between Angelo and Isabella, the Duke and Claudio, Claudio and Isabella, scenes which "overweight" the serious aspects of the play (p. 31)? Is it not strange to attack Isabella for being as destructive as Angelo in her obsessive puritanism (pp. 21, 27); to accuse the Duke of being "inadequate" in his homily on death (pp. 22–23) and of being, though not quite so bad as Lucio paints him, yet "a man of flesh, subject to common lusts and desires" who, in fact, becomes "a fantastical Duke of dark corners" (p. 24); to attack Claudio on the grounds that his cry of "Ay, but to die, and go we know not where" springs "not from a love of life but from horror of death and dread of what comes after," to claim that "to be absolute for life in this way is as perverse as to be absolute for death in the Duke's way" (p. 23)?

Again strange is Mr. Foakes's attempt to link the dark comedies and Shakespeare's tragedies to the satiric drama of Marston and Jonson. There is richness here in the ease with which Mr. Foakes handles the non-Shakespearian drama written for the children's companies of the early 1600s. But there is little connection demonstrated between Jonson's and Marston's plays and those of Shakespeare during this period. More seriously, by accepting Jonson and Marston as experimental and new in their dramas, Mr. Foakes is forced to see *Hamlet* ("one of the last great representatives of a dying mode, heroic tragedy") as "a little old-fashioned even when it was written" (p. 84), a play which appeals to us because of our "nostalgia for the world of certainties" (p. 85) which it represents. By implication, these comments apply as well to *Othello*, *Macbeth*, and *Lear*, since they, too, represent that dying mode of "heroic tragedy." Only the late tragedies—*Timon*, *Coriolanus*, and *Antony and Cleopatra*—"exploit the new possibilities for tragedy opened up" by Marston, Tourneur, and Jonson, claims Mr. Foakes, though his analyses of these plays do not demonstrate just how Shakespeare is using lessons learned from the satirists of the period nor how, as he claims, *Coriolanus* "points the way to a new exploitation of techniques for distancing characters and action," how "the late tragedies, as exemplified by *Coriolanus*, form a natural link between the dark comedies and the last plays" (p. 93). One *feels* that Mr. Foakes is correct in making this final claim, but feeling so is a matter of faith, of trust in the voice of a knowledgeable Shakespearean and in one's own response to Shakespeare's development as a dramatist.

The section on the last plays offers many fine insights, with Mr. Foakes accepting both the concept of the deliberate theatricality of *Cymbeline* and *The Winter's Tale*, and the concept that the characters in these plays do not control their own lives. For those who have not kept up to date on the recent criticism of the last plays, Mr. Foakes's gracefully written statement of these concepts will be particularly welcome. In the analyses of the plays themselves, Mr. Foakes's response to the death-dream-vision aspect of *Cymbeline* (IV.ii and V.iv) is especially good, as is his analysis of the Bohemia section of *The Winter's Tale* and the relationship which he finds there between disguise and deceit and the general theme of art-vs.-nature which dominates the play (see especially pages 114, 118, 136–37). But again there is an overemphasis on hitherto neglected characters (Autolycus in particular), strange readings of certain scenes (he wonders why Leontes, for example, "sees the death of Mamillius as a punishment inflicted on himself, and the death of Hermione likewise, without considering whether these events might be interpretable as punishments inflicted on them" [p. 126]; he claims that Antigonus and his men are "on an errand of mercy" in their journey to abandon Perdita [p. 129]); and his determined attempt to find Imogen comic leads to various misjudgments about her language (p. 110), about her over-concern with herself (p. 111), and about audience response to her. Of course her lament over the headless corpse has its comic aspects, but to claim that, in this most disturbing scene, "Shakespeare wants to ensure that we watch the action with a degree of amused detachment as well as sympathy" (p. 113) is to oversimplify to an incredible degree.

My major disappointment in this last section of the book was his reading of *The Tempest*, a reading which promised to show us how this is "a new departure as a play," linked thematically to *Cymbeline* and *The Winter's Tale* but with its "own distinctive structure . . . [and] its own peculiar pattern of expectations. . ." (p. 144). What we are shown, in fact, is that, according to Mr. Foakes, *The Tempest* is a play about Prospero's desire to return to Milan and rule, a play in which Prospero must learn to rule himself before he can effectively rule others, a play which finds its center in the betrothal masque—a reading that has little to do with "distinctive structure" or "pattern of expectations" and which depends far more on assertion than on demonstration. Mr. Foakes concludes his reading of the play with several related pronouncements about the final scene: "The drive of Prospero to recover rule in himself and in his dukedom has shaped the play, and is now fulfilled" (p. 170); "the drive that sustained him is exhausted"; "the success of his art in completing all his desires is also the completion of his life, in the sense that it leaves him nothing more to live for; which accounts for the sense of melancholy that many people carry away from what is superficially a joyful ending" (p. 172)—a strange way to end the final major section of a book that promises to take us "from satire to celebration." Where, one asks, is the celebration? Certainly not in Mr. Foakes's readings of the last plays.

Rich, strange—and, as I said earlier—disturbing, not only in its peculiar readings of certain plays but also in the carelessness of printing and of footnoting. Some of the mistakes are relatively trivial: on page 19, for example, a needed period is replaced by a comma; on page 21, Claudio becomes Claudius; on page 101, in a discussion of "scene I.vi" of *Cymbeline*, lines quoted from the scene are cited as part of I.v; on the same page, lines quoted from the following scene, which by all rights should be I.vii, are referred to as from I.vi. All in all, very confusing—and symptomatic of a problem that plagues this entire book: namely, that Mr. Foakes never tells us from which edition of a play he is taking his quotes, a galling oversight in a book that depends so heavily on quotations. In the *Cymbeline* problem just cited, for example, he undoubtedly used two editions, one which follows the Folio in giving Act I of *Cymbeline* seven scenes and one of the more customary editions which divides the first act into six scenes. Checking the punctuation of a strangely written quotation from the play against the Folio, Kittredge, Arden, Cambridge, and several other standard editions, I found that he was using none of these. Thus his careful citing of act, scene, and line numbers is essentially useless, unless one just happens upon the edition he used.

The result of this omission on Mr. Foakes's part is that, when one finds a quotation with strange punctuation (and there are many)—for example, from *All's Well* (p. 9),

> Our remedies oft in ourselves do lie.
> Which we ascribe to Heaven.

—one is hard pressed to know whether we have here a typographical error, or whether Mr. Foakes is using an accurate text whose editor had good reason for adopting such odd pointing. Similar questions are raised by renderings of particular lines: e.g., "and make stale / The glistening of this present"—where "glistening" rings very strangely in the ear that has heard only "glistering"—the reading of the Folio, Kittredge, Pafford, *et al.*

A similar carelessness seems to govern the citing of scholarly sources—though here I may easily be mistaken. Mr. Foakes's book is filled with ideas which began to appear in the journals a few years ago and which are in sharp contradiction to his own opinions stated in the 1957 introduction to the Arden *Henry VIII*—yet footnote references are quite sparse. One is astonished to find, for example, no mention of Clifford Leech's essay on the "Structure of the Last Plays" (1958) at critical points where Mr. Foakes seems often to be echoing seminal ideas advanced by Mr. Leech. But ideas and terminology are easily caught things, and those portions of the book that remind me strongly of this author or that may well be examples, not of careless footnoting, but of the fact that certain ideas about the last plays are now so generally accepted as to need no reference.

In summary, Mr. Foakes's book furnishes an interesting, up-to-date introduction to one aspect of Shakespeare's development and should be of interest to the reader who would like a non-thematic approach to some difficult plays. And even for the scholar, if he can put his annoyances aside, overlook the typographical errors, suspend disbelief on certain readings of the plays, and simply relax and enjoy Mr. Foakes's excursions through the land of Shakespeare, expecting not scholarship but gentlemanly gracefulness and ease in handling a mass of material, much pleasure is to be had here.

The Living Image: Shakespearean Essays, by T. R. Henn. Methuen, 1972. Pp. x + 147. $8.00.

Reviewer: Dean Frye

There is an unforgettable footnote on page 92 of this book which may indicate something of its nature and of the kind of effect it produced on at least one urban, North American reader. The discussion concerns the firelock mechanism of the Elizabethan arquebus and caliver and of the "slow-match," which was a "length of string dipped in a solution of saltpetre and alcohol." "I have made this," says the footnote, "by steeping string in the water in which spinach has been boiled." My critical faculties dissolve at such a moment. Here is a writer who has discovered this technique—and how, for heaven's sake?—because slow-matches are a part of his experience, and who apparently assumes that the information will be of use to me in my own experiments with Elizabethan firearms. And this is only a particularly wonderful example. Henn has set springes to catch woodcocks in a garden border at Stratford. More strikingly, for part of his boyhood it "became necessary, for purposes of food, to learn to trap and snare and net" (p. 1), and so he can write with authority about the state in which "the senses are keyed up to receive and register a multitude of small impressions," while "another part of one's mind seems as it were isolated, released" (p. 3). The real subject of this book, many readers will feel, is this sort of interaction between literature and experience of a most specific sort, the experience at first providing significance for the literature; the literature then inviting the search for those particular experiences which will further deepen that significance.

The ostensible subject is Shakespeare's use of imagery from such pursuits as hunting, falconry, horsemanship, and warfare. As Henn points out, facts about these matters and, in some cases, discussions of their relevance to Shakespeare are available in more exhaustive treatments, and what this introductory and rather random study adds in the way of information is the immediacy of personal experience. Much of it was expanded from lectures, and it retains the flavor of the lecture. As an introduction to these subjects, it is more a prospectus than a primer, a taste of the delights in store for the aficionado. As a treatment of some aspects of Shakespearean imagery, it is necessarily incomplete and sometimes fatally idiosyncratic—also necessarily, perhaps, since it is written out of such personal experience of the plays.

It is not merely that metaphoric connections between the managing of horses and of wives are said to be "in the nature of things" (p. 74) or that Henn details an example of the principle that "a wholly extraneous experience may impinge upon us to provide a private interpretation and response" (p. 67) or that, in connection with the galley scene in *Antony and Cleopatra*, we are told that "one's mind turns to another conference (for so the gyres of history work) at which two thirds of the world, having drunk deep in factitious fellowship, gave away to the third sufficient of it to ensure that no peace could be established within their lifetimes" (p. 125). These are frankly personal, if not crotchety, responses which are easily passed over. But the theoretical center of the discussion, in so far as there is one, is a preference for imagery "rooted in the concrete rather than in the abstract" (p. 3), a distinction which amounts to nothing more than "the difference between the contrived and the spontaneous uses of imagery" (p. 26), based on a feeling for "the essential rightness" (p. 6) of some images. "Spontaneous" is used of imagery as though it were a recognized term of clear meaning: "Technical terminology [regarding horsemanship] does enter in, and sometimes it is spontaneous" (p. 70). Yet no real attempt is made to define the term, even for purposes of the argument; spontaneity must simply be sensed, as one senses that Shakespeare uses images from fishing "in a somewhat deliberate and abstract fashion" (p. 55).

Such statements are not necessarily nonsense, but they are at best unhelpful; real communication is possible only with a reader who has already had similar experiences with these images or, for some reason, wishes to have them. And they are based on predilections which are limiting. It is hard to see, for instance, how images from classical mythology—"Mercury, Pegasus, Mars and the rest" (p. 35)—could ever be "living" in the full sense of the title, though it is impossible to pin Henn down on such a point. It is Shakespeare's ability to confirm and deepen experience that is important here, not his ability to enlarge it, and such a subject demands a special kind of criticism—if we are willing today to call it criticism at all—based on a reservoir of shared experiences and assumptions of a sort which certainly does not now bind a tenth of the people who are interested in Shakespeare.

There are intimations of what the reservoir might contain in this case. Henn remarks on the "flat and formalized" imagery from fishing and related areas:

> We may account for this. Hunting and hawking, and horsemanship, were traditionally aristocratic pursuits. They were closely linked to war, diplomacy, and the country gentleman's recreations: they involved the traditional manly qualities of Castiglione's *Courtier*. They were also involved to a greater or lesser degree with the country people, from whom, through the entourage of the Great House, they would have drawn many auxiliaries. One result, as I have pointed out, was a widespread and spontaneous knowledge of the sport: we may suggest some analogy with Irish fox-hounds and harriers today.
>
> (*p. 55*)

Such an explanation for a proposed distinction among Shakespearean images suggests volumes of unexplored assumptions and implications which are prior to the direct experience of the images themselves. No doubt this is to some extent true of all critical statements, but there is an unintimidated trust in private response here which has its weaknesses as well as its strengths.

Full Circle: Shakespeare and Moral Development, by Alan Hobson. Barnes and Noble, 1972. Pp. 232. $9.00.

Reviewer: Gates K. Agnew

It is the author's considerable undertaking in this study to explore the development of Shakespeare's moral awareness and to recommend the emergent process of moral development as a prescription for happiness. Such a program will no doubt strike many Americans in particular as merely arrogant or pretentious, but in my estimate it will be a genuine loss to some who allow themselves to be immediately put off. For Mr. Alan Hobson lives by his own affirmation that "no delicate and beautiful thing, whether in nature or in art, can be received but by the humble and self-disciplined" (p. 59). He is even interesting, perhaps especially interesting, where he fails in humility and discipline or demonstrates the limitations of these virtues. If he is a traditional moralist writing within a traditional British culture, he is also, in Frost's words, "vaguely realizing westward," aware that "man is a maker" who promises not only voyages among the stars but also "new ways of exploring the universe within himself" (p. 226).

In his introduction Hobson lists a variety of traditional moral themes associated with "moral and spiritual transformation" which he will study in "*The Tempest* and other plays." The major focus of his discussion is the development of conscience, which he understands as a progress "from egoism to altruism, and to love, which includes both" (p. 7). Of ten chapters, the first is given over to *King Lear*, the next five to *The Tempest*, and the remainder to *Richard III* (with reference to the *Henry VI* plays), *Macbeth*, *Twelfth Night* (with briefer discussions of several early comedies), and *The Merchant of Venice*. It is difficult in brief compass to give a sense of the expanding analysis of conscience without elaborating discussions of particular texts, and at least in the more successful chapters there is no controversial or "innovative" interpretive argument to be isolated. Hobson seems to me most effective where his interest in conscience directly reflects Shakespeare's interest, notably in *The Tempest, Macbeth,* and *Richard III.* In the lengthy examination of *The Tempest,* the passages on Caliban and Gonzalo and Chapter 5 on dreams are brilliant in their own kind.

It is less difficult to identify certain of the author's assumptions about the purpose and method of reading Shakespeare's plays. Announcing his assumptions is an important means of validating his personal and didactic style, and it gives an appearance of openness and methodological interest all too rare in more "objective" criticism. This book is written in the conviction that "what matters most is the plays and poems we have and what they mean now" (p. 90). The value even of historical and linguistic studies—of which Hobson knows a good deal—is not in establishing "what Shakespeare *was,* but in demonstrating that knowing more of what he was makes us more aware of what he *is.*" These are words Peter Brook might have written, expressing a belief that "the work of art, like pure science, is for the appreciator or student [a] kind of dream whose reality is not established till it has issued in action in the world" (p. 94). The action Hobson has in mind is nothing less than the achievement of a new moral order, and he quotes Jean Piaget to describe the old order in our time of change as "rigid moralities of constraint motivated by fear" (p. 98). This sense of moral purpose in approaching Shakespeare is accompanied by an interest in the way plays are mounted and the ways in which the dramatist manipulates the audience's instinct to identify with his characters. We recognize "a number of ways in which Richard *is* ourselves," for example, before the realities elicited by his dream "make us feel *within* Richard" (p. 125). Where Hobson is not bound by the assumptions of some modern audience, he states his views at length, as in asserting a distinction between Shakespeare's moral assumptions shaped by a Christian culture and the "box-camera mind" of a secular and materialist era which has "grown up thinking of matter and non-matter as sharply distinguishable, and of present, past, and future as clearly separate and distinct" (p. 89). But the readings in this book amount to a test of the usefulness of such assertions rather than imputed proofs of their "truth." In another vein, Hobson challenges the popular assumption that the tragedies are "more convincing" than the comedies, which cannot be credited merely because they end happily (pp. 34–35). His own method of crediting the comedies is less than convincing to me, and it may suggest why these plays still fare better on the stage than in the classroom.

The reference to "development" in the title is related to other assumptions of this study. Development suggests an orientation towards thinking in processes rather than states. And indeed we are told that *King Lear* "does not propound: it explores a process" (p. 31) and later, regarding *Macbeth,* that "the play delineates a process; it would be difficult to maintain that it does not also offer an evaluation" (p. 147). The references, however, are to moral rather than artistic process, which is Hobson's exclusive concern on a conceptual level at least. Another series of assumptions concerning development has to do with the use of psychology in this study. We are told that "the 'inner' life of the mind underlies and conditions the 'outer' life of society and event" (p. 71) and that maturity proceeds with integration. Nevertheless, beyond the brief reference to Piaget, the findings of modern psychology are represented in this book only by John Bowlby's *Child Care and the Growth of Love* (Baltimore: Penguin, 1965) and obliquely through allusions to the poetry of Wordsworth. (Freud and Jung are mentioned once in passing.) Dr. Bowlby's insights are employed with tact in a penetrating analysis of Richard III in comparison with Henry VI (pp. 105 ff.), but the revolutionary perspectives of abnormal and humanistic depth psychology cannot be mediated through a single book on child development. In practice, then, the author's use of psychology is very conservative. He holds that "ceremonies, traditions, social orders exist to reinforce man's flickering altruism or inhibit his egoism, or both" (p. 43), and somewhat like an Elizabethan (wherein lies his value) he gives his attention to the paternal and order-giving, rather than the repressive and neurotic, vision of the social order.

What is impressive to me in these assumptions of the author is the underlying conception of the issues to which a responsible study of moral development in Shakespeare's plays must pay heed. (There you have my prescription.) To be seriously concerned with moral relevance *and* audience response *and* process thinking *and* psychological modes of thought is an heroic enterprise in the present state of culture and criticism (and psychology). Yet no less is required of those moral critics among us, even those cut off from Hobson's supportive, traditional context. Not surprisingly, Hobson's difficulties grow directly out of his rather liberal conservatism, in the presence of which it is easier to make verbal gestures than to pursue certain lines of inquiry. His treatment of the comedies is the major case in point. To deal with comedy within the framework of tragedy and romance has long been a recipe for producing condescension and reductionism, and the assertion that "there is no hard and fast line to be drawn between 'good,' meaning pleasant or desirable, and 'good' meaning 'right' and implying 'ought'" (p. 161) does not alter the traditional subordination of one "good" to the other. The preoccupation with moral experience in the perspective of mature integration of personality inevitably becomes a Procrustean bed which distorts the comedies into variations on the theme of immaturity, moral or otherwise. So Hobson can very sensitively comment upon Prospero's mistreatment of Caliban (pp. 53 ff.) and then act out the same scenario with the characters of *Two Gentleman of Verona and Twelfth Night,* not to mention Falstaff. Here his tone is as shrill and judgmental as before it had been humble and disciplined: "What we have here [in *Two Gentlemen of Verona*] is the spectacle of a sentimental and self-righteous young man offering to hand over the girl he loves, and who loves him, to a proven dastard and liar who merely says he is sorry for what he has done" (p. 172). The author who had discriminated with scrupulous fairness between the forces of life and death in Lady Macbeth concludes querulously that "Julia's love is not quite perfect" (p. 175). Any analysis of the comedies which finds little that can be handled and admired without ethical asbestos gloves beyond Viola and *The Merchant of Venice* is surely itself not quite perfect, showing the actual limits of the author's involvement in audience response, artistic process (the comedies "work" very differently from the tragedies), and psychological insight. The main shortcoming, however, is moral, and the observation that "the Christian myth is itself an illuminating record of human psychology" (p. 105) indicates the first path towards more radical involvement, as in such works as H. A. Williams' *The True Wilderness* (Baltimore: Penguin, 1965) and "Theology and Self-Awareness" in *Soundings* (Cambridge: University Press, 1966). Something important will have happened, a step toward a new moral order will have been taken, when the moral interpreter of Shakespeare allows himself to identify as closely with comic processes and the goodness of pleasure as with the tragic, when he says humbly with the mature Prospero, "this thing of darkness I acknowledge mine."

Scenic Form in Shakespeare, by Emrys Jones. Oxford University Press, 1971. Pp. 269. $9.75.

Reviewer: William Leigh Godshalk

Emrys Jones has written a stimulating and provocative study, not one which the scholarly reader can skim passively, nodding with easy assent at profound commonplaces of description and interpretation. The margin of my copy is crowded with commentary and notes of disagreement.

The study is divided into two parts, each subdivided into four chapters. The first part establishes the principles to be used and the hypotheses to be tested, while the second part focuses on four major tragedies: *Othello, Lear, Macbeth,* and *Antony and Cleopatra.* Jones is chiefly interested in Shakespeare as a maker of scenes. He asserts that, in the great scenes like the banquet scene in *Macbeth,* "what Shakespeare has invented is something—a structure, an *occasion*—which may be said to be (however dangerous the phrase) independent of the words which are usually thought to give the scene its realization. This 'something' we may call a 'scenic form' " (p. 3). The central ideas of the first chapter are the emotional effect of the scene on the audience and Shakespeare's ability to control audience reaction through certain scenic devices, such as tempo.

The discussion of tempo leads smoothly to Jones's distinction between "time" and "continuity" in drama. The nineteenth-century critics developed a theory of double-time, arguing that Shakespeare uses concurrently a "short time" and "long time" in many of his plays. Jones believes that "long time" is generally acceptable but that "short time" is not. In Shakespeare's references to the passage of time we should see only a "sequence" and not a "duration." The dramatist is tying his scenes together sequentially; he is not indicating a definite number of hours and days. Jones believes that an audience is not aware of the passage of "short time" in the plays, and thus it is not valid to calculate it precisely. When Shakespeare wishes the audience to become aware of time passing (as he does in *As You Like It,* V.ii), he works precise time references into the dialogue. But to build a time scheme from Shakespeare's general references to "night" and "day" is to mistake the playwright's intention. He is merely maintaining "scenic continuity."

However, in most of Shakespeare's tragedies there appears to be a break in scenic continuity somewhere in or immediately after the third act. Following George Kernodle and possibly Peter Alexander, Jones argues that Elizabethan plays were built on a five-act structure, but with the first three acts forming an initial movement followed by an intermission or interval. Necessitated by the nature of the drama, the intermission gave Shakespeare a chance to construct two different dramatic worlds for each play, for "if the play has an interval, the imaginative system is dissolved and another one must replace it when the play is resumed after the interval" (p. 71). The two parts of the play may be compared to a sonnet, and Shakespeare will often conclude both parts of the play on a similar note—"it may be considered as a kind of structural rhyme" (p. 76). The climactic sequence of scenes in the third act often mirrors or foreshadows the end of the play.

Jones also investigates what he calls "the growth of scenes," Shakespeare's apparent use of scenes from early plays as paradigms for scenes in the later tragedies. Jones hypothesizes that Shakespeare, when changing his source material into scenes, remembered the structure of the scenes in the earlier plays. These remembered scenes are a kind of structural vocabulary which Shakespeare could and did use again and again. In this connection, the early history plays, *1, 2, 3 Henry VI*, *Richard III*, and *King John* "are of crucial importance for Shakespeare's development as a tragic dramatist. . . . until the end of his career he continued to draw on them as sources of scenic form and contrivance, or in more elusive ways as guides or suggestions for dramatizing narrative materials" (p. 112). On the other hand, Jones admits that we cannot make sweeping generalizations about Shakespeare's progress as a scenic artist. Only by comparing individual scenes can we point to Shakespeare's growing "economy" (p. 113).

In brief outline, these are the ideas which Jones uses to approach the tragedies named above. Although it must be acknowledged that such a summary can only suggest the force of the arguments, still, I think Jones's basic position will be clear. Many of his ideas are extremely compelling. Nevertheless, I would like to indicate some areas where Jones's arguments might have been expanded and others where I have detected possible weaknesses.

In studying Shakespeare as a "scenic poet," Jones emphasizes that Shakespeare was a man of the theater who learned a good deal from his compeers, like Greene, and who took artistic advantage of the exigencies of the Elizabethan stage. However, he does not mention the possible influence of Elizabethan production "plots" on Shakespeare's constructive technique. Apparently it was the custom to make such a plot-outline for each play presented so that the actors or the bookkeeper could keep track of the entrances and the properties. An actor-playwright who daily used a "plot" would naturally, we may suppose, think of a play in visual terms, as a sequence of carefully marked scenes. Even today, if the critic wants to *see* the physical shape of Shakespeare's plays, he can do little better than make a "plot."

However, Jones is primarily interested, not in the physical shape of the scene, but in its emotive power. "A comparison can be drawn with works of music," he believes, "for there is something more than superficially 'musical' about such resilient theatrical works as *Richard III*, *Romeo and Juliet*, *The Merchant of Venice*, and *Hamlet*. When we see them performed what we enjoy is, in part, the process of 'going through' the work, taking pleasure in its texture and structure in a way which critical accounts which limit themselves to interpretation can hardly do justice to" (p. 28). The musical analogy, which is used throughout the study, suggests Jones's emphasis.

Unfortunately, the analysis of the emotional value of a scene or a play appears to be even more open to individual reaction than intellectual interpretation. My emotions while watching a scene may not correspond to yours in any way. Let us take an example from the 1955 production of *Titus Andronicus* by Peter Brook, a "major piece of theatrical resuscitation" in Jones's opinion (p. 8). Jones analyzes the emotional impact of the first scene of Act III on the audience, "an example of what the dramatist can do to bring about a profound emotional experience in his audience" (p. 8). But Richard David's emotions were not engaged by Brook's production ("the evening so unrewarding, the effect so cold"—*ShS*, 10 [1957], 128), while Arnold Szyfman writes, "I recall vividly the Stratford Memorial Theatre performance of *Titus Andronicus* in 1955. This was unforgettable, in which Peter Brook's direction gave the play a completely fresh structural quality" (*ShS*, 13 [1960], 70). Evidently Shakespeare did not uniformly control the emotions of the audience in 1955.

Diversity of reaction to a play is, of course, to be expected, and only because Jones seems to attribute uniformity to an audience do I emphasize the opposite. Jones's description of the audience is almost mystical: "The audience is a mysteriously endowed thing, in some respects slow-witted, in others shrewdly self-possessed and hard to deceive; having what may seem a simpler mental equipment than an intelligent individual, but with different powers and susceptibilities and a different emotional range" (p. 6). This "corporate presence" has an " 'audience mind' " (p. 7). To this audience mind Jones, at certain points in his argument, appeals: "It is surely clear whose response is more to be trusted. . . . the audience must be right, the critics wrong" (p. 56). But this is, just as surely, an appeal to a myth. Messers David and Szyfman were part of an audience; they did not react uniformly. How can we call on their "audience mind" to render judgment on a difficult question of interpretation? Questionnaires might be handed out at performances to ascertain the "truth" about Shakespeare's plays. Although the hazards of such an approach are revealed in I. A. Richard's *Practical Criticism*, some enterprising critic of the future may wish to gather information in this manner and then computerize the data. But would the conclusions be acceptable to anyone, even Jones?

In discussing the emotive power of a play, Jones concentrates on the individual scene at the expense of cumulative effect. Jones's first example of scenic power, *Titus Andronicus*, III.i, will also serve as an example. Jones does an excellent job of showing how the "scene is carefully built in stages" (p. 9), but he neglects to point out, even in passing, that the scene gains emotive force through its relationship with former scenes. Titus' pleading and crawling in this scene is connected, as Judith Karr points out (*SQ*, 14 [Summer 1963], 278–79), with a recurring pattern of kneeling and pleading. The hand which Titus cuts off in this scene as the mutilated Lavinia watches is the same hand which blessed her in the first scene. The action is part of a dismemberment motif which is present throughout the play. My point is that the power of a scene is never simply the product of that particular scene. There is a cumulative power which Jones neglects, in the main, to consider. This is one reason, I believe, why Jones's criticism lacks the sharpness of, say, Anthony Caputi's scenic analyses (see, e.g., "Scenic Design in *Measure for Measure*," *JEGP*, 60 [July 1961], 423–34). Jones might have further sharpened his criticism by adopting Harold Brook's view of scenic structure, which takes into account sub-scenes or *scènes*. Jones apparently lacks the concept of a sub-scene, and this leads to a kind of awkwardness in discussing a long, variegated scene (see, e.g., p. 181).

Jones's distinction between "time" and "continuity" is useful, for Shakespeare's "prime concern is not duration but continuity" (p. 41). In many of his plays, the time scheme may be ignored. We simply need to be aware that time passes and that people and things change. Flux is important, but not the actual clock. Nevertheless, we may not be entirely satisfied that Jones's examples prove his point. "*Julius Caesar*," Jones writes, "deals of course with historical events. . . . We know, just as Shakespeare and many of his audience knew, that the events which are dramatized in these first three acts did not take place on two successive days. . . . Did Shakespeare mean his audience to think that only two days spanned Cassius' first approach to Brutus on the subject of Caesar, and Caesar's assassination? The answer, it seems clear, is that he did not expect his audience to think this. . . . we are not intended to make any inference about the actual period of time which these events historically occupied" (p. 44). Yes, of course, we cannot make historical inferences from Shakespeare's plays, but within the continuity of the play, we do infer that Brutus is seduced by Cassius within two days. Brutus' stoicism has not kept him from committing a rash act, and the rashness of the act is underscored by the brief period needed to seduce him. Jones's example clearly flies in the face of what is indicated by the play. Beyond slipping into the intentional fallacy, he is confusing in his argument *dramatic time* with *historic time*; his contention that the first three acts of *Julius Caesar* do not take place on two successive days is based on historic and not dramatic considerations.

As Jones points out, the most "extreme case" of double-time is *Othello*. He argues that the first part of the play, ending in III.i, has a precise temporal dimension, but the second part—the destruction of Othello and Desdemona—has an indefinite time sequence. There is, he claims, an "absence of any clear indications of a time-scheme governing the new movement" (p. 57). However, there is a clear time reference placed near the beginning of this movement. Desdemona pointedly asks Othello when he will recall Cassio: "to-morrow night, or Tuesday morn, / On Tuesday noon or night, on Wednesday morn" (III.iii.61–62). The attentive playgoer will notice that it is Sunday, that Othello is seduced by Iago on the same day, and that Desdemona is killed that night. That this movement of the play happens on Sunday is both emotionally and intellectually significant. The oath-taking passage (III.iii.464–83) takes on added power when we remember that it is the Sabbath. Is it a kind of Black

Mass, a homosexual marriage ("I am your own for ever"), or Othello's symbolic union with the Evil One? Possibly it partakes of all three. In the last scene Iago admits his diabolic nature. Othello tells him, "If that thou be'st a devil, I cannot kill thee" (V.ii.290), and after an unsuccessful attempt on his life, Iago answers, "I bleed, sir; but not kill'd" (v.ii.292), with the obvious implication. Ironically, the final stage of Iago's infernal plot takes place on Sunday. But his nature suggests something further about the double-time of the play. If Iago is (at least in part) a supernatural villain, possibly he does operate within a double time scheme, and possibly Othello is caught tragically in a diabolic plot from which it is impossible to escape. "Hell and night / Must bring this monstrous birth to the world's light." In trying to dispose of the concept of double-time, Jones should perhaps exempt *Othello*. This "extreme case" is unique among Shakespeare's plays, and its double time scheme should not be neglected.

With Jones's chapter on "The Two-Part Structure," I will not quibble. This chapter and its ramifications in the second part of the study were for me the strong points of Jones's criticism. However, the following chapter, "The Growth of Scenes," was troublesome. Where the former chapters are aimed at audience reaction and the concomitant formal considerations, this chapter is basically historical, aimed at the scholar and not the playgoer. It is out of character. When scenic sources are traced in detail, Jones's valuable insights are "lost in clogging detail" (p. 192, a phrase Jones uses for *Lear*). Some of the comparisons between early scenes and late seem exceptionally forced (see, e.g., pp. 210–11) and not very enlightening. When the comparisons do throw light, it is often of the most diffuse kind: "The banquet scene [*Macbeth*, III.iv] acquires its complex form from being a conflation of two quite different scenic ideas, and perhaps something of its power derives from this diversity of structural sources" (p. 219). Perhaps. But, while diversity may be the attribute of the sources, complexity is by and large added by the playwright.

Moreover, locating scenic paradigms for Shakesepare's mature tragedies becomes an ever larger and more nebulous task as our inquiry becomes more insistent. Shakespeare knew the value of trial scenes and used them in various ways throughout his career, from *Titus* to *Cymbeline*. Each trial scene bears some similarity to its brethren, and to trace the similarities and differences might take a large book. What is the paradigm for Kent's "trial" by Cornwall? Jones answers: ". . . there are signs that *Henry VI, Part Two* furnished some substantial hints" (p. 182). Again, we may grant him a possible affirmative. But after Shakespeare had learned the "vocabulary of scenic forms" (to use Jones's term, p. 96), did he need to return to individual scenes in former plays? When we learn to write a sentence, do we always return to sentences we have written in the past in order to re-use their forms? Shakespeare had learned how to make a scene; he did not need to return to specific scenes in *Henry VI* for paradigms. All in all, the second half of the study is marred for me by this intrusion of scenic comparisons. If Jones wished to include this material, it is unfortunate that he did not confine it to Chapter IV.

I would also like to bring up several minor issues. "*King John* is certainly not very satisfyingly constructed," Jones believes, "and no amount of special pleading could conceal its episodic progress. . . . No one would claim *King John* to be a very successful or satisfying play as a whole" (pp. 83, 103). The verbs "could" and "would" are rather disconcerting since several critics have indeed defended the play. In his seminal essay, Adrien Bonjour reexamined the question of unity in the play (*ELH*, 18 [Dec. 1951], 253–74), and he has been notably followed in different ways by James Calderwood (*UTQ*, 29 [April 1960], 341–56) and John R. Elliot (*ShakS*, 1 [1965], 64–84). Apparently Jones has not seen these essays. Since *King John* is one of the early plays that Jones concentrates on, this is surely a surprising ignorance. But a glance at Jones's index will reveal that very few recent critics are cited and that he relies in the main on A. C. Bradley and Harley Granville-Barker.

Considering the Chorus of *Henry V*, Jones takes an extremely limited view of its function: "the Chorus is a means of ensuring continuity between the acts, smoothing the transitions, and kindling the imagination of the audience" (p. 232). Especially it helps the audience "to rise to the greatness of the occasion" (p. 234). But this interpretation of the Chorus' function does not account for the ironic juxtapositions, the epic voice of the Chorus set against the mundane realities of politics and war. The Chorus is, in a sense, mocked by the scenes which follow; its voice of triumphant nationalism is undercut by the greed of clerics, the cowardice of soldiers, and the horrors of war. The Chorus speaks sentimentally of "A little touch of Harry in the night" (IV.Prologue.47), while the following scene shows Harry quarrelling with his soldiers. Obviously Jones simplifies the complexity of the Chorus, possibly to make it more comparable to some of the devices used in *Antony and Cleopatra*. But this simplification and distortion calls Jones's comparison into question. Perhaps the epic devices of *Antony* are not at all like the Chorus in *Henry V*.

One factual mistake mars Jones's comments on the sequence of heath scenes in *Lear*. Jones writes: "The second [heath scene] (III.iv) moves to the entrance of a hovel. . . . The third and last heath scene (vi) takes place inside the hovel" (p. 185). But Jones apparently misses the significance of Gloucester's words: "I ventur'd to come seek you out, / And bring you where both fire and food is ready" (III.iv.148–49). Gloucester risks his life and his eyes to take Lear to a comfortable shelter he has prepared (not a hovel), and here Lear conducts the "mad trial" in which Goneril and Regan are condemned. Scene iv takes place not on the heath but, as Alexander's text (i.e., the one Jones uses) points out, in an "outhouse of Gloucester's castle." Of course, this is a very minor point, but in context it becomes symbolic of the lack of precision inherent in Jones's criticism. It is similar to the absence of act, scene, and line references following some of the quoted material (see, e.g., pp. 30–40).

These quibbling criticisms notwithstanding, Jones's study deserves several readings. His insights into the individual plays will repay careful attention, and although one may disagree with his premises, "the significance of one dimension of Shakespeare's art has been given some timely emphasis" (*TLS*, 30 June 1972, p. 739). Jones promises a further study of Shakespeare's comedies, and I, for one, look forward to it with expectation.

Our Naked Frailties: Sensational Art and Meaning in "Macbeth," by Paul A. Jorgensen. University of California Press, 1971. Pp. 242. $7.50.

Reviewer: Joan Hartwig

Damnation is not a present experience for most of us: we put it off. Professor Jorgensen demonstrates in his study of *Macbeth* that the play's power is due to the violent and vividly felt presence of hell that Macbeth leads us through. Macbeth's hell is not something that may occur at some later date after he has had time to accumulate his life and perhaps then to confront the possibility that hell is real—it is a surprising phenomenon that happens before he is ready. The realization that future time simply does not exist, that hell's punishments are felt by bodies and minds not yet dead, creates incomparable sensations of horror for Shakespeare's audience.

The "Naked Frailties" of the book's title are ours as much as they are Banquo's or Macduff's or the Macbeths' at the discovery of Duncan's murdered body, and they "suffer in exposure" to the degree that the play engages us. Jorgensen finds that *Macbeth* has a "uniquely tangible impact upon our feelings"—that "Shakespeare disturbs us throughout our nervous system, by exposing to each of us what is within us" (p. 2). The "sensational" art which the book examines refers not only to the spectacular impact of blood, the Weird Sisters, and Banquo's ghost but also to the "violences of imagery, atmosphere, stress, and sensory and mental torment," the subtler artifices of sensation.

In reviewing the assumptions of the Elizabethan-Jacobean playgoer, Jorgensen points out that a general distrust of feeling was due partly to the belief that the sensible soul could lead to sensuality and passion, even though it was potentially capable of noble actions. The imaginative faculty was as suspect as the sensible soul under which it was classified, and the Devil was thought to work principally through the imagination. Jorgensen suggests that such strictures upon the imagination help to explain Macbeth's downfall and suffering, because he yields "directly to the imaginative faculty rather than to the reason and conscience that should control it" (p. 17). In addition to their distrust of the senses and of the imagination, most people were probably aware of the "murder tracts" and the sensational literature dealing with the clinical symptoms of possession by witches. Jorgensen produces a rich background of contemporary and precedent reference for both of these popular journalistic genres, and he speculates that these secular tracts and the contemporary published sermons that emphasized sensory detail in order to evoke guilt must have created a formidable assault on a man's security concerning the state of his soul. The sensational art of *Macbeth* makes a similar assault upon the conscience of its audience.

The condign punishment which Macbeth suffers reinforces the audience's awareness that hell exists here and now. His pain includes more than exact retribution for evil imaginings and ambition; it includes the pain of sense (*poena sensus*) and the pain of loss (*poena damni*), the two ultimate forms of punishment as defined by Aquinas. According to Jorgensen, Macbeth receives pain of sense throughout the first four acts of the play and feels the pain of loss fully only in the final act. We hear him describe the pain of loss after he has murdered Duncan, but, as is often the case with Macbeth, there is a distance between words spoken and words comprehended.

Whereas many critics shy away from defining the evil in the play, Jorgensen attempts to explain features of the evil by examining the dramaturgical techniques that make it mysterious. In Chapter 3 his discussion of Shakespeare's manipulation of language is excellently suggestive. The namelessness of the evil, Lady Macbeth's and Macbeth's refusal to name either the act of murder or its attributes, the blurring of values through vague reference—pronouns without antecedents, euphemisms for "murder" and "blood"—all contribute to the audience's mounting sense of horror. Macduff's linguistic explosion after he discovers Duncan's body penetrates the muted language of the murder scene and defines the evil, at least partially. Jorgensen says, "Its hysterical force is justified for the audience, who have moved too long and too apprehensively in the murky namelessness of the evil and who are grateful to have the horror howled out and named, though imperfectly" (p. 50). Even Macbeth seems released from his inability to consider the deed and describes the murdered king and guards in gory detail. His fervor is such that Lady Macbeth becomes anxious and faints, either, as Jorgensen thinks, because the scene has been too graphically recalled (p. 91) or to prevent her husband from exposing his further guilt (p. 194).

The murder of Duncan is the most tangible form that the mysterious evil of the play takes, and Shakespeare's employment of the rhythms of ritualistic language increases the horror for the audience. The compulsive movement of the language, Macbeth's earlier commitment of "each corporal agent to this terrible feat," the trancelike quality of Macbeth's progress toward the chamber, all lead Jorgensen to view Macbeth as "possessed" during the murder: "He is no longer a human being—the sentient, conscience-tormented, reasoning man of 'If it were done'—but a Frankenstein instrument of murder" (p. 67). The possession theory has been argued before, and Jorgensen argues it well—perhaps with more consideration for its dangers than some. Still, I am not convinced that Shakespeare meant for these effects to be taken as evidence of literal possession. When Macbeth asks why he "could not pronounce 'Amen' " (II.ii.30), his innocence of the meaning that his action contains speaks more forcibly than Jorgensen's explanation (literally applied) that he could not speak "Amen" because "he is in the service of the Devil, because he has closed the eye of his body and of his soul to light, and because he has done the horrid deed" (p. 67). The idea of possession with its attendant terrifying power works at the metaphoric level to enhance our awareness of Macbeth's experience; but to insist on the literality of possession denies Macbeth his human, and therefore pitiable, struggle against his instinctive knowledge of what his actions mean. The argument seems to center on whether Lady Macbeth's and Macbeth's prayers to be unsexed and dehumanized are answered directly by the play's supernatural control or whether their own human wills, through free choice, are allowed to narrow their human natures. I cannot help but feel that the play explores the complexities of the latter.

Shakespeare's thematic use of blood, Jorgensen finds, is most horrible in *Macbeth*, because for the first time in the plays it spreads uncontrollably as a punishment for murder. From the bloody Captain, who, like an ominous prologue, introduces the theme of blood with both his words and his own bleeding, through Lady Macbeth's invocation to "make thick my blood" and the experiential sticky blood of Duncan, to the gory locks of Banquo's ghost, the blood in *Macbeth* spreads until the protagonist wades in it, by choice as well as by necessity. The reality and the guilt of felt blood is something for which Macbeth is not prepared until he sees the "gouts of blood" form on his visionary dagger, despite his previous knowledge of blood in battle—the smoking blood on his warrior's blade that we hear described by the bleeding Captain.

When blood mixes with guilt, it becomes horrible, and thereafter the protagonists work compulsively but futilely to cleanse their hands.

Chapter 8 on the pain of futile labor, doubled and misapplied, is one of the most interesting in the book. Jorgensen sees the continuing struggles of Macbeth and his lady and even of the Witches ("double, double toil") as characteristic of the punishments of hell. Even time grows labored in its motion through Macbeth's "tomorrow" speech. Wasted labor reinforces the sense that Macbeth's efforts are not only lonely in their undertaking and execution but also sterile in their results. The ironic answer to Lady Macbeth's desire to be unsexed is felt nowhere so surely as in her pathetic attempt in the sleepwalking scene to lead her husband "to bed, to bed, to bed."

The denial of procreative action seems inherent in the ambitious murder of Duncan, the meek and gentle dispenser of Grace in Scotland. Images of violated innocence and babies abound in the play (in contrast to the barrenness of the Macbeths), and they encourage the audience to know the experience of hell's punishment applied for and answered within the realm of human action. In discussing Shakespeare's development of the theme of outraged innocence, Jorgensen says that not only Duncan but Malcolm too becomes a personification of innocence—a view with which I do not agree. The questions that Wilbur Sanders raises in *The Dramatist and the Received Idea* (Cambridge: Cambridge Univ. Press, 1968) about the effects of Malcolm's deception of Macduff need to be considered: "Duncan is the lost possibility, Malcolm the diminished necessity. Royalty of nature once slain, only the meaner virtues of circumspection and prudence can survive. . . . The very act of envisaging the corruption of his own nature has tainted him" (pp. 258–62). I would like to see Jorgensen deal with these questions, but he does not. His statement that Malcolm's protestations of innocence make him innocent seems naïve: "Malcolm further protests that he is unknown to women, has never told a lie or broken faith (IV.iii.125–31). At the risk of making his savior of Scotland Innocence personified rather than a real character, Shakespeare lays on the childlike qualities relentlessly" (p. 106). I do not think that Shakespeare asks us first to consider a corrupt Malcolm and then to discard the image without a hangover. Even Macduff has a problem when he tries to do just that: "Such welcome and unwelcome things at once, / 'Tis hard to reconcile" (IV.iii.138). Surely in a play filled with equivocations, Macduff's (and the audience's) experience of this equivocation cannot be divorced from the larger context. Malcolm cannot be the personification of innocence, even if he would be, once he has denied his own purity in such detail and with such pragmatic disregard for truth.

What Jorgensen does best, I think, is to present the "body" of Macbeth in his nervous frayedness so that readers of his book take away an increased awareness of how Shakespeare pushes them toward a personal physical and emotional weariness. The condign punishment that shrinks Macbeth's ability to feel, when he is the "tragic hero whose life as we see it has been most persistently and intensely one of sensation" (pp. 215–16), is ironic and pitiable. It engages us even as Macbeth loses the capacity for feeling—as he discovers that he can no longer feel even the fear which has compulsively driven him to act throughout the play. When he hears the cry of the women that marks his wife's death, he realizes that his sensible perceptors have simply quit responding to horror. The pain that is left to be felt is the pain of loss, not only of renown and grace but finally of human feeling.

Because I like Professor Jorgensen's book, I must say that his final chapter's *apologia* is unworthy of the clear, careful, and often excitingly suggestive study that precedes it.

Jacobean Dramatic Perspectives, by Arthur C. Kirsch. University Press of Virginia, 1972. Pp. 131. $7.50.

Reviewer: John Scott Colley

Since he wrote *Dryden's Heroic Drama* (Princeton: Princeton Univ. Press 1965), Arthur Kirsch has been interested in the "Fletcherian" mode of dramatic construction. He now observes that "the harmonies of plays written on Shakespearean principles and of those written on Fletcherian principles are different both in kind and dimension, and an appreciation of the differences is essential for a just understanding of the history of seventeenth-century drama" (p. 127). These "Fletcherian harmonies," together with their genesis and development in the plays of Jonson, Marston, Middleton, Shakespeare, Webster, and Ford, form the basis of Kirsch's study. It is his hope to note the effects of the revolution of taste and playwriting which resulted in a triumph of the "self-conscious" Fletcherian, not the Shakespearean, mode. Kirsch sees the Jacobean drama stemming from a confluence of forces, notably Guarini's conception of tragicomedy, the new popularity of comical satire, and the impact of the morality play, especially upon Jonson and Middleton. Affecting these dramatic forces were the revival of the children's indoor playing houses and the creation of an "elite" audience. Kirsch chooses not to involve himself directly in an analysis of the rise of the private theaters, a particularly "vexed question" to him, and concentrates instead upon literary and dramatic, rather than purely theatrical forces.

To Kirsch, Guarini's tragicomedy was a conscious attempt to create a modern genre to serve the tastes of a contemporary audience. With his self-conscious concern with plot and his equal concern with style, Guarini produced a form of drama that moved its audience "to admire and wonder not only at the marvelous oppositions and feelings which are depicted but also the art which depicts them" (p. 12). "Self-consciously wonderful," Guarini's tragicomedy "expressed at once the marvelous Providence of nature and art" (p. 15). In Beaumont and Fletcher's plays, a similar heightened display of language and spectacle becomes the only motive of action. Such displays had performed poetic and thematic functions in Guarini's drama.

Jonson was Guarini's English counterpart in that he established a revolutionary dramatic genre: comical satire. The new genre was formed from such diverse elements as the morality play and formal verse satire: "A common denominator of these factors . . . is a pervasive theatrical self-consciousness which seeks at once to involve the spectator in the playwright's art and to oblige him to stand apart and observe it" (p. 23). Satire distances its audience through irony, and the morality calls attention to itself "through an interplay between the audience's latent and conscious senses that the whole of the world is such a stage" (p. 22).

Kirsch feels that Guarini and Jonson laid the groundwork for the experiments of seventeenth-century drama, and that their influence can be seen in Shakespeare as well as the minor dramatists. The stimulus of Marston's achievement in *The Malcontent* is "almost certainly *The Pastor Fido*" (p. 37); Shakespeare's preoccupation with "riddles, oxymorons and paradoxical oppositions" in *All's Well* is an outgrowth of patterns of tragicomedy (p. 57); and "even superficially considered," most of the features of *Cymbeline* "which cause trouble for critics are precisely those which are most typical of self-conscious tragicomedy" (p. 65). On the other hand, Middleton's savage irony can be understood in terms of the morality-satiric tradition he inherited from Jonson (p. 85).

The reasons behind the new Jacobean consciousness are interpreted in terms of intellectual history: When the fate of men had become intelligible as a function of social behavior, rather than of the state of their souls, and when the creative power of the artist ceased to be compared to the creative power of God, "when Providence disappears as a principle of structure as well as belief" (p. 129), the drama begins to reveal the "Fletcherian harmonies" that Kirsch charts in his critical study. As the drama is cut off from the "metaphysical reverberations" of the Elizabethan public theater, both poetry and narrative begin to suffer. Marston, Webster and Ford succeed only when they are able "to unite theatrical self-consciousness with some commitment to traditional ideas of dramatic Providence." The plays in "which this commitment, though invoked, is not real, suffer from preciosity" (p. 131). Shakespearean drama reveals a harmony that stems from the dramatist's sense of the levels of meaning inherent in his dramatic pieces; Fletcher and those like him fail when their self-conscious artifice "goes beyond the traditional capacity of drama to be simultaneously realistic and symbolic"; Shakespeare's vision serves "to make us aware of the analogies between the stage and the world, to involve us in the action and at the same time to keep us detached enough to make judgments about it" (pp. 39–40). "Without either the vision of fortunate suffering which informs Shakespeare's dispassion or the moral clarity which informs Middleton's, the detachment and self-consciousness which Beaumont and Fletcher's style breeds turn in upon themselves when applied to a serious subject; and this was to be a most damaging legacy in seventeenth-century drama, affecting playwrights like Webster, Ford, and Dryden, as well as comparative hacks like Massinger and Shirley" (p. 51).

Kirsch's reading of intellectual and theatrical history results in some definite critical opinions: Middleton has been undervalued; *The Duchess of Malfi*, not *The White Devil*, is Webster's masterpiece; "the old judgment, held by both Coleridge and Eliot, that Beaumont and Fletcher's plays are parasitic and without inner meaning, seems just" (p. 47). Kirsch's negative reaction to Beaumont at least may be modified by Philip J. Finkelpearl's recent "Beaumont and Fletcher and 'Beaumont and Fletcher': Some Distinctions," *ELR*, 1 (Spring 1971), 144–64.

Kirsch presents an intriguing case. Yet his great strengths as a writer—clarity and brevity—do work against him, and what he intends to be clear and concise may appear terse and undeveloped to some readers. His analysis of the relationship between changes in art and in theological perspectives is limited to five concluding pages. Yet it is only in his conclusion that his earlier discussions of the plays begin to make sense. I experienced a sense of Fletcherian wonder on page 128 when I finally realized what had been at the back of his mind as he had discussed those "precious" dramatists. Kirsch may also be guilty of limiting too severely the scope of his inquiry. He had good reason to omit Tourneur, whose role in his scheme is apparent enough, but he does not treat Chapman at all. Nor does he mention why Chapman (certainly one of the significant coterie dramatists) is of no interest to him. Lyly is ignored as well, and it strikes me that a "self-consciousness" of the Guarini-Jonson type was anticipated by Lyly's drama written for the original children's theater. Some consideration of Lyly (and G. K. Hunter's book on him [Cambridge, Mass.:

Harvard Univ. Press, 1962]) would modify Kirsch's arguments. Kirsch also limits the number of plays he treats, and some distortion may result from his economical coverage. He does state sensibly that the entire question is incredibly complex, and, wishing to avoid "reductive formulae," he seeks only "fresh and essential insights into some familiar Jacobean works" (p. 6). That he accomplishes. Yet his insights are so fresh that I wish he had written more than 131 pages on such a challenging subject.

Moreover, he could have strengthened the force of his arguments by placing his work more clearly in the context of recent scholarship on the subject. Glynne Wickham's *Early English Stages*, Volume II, Part 1 (New York: Columbia Univ. Press, 1963) supplies a sustained discussion of the theatrical forces that so interest Kirsch. And Joseph Donohue's *Dramatic Character in the English Romantic Age* (Princeton: Princeton Univ. Press, 1970) studies the persistence of the Fletcherian mode in later drama. And it seems that no discussion of dramatic patterns of "engagement and detachment" is complete without some reference to S. L. Bethell's *Shakespeare and the Popular Dramatic Tradition* (Durham, N. C.: Duke Univ. Press, 1944). Kirsch's brief references to *felix culpa* themes could have been substantiated by citation of Herbert Weisinger's *Tragedy and the Paradox of the Fortunate Fall* (East Lansing: Michigan State Univ. Press, 1953). I mention these works mainly in an attempt to support or augment some of Kirsch's more suggestive historical insights. His sensitive critical responses do stand without props, however, and his chapters on Shakespeare, Middleton, and Webster are especially fine additions to seventeenth-century studies. I still prefer John F. Danby's assessment of Beaumont and Fletcher in *Poets on Fortune's Hill* (London: Faber & Faber, 1952) and Philip Finkelpearl's evaluation of Marston's art in *John Marston of the Middle Temple* (Cambridge, Mass.: Harvard Univ. Press, 1969).

The Multiple Plot in English Renaissance Drama, by Richard Levin. University of Chicago Press, 1971. Pp. xvi + 277. $9.50.

Reviewer: Maurice Charney.

Literary structure still remains the most forbidding of all critical topics, and Richard Levin has made a noble attempt to wrestle with multiple plots in English Renaissance drama. The basic problem is to follow through the Aristotelian distinction (in the *Poetics*) between plot and action. The plot is only the concatenation of events, the framework, the superstructure, which serves the purposes of the "mythos," or action. In this value-laden dichotomy, the plot is the body and the action the soul. The mythos is what the literary work is about. This definition works particularly well for plots that are in themselves mythic or have become so through familiar repetition in Western literature—Oedipus, Prometheus, even King Lear and his daughters. But what about the minor Elizabethan drama Levin is studying? Here nothing can be taken for granted, and you cannot just plunge into an animated discussion of the structure of Heywood's *A Challenge for Beauty*, or Davenport's *The City Nightcap*, or Shirley's *Hyde Park*, or even *The Second Maiden's Tragedy*. The author gets involved in some dreary plot review, which it is difficult to see how he could have avoided. Perhaps the publisher should offer every reader a copy of Karl Holzknecht's genuinely useful and elegant *Outlines of Tudor and Stuart Plays*, which is now unfortunately out of print.

In dealing with a subject so profound as the multiple plot, I sympathize with Mr. Levin's problems without being able to offer any practical solutions. He has the kind of mind admirably suited to his topic: precise, reasonable, masterful in detail, and willing to take pains to make a convincing demonstration. The problems he encounters are those inherent in the subject. Studies of structure tend to be descriptive and compendious, and there is nothing in the method that can really distinguish between good and bad structures, effective and ineffective ones.

There is also the nagging question of what need on the part of readers the structural analyses are answering. Levin's climactic chapter on *A Chaste Maid in Cheapside* and *Bartholomew Fair* is disappointing because it is so painstakingly obvious. It does not seem worth it to undertake an elaborate analysis of *A Chaste Maid* in order to arrive at the following conclusion:

> The four plots, therefore, have been selected and arranged in a scheme that exhausts the possibilities of comic action defined by these variables (understanding that the term "serious" here marks only the upper limit of the comic spectrum, without passing over into a different genre): the first is serious-sympathetic comedy, the second serious-unsympathetic, the third farcical but sympathetic, and the last farcical-unsympathetic. And their outcomes confirm this analysis; both sympathetic actions end very happily for all the major characters concerned except Whorehound (even Moll's parents finally welcome her marriage), while in the other two everyone is forced to accept, more or less grudgingly, some kind of defeat. Whorehound is a special case since he is affected by all four resolutions and cannot react differently to each, as the Yellowhammers do in plots one

> and four; but his downfall is associated primarily with plot two because it is placed in the Allwits' home and their rejection of him is made to seem the last crushing blow.

I know it is unfair to quote a passage like this out of context, but Levin sometimes indulges his delight in symmetries and parallels without any consideration of the hedonistic urges of his readers. In this example, it seems to me, the interest in plot has displaced any interest in mythos or action.

Levin is at his best when he develops points first announced in William Empson's extraordinary essay, "Double Plots: Heroic and Pastoral in the Main Plot and Sub-Plot," in *Some Versions of Pastoral* (London: Chatto & Windus, 1935). One of the most fascinating of these ideas is that of "coverage." A multiple plot presents a number of separate actions that are closely related analogically but are played out on distinctly different social planes. Each action is made to comment on the others. What is essentially a single issue can be divided hierarchically in the social spectrum, so that kings need clowns in order to establish their own dignity, and the middle range serves as a norm by which to understand extremes. There is a copiousness (in Lovejoy's sense of the fullness of the great chain of being) in the social life of a play that makes all the actions mutually interpreting. In this view structure is a metaphor for the world of the play. These postulates about the range and gamut of the play are beautifully demonstrated in Levin's chapter on "Three-Level Hierarchies," especially in *The Atheist's Tragedy*, where the ethical debate is given a new and surprising dimension.

Frankly, I find it difficult to remember and apply the author's large categories for multiple plots. I would be stumped to know whether I was face to face with a genuine three-decker hierarchy or a simple equivalence plot or direct contrast plot. The categories all seem to lap over into each other. The only satisfying category is the one in Chapter 4: "Clown Subplots: Foil, Parody, Magic." The clowns release hidden sources of eloquence in Levin. I am thinking particularly of his splendid discussion of Dampit (from Middleton's *A Trick to Catch the Old One*), who is a grotesque usurer with a smell of hellfire about him. Levin's point (derived ultimately from Empson) is that a figure like Dampit in the clown subplot acts "as a sort of lightning rod attracting to itself and draining away some undesired negative feeling" which might endanger our response to the main plot. Dampit "descends to his death as a nasty, drunken buffoon, too disgusting to arouse even the minimal pathos we feel at the death of an animal and too ridiculous to evoke the serious punitive emotion that attends the death of a villain." The structural purpose of the Dampit episodes is to relieve Lucre and Hoard, the professed usurers of the main plot, from any anticipated stigma of villainy. "Although we are told repeatedly that Lucre and Hoard are usurers, they are not at all like Dampit; in fact compared to him they seem quite human." In this way the subplot draws off the mephitic humors and bad vibrations that might distort the comedy of the main action.

Levin's book draws significantly on Middleton for its examples, while Shakespeare is shrouded in benign neglect. It is heartening to see Middleton praised so enthusiastically as a master of the comic intrigue plot. The whole book is primarily about comedy, since "The multiple plot is apparently more effective in comedy than in tragedy, as some of the better playwrights recognized: Shakespeare used a subplot in only one of his major tragedies, and Jonson, Chapman, and Webster avoided it in theirs. Indeed, the number of multiple-plot tragedies of the first rank in this period is quite small, while it is almost impossible to think of a good single-plot comedy." One might quibble with Levin's terms, since the number of tragedies of the first rank in this period is also exceedingly small, and some of Shakespeare's tragedies—I am thinking particularly of *Hamlet*—have a multiple action, if not a multiple plot.

One could also wish that Levin had extended his idea of structure beyond the literary text to some awareness that his plays were written to be performed in theaters. There is a structural dimension in the presented play that could significantly enrich Levin's account. In the chapter on the clown subplot, for example, Levin might consider the clown's special relation to the Elizabethan audience. As the unromantic representative of common sense, he can control the audience's reactions to the play and thus the pace of the action. The clowns are natural soliloquizers, backbiters, *tu quoque* men, and *quid pro quo*'ers, and they can endow the formal structure of an Elizabethan play with a lively improvisational quality. This is only to suggest one way of expanding the concept of structure in English Renaissance drama. Other readers will naturally think of different expansions, remodelings, and circular staircases for Mr. Levin's attractive edifice.

Christopher Marlowe's Tragic Vision: A Study in Damnation, by Charles G. Masinton. Ohio University Press, 1972. Pp. x + 168. $8.00.

Reviewer: Roy Battenhouse

A reaction against Romantic interpretation of Marlowe's tragic heroes has been building since about 1940. The Romantic view (espoused notably by Ellis-Fermor, Kocher, Poirier, and Levin) accepts at face value the Kyd and Baines reports of Marlowe's atheism and supposes that his dramas are vehicles for expressing his Renaissance yearnings and iconoclastic freethought. The tragic heroes, in this view, are convenient archetypes of Promethean adventure, through which the playwright can reflect in spectacularly heightened form his subjective quest for knowledge and power and his discovery of the mortal limitations which defeat him. On the other hand, a Christian school of interpreters (including Battenhouse, Mahood, and Cole) has been arguing that the structure of the plays gives evidence, rather, of an objective playwright who was delineating in his tragic heroes the course of representative kinds of evil ambition and retribution as understood in the moral literature of Protestant theology. Irving Ribner, when reviewing these two competing approaches in 1964 (in *Tulane Drama Review*), remarked on their incompatibility and the problem this posed. Mr. Masinton, only half-aware of the dilemma, eclectically draws from both approaches while relying chiefly on the second. His focus is on the "damnation" which Marlowe's protagonists suffer as the punishment of aspirations that are more Luciferian than Promethean. His stress is on the ironies with which Marlowe undercuts our sympathy for the heroes, and he holds that Marlowe can most profitably be studied not as a subjective artist but as an objective workman exploring man's nature in accord with concepts largely traditional.

Masinton argues that Marlowe understands the aspiration of his tragic heroes as that of perverted wills, presumptuously reaching for an illusory self which ignores the wisdom of the ages. These heroes generate their own afflictions by freely and arrogantly choosing fantasy ideals, by which they repudiate their humanity and bring down on themselves punishments tantamount to the torments of damnation. They isolate themselves in a psychological wasteland which is analogous to the "pain of loss" which Aquinas ascribes to souls separated from God, the source of divine light. They contain within themselves their own hell. And they are punished, further, by the fire of their own immoderate appetites. Indeed, Marlowe extends this punishment by fire into symbolic temporal manifestations by showing a death by fire or burning in the cases of Tamburlaine, Barabas, Edward II, and Dido. Furthermore, there is a rough parallelism, Massinton suggests (p. 158), between the Seven Deadly Sins and Marlowe's seven plays: Pride, above all, in *1 Tamburlaine*; Wrath in the Tamburlaine of Part II; Covetousness in Barabas; Envy in the Guise; Gluttony in Faustus; Sloth in Edward; and Lechery in Dido. In short, it may be inferred that Marlowe's intent in dramatizing these forms of passion was not to advocate them but to expose, as Masinton says, "the tragic error of judgment" which gives rise to them and brings doom as a consequence. Marlowe's initial reference to *Tamburlaine* as a "tragicke glass" alerts us to expect eventual misery in the hero, and even in Part I the ironic disparity between the hero's lauding of beauty and his slaughter of innocent virgins cannot mean authorial approval of the hero's self-glorifying ambitions.

But these observations by Masinton, most of them dependent on recent commentators, are accompanied also by occasional other lines of reasoning not logically consonant. Can we accept, for instance, his suggestion that Marlowe, although orthodox in the points mentioned above, went beyond orthodoxy in two respects: first, in perceiving damnation as inevitably man's lot, and second, in placing that damnation not in an eternity after death but under temporal and secular conditions? The second of these points rests on a misapprehension of orthodoxy. Orthodoxy has always understood death as beginning (in a spiritual sense) whenever man sins in the course of his temporal and secular life; each sin by its disordering of life introduces an element of death. Masinton himself has quoted Aquinas as saying that damnation is simply the punished state of the soul which attends man's obdurate choice of evil; physical death merely ends the possibility of reversing obduracy. In so far, then, as obduracy prevails before physical death, hell is already being experienced, and that is why we can speak of the "damnation" evident in a Tamburlaine or a Macbeth, whom other persons in these dramas rightly describe as hellish. Dramatists who perceive this fact are not "going beyond" orthodoxy. And as for Masinton's other suggestion, that for Marlowe damnation is man's "inevitable" lot, this is patently untrue as a generalization, since persons such as the Old Man in *Faustus*, or Kent and Edward III, are evidence to the contrary—in fact, Masinton himself speaks of the "moral integrity" of these non-protagonists but neglects to revise his earlier generalization accordingly.

Lack of logical coherence, unfortunately, is frequent in Masinton's book. For instance, after telling us (on page 6) that Marlowe's heroes *freely* chose an illusory state of being, he tells us three pages later that they are *forced* to reach for a false ideal by "passions they cannot control." How would he reconcile these statements? If choice is compelled (a dubious reading of Faustus' choice), in what sense can it be free? Or again, while Masinton tells us that Marlowe's protagonists are "all objects of Marlowe's pity and scorn" (p. 12), he states elsewhere his belief that these protagonists are remarkably like the intellectual rebel Marlowe himself, as reported by Kyd and Baines. Are we to suppose, then, that Marlowe was pitying and scorning imaginative versions of himself? Can we suppose that a reported scorner of God and the Scriptures was, as Masinton elsewhere and in the main argues, understanding scorners as generating their own damnation? Such a combination (or perhaps muddle) of perspectives seems difficult to believe, and Masinton provides no reasoning to make it credible. And perhaps the most striking inconsistency in his book is his following Ribner in claiming that Marlowe *denies* a Providential interpretation of history, while elsewhere Marlowe is said (following Cole and Mahood) to be interpreting the fate of tragic heroes in accord with the views of Augustine (a thoroughgoing Providentialist).

A New Companion to Shakespeare Studies, edited by Kenneth Muir and Samuel Schoenbaum. Cambridge University Press, 1971. Pp. v + 298. $12.50.

Reviewer: David Riggs

The *New Companion to Shakespeare Studies* preserves the format of the original one, which appeared under the editorship of Harley Granville-Barker and G. B. Harrison in 1934, and its chief attraction are those of its predecessor. The eighteen specialist contributors assume that their readers are already conversant with the writings of Shakespeare and his contemporaries and have some background in Shakespeare studies. Moreover, they do not see it as their task merely to recapitulate the lowest common denominator of scholarly consensus within their several areas of study. At their best, these essays succeed as well in giving some sense of the carefully-sifted evidence, the complex hypotheses, and the interpretive choices that must lie behind any real scholarly consensus. The level of accuracy is high and extends to matters of minute detail. (Those who proceed directly from the Reading Lists to the library may be misled by a few misprints: *Jacqnot* for *Jacquot*, *Sarragin* for *Sarrazin*, *Whittaker* for *Whitaker*—but these are rare.) The *New Companion*, in short, should not be confused with the host of Shakespeare guides and reference books to which it bears a superficial resemblance. It has its distinct purposes to fulfill.

Most of the essays are about the historical conditions under which Shakespeare wrote: his life and times; his theatrical, linguistic, and musical heritage; the intellectual, literary, and rhetorical writings that influenced his work; contemporary practices that affected the earliest printing of the texts. There are four separate essays on the plays and poetry. Three other chapters, on stage history and on Shakespeare criticism in early and modern times, round out the collection. Readers will notice that "criticism" figures here as an object of Shakespeare studies rather than as a kind of study in its own right. This is a perfectly reasonable way to limit the scope of the volume. Still, since the editors have commissioned four essays on the poetry and plays, they do entitle us to expect a fair résumé of "the best that has been thought and said" on these texts by critics and scholars alike. That is a large order, and if the overall plan of the volume falters anywhere it is here. The titles of the two chapters on the plays—"Shakespeare the Elizabethan dramatist," "Shakespeare the Jacobean dramatist"—are serviceable enough, but this way of dividing up the canon has not been characteristic of modern Shakespeare studies. Is "dramatist" simply a way of noting that these chapters are about Shakespeare's plays, grouped by historical periods? Or is it meant to evoke some framework of assumptions about *drama* and Shakespeare's way with it? If the word is used in this latter sense (and it is almost impossible to avoid in any case), one may object that the qualifiers "Elizabethan" and "Jacobean" are not really appropriate: the best recent work on Shakespeare's skill as a dramatist has, by and large, concerned itself not with the impress of those historical moments on his art but, rather, with his continuing adaptation and invention of dramatic genres. Granted that no one today would feel comfortable writing about "Shakespeare's dramatic art" (the title of Granville-Barker's essay in the 1934 *Companion*), it might have made more sense to subdivide the plays by genre. The logic of treating the sonnets and the verse in the plays conjointly, in a chapter titled "Shakespeare's poetry," must also remain a bit obscure. Modern criticism has had an enormous amount to say about both the brief lyric verse and the "play as poem," but it has not ordinarily tried to talk about the one in terms of the other. A separate chapter is devoted to J. W. Lever's fine essay on the narrative poems.

Given the intrinsic difficulty of saying anything about these topics in fifteen pages, the contributors discharge their assignments very well. As the author of a book on *Tudor Politics and Drama*, David Bevington has well-formed notions about the circumstances that made Shakespeare an "Elizabethan dramatist," and some of these are aptly reiterated here. He emphasizes the ascendancy, virtually unbroken through the 1590s, of the adult companies and a "public" audience eager for broad comedy, conventional morality, and native subject matter as factors which led Shakespeare to write a drama of "popular consensus" during these years. This framework serves Bevington well for the histories, perhaps less well for the early comedies. The mature comedies are described in unabashedly literary terms as dramas of contrasting worlds, "one earthbound, rational, legalistic, and competitive; the other, distant, improbable, sylvan, and regenerative" (p. 136). This too is Elizabethan art, though its provenance is surely no less courtly than popular. Muriel Bradbrook's account of the "Jacobean dramatist" takes on more cosmic dimensions. "Loss of the royal image symbolized much deeper loss" (p. 143): the great scenes of the Jacobean tragedies "radiate symbolic potency . . . yet they do not belong to a ritual tradition like the early tourneys, coronations, challenges" (p. 145). In short, "Shakespeare had gone off the gold standard of conventional judgments, and had gained a floating position where the audience must follow with its own judgment the natural pulses of sympathy" (p. 149). This way of periodizing Shakespeare's career leans rather heavily on the supposition of a highly traditional Elizabethan Shakespeare, and Professor Bradbrook is accordingly cautious about finding traditional meanings in the later tragedies, even though she does believe that they are there. Her approach brings out, then, a question that has preoccupied modern criticism of Shakespeare's work from *Hamlet* onwards. She is naturally ready to stress all the unconventionality and inventiveness, the bold ironies and oracular simplicities that we readily attribute to a "Jacobean" Shakespeare, and she also means to argue that Shakespeare was doing something other than indulging in complexity-for-its-own-sake. But the second point is hard to formulate clearly, once the first has been given its full weight. Her brief discussion of *Othello* is rewarding precisely because she is able to focus both sides of the problem, the hero who "never holds anything back" (p. 150) yet still remains part of an underlying unity, "the close relation of all characters in one great household" (p. 151).

Inga-Stina Ewbank's chapter on "Shakespeare's poetry" is the one essay in this volume which addresses itself to a specific critical claim. Her point of departure is Eliot's observation that Shakespeare's poetic and dramatic skills manifest themselves "not by a concurrence of two activities, but by the full expansion of one and the same activity." Mrs. Ewbank seeks out the beliefs that make for this deep affinity between poet and dramatist in several places: reflections on poetry and language that crop up in the plays and sonnets; the evolution of Shakespeare's style and the intentions that seem to lie behind it; moments of intense "drama" where the verbal artifice is perfectly adapted to the action, yet still yields to a "poetic" analysis. There is no need to belabor the difficulties that must confront a project such as this. Transition from the aesthetic premise ("Part of Shakespeare's belief is that what *is* cannot always be said," p. 104) to the dramatic moment ("I would not take this from report. It is / And my heart breaks at it") will always seem, in the course of analysis, to divest the dramatic of its full powers. And once the "poetic" has been disengaged from its native contexts, it will always look more commonplace than we had thought at first: "the fusion of subject and style, matter and manner" (p. 103) in language that "enacts" or "embodies" its meaning. More important than the conclusions here is the weight of evidence uncovered by Mrs. Ewbank's scrutiny of particular passages. The case for Shakespeare's self-consciousness about style and for the interplay of his stylistic and dramatic intentions has seldom been made so persuasively.

The rest of the essays may for convenience' sake be divided into two categories. The greater part deal with areas of Shakespearian research that have been well-organized and highly coordinated for half a century or more: there is wide agreement as to what the important questions are, and the contributor's task is to report on the best answers that modern scholarship has found. Set apart from these, both in tone and substance, are four essays on topics that are relatively new to Shakespeare studies. The chapters on the actors and staging, on rhetoric, and on the thought of Shakespeare's age, have no precedent in the 1934 *Companion.* Here the contributors must not only summarize what is known but also offer basic judgments about the content and relevancy of their subject-matter. I take these essays to be the ones that require more extended comment here.

The most controversial of these will be Brian Vickers' discussion of "Shakespeare's use of rhetoric." Much as Sister Miriam Joseph, whose pioneering book on *Shakespeare and the Arts of Language* appeared in 1947, Vickers maintains that the figures of elocution comprise the one part of classical rhetoric that is genuinely relevant to literary studies. Invention and disposition, it is suggested, were not of much use to the poet and dramatist: "what the student and budding writer most wanted from rhetoric-books was a list of the tropes and figures, set out as clearly as possible, and this fact seems to me good evidence for man's intuitive recognition that rhetoric was fundamentally different from logic or philosophy" (p. 85). It follows that the main thing for the modern student is to learn the list for himself—Vickers provides a brief one—and then to discover how the elements function in Shakespeare's style. No doubt this approach would have recommended itself to many Elizabethans; it was in this way, we recall, that Spenser's friend E. K. criticized *The Shepheardes Calender.* But anyone familiar with the work of Ernst Robert Curtius or Rosemond Tuve (both are cited in the Reading List) must have reservations about the proposed severance of *elocutio* from the rest of rhetorical theory. For their achievement has been precisely to stress both the unity of rhetoric as a humanistic discipline and its filiations with philosophy and literature at all levels. As for the specific applications of rhetoric to drama, our best sources of external evidence are still the great sixteenth-century editions of Terence that were designed for use in schools. Vickers does not refer to these texts, which have been carefully studied by T. W. Baldwin and R. W. Herrick. But unless we are to suppose that the humanists who went on preparing them were truly fantastic pedants, utterly cut off from the living art of their day, these indicate clearly that systems of invention and disposition affected conceptions of genre, plot, character, and theme, as well as particular uses of language. One might add that the best recent studies of rhetoric and drama, such as Wolfgang Clemen's book on earlier English tragedy, do not isolate the figures for special attention, nor do they lead us to believe that the playwrights did so themselves. As these comments may suggest, the problem with writing about "Shakespeare and rhetoric" is that the subject is at once so diffuse and so specialized. Diffuse, because the best work often occurs when someone is not writing about rhetoric per se, but draws on it to develop another point or explicate a passage (Clemen's *Commentary on Shakespeare's Richard III* is a perfect case in point); specialized, because the terminology is technical, confusing, and strange, while the whole edifice is so vast and decentralized that scholars often get up only what they need to do their particular work. The merit of Vickers' piece lies in his effective advocacy of one approach to Shakespeare based on rhetoric. His analyses of individual passages are subtle and persuasive; they do represent a real advance over the bare taxonomies which have sometimes passed for scholarship in this field.

Daniel Seltzer's account of "The actors and staging"—which is here taken to mean the style of acting contemporaneous with Shakespeare's plays—surveys yet another branch of study in which modern scholars are still taking their bearings. There are numerous hypotheses, many of which have been argued in considerable detail; but no one has yet assembled a really comprehensive body of information on the subject and presented it in a systematic way. That is precisely what Seltzer ventures to do in this remarkably compact essay, written, we are told, "after close examination of over two hundred texts, from the earliest interludes through the late Jacobean period" (p. 37). Hence, his entire approach, with its wealth of concrete examples and statistical indices, is no less important than his conclusions. But this must be savored by reading the essay for oneself. Seltzer pursues two main lines of argument, both of which bear on the question of whether Elizabethan acting was "formal" or "realistic." If we begin with a technique that we would consider "realistic," the performance of "small" stage business during exchanges of dialogue, there is ample evidence that Shakespeare's actors were extremely adept at it—for example, playwrights who gave them subtly nuanced dialogue to speak while they were adjusting each other's armor must have depended on their having this skill. On the other hand, certain "large" formal gestures, which were used to demonstrate an internalized emotion or motivation, are no less conspicuous in the acting of this period—witness the rolling eye and gnawing of the nether lip that conveys emotional turmoil in a variety of scripts both early and late. The tentative conclusion here is that Elizabethan and Jacobean performances must have been done in what we would regard as a "mix" of naturalistic and formal styles. The "overall view of a mixed stylistic practice" (p. 45) that emerges from a study of stage business should be supplemented, however, by attending to variations in the actor's manner of "address" (i.e. the *direction* of his speech and the dramatic relationships this entails): for here is where "the gradual *change* of style assumed by some critics can be detected" (p. 45). To put it "in the most general terms, an examination of texts dating from 1608 on reveals an increase in the number of 'ensemble' episodes accompanying the decline of soliloquy techniques" (p. 46). This evolution in acting style had to take place, Seltzer suggests, to keep pace with the demands imposed by new scripts. In the case of Shakespeare, the development from a tragic "concentration inward, upon the mind of the hero" to the "more generalized vision" of romance reduced the importance of soliloquy techniques even as it enjoined the dramatist, and so his actors, to discover "ways to compress the rhythms of human speech" (pp. 51, 52). The essay thus comes to rest on a particular moment in the career of Shakespeare and the King's Men. Given limitations of space and the present state of our knowledge, Seltzer does not and could not hope to present a full account of "the actors and staging" in Shakespeare's lifetime. He shows instead what such an account ought ideally to look like, when we finally do arrive at it.

W. R. Elton's essay, "Shakespeare and the thought of his age," organizes a wide spectrum of Renaissance speculation and belief into an Hegelian clash of old and new, writ large in the "ironies and ambivalences" of Shakespeare's drama. The *thesis,* roughly speaking, is "Analogy," a "prevailing intellectual mode" by which traditional thought had joined "faith with knowledge, actuality with metaphysics . . . symbol with concept, the internal with the external world" (p. 181). The *antithesis* is not itself a new intellectual mode so much as it is a whole series of "Transitions" that could not be accommodated within the traditional framework: Calvinism, skepticism, late nominalism, *raison d'etat,* "market value," the "new astronomy," and so forth. If this is basically the historical overview invented by the nineteenth century—an "organic" medieval world overlaid by "mechanical philosophies"—it is a highly serviceable one nonetheless. The chapter, which Elton describes as "condensed notes," is tough but rewarding. It is not always made clear in just what ways we are to draw connections between the older conceptual apparatus on the one hand and new systems of belief on the other (describing the latter as "transitions" does not render the problem any easier). Inevitably, then, to characterize the plays as a "dialectical" confrontation of traditional and "transitional" attitudes is to leave many questions unanswered. The stress falls on Shakespeare's artistic neutrality, but an "ironic and ambivalent" playwright would finally appear to have more in common with, say, Montaigne than with Hooker.

Stanley Wells's account of "Shakespeare criticism since Bradley" manages to combine a studied neutrality with clear, brief appraisals of about seventy titles that have appeared since Bradley's lectures on the tragedies were published in

1904. The stress falls on Bradley's influence as it affected both those who followed him and those who reacted against him. Stoll and Schücking, Granville-Barker, Caroline Spurgeon, and G. Wilson Knight—all of these, we are reminded, were expressly providing what could not be found in his writings. Similarly, modern studies of dramatic genre, which have sometimes prided themselves on being historically correct where Bradley was not, are themselves descended from *Shakespearean Tragedy*. There is a marked absence of special pleading in this essay, but the steady pressure of Wells's own convictions, which comport well with his admiration for Bradley, is clear throughout. He begins by remarking that *Shakespearean Tragedy* conveniently represents the transition from a Shakespeare criticism written by men of letters to one written by university-based specialists for scholarly publications. He ends by invoking Johnsonian standards that are surely no *less* relevant now than they were in 1904: "the best criticism, and that which stands the best chance of survival, is that which combines a balanced approach with the ability to engage and sustain the attention of the reader without excessive concern with local and temporal matters" (p. 261).

Ten contributions remain to be mentioned: "The life of Shakespeare" (Samuel Schoenbaum), "The playhouses and the stage" (Richard Hosley), "Shakespeare's reading" (G. K. Hunter), "Shakespeare and the English language" (Randolph Quirk), "Shakespeare and music" (F. W. Sternfeld), "The historical and social background" (Joel Hurstfield), "Shakespeare's plays on the English stage" (A. C. Sprague), "Shakespeare and the drama of his time" (Peter Ure), "Shakespeare's text: Approaches and problems" (G. Blakemore Evans), "Shakespeare criticism: Dryden to Bradley" (M. A. Shaaber). Were a reviewer to be given space to deal with them all, these essays would present him with scant alternatives. One can search out misprints, trivial omissions, and minor disagreements; or one can commend the assured scholarship and economy of style that characterize them all. At least two of these chapters are especially welcome because they reveal improved avenues of research and study. G. K. Hunter's chapter on "Shakespeare's reading" replaces the one called "Shakespeare's sources" in the 1934 volume, and the change is quite purposeful. Hunter begins by stressing "the problem of what constitutes evidence," and even as he goes over the familiar ground of classical allusions, prose chronicles, romantic narratives, and "old plays" he is continually illuminating about the formative role of cultural and literary traditions. Similarly, Randolph Quirk's discussion of "Shakespeare and the English language" aims "to establish the kind of language study that is most significant for students of Shakespeare" (p. 67). The essay provides, among other things, a whole range of linguistic questions which may profitably be asked of particular words and lines, and it proceeds in every case to demonstrate the interpretive regards that accrue when these are thoughtfully pursued. It is surprising that an age so given to verbal analysis of Shakespeare should have concerned itself so little with Elizabethan English, apart from the occasional recourse to a few standard works of reference. This chapter, along with some recent writings that Quirk cites, suggests that the situation is changing for the better. One other essay, Richard Hosley's description of "The playhouses and the stage," may occasion some second thoughts in the light of Glynne Wickham's latest installment of *Early English Stages,* which appeared at the same time as the *New Companion.* Anyone who is persuaded by Wickham's case for the influence of stage structures at court on those of the public playhouse will be that much less comfortable with Hosley's emphasis on the animal-baiting house and the innyard. But that is a problem for the next *Companion to Shakespeare.*

The Merry Wives of Windsor, edited by H. J. Oliver. The Arden Shakespeare. Methuen, 1971. Pp. lxxxv + 149. $8.00.

Reviewer: Charles R. Forker

This latest addition to a distinguished series must be hailed at once as a triumph not only for Professor Oliver, who has already given us exemplary editions of *Timon of Athens* (The Arden Shakespeare, 1959) and of Marlowe's *Dido* and *The Massacre at Paris* (The Revels Plays, 1968), but for Shakespeareans in general. A model of textual judiciousness and accuracy (three days of spot collation against the folio and quarto texts failed to expose a single error in transmission), of sound historical scholarship, of concise and enlightening commentary, and of critical good sense, it is likely to be regarded as the standard edition of *The Merry Wives* for some time to come.

Oliver accepts the position, now more or less canonical, that the text of 1602 is a bad quarto; he believes with Greg that the actor who played the Host of the Garter was the main reporter but argues in addition that the player who acted Falstaff (and possibly those who acted Pistol and Nym as well) assisted in the memorial reconstruction. Oliver thinks this text represents a version of the comedy deliberately shortened to appeal to a less sophisticated audience than Shakespeare originally addressed (how else account for the omission of entire scenes, such as the Latin lesson, which would be more appropriate for presentation at court?). As editors have long recognized, the Folio text of 1623 is the only good one, and Oliver follows it scrupulously, nevertheless accepting a few readings from Q (but fewer than most of his predecessors) where there is evidence that the folio compositor misread his copy or where dramatic necessity or historical evidence can be shown to validate the reported text.

Q's consistent reading of "Brooke" as compared with F's "Broome" for Ford's alias clearly represents Shakespeare's intention (jokes turn on the pronunciation), and Oliver quite properly restores the name as it appeared in Q. Some notion of the editor's admirable textual conservatism may be conveyed by his decision to retain F's expurgated oaths in preference to the freer language of Q on the ground that actors cannot be relied on for such details. And unlike most earlier editors of this play, Oliver resists the temptation to include lines and phrases from Q that have no counterpart in F (e.g., at I.i.117 and IV.v.97); in such places, the additional words only spell out, sometimes with a loss in subtlety, what F already implies. Since F masses entries at the head of each scene (a feature which argues that a manuscript by Ralph Crane lies immediately behind it), the quarto does have an authority in the matter of stage directions that it lacks in other respects. Accordingly, Oliver relies when possible upon Q to clarify stage action. Why he should unnecessarily alter Q's wording in such cases, however, is not clear. Oliver prints "*Falstaff hides behind the arras*" (III.iii.84) when Q's language ("*Falstaffe stands behind the aras*") gives us more precise information. Moreover, he omits the all-important word ("*stands*") from the textual note that records his debt.

The Arden policy of modernized spelling predictably involves Oliver in a number of unsatisfactory compromises that tend to obscure Elizabethan sound and flavor. Since comprehensibility would in most cases be little affected, it seems a pity to regularize the copy-text so ruthlessly (e.g., "y'are">"you're"; "wiues">"wife's"; "vilde">"vile"; "diuell">"devil"; "ambassie">"embassy"; "strooke">"struck"; "accustrement">"accoutrement"; "Peeble">"pebble"). Mr. Oliver might of course rejoin that the folio text itself is inconsistent with regard to several of these spellings, and that in any case we cannot be sure they represent Shakespeare's preferences rather than Crane's, a particular compositor's, or some irrecoverable mixture of the three possibilities. But one may note that he undercuts to some extent the position such a defense would imply by preserving (correctly, it seems to me) such older spellings as "pumpion" (=pumpkin) and "Cataian" (=Cathaian, Chinese). Since *The Merry Wives* contains relatively little verse, few problems of lineation arise, but Oliver deals sensibly with those that do. In at least one place (IV.vi.25–26) I prefer Malone's arrangement of a hypermetrical passage in three lines rather than the two that Oliver adopts, but it must be conceded that the difference is essentially a visual rather than an aural one, and is therefore of no great moment.

As for emending the folio, Oliver is commendably restrained; when he does depart from his copy, he almost always defends the decision persuasively. His rejection of Quiller-Couch and Dover Wilson's "mate" for F's "meet" at V.v.118, his retention of Caius's "ballow" (F's apparent anglicization of the French *bailler* at I.iv. 82), and his saving of a line (I.i.54) for Slender (it is usually reassigned to Shallow) may be taken as typical of his textual sanity. And he must be praised also for not over-regularizing or correcting Shakespeare's French in the speeches of Dr. Caius except where compositorial error is involved (Professor Harbage in his Pelican edition of *Henry V* has ably defended this hands-off policy). Occasionally one may feel that the editor leans over backwards in his conservatism. He preserves, for example, F's inconsistency in the naming of George Page (Evans calls him "Thomas" at I.i.42) on the ground that the transcriber can hardly have erred on the point and that Shakespeare "was often careless with names" (p. 7); so far as it goes, this argument is irrefragable, but the dramatist's intention can hardly have been to confuse, and it is not unlikely that the discrepancy would have been corrected in performance. Again, Oliver retains F's "slighted" over Q's "slided" (III.v.9) where Falstaff is describing his ducking in the Thames. Oliver admits that "slighted" may be an error in F and suggests, apparently following the New Cambridge editors, that Shakespeare perhaps intended "a kind of pun" on the two words. He could cite eminent authorities to buttress his choice here; but some readers may feel, notwithstanding, that the less obvious, not to say the less graphic, of two possibilities has been preferred. Oliver (probably correctly) preserves F's "in her invention" (III.v.77) over Q's apparently superior "by her inuention" but does not trouble to argue the point.

Nor does Oliver invariably follow F where he might do so in strict obedience to his own principle. Though F's "liue" at I.iii.14 "makes good sense" (p. 21), the editor nevertheless prints Q's "lime." F's "haue scap'd" (II.i.1) may indeed be a compositor's mistake for "have I scaped" (as F3 and, apparently, Oliver suppose), but it is conceivable that Mistress Page, who is alone on stage and talking to herself at this point, omits the personal pronoun as if it were understood. However defensible the emendation may be (and it is not defended), a case might be made for leaving F as it stands. Oliver emends F's "a Mounseur Mocke-water" (the Host's address to Shallow at II.iii.53–54) to "A word, Mounseur Mock-water," supplying the additional word from Q. Since fidelity to the Folio amounts to an article of faith for this editor, he might more consistently have accepted Hanmer's equally sensible substitution of "ah!" for F's "a". In any case, "Mock-water," though Q and F do agree, fails to yield very clear sense, and one wonders whether either Steevens' "Muck-water" or Sisson's "Make-water" would not provide a better solution after all. I raise such possibilities for objection only to indicate the difficulties of textual choice with which any editor of *The Merry Wives* must wrestle. All such points involve details about which intelligent men may differ, and I should add that Oliver's percentage of "right" choices seems to me unusually high.

The annotations constitute in some ways the most satisfying feature of this edition. Oliver has the gift of packing them with valuable observations and of striking a nearly ideal balance between copiousness and economy. Occasionally one would like a phrase more fully explained or a point more amply supported. We are delighted to learn that in Shakespeare's time "a real Garter Inn at Windsor" existed (p. 11), but we should welcome some scholarly verification of the fact. It would be useful to be reminded of the historical (or legendary) source for the Garter motto (*Honi soit qui mal y pense*) at V.v.70. And since Oliver dwells at length in his introduction upon the topicality of the play, it is odd that he does not record William Green's theory, perfectly congruent with his own findings, that Caius's phrase "*la grande affaire*" (I.iv.47) refers to the Garter Feast of 1597 (*Shakespeare's Merry Wives of Windsor* [Princeton: Princeton Univ. Press, 1962], pp. 10–12). Generally Oliver's glosses are superb. A utopian might perhaps regret the absence of an equivalent for "motions" ("bowel movements" with perhaps a quibble on "bodily exercises") at III.i.95, or desire an explanation of exactly why a limekiln should be as malodorous as a prison at III.iii.73. For Slender's "Cain-coloured beard" at I.iv.21 (cf. Rowe's "Cane-colour'd"), Oliver might have cited the New Cambridge editors' gloss ("cane" ="weasel"), for even though his own interpretation (Cain-coloured="red," the traditional color of Cain's beard) is possible, it would seem to conflict with Simple's immediately preceding mention of "a little yellow beard." Only once does Oliver appear to me to offer a superfluous gloss ("give way" for "relent" at II.ii.28).

For his section on the dating and circumstances of the original performance, Oliver builds upon the scholarship of Leslie Hotson (*Shakespeare Versus Shallow* [1931]) and of William Green. The basic contention is that Shakespeare composed *The Merry Wives* (very likely, as Dennis reported in 1702, at the Queen's request) for a Garter Feast held at Whitehall on 23 April 1597; that the dramatist had the additional motive of honoring Lord Hunsdon, the new Lord Chamberlain and patron of the players, who was eager to celebrate his recent election to the prestigious order of knights; that the play was written hurriedly after *1 Henry IV* but before *Henry V*, that is to say *during* the composition of *2 Henry IV* but *before* Shakespeare had reached the rejection scene of the last named play; that the comedy bristles with topicalities that would make a special appeal to its courtly audience (including especially jokes at the expense of Count Mömpelgard, a German prince who had made himself a laughingstock in England by pressuring the Queen to confer the Garter upon him but who, though finally granted the honor, was deliberately excluded from the installation festivities of 1597); that although Shakespeare, perhaps unwittingly, may have offended the powerful Cobham family by applying the pseudonym Brooke to the disguised Ford just as he had earlier offended them by originally naming Falstaff, Oldcastle, the change from Brooke (Q) to Broome (F) probably occurred in 1604, when Sir Henry Brooke, then in disgrace for his part in a plot to depose James I, was expelled from the Order of the Garter. Oliver thinks the name Brooke might have been censored at this time because of the unpleasant associations it would evoke. Though properly skeptical of Hotson's argument that Shallow and Slender caricature William Gardiner (a Surrey justice of the peace) and William Wayte (his stepson) and also of Rowe's belief that Shallow represents a satiric portrait of Sir Thomas Lucy, who had allegedly prosecuted Shakespeare for deer-stealing, he concludes that "if ever there were a place in Shakespeare's art for laughing comment on individuals . . . that place would have been in such a topical play as *The Merry Wives* seems to have been" (pp. li–lii).

Whether one accepts all the evidence, then, or merely part of it, Oliver's case for 1597 is hard to counter. Arguments for a later date rest chiefly on assumptions about the relationship of *The Merry Wives* to the three plays on Henry IV and V (and on their dates of composition), on the supposed influence of Jonson's *Every Man in His Humour* (1598) upon the piece, on certain traits of style, and on Meres' failure to mention the comedy in *Palladis Tamia* (1598). If Oliver cannot precisely be said to have settled the dating problem beyond dispute, he has at least shifted the burden of proof—a heavy burden—to the shoulders of the opposition. No definite sources for the play are known, and Oliver therefore contents himself with pointing to numerous possibilities and analogues. In one sense, the Henry IV plays are "sources," but his introduction begins with a salutary warning against trying to link *The Merry Wives* too systematically to the chronicle sequence. As Oliver points out, there are some superficial cross-references, e.g., Page's remark that Fenton "kept company with the wild Prince and Poins" (III.ii.66–67), but the comedy is essentially contemporary, not medieval in setting, and Pistol refers explicitly to "Our radiant Queen" who "hates sluts and sluttery" (V.v.47).

Oliver's appreciation of the play as literature is as sensitive as it is just. Without insisting on any great profundity in so occasional a piece, he nevertheless points to genuine aesthetic virtues that have too often been overlooked by critics, such as A. C. Bradley and H. B. Charlton, bent upon chastising Shakespeare for a "crime worse than parricide—the slaughter of [his] own offspring [i.e., Falstaff]" (Charlton, *Shakespearian Comedy* [1938], p. 192). Oliver emphasizes the flattery to a sophisticated audience which the Latin lesson, the mangled quotations from Marlowe and Sidney, and the self-parody of Falstaff's narrative speeches imply. He stresses the unusual mixture of rural freshness and a delight in village manners with the plot and character conventions of city comedy—the kind of comedy we normally associate with Dekker and Webster, with Chapman, Jonson, Marston, and, later, with Massinger. The combination helps enforce the theme of "plain 'honesty' or virtue" as naturally superior "to the sophisticated or sophistical arts of the gallant or courtier" (p. lxvii).

Without pretending that the Falstaff, Mistress Quickly, and Bardolph of *The Merry Wives* are precisely the same characters of *1 Henry IV* or that Shallow, Pistol, and Nym are exactly those of *2 Henry IV* and *Henry V*, Oliver minimizes these differences. He reminds us, for instance, that Falstaff undergoes both verbal and physical defeats in the history plays as well as in the citizen comedy. For those who are outraged by the alleged incongruity of the fat knight's "new" role as wooer, Oliver justly points out that Falstaff's motive is pecuniary, not amorous, and that he is no more "in love" than he ever was. One might, of course, reply that if love is not a consideration for the old reprobate, lust is (or at least becomes) one of the enticements (we hear him praying Jove in the final episode for "a cool rut-time" lest he "piss [his] tallow" [V.v.14–15]). Oliver, moreover, is not slow to underscore the point that Falstaff is but one of several victims of deception in the play, including his intended quarry, Mistress Page—that Falstaff's ultimate discomfiture at Herne's oak is qualified by the discomfiture of Slender, Dr. Caius, and Anne Page's parents, none of whom is in any position to laugh at others. Thus Oliver answers the would-be sentimentalizers of Falstaff, and he answers them well; but his argument will not entirely quiet those for whom the more helpless and obtuse knight of *The Merry Wives*—the figure who is gulled successively into a basket of soiled linen, a dress, and a set of antlers—inevitably comes as a disappointment after the ingeniously resourceful liar and verbal Houdini of *1 Henry IV*. The demeaning disguises into which the Falstaff of the Garter Inn is tricked do raise problems of identity that are no part of our response to the lord of misrule who reigned so securely at the Boar's Head Tavern. Oliver evades the root issue here, and indeed he all but admits as much by noticing that the new Falstaff goes in for truth more readily than mendacity, despite the hilarious and authentic idiom in which Shakespeare continues to couch the rogue's speeches.

Oliver's introduction contains good remarks on the more neglected characters, such as the merry wives themselves (they reveal a touch of pathos in their relationship with each other and uphold bourgeois virtue without being too solemn or didactic about it) and Ford, who is much too subtly portrayed (he evinces "a strain of masochism" [p. lxxii]) to be dismissed as a mere humour character or stereotype of the jealous husband. Slender's tenuous proposal to "sweet Anne Page" is aptly compared for comic effect to "Mr. Collins's offer to Elizabeth Bennet in *Pride and Prejudice*" (p. lxxiii). Oliver is perceptive, too, about the play's structure. He points, for instance, to Shakespeare's skillful handling of the two potentially awkward meetings between Falstaff and Mistress Quickly after the episode of the buck basket when the knight is being re-invited to visit Mistress Ford (the dramatist keeps the first very brief and has the second occur offstage). We get a sensible discussion of the links between the two intrigues by which the merry wives outwit Falstaff on the one hand and the young lovers outwit the Pages, Caius, and Slender on the other—of how both lines of action converge satisfyingly in the disclosures of the concluding scene. Oliver shows that some apparent blemishes (e.g., Mistress Quickly's taking the unlikely role of the Fairy Queen in the final scene) disappear if we allow for the convention by which effects of comic realism give way before or blend into those of the more ceremonial masque. Praise of the play's formal excellences (their recognition goes back to Dryden and the critics of the eighteenth century) is welcome if we remember at the same time that a few unusual awkwardnesses of plotting remain to temper our laudations. Loose ends, such as Shallow's threats to make a Star Chamber matter of the wrongs Falstaff has done him and Slender, are left dangling. Also the scene (IV.iii) in which the Host is cozened of his horses is puzzling; ironically one is obliged to consult the corrupt quarto to make sense of it—or else a long footnote explaining that Caius and Evans have apparently commissioned someone to impersonate the visiting Germans and thus take their vengeance by indirection upon the man who had earlier prevented their duel.

Oliver's critique of the play concludes with some considered observations about its verbal and rhythmic patterns (the homely domestic details and the profusion of Biblical allusions, for instance, reinforce the tone of middle-class morality). Oliver's discussion is not quite as useful a synthesis of the criticism of *The Merry Wives* as one could wish. No doubt limited space necessitated some lacunae, but one misses passing reference, at least, to such recent commentators as Northrop Frye, Sherman Hawkins, Bertrand Evans, and Anne Righter, all of whom in one way or another have had stimulating things to say about the comedy, and it is a pity that J. A. Roberts' clever, perhaps overingenious essay on the play (*ShakS*, 6 [1970], 109–23) appeared too late for Oliver to consult.

Such reservations, whether textual, glossarial, or interpretive, as I have been voicing in this review nearly all concern minor points, and the disproportionate space I have allowed them may partly disguise my enthusiasm for Oliver's splendidly meticulous and reliable edition. The book is certain to be used for a long time. It deserves to be used gratefully and with respect.

A Kingdom for a Stage: The Achievement of Shakespeare's History Plays, by Robert Ornstein. Harvard University Press, 1972. Pp. 231. $11.00.

Reviewer: Robert P. Merrix

Since the publication in 1946 of E. M. W. Tillyard's *Shakespeare's History Plays*, which supposedly established an "orthodox" view of the histories, subsequent scholars and critics have attacked that orthodoxy, chipping away, as Gordon Zeeveld recently noted, "at the Tillyardian myth which presumes a monolithic pattern in fifteenth-century history from the deposition of Richard II to the glorious accession of the first Tudor."[1] The most recent critic of the orthodoxy is Robert Ornstein, whose book on Shakespeare's history plays attempts to rescue Shakespeare from Tillyard, Lily Campbell, and other historical scholars and return him to the world of art. "The pity of this scholarly insistence on the conventionality of the History Plays," says Ornstein in his introductory essay ("The Artist as Historian"), "is that it threatens to turn living works of theater into dramatic fossils or repositories of quaint and dusty ideas" (p. 2). He admits, of course, that literary research is "valid and necessary," since only scholarship can give us "accurate texts" or "free us from misconceptions and misinterpretations" (p. 7). Nevertheless, there is "an implicit refusal by historical scholarship to grant that the ultimate standard for the interpretation of art is aesthetic" (p. 8).

Ornstein's approach is ineluctably a part of his thesis. Convinced that Shakespeare's concern was "artistic" rather than didactic, he insists that the critic's task is "to fathom Shakespeare's unique insight and intuition, not to square his plays with a hypothetical norm of Elizabethan attitudes" (p. 12). He bases his theory of Shakespeare's uniqueness on the dearth of pre-Shakespearean history plays, which might have served as models, and on Shakespeare's freedom in the use of his sources. Rejecting the assumption that Shakespeare's histories evolved from plays like *Cambises*, *Jack Straw*, or *The Famous Victories of Henry V*, he asserts that Shakespeare "created the vogue" of the history play and "shaped its tradition" (p. 6). The same artistic independence is true in Shakespeare's use of the Chronicles. Since the Chronicles were "contradictory and inconsistent," dramatists like Shakespeare felt free to alter historical "fact" for artistic purposes. Shakespeare himself, argues Ornstein, maintained ideological freedom from all the Chronicles. Whatever his source—Hall for the first tetralogy and Holinshed for the second—"his interpretation of the past was his own" (p. 23).[2]

In the remaining nine chapters, Ornstein attempts to prove his thesis by analyzing each history play in relation to both its own uniqueness—its evidence of originality or artistic growth for Shakespeare—and its relation to a larger design—for example, the tetralogies, each of which has its own "distinctive architectural unity" while embracing "a multitude of unities" (p. 31).

In his analysis of the first tetralogy, Ornstein accepts A. S. Cairncross' assumptions (in the New Arden editions) that *The True Tragedy* and *The Contention* are memorial reconstructions (Bad Quartos) of *Henry VI, Part II* and *Part III* and that the entire *Henry VI* trilogy was written by Shakespeare in chronological order. Thus Ornstein finds "a natural progression in Shakespeare's art": since *Part I* is more "primitive" than the others, it had to come first. That natural progression, however, is not clearly evident in Ornstein's analysis. He offers no new evidence, being content to attack the theories of those who, like Dover Wilson, believe that *Part I* was written last. He does not rebut Wilson's analysis of inconsistencies in *Part II* (e.g., the lack of allusions in *Part II* to Talbot, one of the great heroes in *Part I*); and, after terming *Part I* "primitive," he exclaims that the Temple Garden scene is "so superior to all else in the play that it makes all else seem less than 'Shakespearean' " (p. 36).

Individually, in *Part I* Ornstein denies the retribution theory as an explanation of Henry's problems: "It is Henry's failure to rule that makes his authority weak, not the flaw in his title that prevents him from ruling effectively" (p. 38). He cites Henry's lack of judgment in wearing the red rose which "antagonizes" York, "the instigator of civil war" (pp. 39–40). Like *Part I, Part II* shows "the betrayal of England's champion [Gloucester, who now plays Talbot's role] by politic noblemen" (p. 43). Artistically, in *Part II* Shakespeare develops his sense of characterization and his "range of poetic and dramatic techniques." Though some of the "bravura" remains, he is now capable of "nuance of tone" and more subtle shadings of emotion (p. 44). In *Part III*, Shakespeare focuses his attention on character. Richard is a "Machiavellian schemer" and Henry a milquetoast, "cowed by his enemies and intimidated by his wife." The characterizations of Margaret (a "sadistic deliberateness"), Clifford (an "individual bloodlust") and Richard are revealed in "perverted and sacrilegious rituals" which permit Shakespeare to emphasize the "moral perversity rather than the physical horror of the crimes" (p. 55).

In *Richard III*, Ornstein again stresses Shakespeare's artistic freedom from his source (essentially More's *History*). Unlike More, who "makes each of Richard's successes an occasion for moral outrage, disgust and scorn," Shakespeare makes Richard "an engaging, heroic and honest villain" (p. 63). Utterly cynical, he is "immensely rational and self-controlled" (until his fall) and "makes a cheerful vocation of the evil to which he is drawn by natural instincts" (p. 63). His fall is not the result of his sins but a "failure of nerve."

Others fare worse. Buckingham is a "comic" errant boy; Hastings is "childish-foolish"; Margaret is a "Senecan Fury" with "warped emotions." Even Richmond, the "spiritual leader" whose claim to the throne is "moral" rather than "genealogical," is a symbol of the national longing for peace rather than a great soldier whose exploits are historically glorified (pp. 80–81).

If *Richard III* dramatizes Richard's failure (rather than Richmond's success), *King John* exposes Shakespeare's. For Ornstein, *King John* is simply an artistic flop. The dramatic action is "clumsy and giddy"; the plot is irregular; and the characterization poor—especially King John's, which is confused and "opaque." Even the Bastard, the "anti-Machiavel" with a "fundamental innocence" (p. 95), suffers moral "amnesia" when he continues to serve John following Arthur's death. While some of these points are certainly interesting and perhaps valid, Ornstein's explanation for Shakespeare's "failure" in *King John* is itself somewhat confusing, especially in view of his original assumptions. Agreeing that Shakespeare's source is the anonymous *Troublesome Reign of King John* (*TR*), which the dramatist was ordered to "revamp," he asserts that Shakespeare "plodded patiently along in its footsteps" (p. 86). *King John's* failure, then, is predetermined, since the *TR*'s "crude" plot is "cranked along by wholly unanticipated turns of events" (p. 87). But later he states that *King John*'s dramatic action is "awkwardly articulated, not because Shakespeare followed his source too closely, but because he made changes in characterizations and plotting which seriously damaged the coherence and unity of plot that exists in *The Troublesome Reign*" (p. 89). Ornstein then suggests that "part of the problem in *King John* may result from Shakespeare's attempt to use an uninteresting assignment for artistic experiments" (p. 91). But finally he concludes that Shakespeare nodded. He was "careless rather than obtuse" and was "bored" with his assignment (pp. 99–101).

Unlike *King John*, *Richard II* represents a Shakespeare "fully in command of his materials," except, as Ornstein notes later, in Act V, where Shakespeare's "artistic interest or energy apparently wanes" (p. 124). In his analysis Ornstein sees the play as symbolic of the medieval ambience. Richard is "the poetic voice of his era," and the characters project "the collective consciousness of an age which treasured formality and order" (p. 102). But even though the rhetoric in the play "seems to body forth the world as emblem," or "Hooker's vision of cosmological order," the dramatic action "mocks" the ideal scheme (p. 105). The play does not dramatize the results of treasonous acts against the status quo (reflecting the Tudor myth) but presents the "convulsion of a still vigorous political order which turns against the king who wantonly threatens its existence" (p. 104). Again Shakespeare's emphasis is on the individual. Richard is a fascinating "contradiction": he is "weak and irresponsible," yet "physically courageous" and "politically tenacious" (p. 107). Bolingbroke is "strong, determined, shrewd and ruthless," but "eminently capable"; if not the "rightful" heir, he is, nevertheless, the "true king" (pp. 122–24).

In the last three plays of the second tetralogy, Ornstein stresses both the "extraordinary artistic achievement" of each play and each play's historical and moral relation to the tetralogy as a whole. The achievement in *Henry IV, Part I* is a unity of "vision and of plot which embraces and demands the interplay of comedy and history" (p. 127). The history provides what political issues Shakespeare wishes to raise, while the comic scenes "ironically scrutinize" the play's central themes of courage and honor. It is again the human quality which Shakespeare emphasizes, "for behind the logic of events in *Henry IV* is always the illogic of human motives" (p. 128). The characters, especially Hal, reflect this illogicality. Not a "Machiavellian," Hal is, nevertheless, "shrewd in his appraisals and thoroughly pragmatic" (pp. 135–38). His controversial soliloquy (I.ii.219–41) is not used as a "Cinderella" motif but as an assurance to the audience "that he is not a prodigal in temperament at all" (p. 137). Artistically, the themes which Shakespeare again develops—the problem of truth, the nature of honor and courage—culminate at Shrewsbury; but the "moral oppositions" are not clear: Is "honor" simply winning? Is Falstaff a coward? It depends "on how heroic we think fat old men ought to be." But when men like Blunt lay down their lives, "there *is* honor for you" (p. 148).

In his treatment of *Henry IV, Part II*, Ornstein rejects the two-part play theory and focuses on the differences between the two plays in terms of mood. Where *Part I* is primarily "gay" and "exuberant," *Part II* is "heavy with the disillusion and deliberation of age" (p. 154). Again, Shakespeare dramatizes the human rather than the specifically political conditions: the "unchanging human realities" are expressed in "opportunistic cynicism and the facile rationalizations" of the politicians, who are "men o' the times," willing either to be totally cynical or "to counter such cynicism with fraud and ruthlessness" (p. 157). For example, the rebels (calculating "businessmen") are "massacred" by "anti-heroes"—a Prince John, "who is capable of greater sanctimony and sharper practice" than they (p. 158). Other characters in *Part II* reflect the changed mood. While Falstaff "is still Falstaff," he is "degraded by the new circumstances of his life." His rejection by Henry V, says Ornstein, is necessary but cold-blooded: we "wince," not because Henry rejects Falstaff, but because "he rejects him without any trace of regret" (p. 169).

Ornstein's chapter on *Henry V* is in some ways his most disappointing. Although his analysis of Henry is sensitive and at times insightful, his treatment of the play itself falls short of revealing its specific "achievement." One problem is his attitude towards the comic plot. While he accepts the parodic function of the comic plot in *Henry IV, Part I* and *Part II* (e.g., the Gadshill robbery is a comic counterpart to the Percy conspiracy), he denies a similar purpose to the comic plot in *Henry V*. He asserts that we should not "equate Harry's goals with Pistol's and Bardolph's." Though the low comic characters "claim a fair portion of the play," they are "not the sordid reality that lurks beneath the glittering moral surface of the crusade"; they are only "parasites swept along on the tide" (p. 185). Also Katherine's English lesson (III.iv), although filled with "charming obscenities," provides merely "comic relief" to Henry's threat of rape and destruction at Harfleur, rather than functioning as a satiric parallel. Even Ornstein's treatment of Henry falters at times. At Harfleur, Henry makes the "terrible threat" because "he does not see the horror of the war feelingly" (p. 190). Yet later Henry "agonizes" because he might be held accountable "for all the suffering in the war itself" (p. 194). Finally the triumph at Agincourt, "which epitomizes the heroic impulse of a people" (p. 31), is cited as evidence that Henry's leadership is "inspiring" and his men "splendid soldiers." But Ornstein admits that the battle action is kept offstage (because Shakespeare wants to "spare us the horror of war" [p. 192]), and he fails to stress that what military action we see involves the degenerate Pistol, whose threat to cut his prisoner's throat adumbrates Henry's own order that "every soldier kill his prisoner."

Ornstein concludes his analysis of the history plays with *Henry VIII*, which, like most critics, he sees as a poor collaborative effort by Fletcher and Shakespeare. The play, "lacking in essential substance," is concerned primarily "with elegantly contrived surfaces." The characters are either "shallow or opaque." This weakness, of course, is Fletcher's since he, unlike Shakespeare, is more concerned with "exquisite gestures of submission," rather than "courageous acts." For example, in "Shakespeare's" Katherine scenes (I.ii and II.iv for Ornstein), the Queen has "the courage of her convictions," while under Fletcher she "lacks the will to defend her place and her dignity" (p. 207). Yet, bad as the play is, we might enjoy it if we see it as a *double-entendre*. Though the play is "shallow in its religious concern," the "spiritually inclined" will find "conventional piety," and the "worldly sophisticate" an "intense preoccupation" with courtly life (p. 213).

In general, Professor Ornstein's book reflects the strengths and weaknesses of his essentially impressionistic approach. He does not discuss the history play as a genre, but he refuses to accept certain pre-Shakespearean plays (e.g., *James IV* and *Edward I*) as being "histories." Though he speaks of Shakespeare's need "to create a suitable dramatic form for the History Plays" (p. 2), he does not really isolate and define that form and refers, instead, to the "Polonian" difficulty of separating history from tragedy (p. 222). At times Professor Ornstein's analysis reveals his own sensitivity to "nuances of language and characterization"; at times there are genuine insights, especially in his analysis of ceremony in *Richard II* and his depiction of York's pragmatism in the Aumerle-York-Henry IV scene (V.iii). At other times we stumble over a variety of critical fallacies, such as Shakespeare's "genius repealing the laws of artistic gravity and discipline" (p. 125); Shakespeare's being "unwilling to trust his audiences' perception of the subtle ironies of his plot" (p. 64); and even (in *Henry IV, Part I*) Shakespeare's plots being "created moment by moment by the characters without the author's intervention" (p. 125). Moreover, in view of Professor Ornstein's fine essay on the comic plot in *Dr. Faustus* ("The Comic Synthesis in *Doctor Faustus*," *ELH*, 22 [Sept. 1955], 165–72), we should expect a more specific and technical analysis of the function of the comic plots in the second tetralogy. We cannot dismiss those in *Henry V* as reflecting merely the "parasitic" side of humanity. On the other hand, in these days of literary "relevance," it is surely important that someone stress Shakespeare's universality, which Professor Ornstein does convincingly. But a universal Shakespeare is not a modern one. And while it is true that we cannot become "Elizabethans" or "alter our moral and emotional responses" to the plays (p. 9), it is also true that we cannot alter Shakespeare's responses, a danger that Professor Ornstein runs in his references to Shakespeare's attitude on war (pp. 191–92).

Finally, Professor Ornstein's attack on historical scholarship is too obvious a critical strawman whose demolition does little to enhance his own critical insight and scholarly sensitivity. There is little to be gained by debating Tillyard for his lack of perspicacity, and recent historical scholars as diverse as Irving Ribner, M. M. Reese, and Eugene Waith have emphasized the limits of Elizabethan world picturism.[3] Shakespeare was not a Tudor absolutist, but he was a man of his age. And, as Professor Ornstein admits, one of scholarship's jobs is to "free us from misconceptions" of that age, misconceptions, we might add, which are made by critics constantly attempting to create Shakespeare in their own image.

Yet Professor Ornstein's original question, as yet unanswered, is still valid: "Can we join historical research and aesthetic awareness" in the interpretation of a Shakespearean play? Today, as in Falstaff's time, it remains "a question to be asked."

Notes:

1. *SQ*, 22 (Autumn 1971), 406.
2. In Ornstein's attack on the Tudor myth, he asserts that it was Holinshed in 1577, not Hall in 1548, who felt free "to weigh rival claims or to assume a legitimist

stance." Hall and other Tudor apologists "had to avoid the issue of legitimacy by proclaiming . . . the sanctity of de facto royal authority" (p. 19). For a similar view see Henry A. Kelly, *Divine Providence in the England of Shakespeare's Histories* (Cambridge, Mass.: Harvard Univ. Press, 1970). Kelly asserts that Hall set forth his theme on a "purely ethical level, with no explicit reference to the providential order" (pp. 110–11). Like Ornstein, Kelly sees several possible myths which he classes as Lancaster, York, and Tudor.

3. See Eugene M. Waith, ed., *Shakespeare: The Histories, Twentieth-Century Views* (Englewood Cliffs, N.J.: Prentice-Hall, 1965), pp. 8–9. Epitomizing the current attacks on historical scholarship and reflecting the professorial confusion between scholarly theory and pedagogical practice is a recent wry article by Daniel L. McDonald entitled "Anyone Can Teach Shakespeare" (*Journal of General Education*, 22 [October 1970] 187–92). In describing his first teaching assignment, McDonald says that he was so busy depicting the Elizabethan world picture, explaining textual variants, etc., that he "forgot" to teach the play.

Shakespeare's History Plays: The Family and the State, by Robert B. Pierce. Ohio State University Press, 1971. Pp. xii + 261. $8.75.

Reviewer: Michael Manheim

That an analogic relationship between the family and the state was a fixture of Renaissance thought is hardly a new idea, nor does Robert B. Pierce, associate professor at Oberlin, suggest that it is. Neither does he claim to be the first to discover that relationship as an important element in the Shakespearean history play. E. M. W. Tillyard, to whom Pierce repeatedly acknowledges his debt, is the best-known twentieth-century interpreter to have articulated both those notions, and many have restated them since. Rather, Pierce says that the purpose of his book, which derives from a doctoral dissertation written under Herschel Baker at Harvard, "is to study how Shakespeare develops this . . . relationship . . . in ever richer and subtler ways through the nine history plays of the 1590s" (p. 4). In order to read Pierce's book, then, with a general feeling of satisfaction (quibbling reserved only for the finer points), one must pretty well accept as axiomatic the Tillyardian "world picture," particularly its fundamental assumption that, to use Pierce's words, "what sounds to us like a mere figure of speech," when we hear, for example, about similarities between family and state, "has metaphysical reality" for the Renaissance mind. I must acknowledge from the start that I cannot read Pierce's book with that kind of satisfaction because I no longer accept Tillyard's theory—no more, I suspect, than do most interpreters of Renaissance literature today. Briefly, and not to add to a critical furor just beginning to show signs of abatement, I believe that whatever "Elizabethan world picture" or Tudor "myth" existed was largely a propagandistic means whereby leaders of the Elizabethan government and church kept the populace in submission and that most thinking men of the period would not have recognized a special "metaphysical reality" in the parallels that existed between the family and the state, any more than do thinking people in our time.

In fact, let me begin this review by saying I am not sure Pierce really subscribes to the Tillyardian theory of "correspondences" either. While he periodically alludes to the family as a microcosm of the state—and is at pains to assert that "in some mysterious but real way the king is indeed a father, the subject a a son, and the order in the family the same as political justice" (p. 219)—the special "metaphysical" relationship of family and state in the plays is left unexplored. More often by far, Pierce treats family values and family life in the plays as figures of speech: conceits and emblems of political life. This is particularly true when he discusses the *Henry VI* plays, where he finds among the symbols of past political solidarity in *Part I*, stable family relationships like that of elder and younger Talbot; and among the symbols of political disintegration in *Parts II* and *III*, the breakdown of practically all family relationships: Henry's and Gloucester's troubles with their wives, the decay of the time-honored principle of inheritance, and the failure of York's sons to uphold their filial obligations with honor. Most important in *Part III*, Pierce observes correctly, is the scene in which Henry watches and comments on father murdering son and son murdering father as emblematic of the political condition of the land. But in all this, little is said about the metaphysical correspondence between family and state, and little more is said on that subject, despite periodic allusions to it, in later chapters.

Though the importance of images dealing with the family, in both the poetry and the action of the *Henry VI* plays, is unquestionable, Pierce has difficulty defining precisely what he means by family imagery, establishing its place among all the images of the plays, and determining the relative importance of individual images. Like other interpreters of Shakespearean imagery, Pierce occasionally gives disproportionate emphasis to images used quite casually in speeches and frequently underestimates the relation of an image to its context. He is more successful in dealing with *Richard III* because that play's chief context is the character of its central figure, and much of its imagery pertains directly to him. Pierce finds that play constructed about the conflict between Richard, who decimates all family values in his conceits as well as his actions, and the chorus of lamenting women, whose function it is, in Senecan style, to enunciate those values and bewail their desecration. Pierce sees the political downfall of Richard figured as a triumph of traditional family values.

Since Pierce says he will find the family-state analogy in "ever-richer and subtler ways" as he works his way through the histories, one would expect him to find the plays which follow *Richard III* more fruitful fields for discovery than the first tetralogy; but that appears to be the case only in the *Henry IV* plays. *King John* and *Richard II*, says Pierce, are "experimental plays" in which Shakespeare seeks a new dramatic form whereby Elizabethans may look to English history for direction in their progress toward the ordered society. In these plays, he points out, family images are important—again helping to contrast things as they are with things as they ought to be. But in both plays, he says, family imagery diminishes as the plays become a "disinterested study of a tyrant's thinking and behavior" (p. 131). Herein lies Pierce's conception of the "experimental" nature of these plays. They are more concerned with the "psychology of kingship" than with the breakdown of family honor and thus of national honor.

The plays for which Pierce's approach seems most successful are the Henry IV plays, because what the concept "family" stands for, which tends to be multi-faceted and at times vague in his discusssion of the earlier plays, is quite precise in his discussion of *Henry IV*. Family here is focused on a father's expectations. Hal, says Pierce, "must transcend his inheritance without denying it" (p. 172). Pierce's discussion of the *Henry IV-Henry V* cycle in these terms is clear and tight, but it is in this discussion that I find my most serious disagreement with him. Hal does indeed transcend his inheritance without denying it; but my question is, what is the nature of that inheritance? At what precisely does Hal surpass his father? Pierce indicates of course that it is at achieving the ordered state in the medieval, hierarchical sense. Like others today, I find another direction in Hal's achievements.

Throughout his discussion from *King John* on, Pierce dismisses the possible impact of Machiavellian thought. He is satisfied to let the image of the Machiavel in drama of the 1590s rest with the monstrous Richard III, without considering the question a number of historians and critics have been asking in recent years. Is the monstrous Machiavel of the English Renaissance the true and only Machiavel of that age? The question might be asked another way. Which Shakespearean monarch would the Machiavelli who wrote *The Prince* be more likely to admire: Richard III or Henry V? If the answer be the latter, which I think is the only one possible, then these plays are directed toward a concept of order quite different from that implicit in Tillyard and Pierce. Hal surpasses Bolingbroke in bringing a semblance of order to their kingdom, but their methods are hardly those which do honor to traditional family values as Pierce sees them. They overpower and outwit their opposition. If one true image of these Lancastrians is that seen at Shrewsbury and Agincourt, another equally true image of them is that seen in Prince John's perfidy at Gaultree Forest and Henry's barbarous threats before Harfleur. Bolingbroke's advice taken most seriously by Hal and most successfully implemented by him is to unify his kingdom by busying "giddy minds with foreign wars." Monarchy thus represented is a far cry from God's deputy putting everything in its proper place in the heavenly hierarchy. Hal does indeed surpass his father, not as medieval monarch, but as Renaissance political realist very much in the image of Machiavelli's prince.

The main trouble with the kind of order-oriented approach to *Henry IV* Pierce's study represents is what it does to Hotspur and Falstaff, both disorderly types as far as the state is concerned. From Pierce's point of view, and quite apart from the family theme, their sacrifice is a necessity rooted in the obvious national benefits it will bring, both men being serious obsbtacles in the smooth functioning of a hierarchical machine. The plays tell me, too, that their sacrifice is a necessity, but a bitter necessity demonstrating that authenticity and individuality are inherently antithetic to rulers who must control countries. I cannot see why, were Pierce's view of these plays entirely accurate, Hotspur and Falstaff would be treated as they are. Why the persistent emphasis on their vitality and energy, even in *Part II* through Lady Percy's remarkable memorial to her dead husband and the increasing rather than decreasing impact of Falstaff's humor? Why have Hotspur and Falstaff been made so dynamic if the message of the plays concerns the blessings their sacrifice will bring? Hardly, I suspect, as a warning against the powerful attractions of the ego and the flesh —though that seems the logical extension of Pierce's approach. In destroying Hotspur and Falstaff, Hal leaves the world a more sterile place (as Pierce observes accurately in *2 Henry IV*), to be only superficially revivified by the magnificently contrived patriotic language and action of *Henry V*. Seeing that final play as the true triumph of the Machiavellian spirit might help Pierce understand why it is, as he says, "good without being great" (p. 225).

Pierce says comparatively early in his book that he cannot discuss his subject "without considering the kind of response that an Elizabethan audience might have given . . ." (p. 30). Yet the possible responses of that audience are what he really does not consider. For all the lip service theatergoers might have given official Tudor propaganda, can anyone doubt the confusion they must have felt when they contrasted the actual existence they knew with the ideal that propaganda promised? Family images are important in the history plays, but as indications of the betrayal, dishonor, and false dealing the audience knew all too well, not as instruments of political persuasion. Shakespeare, like successful dramatists in every age, articulates the unstated, half-realized doubts and fears of his audience. Why must he be singled out, of all dramatists, to be a spokesman for official propaganda? The kind of order represented by the Bolingbrokes was undoubtedly one the audience was coming to accept, but that acceptance was grudging, if these plays are the true reflection of audience feeling that most significant drama is. I wish Pierce had really kept Shakespeare's audience in mind throughout his work, feeling greater empathy perhaps with the humanity of that audience and somewhat less concern for the official political dogmas of the age.

Fulke Greville, Lord Brooke, 1554–1628: A Critical Biography, by Joan Rees. University of California Press, 1971. Pp. xiv + 238. $8.50.

Reviewer: Robert L. Montgomery, Jr.

Students of English Renaissance poetry have for some years been attracted by Fulke Greville's *Caelica,* though only a handful have attempted a searching investigation. Nor has there been, apart from some unpublished dissertations, much effort at a comprehensive study of all his work. The pioneering comments of Morris Croll, Yvor Winters, and Geoffrey Bullough (the editor of the *Poems and Dramas*) have only lately begun to be built upon in books by younger scholars and critics, and Joan Rees is the first of these to publish a book entirely devoted to Greville and the full range of his writings.

Professor Rees asserts that her "main interest is in the poetry" (p. xi), which includes *Caelica,* the plays, "A Treatise of Monarchy," "A Treatise of Humane Learning," "A Treatise of Warres," and "A Treatise of Religion," though four of her nine chapters are devoted to biographical matters. She thus attempts to establish an interplay between certain aspects of Greville's life and the attitudes toward public affairs, moral conduct, and religious questions as they appear in the written material he left behind. This might be thought a generally useful objective, for Greville was an interesting man, as well as an important public servant more or less at the center of affairs off and on through substantial portions of the reigns of Elizabeth and James. Unfortunately, Professor Rees's execution of her task leaves the impression that she cannot make up her mind whether she is writing historical biography, intellectual history, or literary criticism. The result is that she does full justice to none of these.

The book is apt to be most disappointing for readers interested in Greville as a literary artist. Her chapter on the plays indulges in extensive paraphrase (perhaps excusable because they are little read) and settles finally in a discussion of their characters as embodiments of Greville's convictions about princely governance. It would probably be difficult to argue for them as very successful dramas, but one might still wish for a sharper focus than Professor Rees achieves. Similar reservations apply with even greater force to her treatment of *Caelica.*

Caelica is, after all, the one work that establishes Greville's distinction as a poet; yet it would appear to interest Professor Rees less than the discursive poems. In *Caelica* she finds no "recognizable thematic scheme," though "The ambivalence of attitude to love runs throughout" (p. 79). Lacking firm dates for the poems, she seems to assume that their order is almost random, and her discussion thus amounts to scattered comments, a kind of analysis of several poems, and a sustained (pp. 90–103) though uninspiring comment on those poems supposedly written in company and competition with Sidney and Dyer. One misses any critical position; there is simply no coherent viewpoint from which *Caelica* as a whole is examined. Profesor Rees objects to the view that Greville was a practitioner of the "plain style," a position initiated by Yvor Winters and taken up by Douglas Peterson and Thom Gunn (whose edition of *Caelica* she seems to have missed), but she offers us little except her objection. She herself makes only isolated comments on the style, such as her remark on LVIII that "The first two lines are an example of the pastoral imagery drawn evidently from appreciative observation which occurs pleasantly from time to time in *Caelica* and reminds us that Greville was a Warwickshire man" (pp. 80–81). This is the sort of thing one used to find in bad books on Spenser.

Nevertheless, Professor Rees does have a reason for discussing *Caelica,* and this appears in the latter pages of her chapter, where she links Greville's religious attitudes to similar sentiments in "A Treatise of Religion" and "A Treatise of Monarchy": hence her preoccupation with theme throughout her discussions. It is plain that she is really interested in Greville's moral and religious ideas, which she believes were chiefly influenced by his acquaintance with Sidney and by Sidney's death. These ideas are Calvinistic, pessimistic, somewhat anti-intellectual and anti-art. Where we can be sure that his work is fairly late (as in the case of *The Life of Sidney*), we find a nostalgia for the idealism of Sidney and Essex and a sour gloom about the Jacobean era. Professor Rees's best chapter is that on *A Treatie of Humane Learning,* partly because it bears most directly on the issues she is most interested in and partly because she takes the trouble to set Greville's point of view against those of Bacon and Milton. But this chapter is all too brief a moment of reward in a book that generally lacks reference to any method of literary criticism, ignores the context of literary culture in which Greville's works belong, and consistently evades the serious problems posed by looking at Greville, at least in part, as a maker of works of art.

Shakespeare's Heroical Histories: "Henry VI" and Its Literary Tradition, by David Riggs. Harvard University Press, 1971. Pp. viii + 194. $6.50.

Reviewer: C. J. Gianakaris

It would not be surprising for most casual readers of *Shakespeare's Heroical Histories* [:] *"Henry VI" and Its Literary Tradition* to regard it merely as another barrage against Tillyard's approach to Shakespeare's historical drama. For indeed, as appears incumbent upon scholars today scrutinizing the chronicle plays, David Riggs early in his book expresses his suspicion of the theory of "providential history," at least in accounting for the *Henry VI* trilogy. As Professor Riggs observes, "despite the playwright's [i.e., Shakespeare's] readiness to endorse, on occasion, Elibabethan dogma about the moral necessity of hierarchical loyalties, it by no means follows that *Henry VI* exists merely to illustrate the providential ratification of that dogma" (p. 5).

But for us to summarize Riggs's work as anti-Tillyardian also is misleading. We find that by the end of the book, Riggs explicitly acknowledges a providential design in Shakespeare's histories after all, even by the end of the first tetralogy. In concluding his commentary on *Richard III*, which he convincingly argues is the culminating piece in the *Henry VI* set, Riggs identifies as central features those very literary elements to which he denied prominence before in Shakespeare's chronicles: "The playwright's idea of history, like his ideals of personal 'worth,' has undergone a drastic transformation. Coming to terms with one historical tradition, Shakespeare arrives at another, which we may tentatively identify as Christian and providential" (p. 151).

Riggs's seemingly inconsistent attitude towards Tillyard, Dover Wilson, Rossiter, and other scholars treating Shakespeare's histories is a product of his highly selective and meticulous refinement of their postulates to fit them into his own purview. Specifically, Riggs discerns Shakespeare's earliest efforts in *Henry VI* as perfectly comprehendible within the conventional humanistic wisdom of his time. The notion that history plays *must* reflect the Tudor myth and divine retribution for an entire nation was not the governing impulse for Shakespeare's early works, declares Riggs, even if such an objective was evidenced within the chronicles written by Halle and Holinshed. In sorting out the influences impinging on the young playwright around 1590, Riggs suggests that Shakespeare's histories mirrored more faithfully the notions and manners instilled through the "education in rhetoric offered by the Tudor grammar school" and the "education in popular drama offered by the London theater of the late 1580's" (p. 3) than any direct carry-over from the source prose chronicles. Riggs later in his study agrees that Shakespeare does indeed reflect in *Richard III* and in the *Henry IV–V* tetralogy the providential and hierarchical theorems catalogued by Tillyard. But according to Riggs, when he does accommodate those *données* in the later histories, Shakespeare does so only after having developed them gradually within his personal aesthetic matrix. In short, he never simply adopts the providential view out of hand just because the historians of his time pressed that schema.

So much for the axis underlying Professor Riggs's book, wherein he intends to trace the development of Shakespeare's sense of history and drama and to place *Henry VI* within his evolving premises. To begin his scrutiny of the "rhetorical and dramatic antecedents of Shakespeare's earlier histories," the author undertakes a summarization in Chapters 2 and 3 of the academic curricula and the social standards concerning family and honor in Elizabethan England. He remarks that "The purpose of such a survey . . . is to see the trilogy not as the erratic beginning of a remarkable career but, rather, as the sustained effort of one playwright, drawing on the resources of a long and varied humanistic tradition, to assess a literary ideal by setting it within the recent history of his own society" (p. 3). A great deal of valuable study on this general subject has appeared in the last few decades, and Riggs could have strengthened his findings in these chapters by consulting the work done by Hardin Craig and Madeleine Doran (*Endeavors of Art*, especially). But neither is cited in the book in this connection.

If we seem to have expended much effort to establish Riggs's ends and means as he lays them out at the opening of his book, it is only because those interlinked objectives vanish from view on several occasions, even in the short span of 160 pages of text. The problem does not arise from any stylistic deficiency, I hasten to note, for Professor Riggs possesses a splendid talent for writing. With remarkably few exceptions, his diction, phrases, and sentences lucidly and concisely convey his ideas. *Shakespeare's Heroical Histories* stands as a satisfying book in that respect. All the same, it takes on a disjointed quality because, I think, Riggs brings into his dialectic equation too many peripheral factors of admitted individual significance, provocativeness, and hence debatability. The total effect—consequently and unfortunately—is one of fragmentariness.

Riggs's title, for example, invokes several topics, each of which deserves a fully developed commentary. And, in fact, he commences helpfully by defining some of his core terms, such as "heroical-historical drama" (pp. 14 ff.). But his foremost desire to trace Shakespeare's development through the tetralogies is long-delayed by Riggs's extensive side excursions into the unique nature of Marlowe's history pieces, most notably both parts of *Tamburlaine.*

One can, in part, sympathize with the urge to pursue Marlowe's version of plays built on historical figures as a useful tangent, particularly inasmuch as Riggs emphasizes the heroical in his approach to Shakespeare. Once on that tack, of course, the Hercules-as-hero and *virtù* issues lead directly to Eugene Waith's masterful book, on which Riggs draws substantially (pp. 18 ff.). In addition, Riggs intends to utilize the Marlovian method with history as a measuring gauge of Shakespeare's own art: "While Shakespeare shared with his predecessors an idea of history that is rooted in the lives of great individuals, he diverged from them . . . in the degree to which he modified certain received definitions of personal greatness. More precisely, working within the current Marlovian conventions, he reshaped Marlowe's heroic values to the point where they could be accommodated within a portrayal of fifteenth-century English history on the Elizabethan stage" (p. 21). Serious difficulties emerge from this kind of comparison, however, and the Marlowe analogue does not succeed on many points. Most obvious is the fact that the *Tamburlaine* pieces in no way can be considered English "history" plays in the tradition of Shakespeare's tetralogies. *Tamburlaine* concerns a legendary, bloodthirsty warrior of an altogether different epoch and part of the world, and it thus introduces more variable parameters than helpful parallels with the *Henry VI* plays. Then, too, the matter of a soldier's gaining political power involves another set of ethical standards than does usurpation of a throne of and by royal figures.

In conjunction with the Marlovian paradigm, which is woven throughout the book, emerges Riggs's examination of the humanistic underpinnings of the era, found in Chapter 2, "The Rhetorical Basis of the Popular History." Studying the career of a dynamic figure such as Tamburlaine might be profitable if viewed solely within the academic framework Riggs delineates: "Thus history finds its surest field of inquiry in the lives of individuals, or of national types; and those lives are meaningful only when they can be transposed into the received abstractions that delimit the areas of philosophical truth and humanistic value" (p. 37). Nonetheless, the rhetorical regimens Riggs distills from a typical Elizabethan grammar school training appear much too constricting to be reasonably applied to the dramaturgy of either Shakespeare or Marlowe—a point admitted by Riggs himself (p. 43).

Riggs misses a more beneficial discussion by failing to examine Shakespeare's sense and use of history with respect to Plutarch. Shakespeare's methods in adapting Plutarch's noble figures for the Roman plays would be more instructive than the Marlovian modes for comprehending Shakespeare's history pieces. But instead, in Riggs's book Plutarch is mentioned only in passing as providing illustrations of *ethopoeia* and *comparitio* in Tudor rhetorical studies (p. 42). In addition, a scrutiny of Shakespeare's treatment of ancient history in his Roman plays might well have led Riggs to reconsider the argument which props up his chapter on Elizabethan rhetoric: "A formal explanation of why . . . the early Shakespeare, and all of the other playwrights treated here, found it difficult to discern a providential pattern beneath the rises and falls of heroic drama can be deduced from what has already been said: their approach to the past left them without any sense of history as a coherent process" (p. 48).

The remainder of the second chapter and a good deal of the third covering heroic ideals are inordinately concerned with Marlowe, too, thereby staying the reader's approach to the *Henry VI* plays as promised by the book's title. Riggs offers an ostensible reason for devoting so many pages to Marlowe, apparently sensing how his attention to Shakespeare has been postponed: ". . . *Tamburlaine* showed an entire generation of writers how the set procedures of formal rhetoric could be used to fashion imaginative literature" (p. 56). Yet, at the same time, Riggs to his credit acknowledges the limited value of Marlowe as illustrative of rhetorical roots in playwriting: "But no inventory of set speeches can account for the ways in which the strategies of formal rhetoric enable Marlowe to draw out the latent significance of particular dramatic situations" (p. 57—also consider p. 60 on this point).

The topic of Chapter 3 is legitimate and apt, namely, whether one's character is determined by nobleness of birth or by nobleness of one's deeds. Talbot and Richard are properly brought into the discussion (p. 73); all the same, before long the reader begins to suspect that the chapter owes more of its inspiration and relevance to Marlowe than to Shakespeare, for it is Marlowe's dramatic heroes who continue to receive the most systematic attention. Although Riggs admits, "it must be conceded that the connections between heroic aspirations and social ones are usually too oblique to permit the kind of analysis that was attempted a few pages earlier" (p. 71), he yet assures us that from such tentative relationships we will find "an important clue" to the development of heroical characters in drama of the time. From that point on, Marlowe's *Edward III* takes front center stage. Only in the last half dozen pages of the third chapter is a Shakespearean play—*Richard III*—given prominence.

The nominal subject of the book, *Henry VI*, eventually comes into sight on page 93 of this short study, in Chapter 4, called "The Hero in History: A Reading of *Henry VI*." At this stage in Riggs's commentary, it will surprise some to discover that he foregoes his own earlier insistence that the plays produced on London boards in his day were the primary influence on Shakespeare's own dramaturgy. Riggs's analyses become more abstract as he probes the workings of the first tetralogy: "*Henry VI* is designed to disclose a set of exemplary truths drawn from the playwright's reading of fifteenth-century English history" (p. 97)—but *not* necessarily moral history with a providential bias, Riggs immediately adds. When he turns specifically to literary analysis of the pieces in question in the remainder of the book, Riggs proves provocative indeed, as with his insights into Talbot and Joan (p. 101). For instance, Riggs clarifies the full impact of Talbot's emblematic role this way: "At Talbot's last battle, however, the problem of consolation arises in quite a different context. Talbot and his son must die, and Bordeaux will never be retaken. For Shakespeare, this is to be the last battle of the Hundred Years' War and the last stand of English chivalry" (p. 109). In Riggs's interesting interpretation, then, the close of *1 Henry VI* mirrors a failure on the part of the courtly aristocracy to present a proper model of chivalric conduct.

2 Henry VI also receives enlightened attention by Riggs, once he turns his energies to it. For him, *Part II* plays a crucial role in reflecting the continued lowering of courtly standards, whereby "the emphasis has shifted towards a drama of ambition and disruption" (p. 115). Epitomizing the vanishing exemplars needed in a healthy court is Humphrey, Duke of Gloucester, termed by Riggs "a type of the Renaissance governor whom humanists like Ascham and Elyot saw as supplanting such medieval *chevaliers* as Talbot . . ." (p. 119). Gloucester's downfall therefore further signals the enervating erosion of honorable conduct in courtly councils. Within the blueprint Riggs proposes for Shakespeare's early history plays, *3 Henry VI* completes the downward design begun in the two earlier parts, underscoring the "ceaseless deterioration of aristocratic idealism into uncontrolled violence and brutality" (p. 130). Only the most ruthless of rulers can survive in such a milieu, Riggs believes, not those like Henry VI (pp. 138–39). Consequently, in Riggs's view, Richard III appears the natural figure to thrive in the moral wilderness that England had become.

Riggs's final chapter serves a vital purpose because it completes the arc of his hypothesis regarding the pattern developing in Shakespeare's histories. Additionally, Chapter 5 reveals the nature of Riggs's revision and refinement of Tillyard's basic concepts. What Riggs argues is that by the time he came to write *Richard III* and *1 Henry IV*, Shakespeare had altered his vision concerning history and its projection on the boards. Whereas in the *Henry VI* plays Shakespeare anatomized the disintegrating chivalric traditions which established a leader's "nobility" quotient, as it were, *Richard III* and subsequent history plays depend upon "the legend of the hero-king [which] has a life of its own, a currency in popular belief that will outlast any number of 'vile politicians' " (p. 140).

In an effort to distinguish his findings from those of Tillyard regarding *Richard III*, Riggs arrives at an intriguing conclusion in analyzing that play's protagonist: "This movement into a fully providential vision of history does not depend, however, on Richard's simply being reduced to a figure in a pattern. The externalization of moral values on the plane of national history is exactly paralleled, and extended into an individual conscience, when Richard looks within himself" (p. 147). Although not every scholar will concur with such a verdict, Riggs's account does explain in part the special dramatic attraction Richard has held for audiences over the years. One could fault Riggs for confusing irony with humor, farce, and satire in *Richard III*, for to insist that we view Richard as a practical joker stretches one's tolerance level (pp. 144–46).

The great glory of Prince Hal in *1 Henry IV*, asserts Riggs, derives from his avoiding the models of conduct advocated by his father—who emphasizes merely "those tricks of perspective that are to make him the observed of all observers" (p. 156)—or Falstaff's bias towards rascality or Hotspur's myopia concerning valor in the abstract. Riggs sums up the accomplishment of the Prince this way: "By insisting that the aristocratic life be freed from the domain of 'work,' Hal not only restores the prince's integrity, he also manages to redefine the intrinsic political value of chivalry in a world where everything has its market price" (p. 157). It will be noticed that Riggs borrows freely from Dover Wilson, Tillyard, and Barber in placing the Prince in his schema; but that is all to the good, since many provocative suggestions result. Still, one asks why Traversi's book *Shakespeare from "Richard II" to "Henry V"* (1957) was not taken advantage of, since it is ideally appropriate at this juncture.

We have had to detail and quote rather thoroughly in this review, because Professor Riggs marshals a large number of varied materials to support his arguments. In the balance, *Shakespeare's Heroical Histories* furnishes new momentum to the consideration of a portion of Shakespeare's dramatic output often bypassed by viewers. Certain background premises emerge as arbitrary, growing out of his selective documentation concerning the rhetorical learning process of the age. The syntheses involving the many humanistic strands in Elizabethan England as propounded by Craig and Doran might have offered Riggs a firmer cultural-historical base from which to operate. Even more important, possibly with such assistance, the focus of the book could have been better maintained throughout its pages.

Nor was I wholly convinced that an extended scrutiny of Marlowe was required to buttress Riggs's core concepts. The correlations were not always recognizable, and the space given over to Marlowe so generously might better have been utilized in analyses of Shakespeare's pieces themselves—particularly in so brief a study. Besides, Riggs is at his best when treating specific characters and episodes from the plays; many readers will hope with me that Riggs turns his attention to textual interpretations again in later writing. Finally, and most crucial of all, Riggs proposes an approach to the histories which is significant and provocative. His difference with the position represented by Tillyard is in the last analysis more one of degree than of actual substance; as a consequence, the campaign Riggs mounts against the notion of providential history is not required and in fact diverts attention from his own interpretive stance. In a word, the difficulties in Riggs's book all combine to force the reader's consideration *away* from his central vision.

All the same, there is evidence of much learning and thought in this book, and Riggs writes intelligently. Thus, although a casual reader probably will find the book diffused and confused in focus, scholars will satisfy themselves here with many thought-provoking perceptions.

The Imagery of John Donne's Sermons, by Winfried Schleiner. Brown University Press, 1970. Pp. x + 254. $7.50.

Reviewer: Chauncey Wood

The major portion of Professor Schleiner's study of the imagery of Donne's sermons is given over to the exercise of a new critical tool: the "field of imagery." As usual when new critical terms are employed, the study gains in freshness and in intellectual stimulation, but there are times when one wonders whether it is the subject or the instrument that is being examined. The author might have forestalled this criticism by selecting a somewhat less sweeping title for his rather narrowly defined study, but my demurrer is not intended to belittle either his methods or his results. Indeed, without something like this sort of carefully regulated approach, any attempt to deal with the ten volumes of Donne's sermons would seem foredoomed to result in description rather than analysis, in tabulation of effects rather than interpretation of means.

The idea of a field of imagery or *Bildfeld*, on which Professor Schleiner relies so heavily and effectively, originated with Harald Weinrich and is described in his article, "Münze and Wort: Untersuchungen an einem Bildfeld," *Romanica: Festschrift für Gerhard Rohlfs*, ed. H. Lausberg and H. Weinrich (Halle, 1958), pp. 508–21. Prior to Weinrich's study, imagery had ordinarily been studied in terms of the subjects (tenors) and vehicles of tropes. One approached imagery through the point of comparison or common ground between the tenor and the vehicle, or through the vehicles alone or the tenors alone. The first approach, Schleiner points out, lends itself all too easily to subjectivism and to "fruitless speculation." The other methods will take a metaphor such as *leprosy of sin* and will either classify the vehicle (leprosy) along with other diseases used for various metaphorical purposes, or will concentrate on the tenor (sin) and inquire what other vehicles are used to express it elsewhere. Weinrich, however, contends that we can properly speak of metaphorical language only when we keep both the tenors and the vehicles in view simultaneously, and not just their points of intersection. Thus Weinrich would discard terms such as *sea imagery* and *medical imagery* as artificial abstractions. He uses instead the idea of a field of imagery, which "is formed neither by a number of vehicles grouped together according to some scheme borrowed from the natural sciences or theology nor by a group of such vehicles as denote one tenor. Thus *sin* and *sickness* certainly represent spheres of meaning in a language, but separately they do not fall within the realm of metaphor" (p. 67). Rather, there must be both a source of supply and an area of reception, so that we can speak of metaphors of sin *as* sickness. Weinrich himself, discussing the field of imagery in which words are "coins" and people "pay" with words, writes:

> It is only through the establishment of the field of imagery that one area of meaning becomes the image-supplying field, the other the image-receiving field. It would be an unacceptable and deceptive abstraction to isolate the image-supplying from the image-receiving field. Thus all the metaphors concerning matters of finance taken together amount to—nothing. Likewise if one takes together all the metaphors for the *Wortwesen* [i.e., for a certain idea] he gets nothing at all, at least no meaningful structure. As long as one does not keep in view both the image-supplying and the image-receiving fields, he is not speaking of metaphor at all.
>
> (*Quoted in Schleiner, pp. 67–68*)

Although there is some potential for confusion in defining a field of imagery as something that contains two fields—one of supply and one of reception—Weinrich's point is nevertheless well taken. Having accepted Weinrich's definition, Professor Schleiner then examines a number of fields of imagery: Sin as Sickness, Life as a Journey, the Book of the World, the Seal of the Sacrament, Salvation as Purchase, and the Eyes of the Soul. Certainly one of the more interesting results to emerge from his study of these fields of imagery is a rebuttal of some of the psychological interpretations of Donne's imagery. The contention that Donne was preoccupied with medicine has been made by more than one critic, with varying consequent deductions about Donne's psyche. What

Schleiner does in his section on Sin as Sickness, for example, is to show that this particular field of imagery is common in St. Augustine, and thus that Donne's contribution is in fact the furnishing of precise contemporary terminology for the medical side of the field. One should note that this argument is the result of simple historical criticism and does not necessarily depend upon the employment of the field of imagery concept. However, perhaps one of the more important benefits of this critical approach is that it facilitates source study through its superior definition of what it is that the author under study is actually doing.

Professor Schleiner is certainly not contentious, but when he does challenge a statement such as D. C. Allen's claim that Donne "unwinds his medical knowledge to the delight of the hypochondriacs of his parish" (p. 84), the challenge is based on his careful analysis of a field of imagery rather than on Donne's presumed fondness for medical analogies for their own (or his own) sake. Similarly, when Schleiner discusses Donne's marine imagery, he dissents both from William Mueller's view that Donne regularly turned to secular things to illustrate points of religion and from Milton Rugoff's biographical account of Donne's unhappy experiences with sea travel as the source for his generally uneasy marine imagery. Rather, Schleiner identifies Donne's images not as *sea imagery* or *voyage imagery* but as a field in which life is envisioned as a journey. This field, a commonplace in Christian writings because of several Biblical passages, occurs in St. Augustine and other early writers and also in writings more nearly contemporary with Donne: Bernadino Ochino, Thomas Adams, and Marco Antonio de Dominis. Again, the author is simply applying good historical criticism to his text, but that he can do so in such a well-worked area suggests that his concentration on fields of imagery rather than on tenors or vehicles alone facilitates the identification of sources and analogues. Nor has the author had to go very far afield for convincing evidence.

In the section on Salvation as Purchase, Professor Schleiner suggests a correction to the ideas that Donne's use of monetary and commercial images is homely, that it reflects his own special interests, or that it serves as an example of his intention to surprise by using a secular metaphor for a spiritual transaction. Rather, Donne, "like the preachers he imitated, revivified the old metaphor by devising new analogies, by taking in, as it were, new aspects of the secular realm and linking them to the venerable concept" (p. 134.) In this section Professor Schleiner refers to several images (such as Christ as Pay-Master and the Holy Spirit as the reverser of contracts made by a minor) which contribute to his primary argument yet seem to constitute fields or subfields of imagery in themselves. Somewhat further on, the author confronts this ramification of Weinrich's theory directly and argues that "fields of imagery do not lie neatly one beside the other like the compartments of an egg carton; they occasionally overlap" (p. 146). This leads Schleiner to conclude, in his section on Extended Metaphor, that "the existence of substructures, while attesting to the fact that in living language fields of imagery are not tidily discrete, poses some problems for the examination of imagery. Some subjective element in the identification of fields cannot be quite excluded" (p. 156). The field of imagery, then, like all critical tools, requires skill on the part of its user and does not guarantee the reader's assent to the critic's conclusions. Indeed, Schleiner's section on the Seal of the Sacrament, because it does not clearly define the image-supplying and the image-receiving fields, seems less successful than some of the other sections in this chapter. The tool, however, is essentially a sound one, the author has made good use of it, and we can doubtless look forward to the study of Donne's poetic imagery using the same instrument, and indeed to its use for imagery studies generally.

We have examined Professor Schleiner's long and many-sectioned chapter on Fields of Imagery first—in spite of its placement in the middle of the book—because it is the most original part of the work. The author does, of course, examine other aspects of the imagery of Donne's sermons in his first and last chapters. There is for example, a very intelligently managed section in the chapter "Imagery and the Exegesis of Scripture" in which the author notes that Donne, much like a medieval exegete, could develop the symbolic potential of biblical objects. Thus the staff used by Jacob passing over the Jordan can be multiplied with other "staff" metaphors as the preacher examines the actual properties of the thing itself. This approach leads Schleiner to demur from the view that Donne was ostentatious in his use of esoterica. As he puts it, "it is on the basis of passages such as this [on honey, with Pliny's definitions] that the editors of the *Sermons* remark in their introduction that the sermon is marred by the preacher's intent to parade his knowledge. Yet it had been precisely the function of all natural science in the Middle Ages to help explain the Scriptures. All the bestiaries, lapidaries, dictionaries of plants, and all general encyclopedias were designed to fulfill this purpose" (p. 176).

The remaining issue raised by Schleiner with regard to Donne's imagery in the sermons is taken up in the first chapter, "Imagery and Decorum." Rosemond Tuve had argued against the view that the metaphysical poets produced poetic "shocks" and maintained that metaphysical imagery was decorus, basing her judgment on Renaissance books of rhetoric and poetic. Professor Schleiner attempts to carry this judgment along into the realm of prose by examining decorum in the sorts of books a preacher would use: the *artes concionandi.* Although Schleiner readily admits we have no evidence that Donne actually used these works (p. 20), he does make a good case for Donne's awareness of the relative "height" of metaphors by adducing passages in which Donne identifies "high" and "low" comparisons and also discusses propriety. The theoretical aspects of all this are necessarily a bit shaky, forcing the author to rely on phrases such as "the working model in the back of the minds of most writers on ecclesiastical rhetoric when they judge the fittingness of a trope" (p. 17). Nevertheless, he argues as well as he can about theory in view of the paucity of evidence, and his practical applications are arresting. For example, one mode of preaching involves the lowering of style to emphasize the lowliness of subject. Thus, if the subject is sin, the preacher might expand the Psalmist's "Vermis ego et non homo," as Donne does with comparisons of man soaring in his ambition like an eagle yet groveling like a worm, swollen to those beneath him yet so shallow his dog can step over him (p. 34). Thus even the seemingly indecorous image of man as excremental nails or excremental hairs can be shown to be the result of a controlled stylistic exercise and not the manifestation of an unhealthy subconscious (p. 36). As Schleiner puts it, "some of these macabre images, which have sometimes been taken as indicating a strange temperament if not a morbid preoccupation with the gruesome, are nothing but the result of . . . consistent diminution" (p. 41).

Overall, then, this work is a valuable contribution to our understanding of some ways in which imagery works in Donne's sermons, providing in this narrow confine an analytical tool for discussing imagery that will doubtless prove to be of great value in wider contexts. While the three analytical chapters of the book are not very well joined together, each is well managed in itself and ably written. The author often regards Donne from a medieval perspective, which seems to turn out well, and the author himself has learned from the medieval rhetoricians a proper regard for *divisio*. That is, he always advises us as to what matters are agreed upon and what contested and announces what points he will take up. The book has been attractively printed by Brown University Press, although all readers will join with the reviewer in regretting the rustication of the footnotes to the end of the volume.

The Boar's Head Theatre: An Inn-Yard Theatre of the Elizabethan Age, by C. J. Sisson (edited by Stanley Wells). Routledge and Kegan Paul, 1972. Pp. xx + 96. $7.50.

Reviewer: G. E. Bentley

This book is based almost entirely on unpublished suits and records discovered by Professor Sisson during many years of diligent investigation, mostly in the Public Record Office. He was already a master of Public Record Office research when I first met him in 1927, and he was still a reader there until almost the time of his death in 1966. So far as I know, in the field of literature only Leslie Hotson and perhaps C. W. Wallace could approach his familiarity with that vast agglomeration in Chancery Lane.

No one who has subjected himself to the endless frustration of seeking records of a single man or a single building or tried merely to disentangle the contradictory statements of a single suit in Chancery can fail to be impressed by the number of records pertaining to the Boar's Head tracked down by Professor Sisson. In this little book he cites some thirty-five Chancery documents and seven suits in the Star Chamber, as well as other manuscript records from the Court of Requests, the Exchequer, and the Guild Hall. A most impressive harvest!

Stanley Wells, who has edited Sisson's book, indicates that the author had essentially completed the work:

> Though the typescript was complete, there were some puzzles of the kind that would probably have been resolved by the author as the book went through the printing press. . . . In preparing Sisson's typescript for the press, I have checked the quotations from printed sources and supplied a few additional references. I have not attempted to follow Sisson's footsteps in his researches. In no case have I modified his treatment of the evidence. I have checked quotations from the more important legal documents, of which Sisson's photostats are on deposit in the Paleography Room of the Goldsmith's Library, University of London.

The inn-theater which is the subject of Sisson's research had been vaguely known before from several casual allusions, though there was great uncertainty because, as Sir Edmund Chambers noted (*Elizabethan Stage*, II, 443) there were at least six inns in London called the Boar's Head. Sisson has now shown from a number of statements in the law suits that the theatrical Boar's Head was on the north side of Whitechapel Street in the parish of St. Mary Matfellon, or Whitechapel, without Aldgate. It was presumably at this inn that a performance of the lost anonymous *A Sackfull of News* was suppressed by the Privy Council in 1557, and probably it was the inn referred to by the Duke of Newcastle about 1660 in his list of old London playing places. It was certainly the theater referred to by Joan Alleyn in a letter to her husband on 21 October 1603, "Browne of the Boars head is dead & dyed very pore." And with equal certainty it can now be shown that it was the theater referred to in the draft patent for Queen Anne's Men of about 1604 as "there now vsuall Howsen, called the Curtayne and the Bores head."

Sisson's evidence shows that there was a good deal of construction work done in this inn and its yard from 1594 to 1599. In effect, a permanent year-round theater was built in the innyard, with a raised stage, galleries, tiring rooms, and apparently a balcony over the tiring rooms. This information is collected from incidental statements in the protracted litigation about costs, rents, and ownership. Clearly the Boar's Head theater did not conform to our old idea of an innyard theater with a temporary stage set up in the yard of a carrier inn and used for performances on days when the carriers and their horses and wagons had not taken over. Obviously no carriers could have used the yard at the Boar's Head after the elaborate constructions had been erected by Woodlif, Poley, Samwell, Mago, and the others. Indeed, as Sisson says, "With the Boar's Head, we are dealing with an inn converted into a theatre as a permanent home for a company of actors."

So much is clear and well established from the testimony in the numerous suits about the ownership and alterations in the Boar's Head. Unfortunately, the author makes too many other claims which are not supported by the evidence cited. After noting that there is little information about the Boar's Head from 1557 to 1594, he continues (p. 35): "But all the evidence suggests a reasonable conclusion that the Boar's Head had continued to be in use as at least an occasional theatre before Woodlif took possession" (1594). Since there are no references at all to the Boar's Head in a theatrical context for a period of thirty-seven years when theatrical allusions are proliferating in London records and publications and when the printing of plays is becoming common, this statement is a very dubious use of "all the evidence suggests."

Very annoying for the scholar is Sisson's habit of making assertions about facts established by the testimony in his lawsuits without quoting them. When he does quote, the passage is generally a phrase or two and the reader can tell nothing of the context. "The elder Samwell, in a Star Chamber suite of 1600, estimated his expenditure upon the galleries at £300 and more. It is apparent that these structures were built on an important scale" (p. 44; no reference). Sometimes, though there is no proper quotation, there is a reference, but the reference is inaccessible to most scholars.

> The theatre was newly and handsomely equipped with stands for spectators, and with all the structures required by the actors for the production of plays. It was equipped for winter use, as an all-weather theatre, as appears in the evidence of John Mago."
>
> (Note 1, p. 46: "C 24/304/27 Interrogatory 14")

An appendix of important passages from the suits would have been a great help and would not have made a very bulky volume, since the present text is only 96 + xx pages.

The organization of *The Boar's Head Theatre* makes for rather pleasant superficial reading, but for the scholar who wants to set straight the facts about this important enterprise it is chaotic. These facts are scattered here and there through the book, and the index is inadequate for reordering them. A central difficulty with the book is that the material is of interest primarily for the stage historian or the student of Elizabethan drama, but the organization is that of a narrative for a dilettante. The same difficulty is apparent in Sisson's two articles incorporating part of this material, which the author published long since.

"Mr. and Mrs. Browne of the Boar's Head," *Life and Letters Today*, 15 (1936), 99–107.

"The Red Bull Company and the Importunate Widow," *Shakespeare Survey*, 7 (1954), 57–68.

Three years after Sisson's death and three before the publication of this book, Professor Herbert Berry of the University of Saskatchewan published an article on the same material: "The Playhouse in the Boar's Head Inn, Whitechapel" in *The Elizabethan Theatre*, edited by David Galloway: (Toronto: Univ. of Toronto Press, 1969), pp. 45–73. He uses almost all of Sisson's documents and a few more. His work is much better organized, less speculative, and better documented than *The Boar's Head Theatre*. Berry has said that he intends to publish further material on this theater. Generally speaking, the picture that Berry pieces together from the testimony, though much clearer and more succint than Sisson's, does not differ greatly in detail about the theater as distinct from the inn, except that Berry finds no evidence for an independent balcony or upper stage.

Memorial Transmission and Quarto Copy in "Richard III": A Reassessment, by Kristian Smidt. Norwegian Studies in English, No. 16. Universitetsforlaget, Oslo, and Humanities Press, New York, 1970. Pp. 93. $6.75.

Reviewer: Christopher Spencer

If one reads the first act of Shakespeare's *Richard III* in G. B. Harrison's edition of *The Complete Works* and then reads the same act in *The Complete Pelican Shakespeare*, he will have read (in the speeches alone) almost three hundred words in the former that do not appear in the latter and, in their stead, almost as many in the latter that do not appear in the former. If the different words were distributed evenly, there would be one in every three and one-half lines. Almost all of these variants result from differing evaluations of the original texts: Harrison is heavily indebted to the First Quarto, and G. Blakemore Evans in the *Pelican* relies upon the First Folio. Although any text prepared today would be based upon the Folio, we still do not have a satisfying explanation of the nature of the copy for either text, and, therefore, we are still uncertain how much or what should be borrowed from the Quarto. The prevailing opinion today is that the Quarto text is a reconstruction from memory of an acting version of the play made by some members of Shakespeare's company, perhaps when they were on tour in the provinces; it is thus a "bad" quarto, though its text is less corrupt than that of most of the "bad" quartos. The Folio is generally thought to have been printed from pages of one or more of the six quarto editions published before 1623 which had been collated with an authoritative manuscript. There has been much discussion whether the quarto pages came from Q6 (1622) or Q3 (1602) or a combination of both—possibly even with other quartos.

Kristian Smidt has wrestled with this problem before in *Iniurious Impostors and "Richard III"* (1964) and has also published a useful edition of Quarto and Folio texts of the play on facing pages (1969). In *Memorial Transmission and Quarto Copy in "Richard III"* he modifies his earlier views. In 1964 he doubted that the Quarto was either an acting version or a memorially reconstructed text. Now he agrees that there are "marks of theatrical adaptation" in Q1, though he does not think it has "come straight from the theatre" (p. 14); and he concurs also that "memorial transmission played an important part in the constitution of the Q text" (p. 25), though he argues that the copy for Q1 had been "revised and completed . . . by collation with a sound manuscript" (p. 46)—perhaps Shakespeare's foul papers. Included in his evidence for written transmission behind Q1 are the inconsistent use of the names "Stanley" and "Derby" much as in the Folio, the use of parentheses at the same places in the two texts, the examples supplementing E. A. J. Honigmann's[1] of greater closeness to the sources in the Quarto than in the Folio, and the proof correction of "greatest" to "utmost" in three copies of Q1 (where Qq2–6 read "greatest" but the Folio reads "utmost"). He remarks that some Quarto-Folio variants may be alternative readings from Shakespeare's revision of the play. As for the Folio text, Smidt earlier thought it to be printed from a difficult manuscript with some consultation of the quarto editions that the printer had available. Now he believes that the Folio was printed from a manuscript prepared from Shakespeare's fair copy (or a transcript of it), collated with one or more of the quarto editions and with pages from Q3 filling lacunae in Shakespeare's fair copy (or transcript).

Smidt maintains that such a manuscript would be easier printer's copy—even for casting off—than heavily marked quarto pages. He points out that the two passages in the Folio that are close to Q3 correspond in the first instance with Qq3–6 pages and in the second with Q6 (only) pagination, and from this observation he suggests that the manuscript prepared for the Folio was divided "into pages matching those of Q6 in order to facilitate casting-off" (p. 78). The observation is indeed interesting, but the explanation (or at least the alleged reason for it) is unlikely: since each text—Quarto and Folio—contains lines not in the other, the Folio text arranged in Quarto pages would not produce the regular number of lines per page that would be useful for casting off.

If Smidt is indeed correct in his general explanation of the texts, both Quarto and Folio are better than we have thought—the Quarto because of the influence of the written text and the Folio because a manuscript with quarto corrections made on it is likely to be more independent of the quarto tradition than quarto pages with corrections from the manuscript made on them. In general, an editor of the play would be encouraged to produce a text that is more eclectic but that has fewer emendations—a direction already taken by Honigmann.[2]Although more Quarto readings would be attractive, some Folio readings might also gain support For example, in I.iv.101 the Second Murderer asks, "What, shall we stab him [Clarence] as he sleepes[?]" in the Folio. Qq3–6, Ff1–4, all editors recorded in the Furness *Variorum* of 1908, and some modern editors (including Kittredge, Irving Riber in his revision of Kittredge, and Mark Eccles in the Signet edition) read "we," whereas Qq1–2 and most modern editors (including John Dover Wilson, Peter Alexander, C. J. Sisson, Evans, and Honigmann) read "I". "I" can be supported on the grounds that the Folio has no authority here, since if it was printed from pages of a later quarto, it was taking over the unauthoritative reading ("we") of its copy, which may well have been left uncorrected inadvertently. "We" might be favored on the grounds that the Murderers are supposed to do the job together (and later the First Murderer stabs Clarence). Smidt's theory provides a textual justification for "we," since it seems likely that "we" was the reading of the manuscript behind the Folio (or at least that it was deliberately copied by the collator into the manuscript behind the Folio) and so would have authority in what is generally the better text.

Not only does Smidt perform a useful service in reordering the evidence and injecting fresh suggestions into the stream of scholarly opinion, but his theories are attractive and are supported by much of the evidence. Unfortunately, they are not compelled by it. The mass of many hundreds of variants of different kinds, the ambiguity of most of them in the face of the possible alternatives, and the overlay of collation in Folio copy—to say nothing of the possibility of Shakespeare's own revisions—make a confident solution extraordinarily difficult to achieve.

Notes:

1. "The Text of *Richard III*," *Theatre Research*, 7 (1965), 48–55.
2. E. A. J. Honigmann, ed., *King Richard the Third*, New Penguin Shakespeare (London: Penguin, 1968). See especially page 244.

Shakespeare and the Nature of Time: Moral and Philosophical Themes in Some Plays and Poems of William Shakespeare, by Frederick Turner. Clarendon Press, 1971. Pp. 193. $6.25.

Reviewer: R. W. Dent

This is a troublesome book to evaluate. In many obvious respects it is extremely vulnerable, and one may run the danger of too quickly assuming it lacks compensating virtues.

First of all—and I do not mean this as a value judgment, basically—the sporadic resemblances to conventional historically oriented scholarship or criticism should be largely dismissed as unfortunate intrusions. The author's interests lie elsewhere. The book would make a better impression without, for example, its quasi-scholarly (but typically undocumented) appendix on Time from "Herakleitos" to the Renaissance, doubly so since he makes so little use of it. That Turner has no serious interest in the "multitude of channels" by which Shakespeare had access to Greek thought is probably implicit in the two such "channels" he specifies, getting La Primaudaye slightly wrong on author, title, and date, and misdating Googe's Palingenius by more than a quarter of a century (p. 177). On channels to Rome he is more embarrassing. Somehow the only relevant Roman philosopher before Plotinus, Marcus Aurelius, was "directly available to Shakespeare. . . . The 'Golden Boke' of Marcus Aurelius Antonius [*sic*, but correct elsewhere] (A.D. 121–80) as the *Meditations* were called, was translated by John Bourchier in 1534; it went through ten editions by 1586" (p. 178). Even the STC could have done more for Turner than enlarge the number of editions. It could have warned him that Lord Berners' popular translation was of Antonio de Guevara, not of Marcus Aurelius (at a time when the *Meditations* were not even known). Turner's bibliography, or "List of Works Consulted," is honest; Palingenius, La Primaudaye, and the "Golden Boke" are absent. His limited interest in the history of Renaissance ideas, or in the meanings of Renaissance words for that matter, is typically reflected on page 132, after a quotation from the *Faerie Queene*'s description of Phantastes: "We can infer that Spenser identifies that human faculty which deals with the future, with the fancy or imagination. Whether Shakespeare borrowed this idea, or whether it was an Elizabethan commonplace, he seems to use it where he deals with the Witches [in *Macbeth*]. The Witches are termed 'fantastical'. . . ." Fantastic.

As a former Shakespeare bibliographer, I find it considerably more difficult to forgive Turner's obvious indifference to bibliographical resources and to the reasons for their existence. Professedly anxious to see "criticism . . . improve and progress" (page 1), he nevertheless reflects very little concern with the present state of criticism on his subject. Clearly he has made no serious effort whatever to discover what others have written on Time, or Time in Literature, or his own professed topic, "Shakespeare and the Nature of Time." He has not bothered to look up "Time" (let alone "Witches," or "Imagination") in Gordon Ross Smith or John Velz or the annual *Shakespeare Quarterly* bibliography, and he by no means sounds so steeped in Shakespeare studies as to make such consultation superfluous. The few obviously pertinent titles in his "List of Works Consulted" appear as if by accident. That list, incidentally, includes only three articles: one on *Tristram Shandy*, one by E. E. Stoll garnered from J. I. M. Stewart, and a third which he casually dismisses in a footnote: "Since writing this chapter ['The Speech of "Time" in *The Winter's Tale*'], I have discovered I. S. Ewbank's article (in the *Review of English Literature*, 5, 1964), 'The Triumph of Time in the Winter's Tale' [sic]. Its methods and conclusions are largely different from mine." Presumably Turner's book went to press without his discovering many another relevant-irrelevant article or book (e.g., those by Tom Driver). Yet he is willing to begin this chapter with a paragraph on how Time's speech "has divided its commentators"—with the latest "commentator" Henry Hudson in 1880!—and then proceed with no signs of misgiving other than an habitual "perhaps" to a "new vision" of the speech and the play. Small wonder that much sounds far from new, especially on Time's speech. Indeed, Turner does not *sound* as if he looked even at Pafford's Arden edition of 1963, which renders superfluous a good deal he has to say. What is true for this chapter is true elsewhere. Turner does have some fresh things to say and, in part, a fresh point of view. But the fresh commonly gets buried under the unduly familiar, even the stale or antiquated, and too often he sounds unaware of the fact.

The explanation, I suspect, is that Turner legitimately felt he had a largely fresh approach to some familiar aspects of Shakespeare, an approach based on current studies in the social sciences, especially anthropology, but that he seriously failed ever to clarify (perhaps even for himself) precisely what that approach was or precisely what it sought to accomplish. A far too brief "Introduction" has only two loosely-written pages on his purposes before it leaps into a cryptic catalogue of the ten aspects of "time" he will consider. From these first two pages, however, we infer that what Shakespeare "captured in parable and symbol" has "later become accessible to analysis and exposition" and that thanks to new ways of viewing reality in the physical, biological, and social sciences we "are now in a position to understand theoretically much [in Shakespeare] that was exciting but obscure before." Turner continues: "I have not attempted to 'apply' modern philosophical or scientific concepts of time to the works of a man who never heard of either; rather, I have tried to suggest what Shakespeare and the twentieth century have in common in this respect, and cast light on my object of study by their juxtaposition."

This sounds legitimate enough, however ambitious. But the average reader—if I am at all average—will rarely be aware that Turner subsequently endeavors to fulfill this promise. Eliot's "illuminating" *Four Quartets* are repeatedly cited, usually as if the illumination provided were too self-evident to deserve any comment, but there is rarely any explicit reference to "modern philosophical or scientific concepts of time." The index is symptomatic. Of its seven entries under "science," three are to pages 1–3; the next three guide one to brief, loose, undocumented, undeveloped allusions (to "increase of entropy," something "the biologists tell us," and "Planck and Einstein"; Heisenberg on page 37 should be similarly indexed); the seventh, mysteriously, refers us to a page of quotations from Heraclitus. On such aspects of his professed topic, once again one suspects that Turner had only a peripheral interest.

The prime clues to his actual centers of interest probably lie in his "Acknowledgments" ("I cannot express my gratitude to my father, Mr. Victor Turner, of the Committee on Social Thought at Chicago"—something I mistakenly thought a gracious familial acknowledgement like that to his wife, but no more than that) and in his "List of Works Consulted" (where, rather than many an expected Shakespeare study, one sees two books by psychologist R. D. Laing, one by anthropologist E. R. Leach, and three by V. W. Turner based on his studies of Ndembu ritual). In the text Leach is mentioned but once (a 1961 essay seen "since writing this book . . . may suggest [in ways I do not quite understand after reading the essay] further elaborations of my approach"),

Laing but twice (in two brief footnotes, one of them indexed), Turner, Sr., not at all. It becomes increasingly clear, however, that Turner, Jr., assumes in his readers a considerable familiarity with these authors, or at least with ideas they have helped to advance, and apparently with several more whom I cannot yet identify—although I am almost certain that Martin Buber (especially *I and Thou*?) and Mircea Eliade (especially *Images and Symbols*?) stand high in the list. Neither is ever mentioned, and in my ignorance I have been led to them only by the pleasure of reading V. W. Turner's *The Ritual Process*, a fascinating study that could have encouraged even me to write on the "liminality" of Act IV in *The Winter's Tale*. Turner, Jr., told me that in using the word "liminal" he was borrowing "a term from Social Anthropology" (p. 161, unfootnoted). It came as a bit of a shock, nevertheless, to discover that Turner, Sr. had devoted half a book to "liminality," and that within the book one would find the basic authority for page 161's views on "the power of sacred weakness" and on "*comitatus*."

Which brings me to the index. In reading this particular book, Mortimer Adler notwithstanding, it is probably best to start with the index, which, despite many many omissions of both headings and references, is nevertheless the easiest guide to Turner's central concerns, especially if one pays attention to those entries with most page references or most cross references. For example:

liminality, 160 (*see* 'common humanity', 'power of the weak', 'holiday', etc.)
comparison, 27 [still baffles me], 37–38 [page 37 implies a definition which makes intelligible such later statements as "one cannot compare persons; one can only compare things" (p. 102)], 102, 116 [a reference to "Iago's perpetual comparatives," the point of which initially escaped me], 155 ["in matters of love comparison must be irrelevant," etc.], 157 ["Leontes' obsessive comparisons"; cf. on Iago above]
imprisonment [twelve entries, of which I now understand at least half; page 22's unindexed reference to "the prison of behavioural determinism" may be a clue]

And so on. The entries with most references include "externals," "faith," "freedom," "love," "masks . . . (*see* 'appearances', 'externals', 'holiday', etc.)," "perception," "present moment" (probably the most important, and least adequately indexed, of all major entries; I am still far from certain I really understand the concepts involved), "reason . . . (*see* 'reification', 'time as cause and effect')," "ritual, *see* 'ritual mask', 'dance', 'holiday', 'burial'," "timeless . . . (*see* 'eternal', 'present moment')," and of course several of the subdivisions under "Time," especially the one just named: "as cause and effect." One entry continues to intrigue me in my ignorance: "intellect that kills, *see* 'reason'." The expression twice appears in Turner's text (pp. 155, 167), each time as a quotation; if I knew its specific origin, I suspect I would have one more clue to understanding the purposes and theses of this book. My colleagues in English have proved no help whatever.

As I have repeatedly implied, this is scarcely a book for browsers—unless those browsers are by previous reading well initiated into Turner's principal concerns and concepts. The roughly chronological organization (with a chapter for the *Sonnets*, for *As You Like It*, for *Twelfth Night*, for *Hamlet*, for three "Tragedies of Love and Time" [*Romeo and Juliet*, *Troilus and Cressida*, *Othello*], for *Macbeth*, and two for *The Winter's Tale*) might encourage anyone especially interested in but a single play to look only at the relevant chapter. If interested in *Henry the Fourth, Part One* or *Antony and Cleopatra*, one could at least discover at once that he had the wrong book (Harry Hotspur, to my great frustration, never gets even a passing allusion, although he seems to me extremely pertinent to many of Turner's major themes). If, on the other hand, the book does provide a chapter to match the reader's interest, he should probably resist the temptation to turn to it. Otherwise, in most cases a great deal of what he reads will *sound* inexcusably trite, whether acceptable or not, and often it will *sound* either wholly irrelevant to "Time" or forced into some species of pseudo-relevance. In a good many cases such judgments prove unfair once one recognizes Turner's key terminology or begins to comprehend his rationale for the book as a whole. More seriously disturbing, however, are assertions that *sound*—to the uninitiated—excessively subjective, idiosyncratic, and either unsupportable or unintelligible. On *Othello*, for instance: "Othello participates in his tragedy not by reifying himself, but by reifying Desdemona. . . . Othello *must* turn Desdemona into a thing, because otherwise he would not be able to believe in her unfaithfulness. It is *humanly* impossible for Desdemona to be unfaithful: therefore she must be imagined as less than human" (pp. 104–5). After my browsings provoked by trying to review this book, I still do not agree with Turner on the aspect of *Othello* with which the above sentences are concerned. But at least I can now understand what he is saying, and my original irritation has been replaced by a desire to reconsider my own interpretation of the play in the light of his. Or take *Twelfth Night*. Here, all that's new in Turner's chapter seems to me built on a readily intelligible but wholly indefensible statement, one that muddles the characters in the play with those possibly in its original audience: "The people in *Twelfth Night* are on holiday" (p. 46). Conceivably, for the initiated this has some valid meaning, although I doubt it. In any case, Turner—and his editors, regrettably—seems to have had very little awareness of where further explication was essential for the average reader, and of where it was not.

It does not greatly help, therefore, to begin this book at the beginning. By the time I reached the above quotation from pages 104–5, I had apparently more than once been introduced to its central concepts without knowing it. Sonnet 129, for example, is, according to page 104, similarly concerned with making "the individual into a thing rather than a person; and things come under time's jurisdiction," but if the discussion of this sonnet earlier makes any such point, it does so in very different terms (and the index's first entry for "reification" refers to this present discussion, pages 102–5). Clearly, Turner did far too little thinking about the problems which would face his average reader, and in revising chapters presumably written at quite different times he did far too little to fuse the parts into a coherent and lucid whole. Probably he could have written a much better book, one much more immediately appealing and challenging, if he had organized it around his central themes rather than around individual plays. And if some of these themes had little relationship to "Time"—so be it. (I may be very wrong, but I suspect that Turner made a serious mistake in trying to unify his subtitle's concerns so exclusively under his main title. I, for one, would be thoroughly willing to forego some of the peripheral paragraphs made possible by that main title—especially the suggestion that the use of "come" by Rosalind and by Cleopatra is somehow connected to "the virtues of timing in love-making" familiar to us through "modern manuals on sex" [p. 41].)

Predictably, given all the foregoing, after studying the index one should probably begin with the final chapter, nominally on *The Winter's Tale* but at the same time Turner's most lucid treatment of many of his principal themes. Despite all the complaining of which I have been guilty, I sincerely hope the following example (from pp. 171–72) will encourage readers to give Turner's book the serious consideration some parts of it deserve. If what follows sounds unduly "subjective"—in a non-Laing, non-Turner sense—you, too, are uninitiated.

> The true sight which Leontes has gained is perhaps the capacity to see that which is timeless in the flux of time; based on a moral vision which is itself uncorrupted by those aspects of time that can destroy the inner spirit. In human relationships, to see the person rather than the thing is to see something which is not entirely of the temporal world, something not completely limited by the confines of time. A person can grow, and contradict the law of time that rules that all things must decay; and the actions of a person cannot be explained only by the temporal laws of cause and effect.

> Again, to see human beings not only with the eye of reason, but also with the eye of faith, is to use a faculty which is in some respects beyond the touch of time. Reason is based on temporal relations which become a logic; faith is closer to the inner self of a man, so that we can say that what a man reasons, he knows; but what a man believes, he is. Faith can endure blows that would shatter a concept based merely on reason. And faith is the only ultimate basis of human relationships. The third distinction between true and false sight that we saw in the test of Leontes was the difference between seeing a thing as a link in a causal chain, and seeing it as itself. . . .

While misprints, slips, and inconsistencies are irritatingly frequent in the bibliography and index, the text itself is generally careful. Rarely is anything more than mere distraction involved. In an unusually sloppy paragraph on page 125, for example, "as" is surely just a slip for "are," and "casual" is almost as surely twice a slip for "causal" (I am not absolutely certain); but the final clause (although its use of "insane" and "to" continues to baffle me) is probably correct: "Othello becomes objective, insane to his former lucid subjectivity." (Cf. page 95 on Hamlet's leaping into the grave: "For the first time in the play he loses control and becomes sane.") Page 28 causes me less difficulty. There "pité" should probably be "piété" (or "pitié," less plausibly), but is conceivably some term familiar to anthropologists but new to me; characteristically, Turner gives the reader no hint as to why he introduces the word at all. It's a pity.

Books Received

(Inclusion of a book in this list does not preclude its being reviewed in this or a subsequent volume.)

Adelman, Janet. *The Common Liar: An Essay on "Anthony and Cleopatra."* New Haven: Yale Univ. Press, 1973. Pp. x + 235.

Aretino's Dialogues. Trans. Raymond Rosenthal. New York: Stein & Day, 1971. Pp. 384.

Ariosto, Ludovico. *Orlando Furioso,* trans. Sir John Harrington (1591). Ed. Robert McNulty. Oxford: Oxford Univ. Press, 1972. Pp. liv + 588.

Aronson, Alex. *Psyche and Symbolism in Shakespeare.* Bloomington: Indiana Univ. Press, 1972. Pp. vi + 343.

Arthos, John. *Shakespeare: The Early Writings.* Totowa, N.J.: Rowman and Littlefield, 1972. Pp. 264.

Avery, Catherine B., ed. *The New Century Italian Renaissance Encyclopedia.* New York: Appleton-Century-Crofts, 1972. Pp. xiii + 978.

Badawi, M. M. *Coleridge: Critic of Shakespeare.* Cambridge: Cambridge Univ. Press, 1973. Pp. viii + 222.

Bender, John B. *Spenser and Literary Pictorialism.* Princeton: Princeton Univ. Press, 1972. Pp. vii + 218.

Benson, Thomas W., and Michael H. Prosser, eds. *Readings in Classical Rhetoric.* Bloomington: Indiana Univ. Press, 1972. Pp. ix + 339.

Bergeron, David. *Twentieth-Century Criticism of English Masques, Pageants, and Entertainments, 1558–1642.* San Antonio, Trinity Univ. Press, 1972. Pp. 67.

Berman, Ronald. *A Reader's Guide to Shakespeare's Plays,* rev. ed. Glenview, Ill.: Scott, Foresman, 1973. Pp. 167.

Berry, Ralph. *The Art of John Webster.* Oxford: Clarendon Press, 1972. Pp. vii + 174.

———. *Shakespeare's Comedies: Explorations in Form.* Princeton: Princeton Univ. Press, 1972. Pp. 214.

Birney, Alice Lotvin. *Satiric Catharsis in Shakespeare: A Theory of Dramatic Structure.* Berkeley: Univ. of California Press, 1973. Pp. xi + 176.

Bremner, Robert. *The Harpsichord or Spinnet Miscellany.* Charlottesville: Univ. Press of Virginia, 1972. Pp. vi + 26.

Brooke, Nicholas, ed. *Shakespeare: Richard II, A Casebook.* London: Macmillan, 1973. Pp. 256.

Brown, Howard Mayer, and Joan Lascelle. *Musical Iconography: A Manual for Cata-*

loguing Musical Subjects in Western Art before 1800. Cambridge, Mass.: Harvard Univ. Press, 1972. Pp. xiii + 220.

Bullough, Geoffrey. *Narrative and Dramatic Sources of Shakespeare.* Vol. VII: Major Tragedies. New York: Columbia Univ. Press, 1973. Pp. xvi + 600.

Bursill-Hall, G. L. *Speculative Grammars of the Middle Ages.* The Hague: Mouton, 1971. Pp. 424.

Burton, Dolores M. *Shakespeare's Grammatical Style.* Austin: Univ. of Texas Press, 1973. Pp. xviii + 364.

Caldwel, Harry B., and David L. Middleton, eds. *English Tragedy, 1370 to 1600: Fifty Years of Criticism.* San Antonio: Trinity Univ. Press, 1971. Pp. 89.

Charney, Maurice. *How to Read Shakespeare.* New York: McGraw-Hill, 1971. Pp. x + 149.

Chaucer, Geoffrey. *The Canterbury Tales.* (A facsimile of Pepys's copy.) Cambridge: Cornmarket Reprints, 1972. Pp. unnumbered.

Clarkson, L. A. *The Pre-Industrial Economy in England, 1500–1750.* New York: Schocken Books, 1972. Pp. 268.

Clemen, Wolfgang. *Shakespeare's Dramatic Art.* London: Methuen, 1972. Pp. vii + 236.

Clogan, Paul Maurice, ed. *Medievalia et Humanistica: Studies in Medieval and Renaissance Culture.* New Series, No. 2. Cleveland: Case Western Reserve Univ. Press, 1971. Pp. viii + 223.

Cockburn, J. S. *A History of English Assizes, 1558–1714.* Cambridge: Cambridge Univ. Press, 1972. Pp. xviii + 327.

Collins, Fletcher, Jr. *The Production of Medieval Church Music-Drama.* Charlottesville: Univ. Press of Virginia, 1972. Pp. 356.

Collins, R. G., ed. *From an Ancient to a Modern Theatre.* Winnipeg: Univ. of Manitoba Press, 1972. Pp. xiv + 170.

Cooke, Katharine. *A. C. Bradley and his Influence in Twentieth-Century Shakespearean Criticism.* Oxford: Oxford Univ. Press, 1972. Pp. xiv + 243.

Council, Norman. *When Honour's at the Stake: Ideas of Honour in Shakespeare's Plays.* New York: Barnes & Noble, 1973. Pp. 165.

Coupe, W. A. *A Sixteenth-Century German Reader.* Oxford: Oxford Univ. Press, 1972. Pp. xxiii + 362.

Covatta, Anthony. *Thomas Middleton's City Comedies.* Lewisburg, Pa.: Bucknell Univ. Press, 1973. Pp. 187.

Crane, Milton, ed. *Shakespeare's Art: Seven Essays.* The Tupper Lectures on Shakespeare at George Washington University. Chicago: Univ. of Chicago Press, 1973. Pp. 168.

Cutts, John P. *The Left Hand of God: A Critical Interpretation of the Plays of Christopher Marflowe.* Haddonfield, N.J.: Haddonfield House, 1973. Pp. ix + 254.

Damrosch, Leopold, Jr. *Samuel Johnson and the Tragic Sense.* Princeton: Princeton Univ. Press, 1972. Pp. xii + 267.

Duncan, Joseph E. *Milton's Earthly Paradise: A Historical Study of Eden.* Minneapolis: Univ. of Minnesota Press, 1972. Pp. viii + 329.

Eckert, Charles W. ed. *Focus on Shakespearean Films.* Englewood Cliffs, N.J.: Prentice-Hall, 1972. Pp. viii + 184.

Economou, George D. *The Goddess Natura in Medieval Literature.* Cambridge, Mass.: Harvard Univ. Press, 1972. Pp. ix + 213.

Edwardes, Michael. *Ralph Fitch, Elizabethan in the Indies.* London: Faber & Faber, 1973. Pp. 184.

Ellis-Fermor, Una. *Shakespeare the Dramatist.* 1961; rpt. London: Methuen, 1973. Pp. 188.

English Literature, 1660–1800: A Bibliography of Modern Studies. Vols. V & VI. Princeton: Princeton Univ. Press, 1972. Pp. xi + 1293.

Farnham, Willard. *Shakespeare's Tragic Frontier.* 1950; rpt. New York: Barnes & Noble, 1973. Pp. 289.

Farr, Dorothy M. *Thomas Middleton and the Drama of Realism.* New York: Barnes & Noble, 1973. Pp. viii + 139.

Felperin, Howard. *Shakespearean Romance.* Princeton: Princeton Univ. Press, 1972. Pp. vii + 317.

Fiedler, Leslie A. *The Stranger in Shakespeare.* New York: Stein & Day, 1972. Pp. 263.

Fielding, Henry. *The Grub-Street Opera.* Ed. J. L. Morrissey. Fountainwell Drama Texts. Edinburgh: Oliver & Boyd, 1973. Pp. 133.

Fisch, Harold. *Hamlet and the Word.* New York: Frederick Ungar, 1971. Pp. viii + 248.

Folger Shakespeare Library. *Catalog of the Shakespeare Collection.* Vols. I & II. Boston: G. K. Hall, 1972. Pp. iii + 697; iii + 369.

Fraser, Russell. *The Dark Ages and the Age of Gold.* Princeton: Princeton Univ. Press, 1973. Pp. xi + 425.

French, A. L. *Shakespeare and the Critics.* Cambridge: Cambridge Univ. Press, 1972. Pp. v + 239.

French, Peter J. *John Dee: The World of an Elizabethan Magus.* London: Routledge & Kegan Paul, 197. Pp. xii + 243.

Fruman, Norman. *Coleridge: The Damaged Archangel.* New York: George Braziller, 1971. Pp. xxiii + 607.

Galloway, David, ed. *The Elizabethan Theater III.* Hamden, Conn.: Shoe String Press, 1973. Pp. xvi + 149.

Garton, Charles. *Personal Aspects of the Roman Theatre.* Toronto: Hakkert, 1972. Pp. xv + 338.

Gaskell, Philip. *A New Introduction to Bibliography.* Oxford: Oxford Univ. Press, 1972. Pp. 438.

Gillie, Christopher. *Longman Companion to English Literature.* London: Longman, 1972. Pp. xi + 880.

Godschalk, William Leigh. *Patterning in Shakespearean Drama.* The Hague: Mouton, 1973. Pp. 199.

Goldman, Michael. *Shakespeare and the Energies of Drama.* Princeton: Princeton Univ. Press, 1972. Pp. vii + 176.

Gombrich, E. H. *Symbolic Images: Studies in the Art of the Renaissance.* London: Phaidon Press, 1972. Pp. viii + 247.

Gottschalk, Paul. *The Meanings of Hamlet: Modes of Literary Interpretation since Bradley.* Albuquerque: Univ. of New Mexico Press, 1972. Pp. 197.

Greene, Robert. *James the Fourth.* Ed. Norman Sanders. Revels Plays. London: Methuen, 1973. Pp. lxiii + 154.

Grose, Christopher. *Milton's Epic Process.* New Haven: Yale Univ. Press, 1973. Pp. 268.

Guerinot, J. V., ed. *Pope: A Collection of Critical Essays.* Englewood Cliffs, N.J.: Prentice-Hall, 1973. Pp. 184.

Hale, J. R. *Renaissance Venice.* Totowa, N. J.: Rowman & Littlefield, 1973. Pp. 483.

Harbage, Alfred. *Shakespeare without Words and Other Essays.* Cambridge, Mass.: Harvard Univ. Press, 1972. Pp. viii + 229.

Hargreaves-Mawdsley, W. N. *Oxford in the Age of John Locke.* Norman: Univ. of Oklahoma Press, 1973. Pp. xi + 132.

Havran, Martin J. *Caroline Courtier: The Life of Lord Cottington.* Columbia: Univ. of South Carolina Press, 1973. Pp. xviii + 232.

Heywood, Ellis. *Il Moro.* Ed. and trans. Roger L. Deakins. Cambridge, Mass.: Harvard Univ. Press, 1972. Pp. xxxvii + 118.

Hodges, C. Walter. *Shakespeare's Second Globe: The Missing Monument.* Oxford: Oxford Univ. Press, 1973. Pp. 100.

Holmes, Martin. *Shakespeare and his Players.* New York: Charles Scribner's Sons, 1972. Pp. x + 212.

Honig, Edwin. *Dark Conceit: The Making of Allegory.* Providence, R.I.: Brown Univ. Press, 1972. Pp. xii + 210.

Howard-Hill, T. H., ed. *Oxford Shakespeare Concordances*: Cymbeline. Oxford: Oxford Univ. Press, 1972. Pp. xiii + 364.

———. *Oxford Shakespeare Concordances*: Hamlet. Oxford: Oxford Univ. Press, 1973. Pp. xiv + 438.

———. *Ralph Crane and Some Shakespeare First Folio Comedies.* Charlottesville: Univ. of Virginia Press, 1972. Pp. ix. + 190.

Hurstfield, Joel, and Alan G. R. Smith, eds. *Elizabethan People: State and Society.* New York: St. Martin's Press, 1972. Pp. ix + 168.

Hurstfield, Joel. *Freedom, Corruption and Government in Elizabethan England.* Cambridge, Mass.: Harvard Univ. Press, 1973. Pp. 368.

———. *The Queen's Wards: Wardship and Marriage under Elizabeth I.* 1958: rpt. London: Frank Cass, 1973. Pp. xxii + 366.

Johan Johan the Husband. Ed. G. R. Proudfoot. Malone Society Reprints. 1967; rpt. Oxford: Oxford Univ. Press, 1972. Pp. x + text.

Johnson, Paula. *English Renaissance: Form and Transformation in Music and Poetry of the English Renaissance.* New Haven: Yale Univ. Press, 1972. Pp. 170.

Jones-Davies, Marie-Thérèse. *Ben Jonson: Théâtre de tous les temps.* Paris: Seghers, 1973. Pp. 192.

Jonson, Ben. *Bartholomew Fair.* Ed. Douglas Duncan. Fountainwell Drama Texts. Edinburgh: Oliver & Boyd, 1972. Pp. 159.

Kennedy, Judith M., and James A. Reither. *A Theatre for Spenserians.* Toronto: Univ. of Toronto Press, 1973. Pp. ix + 144.

Kennedy, Arthur G. and Donald B. Sands. *A Concise Bibliography for Students of English.* Rev. William E. Colburn. Stanford: Stanford Univ. Press, 1972. Pp. 300.

Kinney, Arthur F. *Titled Elizabethans.* Hamden, Conn.: Shoe String Press, 1973. Pp. ix + 89.

Larkin, James F., and Paul L. Hughes, eds. *Stuart Royal Proclamations.* Vol. I. Oxford: Clarendon Press, 1973. Pp. xxxiv + 679.

Lascelles, Mary. *Notions and Facts: Collected Criticism and Research.* Oxford: Oxford Univ. Press, 1972. Pp. xi + 264.

Lawry, Jon S. *Sidney's Two "Arcadias": Pattern and Proceeding.* Ithaca: Cornell Univ. Press, 1972. Pp. xiii + 304.

Leacroft, Richard. *The Development of the English Playhouse.* Ithaca: Cornell Univ. Press, 1973. Pp. xiii + 354.

Leech, Clifford, and J. M. R. Margeson, eds. *Shakespeare 1971:* Proceedings of the World Shakespeare Congress, Vancouver, August, 1971. Toronto: Univ. of Toronto Press, 1972. Pp. vi + 298.

Levy, Bernard S., ed. *Developments in the Early Renaissance.* Albany: State University of New York Press, 1972. Pp. 223.

Lloyd, Joan Barclay. *African Animals in Renaissance Literature and Art.* Oxford: Oxford Univ. Press, 1972. Pp. xi + 145.

Loftis, John. *The Spanish Plays of Neoclassical England.* New Haven: Yale Univ. Press, 1973. Pp. xiii + 263.

Logan, Terence P., and Denzell S. Smith, eds. *The Predecessors of Shakespeare.* Lincoln: Univ. of Nebraska Press, 1973. Pp. xiv + 348.

Mack, Maynard, Jr. *Killing the King: Three Studies in Shakespeare's Tragic Structure.* New Haven, Conn.: Yale Univ. Press, 1973. Pp. viii + 210.

Macrae-Gibson, O. D., ed. *Of Arthour and of Merlin.* Early English Text Society. Oxford: Oxford Univ. Press, 1973. Pp. xiv + 367.

Manheim, Michael. *The Weak King Dilemma in the Shakespearean History Play.* Syracuse: Syracuse Univ. Press, 1973. Pp. x + 198.

Manvell, Roger, and Heinrich Fraenkel. *The German Cinema.* New York: Praeger, 1972. Pp. 159.

Marlowe, Christopher. *The Complete Works.* 2 vols. Ed. Fredson Bowers. Cambridge Cambridge Univ. Press, 1973. Pp. xi + 417; 541.

The Marriage Between Wit and Wisdom. Ed. Trevor N. S. Lennam. Malone Society Reprints. 1966; rpt. Oxford: Oxford Univ. Press, 1971. Pp. xi + 59.

Martin, Philip. *Shakespeare's Sonnets: Self, Love, and Art.* Cambridge: Cambridge Univ. Press, 1972. Pp. 169.

Maskell, David. *The Historical Epic in France, 1500–1700.* Oxford Oxford Univ. Press, 1973. Pp. x + 263.

McCollom, William G. *The Divine Average: A View of Comedy.* Cleveland: Case Western Reserve Univ. Press, 1971. Pp. viii + 231.

McElroy, Bernard. *Shakespeare's Mature Tragedies.* Princeton: Princeton Univ. Press, 1973. Pp. ix + 256.

McFarland, Thomas. *Shakespeare's Pastoral Comedy.* Chapel Hill: Univ. of North Carolina Press, 1972. Pp. x + 218.

McLean, Antonia. *Humanism and the Rise of Science in Tudor England.* New York: Neale Watson Academic Publications, 1972. Pp. 258.

Means, Michael. *The Consolatio Genre in Medieval English Literature.* Univ. of Florida Humanities Monograph 36. Gainesville: Univ. of Florida Press, 1972. Pp. v + 105.

Medieval Drama. Ed. Malcolm Bradbury, David Palmer, and Neville Denny. Stratford-Upon-Avon Studies 16. New York: Crane, Russak, 1973. Pp. 254.

Miller, John. *Popery and Politics in England, 1660–1688.* Cambridge: Cambridge Univ. Press, 1973. Pp. xiii + 288.

Milward, Peter. *Shakespeare's Religious Background.* Bloomington: Indiana Univ. Press, 1973. Pp. 312.

Miner, Earl. *English Criticism in Japan.* Tokyo: Univ. of Tokyo Press, 1972. Pp. xxiii +3d.

Molnar, John W. *Songs from the Williamsburg Theatre.* Charlottesville: Univ. Press of Virginia, 1972. Pp. xix + 227.

Morgann, Maurice. *Shakespearean Criticism.* Ed. D. A. Fineman. Oxford: Oxford Univ. Press, 1972. Pp. xiv + 444.

Morison, Stanley. *Politics and Script.* Oxford: Oxford Univ. Press, 1972. Pp. 361.

Morris, David B. *The Religious Sublime: Christian Poetry and Critical Tradition in Eighteenth-Century England.* Lexington: Univ. Press of Kentucky, 1972. Pp. ix + 261.

Morris, Wesley. *Toward a New Historicism.* Princeton: Princeton Univ. Press, 1972. Pp. xii + 265.

Muir, Kenneth. *Shakespeare's Tragic Sequence.* New York: Hillary House Publishers, 1972. Pp. 207.

Murphy, James J. *Medieval Rhetoric: A Select Bibliography.* Toronto: Univ. of Toronto Press, 1972. Pp. xvi + 100.

Naugle, Helen H. *A Concordance to the Poems of Samuel Johnson.* Ithaca: Cornell Univ. Press, 1973. Pp. xxx + 578.

Nemerov, Howard. *Reflexions on Poetry and Poetics.* New Brunswick, N.J.: Rutgers Univ. Press, 1972. Pp. xii + 233.

Nevo, Ruth. *Tragic Form in Shakespeare.* Princeton: Princeton Univ. Press, 1972. Pp. 412.

Nilsson, Martin. *The Mycenaean Origin of Greek Mythology.* Berkeley: Univ. of California Press, 1973. Pp. xv + 258.

Olsen, V. Norskov. *John Foxe and the Elizabethan Church.* Berkeley: Univ. of California Press, 1973. Pp. xii + 264.

Orgel, Stephen, and Roy Strong. *Inigo Jones: The Theatre of the Stuart Court.* 2 vols. Berkeley: Univ. of California Press, Pp. xx + 843.

Orme, Nicholas. *English Schools in the Middle Ages.* London: Methuen, 1973. Pp. xiii + 369.

Osbourn, James M. *Young Philip Sidney, 1572–1577.* New Haven: Yale Univ. Press, 1972. Pp. xxiv + 565.

Owsei, Temkin. *The Falling Sickness: A History of Epilepsy from the Greeks to the Beginnings of Modern Neurology.* Baltimore: Johns Hopkins Press, 1971. Pp. xv + 467.

Partridge, A. C. *Tudor to Augustan English.* London: André Deutsch, 1969. Pp. 242.

A Pepysian Garland: Black Letter Broadside Ballads of the Years 1595–1639. Ed. Hyder E. Rollins. 1922; rpt. Cambridge, Mass.: Harvard Univ. Press, 1971. Pp. xxxvi + 491.

Phillips, O. Hood. *Shakespeare and the Lawyers.* London: Methuen, 1972. Pp. ix + 214.

Pill, David H. *The English Reformation.* Totowa, N.J.: Rowan & Littlefield, 1973. Pp. 224.

Poetics: International Review for the Theory of Literature 7. Ed. Siegfried J. Schmidt. The Hague: Mouton, 1973. Pp. 148.

Prest, Wilfrid R. *The Inns of Court under Elizabeth I and the Early Stuarts, 1590–1640.* Totowa, N.J.: Rowman & Littlefield, 1972. Pp. xii + 263.

Prior, Moody E. *The Drama of Power.* Evanston, Ill.: Northwestern Univ. Press, 1973. Pp. xvi + 410.

Quinones, Richard J. *The Renaissance Discovery of Time.* Cambridge, Mass.: Harvard Univ. Press, 1972. Pp. xvi + 549.

Rajan, Balachandra, ed. *The Prison and the Pinnacle.* Toronto: Univ. of Toronto Press, 1973. Pp. 163.

Raleigh, Sir Walter. *The History of the World.* Ed. C. A. Patrides. Philadelphia: Temple Univ. Press, 1971. Pp. xvi + 418.

Rebholz, Ronald A. *The Life of Fulke Greville, First Lord Brooke.* Oxford: Clarendon Press, 1971. Pp. xvii + 384.

Renaissance Drama. New Series IV (1971) & V (1972). Ed. Samuel Schoenbaum and Alan C. Dessen. Evanston, Ill.: Northwestern Univ. Press, 1972 & 1973. Pp. 248; 246.

Renaissance Papers. Ed. Dennis G. Donovan and A. Leigh Deneef. Southeastern Renaissance Conference, 1972. Pp. vi + 63.

Ridley, Jasper. *The Life and Times of Mary Tudor.* London: Weidenfeld & Nicolson, 1973. Pp. 224.

Rist, J. M. *Epicurus, an Introduction.* Cambridge: Cambridge Univ. Press, 1972. Pp. xiv + 185.

Robinson, Forrest G. *The Shape of Things Known: Sidney's "Apology" in its Philosophical Tradition.* Cambridge, Mass.: Harvard Univ. Press, 1972. Pp. xi + 230.

Rogers, Thomas. *Leicester's Ghost.* Ed. Franklin B. Williams, Jr. Chicago: Chicago Univ. Press, 1972. Pp. xxiii + 94.

Rose, Mark. *Shakespearean Design.* Cambridge, Mass.: Harvard Univ. Press, 1972. Pp. xi + 190.

Rosenberg, Marvin. *The Masks of King Lear.* Berkeley: Univ. of California Press, 1972. Pp. 431.

Rosenfeld, Sybil Marion. *A Short History of Scene Design in Great Britain.* Totowa, N.J.: Rowman & Littlefield, 1973. Pp. xviii + 214.

Rousseau, G. S., ed. *Organic Form: The Life of an Idea.* London: Routledge & Kegan Paul, 1972. Pp. xii + 108.

Salgado, Gamini, ed. *Cony-Catchers and Bawdy Baskets: An Anthology of Elizabethan Low Life.* Baltimore: Penguin Books, 1973. Pp. 389.

Schrader, Richard J., ed. *The Reminiscences of Alexander Dyce.* Columbus: Ohio State Univ. Press, 1972. Pp. xiii + 267.

A Shakespeare Bibliography: The Catalogue of the Birmingham Shakespeare Library. 8 vols. London: Mansell, 1971. Pp. 2753.

Shakespeare Survey 25 & 26. Ed. Kenneth Muir. Cambridge: Cambridge Univ. Press, 1972 & 1973. Pp. viii + 205; viii & 189.

Shakespeare, William. *The Comedy of Errors.* Ed. Stanley Wells. New Penguin Shakespeare. Baltimore: Penguin Books, 1972. Pp. 189.

———. *The Complete Works.* Rd. Hardin Craig and David Bevington. Glenview, Ill.: Scott, Foresman, 1973. Pp. ix + 1447.

———. *King Lear.* Ed. J. L. Halio. Fountainwell Drama Texts. Edinburgh: Oliver & Boyd, 1973. Pp. 192.

———. *Macbeth.* Ed. J. L. Halio. Fountainwell Drama Texts. Edinburgh: Oliver & Boyd, 1972. Pp. 137.

———. *The Riverside Shakespeare.* Ed. G. Blakemore Evans et al. Boston: Houghton Mifflin, 1974. Pp. xvi + 1902.

———. *The Tragedy of King Lear.* Ed. E. A. Horsman. New York: Bobbs Merrill, 1973. Pp. xxix + 239.

———. *The Two Gentlemen of Verona.* Ed. Clifford Leech. The Arden Shakespeare. New York: Barnes & Noble, 1973. Pp. 122.

Shakespearean Comedy. Ed. Malcolm Bradbury and David Palmer. Stratford-upon-Avon Studies 14. New York: Crane, Russak, 1973. Pp. 247.

Shumaker, Wayne. *The Occult Sciences in the Renaissance.* Berkeley: Univ. of California Press, 1972. Pp. xxi + 284.

Shurr, William H. *The Mystery of Iniquity: Melville as Poet, 1857–1891.* Lexington: Univ. Press of Kentucky, 1972. Pp. ix + 283.

Smith, Hallett. *Shakespeare's Romances: A Study of Some Ways of the Imagination.* San Marino, Calif.: Huntington Library, 1972. Pp. xiii + 244.

Soellner, Rolf. *Shakespeare's Patterns of Self-Knowledge.* Columbus: Ohio State Univ. Press, 1972. Pp. xxi + 454.

Southall, Raymond. *Literature and the Rise of Capitalism: Critical Essays Mainly on the Sixteenth and Seventeenth Centuries.* London: Laurence & Wishart, 1973. Pp. 175.

Southern, Richard. *The Staging of Plays before Shakespeare.* New York: Theatre Arts Books, 1973. Pp. 603.

Spevack, Marvin. *The Harvard Concordance to Shakespeare.* Cambridge, Mass.: Harvard Univ. Press, 1973. Pp. ix + 1600.

Sticca, Sandro, ed. *The Medieval Drama.* Albany: State University of New York Press, 1972. Pp. xii + 154.

Stilwell, Margaret Bingham. *The Beginning of the World of Books, 1450–1470.* New York: Bibliographical Society of America, 1972. Pp. xxviii + 112.

Stone, Lawrence. *Family and Fortune: Studies in Aristocratic Finance in the Sixteenth and Seventeenth Centuries.* Oxford: Oxford Univ. Press, 1973. Pp. xviii + 315.

Tailor, Robert. *The Hogge Hath Lost his Pearl.* Ed. D. F. McKenzie. Malone Society Reprints. 1967; rpt. Oxford: Oxford Univ. Press, 1972. Pp. xvii + text.

Thirsk, Joan, and J. P. Cooper, eds. *Seventeenth Century Economic Documents.* Oxford: Oxford Univ. Press, 1972. Pp. ix + 849.

Thorpe, James. *Principles of Textual Criticism.* San Marino, Calif.: Huntington Library, 1972. Pp. ix + 209.

Tidworth, Simon. *Theatres: An Illustrated History.* London: Pall Mall Press, 1973. Pp. 224.

Topsell, Edward. *The Fowles of Heaven, or History of Birdes.* Ed. Thomas P. Harrison and F. David Hoeniger. Austin: Univ. of Texas Press, 1972. Pp. xxxvi + 332.

Toynbee, J. M. C. *Animals in Roman Life and Art.* Ithaca: Cornell Univ. Press, 1973. Pp. 431.

The Tragedy of Master Arden of Faversham. Ed. M. L. Wine. Revels Plays. London: Methuen, 1973. Pp. xcvi + 180.

Van Eerde, Katherine S. *Wenceslaus Hollar, Delineator of His Time.* Charlottesville: Univ. Press of Virginia, 1970. Pp. xiv + 122.

Vessey, David. *Statius and the "Thebaid."* Cambridge: Cambridge Univ. Press, 1973. Pp. viii + 358.

Viator: Medieval and Renaissance Studies. Vol II (1971). Ed. Lynn White, Jr. Berkeley: Univ. of California Press, 1972. Pp. vi + 397.

Wait, R. J. C. *The Background to Shakespeare's Sonnets.* New York: Schocken Books, 1972. Pp. 208.

Warren, H. L. *Henry II.* Berkeley: Univ. of California, 1973. Pp. 710.

Washington, Mary A. *Sir Philip Sidney: An Annotated Bibliography of Modern Criticism, 1941–1970. Columbia:* Univ. of Missouri Press, 1972. Pp. 199.

Webster, John. *The Devil's Law Case.* Ed. Frances A. Shirley Regents Renaissance Drama Series. Lincoln: Univ. of Nebraska Press, 1972. Pp. xxv + 149.

Whitbread, Leslie George. *Fulgentius the Mythographer.* Columbus: Ohio State Univ. Press, 1971. Pp. x + 258.

Wickham, Glynne. *Early English Stages, 1300 to 1600.* Vol. II: 1576 to 1600, Part II. New York: Columbia University Press, 1972. Pp. xii + 266.

Wilson, Elkin Calhoun. *Shakespeare, Santayana and the Comic.* Tuscaloosa: Univ. of Alabama Press, 1973. Pp. v + 191.

Woodman, David. *White Magic and English Renaissance Drama.* Rutherford, N.J.: Fairleigh Dickerson Univ. Press, 1973. Pp. 148.

Yates, Frances A. *The Rosicrucian Enlightenment.* London: Routledge & Kegan Paul, 1972. Pp. xv + 269.

Young, David. *The Heart's Forest: A Study of Shakespeare's Pastoral Plays.* New Haven: Yale Univ. Press, 1972. Pp. xii + 205.